In the nam … Merciful

IN THE SHADE OF
THE QUR'ĀN

Fī Ẓilāl al-Qur'ān

Revised Edition

VOLUME I

SŪRAHS 1–2

Al-Fātiḥah – Al-Baqarah

Translated and Edited by
Adil Salahi & Ashur Shamis

THE ISLAMIC FOUNDATION

Published by
THE ISLAMIC FOUNDATION
Markfield Conference Centre,
Ratby Lane, Markfield, Leicester LE67 9SY, United Kingdom
Email: publications@islamic-foundation.com
Website: www.islamic-foundation.com

Quran House, PO Box 30611, Nairobi, Kenya

PMB 3193, Kano, Nigeria

Distributed by
KUBE PUBLISHING LTD.
Tel: +44(0)1530 249230, Fax: +44(0) 1530 249656
Email: info@kubepublishing.com
Website: www.kubepublishing.com

Revised Edition 2003/1424 AH
2nd impression 2011/1432 AH

British Library Cataloguing-in-Publication Data
Qutb, Sayyid, 1903–1966
In the shade of the Qur'an: Fi zilal al-Qur'an,
Vol. 1: Surah 1-2: Al-Fatihah - Al-Baqarah
1. Koran - Commentaries
I. Title II. Salahi, Adil III. Shamis, Ashur
IV. Islamic Foundation V. Fi zilal al-Qur'an
297.1'227

ISBN 978-0 -86037-303-2 *casebound*
ISBN 978-0-86037-397-1 *paperback*

Typesetting by: N.A. Qaddoura
Cover design by: Imtiaze A. Manjra

بسم الله الرحمن الرحيم

Contents

Transliteration Table

Consonants. Arabic

initial: unexpressed medial and final:

ء	’	د	d	ض	ḍ	ك	k
ب	b	ذ	dh	ط	ṭ	ل	l
ت	t	ر	r	ظ	ẓ	م	m
ث	th	ز	z	ع	ʿ	ن	n
ج	j	س	s	غ	gh	هـ	h
ح	ḥ	ش	sh	ف	f	و	w
خ	kh	ص	ṣ	ق	q	ي	y

Vowels, diphthongs, etc.

Short:	ـَ	a;	ـِ	i;	ـُ	u.		
long:	ـَا	ā;	ـُو	ū;	ـِي	ī;	ىّ	īy
diphthongs:			ـِوْ	aw;				
			ـَىْ	ay				

Preface to the First Edition

The influence of the Qur'ān in shaping the paradigm and ethos of Muslim culture and civilization has been overpowering. It is because of the Qur'ān that the Muslim community, or *ummah,* rose to power and prominence in different periods of history and it is because of their neglect of this divine revelation that they have suffered humiliation and ignominy. The rise and fall of the Muslim individual and community is, therefore, intrinsically linked with the principles and values given by the Qur'ān. It is not without significance that God describes the Qur'ān as a 'light' which enables people to find their way in the darkness of ignorance and prejudice, a 'healing' for the ailments of the soul, a 'criterion' to distinguish between right and wrong and, above all, a 'book of guidance' to lead humanity to its destiny along a path which is characterized as 'straight'.

Islam looks at life as a composite whole. Therefore, it is appropriate that God provides all the necessary guidance through the Qur'ān and its interpreter, the Prophet Muḥammad (peace be upon him) and does not leave any aspect of life unguided whether it is private or public, individual or collective, spiritual or mundane, national or international, this-worldly or that-worldly. It is no surprise that Muslim scholars and students of the Qur'ān spend their life with great devotion in understanding and interpreting the Qur'ān to derive guidance in the comprehensive sense of the term. The effort to study and understand the meaning and teachings of the Qur'ān has given rise to the specialized discipline of *tafsīr,* or Qur'ānic commentary. Over the period of fourteen centuries a large number of commentaries, or *tafsīr*, in Arabic alone and a similar, if not greater, number in other world languages have been produced. The effort to appreciate the message of the Qur'ān and derive guidance on contemporary and civilizational issues continues as does the proliferation of *tafsīr* literature in Arabic and other world languages.

Sayyid Quṭb's *tafsīr,* entitled in Arabic, *Fī Ẓilāl al-Qur'ān,* has been acclaimed as one of the best contemporary commentaries on the Qur'ān in any language and one that has passed through several editions and reprints and been translated into several languages including Urdu, Bengali, Persian, Indonesian and Turkish. Sayyid Quṭb's *tafsīr,* in fact, is not a *tafsīr* in the traditional sense of the term. It is more than that. It is an effort to reflect on the dynamic and revolutionary message of the Qur'ān in its comprehensive sense and invite not only Muslims but all of humanity to come and enjoy the shade and blessings of the Qur'ān. The title *Fī Ẓilāl al-Qur'ān* or 'In the Shade of the Qur'ān' is, therefore, not without significance. The author acknowledges this fact and regards it a privilege and a great blessing to be able to live in the shade of the Qur'ān and gain the uplifting experience and appreciate the power of the Qur'ān in transforming human perception, experience and history. One cannot but sympathize with him when, commenting on the contemporary world situation he asks with a sense of anxiety, "how has life been allowed to degenerate into such darkness and despair, while this rich treasure of guidance and enlightenment is readily available?" He therefore takes upon himself the task of explaining the meaning and message of the Qur'ān to the people at large, suggesting that it can only be enjoyed and its concomitant spiritual contentment achieved if one is prepared to live in the shade of the Qur'ān, internalizing its message to the best of one's ability.

The process of writing a commentary on the Qur'ān is so involved and engaging that the author often feels the need to revise, edit, improve and add to what he has written. This is particularly true in the case of Sayyid Quṭb and his life experience, especially his long periods in prison under extremely harsh conditions, for no crime other than his writings. That gave him a profound insight into the nature of injustice and the central aim of Islam to liberate mankind from all forms of injustice.

Sayyid Quṭb, in fact, started writing this *tafsīr* for the monthly journal *al-Muslimūn* towards the end of 1951 when it was serialized up to verse 103 of *Sūrah* 2. Within a few months he realized that although serialization of *tafsīr* in a monthly journal is an effective method of disseminating the message of the Qur'ān to a selective audience, it is rather a slow process and perhaps it does not reach the wider audience it is meant for. He, therefore, decided to publish his commentary separately in book form with the result that in October

1952 he was able to bring out its first volume and within a short period of one year and four months (October 1952–January 1954) he published additional volumes containing commentary of some fourteen out of thirty parts (*ajzā'*) of the Qur'ān. Like his illustrious contemporary *mufassir* of the Indo-Pak subcontinent, Mawlānā Mawdūdī (1903–1979) he, too, completed and revised the major part of his *tafsīr* while in prison (1954–1964). The commentary on *Sūrahs* 1–32 was written before the author's first imprisonment in 1954. While in prison, the author adopted a more penetrating, expansive and trenchant approach, evident in his commentary on *Sūrahs* 33–114. He then embarked on re-writing the commentary on *Sūrahs* 1–32 using the new approach but, having been denied all writing facilities, he was only able to do so up to *Sūrah* 15, leaving the commentary on the remaining *Sūrahs* (16–32) in the original succinct style.

Like Mawdūdī, Sayyid Quṭb has provided a very useful introduction to most of the *sūrahs* of the Qur'ān, summarizing the main message of the *sūrah* in such a profound and masterly way that it opens the 'gate of understanding' even for the uninitiated reader. Moreover, for the better understanding of the message of the Qur'ān he divides the chapters into lessons or topical units and also makes his work distinguishable from others by highlighting the link of the beginning of a *sūrah* with its conclusion and thereby showing the harmonized structure or interlinking of the message with the verses and the *sūrahs*. Some other distinguishing features of this monumental *tafsīr* are that it avoids relying on Biblical material, known as *Isrā'iliyyāt* and does not delve too much into *fiqhī* or jurisprudential discussion, unless it is essential to clarify the point under discussion. Similarly, on matters where the Qur'ān does not provide more than basic information and the Prophet has also not provided any clear indication or details, unlike some *mufassirīn*, he scrupulously avoids speculation, and refrains from putting forward any subjective judgements or opinions. Not only does he carefully avoid unnecessary legal polemics, he also refuses to engage in speculative *tafsīr* arguing for or against various schools of philosophical thought, his main concern being to present the clear message of the Qur'ān as expounded by the Prophet, his companions, and scholars of the earlier generations. Using a lively and refined literary style, he presents the commentary on the Qur'ān in such a modern and forceful way that the reader feels captivated and eventually motivated to devote his life to the active struggle to make Islam a living reality in the world and share its blessings with those who have not been fortunate enough to benefit from its 'shade'.

First and foremost we would like to record our special gratitude to Professor Muḥammad Quṭb and the members of the Quṭb family for granting the Islamic Foundation the permission and the honour of publishing this work. We are likewise grateful to Mr. Adil Salahi and Mr. Ashur Shamis, for undertaking the difficult task of translating and editing the work from Arabic to English and offering all possible help to the Foundation for the publication of this monumental work, planned to be completed in some eighteen volumes. The English-speaking world had its first taste of this remarkable commentary when the translation of the 30th part, or *juz'*, was serialized in the FOSIS's monthly journal *The Muslim* and later published in book form by the Muslim Welfare House, London in 1979. Since then, English readers have been eagerly waiting to read the remaining 29 parts in English. Although it is long overdue, the publication of the present volume will breathe some fresh air and generate some realistic hope that it will not be long before the whole *tafsīr* will, *inshā' Allāh*, see the light of day and benefit a large section of English-speaking humanity. We hope and pray to God, *subḥānahū wa ta'ālā*, to enable us to publish the complete work within the next few years, a target not impossible to achieve. We request our readers to have patience and forbearance and pray that we accomplish this rewarding task as planned and earn God's blessings in this world and in the hereafter.

I will be failing in my duty if I do not mention and thank my colleagues who have worked tirelessly to make this publication possible. My special thanks go to Mr. E.R. Fox who, in copy editing, proof-reading and indexing, has devoted so much attention to this noble project. My other colleague, Br. Naiem Qaddoura, among many others, deserves special thanks and appreciation for his hard work and computer skills in the design and page layout. My thanks are also due to Dr. A.R. Kidwai, Dr. A.K. Chachi, Mrs. Deborah Robb and Mr. Imtiaze Ahmed Manjra for their help and assistance provided in various ways.

Rabī' al-Awwal, 1420 AH
July 1999

M. Manazir Ahsan
Director General

Preface to the Second Edition

It is gratifying to note that in less than four years of its publication, need has arisen to bring out the second edition of the first volume of 'In the Shade of the Qur'ān'. This reflects not only the popularity of the work but also gives us an opportunity to gratefully acknowledge some of the suggestions and comments offered by readers and reviewers of the volume.

Readers of this edition will therefore note that it is set differently from the first edition, mainly to accommodate feedback concerning our approach in the first edition. Many readers felt that our treatment of the complete *Sūrah* 2 in one large unit made it difficult for them to consult the work, when they needed to refer to a particular verse.

The author divides long *sūrahs* into passages, and discusses each passage as a unit. His division follows his own understanding of how the *sūrahs* treats its central theme and the angles from which it tackles that theme. Our approach of overriding this division and treating each *sūrah* as a single indivisible unit forced some abridgement of the commentary text at certain points, particularly in the 'Overview' of each passage.

This edition goes back to the author's arrangement, thus bringing the English edition in line with the Arabic original. The same method is followed in all the other volumes published so far, and will be followed in the rest of the work, God willing.

We in the Islamic Foundation are grateful to God Almighty for enabling us to achieve the goal we set for ourselves about the rest of the work. At the moment of writing 6 volumes have already been published, covering almost 9 volumes of the Arabic edition. This is due to the fact that in the English edition we have not followed the division of the Qur'ān into 30 parts, or *ajzā'*, of equal length, because that division aims only to enable a person to read all the Qur'ān in one month, reading an equal portion each day. In the English edition we follow the Qur'ānic arrangement into *sūrahs*, each forming an independent unit. Thus, this volume covers 2.4 volumes of the Arabic edition. We have been working on publishing at least two volumes a year and, by God's grace, we have been able to meet this target. Volume 7 is already close to completion, and we hope that it will be with the readers within the next few weeks, God willing. Work on Volume 8 is already in progress. Contrary to our earlier expectations to manage the entire *tafsīr* in 15 volumes, the complete work will now Insha' Allah be published in 18 volumes in its English version. We also intend to bring out a revised edition of the last volume, published in 1979 as Volume 30. It is hoped that its new edition will be ready within the next few months.

In the team which has been helping us in the editing, typesetting and publication of this and other volumes, I am delighted to add the names of Dr. Suzanne Thackray and Nasir Kadir as their help in the editing and typesetting has been immense. I am also grateful to 'IslamOnLine of al-Balagh Cultural Society, Qatar' for their generous support to this rewarding project.

Dhū al-Qaʿdah, 1423
January 2003

M. Manazir Ahsan
Director General

Foreword

By
Professor Muḥammad Quṭb*

It gives me great pleasure to write this Foreword to *In the Shade of the Qur'ān* in its English version. The book is the fruit of the most productive years of its author's intellectual life and, at the same time, a vivid expression of the sacred battle which he fought and which culminated in his martyrdom in 1966.

The larger part of this work was written when the author was in jail in the period 1954–1964. This was a period of complete solitude, when writing was the main preoccupation of the author and during which he lived totally 'in the shade of the Qur'ān'.

The author's vigorous struggle, for which he was imprisoned, then killed, was, at the practical level, an attempt to achieve the implementation of Islam in the shape of a community which practises Islam in its life and preaches the need for its realization until it becomes the actual code of practice for the society as a whole. At the intellectual level, however, the author's life struggle is embodied in a collection of books devoted to explaining the true nature of Islam, its fundamentals, values and laws. The largest and most important of these works is undoubtedly *In the Shade of the Qur'ān.*

The book is a 'campaign of struggle' because it is, indeed, much more than a commentary on the Qur'ān.

The Qur'ān is the book of Islam. Hardly a generation has passed since the dawn of Islam without the appearance of one or more commentaries which explain the meaning of the Qur'ān. Having spent a considerable part of his life 'in the shade of the Qur'ān' and, having joined the struggle for the sake of Islam, the author of this work did not intend to write just another commentary. He had a different objective which he felt could be attained through writing his commentary.

---

* Professor Muḥammad Quṭb is the author's brother and formerly Professor of Islamic Studies, at Umm al-Qurā University, Makkah, Saudi Arabia. He himself has written several books on Islam, some of which have been translated into English and other languages. He is one of the most distinguished contemporary writers on Islam.

Our present age has its own features which, perhaps, have never existed in any period of history. They are the ones which give this commentary its own colouring and determine its points of emphasis.

Muslims, for their part, are now far removed in their practical life from the true nature of Islam. The image of Islam they present by their way of life is nothing more than the indistinguishable negative of the true image of Islam as it was practised by the early Islamic generations, who perfectly fulfilled God's own description of them:

"You are the best community that has ever been raised up for mankind: you enjoin the doing of what is right and forbid what is wrong, and you believe in God." (3: 110) Hence they were able to write that incomparable page in human history. They established truth and justice on earth and raised for mankind an inimitable civilization which builds up its structure in the material and spiritual worlds at the same time. It is a civilization which unites the two worlds and achieves harmony between body and soul, religion and politics, faith and science, the present life and the hereafter, the practical and the ideal.

Non-Muslims, on the other hand, confront humanity with a host of philosophical, social, political and economic doctrines which banish religion from practical life. At best, such doctrines restrict religion to a tiny corner of man's conscience so that it may become purely a relationship between the individual and his Lord that has no bearing whatsoever on society and its active life, or, at worst, fight it tooth and nail and bar its very existence. As a result, human life is full of many sorts of political, social and economic injustice which know no limits. It witnesses various types of intellectual and moral perversion unknown in history. The advocates of such perversion and deviation try nevertheless to dress their erring ways in a scientific garment and they hold to them as if they were truth itself or the ideal sought after. This they do despite all that they suffer in consequence of nervous and psychological diseases – worry and restlessness, madness and suicide, alcoholism, drug addiction and crime.

What is worse is that these deviant philosophical, social, political and economic doctrines now dominate the lives of contemporary Muslims, wearing the false disguise of a 'modern' human civilization. Thus they poison the lives of the Muslim peoples to a larger degree than they do the life of the West because the Muslims of today have deserted Islam and are unaware of its true nature and fundamental value.

Hence the vigorous intellectual and practical 'campaign of struggle' to which the author devoted himself was an attempt to explain to contemporary Muslims the true nature of Islam. His driving objective was that the Muslims of today should be able to live and practise true Islam in the same way as the early Islamic generations. They would then rescue themselves and would be able to show all mankind the road to salvation.

The Qur'ān is the constitution revealed by God to regulate and govern human life. It is the book which educated the Islamic nation until it attained the standard which earned it the title 'the best community ever raised up for mankind'. Light should, therefore, be thrown on it from two angles. The first is the angle of education: this shows how the Qur'ān, at the levels of the individual, the family, the community and the nation, leads man to achieve the highest degree of moral and spiritual nobility possible in this life. The other angle is that of the practical code which regulates human life in its noblest form and in all its spheres: political, economic, social, intellectual and moral; that is, a life which is befitting to man whom God has ennobled and raised above all species of His creation and entrusted with the task the heavens, the earth and the mountains have all dreaded to shoulder.

This is the method the author has followed in explaining the meanings of the Qur'ān. He does not dwell long on individual words or expressions, unless there is a special need for that. Rather, he takes the whole verse or a number of verses and explains their relevance to the education of man according to the divine method, or to the practical code which regulates the life of Islamic society in all spheres.

Faith is the central point of Islamic education and the Islamic practical code. It takes up the larger part of the Qur'ān and its *sūrahs.* Consequently, it takes up the larger part of *In the Shade of the Qur'ān.* As presented by the Qur'ān, faith is not merely a word to be uttered and then forgotten as man goes about his diverse practical affairs, heedless of the significance of faith and its controls. Faith is indeed the pivot around which all life turns: the conscience, the intellect and the practical sense alike.

The belief in the unity of God goes deep into the very structure of the universe as well as into the human self. It provides a complete conception of life and human existence which differs greatly, in fundamentals and in details, from any concept which is not based on the same essential fact.

The believer, in whose heart this fundamental fact is firmly established, finds that his feelings, ideas and concepts as well as his private and social actions, are totally different from those of a man who conducts his life affairs on a different basis or who views faith as an abstract, philosophical idea which has little or no influence on his life. The same applies to the community whose life is governed by faith. Its aims, ambitions, behaviour and practical achievements are different from those of any other community which does not share its Islamic concepts of God, the universe, life and man.

The Qur'ān projects this in full detail and in two images. The first is the image of the believer as his or her soul is moulded by the acceptance of the reality of the unity of God, in contrast with the erring soul who does not submit to this cardinal truth. The second is the image of the faithful community which conducts its life on the basis that there is no deity but God, in contrast with the erring communities which adopt different doctrines and ignoble values. Through this projection the Qur'ān educates the individual believer and the community of believers so that they may attain their highest standards. It then provides them with the practical code which regulates the various aspects of life and establishes 'the best community ever raised up for mankind'.

The author actually lives with the Qur'ān as it projects these images. He then tries to show his reader the image of a believer content with his faith, delineating the feelings, ideas, values, concepts as well as the practical conduct of the believer as described in the Qur'ān. He also tries to explain the practical code God has laid down for human life. This is indeed the basic theme of this work: *In the Shade of the Qur'ān.*

It dwells at length on faith and how it penetrates the human self, as well as on its influence on the various aspects of life, especially in the area of the implementation of divine legislation. There are two reasons for this: the first is that the Qur'ān itself dwells for long on all these aspects. It describes how faith leaves its mark on *all* human actions, in all situations and conditions: in security or fear, in ease or hardship, in wealth or poverty, in society or solitude, in peace or war, in strength or weakness, in resisting personal desires or struggling against the enemies. The Qur'ān also repeatedly declares in clear terms that accepting the faith means submission to the divine law and the rejection of all other laws. Failing that submission the declaration of faith by any person becomes a hollow statement, with no real substance and unacceptable to God. The other reason is that these very implications are the ones that have been forgotten by, or are completely unknown to, the Muslims of today. This applies more particularly in the case of submission to the divine law as an essential part of faith, without which one's faith is incomplete and faulty. For unless the divine law is upheld, the true image of Islam remains non-existent at both the individual and the social levels.

The author also speaks at length on the numerous signs in the universe which indicate the divine existence, making occasional but cautious use of some of the conclusions arrived at by modern science. This he does because the Qur'ān often dwells on these signs since they are sure to stimulate the human heart to conscious recognition of the unity of the Creator and His infinite majesty and greatness and, consequently to worship and submit to Him alone. He also describes scenes of the hereafter, because the Qur'ān paints these in great detail as they are important means to awaken the religious conscience of man and to establish a dual relationship between God and man based on the two strongest and parallel feelings in man, namely, fear and hope.

He also dwells a great deal on the various Islamic systems, in their basic, unchangeable principles, as opposed to the multitude of deviant and *jāhiliyyah* systems which rule the earth today. His aim here is to show how wide the gulf is between the rule of God and that of *jāhiliyyah,* a state of mind reflecting essential ignorance. He explains the serious consequences of man's refusal to comply with the divine instructions, his obstinate disregard of God's wisdom and his spurning of divine revelations, claiming at the same time that he knows his needs and can judge what is most suitable for him better than God.

The author also speaks comprehensively on the Islamic method of educating the individual and the community, with the dual purpose of shedding light on the Qur'ānic instructions on the one hand and on the other enriching the contemporary Islamic revivalist movement in this field. This enrichment is badly needed at this particular stage as the Islamic movement strives to establish an Islamic presence in the midst of hostile *jāhiliyyah* surroundings which try to suppress Islam or, at least, to move away from it. In this area the author lays strong emphasis on 'education through events' to delineate the Qur'ānic method of making use of great events in disciplining the human soul, so that it may be moulded in the required shape while it is still vividly impressed by the event. Thus, it takes the right mould permanently and becomes immune to deviation.

These are the main themes of this work. As the reader undoubtedly realizes, they are not merely a 'commentary' on the Qur'ān. Should we, however, wish to use the term, we need to qualify it by saying it is a commentary with a definite aim. Its aim is to disseminate the Islamic call and to delineate its system of education and discipline which is essential for its continuity and progress today as it was essential for its prosperity throughout its unique history.

Special mention should be made of a unique characteristic in this 'commentary', of which the author was aware and to which he draws the attention of his reader. It is indeed the net result of his own active involvement in the advocacy of Islam and the trials he had to endure for such involvement. It is the fact the Qur'ān cannot be truly and correctly understood and it does not produce all its dynamic effect except through the practical and active participation in the campaign of 'no deity but God'. For 'no deity but God' represents a massive campaign within the human conscience and in the social set-up of human communities. It is not something static which may be put in a special corner where it settles down. It is a dynamic, ever-active force which never weakens or subsides. Internally, within the individual, it is a self-sustaining force which tries to elevate man above worldly desires and enable him to lead a life which is pure, elevated, noble and consistent, through his continuous attempt to draw nearer to God, seeking His pleasure and avoiding His anger. In society, it is a permanent movement which aims to make all mankind submit to the divine constitution: *"until there is no more oppression, and all submission is made to God alone."* (8: 39)

If one reads the Qur'ān in a sort of a passive, detached state one is sure to miss a lot of its indications and purposes. But when one reads it while actually involved in the cause trying to establish that 'there is no deity but God', one's heart will open to receive its meanings which one would otherwise have missed, and will draw inferences of which one has been totally unaware. The present work is itself a proof of this fact. The author wrote the earlier edition of a number of volumes before he engaged in the real battle, when he had not yet devoted himself fully to the campaign of 'no deity but God'. Then he rewrote the early volumes from within. The difference between the two editions cannot be exaggerated. It is a difference produced by the new light shed by actually practising the meanings of the Qur'ān.

Another arresting feature of this 'commentary', in its Arabic original at least, is its literary style. The author started his life as a man of letters, preoccupied with the artistic side of life. His attitude to life and to the universe was that of a keen artist who has a lively and genuine response to whatever is beautiful and who goes through the practical life with an idealistic outlook. This, however, did not prevent him from becoming involved in the political issues of the day. The latter part of his life, on the other hand, was devoted to his vigorous struggle for the cause that had become his sole preoccupation. To the cause of Islam he devoted his thoughts and his feelings, his nights and his days, and indeed his whole life. But did he ever lose his artistic feeling which was so prominent in his earlier career? Indeed not. The Qur'ān itself, in whose shade the author has lived, is characterized by a fine style of surpassing excellence, even as it portrays the on-going battle of 'no deity but God'.

I extend my greetings to the readers of this English translation hoping that they will live with the author 'In the Shade of the Qur'ān'.

Introduction

To live "in the shade of the Qur'ān" is a great blessing which can only be fully appreciated by those who experience it. It is a rich experience that gives meaning and blessing to life and makes it worth living. I am deeply thankful to God Almighty for blessing me with this uplifting experience over a considerable time, which was the happiest and most fruitful period of my life – a privilege for which I am eternally grateful.

It is a great honour to feel that God Almighty should be addressing me, a humble and insignificant human being, with the blessed and inspiring words of the Qur'ān. They lifted my spirits, and I was raised to a unique vantage point from where I could observe the tumult of human life. I was able to gain a new perspective into man's endless quest for the trivial and the mundane, and the clamour for ephemeral and childish pursuits. I was astounded by the extent of our ignorance and our neglect of the sublime and divine message of the Qur'ān which has the power to uplift and entirely transform human perception, experience and history on this earth.

I had the opportunity to study the Qur'ān at length and ponder over its clear and full conception of creation and existence, and their purpose. I could compare the impact of those ideas with that of others put forward by men throughout history. And I wondered: How has life been allowed to degenerate into such darkness and despair, while this rich treasure of guidance and enlightenment is readily available?

I lived in the shade of the Qur'ān, filled with appreciation of that perfect harmony and balance inherent in God's creation, between man's actions and the movement of the universe around him. I was able to see clearly the dire consequences of the conflict between the two. I could see the folly, indeed the catastrophe, to which humanity is being driven by wicked and ungodly miscreants. Pity the human race, indeed!

In the shade of the Qur'ān I saw this world of ours expanding far outside what we can see or define. Beyond the visible world lies an unseen dimension which encompasses this life and the life hereafter. Man's origins extend back into the dim and distant past, and death is not the end of our perennial journey but a passing phase of a long journey that stretches to infinity. What we earn in the temporal world is but a small portion of what is our due; the rewards or punishments we miss or escape here we shall duly meet in the life to come, and justice shall be done.

Nevertheless, our brief life on this earth is real. The world we live in is essentially friendly and hospitable, and its spirit interacts fully with ours. Like us, it turns to the One Creator in total submission and reverence. *"All that is in the heavens and the earth, and their own shadows, prostrate themselves before God, willingly and unwillingly, morning and evening."* (13: 15) *"The seven heavens, the earth, and all that is in them, glorify Him; there is nothing but celebrates His praises."* (17: 44) Such a powerful, outward-looking, all-embracing and optimistic vision inspires utter confidence within the human heart and fills the soul with total inner peace and security.

I lived in the shade of the Qur'ān to see man being given the respect and reverence never accorded him by any other philosophy or ideology before or since. Man's *raison d'être* emanates from the divine spirit God breathed into him. The Qur'ān tells us that during the creation of man, God said to the angels, *"When I have fashioned him [man] and breathed into him of My spirit, prostrate yourselves before him."* (15: 29; 38: 72)

By virtue of this divine breath, man was destined and commissioned to be God's representative on earth, where he was given access to, and authority and control over, everything. As a consequence of the high esteem in which man is held, God has ordained that ties of belief and faith are the only worthy and legitimate ties that can bring men together. They override all other incidental ties of nationality, race or ancestry.

The Qur'ān has also taught me that the believer in the One God is the descendant of a long and noble line of faithful ancestors that include great figures such as Noah, Abraham, Ishmael, Isaac, Jacob, Joseph, Moses, Jesus and Muḥammad (peace be upon them all). The Qur'ān states, *"This community of yours is one single community and I am your Lord; therefore fear Me alone."* (23: 52; see also 21: 92)

The Qur'ān makes it clear that in this long procession which began at the very moment man appeared on earth, all believers have had to face similar challenges and ordeals: oppression, persecution and threats of annihilation and dispersion. Nevertheless, the procession continues along its well-defined path with a steady step and a calm heart, ever confident that God's will shall prevail and His promise shall be fulfilled. *"The unbelievers said to their messengers, 'Return to our religion, or we will banish you from our land.' But their Lord revealed His will to them [the messengers], saying, 'Most certainly shall We destroy the wrongdoers, and shall cause you to dwell in the land long after they are gone. This I promise to all who stand in awe of My presence, and stand in awe of My warnings.'"* (14: 14)

Throughout human history believers have upheld similar convictions and ideals, faced similar enemies and threats, undergone similar experiences, and enjoyed similar triumphs and rewards.

In the shade of the Qur'ān I learned that in this existence there is no room for blind coincidence or haphazard events: *"We have created everything according to a measure."* (54: 49) *"He has created all things and assigned everything its appropriate measure."* (25: 2) Everything is there for a purpose, but the true and deep wisdom underlying our existence may not always be apparent to the limited human mind. The Qur'ān says: *"It may well be that you are averse to something in which God has placed much good."* (4: 19) *"It may well be that you hate a thing although it is good for you, and love a thing although it is bad for you. God knows, whereas you do not know."* (2: 216)

Causes, as known to man, may or may not lead to their usual, logical effects. Assumptions perceived as essentially inevitable may or may not lead to their conventionally expected consequences. This is so because causes and assumptions do not, in or by themselves, determine actions and events, since cause and effect are both determined by God's absolute will. The Qur'ān says: *"You never know; it may be that God will after that bring something new to pass."* (65: 1) *"Yet you cannot will except by the will of God."* (76: 30)

In performing any deed, the believer must prepare and carry out his actions, and leave God to determine the results and consequences of those actions. To trust in God's mercy, justice, wisdom and knowledge is the only safeguard against uncertainty and fear of the future. The Qur'ān says: *"Satan promises you poverty and bids you to commit indecency, whereas God promises you His forgiveness and bounty. God is Munificent, All-Knowing"* (2: 268)

In the shade of the Qur'ān I have, therefore, felt totally contented and reassured. I could see God's hand in every event and everything. I lived in God's care and custody. His attributes, as given in the Qur'ān, came alive before my eyes.

> *Who else would answer the constrained when he cries out to Him and alleviates affliction?* (27: 62)
>
> *He alone holds sway over all His creatures, and He alone is truly wise, all-aware.* (6: 18)
>
> *God prevails in His purpose, though most people do not know it.* (12: 21)
>
> *Know that God comes in between a man and his heart, and that to Him you shall all be gathered.* (8: 24)
>
> *[God] is the doer of what He wills.* (85: 16)
>
> *Whoever fears God, He will find a way out for him, and He will provide for him in a way he had never reckoned on. He who puts his trust in God, God will suffice for him. God is sure to bring about whatever He decrees.* (65: 2–3)
>
> *There is no living creature which He does not hold by its forelock.* (11: 56)
>
> *Is God not enough for His servant? Yet they [the unbelievers] would frighten you with those [they worship] instead of Him!* (39: 36)
>
> *He whom God shall disgrace will have none who could bestow honour on him.* (22: 18)
>
> *Whoever God lets go astray shall have none to guide him.* (13: 33)

The destiny of the universe is not left to the mercy of some blind laws. Behind the physical laws there is an active will, the absolute power of God that creates and decides.

I also learned that God's hand acts in all things in a manner that is unique to Him. We humans have no power to either force God's hand or rush His actions or anticipate His will.

The Divine scheme, as outlined in the Qur'ān, is designed to operate equally well under all circumstances and at all stages of human development, on the macrocosmic as well as the microcosmic scale. It makes full allowance for man's own abilities and potential for improvement, and gives careful consideration to his strengths and weaknesses. It neither devalues man's role on earth nor denigrates his status as an individual or as a member of society.

In its view of man, God's scheme is neither idealistic, raising man far above his deserved position, nor does it describe man as worthless or dispensable.

Man is a unique creature who can, through his natural talents and innate abilities, adapt himself to the Divine order of life and so rise to the highest levels of progress and achievement. The Divine order is a universal plan for the long term. It is neither oppressive nor arbitrary. Its perspectives and prospects are broad and not restricted to the life or interests of one individual: it looks far into the future. Human ideologies, on the other hand, are usually limited to the life span of their proponents, who are bent on achieving all their ambitions and settling all their scores within a single generation. This inevitably comes into conflict with human nature, resulting in oppression, conflict, bloodshed, and the destruction of human values and civilization.

Islam adopts a very gentle approach towards human nature, encouraging, prodding, pampering, cajoling, reprimanding and, where necessary, disciplining and restraining. It prefers the patient, caring attitude, confident of the eventual outcome. It is a continuous process of growth and development that can only get better as time goes on. Islam, like the oak tree, starts slowly and grows gradually, steadily overcoming all difficulties, vicissitudes and adversities. There is no need for compromises, half-hearted solutions, or arbitrary or foolish measures. In God's scheme, things must be allowed to take their natural course. *"No change will you ever find in God's way."* (35: 43)

Another feature of the universal divine order is that it is inherently built on a universal truth. This, again, has not come about by pure chance or as a result of coincidence. God Himself is the Truth, and from Him, as the Qur'ān affirms, emanates all existence: *"It is because God is the Truth and all that they evoke beside Him is false. He is most high, supreme."* (22: 62)

The Universe was created in truth: *"God has created none of this otherwise than in accordance with the truth."* (10: 5) Believers confirm this, saying: *"Our Lord, You have not created all this in vain. Limitless are You in Your glory."* (3: 191)

Truth is the mainstay of all existence and should the world deviate from the truth, it would decay and fall apart: *"Had the truth followed their [the unbelievers'] caprice, the heavens, the earth, and all that lives in them would have surely been corrupted."* (23: 71)

Hence, regardless of how things may seem, the truth will eventually become manifest. The Qur'ān asserts: *"We hurl the truth against falsehood, and it crushes the latter, and behold, it withers away."* (21: 18)

Likewise, goodness and righteousness are inherent and permanent in the cosmic superstructure. The Qur'ān alludes to this fact in saying: *"He sends down water from the sky, so that riverbeds flow according to their measure, and the torrent bears a swelling foam. Likewise, from what people smelt in the fire to make ornaments or utensils rises similar foam. Thus does God illustrate truth and falsehood. The scum is cast away, while that which is of benefit to mankind remains behind on earth. Thus does God set forth His parables."* (13: 17) It also says: *"Do you not see how God compares a good word to a good tree? Its roots are firm and its branches reach to the sky; it yields its fruits at all times by its Lord's leave. Thus does God set parables for people so that they may reflect. And an evil word is like a bad tree, uprooted from the face of the earth. It cannot have a stable position. God will strengthen the believers through the true, unshakeable word in both this life and the life to come. God lets the wrongdoers go astray. God does whatever He wills."* (14: 24–27)

This clear and forceful belief brings infinite reassurance and fills the human heart and soul with peace and tranquillity. It reinforces man's trust in truth, goodness and righteousness, and gives the human conscience the dignity and the confidence to transcend the limits of its environment.

My study of the Qur'ān has led me to the firm conviction that humanity will see no tranquillity or accord, nor can peace, progress or material and spiritual advances be made, without total recourse to God.

This, from the Qur'ānic point of view, can mean only one thing: the organization of all aspects of human life in accordance with the precepts and directions of the way of life the Qur'ān outlines for humanity. The alternative would be corruption, regression and misery. The Qur'ān puts it thus: *"If they do not respond to you, know that they only follow their vain desires. And who is in greater error than he who follows his own vain desires and has no guidance from God? God does not guide the transgressors."* (28: 50)

Adopting this way of life is an inevitable obligation on man, without which he would have no faith. The Qur'ān says: *"It is not for any believer, male or female, to have any choice in a matter once God and His Messenger pass judgement on it."* (33: 36) *"Now We have set you [Muḥammad] on a path which you should follow and do not yield to the desires of the ignorant ones. They can avail you nothing against God. Transgressors are patrons one to another, while the righteous have God for a patron."* (45: 18–19)

It is, then, an extremely serious matter that concerns the very foundations of faith in God and the happiness and well-being of mankind.

The secrets of man's talent and potential can only be unlocked by God, his creator, who alone can prescribe the cure for man's ills. The key to man's happiness is in God's hands. God says: *"We bestow of the Qur'ān from on high what serves as a healing and a blessing to true believers."* (17: 82) *"This Qur'ān shows the way to that which is most upright"* (17: 9)

However, man tends not to follow the logical and sensible course of action, which is to refer matters concerning his guidance and direction to God, who knows the secrets and the limitations of man's being.

This fundamental error of judgement on man's part is the cause of all the misery and confusion humanity has seen. The isolation of Islam from the active leadership of mankind has been a watershed in human history, and by far the worst setback humanity has suffered.

Islam assumed the leadership of humanity at a time of grave decline, when corruption and decadence were rife and injustice rampant. The revelation of the Qur'ān and the advent of Islam, which was based on it, marked a rebirth of man far more significant than even his first one.

Islam gained that leadership by virtue of the original concepts and laws outlined in the Qur'ān, which introduced a fresh understanding of life and its values, and of the whole world order. These concepts brought about new and exciting realities hitherto unknown in human society, characterized by purity and beauty, and a healthy and positive attitude towards life and the world.

Then came the tragedy that removed Islam from its position of leadership, which then fell into the hands of various man-made ideologies, dominated in the main by materialism.

There have always been cynics who claim that humanity has to choose between the adoption of either a God-given system which negates all the material achievements of man, or a system based entirely on man's own intellectual abilities and accomplishments which has no room for divine intervention whatsoever.

This is a most vile and misleading view. The question is never put in such terms. The way of life outlined by Islam is not antagonistic to human innovation and achievement. It is, in fact, the progenitor and patron of the very spirit of that creativity which is the driving force behind man's fulfilment of his role as God's vicegerent on earth. God has endowed man with all the necessary faculties, talent and skills to carry out that most noble role, and He has harnessed for his benefit all the natural laws and forces that can help him in fulfilling that task. God has ensured a certain harmony and coordination between man and his environment that can enhance man's performance and creativity and raise the quality of his life. Man's own achievement, material or otherwise, thus becomes itself an expression of gratitude to God, and a spur to further constructive activity.

The argument that a God-given way of life and man's ability to advance and improve are mutually exclusive, stems from evil motives and bad faith. It can only add to man's confusion, bewilderment and misery.

However, the argument is sometimes advanced in response to people's fascination with the astonishing achievements made by man, especially in the fields of science and material progress, rather than as a consequence of ignorance or bad faith. Being so much in awe of man's achievement, some are easily tempted to separate natural forces and religious values, claiming that they are mutually exclusive and operate in totally separate spheres. This basically flawed argument leads to the distorted concept that material progress can be achieved without the need for religious values, and that the consequences of the interaction of natural laws are inevitable regardless of whether people believe in God or not, and whether they have adopted the imperatives of a God-given system or a man-made one.

This is what we may describe as the grand illusion. It tries to separate two types of natural laws that are, in fact, inseparable. Both religious values and natural laws are indeed aspects of divine law operating in the universe. They interact all the time and coalesce at several points, and they are both ultimately controlled by the power of God. There is, therefore, no justification for separating these two sets of forces in man's consciousness. This is the rational and intelligent understanding that the Qur'ān tries to instil in man's mind when it says:

> *If only the people of earlier revelations would believe and be God-fearing, We should indeed efface their past bad deeds, and bring them into gardens of bliss. If they would observe the Torah and the Gospel and all that has been revealed to them by their Lord, they would indeed be given abundance from above and from beneath.* (5: 65–66)
>
> *Seek forgiveness of your Lord; He is ever ready to forgive. He will send abundant water from the sky for you and bestow upon you wealth and offspring. He will provide you with gardens and flowing rivers.* (71: 10–12)
>
> *God does not change a people's condition unless they first change what is in their hearts.* (13: 11)

To believe in God, and to worship Him with full sincerity, and to implement His prescribed order in society, are all manifestations of submission to God's universal order. The laws governing this order have a positive effect on human life and relate back to the same origin of all the natural, human and physical laws that we observe and experience every day.

It is true that at times we are confused by certain paradoxes we observe in nature as well as in society. Sometimes it seems that discarding religious values and relying solely on materialistic laws leads to success. But this is a very short-sighted view, because the outcome in the long term is quite the opposite. That is true in the case of Muslim civilization itself. It grew and prospered when religious values and materialistic principles were brought together, while its decline began exactly at the moment when they began to diverge. Muslim civilization has yet to recover from that catastrophic reversal in its history.

In contrast, we have today's materialistic civilization which is like an albatross flying with only one wing; the huge advances it registers on the material scale are undermined by its reverses on the humanitarian, psychological and spiritual one.

God's law forms only part of His overall universal order, and the implementation of the divine law in society acts as a catalyst in bringing harmony and balance into man's relationship with the world around.

But the implementation of the divine law must be built on faith in God. It is designed for application within an Islamic society, to whose building and progress it in turn contributes.

Islamic law is totally complementary to Islam's overall view of man, nature and the world. This view is based on a comprehensive and integrated concept that unites such elements as fear of God, conscientiousness, purity of feeling, broadness of concern, high moral standards and upright behaviour. Within such a view compatibility is easily achieved between the so-called "natural laws" and "human values", which are perceived as different aspects of a single universal structure.

Man is seen as another active force in this structure. His will and his actions, his faith and his well-being, his submission to God and his contribution are all forces that exercise a positive influence on life and the world. They also are influenced and controlled by the principles and precepts of God's universal scheme. These forces produce results and multiply when they act in harmony, but they can result in suffering, corruption and strife when they do not: *"God would never alter the favours He bestows on a community unless they change what is in their hearts."* (8: 53)

The link between man's actions and his feelings on the one hand, and God's universal order on the other, is real and constant. No one would wish for this relationship to be broken or undermined, unless they wish ill for man and his future.

These are but a few general observations that living "in the shade of the Qur'ān" has inspired within me. I humbly pray to God that they may be of benefit to the reader.

Cairo
1959

Sayyid Quṭb

*SŪRAH** 1

Al-Fātiḥah

(The Opening)

Al-Fātiḥah (The Opening)

In the Name of God, the Merciful, the Beneficent. (1)

Praise be to God, the Lord of all the worlds. (2)

The Compassionate, the Merciful. (3)

Master of the Day of Judgement. (4)

You alone do we worship and to You alone do we turn for help. (5)

Guide us on the straight path. (6)

سُورَةُ الفَاتِحَةِ

بِسْمِ ٱللَّهِ ٱلرَّحْمَٰنِ ٱلرَّحِيمِ ١

ٱلْحَمْدُ لِلَّهِ رَبِّ ٱلْعَٰلَمِينَ ٢

ٱلرَّحْمَٰنِ ٱلرَّحِيمِ ٣

مَٰلِكِ يَوْمِ ٱلدِّينِ ٤

إِيَّاكَ نَعْبُدُ وَإِيَّاكَ نَسْتَعِينُ ٥

ٱهْدِنَا ٱلصِّرَٰطَ ٱلْمُسْتَقِيمَ ٦

---

* *Sūrah* is the name of a unit of the Qur'ān. The nearest English word is 'chapter', but since '*sūrah*' is used in Arabic to denote only units of the Qur'ān, it has been retained in English. The Qur'ān has 114 *sūrahs* of varying length.

The path of those on whom You have bestowed Your favours, not those who have incurred Your wrath, nor those who have gone astray. (7)	صِرَٰطَ ٱلَّذِينَ أَنۡعَمۡتَ عَلَيۡهِمۡ غَيۡرِ ٱلۡمَغۡضُوبِ عَلَيۡهِمۡ وَلَا ٱلضَّآلِّينَ ٧

Overview

Every Muslim recites this short *sūrah* of seven verses at least seventeen times a day. An authentic *ḥadīth* of the Prophet Muḥammad (peace be upon him), says: "A prayer by one who does not read the *Fātiḥah* is invalid."

This short *sūrah* contains a great deal of the central basic ideas of Islam, its beliefs and concepts. It outlines many of its essential perceptions and attitudes. All this makes it clear why it is chosen for frequent recitation and why it is essential for the validity of prayer.

The *sūrah* opens with the phrase:

In the name of God, the Compassionate, the Merciful. (Verse 1)

This is recognized by the majority of scholars as a verse of the *sūrah*, in its own right, completing its verses into seven. There is, however, a difference of opinion over whether this is so with respect to all other *sūrahs* of the Qur'ān in which the same words appear as the opening phrase. Some scholars maintain that it is to the *Fātiḥah* that the following Qur'ānic statement refers: *"We have given you seven oft-repeated verses and this sublime Qur'ān."* (15: 87)

The very first verses of the Qur'ān revealed to Prophet Muḥammad, which begin with: *"Read in the name of your Lord ..."* (96: 1) establish the Islamic etiquette of invoking the name of God at the beginning of every action. This is also in line with the fundamental Islamic principle that God is *"the first and the last, the outward and the inward."* (57: 3) He is indeed the real being, the origin and the *raison d'être* of all that exists. In His name, therefore, every movement and action is made, and in His name everything begins.

The divine attributes of the Compassionate, *al-Raḥmān*, and the Merciful, *al-Raḥīm*, encompass all aspects and meaning of mercy, and can only be used together with respect to God Almighty. It would be appropriate to use the attribute of *al-Raḥīm* in reference to a human being, but the Islamic faith requires that use of *al-Raḥmān* is exclusive to God. As for the debate over which of the two adjectives denotes the wider meaning of mercy and compassion, it does not concern us here. We can conclude, however, that when combined, they encompass all aspects and dimensions of mercy.

As the invocation of God's name at the beginning of every action constitutes the first fundamental principle of the Muslim faith, the restriction of the use of *al-Raḥmān* and *al-Raḥīm* to God alone constitutes the second principle and defines the relationship between God and man.

Having invoked God's name and acknowledged His infinite mercy, one is directed to praise God and recognize His absolute sovereignty over all beings:

> *Praise be to God, the Lord of all the worlds.* (Verse 2)

Praise of God is the first feeling aroused in a believer's heart at the mention of God. For man's own existence is an aspect of God's infinite grace, which engenders gratitude and reverence towards God. The manifestations of God's munificence and generosity to man and other creatures abound everywhere and can be seen at every moment. To praise God at the beginning and at the end of every action is another fundamental principle of the Islamic faith. The Qur'ān says: *"He is God; there is no deity but He. To Him belongs praise in the first and in the last ..."* (28: 70)

Nevertheless, God's grace is such that when a believer says, 'praise be to God,' it is recorded for him as a good deed outweighing everything. 'Umar ibn al-Khaṭṭāb, the Prophet's Companion, relates that the Prophet (peace be upon him) told how a man once said, "Lord, I praise You as befits the majesty of Your face and the greatness of Your power." The two angels accompanying that man could not evaluate the remark and referred to God Almighty, who commanded them: "Register it in his record as he said it, and I shall reward him as he deserves when he returns to Me."

The last part of this verse, *"Lord of all the worlds"*, expresses the belief in absolute universal Godhead which is at the very core of the Islamic concept of God. God is the sole, absolute and ultimate owner with full independent authority to act in the whole cosmos. He is the overall supreme master who has created the world and continues to watch over it, take care of it, and ensure its stability and well-being. This living and dynamic relationship between the Creator and the created is the perpetual fountain of life for all creation. God has not created the world and abandoned it to its own devices. He continues to be an active living authority over His creation, giving it what it needs for its continued and meaningful life. This applies to all God's creation.

Acknowledging God's absolute Lordship makes all the difference between clarity and confusion with regard to God's absolute oneness. People often combined their acknowledgement of God as the sole creator with belief in multiple deities having authority in their life. It may seem absurd that people should ever hold such a belief, but this was true in the past and is still true today. The Qur'ān speaks of those who claim that they *"only worship them [minor gods] so that they may bring us nearer to God."* (39: 3) It also mentions that some Jewish and Christian groups who *"have taken their rabbis and priests as gods alongside God."* (9: 31) Polytheism, or the worship of several deities or demigods besides the perceived 'Grand Deity', was widespread when Islam emerged in the 7th century in Arabia.

The affirmation of the absolute sovereignty and active authority of the One God over all creation was necessary to ensure man's rationality and peace of mind, and to relieve him from the cruel bewilderment of polytheism. Man must be reassured that a vigilant and caring God is in charge of this world and will never abandon or forsake it.

At the advent of Islam, the world was full of erroneous beliefs and philosophies, and of false religions based on superstition, legend and mythology. Very little of it was true or even rational. As far as the concept of God and His relationship with man and the world was concerned, there was plenty of miserable confusion. This in turn led to confusion in man's understanding of the world and of his own position and role within it.

The need for a rational, clear and consistent system of beliefs only becomes apparent when we study those dark periods of human history when there was no such system. We then realize how heavily such great myth and false beliefs weigh on man. There will be more on this when we come to study specific instances in the Qur'ān.

It is in the light of such need that Islam has taken great care to correct man's beliefs and define very clearly the concept and nature of

God and His attributes, and the relationship between Creator and creation.

This is embodied in the Islamic concept of God's oneness, the essence and most fundamental principle of Islam. Much care has been devoted to establishing and elucidating the affirmation that God is the One, absolute and transcendent Lord and Master of all that exists. The other aspect of this concept to which Islam has given its greatest attention is the definition of God's attributes, which has been the cause of much confusion, obfuscation and muddled religious and philosophical thinking through the ages.

The intensity, emphasis and detail with which Islam has dealt with the concept of God's oneness, and all subjects related to it, can only be appreciated against the background of the great mass of erroneous beliefs and confused theologies that had accumulated in the course of history. From this perspective, Islam can readily be seen as a profound and timely act of divine mercy bestowed on humanity – mercy that is given with beauty, simplicity, clarity, harmony and full accordance with human nature.

The Compassionate, the Merciful. (Verse 3)

These are two attributes that encompass all meanings and aspects of mercy and compassion, and epitomize mercy as a property of God Almighty. These two attributes define the link between the Lord as Creator and His creation. It is a link based entirely on love, peace, reassurance and care, and which inspires within man a spontaneous feeling of gratitude and praise towards God.

Unlike Greek mythology or the Old Testament (Genesis, 4: 11–12), Islam does not depict God as an enemy who pursues man with relentless vengeance, or plots and schemes against His creation with spite and vindictiveness.

Master of the Day of Judgement. (Verse 4)

This verse states a fundamental Islamic principle that has a most profound influence on human life: belief in the hereafter. The Qur'ān comments on the curious fact that people have often believed in God as Creator but have failed to believe in a Day of Judgement, in a life to come, when reward and punishment are meted out to restore the balance of justice. It is in reference to these that the Qur'ān says: *"If you ask them, 'Who is it that created the heavens and the earth?' they will surely answer, 'God.'"* (31: 25) Elsewhere the Qur'ān says of such people: *"They deem it strange that a warner should have come to them from their own midst. Thus, the unbelievers say, 'A strange thing is this! [Are we to be resurrected] after we have died and become mere dust? Such a return seems far-fetched indeed!'"* (50: 2–3)

Belief in the hereafter is essential because it engages the human soul and mind and concentrates man's attention on a future existence. This in turn helps to rein in man's obsession with the present life, and to transcend his immediate earthly desires. He is no longer anxious to reap all his rewards here and now; he can conquer his selfishness and develop altruistic feelings and interests. Man is able to go through life as a motivated, tolerant, confident and optimistic being.

This central Islamic belief distinguishes clearly between aspiring to gain the moral and intellectual freedom that man needs and deserves, and capitulation to worldly and selfish desires and pleasures. It marks the difference between a well-balanced and conscientious humanity and an egotistic, self-seeking one.

Human life can never be balanced and equitable until people believe that what they earn in this transient life is not the be-all and the end-all. Man needs to have the incentive of a confident belief that another life awaits him, which is worth the struggle and the sacrifices and the effort he may have to make here in this short one. This belief brings a fundamental difference in the feelings, attitudes and behaviour of those who uphold it.

> *You alone do we worship and to You alone do we turn for help.* (Verse 5)

This verse expresses another fundamental principle that follows logically from the preceding ones. It is also a decisive and crucial principle that draws a line between the freedom man gains in submitting to God and the abuse and debasement implicit in man's servitude to man.

Once man has submitted himself to God and sought help and guidance from Him alone, he has achieved total liberation from the tyranny of all religious, intellectual, moral and political powers.

To the believer in Islam, human power falls into two categories: a rightly guided power that recognizes God and abides by His directions, and an arrogant, rebellious one that does not admit to God's sovereignty and authority. A Muslim is required to support and endorse the former, no matter how weak or disadvantaged it may be, and to reject and oppose the latter, regardless of its strength or dominance. The Qur'ān says: *"Many a small band, by the grace of God, has vanquished a large one."* (2: 249) Such victory of the apparently weaker host could only be achieved when it relies on God, the source of all power.

Towards natural forces, a Muslim's attitude is one of curiosity and friendliness rather than fear or hostility. The powers of man and the powers of nature are perceived as by-products of God's own power, and subject to His will. They are, therefore, perfectly complementary and interdependent.

Islam teaches that God has created the physical world and all its forces for man's own use and benefit. Man is specifically taught and directed to study the world around him, discover its potential and utilize all his environment for his own good and the good of his fellow humans. Any harm that man suffers at the hands of nature is a result only of his ignorance or lack of understanding of it and of the laws governing it. The more man learns about nature, the more peaceful and harmonious his relationship with nature and the environment.

Hence the notion of "conquering nature" can readily be seen as cynical and negative. It is alien to Islamic perceptions and betrays a shameless ignorance of the spirit in which the world has been created and the divine wisdom that underlies it.

Being always aware of God's hand and role in shaping and running the world, Muslims have a positive, friendly and constructive outlook on man's relationship with nature. Simply stated, it acknowledges God as the origin and Creator of all these forces, on the basis of the same set of axioms and laws. They are designed to function together, for a common purpose, in harmony, compatibility and mutual support. The forces of nature are essentially subservient to man, who is mentally and physically equipped to discern them, unravel their secrets, comprehend the laws governing them and, subsequently, to harness them to improve the quality of life on earth. The Qur'ān asserts: *"He has all that is on the earth subservient to you."* (45: 13)

Such an outlook eliminates all traces of fear or isolation and allows, instead, a profound sense of belonging in which man is seen not only as an integral part of the overall design of the world, but also an essentially effective and influential one. Thus, his world becomes a friendly one. This is best expressed by the Prophet when he once faced Mount Uḥud, the scene of a bitter defeat for Muslims, and said, "How we love this mountain, and how it loves us!" This expresses in a nutshell the affinity the Prophet felt towards nature even in its most rugged forms.

Having established these fundamental principles, the *sūrah* points the way to certain practical means of responding to them, foremost among which is prayer:

> *Guide us on the straight path; the path of those on whom You have bestowed Your favours, not those who have incurred Your wrath, nor those who have gone astray.* (Verses 6–7)

With these words a believer pleads to be shown the Right Way and to be helped along it, which cannot be achieved without God's guidance, care and mercy. To acknowledge that is in itself a recognition of God's sovereignty and dominance over all things and events.

Guidance to the right way of life guarantees man's happiness in this world and in the hereafter. It comes about, in effect, by guiding human nature and man's instincts, desires and inspirations towards the recognition and comprehension of the divine will, so bringing human activity into rhythm with the natural order and the physical world.

The *sūrah* reveals the nature of the "straight path" as being one taken by those whom God has favoured, not the way of those who have earned His displeasure by their deviation from the Truth, nor that of the heedless who have no knowledge of the truth. It is the path of happiness and salvation.

This, then, is *al-Fātiḥah*, the *sūrah* selected for frequent daily recitation, without which Islamic prayers are invalid. Despite its brevity, it contains some of the most fundamental principles of the Islamic faith and certain insights that arise from them.

The Prophet Muḥammad is reliably reported to have quoted God as saying that the fruits of "prayer are shared equally between Me and My servant, and My servant will be granted what he asks for. As the worshipper recites [in Prayer]: *'Praise be to God, the Lord of all the worlds,*' God will say: 'My servant has praised Me.' As he recites: *'The Compassionate, the Merciful,'* God will say: 'My servant has thanked Me.' As he recites: *'Master of the Day of Judgement,'* God will say: 'My servant has glorified Me.' As he says: *'You alone do we worship, and to You alone do we turn for help,'* God will say: 'This is between Me and My servant, and My servant will receive what he asks for.' And, as he says: *'Guide us on the straight path, the path of those on whom You have bestowed Your favours, not those who have incurred Your wrath, nor those who have gone astray,'* God will say: 'This is for My servant, and he will be granted his wish.'"

This *ḥadīth* explores some of the meanings of *al-Fātiḥah*. The reader will perhaps find it helpful in understanding why God has chosen this *sūrah* for recitation by Muslims at least seventeen times a day, as they stand up for their obligatory prayers, spread over the night and day, and even more frequently, whenever they offer voluntary prayers.

SŪRAH 2

Al-Baqarah

(The Cow)

Prologue

This *sūrah* is one of the earliest to be revealed soon after the migration of the Prophet Muḥammad and his companions from Makkah to Madinah in 622 CE. It is the longest *sūrah* in the Qur'ān.

From the varied and wide-ranging context of its verses, it is safe to assume that they were not all revealed in sequence. A common feature of the long Madinan *sūrahs* is that their verses were not revealed in consecutive order. Sometimes, passages of one *sūrah* were revealed before the completion of an earlier one. Hence, the convention in deciding the chronological order of the *sūrahs* has been based on the dates of the revelation of the opening passages, and not of the complete *sūrah*. In this instance, we find that Verses 275–280, prohibiting usury, were among the last Qur'ānic revelations, while the opening parts of the *sūrah* were revealed early in the Madinah period.

The composition and arrangement of the verses within each *sūrah* of the Qur'ān is fixed by God and was directly intimated to Prophet Muḥammad. Al-Tirmidhī reports that 'Abdullāh ibn 'Abbās, a close and learned Companion of the Prophet, said that he had asked 'Uthmān ibn 'Affān, the third Caliph who is universally recognized as having authorized the compilation of the Qur'ānic text as we have it today, why *Sūrah* 8, al-Anfāl, consisting of less than 100 verses, was placed before *Sūrah* 9, al-Tawbah, which comprises over 100 verses, and which, unlike other *sūrahs*, does not contain the usual opening phrase of *"In the name of God, the Compassionate, the Merciful"*? He further enquired from him why *Sūrah* 8 was grouped with the seven long *sūrahs* [that appear at the beginning of the Qur'ān]?

'Uthmān answered, "The Prophet (peace be upon him) used to receive verses or passages from several *sūrahs* at the same time. He would call the scribes and instruct them to put specific verses at specified places in their respective *sūrahs*. Al-Anfāl was one of the earliest *sūrahs* revealed in Madinah while al-Tawbah was one of the latest, but their subject matter was very similar that I suspected they might be one *sūrah*. The Prophet passed away without clarifying this particular point. Therefore, I placed them one after the other without separation."

This account makes it clear that the arrangement of the verses within every *sūrah* was decided on the Prophet's instructions.

Furthermore, authentic *aḥādīth* related by al-Bukhārī and Muslim mention that the Prophet used to recite the Qur'ān for the Archangel Gabriel every night during the month of Ramaḍān, and that both the Prophet and Gabriel recited the whole Qur'ān for each other. Needless to say, he recited the Qur'ān in the right arrangement of its verses and *sūrahs*.

Anyone who studies the Qur'ān closely, and tastes the unique and rich experience of living within its ambience, will immediately identify the distinct character of every one of its *sūrahs*. Every *sūrah* has an aura and a personality of its own, with unique and well-defined features, and a feel that makes it stand apart from all the rest. Moreover, every *sūrah* revolves around a central theme, or a number of major themes related to one another by a common thread or idea. Every *sūrah* radiates its own atmosphere of meaning and essence, within which its theme, or themes, are discussed using the same well integrated and well coordinated style and approach. It also has its own special rhythm and musical pulse which accord with the meaning and context of its topics and content.

These general outstanding features are common to all *sūrahs*, including the longer ones, such as the present one.

This *sūrah* deals with several issues which revolve in total harmony around closely interrelated twin central lines. On the one hand, the *sūrah* discusses the attitude of the Israelites towards Islam and the burgeoning Muslim community in Madinah. It describes aspects of the hostile reception they gave the new religion and their reaction to the Prophet Muḥammad and the growing community of his followers. It explores the close and unholy alliance that had developed between the Jews and the hypocrites of Madinah, professing belief in Islam, on the one hand, and between the Jews and the Arab idolaters of the rest of Arabia, on the other.

On the other hand, the *sūrah*, having established the Israelites' failure to uphold God's trust and honour their covenant with Him, discusses the vicissitudes faced by the Muslim community during its formative years, and the manner and environment in which it developed, and prepared and mobilized itself for the great task of inheriting the trust of the establishment of God's sovereignty on earth. The *sūrah* decisively and swiftly strips the Israelites of their association with Abraham, the great proponent of monotheistic belief, and the source of all the honours and privileges that go with it.

This two-fold central theme forms the backbone of the *sūrah*'s subject matter as a whole and shadows the growth and progress of Islam and the Muslim community in Madinah during the period from 622 to 632 CE.

To set the contents of this *sūrah* in their appropriate context, it would be pertinent to throw more light on the historic environment and the religious and social setting in which the verses were revealed. Before we do that, however, it is important to point out that, in general terms, what the Muslims had to face in those early days was a miniature of, and a rehearsal for, what has occurred throughout the later history of Islam, albeit with some variations of scope and detail. The setbacks and the achievements, the allies and the opponents have invariably been the same.

This fact highlights the role and status of the Qur'ān as the unchallenged, immutable and incontrovertible authoritative reference for the religious, ethical and legislative principles and systems of Islam. It further affirms the unique property of the Qur'ānic text as being ever fresh and responsive to the inevitable changes that come with the perpetuation and progress of human life.

With these qualities, the Qur'ān remains the eternal guiding light for Muslims, despite the difficulties and hardships they have to suffer or the animosity and hostility they have to face. This, in itself, is an aspect of the inimitability and unsurpassed veracity and beauty of every verse in the Qur'ān.

Seeking a Secure Base

The Prophet Muḥammad's migration from Makkah to Madinah in 622 CE was undertaken after meticulous planning and with appropriate care and attention to detail. Leaving Makkah had become unavoidable in consequence of events: the indigenous Quraysh Arabs of Makkah were pursuing a relentlessly hostile and oppressive campaign against the Prophet personally, and his mission and followers in general. This campaign had intensified following the double personal tragedy of 619 CE in which the Prophet had lost his wife Khadījah, who had been to him a pillar of personal support and strength, and his uncle Abū Ṭālib, his guardian and protector. This tragedy greatly restricted Muḥammad's movement and his followers' activities in and around Makkah.

While the conflict between Muḥammad and his tribal cousins, led by Abū Lahab, ʿAmr ibn Hishām and Abū Sufyān ibn Ḥarb, reached a stalemate within Makkah, his message was gaining converts and supporters outside it. The majority of provincial Arabs, however, elected to watch from a distance what they viewed as a purely internal dispute over power within the Quraysh. It would not do for them to become embroiled in supporting the religion of a man whose own tribe had denounced him, especially since that tribe held the custodianship of the sacred Kaʿbah and assumed supreme religious authority for the whole of Arabia.

The Prophet had to seek an alternative home for his new faith, and a base where he could be protected, so that he could break the deadlock he had reached in Makkah, and be allowed to pursue his commission unimpeded. This, in my view, was the first and most important reason for leaving Makkah.

Before Madinah, other destinations had been proposed and tried as alternatives to Makkah. In 615, only a few years after Muḥammad's call to prophethood in 610 CE, a number of early Muslims had emigrated to Abyssinia. It would not be correct to say that they had gone there for reasons of personal safety alone. Had this been the case, the emigrants would have included the weakest and least supported elements among the Muslims. These were the ones at the receiving end of a sustained persecution campaign. But the reverse was the case. The emigrants included some of the most powerful of the Prophet's followers and tribesmen. The majority of them were from the tribe of Quraysh, including Ja'far ibn Abī Ṭālib, and a number of young men who were accustomed to providing protection to the Prophet, such as al-Zubayr ibn al-'Awwām, 'Abdur Raḥmān ibn 'Awf, Abū Salamah al-Makhzūmī, 'Uthmān ibn 'Affān, to mention but a few. There were women belonging to some of the most prominent families of the Quraysh, such as Umm Ḥabībah, daughter of Abū Sufyān, the Quraysh's unrivalled non-Muslim leader. Such women would never be persecuted in Makkah.

There were, no doubt, other reasons for the Muslims' emigration to Abyssinia. There was the need to shake the religious and social foundations of the Quraysh's most noble and powerful families. There could be no greater insult or threat to the Quraysh dynasties than seeing their proudest and most noble sons and daughters running away for conscientious and religious reasons, leaving their cultural heritage and tribal homeland behind.

Whatever other reasons there might have been for the Muslims' emigration to Abyssinia, the fact remains that the search had started very early on for a safe haven for Islam, or a secure base where it could flourish and spread freely. This is further supported by reports of the Negus of Abyssinia's conversion to Islam, which only the threatened rebellion of his patriarchs prevented him from making public, as some reliable accounts confirm.

Following the death of his uncle, Abū Ṭālib, in 619 CE and as a result of the Quraysh's growing hostility, the Prophet sought help from the Thaqīf tribe who lived in the town of Ṭā'if, some 90 km east of Makkah. The effort ended in failure because the Thaqīf gave him a most hostile reception. They mocked him and heaped scorn on him. They let loose their louts and their children to chase him and throw stones at him, causing his feet to bleed.

The Prophet's biographers tell us that he took refuge in an orchard belonging to 'Utbah ibn Rabī'ah and his brother Shaybah, where he made a most moving and emotional appeal to God, saying, "To You, my Lord, I complain of my weakness, lack of support and the humiliation I am made to receive. Most compassionate and merciful! You are the Lord of the weak, and You are my Lord. To whom do You leave me? To a distant person who receives me with hostility? Or an enemy to whom You have given power over me? If You are not displeased with me I do not care what I face. I would, however, be much happier with Your mercy. I seek refuge in Your face by which all darkness is dispelled and both this life and the life to come are put in their right courses against incurring Your wrath or being the subject of Your anger. To You I submit, until I earn Your pleasure. Everything is powerless without Your support."

A Major Breakthrough

Not long after that, the Prophet's, and Islam's, fortunes suddenly changed for the better. At a place called 'Aqabah near Makkah, the Prophet had two crucial historic meetings in 621 and 622 CE with a group of Arabs from Madinah, during which they pledged their allegiance and support. This was to have a profound and far-reaching effect on the whole future of Islam and the Muslim community.

Towards the end of the Makkan period, the Prophet Muḥammad embarked on a concerted effort of making contact with various influential Arab communities and tribes to introduce Islam to them and seek their following and support.

The Khazraj and the Aws, the two Arab tribes of Madinah, having lived side by side with the Jews, had often heard them boast about "the Prophet who will come soon" and "whose day is at hand", who would lead the Jews to victory over the Arabs. A group of the Khazraj pilgrims met the Prophet who explained to them his message. They immediately realized that he was the very Prophet the Jews were talking about. They were determined to get to him before the Jews did. Having met him and listened to what he had to say, they accepted him and became Muslims. They said to him: "We have left our people in an unprecedented state of mutual hostility. May God make you the cause of their unity." On their return home, they reported what they did to their people who approved their action.

The following year a delegation comprising members of the two tribes of the Aws and the Khazraj, arrived in Makkah to meet the Prophet. They declared their acceptance of Islam and their allegiance. He sent them back with one of his senior companions to teach them the Qur'ān and instruct them in their new religion.

At the following annual Pilgrimage, a larger group from both tribes came to Makkah, and offered to make a covenant with the Prophet Muḥammad. This was attended by his then non-Muslim uncle al-'Abbās. The covenant bound them to support Muḥammad and defend him as they would their own families and property. This is known as the second 'Aqabah covenant.

'Abdullāh ibn Rawāḥah of the Madinah people is reported to have stood up and asked the Prophet to "put forward your Lord's and your own conditions."

Muḥammad replied, "My Lord's condition is that you worship Him alone and take no other gods beside Him. As for myself, my condition is that you give me the protection you would give yourselves and your property."

'Abdullāh asked, "What do we receive in return?"

"Paradise!" the Prophet replied.

They said, "This is a profitable deal on which none will go back."

Thus the Arabs of Madinah committed themselves to Islam and to following Muḥammad and defending him. Islam was to spread rapidly and entrench itself among them. The Muslims of Makkah began to arrive in Madinah in droves, abandoning their belongings and material possessions and taking only their faith. They were warmly welcomed by their fellow Muslims, who offered to share with them everything they had.

Eventually the time came for the Prophet himself to migrate to Madinah. He was accompanied by his close and trusted companion Abū Bakr. At last Muḥammad had found the safe haven he had been looking for all those years, where he and his followers would be free to proclaim the faith and establish their community. The Prophet's arrival in Madinah was to prove a crucial turning point in the history of Islam.

The Making of a Unique Community

The community taking shape in Madinah was a unique and distinguished one, praised repeatedly throughout the Qur'ān. This *sūrah* opens with a concise, generally applicable, definition of true believers. Nevertheless, it refers specifically to those early pioneers of Islam: *"This is the Book; there is no doubt about it, a guidance for the God-fearing. Those who believe in what lies beyond the reach of human perception, observe Prayer and give of what We bestow upon them. Those who believe in what has been revealed to you and what was revealed before you, and are certain of the Hereafter. Those follow their Lord's guidance, and they shall surely prosper."* (Verses 1–5)

In contrast, we are immediately given a description of the unbelievers, which is again general and universal but applies specifically to those who rejected Islam and opposed it, in and around both Makkah and Madinah: *"For the unbelievers, it is alike whether you forewarn them or not, they will not accept the faith. God has sealed their hearts and ears; their eyes are covered; and a grievous punishment awaits them."* (Verses 6–7)

In Madinah, a third group emerged, the hypocrites, or *al-Munāfiqūn*. This faction had not been noticeable in Makkah; its rise was prompted by the Prophet's arrival and settlement in Madinah, as outlined earlier. That was because in Makkah, Islam had no sovereign political entity or force, and the Muslims remained soft targets for persecution and repression by the rest of the Arabs. Those who accepted Islam had to be brave and sincere, prepared to endure all kinds of hardship and terror.

In Madinah, hitherto known as Yathrib, the picture was very different. Islam was gradually gaining strength and the Muslims were developing into a dominant force. This became even more evident following their decisive victory over the non-Muslim Arabs at Badr, 125 kms south of Madinah, in February of 624 CE. This caused some people, including a number of leading and privileged figures, to feign acceptance of Islam merely to save their position and protect their social and tribal status and interests. Thus they came to be known as the 'hypocrites' in Islamic terminology. One of the most prominent of these was 'Abdullāh ibn Ubayy ibn Salūl who, prior to the Prophet's arrival in Madinah, was about to be crowned as a king of the city.

At the beginning of the *sūrah*, we find a detailed description of the hypocrites (Verses 8–20) from which it can easily be seen that they included those who had reluctantly embraced Islam and had not totally relinquished their self-pride and arrogance.

We also find a reference to their 'evil companions', which the context of the *sūrah* indicates to be the Jews, who were at the forefront of opposition and hostility to Islam. The *sūrah* devotes a fair amount of space to a series of stinging attacks on the Jews who were ranged against Islam and the Prophet Muḥammad.

The Jews were the first community to confront Islam in Madinah, for several reasons. As a people with an established religious heritage and culture, the Jews enjoyed a privileged and highly esteemed position among the illiterate Arabs of Madinah from both tribes of the Aws and the Khazraj. However, the pagan Arabs had not shown any great enthusiasm or inclination to embrace the Jewish religion. Nevertheless, they acknowledged that the Jews were better versed in matters of religious wisdom than they were. Moreover, the tense, and at times bloody, rivalry existing between these two tribes provided the Jews with an ideal environment for manipulation and exploitation.

When Islam came to Madinah, those advantages and privileges came under threat. Not only did Islam come to embrace and endorse Jewish Scriptures and beliefs, but it immediately aimed to eliminate the existing feuds and divisions between the Arab tribes and integrate them into a unified and harmonious community, unique in the whole history of mankind.

Above all, the Jews had claimed to be God's own chosen people, heirs of earlier prophets, true inheritors and custodians of the divine message, and the people from among whom the new Prophet, foretold in their own scriptures, was most likely to be selected. When an Arab prophet emerged, they expected him to discredit them and restrict the new religion to his own people, the Arabs. But, as Muḥammad went on to introduce his message to the Jews, as recipients of earlier revelations and therefore more likely to respond and give him their support, they became arrogant and self-important and took offence.

They were overwhelmed with envy and jealousy towards Muḥammad on two grounds: first, for being chosen as God's Messenger and, second, for the rapid and growing success he was having in and around Madinah.

But, of course, there was another very important reason for their unease and hostility. They had seen the threat of becoming marginalized and isolated within Madinah itself, where they had held spiritual as well as commercial sway for such a long time. The alternative would be to embrace the new faith and become assimilated into the Muslim community, losing their identity and separate existence for ever. Their options were thus severely restricted.

These factors explain the stance taken by the Jews towards Islam; a stance which has been extensively explored on several occasions in the Qur'ān. In this *sūrah*, we find the Qur'ān appealing to the Israelites, reminding them of the attitudes and conduct of their ancestors towards earlier Prophets, and recalling their stubbornness and intransigence, and their betrayal of God's trust and covenant.

The images and examples cited from the chequered and turbulent Jewish past were familiar in Muḥammad's time, and reflected the true nature of the Jewish psyche and attitude. Those features have accompanied the Jews in every generation and remain typical of their behaviour even today. For this reason, the Qur'ān has adopted a unique and revealing style in addressing all Israelite generations as one and the same, which again makes these accounts relevant for all time: past, present and future. Thus, the Qur'ānic words shall remain a timely and pertinent guide, and a warning, to Muslims in every generation with respect to the identity and potential intrigues of the enemies of their faith.

The *Sūrah*'s Central Theme

A significant part of the *sūrah* is devoted to the foundation and essential preparation of the Muslim community which was to carry God's message to the world, the Israelites having notably failed to undertake that noble task. Indeed, they were now in opposition to its final version, Islam.

Having introduced the three main types of humanity: believers, unbelievers and hypocrites, and having made a clear though implicit reference to the 'evil ones', the *sūrah* addresses mankind as a whole, asking them to worship the One God and fully acknowledge the revelations He has bestowed on His Messenger. It affirms God's favour and wisdom in creating the earth and the heavens, and all that is in them, for the use and benefit of man. (Verses 21–29)

This is followed by an account of the occasion when God appointed man as His vicegerent and representative on earth, outlining the terms and conditions of that auspicious appointment. (Verses 30–39)

The following section of the *sūrah* is devoted entirely to an extensive and wide-ranging debate with the Israelites, dealing critically with various aspects of their religious and historic record. (Verses 40–141)

The discussion focuses on the Israelites' reception of Islam in Madinah. They were the first to actively reject it. They deliberately confused and concealed facts. They adopted a two-faced attitude towards faith and attempted to distort God's words. They cheated, lied and broke faith with the Muslims in the hope of turning them away from their religion. They claimed the exclusive possession of God's trust and a monopoly of righteousness. They became envious of the Muslims and spared no effort to undermine their existence and cause them harm. Last, but not least, they allied themselves with Islam's enemies, the hypocrites and pagan Arabs, and were prepared to conspire with them against the Muslim community.

In consequence, the *sūrah* launches a bitter and fierce attack on the Jews, drawing its justification from their behaviour towards Moses and their reaction to the laws given them by God and the prophets and messengers He sent them. All generations of the Jewish nation are addressed as one group.

The attack ends with an admonition to the Muslims never to hold any hope that the Jews will ever reconcile themselves to accepting or acknowledging Islam. It goes on to lambast the Jewish claim to the monotheistic legacy of Abraham, and to establish Muḥammad and his followers as the true heirs of Abraham's faith who are entitled to inherit his covenant with God. It affirms that the inheritance by Muslims of the guardianship of God's message to man had come as a fulfilment of Abraham's and Ishmael's prayers to God while constructing the Ka'bah, the symbol of surrender and the Sacred House devoted to the worship of the One God.

From then on, the *sūrah* addresses the Muslims, instructing them how to fulfil their role as guardians and carriers of God's Message to mankind. It offers guidance on the beliefs and concepts that were to distinguish the Muslim faith and way of life for all time to come. (Verses 142–283)

This part begins by defining the *qiblah*, the direction to which Muslims should turn when praying. It was to be the sacred site at Makkah housing the Ka'bah, the House of God built by Abraham and Ishmael, its first keepers and custodians. The *sūrah* tells us that even while the Muslims had been praying towards Jerusalem, the centre of Judaism, Muḥammad was privately yearning for the Ka'bah to become the exclusive direction for the Muslims during Prayer. (Verse 144)

The *sūrah* goes on to outline the principles and systems of Islam in several fields including faith and outlook, rites of worship and religious matters, personal and public behaviour and conduct. It teaches the Muslims that those who give their lives for the cause of God never die; that insecurity, hunger and poverty are not necessarily evil in themselves, but are means to test the believers, to assess their potential and refine and strengthen their capacity to advance God's cause in the world. It reassures Muslims that God is their patron and will always be on their side, while their detractors and opponents will be led astray into a wilderness of darkness by impostors, false mentors and bogus leaders. The *sūrah* outlines aspects of lawful and unlawful food and drink, penal measures, rules governing wills, fasting, war, and pilgrimage. It dwells at length on the regulation and organization of family affairs, including marriage and divorce, and covers rules governing spending, usury, lending and trade.

Although during this extensive discussion the *sūrah* refers, from time to time, to instances and glimpses from Jewish history, the main body of the second part deals basically with the structure and organization of the Muslim community, and the essential features and qualifications it requires to uphold God's message and fulfil its prime role as His trustee and the custodian of His message for all time to come.

The following section of the *sūrah* is almost entirely devoted to the education, formation and building of the Muslim community, which was destined to take up the task of expounding God's message to the rest of humanity. We continue, from time to time, to come across discourses and arguments dealing with those opposed to Islam, especially the Israelites, and their plots and schemes to thwart its progress and stifle the growth of the Muslim community. There are also instructions to the Muslims on how to fight back and what precautions to take in order to avoid their traps.

Nevertheless, the chief concern of this section, and of the rest of the *sūrah*, remains the establishment and codification of the distinguishing qualities and features of the Muslim community. It is a community that has its own laws, confirming and succeeding those of earlier Divine Revelation, its own *qiblah*, and above all its distinct and original outlook on the world and life as a whole. It is a community that is fully cognizant of its relationship with God and of its leading role in the world, and the responsibilities and obligations stemming from that role. It is a community that is confidently and loyally poised to submit fully to God's will and command, as ordained and articulated in the Qur'ān and the teachings and work of the Prophet Muḥammad, God's peace and blessings be upon him.

We learn that the *qiblah* issue is related to the fact that the Muslim community is a moderate and middle-of-the-road community. By virtue of their message and role in the world, Muslims shall be God's witness to the rest of mankind, while Muḥammad shall be a witness to them. The Qur'ān accords the Muslims a leading status in the world, and calls on them to work hard, persevere and make all the sacrifices that are required of them to earn that status and fulfil their role, putting their trust fully in God's will and wisdom.

We come across some important elaboration of basic Islamic concepts such as *taqwā*, fearing God, and *'amal ṣāliḥ*, good works. This comes in the course of refuting Jewish arguments concerning the change of the *qiblah*, which are based on distortion of the facts and faulty interpretations of Divine instructions.

The *sūrah* then turns to setting out rules and regulations for the religious and practical life of the community. These include penalties for capital offences and rules relating to wills, fasting during the month of Ramaḍān, going to war during the sacred months and within the surrounds of the Ka'bah, the *Ḥajj*, or Pilgrimage, drinking and gambling, and family affairs. The common denominator underpinning all these duties and regulations is sound belief and strong faith in God Almighty.

The section contains a discussion on *jihād*, citing an important episode from the history of the Israelites after Moses, during the reign of the Prophet David, which has many essential lessons for the Muslims as heirs of Abraham's religious tradition and the responsibility of world leadership.

The *sūrah* has given us a good idea of the nature of the battle the Qur'ān was fighting and the environment it was fighting in while it was being revealed, and the objectives it was aiming to achieve in raising and building the Muslim community in the 7th century CE. The atmosphere among the Makkan Arabs was one of intrigue, mischief, confusion and falsehood. Human weakness and greed also had to be taken into account.

Above all, the Qur'ān was aiming to establish and articulate upright concepts and sound principles on which the community could be raised, and to chart for it a course for a righteous and dignified leadership of the world.

The enduring qualities of the Qur'ān are vindicated by the fact that the principles, rules and instructions it propounded fourteen centuries ago remain today, and for all time to come, essential for the regeneration and reconstruction of Muslim society. The battles and the issues and the controversies remain the same. The enemies, and the means and weapons used against the Qur'ān and its followers also remain fundamentally the same. To fight and win today's battles, Muslims will need to follow the Qur'ānic principles and teachings which shaped and guided that pioneering Muslim community of Madinah.

Muslims today need the Qur'ān for a better and a more realistic understanding of the world and their role in it. No other source exists that can provide them with the inspiration, the practical guidance and the complete way of life they need to forge ahead and assume the leadership of the world again.

The closing two verses take us full circle to the opening of the *sūrah*, affirming the Muslim world community's eternal belief in all Prophets and messages sent by God to man, without exception, and in what lies beyond the reach of human perception. They assert the Muslims' total unqualified faith in, and submission to, the One God.

Thus, the ending of the *sūrah* coalesces smoothly with its beginning, as the subject matter is shaped and honed to give a complete and superb example of the Qur'ān's inimitable and powerful style.

I

The Message Spelt Out

Al-Baqarah (The Cow)

سُورَةُ البَقَرَةِ

In the Name of God, the Merciful, the Beneficent.

بِسۡمِ ٱللَّهِ ٱلرَّحۡمَٰنِ ٱلرَّحِيمِ

Alif, lām, mīm. (1)

الٓمٓ ﴿١﴾

This is the Book; there is no doubt about it, a guidance for the God-fearing. (2)

ذَٰلِكَ ٱلۡكِتَٰبُ لَا رَيۡبَۛ فِيهِۛ
هُدٗى لِّلۡمُتَّقِينَ ﴿٢﴾

Those who believe in what lies beyond the reach of human perception, observe Prayer and give of what We bestow upon them. (3)

ٱلَّذِينَ يُؤۡمِنُونَ بِٱلۡغَيۡبِ وَيُقِيمُونَ ٱلصَّلَوٰةَ
وَمِمَّا رَزَقۡنَٰهُمۡ يُنفِقُونَ ﴿٣﴾

Those who believe in what has been revealed to you and what was revealed before you, and are certain of the Hereafter. (4)

وَٱلَّذِينَ يُؤۡمِنُونَ بِمَآ أُنزِلَ إِلَيۡكَ وَمَآ أُنزِلَ
مِن قَبۡلِكَ وَبِٱلۡأٓخِرَةِ هُمۡ يُوقِنُونَ ﴿٤﴾

Those follow their Lord's guidance, and they shall surely prosper. (5)

أُوْلَٰٓئِكَ عَلَىٰ هُدٗى مِّن رَّبِّهِمۡۖ وَأُوْلَٰٓئِكَ هُمُ
ٱلۡمُفۡلِحُونَ ﴿٥﴾

For the unbelievers, it is alike whether you forewarn them or not, they will not accept the faith. (6)

إِنَّ ٱلَّذِينَ كَفَرُوا۟ سَوَآءٌ عَلَيْهِمْ
ءَأَنذَرْتَهُمْ أَمْ لَمْ تُنذِرْهُمْ لَا يُؤْمِنُونَ ﴿٦﴾

God has sealed their hearts and ears; their eyes are covered; and a grievous punishment awaits them. (7)

خَتَمَ ٱللَّهُ عَلَىٰ قُلُوبِهِمْ وَعَلَىٰ سَمْعِهِمْ ۖ
وَعَلَىٰٓ أَبْصَٰرِهِمْ غِشَٰوَةٌ ۖ وَلَهُمْ عَذَابٌ
عَظِيمٌ ﴿٧﴾

There are some who say: 'We believe in God and the Last Day', yet, in truth, they do not believe. (8)

وَمِنَ ٱلنَّاسِ مَن يَقُولُ ءَامَنَّا بِٱللَّهِ وَبِٱلْيَوْمِ
ٱلْءَاخِرِ وَمَا هُم بِمُؤْمِنِينَ ﴿٨﴾

They seek to deceive God and the believers, but they are only deceiving themselves, though they may not realize it. (9)

يُخَٰدِعُونَ ٱللَّهَ وَٱلَّذِينَ ءَامَنُوا۟
وَمَا يَخْدَعُونَ إِلَّآ أَنفُسَهُمْ
وَمَا يَشْعُرُونَ ﴿٩﴾

There is sickness in their hearts, and God has aggravated their sickness. Painful suffering awaits them for the lies they keep telling. (10)

فِى قُلُوبِهِم مَّرَضٌ فَزَادَهُمُ ٱللَّهُ
مَرَضًا ۖ وَلَهُمْ عَذَابٌ أَلِيمٌۢ بِمَا
كَانُوا۟ يَكْذِبُونَ ﴿١٠﴾

When it is said to them: 'Do not spread corruption in the land', they say: 'We are but doers of good.' (11)

وَإِذَا قِيلَ لَهُمْ لَا تُفْسِدُوا۟ فِى ٱلْأَرْضِ قَالُوٓا۟
إِنَّمَا نَحْنُ مُصْلِحُونَ ﴿١١﴾

But, they indeed are the ones who do spread corruption, though they do not realize it. (12)

أَلَآ إِنَّهُمْ هُمُ ٱلْمُفْسِدُونَ وَلَٰكِن
لَّا يَشْعُرُونَ ﴿١٢﴾

When it is said to them, 'Believe as other people have believed', they say, 'Are we to believe as the fools believe?' It is indeed they who are fools, though they do not know it. (13)

وَإِذَا قِيلَ لَهُمْ ءَامِنُوا۟ كَمَآ ءَامَنَ ٱلنَّاسُ قَالُوٓا۟
أَنُؤْمِنُ كَمَآ ءَامَنَ ٱلسُّفَهَآءُ ۗ أَلَآ إِنَّهُمْ هُمُ
ٱلسُّفَهَآءُ وَلَٰكِن لَّا يَعْلَمُونَ ﴿١٣﴾

When they meet the believers, they say, 'We believe', but when they are alone with their devilish allies, they say, 'We are with you, we are only mocking.' (14)

وَإِذَا لَقُوا۟ ٱلَّذِينَ ءَامَنُوا۟ قَالُوٓا۟ ءَامَنَّا وَإِذَا
خَلَوْا۟ إِلَىٰ شَيَٰطِينِهِمْ قَالُوٓا۟ إِنَّا مَعَكُمْ إِنَّمَا
نَحْنُ مُسْتَهْزِءُونَ ﴿١٤﴾

God will put them to derision and let them continue their transgression, blundering blindly along. (15)

ٱللَّهُ يَسْتَهْزِئُ بِهِمْ وَيَمُدُّهُمْ فِى طُغْيَٰنِهِمْ
يَعْمَهُونَ ﴿١٥﴾

These are the ones who barter away guidance for error. Their transaction is profitless and they will receive no guidance. (16)

أُو۟لَٰٓئِكَ ٱلَّذِينَ ٱشْتَرَوُا۟ ٱلضَّلَٰلَةَ
بِٱلْهُدَىٰ فَمَا رَبِحَت تِّجَٰرَتُهُمْ وَمَا كَانُوا۟
مُهْتَدِينَ ﴿١٦﴾

They are like one who sought to kindle a fire, and as it lit up all around him God took away their light and left them in darkness, unable to see anything. (17)

مَثَلُهُمْ كَمَثَلِ ٱلَّذِى ٱسْتَوْقَدَ نَارًا فَلَمَّآ
أَضَآءَتْ مَا حَوْلَهُۥ ذَهَبَ ٱللَّهُ بِنُورِهِمْ
وَتَرَكَهُمْ فِى ظُلُمَٰتٍ لَّا يُبْصِرُونَ ﴿١٧﴾

Deaf, dumb and blind, they can never return to the right path. (18)

صُمٌّۢ بُكْمٌ عُمْىٌ فَهُمْ لَا يَرْجِعُونَ ﴿١٨﴾

Or, when there is a storm-cloud, dark, charged with thunder and lightning, they thrust their fingers in their ears at every thunder-clap, for fear of death; but God encompasses the unbelievers. (19)

أَوْ كَصَيِّبٍ مِّنَ ٱلسَّمَآءِ فِيهِ ظُلُمَٰتٌ
وَرَعْدٌ وَبَرْقٌ يَجْعَلُونَ أَصَٰبِعَهُمْ فِىٓ
ءَاذَانِهِم مِّنَ ٱلصَّوَٰعِقِ حَذَرَ ٱلْمَوْتِ ۚ
وَٱللَّهُ مُحِيطٌۢ بِٱلْكَٰفِرِينَ ﴿١٩﴾

The lightning all but snatches away their sight; whenever it flashes over them they walk on, but when darkness overtakes them they stand still. Should God will it, He would take away their hearing and their sight, for God has power over all things. (20)

يَكَادُ ٱلْبَرْقُ يَخْطَفُ أَبْصَٰرَهُمْ ۖ كُلَّمَآ أَضَآءَ
لَهُم مَّشَوْا۟ فِيهِ وَإِذَآ أَظْلَمَ عَلَيْهِمْ قَامُوا۟ ۚ وَلَوْ
شَآءَ ٱللَّهُ لَذَهَبَ بِسَمْعِهِمْ وَأَبْصَٰرِهِمْ ۚ
إِنَّ ٱللَّهَ عَلَىٰ كُلِّ شَىْءٍ قَدِيرٌ ﴿٢٠﴾

Mankind, worship your Lord who has created you and those who lived before you, so that you may become God-fearing. (21)

يَٰٓأَيُّهَا ٱلنَّاسُ ٱعْبُدُوا۟ رَبَّكُمُ ٱلَّذِى خَلَقَكُمْ
وَٱلَّذِينَ مِن قَبْلِكُمْ لَعَلَّكُمْ تَتَّقُونَ ﴿٢١﴾

He made the earth a couch for you, and the heavens a ceiling. He sent down water from the sky to bring forth fruits for your sustenance. Do not, then, knowingly set up equals to God. (22)

ٱلَّذِى جَعَلَ لَكُمُ ٱلْأَرْضَ فِرَٰشًا وَٱلسَّمَآءَ
بِنَآءً وَأَنزَلَ مِنَ ٱلسَّمَآءِ مَآءً فَأَخْرَجَ بِهِۦ مِنَ
ٱلثَّمَرَٰتِ رِزْقًا لَّكُمْ ۖ فَلَا تَجْعَلُوا۟ لِلَّهِ
أَندَادًا وَأَنتُمْ تَعْلَمُونَ ﴿٢٢﴾

If you are in doubt as to what We have revealed to Our servant, then produce one sūrah comparable to it and call upon all your witnesses, other than God, if what you say is true. (23)

وَإِن كُنتُمْ فِى رَيْبٍ مِّمَّا نَزَّلْنَا عَلَىٰ
عَبْدِنَا فَأْتُوا۟ بِسُورَةٍ مِّن مِّثْلِهِۦ وَٱدْعُوا۟
شُهَدَآءَكُم مِّن دُونِ ٱللَّهِ إِن كُنتُمْ
صَٰدِقِينَ ﴿٢٣﴾

But if you fail, as you will certainly do, then guard yourselves against the fire, fuelled by men and stones, prepared for the unbelievers. (24)

فَإِن لَّمْ تَفْعَلُوا۟ وَلَن تَفْعَلُوا۟ فَٱتَّقُوا۟ ٱلنَّارَ
ٱلَّتِى وَقُودُهَا ٱلنَّاسُ وَٱلْحِجَارَةُ ۖ أُعِدَّتْ
لِلْكَـٰفِرِينَ ﴿٢٤﴾

To those who believe and do good deeds give the good tidings that they shall reside in gardens through which running waters flow. Whenever they are offered fruits therefrom, they say, 'We have been given the same before', for they shall be provided with what looks similar. They shall also have pure spouses and they shall reside there for ever. (25)

وَبَشِّرِ ٱلَّذِينَ ءَامَنُوا۟ وَعَمِلُوا۟ ٱلصَّـٰلِحَـٰتِ
أَنَّ لَهُمْ جَنَّـٰتٍ تَجْرِى مِن تَحْتِهَا ٱلْأَنْهَـٰرُ ۖ
كُلَّمَا رُزِقُوا۟ مِنْهَا مِن ثَمَرَةٍ رِّزْقًا ۙ
قَالُوا۟ هَـٰذَا ٱلَّذِى رُزِقْنَا مِن قَبْلُ ۖ وَأُتُوا۟ بِهِۦ
مُتَشَـٰبِهًا ۖ وَلَهُمْ فِيهَآ أَزْوَٰجٌ مُّطَهَّرَةٌ ۖ
وَهُمْ فِيهَا خَـٰلِدُونَ ﴿٢٥﴾

God does not disdain to give a parable of a gnat, or a higher creature. Those who believe know that it is the truth from their Lord, while the unbelievers ask, 'What could God mean by such a parable?' In this way, God lets many go astray and gives guidance to many others, but none does He leave to go astray except the evildoers. (26)

إِنَّ ٱللَّهَ لَا يَسْتَحْىِۦٓ أَن يَضْرِبَ مَثَلًا
مَّا بَعُوضَةً فَمَا فَوْقَهَا ۚ فَأَمَّا ٱلَّذِينَ
ءَامَنُوا۟ فَيَعْلَمُونَ أَنَّهُ ٱلْحَقُّ مِن
رَّبِّهِمْ ۖ وَأَمَّا ٱلَّذِينَ كَفَرُوا۟
فَيَقُولُونَ مَاذَآ أَرَادَ ٱللَّهُ بِهَـٰذَا مَثَلًا ۘ
يُضِلُّ بِهِۦ كَثِيرًا وَيَهْدِى بِهِۦ كَثِيرًا ۚ
وَمَا يُضِلُّ بِهِۦٓ إِلَّا ٱلْفَـٰسِقِينَ ﴿٢٦﴾

Who violate God's covenant after having accepted it, and cut asunder what He has ordered to be joined, and spread corruption in the land. They are the losers. (27)

ٱلَّذِينَ يَنقُضُونَ عَهْدَ ٱللَّهِ مِنۢ بَعْدِ
مِيثَـٰقِهِۦ وَيَقْطَعُونَ مَآ أَمَرَ ٱللَّهُ بِهِۦٓ أَن
يُوصَلَ وَيُفْسِدُونَ فِى ٱلْأَرْضِ ۚ
أُو۟لَـٰٓئِكَ هُمُ ٱلْخَـٰسِرُونَ ﴿٢٧﴾

How can you reject God who has given you life after you were dead? He will cause you to die again then He will bring you back to life. To Him you shall return. (28)

كَيْفَ تَكْفُرُونَ بِٱللَّهِ وَكُنتُمْ
أَمْوَٰتًا فَأَحْيَٰكُمْ ۖ ثُمَّ يُمِيتُكُمْ
ثُمَّ يُحْيِيكُمْ ثُمَّ إِلَيْهِ تُرْجَعُونَ ﴿٢٨﴾

It is He who created for you all that is on earth. He then turned to heaven and fashioned it into seven heavens. He has knowledge of all things. (29)

هُوَ ٱلَّذِى خَلَقَ لَكُم مَّا فِى ٱلْأَرْضِ
جَمِيعًا ثُمَّ ٱسْتَوَىٰٓ إِلَى ٱلسَّمَآءِ
فَسَوَّىٰهُنَّ سَبْعَ سَمَٰوَٰتٍ ۚ وَهُوَ بِكُلِّ
شَىْءٍ عَلِيمٌ ﴿٢٩﴾

Overview

This opening passage of the *sūrah* outlines the essential features of the religious groups the Muslim community faced in Madinah, with the exception of the Jews, to whom only a brief, but adequate, reference is made. They are described as the 'satans' or 'evil companions' of the hypocrites; a description that says a great deal about their qualities and the nature of their role. They are dealt with in more detail later on in the *sūrah*.

In delineating the features of these groups, the special characteristics of the Qur'ānic style are clearly displayed. Words are used as an artist uses lines and colours, and through them images slowly begin to take on shape and life.

At the outset, in a few words and sentences, profiles of three types of people emerge, each a true representation of a group of human beings such as recurs in every day and age. Indeed, all mankind in all ages and places can be classified into these types. This is a fine example of the eloquence and power of the Qur'ānic style.

In these brief and highly informative sentences and verses, pictures are brought to life with a power and focus that no lengthy or elaborate rendition could ever provide. A few rapid touches combine with the beauties of style and rhythm to supreme effect.

Following this concise and powerful introduction, the *sūrah* addresses all people in the world, calling on them to belong to the first category of mankind. It urges man to believe in the One God, the Creator, Sustainer and Provider, who has no equals or partners. It challenges those sceptics who doubt the truth of the Prophet Muḥammad's message, and of the revelations he received, to come up with a single *sūrah* to compare with the Qur'ān. It complements the challenge with a severe warning of horrible punishment for those who reject God's message, and a promise of everlasting bliss and happiness for those who trust and believe in God and His revelations.

The passage then responds to certain Jews and hypocrites who had questioned the use of parables in the Qur'ān, which they used as an excuse to doubt the truth and validity of Divine revelations altogether. It gives them a stern warning that they are departing from God's path, in contrast to the believers, who are drawn closer to God and strengthened in faith. It denounces their denial of God who gives life and takes it away, the Creator who controls all and whose knowledge of things and events in this vast universe is all-embracing and comprehensive. It is God who has bestowed His grace on mankind by making the earth and all that it contains, to be under their control and for their benefit.

These are the main themes of this opening passage of the *sūrah*, and we shall now go on to look into them in more detail.

The Qualities of True Believers

The *sūrah* opens with three Arabic letters: *"Alif, lām, mīm."* (Verse 1) This is immediately followed by the statement: *"This is the Book, there is no doubt about it, a guidance for the God-fearing."* (Verse 2)

Several *sūrahs* in the Qur'ān begin with a combination of Arabic letters in this way, and interpretations of these abstract openings vary quite widely. The one we tend to favour is that these are meant to emphasize the fact that the Qur'ān is a book composed of the letters of the Arabic language, in the same way as they are used by the Arabs who were the first people addressed by this divine revelation. Nevertheless, it is such an unparalleled and transcendent work that no Arab writer, using the same letters and the same language, could ever match its majesty and power. Rivals are repeatedly challenged to compose a book similar to it, or only ten *sūrahs*, or even a single *sūrah*, of matching quality. No one has ever been able to take up the challenge.

This is true for all God's creation. Soil, for example, is made up of elements of known properties. The best man has been able to make out of soil is bricks, tiles, vessels and structures of various types and uses, which are in some cases very sophisticated. But using these same elements, God has created life, the one outstanding secret that remains far beyond man's intellectual and creative abilities.

Similarly, the same letters and words that ordinary people, speaking the language of the Qur'ān, use to articulate expressions and convey meanings and concepts, are used by God to produce the Qur'ān as a definitive book stating the final and absolute distinction between truth and falsehood. A comparison between man's work and the work of God is simply not possible; it is a comparison between the image and the reality, between the dead body and the living soul.

"This is the Book; there is no doubt about it." (Verse 2) How can there be any doubt about it when the evidence for its truth and veracity is given in these very letters with which the *sūrah* opens? Evidence is implicit in the total inability of the Arabs to produce anything matching the Qur'ān, despite their proficiency and excellence in the use of their own language which is comprised of the same letters and words.

"This is the Book; there is no doubt about it, a guidance for the God-fearing." (Verse 2) The key word in this statement is 'guidance'. It expresses the essence and the nature of the Qur'ān. But guidance for whom? Who are the people who will find that this Book provides them with light, direction and true counsel? They are the God-fearing.

Once a man's heart is filled with the fear of God, he will benefit by the Qur'ān. Fear and consciousness of God is the quality that opens one's mind to the true guidance contained in the Qur'ān and allows it to have its proper effect on one's life. It is the factor that causes one's heart and mind to become sensitive and receptive to God's guidance and enables one to respond to His call and His instruction.

Anyone seeking the benefit and Godly wisdom of the Qur'ān must approach it with an open mind and a pure heart. One must also approach it with perception and sensitivity, and with a determination not to fall by the wayside or be tempted away from God. Then, and only then, will the marvels and treasures of the Qur'ān be opened and revealed, and their light and wisdom will pour into this apprehensive, alert and welcoming heart.

It is reported that 'Umar ibn al-Khaṭṭāb, a close companion of the Prophet and his second successor, asked the learned Companion, Ubayy ibn Ka'b, about the true meaning of 'fear of God'.

Ubayy asked 'Umar, "Have you ever walked along a thorny road?"

"Yes, certainly," 'Umar replied.

Ubayy asked again, "How did you manage to get through it?"

'Umar replied, "I gathered up my clothes and tried my best to avoid the thorns."

"That is precisely what God-fearing is like," said Ubayy.

Fear of God, then, is to have a sensitive conscience, clear feelings, a continuous concern, vigilance and alacrity, and a yearning for the correct path in life. It is a feeling that is ever alive, a feeling of being aware of life's temptations and pitfalls; and the ambitions and hopes, and the worries and fears that come with it. It is a feeling of being able to discern false hopes and unwarranted fears that one associates with individuals or powers that could neither bring benefit nor cause harm. Above all, the journey of life is full of many other kinds of thorns and nettles one must be aware of and strive to avoid.

Believing in the Imperceptible

The *sūrah* then gives a description of those who are God-fearing. In doing so it presents the early model of believers in Madinah, which was also to be the universal one for all future generations of Muslims: *"Those who believe in what lies beyond the reach of human perception, observe Prayer and give of what We bestow upon them. Those who believe in what has been revealed to you and what was revealed before you, and are certain of the Hereafter."* (Verses 3–4)

The most essential quality of the God-fearing believers is their conscious, active moral unity that enriches their souls with profound belief in the imperceptible, or *ghayb*, dedication to their religious obligations, recognition of all God's messengers, and unshakeable certainty in the hereafter. Such are the ingredients that make the Muslim faith a complete whole and distinguishes believers from unbelievers. Such a thorough outlook is worthy of God's final message to man, which was intended as a focus and a guide for all human endeavour on this earth. Man is called upon to adopt this message and lead a complete and wholesome life, guided by its light which shapes man's feelings, actions, beliefs and ways of living and behaviour.

Looking more closely at each of these qualities, one discovers a number of essential values that are fundamental to human life.

"Who believe in what lies beyond the reach of human perception." (Verse 3) The limits of human perception do not prevent believers' souls from reaching their Creator, the omnipotent power behind the universe and all existence. Their limited natural senses do not stand in the way of their desire to reach beyond the physical world or their pursuit of the ultimate truths of life.

Belief in the imperceptible is a major threshold in human understanding, and crossing it elevates man above animals and takes him far beyond the physical world of the senses or all the devices that may extend their function. It raises human consciousness to a level where a wider and fuller world can be perceived. Such a step has far-reaching effects on man's understanding of his own existence and the existence of everything else around him. It provides him with a totally new awareness of the realities of the interacting energies and forces that are at play in this complex world, and of the way he conceives of them. It also affects his behaviour and life on earth in general.

There is a vast difference between the thinking that is trapped within the parochial materialist world of the senses, and that which is based on the awareness of an infinite world of existence and which can, through the soul and the instinctive mind, deeply and intensely feel its energies and the forces governing it. Time and space extend far beyond what can be determined or comprehended within the short span of life. Man will come to recognize the great and ultimate truth that underpins the whole cosmos and sustains all existence, seen as well as unseen. It is the Divine Being that the human eye cannot see, nor the mind perceive.

This belief has the vital role of preserving man's finite mental and intellectual powers and saving them from being wasted, abused or misdirected. These faculties have been bestowed on man to enable him to properly discharge his obligations as God's vicegerent on earth. In the present life, the domain for man's activities of procreation, construction, innovation and excellence is limited. His intellectual power needs to be strengthened and complemented by spiritual power which stems directly from God and is thereby linked to the whole of existence.

Any attempt to comprehend the world from another perspective is futile and foolish, because it resorts to the wrong tools and defies the fundamental truth that the finite cannot fathom the infinite. Man's limited sensory and intellectual capabilities do not enable him to understand the absolute meaning of things.

This inherent human deficiency, however, in no way prevents man from believing in the imperceptible and accepting that it is the prerogative of the Divine. Man should leave these matters to God, the Omniscient, and should turn to Him for meaning, information, understanding and explanation. Recognition of this fact is the greatest prize the human mind can win, and is the first and foremost mark of the God-fearing believer.

The concept of the imperceptible is a decisive factor in distinguishing man from animals. Materialist thinking, ancient as well as modern, has tended to drag man back to an irrational existence, with no room for the spiritual, where everything is determined by sensory means alone. What is peddled as 'progressive thought' is no more than dismal regression. God has protected believers against such an error by describing them as those who believe in the imperceptible. For that alone they should be deeply grateful.

Those who *"observe prayer,"* revere and worship none but God Almighty. They never debase themselves by worshipping anyone or anything else. They turn to the real and ultimate power in this world, humbling their hearts and souls to Him alone. In this way they link up to the cause and origin of existence; their lives assume real meaning and noble purpose, transcending the crude and trivial pursuits and needs of worldly living. Their ties with God give them power over other creatures and feed their conscience with moral strength and fear of God. Prayer is an essential element in the building of a believer's character and shaping his concepts, feelings and behaviour and in linking them directly with God.

"And give of what We bestow upon them." (Verse 3) This implies the believers' recognition that what they own and possess is a gift and a favour from God. It is not of their own making. Such a belief brings mercy and benevolence towards the weak and the poor, and mutual fellowship and a true spirit of brotherhood and human community among all. The outcome is to eliminate greed and fill people's hearts with compassion and humanity, making life an opportunity for cooperation rather than an arena for conflict and confrontation. The sick, the weak and the young and helpless in society are given security, so that they feel they are living among human beings with

compassionate hearts and scrupulous souls, rather than selfish beasts with nothing but claws and teeth.

This kind of benevolent spending comprises the obligatory *zakāt*, as well as the giving of alms, voluntary donations and all other forms of charitable offerings. The latter had been instituted in Islam long before *zakāt*, because they are more general and wide-ranging than *zakāt*, which relates to the obligatory aspect of charitable spending. Fāṭimah bint Qays quotes the Prophet Muḥammad as saying: "There is a rightful claim to people's money, other than *zakāt*." [Related by al-Tirmidhī] This statement by the Prophet clearly establishes the general principle with respect to financial obligations.

"Who believe in what has been revealed to you and what was revealed before you." (Verse 4) This is a characteristic of the Muslim community, or *ummah*, the rightful heir to, and custodian of, God's message and the legacy of all prophets since the dawn of human life, and the leader of mankind. This characteristic embodies such concepts as the unity of man, the oneness of God, the unity of the divine faith and God's messengers. It purges man's soul of bigotry and petty fanaticism. It reassures us of God's everlasting grace and protection which He has shown by sending successive messengers preaching one and the same faith and offering the same guidance to all mankind. It allows us to feel proud of being the recipients of God's pure and universal guidance, which remains a bright shining star that is never extinguished, even in the darkest days of human history.

"And are certain of the Hereafter." (Verse 4) This characteristic of the God-fearing links the present life with the life to come; the beginning with the end; deed with reward. It provokes in man the feeling that he is no mere useless being, created without a purpose and left to wither away. It comforts him by affirming that full justice is certain to come, and thus inspires man to seek to do good, with total confidence in God's justice and mercy.

Belief in the hereafter is the point of departure between those who conceive only of the confines of the physical world and those who appreciate the limitless expanse of existence; those who believe that worldly life is the be-all and end-all, and those who see it merely as a testing arena where the ultimate reward is earned. This latter group realize that true life is there, beyond the limited confines of this earthly existence.

Each of these interrelated characteristics carries certain values for human life, and they form one harmonious entity.

Fear of God is an inner feeling, a state of mind, a source of human action and behaviour. It binds inner feeling with outer action, and brings man into constant contact with God, in private and in public. This contact extends into the deeper recesses of meaning and consciousness, penetrating barriers of knowledge and feeling, making acceptance of the belief in the unseen a plausible and natural outcome and bringing total peace and tranquillity to man's soul.

Fear of God and belief in what is beyond human perception go hand in hand with acts of worship, in accordance with the manner prescribed by God Almighty in order to link man the servant with God the Lord and Master.

Then comes the giving of part of one's wealth to charity, in acknowledgement of God's favour and as an expression of human fraternity and compassion. This is followed by a broad, all-embracing fellowship with all believers in God, and acceptance of His message and all the Prophets and messengers who preached it. Finally comes an unswerving belief in the hereafter.

These qualities were true of the first Muslim community which emerged in Madinah at the time these verses were revealed. It consisted of the *Muhājirūn*, who had migrated from Makkah, and the *Anṣār*, the natives of Madinah who welcomed them. Members of this model community displayed these profound characteristics of faith in their personal and public conduct. Thus they were capable of great achievements, with far-reaching effects on human life and civilization as a whole.

The passage aptly concludes with the comment: *"Those follow their Lord's guidance, and they shall surely prosper."* (Verse 5) Indeed, they adhered to God's guidance and they were successful. For those who wish to follow in their footsteps, the route remains clearly marked.

A Contrasting Picture

The next human model we are presented with is that of the unbelievers. *"For the unbelievers, it is alike whether you forewarn them or not, they will not accept the faith. God has sealed their hearts and ears; their eyes are covered; and a grievous punishment awaits them."* (Verses 6–7)

The contrast with the previous group is total. While God's Book in itself is a guide for the God-fearing, no warning to the unbelievers has any effect at all. The receptivity of the believer contrasts with the unbeliever's total unreceptivity; here the ties that bind the believer to God and the world around, and link the seen with the unseen and the overt with the covert, are completely absent. Their hearts are firmly shut and their ears can hear nothing. They are utterly incapable of receiving guidance or discovering the truth. Moreover, *"their eyes are covered."* (Verse 7) They are in total darkness, with no light to guide them anywhere. All this is their just reward for ignoring God's warnings.

The verses paint a grim and lifeless picture of these people on their way to *"a grievous punishment"*, which is a fitting and proper reward for obstinacy and disbelief.

The Mark of Hypocrisy

We now move on to the third model. The picture that the verses paint of this type of people is neither as bright and noble as the first nor as dark and base as the second. It is an elusive, evanescent image, constantly changing. These are the hypocrites: *"There are some who say: 'We believe in God and the Last Day', yet, in truth, they do not believe. They seek to deceive God and the believers, but they are only deceiving themselves, though they may not realize it. There is sickness in their hearts, and God has aggravated their sickness. Painful suffering awaits them for the lies they keep telling. When it is said to them: 'Do not spread corruption in the land', they say: 'We are but doers of good.' But, they indeed are the ones who do spread corruption, though they do not realize it. When it is said to them, 'Believe as other people have believed', they say, 'Are we to believe as the fools believe?' It is indeed they who are fools, though they do not know it. When they meet the believers, they say, 'We believe', but when they are alone with their devilish allies, they say, 'We are with you, we are only mocking.' God will put them to derision and let them continue their transgression, blundering blindly along. These are the ones who barter away guidance for error. Their transaction is profitless and they will receive no guidance."* (Verses 8–16)

This was a description of a number of people in Madinah, but the picture can be identified in every human generation. Such people are to be found among the élite of society who lack the moral courage to either openly accept the truth or clearly reject it. They are ever assuming the moral high ground, placing themselves above all others, deriding their understanding. We should, therefore, take these verses in their absolute sense, as being descriptive of hypocrites in all generations. They indeed address the human soul which is one in all societies.

Typically, the hypocrites claim belief in God and the Last Day when they in fact entertain no such belief. They simply do not possess the resolve to declare their true feelings and convictions.

They delude themselves into thinking that they are so clever and cunning as to be able to deceive the 'naïve' believers, but God uncovers the truth about their actions. They are trying to deceive not only believers, but God Himself: *"They seek to deceive God and the believers."* (Verse 9)

This and similar Qur'ānic verses reveal a great truth and an honour that God has bestowed on believers, for they emphasize the special relationship He has with them. God always takes the believers' side and makes their concern His concern. He protects them and stands against their enemy, and repels any attacks directed at them. This great honour elevates the status of believers among the rest of mankind, and affirms the fact that belief in God is the noblest and most honourable of all concepts in this life. It is the source of boundless reassurance to the believer that God supports his cause, nurtures him and fights on his side. The scheming and intrigue of other mortals is not to be feared.

This statement also carries a stiff warning to those who seek to deceive believers, harm them or scheme against them. It tells them that they will have to confront not only believers, but God Almighty. Waging war against believers means having to fight against God Himself and face His wrath and His retribution.

Both aspects of this fact should be appreciated and carefully considered by believers, so that they may be fully satisfied and reassured of their ultimate success. They need not be perturbed by the scheming and hostility of their detractors or the harm that these people may inflict upon them. Equally, the enemies of the believers should reflect on them, in order to appreciate the true nature and magnitude of the force they are contending with.

Going back to the verse, we find that it mocks their behaviour, pointing out that *"they are only deceiving themselves, though they may not realize it."* (Verse 9) They are so oblivious of the reality of their position, and so careless, that they deceive no one but themselves. God is aware of their schemes and deception. The believers are under God's protection. The thinking of these foolish hypocrites is so warped that they believe they have triumphed and achieved their goal, whereas in fact they have earned themselves nothing but doom and have condemned themselves to a terrible fate.

But why, we may ask, do these hypocrites resort to such behaviour? The answer is: *"There is sickness in their hearts."* (Verse 10) There is something wrong with their attitude and their hearts are not pure, which causes them to deviate and incur further displeasure from God, who has *"aggravated their sickness."* (Verse 10)

This type of sickness begins as a minor deviation and grows gradually, according to the established laws of human social and psychological behaviour. Predictably, such behaviour will only lead to one end, as befits those who deceive God and the believers: *"Painful suffering awaits them for the lies they keep telling."* (Verse 10)

Other characteristics of the hypocrites, which were certainly evident in the case of those notorious ones encountered by the early Muslims at Madinah, such as ʿAbdullāh ibn Ubayy ibn Salūl, is obstinacy and justification of their corrupting behaviour, together with an arrogant belief that they will escape punishment. *"When it is said to them: 'Do not spread corruption in the land', they say: 'We are but doers of good.' But, they indeed are the ones who do spread corruption, though they do not realize it ..."* (Verses 11–12) It is not sufficient for them simply to tell lies and resort to deception. They have to make false claims, adding insult to injury.

People of this type can be found in every generation. They perpetuate evil and corruption but claim to be proponents of reform and proper behaviour. Their standards of responsibility towards society and dedication to the common interest are distorted, and so is their evaluation of good and evil. Lack of faith and sincerity towards God blurs their vision of right and wrong, allowing their actions to be influenced by personal whims and desires. Their criteria of good and evil, right and wrong, are not dictated by the standards laid down by God. Therefore they are strongly and severely reprimanded: *"They indeed are the ones who do spread corruption, though they do not realize it."* (Verse 12)

Hypocrites are also distinguished by their arrogance, their contempt for other people and their pretence to be what they are not. The description continues: *"When it is said to them, 'Believe as other people have believed', they say, 'Are we to believe as the fools believe?' It is indeed they who are fools, though they do not know it."* (Verse 13)

It is clear that what the hypocrites of Madinah were being called on to demonstrate was sincere, unwavering faith, free of personal desire or caprice. They were being urged to join those who accepted Islam in its totality, submitted themselves completely to God, and opened their hearts and minds to the teachings and instructions of the Prophet Muḥammad (peace be upon him).

But it is also clear that they were too proud to accept. They thought of Islam as a religion for the meek and the poor in society, which did not become the lofty élite. This was reflected in their response. They are quoted as saying: *"Are we to believe as the fools believe?"*, which is appropriately met by: *"It is indeed they who are fools, though they do not know it."* (Verse 13) Fools are seldom aware of their predicament and are always willing to delude themselves that they are righteous and proper.

Then comes the last characteristic, which reveals the common ground that the hypocrites of Madinah shared with the grudging Jews. Their lies and deceptions are compounded by treachery and murky scheming against the Muslims: *"When they meet the believers, they say, 'We believe', but when they are alone with their devilish allies, they say, 'We are with you, we are only mocking.'"* (Verse 14)

To some people wickedness means strength and scheming is an art; yet the opposite is true. A strong person never feels the need to resort to treachery or intrigue. The hypocrites were too cowardly to come into the open and could only adopt a two-faced attitude. With the Muslims they professed belief in order to protect themselves and have access to the Muslim community and undermine it from within, but with their allies, who were often the Jews, they would say otherwise. Their rapport was matched by their cooperation in wicked schemes.

As soon as this aspect of their conduct is revealed, God delivers the sternest warning of all: *"God will put them to derision and let them continue their transgression, blundering blindly along."* (Verse 15)

What a degrading, humiliating and terrifying end: they are left wandering heedlessly, without guidance or direction, until the hand of God picks them up again, like feeble mice walking unawares into a trap. This is the true irony of their situation, which makes their mockery of the believers appear even more petty and ignoble.

Here again we are faced with the timeless truth mentioned earlier: that God always takes care to defend the believers, reassuring them and thwarting their enemy, who will blunder arrogantly in the dark, deceived by God's temporary clemency and brief remission, towards their inevitable and dreadful fate.

Then comes a final statement to sum up: *"These are the ones who barter away guidance for error. Their transaction is profitless and they will receive no guidance."* (Verse 16) They spurned the opportunity to be rightly guided, and forfeited their right to it. They are left miserable and totally lost on all counts.

The Enemy Within

We note that more space is devoted to the delineation of the character of the third group, the hypocrites, than to either of the preceding ones. This is because each of the first two types is, in a sense, simple and straightforward. The first picture shows people with clear vision and honest purpose, while the second paints those moving aimlessly, devoid of guidance. In the third picture we see those with a devious, restless, complex and sick disposition. Its delineation requires more touches and finer detail to be clearly and fully defined.

A detailed description of this third group also suggests that the role played by the hypocrites in Madinah in undermining the Muslim community during those formative years was a very serious one, and that they instigated trouble and instability in that community. It is also an indication of how far-reaching a role hypocrites can play in any Muslim community, and that there is a need to expose their activities and maleficent scheming against the Muslims.

Further examples are given to add more clarification and expose the nature of hypocrisy: *"They are like one who sought to kindle a fire, and as it lit up all around him God took away their light and left them in darkness, unable to see anything. Deaf, dumb and blind, they can never return to the right path."* (Verses 17–18)

Unlike the unbelievers, the hypocrites did not turn away from divine guidance in the first instance. They did not block their ears or refuse to listen or understand. They simply elected to turn away from God's guidance, after having considered and understood it. They sought the light and saw it, but they did not benefit from it. It was for this reason that *"God took away their light and left them in darkness, unable to see anything."* (Verse 17) This is a punishment for their deliberate rejection of God's guidance.

Man's senses are meant to enable him to perceive and receive God's Guidance, but the hypocrites wilfully closed off their senses, rendering themselves deaf, dumb and blind. Thus they are no longer able to see the light, nor can they find the right path again. They are lost.

Another description of their wavering and loss of direction tells us that: *"Or, when there is a storm-cloud, dark, charged with thunder and lightning, they thrust their fingers in their ears at every thunder-clap, for fear of death; but God encompasses the unbelievers. The lightning all but snatches away their sight; whenever it flashes over them they walk on, but when darkness overtakes them they stand still. Should God will it, He would take away their hearing and their sight, for God has power over all things."* (Verses 19–20)

It is a fascinating scene, full of life and movement, overshadowed by confusion. It is remarkable for the sense of loss, panic and perplexity it conveys. There is light and sound, dark stormy clouds bringing heavy rain, intermittent spells of light and darkness. People walking in all directions, not knowing where to go, and stopping abruptly in terror as the light disappears, covering their ears against the piercing sound of thunder that could well-nigh kill them.

The interaction between the various dynamic elements of this awesome scene perfectly reflects the confused and perplexed state of mind of the hypocrites, their double-faced way of life and their wavering and equivocating attitude towards others. It is a vivid picture of the psychological condition of those people, eloquently expressed in the rich inimitable style of the Qur'ān.

Having clearly defined these three types of people, the *sūrah* goes on to address mankind as a whole with an exhortation to seek to be of the pure, constructive and honest type in order to attain happiness and prosperity. *"Mankind, worship your Lord who has created you and those who lived before you, so that you may become God-fearing. He made the earth a couch for you, and the heavens a ceiling. He sent down water from the sky to bring forth fruits for your sustenance. Do not, then, knowingly set up equals to God."* (Verses 21–22)

The call is addressed to all mankind to worship God, the sole Creator of all beings. He alone is the Creator, and He alone must be worshipped. Man's worship of God fulfils a definite purpose, namely, to make man God-fearing. It is through worship that people can attain the honourable status of believing in, and fearing none other than God. Thus, they fulfil their obligations towards the One God, Lord of the living and the dead, past and present, and the sole sustainer and provider of all that is in the heavens and the earth.

"He made the earth a couch for you." (Verse 22) The tone here emphasizes the element of ease in human life. Planet earth has been prepared as a suitable place for living, providing comfortable shelter for man. Long familiarity, however, tends to make people take this ease and comfort for granted and to overlook the meticulous care and balance involved in providing the means to sustain human life on earth. Should only one of the elements necessary for life on this planet fail or run short, life itself would disappear or become impossibly hard.

"And the heavens a ceiling", solid and well coordinated. Man's life on earth is strongly linked to the skies and what they provide: heat, light, gravity, stars and planets. The forces that preserve this delicate coherence and harmony between the earth and the rest of the universe are vital to enable and sustain man's life. It is no surprise, therefore, that this should be mentioned within the context of God's power and grace, emphasizing man's duty to worship and submit to Him.

"He sent down water from the sky to bring forth fruits for your sustenance." (Verse 22) This is a recurring theme in the Qur'ān, especially in the context of reminding man of God's power and grace. Water is the essence of all life on earth. God says elsewhere in the Qur'ān: *"We have made out of water every living thing."* (21: 30) Causing plants to grow, running into rivers, forming lakes, permeating the soil to form underground reservoirs then springing out or drilled up, water remains the most vital substance for life.

Water as a phenomenon, and its role on this earth, are wonders that no one can deny or overlook. To assert God's power and grace, it is sufficient simply to point them out as an example.

Two fundamental Islamic principles emerge from this passage. The first is God's oneness as the Creator of all beings; the other is the unity of the universe and its internal cohesion, and its fitness for man and for all life. The earth is stretched out for our ease and comfort and the skies support their marvellous systems above us, while water brings forth crops and fruits to sustain mankind. All this is by the grace of God, the sole Creator. Therefore the *sūrah* continues: *"Do not, then, knowingly set up equals to God."* (Verse 22)

Knowing that God has created us and those who came before us, and knowing that He prepared the earth for us to live on and built the skies above us, single-handedly and without a partner or helper, and provided us with water, the essence of life, how can we ever deny Him, set up equals to Him, or worship others as gods beside Him?

The concept of "setting up equals to God" which the Qur'ān frequently and strongly condemns need not necessarily refer to the worship of idols or figurines or statues, normally associated with pagan religious practice and observed by the Arab idolaters. It could very well take other forms, some of which are very subtle indeed. To pin one's hopes on anyone other than God, to fear someone other than Him, to believe that others can bring fortune or cause harm, are all infringements of monotheistic belief and, therefore, forms of idolatry or, to use Islamic terminology, *shirk*.

The Prophet's learned companion, 'Abdullāh ibn 'Abbās, said: "Setting up equals to God is a subtle form of idolatry, or *shirk*. It is more subtle than an ant stealthily walking on a smooth black surface in the thick of darkness. It is when someone swears by something other than the name of God or believes that dogs or ducks keep the thief away. It is when someone says, 'By the will of God and the will of man' or, 'Were it not for God and you ...'" It is also reported that a man once came up to the Prophet and said: "Whatever you and God will." The Prophet replied: "Do you take me as an equal to God?"

The early Muslims were extremely sensitive and alert to these subtle forms of idolatry. We today have to reflect on our own attitude towards this matter and determine how true and faithful we are to the pure and fundamental principle of God's oneness.

A Divine Challenge

The Jews of Madinah used to raise doubts about the truth of the Prophet Muḥammad's message, while the hypocrites, like the pagan Arabs of Makkah, were sceptical and called it into question. Therefore we find the Qur'ān challenging them all, as indeed it challenges mankind in general, saying: *"If you are in doubt as to what We have revealed to Our servant, then produce one sūrah comparable to it and call upon all your witnesses, other than God, if what you say is true."* (Verse 23)

The challenge starts off with emphasizing an important fact by describing the Prophet Muḥammad as God's 'servant'. This description is significant in a number of ways: it is, first, an honour to the Prophet himself and an indication that to be a 'servant' of God is the highest honour a human being can attain. Second, it affirms the essence of servitude to God in the universal human context, calling on all men to submit only to God and renounce all partners that may be associated with Him. The Prophet Muḥammad, who attained the highest position of honour as a recipient of divine revelations, is also honoured by being described as a servant of God.

The challenge is also related to the opening of this *sūrah*, which points out that the Qur'ān was composed of the very same letters the Arabs were familiar with in their language. If they were in any doubt as to its truth or veracity, they were free to produce anything, even one *sūrah*, comparable to it, and they could call any witnesses they wished to testify in their favour. The Prophet's claim had already been supported by God.

This challenge remained open throughout the Prophet's life, and has done so ever since. The Qur'ānic argument stands just as firmly today as it has through the centuries. The Qur'ān remains today the unique work it was on the first day it was revealed, clearly distinguished from anything men can ever produce. Thus, God's words, and His warning, remain true: *"But if you fail, as you will certainly do, then guard yourselves against the fire, fuelled by men and stones, prepared for the unbelievers."* (Verse 24)

It is a remarkable challenge indeed, but what is even more remarkable is the absolute certainty with which it is made. Were any of the unbelieving Arabs able to take up the challenge, they would not have hesitated for a moment. The Qur'ānic assertion of the futility of their task, and the endurance of that assertion, are in themselves manifest and irrefutable proof of its superior nature.

The opportunity remains wide open for anyone or any group to pick up the gauntlet and try their best to match the Qur'ān and refute its claims of divinity and superiority. But this has not happened and, as the Qur'ān clearly states, will never happen. That is the Qur'ān's final word for posterity.

Anyone with any real knowledge or appreciation of literary styles, or expertise in philosophy, psychology, social science, or any other science at all, will not fail to recognize that whatever the Qur'ān has to say in any field of knowledge is something unique, unlike anything human beings would say. Argument over this fact can only arise from blind ignorance or sheer prejudice.

The stern warning to *"guard yourselves against the fire, fuelled by men and stones"* should, therefore, come as no surprise to those who may fail in their challenge to God but persist, nevertheless, with their rejection of the truth.

The use of the word 'stones' here is intriguing. This fire is prepared for the unbelievers, described earlier in the *sūrah* as those whom *"God has sealed their hearts and ears"* and whose *"eyes are covered."* (Verse 7) They are the ones who have failed to take up God's challenge, and persisted, nevertheless, in their rejection of His message. They are effectively stone-like, although they have a human form. Hence the connection between humans and stones in this verse. The expression amply conveys the horror of the awesome scene in which people and stones are consumed by fire.

In total contrast, we are given the scene of bliss which awaits the believers: *"To those who believe and do good deeds give the good tidings that they shall reside in gardens through which running waters flow. Whenever they are offered fruits therefrom, they say, 'We have been given the same before', for they shall be provided with what looks similar. They shall also have pure spouses and they shall reside there for ever."* (Verse 25)

The interesting aspect of this life of eternal bliss, besides the chaste, pure spouses, is the similar types of fruit offered to the believers, which they somehow feel they were given previously, either in this world or in heaven. This apparent similarity seems to introduce an element of recurring surprise; every time the fruits are found to be different, adding to an atmosphere already filled with pleasure, abundance and enjoyment.

The combination of apparent similarity and difference of essence is a phenomenon clearly discernible in God's creation, indicating, for one thing, that the world we know is much greater than it seems to us. Take man as an example. Overall, people look the same and possess the same limbs and organs, with essentially the same physical, biological and chemical constitution. But how far does this similarity go? How different can people be in their habits and aptitudes? For, despite the striking physical similarity, such differences can be vast indeed.

Variety and diversity in God's creation can be great indeed. There is variety in living species and in human races; there is diversity in shapes and features, as well as qualities and characteristics. Yet, this vast, multitudinous, diversified and inexhaustible universe goes back to a basic single cell which is made up of the same constituent parts.

Who, with all these manifest marvels and astounding proofs of God's power and omnipotence, dare reject God and fail to submit to Him alone in total awe and reverence?

The Use of Parables in the Qur'ān

At this point the *sūrah* speaks of the Qur'ānic use of parables: *"God does not disdain to give a parable of a gnat, or a higher creature. Those who believe know that it is the truth from their Lord, while the unbelievers ask, 'What could God mean by such a parable?' In this way, God lets many go astray and gives guidance to many others, but none does He leave to go astray except the evildoers, who violate God's covenant after having accepted it, and cut asunder what He has ordered to be joined, and spread corruption in the land. They are the losers."* (Verses 26–27)

Earlier in the *sūrah*, the hypocrites were shown in derogatory situations. They also realized that the Qur'ān uses parables referring to insignificant creatures. One of these compares unblievers to spiders: *"Those who take beings other than God for their protectors are like a spider which makes for itself a house. The frailest of all houses is the spider's house. Could they only understand."* (29: 41) Similarly the Qur'ān cites a parable showing the powerlessness of their false deities: *"Mankind! An aphorism is set forth; hearken, then, to it. Those beings whom you invoke instead of God cannot create a fly, even though they were to join all their forces to that end. If a fly robs them of anything, they cannot rescue it from him! Weak indeed is the seeker, and weak the sought!"* (22: 73)

This passage suggests that the hypocrites in Madinah, and probably the Jews and the polytheists, were, in their clumsy and confused campaign against Islam, trying to exploit such use of parables to raise doubts about the Qur'ān's divine origins, claiming that God would not speak about such insignificant creatures as spiders and flies. They thus hoped to undermine the authority and authenticity of the Qur'ān.

These verses serve to refute that argument and explain the wisdom underlying the use of such parables, while warning unbelievers against taking up such a line of argument and reassuring believers that they will strengthen their faith.

"God does not disdain to give a parable of a gnat, or a higher creature." (Verse 26) God is the Lord of all creatures, big and small. Every single creature, regardless of shape or size, is a marvel to behold, embodying the greatest secret of life, which is known only to God. Besides, parables are used to explain and illustrate concepts and ideas, and the size or shape of their subjects is irrelevant; in no case should they be slighted or scoffed at. Moreover, God, in His infinite wisdom, makes use of such parables to assess and test people's faith. *"Those who believe know that it is the truth from their Lord ..."* (Verse 26)

Since they believe in God, they accept what He sends with the reverence that is due to Him and with respect for His wisdom, which they do not question. The faith He bestowed upon them enlightens believers' hearts, enhances their spirits, opens their minds, brings them closer to God and makes them more sensitive and receptive to what they receive from Him.

"While the unbelievers ask, 'What could God mean by such a parable?'" (Verse 26) Apart from being an impertinent and inappropriate question, this reveals the unbelievers' ignorance and their exclusion from God's light and guidance. They have no reverence for God and no trust in His revelations.

Accordingly, the answer comes in the form of a swift warning: *"In this way, God lets many go astray and gives guidance to many others, but none does He leave to go astray except the evildoers."* (Verse 26)

God tests people in various ways and with varying degrees of difficulty and rigour, but the effect is not the same. Ordeals and tribulations can only bring a believer much closer to God and enhance his God-fearing sense and his submission to Him, while they will shake and confound an unbeliever or a hypocrite. It is the same with prosperity and good fortune. A believer will become more conscious of, and thankful to God, while an unbeliever or a hypocrite will grow more arrogant, inconsiderate and irresponsible.

Thus parables are used by God to test people's faith, so that *"In this way, God lets many go astray and gives guidance to many others, but none does He leave to go astray except the evildoers."* (Verse 26) In consequence of their attitudes and actions, the evildoers are given even more freedom to pursue the route they have chosen for themselves.

God's Covenant with Man

We have not completely departed from the subject of the beginning of the *sūrah*: the presentation of the main types of people found in every human society. So the text turns to speak in more detail of the "evildoers". They are those *"who violate God's covenant after having accepted it, and cut asunder what He has ordered to be joined, and spread corruption in the land. They are the losers."* (Verse 27)

The text speaks in very general terms, without specifying the 'covenant' or the thing they cut asunder, or the type of 'corruption' they spread. Priority is given to defining the overall profile of this type of people rather than recording any particular incidents or examples. They have lost God's trust, severed all the ties He commanded to be maintained, and they are capable of perpetrating every kind of corruption or evil. These are people condemned to confusion and loss of guidance; their basic human nature has been corrupted and perverted. They are like a prematurely picked fruit that has rotted and withered away. Their minds and outlook on life are totally distorted, so that whatever gives believers guidance and direction only confounds them and sends them further towards ruin and damnation.

Here, we may care to reflect briefly on the destructive effect of the activities of this type of people, as represented by the Jews, the hypocrites and the idolaters, on the young Muslim community of Madinah; and on subsequent Muslim societies everywhere, although under different guises and names.

Those *"who violate God's covenant after having accepted it"*. (Verse 27) The 'covenant' is in fact several covenants, the fundamental one being man's obligation to acknowledge his Creator and turn to Him in worship and submission. Belief in God is a basic human need that must be fulfilled; but it can be abused and misdirected, so that a person sets up partners or equals to God and turns to them.

There is the covenant made with Adam on behalf of all mankind, establishing man's role on earth and defining his rights and obligations, as we shall discuss presently.

There are numerous covenants and agreements, conveyed through Prophets and Messengers at different stages of human history, with various communities and human groups, committing them to the belief in the One God and implementation in their daily life of His laws and teachings. Evildoers, throughout history, have violated these covenants, and once they renege on their basic and fundamental obligations towards God, there is nothing to deter them from violating laws and norms of every kind, thereby wreaking havoc and destruction on all forms of life.

"And cut asunder what He has ordered to be joined." (Verse 27) Such ties are also numerous, and include family ties between kindred and relations as well as humanitarian ties within the larger human family. First and foremost, God has enjoined the maintenance of man's relationship with God and his fellow believers, which underpins all other ties and relationships. When these ties are broken or dissolved, societies fall apart and chaos and corruption run rampant.

"And [they] spread corruption in the land". (Verse 27) This corruption also takes numerous forms and manifestations, but it stems from one major evil: deviation from God's word and violation of His covenant, severing the ties and relations He has commanded to be maintained. The root of all evil and corruption on earth is deviation from God's laws which He has laid down for the conduct and organization of human life. This is a departure that will surely lead to ruin and destruction.

Human life cannot be built on sound and healthy foundations as long as God's laws, commands and teachings are discarded or ignored or given second place. Once this vital bond between God and man is broken, human and natural destruction becomes inevitable. Therefore, those who advocate such deviation from God's path and perpetrate corruption and ungodliness deserve to be left to stray and to be utterly confounded. Their confusion is caused by the same thing that provides guidance to those who are God-fearing.

Giving Life after Death

The *sūrah* then addresses all mankind, denouncing their disbelief in God who gives life and takes it away, and who provides for all and has full control over the whole universe: *"How can you reject God who has given you life after you were dead? He will cause you to die again then He will bring you back to life. To Him you shall return. It is He who created for you all that is on earth. He then turned to heaven and fashioned it into seven heavens. He has knowledge of all things."* (Verses 28–29)

Denial or rejection of God after seeing all these manifest signs is certainly despicable and utterly unjustifiable. The Qur'ān here faces mankind directly with facts they cannot deny or question. It refers to their life and the phases of human existence. God brought man out of a state of death and gave him life. This transformation is a fact that cannot be ignored or denied, and can only be explained by acknowledging the creative power of God. Life is not an illusion, but how has it come about? Who has initiated this unique phenomenon we call life, which distinguishes the living from the dead in this world? Life represents an extraordinary dimension that is the complete antithesis of death, but where does it originate?

It is a question that has to be faced and answered in a way that will satisfy man's curiosity and put his heart and mind at rest. It is simply not enough to dismiss it or attribute life to anything other than a creative power that is itself totally different from creation. The immediate answer to this question is that life comes from God. Let those who dispute this come up with another answer.

The verse questions man's denial of, and disbelief in, God *"who has given you life after you were dead"*. (Verse 28) How impertinent of man to reject God, the origin and the cause of life. It affirms that God *"will cause you to die again"*, a fact that is beyond dispute and of which we are constantly reminded. It adds that *"[He] will bring you back to life"*, which has been, and still is today, a matter for endless argument and debate. Yet, if people would only reflect on how man came to be in the first instance, there would be no reason for bewilderment or rejection of life after death.

"And to Him you shall return." (Verse 28) As it was from Him you have come, to Him you shall return, in total fulfilment of His will and purpose.

Thus, in one short verse, the whole book of life is opened and closed. The whole story of man's existence on this earth is reviewed. It begins, by the will of God, with a state of death and ends with death, after which God will restore life again, and the ultimate return thereafter shall be to Him from whom life originated. In this brief picture, we can visualize God's awesome power and appreciate its deep impact on our hearts and minds.

This is complemented by another powerful affirmation: *"It is He who created for you all that is on earth. He then turned to heaven and fashioned it into seven heavens. He has knowledge of all things."* (Verse 29)

Commentators and scholars have spoken at length about the origin and creation of the heavens and the earth. They have spoken about the order in which various parts of the universe were created. They have delved deep into the possible ways in which God could have 'turned' to heaven and 'fashioned' it. However, they overlook the fact that such dimensions of time and space are meaningless in relation to God. These are linguistic terms used to bring infinite concepts into the sphere of our finite minds. Endless disputes have periodically erupted among Muslim scholars about these and similar terms, over many centuries. These are part of the unfortunate legacy of Greek philosophy and Jewish and Christian theological and scholastic arguments that had crept into Arabic and Islamic thought and theology. Today, we would be better advised to avoid engaging in such futile debates, which can only mar the clarity of faith and destroy the beauty of the Qur'ān.

We should, therefore, look for those facts, ideas and concepts that lie beyond these Qur'ānic expressions and relate to the creation of all that is on the earth for the benefit of man. Let us look into the purpose of human existence and man's great role on this earth, and its value in the sight of God. What value does Islam attach to human beings, and what role does it assign to them in the social system?

"It is He who created for you all that is on earth." (Verse 29) The key words in this sentence are: *"for you"*. They explicitly assert that God created man for a momentous and important purpose, placing him in charge of the earth's affairs: to own it and to play an effective part in it.

Man is the master of this expansive earthly realm, and his role in its development and well-being is the most crucial of all. Man is the master on earth, and he is the master of the tools that are available to him on it. He cannot become a slave to these tools, as he is perceived to be by modern materialistic thinking. Nor is he subservient to, or dependent on, the changes or developments brought about by technology and their influence on human relations and societies, as materialists today would have us believe. Such thinking belittles man's role, lowers his status in the world, and renders him inferior to machines instead of being their master.

No material value should ever supersede human values, or subjugate or dominate man. Any cause that aims to depreciate man's worth is anti-human, no matter how much material advantage it achieves. Man's dignity and integrity override all material values and ideals, which are of secondary importance.

The grace and honour implied in these verses, of which God reminds mankind, even while He denounces their rejection of Him, are not only reflected in the fact that He has provided them with all that is on earth, but also that He has appointed man its master and set him above everything else on it. This honour is represented by the fact that man has been delegated by God to rule over the earth.

"He then turned to heaven and fashioned it into seven heavens." (Verse 29) This can only be interpreted in the sense that God has total control over everything, and with Him rests the will and decision of creating and shaping things. There is no need to dwell on the precise meaning, shape or dimensions of the 'seven heavens' referred to here. It is sufficient to point out the overall import of the text as outlined above.

"He has knowledge of all things." (Verse 29) He is the Creator of everything and has control over all things. God's omniscience and omnipotence are strong incentives for man to believe in Him, acknowledge His favours and worship Him alone.

This brings us to the end of the first section of the *sūrah*, which has focused mainly on belief in God and on urging mankind to join the ranks of God-fearing believers.

2

Man in Charge of the Earth

Your Lord said to the angels, 'I am appointing a vicegerent on earth.' They said, 'Will You appoint on it someone who would spread corruption and shed blood, whereas we celebrate Your praises and extol Your holiness?' He said, 'I surely know that of which you have no knowledge.' (30)

وَإِذْ قَالَ رَبُّكَ لِلْمَلَٰٓئِكَةِ إِنِّى جَاعِلٌ
فِى ٱلْأَرْضِ خَلِيفَةً ۖ قَالُوٓا۟ أَتَجْعَلُ فِيهَا
مَن يُفْسِدُ فِيهَا وَيَسْفِكُ ٱلدِّمَآءَ
وَنَحْنُ نُسَبِّحُ بِحَمْدِكَ وَنُقَدِّسُ لَكَ ۖ
قَالَ إِنِّىٓ أَعْلَمُ مَا لَا تَعْلَمُونَ ﴿٣٠﴾

And He taught Adam the names of all things and then turned to the angels and said, 'Tell Me the names of these things, if what you say is true.' (31)

وَعَلَّمَ ءَادَمَ ٱلْأَسْمَآءَ كُلَّهَا ثُمَّ عَرَضَهُمْ عَلَى
ٱلْمَلَٰٓئِكَةِ فَقَالَ أَنۢبِـُٔونِى بِأَسْمَآءِ هَٰٓؤُلَآءِ
إِن كُنتُمْ صَٰدِقِينَ ﴿٣١﴾

They said, 'Limitless are You in Your glory! We only know what You have taught us. Indeed, You alone are All-Knowing, Wise.' (32)

قَالُوا۟ سُبْحَٰنَكَ لَا عِلْمَ لَنَآ إِلَّا مَا عَلَّمْتَنَآ
إِنَّكَ أَنتَ ٱلْعَلِيمُ ٱلْحَكِيمُ ﴿٣٢﴾

He said, 'Adam! Tell them their names.' When he had told them all their names, He said, 'Have I not said to you that I know the secrets of what is in the heavens and the earth, and I know all that you reveal and conceal?' (33)

قَالَ يَٰٓـَٔادَمُ أَنۢبِئْهُم بِأَسْمَآئِهِمْ ۖ فَلَمَّآ أَنۢبَأَهُم
بِأَسْمَآئِهِمْ قَالَ أَلَمْ أَقُل لَّكُمْ إِنِّىٓ أَعْلَمُ غَيْبَ
ٱلسَّمَٰوَٰتِ وَٱلْأَرْضِ وَأَعْلَمُ مَا تُبْدُونَ
وَمَا كُنتُمْ تَكْتُمُونَ ﴿٣٣﴾

When We said to the angels, 'Prostrate yourselves before Adam', they did so except for Iblīs who refused, swelled in insolence, and was thus an unbeliever. (34)

وَإِذْ قُلْنَا لِلْمَلَٰٓئِكَةِ ٱسْجُدُوا۟ لِءَادَمَ
فَسَجَدُوٓا۟ إِلَّآ إِبْلِيسَ أَبَىٰ وَٱسْتَكْبَرَ
وَكَانَ مِنَ ٱلْكَٰفِرِينَ ﴿٣٤﴾

And We said to Adam, 'Dwell you with your spouse in Paradise and eat freely whatever you wish of its fruit, but do not come near this one tree, lest you would be wrongdoers.' (35)

وَقُلْنَا يَٰٓـَٔادَمُ ٱسْكُنْ أَنتَ وَزَوْجُكَ ٱلْجَنَّةَ وَكُلَا
مِنْهَا رَغَدًا حَيْثُ شِئْتُمَا وَلَا تَقْرَبَا هَٰذِهِ
ٱلشَّجَرَةَ فَتَكُونَا مِنَ ٱلظَّٰلِمِينَ ﴿٣٥﴾

But Satan lured them away from it [Paradise] and thus caused them to be ousted from where they had been. We said, 'Get you down. You shall be enemies to one another. On earth you shall have an abode and sustenance, for a while.' (36)

فَأَزَلَّهُمَا ٱلشَّيْطَٰنُ عَنْهَا فَأَخْرَجَهُمَا مِمَّا كَانَا
فِيهِ ۖ وَقُلْنَا ٱهْبِطُوا۟ بَعْضُكُمْ لِبَعْضٍ عَدُوٌّ ۖ وَلَكُمْ
فِى ٱلْأَرْضِ مُسْتَقَرٌّ وَمَتَٰعٌ إِلَىٰ حِينٍ ﴿٣٦﴾

Thereupon Adam received from his Lord certain words, and He accepted his repentance; for He alone is the One who accepts repentance, the Merciful. (37)

فَتَلَقَّىٰٓ ءَادَمُ مِن رَّبِّهِۦ كَلِمَٰتٍ فَتَابَ عَلَيْهِ ۚ إِنَّهُۥ
هُوَ ٱلتَّوَّابُ ٱلرَّحِيمُ ﴿٣٧﴾

We said, 'You shall all descend from it [Paradise]. Guidance shall reach you from Me. Those who follow My guidance shall have nothing to fear nor shall they grieve, (38)

قُلْنَا ٱهْبِطُوا۟ مِنْهَا جَمِيعًا ۖ فَإِمَّا يَأْتِيَنَّكُم مِّنِّى
هُدًى فَمَن تَبِعَ هُدَاىَ فَلَا خَوْفٌ عَلَيْهِمْ
وَلَا هُمْ يَحْزَنُونَ ﴿٣٨﴾

but those who deny and gainsay Our revelations shall have the fire, wherein they shall abide.' (39)

وَٱلَّذِينَ كَفَرُوا۟ وَكَذَّبُوا۟ بِـَٔايَٰتِنَآ أُو۟لَٰٓئِكَ
أَصْحَٰبُ ٱلنَّارِ ۖ هُمْ فِيهَا خَٰلِدُونَ ﴿٣٩﴾

Overview

Stories and narratives are a familiar part of the Qur'ān, recurring with varying emphasis and detail. The context within which a narrative or story is given normally dictates the main line and content of the story, as well as the style and form in which it is presented. All these factors are chosen to blend in with the spiritual and intellectual background of the text, as well as its artistic aspects. In this way, a story or narrative serves its intended purpose and produces the desired psychological effect.

Some people are of the view that there is much repetition in the Qur'ān, as some stories are related in more than one *sūrah*. But on deeper reflection, one finds that not a single story or episode is ever related twice in exactly the same way. There are obvious variations of detail, style and format. Every time a story is told, it has something new to say. The criticism of repetitiveness does not stand.

Some have gone so far as to suggest that there is a certain amount of invention or manipulation of detail and events, with a tendency to artistic licence that does not adhere to historical facts. But anyone studying the Qur'ān objectively, with an honest and open mind, will see clearly that the circumstances in which a story is related determine the aspects and amount of detail given in each specific instance. These also usually dictate the style and the way in which it is presented.

The Qur'ān is a book with a message. It lays down a constitution and provides an outline for a complete way of life. Its purpose is not to relate a story or to give an account of historical events for pure intellectual enjoyment. The extent of narrative detail chosen is determined by the message and the context in which it is used, while seeking also to attain and preserve beauty of style and power of expression, without exaggeration or false embellishment. The Qur'ānic style relies purely on faithful representation of the facts with characteristic power and beauty.

Historical accounts of earlier Prophets, as related in the Qur'ān, portray the long procession of the faithful through the ages, and the reaction of mankind to God's messages, generation after generation. They also give us a glimpse of faith in God as experienced and interpreted by that select group of human beings, the messengers, whom God has chosen for the great honour of conveying His message to mankind. For believers, reading these rich and vivid accounts can be heart-warming and reassuring, reaffirming the essence and value of faith and its profound role in human life. They also help define the believer's outlook on life, as established by the belief in God, and distinguish it from other man-made concepts. It is for these reasons that such historical narratives form a significant part of the Qur'ānic text.

Against this background, we now look at the story of Adam, or that part of it that is related in this *sūrah*.

The overall context, we may recall, is a review of human life in general and of the phenomenon of existence as a whole. It talks about planet earth, emphasizing the grace of God, who created everything on it for man's benefit. It then moves on to tell us about Adam's arrival on earth and his appointment as master over it, in full charge of its affairs, subject to certain conditions. It mentions that God has provided him with the tools of knowledge that would qualify and enable him and his descendants to fulfil their mission. This also serves as an interlude to the account that will follow, relating the assignment of the Israelites to take charge of God's message on earth, their covenant with Him, and their subsequent discharge and replacement by the followers of Islam, the loyal and true keepers of God's covenant.

Thus we find that the account of Adam fits in very well with the whole drift of the *sūrah* and forms a perfect link between the sections that precede and follow it, as we shall now see in more detail.

Establishing Man's Authority

The opening scene is an awesome one. We are in the presence of God Almighty and the Supreme Society of the angels: *"Your Lord said to the angels, 'I am appointing a vicegerent on earth.' They said, 'Will You appoint on it someone who would spread corruption and shed blood, whereas we celebrate Your praises and extol Your holiness?' He said, 'I surely know that of which you have no knowledge.'"* (Verse 30)

God, in His infinite wisdom, decided to hand over the earth's affairs and destiny to man and give him a free hand to use, develop and transform all its energies and resources for the fulfilment of God's will and purpose in creation, and to carry out the pre-eminent mission with which he was charged.

It may be assumed, then, that man has been given the capability to take on that responsibility, and the necessary latent skills and energies to fulfil God's purpose on earth.

It may, therefore, be concluded that a perfect harmony exists between those laws that govern the earth and the universe, and those governing man's powers and abilities. The aim of this harmony is to eliminate and avoid conflict and collision, and to save man's energies from being overwhelmed by the formidable forces of nature.

This clearly indicates that man is held in high regard in God's sight, and occupies a prominent position in the system of the universe, bestowed on him by God Himself. This is neatly encapsulated in the glorious statement: *"I am appointing a vicegerent on earth."* (Verse 30) The impact of this statement becomes even more profound and impressive, as we reflect on man's contribution and achievement on earth and beyond.

"They said: 'Will You appoint on it someone who would spread corruption and shed blood, whereas we celebrate Your praises and extol Your holiness?'" (Verse 30) The angels' reply suggests that they were aware of man's nature and disposition, either through some past experience on earth or special inspiration or direct information. Thus, they were able to surmise that he would spread corruption and shed blood on earth. Furthermore, by nature, angels can think only of absolute goodness and complete peace. Hence, they perceive that total dedication to the praise of God should be the sole and ultimate purpose of existence. They were already carrying out this purpose, extolling God's praises and glorifying Him at all times.

The angels were not privy to God's will and His purpose in setting up the earth and creating the various forms of life on it. They were not aware of God's plan to have the earth developed, cultivated and enriched at the hands of man, His vicegerent there. It is true that man would commit corruption and shed blood, but even this apparently evil aspect of his function turns out to be for the best. It is a necessary consequence of perpetual progress and development, and the changes brought about by a ceaseless endeavour in pursuit of better and higher things in this world.

Thus, they are given God's answer which settles the matter: *"He said: 'I surely know that of which you have no knowledge.'"* (Verse 30) *"And He taught Adam the names of all things and then turned to the angels and said, 'Tell Me the names of these things, if what you say is true.' They said, 'Limitless are You in Your glory! We only know what You have taught us. Indeed, You alone are all-knowing, wise.' He said, 'Adam! Tell them their names.' When he had told them all their names, He said, 'Have I not said to you that I know the secrets of what is in the heavens and the earth, and I know all that you reveal and conceal?'"* (Verses 31–33)

The passage takes us right into the very scene in which we can see the angels in God's presence, and witness how He entrusts man with the task of God's vicegerent on earth. He has given man the great secret of knowledge and cognition, as well as the ability to assign names to persons and objects which serve as symbols denoting whatever they are assigned to, even though they are no more than sounds and words. The ability to know and name objects has had the most profound effect on man's life on earth. We can only imagine what life would have been like without this communication tool to appreciate its value. Indeed, without it, human life and interaction would have been unthinkable, and there would have been no progress beyond a very primitive state. Without such ability, all communication would have necessitated the presence of the subject matter. Thus, if a group want to discuss something related to a tree, a mountain, or a particular person, then that person should be brought before the group, or they should all go to the tree or mountain. Indeed, without the ability to use names and symbols, human life could not function.

The angels have no use for such an ability because it is not required for their role. Therefore, they have not been given it. When God, having bestowed this great honour on Adam, asked the angels to identify certain objects, they could not because they did not possess the ability to use symbols and assign names or titles to things. They admitted their inability and recognized the limits of their knowledge, prompting the comment that followed: *"He said, 'Have I not said to you that I know the secrets of what is in the heavens and the earth, and I know all that you reveal and conceal?'"* (Verse 33)

Man's First Test

The story continues: *"When We said to the angels, 'Prostrate yourselves before Adam', they did so."* (Verse 34) This is undoubtedly the highest accolade bestowed upon man. For, despite the fact that he would commit corruption on earth and shed blood, he was elevated above the angels, endowed with the secrets of knowledge, and given a free and independent will to choose his destiny. Man's dual nature, his ability to determine his own course of action, and the trust he carries to pursue God's guidance by his own means are all aspects of the high esteem in which he is held. The angels prostrated themselves before Adam in obedience to God's command, *"except for Iblīs who refused, swelled in insolence, and was thus an unbeliever."* (Verse 34)

Here we see evil manifested in Satan's behaviour as he disobeys God Almighty, vainly refuses to recognize honour where it is due, persists in his error and closes his mind to the truth.

The general drift of the narration suggests that *Iblīs* was not one of the angels; rather, he was with them. For, had he been an angel, he would not have disobeyed God, since the angels' foremost characteristic is that they *"do not disobey God in whatever He commands them and always do what they are bidden."* (66: 6) The fact that the Arabic construction here makes an exception in relation to *Iblīs* does not mean that he is, or was, one of the angles. The exception is justified on the basis that he was with the angles. This is perfectly acceptable in Arabic, which allows the construction "the whole clan arrived but not Ahmad" without implying that Ahmad is a member of the clan.

Furthermore, the Qur'ān specifically identifies *Iblīs* as belonging to another type of extra-terrestrial creatures, the *jinn*, who are created out of fire, eliminating the idea that he was, at any time, an angel. (See 15: 27, 18: 50, and 55: 15)

The battle lines are drawn, and the long struggle commences between *Iblīs*, the epitome of evil, and man, God's vicegerent on earth.

This battle is fought within man's own conscience. Its outcome will be in man's favour as long as he exercises his will and remains faithful to his covenant with God. Evil will triumph only if man succumbs to his own desires and alienates himself from his Lord.

"And We said to Adam, 'Dwell you with your spouse in Paradise and eat freely whatever you wish of its fruit, but do not come near this one tree, lest you would be wrongdoers.'" (Verse 35)

They had been allowed access to all the fruits of Paradise with the exception of one tree. That tree may be seen as a symbol of the things forbidden to man on earth, without which there would be no free-will for him to exercise. Man would have been indistinguishable from animals, acting on mere instinct. Without forbidden things, there would be no way of testing man's willpower and resolve in fulfilling his covenant with God. The human will is the deciding factor, and those who do not exercise their will, despite their human form, belong with animals and irrational creatures.

"But Satan lured them away from it [Paradise] and thus caused them to be ousted from where they had been." (Verse 36) So graphic and expressive is the Arabic word, *azallahumā*, used here to express the act of luring away. We almost visualise the scene of Adam and Eve being tempted and manoeuvered so that they slip and fall out of Paradise.

Thus the test is over. Adam forgot his covenant and yielded to temptation, invoking God's inevitable judgement that they should be sent down to earth. *"We said, 'Get you down. You shall be enemies to one another. On earth you shall have an abode and sustenance, for a while.'"* (Verse 36) This was the signal for the battle between man and Satan to commence and continue until the end of time.

But Adam, by virtue of his basically good and sound human nature, was awakened to his oversight and was saved by God's boundless mercy, which is always close at hand for the repentant to seek. *"Thereupon Adam received from his Lord certain words, and He accepted his repentance; for He alone is the One who accepts repentance, the Merciful."* (Verse 37)

God's final word has been spoken, and His full covenant with Adam and his offspring as His vicegerents on earth has been sealed and brought into effect. This covenant outlines the conditions that bring mankind prosperity and those that lead people to ruin. *"We said, 'You shall all descend from it [Paradise]. Guidance shall reach you from*

Me. Those who follow My guidance shall have nothing to fear nor shall they grieve, but those who deny and gainsay Our revelations shall have the fire, wherein they shall abide.'" (Verses 38–39)

Thus the battlefield was transferred to its proper location, the planet earth, and the battle was to rage on unabated. From that early moment man was taught how to triumph over evil, and what would bring about his defeat and condemnation. It is now for him to choose how to act.

Points to Consider

It is quite clear that when God told the angels that He was appointing a vicegerent on earth, He intended Adam and his descendants to settle there. Hence, the question arises about the purpose behind the forbidden tree and the ordeal that Adam and his wife had to endure. Why was it all necessary to justify Adam's coming to earth, since he was meant to live on it in the first instance?

It seems that all this was part of Adam's training and preparation for the task ahead. The test was necessary in order to awaken his inner powers and latent ability to face up to temptation, so that he could see for himself the consequences of his actions and bear responsibility for them. It was also necessary to let man identify his enemy, and to give him a taste of repentance so that he would feel the need to return to God and seek His help and forgiveness.

The forbidden fruit, Satan's deception, Adam's disregard of his covenant with God, his grave error, subsequent realization and profound sorrow for what he had done, and his pleading for God's forgiveness, encapsulate the ever-recurring cycle of human experience.

God Almighty, in His infinite wisdom and mercy, has seen fit that man should undergo this experience before he came to settle on earth, where he was to be the master. Man was going to face this experience time and again in order to be properly equipped to cope with the rigours of his fight with Satan and the evil he represented.

We may also ask: Where did all that happen? What was this 'paradise' where Adam and his spouse had lived for some time? Who were the angels? Who was *Iblīs*? How did God communicate with them all, and how did they speak to Him?

Knowledge of these and other similar matters found in the Qur'ān is exclusive to God Almighty. God, in His infinite wisdom, knows that such details, and similar information, are of little consequence in the fulfilment of man's mission as God's vicegerent on earth. Just as God has favoured man with the secrets of many physical laws and control over many physical events, He has withheld certain others as they are of no immediate benefit to man.

Thus, despite the vast and amazing knowledge of life and the universe that he has been able to accumulate, man remains completely ignorant of what lies beyond the present moment. None of the tools of knowledge, intuition or technology enable him to gain knowledge of the immediate future in any degree of certainty. No human being can even know if his next breath will be his last. This is a typical example of the kind of knowledge that is withheld from man because it is not needed for the discharge of his duties as God's vicegerent. Indeed, were man to have access to such knowledge, it could well impede the fulfilment of those duties.

For this reason it would be futile for man to persist in pursuing such knowledge, since he does not have the means to obtain it. All efforts expended in this direction will be fruitless and would simply lead nowhere.

On the other hand, the lack of licence to penetrate the unknown does not give man the right to deny it. Denial is in itself a judgement which must be based on knowledge, but this is out of bounds for the human mind because it is not a prerequisite for man's life and role on earth.

To succumb to myth and superstition is extremely serious and harmful, but it is even more serious to deny the unknown or refuse to take it into account simply because it is beyond the limits of human perception and understanding. Such an attitude reduces man to the level of animals which can only live within the realm of the material world of the senses and are not capable of going to the wider universe beyond.

We ought, therefore, to leave the knowledge of the unknown to God and be satisfied with whatever glimpses He allows us into it that would improve our understanding and the quality of our life and behaviour. With accounts such as that of Adam and Eve, we must reflect on the universal and human truths, concepts, morals and impressions the story conveys and on man's nature and values, and their place within the context of the wider existence. That should prove a far more useful pursuit.

Man, the Master on Earth

With that in mind, we shall now have a close, but brief, look at the concepts, facts and ideas that can be derived from this story.

Foremost among these is the great value Islam assigns to man, his role on earth and his position in the universal system as well as the values by which he will be judged. Equally important is man's commitment to God's covenant which forms the basis upon which man's mission on earth is founded.

The high regard in which man is held in God's universe is manifested in the divine will to declare man a vicegerent on earth and in the symbolic gesture of ordering the angels to prostrate themselves before him, and the subsequent condemnation of *Iblīs* who refused to join them. It is also evident in the care and the kindness with which God has blessed man from the start.

From this emerge a number of fundamental concepts and considerations which are relevant to both intellectual and practical aspects of human life.

The first of these is that man is the master over this earth; everything in it has been created for his benefit and pleasure. This elevates man above all other beings and forbids his subjugation or humiliation for the sake of material achievement. Man's humanity must be respected and safeguarded; none of his fundamental rights or values should for any reason be violated or abused. Material things are meant to serve man and are made to promote his humanity and enhance his existence. It, therefore, stands to reason that achievements must not come at a price that would undermine fundamental human values, or at the expense of man's dignity or integrity.

Secondly, man's role on earth is of the highest importance. Man, rather than the means of production or distribution, is the force of change on this earth; he influences and alters the course of all life on it. Contrary to the materialistic view, man is the master, not the slave, of the machine.

The Qur'ānic view of man as a vicegerent on earth accords him a distinguished status and a central position in the divine world order. Through a number of vital and complex relationships, man's commission on earth is closely linked to other parts and forces of the physical world such as the stars and planets, the wind and the rain, the sun and the skies. All these phenomena are evidently designed, and are made to interact and converge, to serve the purpose of sustaining life on earth and to assist man in fulfilling the purpose of his existence on it. This view of man is easily distinguished from, and vastly superior to, the feeble and negative role assigned to him by materialistic philosophies.

All such views advocate their own means to promote, develop and preserve human life and values. The erosion of human freedom, dignity and values we see in materialistic societies as a result of the relentless drive towards material prosperity and progress, is but one facet of their godless view of man and his role on earth.

The Islamic view, on the other hand, leads to a deeper appreciation of moral values and ethical behaviour. It teaches man to appreciate highly such virtues as religious belief, righteousness and honesty, which are indeed the terms on which his covenant with God was originally based. These virtues and values supersede and override all material ones. This is not to say that material objectives and considerations are unimportant; indeed, they are vital for the fulfilment of man's commission as God's vicegerent on earth. But they must not be allowed to overshadow or usurp the fundamental higher ones. Unlike materialistic creeds and principles that dismiss spiritual values, Islam aims to always guide man towards a decent and moral life. Production, consumerism and the satisfaction of man's carnal instincts and desires are not all that life is about.

The Islamic view clearly accords to human will a lofty position, as the cornerstone in man's covenant with God. Free-will is also seen as the essence of man's responsibility and accountability. Man can attain a status higher than that of the angels by remaining, through his own choice and free-will, true to his covenant with God, and by not yielding to his desires or succumbing to temptation. However, he can also debase himself by allowing his desires to get the better of his will, and temptation to overcome faith and common sense, and by neglecting his commitments towards God Almighty.

This way of looking at man and his place in the world accords the human species further honour and esteem, and reminds us constantly of what leads to happiness and fulfilment and what ends in misery and degradation.

We are also constantly reminded through Adam's story of the nature of the battle between belief and denial, truth and falsehood, guidance and error. Man's own soul is part of the battleground, while man himself is the protagonist who may either win or lose.

The Concept of Sin

Finally, we have the Islamic view of sin and repentance. This view is very clear and simple, with no mysteries or complications. Sin and repentance are two very personal acts. Contrary to the Christian doctrine of 'original sin', no sin is ever imposed on a person prior to his or her birth. Nor, as the Church claims, is there 'divine' atonement in which Jesus, whom they allege to be the son of God, was crucified to free humanity of Adam's sin. Adam took full responsibility for his sin, which he personally committed. Having repented, he was simply and easily absolved of it. Any sins committed by Adam's offspring would likewise be totally personal. The gateway to repentance and forgiveness is open to all, without restriction or discrimination.

It is a simple and straightforward concept that puts everyone's mind and heart at rest, and inspires man to do his utmost to succeed and save his soul, and never to despair or give up. Everyone shall be held responsible for what he or she does; none shall carry the burden of another.

These are some of the impressions that the story of Adam, as related in the Qur'ān, evokes. They are rich with meaning and ideas, inspiration and generous advice that can underpin a social system built on virtue and morality. They highlight the significance of such accounts as we find in the Qur'ān, and reinforce the concepts and precepts of the Islamic view and the values on which it is based.

These values originate with God Almighty and are bound to lead to Him in the end. God's covenant with man is based on man receiving God's guidance and abiding by its imperatives and principles. The decisive factor is man's choice either to adhere to and obey God's commands, or to hanker after Satan's deceptive allurements. There can be no third way. This foremost and fundamental truth is emphasized throughout the Qur'ān, and it is the foundation on which all human concepts and systems are established.

3

Glimpses of Israelite History

Children of Israel! Remember My favour which I have bestowed on you. Fulfil your covenant with Me and I will fulfil Mine with you; and of Me alone stand in awe. (40)

يَٰبَنِيٓ إِسۡرَٰٓءِيلَ ٱذۡكُرُواْ نِعۡمَتِيَ ٱلَّتِيٓ أَنۡعَمۡتُ
عَلَيۡكُمۡ وَأَوۡفُواْ بِعَهۡدِيٓ أُوفِ بِعَهۡدِكُمۡ وَإِيَّٰيَ
فَٱرۡهَبُونِ ﴿٤٠﴾

Believe in what I have revealed, confirming that which you already have, and be not the first to reject it. Do not barter away My revelations for a paltry price, and fear Me alone. (41)

وَءَامِنُواْ بِمَآ أَنزَلۡتُ مُصَدِّقٗا لِّمَا مَعَكُمۡ
وَلَا تَكُونُوٓاْ أَوَّلَ كَافِرِۭ بِهِۦۖ وَلَا تَشۡتَرُواْ بِـَٔايَٰتِي
ثَمَنٗا قَلِيلٗا وَإِيَّٰيَ فَٱتَّقُونِ ﴿٤١﴾

Do not overlay the truth with falsehood, nor knowingly suppress the truth. (42)

وَلَا تَلۡبِسُواْ ٱلۡحَقَّ بِٱلۡبَٰطِلِ وَتَكۡتُمُواْ ٱلۡحَقَّ
وَأَنتُمۡ تَعۡلَمُونَ ﴿٤٢﴾

Attend regularly to your prayers, pay your *zakāt*, and bow down in prayer with those who bow down. (43)

وَأَقِيمُواْ ٱلصَّلَوٰةَ وَءَاتُواْ ٱلزَّكَوٰةَ وَٱرۡكَعُواْ
مَعَ ٱلرَّٰكِعِينَ ﴿٤٣﴾

How can you bid others to be righteous and forget yourselves, even when you read the Scriptures? Do you not understand? (44)

أَتَأۡمُرُونَ ٱلنَّاسَ بِٱلۡبِرِّ وَتَنسَوۡنَ أَنفُسَكُمۡ
وَأَنتُمۡ تَتۡلُونَ ٱلۡكِتَٰبَۚ أَفَلَا تَعۡقِلُونَ ﴿٤٤﴾

Seek strength in patient perseverance and in prayer, which is indeed a demanding task except for the devout. (45)

وَٱسْتَعِينُوا۟ بِٱلصَّبْرِ وَٱلصَّلَوٰةِ ۚ وَإِنَّهَا
لَكَبِيرَةٌ إِلَّا عَلَى ٱلْخَٰشِعِينَ ﴿٤٥﴾

who know that they shall meet their Lord and to Him they shall ultimately return. (46)

ٱلَّذِينَ يَظُنُّونَ أَنَّهُم مُّلَٰقُوا۟ رَبِّهِمْ وَأَنَّهُمْ
إِلَيْهِ رَٰجِعُونَ ﴿٤٦﴾

Children of Israel! Remember My favour which I bestowed on you, and that I have preferred you over all people. (47)

يَٰبَنِىٓ إِسْرَٰٓءِيلَ ٱذْكُرُوا۟ نِعْمَتِىَ ٱلَّتِىٓ أَنْعَمْتُ
عَلَيْكُمْ وَأَنِّى فَضَّلْتُكُمْ عَلَى ٱلْعَٰلَمِينَ ﴿٤٧﴾

Fear the day when no soul shall avail another in any way, nor shall intercession be accepted from any of them, nor ransom taken from them, and none shall receive help. (48)

وَٱتَّقُوا۟ يَوْمًا لَّا تَجْزِى نَفْسٌ عَن نَّفْسٍ شَيْـًٔا
وَلَا يُقْبَلُ مِنْهَا شَفَٰعَةٌ وَلَا يُؤْخَذُ مِنْهَا
عَدْلٌ وَلَا هُمْ يُنصَرُونَ ﴿٤٨﴾

And remember how We delivered you from Pharaoh's people, who afflicted you with cruel suffering, killing your sons and sparing only your women. That was a grievous trial from your Lord. (49)

وَإِذْ نَجَّيْنَٰكُم مِّنْ ءَالِ فِرْعَوْنَ
يَسُومُونَكُمْ سُوٓءَ ٱلْعَذَابِ يُذَبِّحُونَ
أَبْنَآءَكُمْ وَيَسْتَحْيُونَ نِسَآءَكُمْ ۚ وَفِى
ذَٰلِكُم بَلَآءٌ مِّن رَّبِّكُمْ عَظِيمٌ ﴿٤٩﴾

We parted the sea for you, led you to safety and drowned Pharaoh's people before your very eyes. (50)

وَإِذْ فَرَقْنَا بِكُمُ ٱلْبَحْرَ فَأَنجَيْنَٰكُمْ
وَأَغْرَقْنَآ ءَالَ فِرْعَوْنَ وَأَنتُمْ تَنظُرُونَ ﴿٥٠﴾

And [remember, too], when We appointed for Moses forty nights, and in his absence you took to worshipping the calf, and thus became wrongdoers. (51)

وَإِذْ وَٰعَدْنَا مُوسَىٰٓ أَرْبَعِينَ لَيْلَةً ثُمَّ ٱتَّخَذْتُمُ
ٱلْعِجْلَ مِنۢ بَعْدِهِۦ وَأَنتُمْ ظَٰلِمُونَ ٥١

Yet even after that We pardoned you, so that you might be thankful. (52)

ثُمَّ عَفَوْنَا عَنكُم مِّنۢ بَعْدِ ذَٰلِكَ لَعَلَّكُمْ
تَشْكُرُونَ ٥٢

We gave Moses the Scriptures and the Standard [by which to distinguish right from wrong], so that you might be rightly guided. (53)

وَإِذْ ءَاتَيْنَا مُوسَى ٱلْكِتَٰبَ وَٱلْفُرْقَانَ
لَعَلَّكُمْ تَهْتَدُونَ ٥٣

Moses said to his people, 'You, my people, have wronged yourselves by worshipping the calf. Turn, then, in repentance to your Maker and slay one another. That will be better for you in your Maker's sight.' Thus, He accepted your repentance; for He is the One to accept repentance, the Merciful. (54)

وَإِذْ قَالَ مُوسَىٰ لِقَوْمِهِۦ يَٰقَوْمِ إِنَّكُمْ
ظَلَمْتُمْ أَنفُسَكُم بِٱتِّخَاذِكُمُ ٱلْعِجْلَ
فَتُوبُوٓا۟ إِلَىٰ بَارِئِكُمْ فَٱقْتُلُوٓا۟ أَنفُسَكُمْ
ذَٰلِكُمْ خَيْرٌ لَّكُمْ عِندَ بَارِئِكُمْ فَتَابَ
عَلَيْكُمْ ۚ إِنَّهُۥ هُوَ ٱلتَّوَّابُ ٱلرَّحِيمُ ٥٤

And [remember] when you said, 'Moses, we will not believe in you until we see God in person.' You were then struck by a thunderbolt while you were looking on. (55)

وَإِذْ قُلْتُمْ يَٰمُوسَىٰ لَن نُّؤْمِنَ لَكَ حَتَّىٰ نَرَى
ٱللَّهَ جَهْرَةً فَأَخَذَتْكُمُ ٱلصَّٰعِقَةُ وَأَنتُمْ
تَنظُرُونَ ٥٥

But We raised you again after you had been as dead, so that you might be thankful. (56)

ثُمَّ بَعَثْنَٰكُم مِّنۢ بَعْدِ مَوْتِكُمْ لَعَلَّكُمْ
تَشْكُرُونَ ٥٦

وَظَلَّلْنَا عَلَيْكُمُ ٱلْغَمَامَ وَأَنزَلْنَا عَلَيْكُمُ
ٱلْمَنَّ وَٱلسَّلْوَىٰ ۖ كُلُوا۟ مِن طَيِّبَٰتِ مَا
رَزَقْنَٰكُمْ ۖ وَمَا ظَلَمُونَا وَلَٰكِن كَانُوٓا۟
أَنفُسَهُمْ يَظْلِمُونَ ﴿٥٧﴾

We caused the clouds to provide shade for you, and sent down for you manna and quails. 'Eat of the good things We have provided for you.' Indeed, to Us they did no harm, but themselves did they wrong. (57)

وَإِذْ قُلْنَا ٱدْخُلُوا۟ هَٰذِهِ ٱلْقَرْيَةَ فَكُلُوا۟ مِنْهَا
حَيْثُ شِئْتُمْ رَغَدًا وَٱدْخُلُوا۟ ٱلْبَابَ سُجَّدًا
وَقُولُوا۟ حِطَّةٌ نَّغْفِرْ لَكُمْ خَطَٰيَٰكُمْ ۚ وَسَنَزِيدُ
ٱلْمُحْسِنِينَ ﴿٥٨﴾

And [remember] when We said, 'Enter this city, eat of its abundant food as you may desire, prostrate yourselves as you enter the gates and say: "Lord, relieve us of our burden." We will then forgive your sins and We will richly reward those who do good.' (58)

فَبَدَّلَ ٱلَّذِينَ ظَلَمُوا۟ قَوْلًا غَيْرَ ٱلَّذِى
قِيلَ لَهُمْ فَأَنزَلْنَا عَلَى ٱلَّذِينَ ظَلَمُوا۟
رِجْزًا مِّنَ ٱلسَّمَآءِ بِمَا كَانُوا۟ يَفْسُقُونَ ﴿٥٩﴾

But the wrongdoers among them substituted other words for those which they had been given. Therefore, We let loose against them a scourge from heaven in requital for their transgression. (59)

وَإِذِ ٱسْتَسْقَىٰ مُوسَىٰ لِقَوْمِهِۦ فَقُلْنَا ٱضْرِب
بِّعَصَاكَ ٱلْحَجَرَ ۖ فَٱنفَجَرَتْ مِنْهُ ٱثْنَتَا
عَشْرَةَ عَيْنًا ۖ قَدْ عَلِمَ كُلُّ أُنَاسٍ مَّشْرَبَهُمْ ۖ
كُلُوا۟ وَٱشْرَبُوا۟ مِن رِّزْقِ ٱللَّهِ وَلَا تَعْثَوْا۟
فِى ٱلْأَرْضِ مُفْسِدِينَ ﴿٦٠﴾

And [remember] when Moses prayed for water for his people We said to him, 'Strike the rock with your staff.' Twelve springs gushed forth from it. Each tribe knew their drinking place. Eat and drink of what God has provided and do not persistently spread corruption in the land. (60)

And [remember] when you said, 'Moses! We can no longer put up with one kind of food. Pray to your Lord, then, to bring forth for us some of what the earth produces of green herbs, cucumber, garlic, lentils and onions.' He said, 'Would you take a lesser thing in exchange for what is much better? Go down to any land and you shall have what you asked for.' Ignominy and humiliation were stamped upon them and they incurred the wrath of God, because they denied His revelations and slew prophets against all right, and because they persisted in their disobedience and transgression. (61)

وَإِذْ قُلْتُمْ يَٰمُوسَىٰ لَن نَّصْبِرَ عَلَىٰ طَعَامٍ
وَٰحِدٍ فَٱدْعُ لَنَا رَبَّكَ يُخْرِجْ لَنَا مِمَّا تُنۢبِتُ
ٱلْأَرْضُ مِنۢ بَقْلِهَا وَقِثَّآئِهَا وَفُومِهَا
وَعَدَسِهَا وَبَصَلِهَا ۖ قَالَ أَتَسْتَبْدِلُونَ
ٱلَّذِى هُوَ أَدْنَىٰ بِٱلَّذِى هُوَ خَيْرٌ ۚ ٱهْبِطُوا۟
مِصْرًا فَإِنَّ لَكُم مَّا سَأَلْتُمْ ۗ وَضُرِبَتْ
عَلَيْهِمُ ٱلذِّلَّةُ وَٱلْمَسْكَنَةُ وَبَآءُو
بِغَضَبٍ مِّنَ ٱللَّهِ ۗ ذَٰلِكَ بِأَنَّهُمْ كَانُوا۟
يَكْفُرُونَ بِـَٔايَٰتِ ٱللَّهِ وَيَقْتُلُونَ
ٱلنَّبِيِّۦنَ بِغَيْرِ ٱلْحَقِّ ۗ ذَٰلِكَ بِمَا عَصَوا۟ وَّكَانُوا۟
يَعْتَدُونَ ﴿٦١﴾

Those who believe, and those who are Jews, and the Christians and the Sabaeans – anyone who believes in God and the Last Day, and does what is right, shall have their reward with their Lord. They have nothing to fear nor shall they grieve. (62)

إِنَّ ٱلَّذِينَ ءَامَنُوا۟ وَٱلَّذِينَ هَادُوا۟
وَٱلنَّصَٰرَىٰ وَٱلصَّٰبِـِٔينَ مَنْ ءَامَنَ
بِٱللَّهِ وَٱلْيَوْمِ ٱلْءَاخِرِ وَعَمِلَ صَٰلِحًا
فَلَهُمْ أَجْرُهُمْ عِندَ رَبِّهِمْ وَلَا خَوْفٌ
عَلَيْهِمْ وَلَا هُمْ يَحْزَنُونَ ﴿٦٢﴾

We accepted your solemn pledge and raised Mount Sinai above you, saying, 'Take with firmness and strength what We have given you, and bear in mind all its contents, so that you may remain God-fearing.' (63)

وَإِذْ أَخَذْنَا مِيثَٰقَكُمْ وَرَفَعْنَا فَوْقَكُمُ
ٱلطُّورَ خُذُوا۟ مَآ ءَاتَيْنَٰكُم بِقُوَّةٍ وَٱذْكُرُوا۟
مَا فِيهِ لَعَلَّكُمْ تَتَّقُونَ ﴿٦٣﴾

ثُمَّ تَوَلَّيْتُم مِّنۢ بَعْدِ ذَٰلِكَ ۖ فَلَوْلَا فَضْلُ ٱللَّهِ
عَلَيْكُمْ وَرَحْمَتُهُۥ لَكُنتُم مِّنَ ٱلْخَٰسِرِينَ ﴿٦٤﴾

Yet after that you turned away, and but for God's grace and mercy you would have surely been among the losers. (64)

وَلَقَدْ عَلِمْتُمُ ٱلَّذِينَ ٱعْتَدَوْا۟ مِنكُمْ
فِى ٱلسَّبْتِ فَقُلْنَا لَهُمْ كُونُوا۟ قِرَدَةً
خَٰسِـِٔينَ ﴿٦٥﴾

You are well aware of those of you who broke the Sabbath. To them We said, 'Be as despicable apes.' (65)

فَجَعَلْنَٰهَا نَكَٰلًا لِّمَا بَيْنَ يَدَيْهَا
وَمَا خَلْفَهَا وَمَوْعِظَةً لِّلْمُتَّقِينَ ﴿٦٦﴾

Through that [punishment] We set an example to their own time and for all times to come, and an admonition to the God-fearing. (66)

وَإِذْ قَالَ مُوسَىٰ لِقَوْمِهِۦٓ إِنَّ ٱللَّهَ يَأْمُرُكُمْ
أَن تَذْبَحُوا۟ بَقَرَةً ۖ قَالُوٓا۟ أَتَتَّخِذُنَا هُزُوًا ۖ قَالَ
أَعُوذُ بِٱللَّهِ أَنْ أَكُونَ مِنَ ٱلْجَٰهِلِينَ ﴿٦٧﴾

When Moses said to his people, 'God commands you to sacrifice a cow,' they said, 'Are you mocking at us?' He said, 'God forbid that I should be so ignorant.' (67)

قَالُوا۟ ٱدْعُ لَنَا رَبَّكَ يُبَيِّن لَّنَا مَا هِىَ ۚ قَالَ إِنَّهُۥ
يَقُولُ إِنَّهَا بَقَرَةٌ لَّا فَارِضٌ وَلَا بِكْرٌ عَوَانٌۢ
بَيْنَ ذَٰلِكَ ۖ فَٱفْعَلُوا۟ مَا تُؤْمَرُونَ ﴿٦٨﴾

They said, 'Pray on our behalf to your Lord to make plain to us what kind of cow she should be.' He said, 'He says let her be neither an old cow nor a young heifer, but of an age in between. Do, then, as you are commanded.' (68)

قَالُوا۟ ٱدْعُ لَنَا رَبَّكَ يُبَيِّن لَّنَا مَا لَوْنُهَا ۚ
قَالَ إِنَّهُۥ يَقُولُ إِنَّهَا بَقَرَةٌ صَفْرَآءُ فَاقِعٌ
لَّوْنُهَا تَسُرُّ ٱلنَّٰظِرِينَ ﴿٦٩﴾

They said, 'Pray on our behalf to your Lord to make clear to us of what colour she should be.' [Moses] replied, 'He says let her be a yellow cow, bright of hue, pleasing to the beholder.' (69)

They said, 'Pray on our behalf to your Lord to make plain to us of what exact type she should be, for to us cows are much alike. We shall, God willing, be guided aright.' (70)

قَالُوا ادْعُ لَنَا رَبَّكَ يُبَيِّن لَّنَا مَا هِيَ إِنَّ الْبَقَرَ
تَشَابَهَ عَلَيْنَا وَإِنَّا إِن شَاءَ اللَّهُ
لَمُهْتَدُونَ ﴿٧٠﴾

[Moses] answered, 'He says let her be a cow, not broken-in to plough the earth or water the tillage, free of all fault, without markings of any other colour.' Said they, 'Now you have given the right description.' They sacrificed her, although they had almost left it undone. (71)

قَالَ إِنَّهُ يَقُولُ إِنَّهَا بَقَرَةٌ لَّا ذَلُولٌ تُثِيرُ
الْأَرْضَ وَلَا تَسْقِي الْحَرْثَ مُسَلَّمَةٌ لَّا شِيَةَ
فِيهَا قَالُوا الْآنَ جِئْتَ بِالْحَقِّ فَذَبَحُوهَا
وَمَا كَادُوا يَفْعَلُونَ ﴿٧١﴾

Having slain a human being, you cast the blame on one another for this [murder]. God would definitely reveal what you have concealed. (72)

وَإِذْ قَتَلْتُمْ نَفْسًا فَادَّارَأْتُمْ فِيهَا وَاللَّهُ
مُخْرِجٌ مَّا كُنتُمْ تَكْتُمُونَ ﴿٧٢﴾

We said, 'Strike him with a piece of it. Thus God brings the dead back to life and shows you His signs, so that you may use your reason.' (73)

فَقُلْنَا اضْرِبُوهُ بِبَعْضِهَا كَذَلِكَ يُحْيِي
اللَّهُ الْمَوْتَى وَيُرِيكُمْ آيَاتِهِ
لَعَلَّكُمْ تَعْقِلُونَ ﴿٧٣﴾

Yet after all this, your hearts hardened until they were as hard as rocks or even harder; for there are rocks from which rivers gush forth; others split so that water flows through them, and some other rocks fall down for fear of God. Indeed, God is not unaware of what you do. (74)

ثُمَّ قَسَتْ قُلُوبُكُم مِّن بَعْدِ ذَلِكَ فَهِيَ
كَالْحِجَارَةِ أَوْ أَشَدُّ قَسْوَةً وَإِنَّ مِنَ
الْحِجَارَةِ لَمَا يَتَفَجَّرُ مِنْهُ الْأَنْهَارُ
وَإِنَّ مِنْهَا لَمَا يَشَّقَّقُ فَيَخْرُجُ مِنْهُ
الْمَاءُ وَإِنَّ مِنْهَا لَمَا يَهْبِطُ مِنْ خَشْيَةِ
اللَّهِ وَمَا اللَّهُ بِغَافِلٍ عَمَّا تَعْمَلُونَ ﴿٧٤﴾

Overview

At this point, the *sūrah* begins its address to the Children of Israel, represented by the Jews of Madinah, who posed the stiffest opposition to the Islamic message the moment it arrived there. They launched a relentless campaign of overt and covert resistance as soon as they realized that it had come to stay and to take control of the city and its population. They felt that Islam was bound to deprive them of the moral and economic hegemony they had so far enjoyed. Slowly, Islam began to heal the rifts that had existed between Madinah's two main rival Arab tribes, the Aws and the Khazraj, thus ending the disputes that the Jews had been able to exploit. At the same time it provided Madinah with an independent code of conduct, based on the Qur'ān.

The war the Jews began to wage against Islam and Muslims in those early days has raged on to the present day. The form and appearance may have changed, but the nature and means remain the same. This is in spite of the fact that the Jews, who have been widely persecuted throughout their history, have always been welcomed and accommodated by Muslim communities. Indeed, Muslim communities have no history of religious or racial intolerance, discrimination or persecution. They are known to welcome peaceful outsiders who have no intention to undermine Islam or harm its people.

It was thought that the Jews of Madinah would be the first to welcome Islam and embrace the new religion and its advocate, the Prophet Muḥammad. The Qur'ān had already given a general endorsement to the Torah; while the Jews had been bidden by their own Scriptures to await the emergence of a new Messenger, whom their own prophets had described. In fact, they had been boasting about his impending arrival to the pagan Arabs.

This section of the *sūrah* constitutes the opening chapter in a wide-ranging campaign aimed at exposing the scheming and hostile stance of the Jews towards Islam. This counter-attack, however, was launched only after all means of persuasion to get them to accept Islam and join its ranks had been used without success.

The passage opens with a majestic call to the Israelites, reminding them of God's grace and inviting them to fulfil their part of the covenant with God so that He will fulfil His. It calls on them to be fearful of God and submit to Him, as a prelude to appealing to them to accept the new revelations. It then goes on to condemn them for being among the first to reject it. It censures their deliberate confusion of truth with falsehood and their efforts to obfuscate and conceal the truth contained in their Scriptures. It denounces their attempts to mislead others, particularly those who had recently embraced the new religion, and to foment conflict and strife in the burgeoning Muslim community. It invites them to join the ranks of the believers, observe prayers, and pay their religious dues. Through perseverance and prayer, they seek to overcome their intransigence and arrogance that have prevented them from acknowledging and embracing the new religion. It denounces their two-faced attitude of calling on the Arab idolaters to believe in God while they themselves refuse to accept Islam.

The *sūrah* goes on to recall for the Jews the long list of favours God had bestowed on them all through their long history. In its unique style, the Qur'ān addresses the Jewish contemporaries of Muḥammad as if they were the contemporaries of Moses who lived centuries earlier, and treats them as one and the same community. Indeed, their attitude and behaviour have been remarkably the same through the ages.

The Qur'ān also reminds them of the horrors of Resurrection Day, when every soul has to defend itself, no intercession or ransom shall be accepted, and no one shall save them from God's wrath and punishment.

It recalls in vivid detail their ancestors' confrontation with, and subsequent escape from, Egypt's Pharaoh, and all the favours God blessed them with afterwards. It reminds them of their lack of gratitude, their relapses and frequent deviations, and their insistence on committing the same errors again and again. It stresses their stubbornness, deviousness, lack of resolve, inability to shoulder responsibility, dishonesty and unfaithfulness to their covenants with God and their own Prophets, some of whom they even killed. They defied God and rejected His messages, worshipped the golden calf, made impossible demands on their prophets and violated almost every commandment they received from God.

The Jews, according to the Qur'ān, have done all this while insisting that they are the only rightly-guided nation in the world and the exclusive recipients of God's guidance and blessings, and arguing that their religion is the only true one. However, as we shall see in the following pages, the Qur'ān refutes this claim and declares that all believers in God who adhere to His commands shall receive their deserved reward and shall have nothing to fear or regret.

This campaign to uncover the destructive machinations of the Jews was unavoidable for two main reasons. First, it was essential to demolish their arguments, expose their intrigues and reveal their true intentions towards Islam and the Muslims. This would make Muslims fully aware of what was being done behind their backs to undermine the foundations of their fledgling community.

Second, it was necessary as a warning to the Muslims themselves to avoid the pitfalls into which earlier recipients of God's message, had fallen. As a result, such communities were stripped of the honour of having custody of the divine message and of the leadership of mankind. A number of specific instructions to this effect, some implicit and some explicit, can be found throughout the present passage.

There is no doubt that the Muslim community in Madinah at the time, and Muslims in subsequent generations, are in need of such warnings and admonitions. Muslims always need to study the Qur'ān very closely in order to discern and understand the divine instructions that will help them fight their habitual enemies, and to find out how to combat their insidious scheming.

Without God's guidance and the light of faith, human beings can never recognize all the perils or fathom the wickedness of their enemies.

We can see very clearly here how, in the unique Qur'ānic style, the story of the Jews dovetails with that of Adam and Eve. This reflects an aspect of the integrity and the complementary nature of the topics with the context in which they are presented.

If we go back a little we find that the *sūrah* had established that God created everything on earth for the benefit of man. It then went on to relate how Adam, father of the human race, was given a covenant as God's vicegerent on earth, how he was honoured by the angels falling prostrate before him, the brief he received from God, how he overlooked it, regretted his error and repented. We have also been told how he was forgiven and provided with divine guidance to ensure his success in this life. We have seen how that experience was in fact the prelude to the continuous conflict that was to take place on earth between the forces of evil and destruction, represented by *Iblīs*, and the forces of goodness and construction, represented by God-fearing man.

This is followed by an account of the history of the Israelites which records their covenant with God and how they violated it, as well as the favours God had bestowed on them and their ingratitude. As a result God withdrew His trust from them, allowing them to live in humiliation. The account warns Muslims against the evil designs of the Israelites and against following their example.

There is a clear link between the assignment of Adam as God's vicegerent on earth and the choice of the Israelites as custodians of God's message. The subject matter and the message flow in total harmony with the style employed.

The Qur'ān is not concerned with the chronology of the history of the Israelites. It is only recalling certain events or actions in as much or as little detail as is appropriate. Various other episodes of the story of the Israelites are related in other *sūrahs*, revealed earlier in Makkah, but for a different purpose. The aim there was to inspire and reassure that small group of the early Muslims in Makkah, and show them how to cope with their situation and learn from the strong faith and courage of earlier believers.

In the present context, however, the aim is to expose the real intentions and plans of the Jews, to describe their methods, and to warn the Muslim community about their scheming, as well as against repeating their mistakes. The difference between the Makkan and Madinan styles of the Qur'ān, which will become clear later when we study the Makkan *sūrahs*, is reflected in the emphasis and the presentation of the same topics.

On reviewing the passages where the story of the Israelites occurs in the Qur'ān, one finds that the details fit perfectly into the context to reinforce the argument or the point that is being made. It is also the case in this instance, as already explained.

The story of the Israelites is the one most frequently mentioned in the Qur'ān. The special care and attention with which it is told is indicative of God's great wisdom in the way He deals with the Muslim community and how He prepares it to assume the all important task of the leadership of mankind.

God's Covenant with the Israelites

Children of Israel! Remember My favour which I have bestowed on you. Fulfil your covenant with Me and I will fulfil Mine with you;

and of Me alone stand in awe. Believe in what I have revealed, confirming that which you already have, and be not the first to reject it. Do not barter away My revelations for a paltry price, and fear Me alone. Do not overlay the truth with falsehood, nor knowingly suppress the truth. Attend regularly to your prayers, pay your zakāt, and bow down in prayers with those who bow down. How can you bid others to be righteous and forget yourselves, even when you read the Scriptures? Do you not understand? Seek strength in patient perseverance and in prayer, which is indeed a demanding task except for the devout, who know that they shall meet their Lord and to Him they shall ultimately return. (Verses 40–46)

Any review of Jewish history would immediately fill one with amazement at the host of favours and blessings God has bestowed on these people. Nor could one fail to be amazed at how persistently they have shown total ingratitude in return. In this opening announcement, God makes a general reference to those special favours before going on to speak about some of them in greater detail. As He does so, God again calls on the Israelites to fulfil their pledges and the commitments they made to Him. If they do, He will bless them with more favour and grace.

What is this covenant? Is it the original one made with Adam: *"Guidance shall reach you from Me. Those who follow My guidance shall have nothing to fear nor shall they grieve, but those who deny and gainsay Our revelations shall have the fire, wherein they shall abide."* (Verses 38–39) Or, is it the universal covenant made between God and human nature, which binds man to seek the Lord and worship Him alone, associating no partners with Him? The latter needs no qualification or justification, as man perceives it instinctively and naturally, as long as his basic nature is free of capricious and deviant influences. Or does the verse refer to the covenant made with Abraham, the patriarch of Israel: *"When his Lord tested Abraham with certain commandments and he fulfilled them, He said, 'I have appointed you a leader of mankind.' Abraham asked, 'And what of my descendants?' God said, 'My covenant does not apply to the wrongdoers.'"* (Verse 124) Is it, on the other hand, the covenant made with the Israelites on Mount Sinai, when the mountain was raised over their heads? They were ordered then to take it up with strength and dedication, as will be later explained.

In fact, all these are essentially one covenant. Their essence is man's total submission to God and adherence to the one true faith He sent to humanity through His messengers, in a long and honourable procession throughout history.

In fulfilment of this covenant, God calls on the Israelites to fear Him alone, and to believe in and accept what He has revealed to His Messenger, Muḥammad, confirming and endorsing their own Scriptures. They are urged not to hasten into rejecting it but to be among the first to believe in it: *"Believe in what I have revealed, confirming that which you already have, and be not the first to reject it."* (Verse 41)

Islam, as propounded by Prophet Muḥammad, was no more than God's one eternal religion given its final form. It is a continuation of the same message and the complement of the covenant God made with man in the beginning. It embraces past revelations and provides guidance for mankind in future generations. It brings together the Torah of the Old Testament and the Gospel of the New Testament, and adds what is required to lead mankind to further prosperity, unity and progress. Its aim has been to achieve the true brotherhood of man, eliminate racial and ethnic divisions and discrimination, and unite humanity in its submission to God under the covenant with Him.

God warns the Israelites against rejecting His final message in pursuit of temporal gain or narrow interests, such as the privileges and the status enjoyed by the rabbis through their religious function in the community: *"Do not barter away My revelations for a paltry price, and fear Me alone."* (Verse 41)

Money, wealth and worldly aggrandizement have been the delight of the Jews since their early days. This verse could be referring to the fees and taxes imposed on ordinary Jews by their rabbis and clerics in return for religious services. These people were known, as stated elsewhere in the Qur'ān, to have had a monopoly on the interpretation of the Scriptures which enabled them to issue biased and tendentious rulings favouring the rich and powerful. To maintain this monopoly, Jewish elders and religious leaders would be inclined to urge their people to reject Islam and refuse to recognize it.

Commenting on this verse, some companions of the Prophet and later scholars have pointed out that when compared to belief in God's revelations and the promised rewards of the hereafter, the world and all its treasures are worthless.

The *sūrah* goes on to censure the Israelites for deliberately confusing truth with falsehood in order to create confusion, doubt and discord among the Muslims. *"Do not overlay the truth with falsehood, nor knowingly suppress the truth."* (Verse 42)

The Qur'ān abounds with reports of how the Jews of Madinah would seize every opportunity to antagonize its Muslims, create distractions and spread false ideas and malicious rumours among them. They had a notorious reputation, as we shall see, for causing division and making mischief within the Muslim community.

The *sūrah* then invites the Israelites to join the Muslims in their religious practices, and abandon their prejudices and ethnocentric tendencies. *"Attend regularly to your prayers, pay your zakāt, and bow down in prayer with those who bow down."* (Verse 43)

Matching Words with Deeds

The *sūrah* refutes their pretence, particularly that of their elders and rabbis, of piety and godliness which they claim simply on the basis of having received divine revelations. The fact is that they continued to reject the new revelations which confirm their own. The *sūrah* asks them disapprovingly: *"How can you bid others to be righteous and forget yourselves, even when you read the Scriptures? Do you not understand?"* (Verse 44)

This may well have been directed at the Jews of Madinah on some specific occasions, but it applies to all believers and religious leaders of all groups and generations.

When religious teaching becomes a mere profession, it loses its fervour. Those who take it up begin to say things they do not believe and their actions tend to become divorced from their words. This can lead them to twist facts and compromise ideas and principles to serve their interests and desires. Their rulings, pronouncements and opinions, or *fatwās*, may sound convincing but they are far removed from the spirit and the letter of the religion.

The double standards of those who claim to represent a certain religion or ideology not only harm them personally, but also undermine the ideas and the religions they are advocating. Thus people would hear fine words, contradicted by foul deeds. The become confused and the light generated by faith in their hearts becomes dim. Having lost trust in religious preachers, they now lose trust in the religion itself.

When they are not uttered with sincerity and conviction, words lose their impact. A man's beliefs are meaningless unless his actions and behaviour become a practical translation of those beliefs. When a man's conduct reflects his words, no matter how plain and ordinary these words are, people will trust him and take him seriously. His words draw their power and effect from the sincerity and honesty with which they are being uttered, not from the rhetoric or eloquence in which they are delivered. They assume a force of their own.

To match one's actions to one's words is not easy to achieve. It requires cultivation, discipline and constant contact with God. Life's preoccupations are normally distracting, and man is weak unless he remains in touch with God's omnipotent power. The forces of evil and temptation can also overwhelm him sometimes, and a brief moment of carelessness can damage the entire course of his life. But, supported by God's invincible power, man can conquer his desires, overcome his weaknesses and overpower his opponents, powerful as they may be.

Thus the Qur'ān directs the Jews of Madinah and, by implication, all mankind, to seek support and strength through perseverance and prayer. The Jews were being asked to give up the privileged status they enjoyed in Madinah and the material benefits obtained from their religious functions, and to accept the new revelations which they knew to be true. Such great sacrifices require strength, courage and devotion. Hence the directive: *"Seek strength in patient perseverance and in prayer, which is indeed a demanding task except for the devout, who know that they shall meet their Lord and to Him they shall ultimately return."* (Verses 45–46)

It demands courage, honesty and tenacity, as well as the power of prayer and perseverance.

Two Sources of Strength

Reference to perseverance is quite frequent in the Qur'ān, which presents it as crucial and indispensable in enduring hardship and making momentous decisions. One of the most difficult moments anyone can encounter is having to acknowledge the truth and relinquish power and material privilege as a result.

But what do we understand from the directive to *'seek strength in ... prayer'*?

Prayer is seen by Islam as a link between man and his Lord and Master, through which the human heart draws strength and fortitude. It generates life and energy in the human soul. Despite his unique relationship with God and the lofty level of spiritual piety he attained, the Prophet Muḥammad was known to resort to prayer every time he experienced distress or anxiety. Prayer remains an inexhaustible fountain of peace, comfort and spiritual uplift for every believer.

A prerequisite of perseverance, or *ṣabr*, and fear of God, or *taqwā*, is the absolute and unshakeable belief in man's return to God when his actions will be reckoned and he will be judged. This is also an essential requirement for the establishment of values for this life and the life to come. Once the right criteria to judge these values are set, the world and all its treasures and riches are seen as worth very little when compared to the rewards in the hereafter.

What started as a simple instruction initially directed at the Jews of Madinah turns out to be a permanent and enduring lesson for all mankind.

The following verse is yet another reminder from God to the Israelites of His grace and generosity towards them, and a general admonition to them about the resurrection that is certain to come: *"Children of Israel! Remember My favour which I bestowed on you, and that I have preferred you over all people. Fear the day when no soul shall avail another in any way, nor shall intercession be accepted from any of them, nor ransom taken from them, and none shall receive help."* (Verses 47–48)

The preferred position granted to the Israelites was limited to the time of their mandate as custodians of God's message on earth. As soon as they betrayed their trust, disobeyed their prophets, denied God's favours and abandoned their commitment to God, they incurred His wrath, and were condemned to a life of humiliation, misery and exile.

When Every Soul Stands Alone

The statement was meant to remind them of that glory and privilege in order to encourage them to seize the fresh opportunity presented to them by Islam to rejoin the community of believers and renew their covenant with God. But they are also being warned about *"a day when no soul shall avail another in any way,"* and no individual can save another.

This is one of the most important Islamic principles. Responsibility and accountability are personal and not collective, and are directly related to an individual's will and freedom of choice. They are also based on divine justice.

It is a principle that upholds the dignity and integrity of man and cultivates and strengthens his conscience. It raises his standards of morality and behaviour and enriches his wealth of values with which Islam has honoured him.

The verse further stresses that on that day, no intercession *"shall be accepted..., nor ransom taken"* from, or on behalf of, anyone. Unless a person has a record of faith and good deeds, nothing can save him or absolve his misdemeanours or intransigence towards God. Furthermore, he shall receive no support of any kind from anyone else.

A Long List of Favours

The *sūrah* proceeds to enumerate the favours God had extended to the Israelites, the most significant of which was their deliverance from the tyranny and persecution of the Pharaoh. It portrays their response to these favours which was marked with lack of appreciation and flagrant violation of God's commandments. *"And remember how We delivered you from Pharaoh's people, who afflicted you with cruel suffering, killing your sons and sparing only your women. That was a grievous trial from your Lord. We parted the sea for you, led you to safety and drowned Pharaoh's people before your very eyes."* (Verses 49–50)

The Qur'ān graphically recalls the ordeals suffered by the Israelites' forefathers, as if the later Jews themselves had undergone those experiences. It stresses the act of deliverance as well as the torment and the persecution that preceded it. It makes the specific point that the whole experience contained an element of trial by God to the Israelites, testing their faith and resolve, and their trust in the Lord. The expression used in this verse in reference to the suffering adds connotations that the suffering was like food given regularly. It highlights one aspect of that suffering, which is the killing of young men and leaving women alone. This was meant to weaken the Jews and exhaust their strength.

The verse seeks to impress upon the listener that when ordained by the will of God, hardship, misfortune and tribulation will not be in vain. Once aware of this fact, one will develop more resilience and moral strength that will enable one to endure pain and overcome it much more easily. The experience will inspire one to draw closer to God and seek His mercy and help, and raise one's capacity to cope with life's difficulties as well as one's credit for reward in the hereafter. Hence the telling comment: *"That was a grievous trial from your Lord."* (Verse 49)

Having recalled the painful part of the episode, the *sūrah* portrays the scene of delivery when God *"parted the sea for you, led you to safety and drowned Pharaoh's people before your very eyes."* (Verse 50)

More detailed accounts of this event, already familiar to the Jews from their own Scriptures, are given in several Makkan *sūrahs* of the Qur'ān. Here, in typical Qur'ānic style, we get only a brief reference to it, but in the most vivid terms, addressing the Jews of Madinah as if they were present at the scene, for a heightened effect and greater impact.

Ingratitude at Its Worst

The Jews have left Egypt and, through God's grace and mercy, crossed the Red Sea safely. The *sūrah* picks up the story: *"And [remember, too], when We appointed for Moses forty nights, and in his absence you took to worshipping the calf, and thus became wrongdoers. Yet even after that We pardoned you, so that you might be thankful. We gave Moses the Scriptures and the Standard [by which to distinguish right from wrong], so that you might be rightly guided. Moses said to his people, 'You, my people, have wronged yourselves by worshipping the calf. Turn, then, in repentance to your Maker and slay one another. That will be better for you in your Maker's sight.' Thus, He accepted your repentance; for He is the One to accept repentance, the Merciful."* (Verses 51–54)

The episode of the calf is covered in more detail in verses 87–98 of *Sūrah* 20, revealed earlier in Makkah. It is a well-known chapter of Jewish history. When their Prophet left them for a while, they sank as low as worshipping an inanimate object, in total disregard of the instructions of the Prophet who saved them, by God's grace, from Pharaoh and his army. Their attitude is described in its true colours:

"You took to worshipping the calf, and thus became wrongdoers." (Verse 51) Who could be a worse wrongdoer than one who worships the model of a calf after God had saved him from idolaters?

Nevertheless, God pardoned them and gave their Prophet, Moses, the Torah as a source of guidance for them. However, there was need for a thorough cleansing of ranks. Such a shaky nature could only be steadied by a very stringent atonement: *"Moses said to his people: 'You, my people, have wronged yourselves by worshipping the calf. Turn, then, in repentance to your Maker and slay one another. That will be better for you in your Maker's sight.'"* (Verse 54) Thus, the order was given to kill those who went far astray as a means of cleansing for the whole community.

No doubt it was a heavy responsibility, for killing members of their community was like killing themselves; but it was inescapable in order to preserve the purity and righteousness of the rest of the community. It was a punishment commensurate with the vile transgression perpetrated. Had they counselled one another against transgression, they would not have worshipped the calf. Hence, the punishment to reform their nature.

Once punishment has been meted out, God's mercy descends afresh. *"Thus, He accepted your repentance; for He is the One to accept repentance, the Merciful."* (Verse 54)

Yet, true to form, their stubbornness and obduracy had the better of the Israelites. They now demanded to see God Himself. The demand was made by the seventy individuals who, as detailed in the earlier Makkan *sūrahs*, had been chosen by Moses to represent his people. They went further than that, making their belief in Moses and his message conditional on their seeing God in person. Obviously, this is mentioned here for comparison with the attitude of the Prophet Muḥammad's Jewish contemporaries, who were demanding impossible proof to verify the truth of his claim to prophethood.

> *And [remember] when you said, 'Moses, we will not believe in you until we see God in person.' You were then struck by a thunderbolt while you were looking on. But We raised you again after you had been as dead, so that you might be thankful. We caused the clouds to provide shade for you, and sent down for you manna and quails. 'Eat of the good things We have provided for you.' Indeed, to Us they did no harm, but themselves did they wrong.* (Verses 55–57)

Neither the signs and favours nor God's forgiveness and generosity had any effect on the Israelites' obdurate, materialistic and cynical nature. The prolonged and harsh persecution they had endured under the tyranny of the Pharaoh seems to have finally corrupted their souls, so that they would yield only to force. Nothing corrupts souls and natures than writhing under tyranny for a long time. They had acquired the slave characteristics of being submissive when overpowered and subjugated, but vicious and revengeful when not under threat. Over the centuries, this became, and remains today, a defining character of the Jewish people.

While on Mount Sinai, the Israelites had the audacity to demand from Moses that they should see God in person, to which God responded by striking them with a thunderbolt that left them as dead. Nevertheless, God was again merciful towards them and restored them to consciousness, so that they might appreciate His kindness and show gratitude.

God also recalls for them how He had taken care of their forefathers when they were lost in the wilderness, providing them with food and protecting them against the scorching heat of the sun. Historic records indicate that the Israelites, on leaving Egypt, crossed the Red Sea into the Sinai desert. It was hot and without water, which put them in danger of dying of starvation. But, God bestowed His grace on them and provided them with a special type of food, as sweet as honey, which they called manna. God also sent them flocks of quail which they could easily catch and eat. Clouds would gather above them to protect them from the heat of the desert sun. Thus God alleviated their suffering in the wilderness, but, as the verse comments, they showed no appreciation or gratitude. As such, they were the losers: *"Indeed to Us they did no harm, but themselves did they wrong."* (Verse 57)

Inviting God's Punishment

The *sūrah* reminds the Children of Israel of more of their acts of intransigence and heartless behaviour: *"And [remember] when We said, 'Enter this city, eat of its abundant food as you may desire, prostrate yourselves as you enter the gates and say: "Lord, relieve us of our burden." We will then forgive your sins and We will richly reward those who do good.' But the wrongdoers among them substituted other words for those which they had been given. Therefore We let loose against them a scourge from heaven in requital for their transgression."* (Verses 58–59)

Some reports indicate that the city referred to here is Jerusalem, the holy city which, not long after the Jewish exodus from Egypt, God commanded the Israelites to enter, driving out its inhabitants who were a race of giants. They refused and asked Moses to do that by himself while they waited outside the city. This episode is discussed fully in verses 20–26 of *Sūrah* 5, where, in an attitude of unmatched insolence, they say to Moses: *"Mighty people dwell in that land, and we will surely not enter it unless they depart from it. If they do depart, then we will enter."* (5: 22) *"Moses, we will never go in so long as they are in it. Go forth, then, you and your Lord, and fight. We shall stay here."* (5: 24)

As punishment they were lost for forty years in the wilderness of the Sinai desert, until a new generation had grown up who, led by the Prophet Joshua, son of Nūn, conquered the city. However, instead of entering Jerusalem, prostrating themselves in humility, and praying God to remove their burden of sin and forgive them, they took a totally different attitude and said different words.

Although these events occurred at a time much later than the one described at the beginning of this section of the *sūrah*, it can be seen clearly that, throughout their history, the Children of Israel displayed the same characteristics of insolence, rebellion, and stubborn deviation.

The Qur'ān was relating to the Jews of Madinah events and episodes of their history well known to them, reminding them of the victory God granted to their forefathers, God's help in bringing them to the holy city of Jerusalem, and their ingratitude and disobedience towards God. *"But the wrongdoers among them substituted other words for those which they had been given. Therefore, We let loose on them a scourge from heaven in requital for their transgression."* (Verse 59)

'Wrongdoers', as used in this verse, could be a reference to a small group among the Israelites or to the whole community, depending on who perpetrated the misdemeanours and rebelled against God and Moses.

In addition to the above, God had also blessed the Israelites while they were in the wilderness by providing them with water. The Qur'ān reminds the Jews of Madinah of this also, and of their forefathers' response to it. *"And [remember] when Moses prayed for water for his people We said to him, 'Strike the rock with your staff.' Twelve springs gushed forth from it. Each tribe knew their drinking place. Eat and drink of what God has provided and do not persistently spread corruption in the land."* (Verse 60)

The Israelites descended from twelve tribes who went back to the twelve sons of Jacob, or Israel, father of the Jews. When they needed water in the desert, they asked Moses to provide it for them, and he turned to God for help. God answered his prayers, and asked Moses to strike a rock with his stick, whereupon twelve springs, one for each tribe, spurted out with enough water for all their needs. They were given all this by God's grace, but they were also warned against spreading corruption: *"Eat and drink of what God has provided for you and do not persistently spread corruption in the land."* (Verse 60)

Unhappy with God's Bounty

Let us recall the scene. The Israelites have fled from persecution and have journeyed into a desert of sand and rocks. The sun beats down all day and the sky will yield no rain. While they endure these desperate and hostile conditions, water springs out of the rocks, honey-tasting manna falls from the sky and quails begin to arrive in multitudes.

But despite all this, the people's minds remained closed, their hearts intractable and their attitude rigid. They could not rise to the occasion or appreciate the purpose of their flight from Egypt. God had delivered them from the humiliation and persecution of the Pharaoh in order to restore their honour, dignity and freedom. Needless to say, there was a price to be paid. They were to inherit the holy city of Jerusalem; but they had to capture it first.

The Israelites did not seem to appreciate that honour or to be ready to make the necessary sacrifices. They simply were not up to the commitment and the responsibility that God had entrusted them with. They were not prepared even to sacrifice the most mundane of their daily needs and habits, so that they might undertake the brief but harsh journey across the desert, on their way to glory, freedom and dignity.

The Qur'ān reminds the Jews of Madinah of what their forefathers had asked of Moses and addresses the early Israelites, saying: *"And [remember] when you said, 'Moses! We can no longer put up with one kind of food. Pray to your Lord, then, to bring forth for us some of what the earth produces of green herbs, cucumber, garlic, lentils and onions.' He said, 'Would you take a lesser thing in exchange for what is much better? Go down to any land and you shall have what you asked for.' Ignominy and humiliation were stamped upon them and they incurred the wrath of God, because they denied His revelations and slew prophets against all right, and because they persisted in their disobedience and transgression."* (Verse 61)

It is clear that Moses himself was aghast at their ignoble demands. His response was that what they were asking for was worthless and could be found anywhere. In its Arabic form, Moses's response could be interpreted in one of two ways. It could mean that their request is so mundane and available everywhere. So wherever they wish to stay, they could find what they asked for. Alternatively, Moses is telling them to go back to Egypt and resume their servile, humble, humdrum life where they can have their cucumber, lentils, garlic and onion. They would not, it seems, be strong enough for the great and noble task God had called on them to undertake.

Contrary to some commentators, I favour this second meaning because it reminds the Israelites of their misery and humiliation in Egypt, as it says: *"Ignominy and humiliation were stamped upon them and they incurred the wrath of God."* (Verse 61) Historically, this came later as a result of their disbelief in God's revelations, their killing of some of their prophets, and their general disobedience. These developments occurred several generations after Moses, but *"ignominy and humiliation"* are mentioned here because they fit the context of their condescension and insolence. Moses reminded them of the suffering and the distress they had undergone in Egypt and of God's kindness in delivering them from the Pharaoh.

Boastful Claims by the Jews

No other nation in history has shown more intransigence and obstinacy than the Jews. They viciously and mercilessly killed and mutilated a number of prophets and messengers. They have over the centuries displayed the most extreme attitudes towards God, and towards their own religion and people.

Nevertheless, they have always boasted of their virtue and made the implausible claims of being the most rightly-guided nation, the chosen people of God and the only people that shall be saved. Such claims are totally refuted by the Qur'ān which, in this *sūrah,* goes on to stress the most basic and all-embracing principle of the unity of God's religion. It establishes that belief in God is one and the same for all groups and nations, and that it will lead to righteousness and good deeds. God's grace and mercy are not the monopoly or the privilege of any particular racial or ethnic group. They are extended to all believers at all stages of human history, in succession, until the arrival of God's final message, which would unite all believers. *"Those who believe, and those who are Jews, and the Christians and the Sabaeans – anyone who believes in God and the Last Day, and does what is right, shall have their reward with their Lord. They have nothing to fear nor shall they grieve."* (Verse 62)

'Those who believe', as used here refers to the Muslims, while "Sabaeans" probably refers to a pre-Islamic religious group among the Arabs who were unhappy with idolatry and sought belief in the one God of Abraham, cutting themselves off from the pagan Arabs. Their name comes from the Arab word *saba',* describing a person who has abandoned the religion of his forefathers. In some commentaries, they are confused with the followers of Sabaism, who worshipped stars.

The verse affirms that all of those religious communities who believe in God and the Last Day shall obtain their reward with God and may rest assured that they will be saved. The main criterion is religious belief rather than ethnic or national affiliation. With the advent of Islam this comes into sharper focus, because the final version of divine faith has been established.

The *sūrah* continues to recall to the Jews of Madinah incidents from the history of their forefathers. *"We accepted your solemn pledge and raised Mount Sinai above you, saying, 'Take with firmness and strength what We have given you, and bear in mind all its contents, so that you may remain God-fearing.' Yet after that you turned away, and but for God's grace and mercy you would have surely been among the losers."* (Verses 63–64)

Details of the 'pledge' are given later on in this *sūrah* and elsewhere in the Qur'ān. The emphasis here is on recalling the scene, in words that well suit the awesome atmosphere in which the covenant was delivered, and lend particular stress to the solemnity and significance of the occasion. God's covenant with the Israelites was not a matter that could be taken lightly; no half-heartedness, equivocation or wavering. It is the most momentous, gravest enterprise that can be contracted between God and man, and it carries a heavy responsibility indeed. Those chosen to give such a pledge must have total determination and devotion to be able to fulfil its obligations. The Israelites are therefore told: *"Take with firmness and strength what We have given you, and bear in mind all its contents, so that you may remain God-fearing."* (Verse 63)

When Prophet Muḥammad was assigned prophethood he said to his wife Khadījah, "There is no longer any time for relaxation", for he had already been told in the Qur'ān: *"We are about to address you with grave and weighty words."* (73: 5)

Having given their pledge, it was essential that the Israelites should understand its implications, appreciate its reality and prepare to meet its demands. What is particularly important is that there should be no short-lived enthusiasm. Such a pledge means, in essence, a whole new way of life for them. As they go about implementing it, it generates new feelings, establishes a new system and observes a new morality. The end result is an attitude based on fearing God, always remembering that He sees us and knows our feelings and motives.

Alas, what a disappointment! The Israelites failed to live up to that responsibility. *"Yet after that you turned away."* (Verse 64) Nevertheless, God did not withhold His grace and mercy from them: *"but for God's grace and mercy you would have surely been among the losers."* (Verse 64)

Where Mockery Is Inadmissible

The *sūrah* moves on to yet another manifestation of their violations of their covenant with God, and their failure to fulfil its requirements. This time it takes the form of weakness in the face of temptation and the prospect of short-term gain. *"You are well aware of those of you who broke the Sabbath. To them We said, 'Be as despicable apes.' Through that [punishment] We set an example to their own time and for all times to come, and an admonition to the God-fearing."* (Verses 65–66)

Elsewhere in the Qur'ān we have the details of their violation of the Sabbath: *"Ask them about the town which stood by the sea: how its people profaned the Sabbath. Each Sabbath their fish appeared before them breaking the water's surface, but they would not come near them on other than Sabbath days."* (7: 163) They had requested that a day should be assigned to them for rest. God set them Saturday as a day when they do not work for a living. He then put them to a clear test when fish would come to the shore in large numbers on the Sabbath but not on other days of the week. Overwhelmed by greed, the Israelites were not able to pass that test. It was not in their nature to let such an opportunity go by for the sake of such a trivial matter as the observance of a certain covenant made with God!

Thus, deviously and flagrantly, they violated the Sabbath by trapping the fish when they came to the shore and waiting until the next day, when the Sabbath was over, to collect them. As a consequence, they were severely reprimanded and rated as no more than *'despicable apes',* since their mentality and behaviour had sunk to utterly revolting depths.

They had earned their due punishment for breaching the trust God had placed in them, abased their humanity by losing their self discipline and control, and descended to the lowest level of animals who have no free will of their own, but are driven by their needs and desires. It is not imperative that they should be physically changed into apes, as the Arabic text may be taken to mean. They had already sunk into that level by thought and spirit.

This episode was marked in their history as a useful lesson for them and for the generations of believers that would come after them.

The Episode of the Cow

The present passage is rounded off by the story of the cow, told here in full since it is not mentioned elsewhere in the Qur'ān. The story depicts the Israelites as shifty and stubborn people, ever looking for excuses and justification for their failures.

> *When Moses said to his people, 'God commands you to sacrifice a cow,' they said, 'Are you mocking at us?' He said, 'God forbid that I should be so ignorant.' They said, 'Pray on our behalf to your Lord to make plain to us what kind of cow she should be.' He said, 'He says let her be neither an old cow nor a young heifer, but of an age in between. Do, then, as you are commanded.'*

> *They said, 'Pray on our behalf to your Lord to make clear to us of what colour she should be.' [Moses] replied, 'He says let her be a yellow cow, bright of hue, pleasing to the beholder.'*
>
> *They said, 'Pray on our behalf to your Lord to make plain to us of what exact type she should be, for to us cows are much alike. We shall, God willing, be guided aright.' [Moses] answered, 'He says let her be a cow, not broken-in to plough the earth or water the tillage, free of all fault, without markings of any other colour.' Said they, 'Now you have given the right description.' They sacrificed her, although they had almost left it undone.*
>
> *Having slain a human being, you cast the blame on one another for this [murder]. God would definitely reveal what you have concealed. We said, 'Strike him with a piece of it. Thus God brings the dead back to life and shows you His signs, so that you may use your reason.'* (Verses 67–73)

This brief account highlights a number of issues, including the nature and disposition of the Israelite mentality, God's power, life after death, and the nature of life and death. Moreover, we may reflect on the stylistic touches in the way the story is told, which fit it perfectly into the context of the *sūrah*.

The Israelite character comes through very clearly in this story, reflecting lack of faith or trust in God, reluctance to believe their Prophets and hesitation in responding to them, and a tendency to mock and ridicule what they are told, coupled with impertinence.

God's directive, as conveyed to them by Moses was clear and simple: *"sacrifice a cow"*. It hardly needed elaboration, nor was it difficult to carry out. Moses, after all, was the man who had led them out of Egypt and, by the grace of God, brought them to safety. He made it clear that he was simply conveying a commandment from God. Not only was their response insolent and brazen, but they also accused Moses of jesting and making fun of them.

Moses was clearly perturbed and made it immediately clear that he entertained no such idea: "*He said: 'God forbid that I should be so ignorant.'*" (Verse 67) His gentle, polite response was sufficient to prompt them to reconsider and act upon God's order. He makes it clear to them that mocking at others is unbecoming of anyone other than a person who does not know recognize God's position.

Up to that point, it was still possible for them to sacrifice any cow to fulfil God's order as given to them by His Messenger, but their devious and hesitant nature got the better of them and they came up with an unnecessary demand: *"They said: 'Pray on our behalf to your Lord to make plain to us what kind of cow she should be.'"* (Verse 68)

The way this question is phrased suggests that they still suspected Moses of making fun of them. Their use of the phrase 'your Lord' when addressing Moses also indicates their indifference towards the whole affair which, they inferred, concerned only Moses and *his* Lord. Moreover, their question regarding the type of cow to be sacrificed is also indicative of their total lack of interest and their tendency to ridicule. Moses had already told them to sacrifice a cow, and any cow would have sufficed.

Moses persisted with his patient approach and tried to steer the dialogue back to a sensible level and away from argument on formality and technicality. He gives them another straight and clear answer: "*He says let her be neither an old cow nor a young heifer, but of an age in between.*" (Verse 68) He follows that with a clear, authoritative advice: *"Do, then, as you are commanded."* (Verse 68)

That should have been more than adequate for them to choose a cow and carry out the order, discharging their obligation and sparing themselves further complication by narrowing their choices even further. Nevertheless, they insisted on asking more questions: "*They said: 'Pray on our behalf to your Lord to make clear to us of what colour she should be.'*" (Verse 69) Since they asked, they received an answer: "*[Moses] replied: 'He says let her be a yellow cow, bright of hue, pleasing to the beholder.'*" (Verse 69)

The choices are narrowing and the task of finding the right kind of beast that would meet this now elaborate description has become more difficult than ever. It is no longer simply the first available cow, but it has to be one of middle years, neither very old nor very young, of bright yellow colour, not too fat nor too lean, and, most difficult of all, 'pleasing to the beholder'. This means that the cow must be bright, lively and vigorous; because such are the qualities that people are pleased to see. On the other hand, people dislike to look at a thin, weak or deformed animal.

Yet those Jews were not finished. They continued to make matters difficult for themselves. Once again they ask about the type of cow they should sacrifice, justifying their new request on grounds that they had a problem of choice: *"They said: 'Pray on our behalf to your Lord to make plain to us of what exact type she should be, for to us cows are much alike. We shall, God willing, be guided aright.'"* (Verse 70)

There was now no escaping severe complication and restriction of choice, as more and more features were specified: *"[Moses] answered: 'He says let her be a cow, not broken-in to plough the earth or water the tillage, free of all fault, without markings of any other colour.'"* (Verse 71)

It was no longer an ordinary, average cow that could be easily found anywhere, but one with a specific description and an unusual combination of features. Then, just as the matter became unduly complicated and the choice really hard, the people relented: *"Said they: 'Now you have given the right description.' They sacrificed her, although they had almost left it undone."* (Verse 71)

It was as though Moses had not, up to that point, been telling them the truth, or they had not been disposed to believe him.

A Murdered Man Brought Back to Life

As soon as they carried out the command, God revealed to them its purpose: *"Having slain a human being, you cast the blame on one another for this [murder]. God would definitely reveal what you have concealed. We said, 'Strike him with a piece of it. Thus God brings the dead back to life and shows you His signs, so that you may use your reason.'"* (Verses 72–73)

This is the second aspect of the story, which highlights God's power, the reality of resurrection and the nature of life and death. The mode changes from narration to direct speech. God has revealed to the Israelites under Moses the wisdom behind asking them to slaughter a cow. A man had been murdered and, with no witnesses available, they were blaming one another for his murder. God wanted to demonstrate to them that He could bring the victim back to life to identify his killer or killers. This was achieved by striking the dead man's body with a piece of the sacrificial cow. The mystery was solved and justice was done.

The question here is why this approach should be necessary when God can restore the dead to life without the need for anything in particular. What possible relationship could there be between the sacrificed cow and the murdered person being restored to life?

The Jews were accustomed to sacrificing cows, but why should a piece of meat restore life to a dead body when it had no life and no ability to give life? The logical answer is that the whole event was symbolic, intended to demonstrate God's power, the workings of which human beings cannot comprehend. We see the effects of God's power around us all the time, but we are not able to grasp its reality or the way it works.

"Thus God brings the dead back to life ..." – just as effortlessly and readily as they had seen, though they could not understand how it happened.

To the human mind, the contrast between the reality of life and the mystery of death cannot be more bewildering, but to God Almighty the matter poses no problem whatsoever. But, how is that so? This is the greatest mystery that no creature can, or ever will, unravel. It is the secret that only the Supreme Being knows, but whose significance and outcome the human mind is able to appreciate and comprehend, because God *"shows you His signs, so that you may use your reason."* (Verse 73)

As given in the Qur'ānic superior style, the narrative takes us on a short mystery tour with a story that begins with a command from God to the Israelites to sacrifice a cow, without at first telling them, or the reader, of the purpose behind it. It was simply a test of faith and obedience.

We are only given the dialogue that takes place between Moses and his people. At no time is the story interrupted to tell us what words were exchanged between God and Moses. We only know that every time the Israelites asked Moses to refer to "his Lord", he did so and came back to them with an answer. We are not told how that communication was conducted or what was said by either God or Moses. This omission is most befitting of God's greatness, who should be revered and not insulted with pointless arguments such as those Jews were making.

The story concludes with an event as astounding for us as it was for the Israelites themselves: a dead man brought back to life simply by striking his corpse with a piece of a dead cow. That is most amazing!

The artistic method employed here combines with the purpose of the narration to a most significant and successful effect in one of the shortest and finest stories told in the Qur'ān.

The final scene in the story should have been awesome enough to inspire faith, submission and fear of God in the hearts of the Children of Israel. But despite all the lessons they might have learnt from earlier encounters related in the *sūrah*, there is a gloomy, disappointing conclusion that comes as a complete surprise: *"Yet after all this, your hearts hardened until they were as hard as rocks or even harder; for there are rocks from which rivers gush forth; others split so that water flows through them, and some other rocks fall down for fear of God. Indeed, God is not unaware of what you do."* (Verse 74)

Their hearts are compared here to hard rocks, but even more difficult to subdue. The similes given were not altogether unfamiliar to the Israelites, for when they needed water they had seen it gush forth from one solid rock, in twelve springs. They had witnessed how a Mountain crashed down when God revealed His glory there, as told in *Sūrah* 7, Verse 143. Their hearts, however, remained rigid and inflexible, totally devoid of faith and fear of God, harsh, barren and unbending. But they are warned that *"God is not unaware of what you do."* (Verse 74)

This concludes an episode of the Israelites' rich and chequered history; a history fraught with denials, deviousness, scheming, stubbornness, corruption and flagrant rebellion.

4

Covenants Breached All the Time

Do you hope that they will accept your message when some of them would listen to the word of God then, having understood them, knowingly distort it? (75)

أَفَتَطْمَعُونَ أَن يُؤْمِنُوا۟ لَكُمْ وَقَدْ كَانَ
فَرِيقٌ مِّنْهُمْ يَسْمَعُونَ كَلَـٰمَ ٱللَّهِ
ثُمَّ يُحَرِّفُونَهُۥ مِنۢ بَعْدِ مَا عَقَلُوهُ
وَهُمْ يَعْلَمُونَ ﴿٧٥﴾

When they meet the believers, they say, 'We believe,' but when they find themselves alone, they say to one another, 'Need you inform them that which God has disclosed to you? They will only use it in argument against you before your Lord? Will you not use your reason?' (76)

وَإِذَا لَقُوا۟ ٱلَّذِينَ ءَامَنُوا۟ قَالُوٓا۟ ءَامَنَّا وَإِذَا
خَلَا بَعْضُهُمْ إِلَىٰ بَعْضٍ قَالُوٓا۟ أَتُحَدِّثُونَهُم
بِمَا فَتَحَ ٱللَّهُ عَلَيْكُمْ لِيُحَآجُّوكُم بِهِۦ
عِندَ رَبِّكُمْ ۚ أَفَلَا تَعْقِلُونَ ﴿٧٦﴾

Do they not know that God is well aware of all that they conceal and all that they reveal? (77)

أَوَلَا يَعْلَمُونَ أَنَّ ٱللَّهَ يَعْلَمُ مَا يُسِرُّونَ
وَمَا يُعْلِنُونَ ﴿٧٧﴾

There are among them illiterate people who have no real knowledge of the Scriptures, entertaining only wishful beliefs and conjecture. (78)

وَمِنْهُمْ أُمِّيُّونَ لَا يَعْلَمُونَ ٱلْكِتَـٰبَ
إِلَّآ أَمَانِىَّ وَإِنْ هُمْ إِلَّا يَظُنُّونَ ﴿٧٨﴾

Woe, then, to those who write down, with their own hands, [something which they claim to be of] the Scriptures, and then say, 'This is from God', in order to get for it a trifling price. Woe to them for what their hands have written and woe to them for what they earn. (79)

فَوَيۡلٞ لِّلَّذِينَ يَكۡتُبُونَ ٱلۡكِتَٰبَ بِأَيۡدِيهِمۡ
ثُمَّ يَقُولُونَ هَٰذَا مِنۡ عِندِ ٱللَّهِ لِيَشۡتَرُواْ
بِهِۦ ثَمَنٗا قَلِيلٗاۖ فَوَيۡلٞ لَّهُم مِّمَّا كَتَبَتۡ
أَيۡدِيهِمۡ وَوَيۡلٞ لَّهُم مِّمَّا يَكۡسِبُونَ ٧٩

They declare, 'The fire will not touch us except for a few days.' Say, 'Have you received such a promise from God – for God never breaks His promise – or do you attribute to God something of which you have no knowledge?' (80)

وَقَالُواْ لَن تَمَسَّنَا ٱلنَّارُ إِلَّآ أَيَّامٗا
مَّعۡدُودَةٗۚ قُلۡ أَتَّخَذۡتُمۡ عِندَ ٱللَّهِ عَهۡدٗا
فَلَن يُخۡلِفَ ٱللَّهُ عَهۡدَهُۥٓۖ أَمۡ تَقُولُونَ عَلَى
ٱللَّهِ مَا لَا تَعۡلَمُونَ ٨٠

Indeed, those who earn evil and become engulfed by their sin are destined for the fire where they shall abide, (81)

بَلَىٰ مَن كَسَبَ سَيِّئَةٗ وَأَحَٰطَتۡ بِهِۦ
خَطِيٓـَٔتُهُۥ فَأُوْلَٰٓئِكَ أَصۡحَٰبُ ٱلنَّارِۖ
هُمۡ فِيهَا خَٰلِدُونَ ٨١

but those who believe and do righteous deeds are destined for Paradise where they shall abide. (82)

وَٱلَّذِينَ ءَامَنُواْ وَعَمِلُواْ ٱلصَّٰلِحَٰتِ
أُوْلَٰٓئِكَ أَصۡحَٰبُ ٱلۡجَنَّةِۖ هُمۡ فِيهَا
خَٰلِدُونَ ٨٢

We made this covenant with the Children of Israel: 'Worship none but God; show kindness to parents and kinsfolk and to the orphans and the poor; speak kindly to all people; attend

وَإِذۡ أَخَذۡنَا مِيثَٰقَ بَنِيٓ إِسۡرَٰٓءِيلَ
لَا تَعۡبُدُونَ إِلَّا ٱللَّهَ وَبِٱلۡوَٰلِدَيۡنِ
إِحۡسَانٗا وَذِي ٱلۡقُرۡبَىٰ وَٱلۡيَتَٰمَىٰ
وَٱلۡمَسَٰكِينِ وَقُولُواْ لِلنَّاسِ

regularly to your prayers and pay the obligatory alms.' But, except for a few, you turned away and paid no heed. (83)

حُسْنًا وَأَقِيمُوا۟ ٱلصَّلَوٰةَ وَءَاتُوا۟
ٱلزَّكَوٰةَ ثُمَّ تَوَلَّيْتُمْ إِلَّا قَلِيلًا
مِّنكُمْ وَأَنتُم مُّعْرِضُونَ ﴿٨٣﴾

We made a covenant with you that you shall not shed your own blood or drive yourselves out of your own homeland. You acknowledged all that and bore witness to it. (84)

وَإِذْ أَخَذْنَا مِيثَٰقَكُمْ لَا تَسْفِكُونَ
دِمَآءَكُمْ وَلَا تُخْرِجُونَ أَنفُسَكُم
مِّن دِيَٰرِكُمْ ثُمَّ أَقْرَرْتُمْ وَأَنتُمْ
تَشْهَدُونَ ﴿٨٤﴾

Yet there you are, slaying yourselves, and driving some of your own people out of their homes, collaborating against them in sin and injustice. Had they come to you as captives you would have ransomed them. Their expulsion is indeed forbidden to you. Do you, then, believe in some parts of the Scriptures and deny others? Those of you who do this will have nothing for their reward other than ignominy in this life and, on the Day of Resurrection, they shall be committed to a most grievous suffering. For God is not unaware of what you do. (85)

ثُمَّ أَنتُمْ هَٰٓؤُلَآءِ تَقْتُلُونَ أَنفُسَكُمْ
وَتُخْرِجُونَ فَرِيقًا مِّنكُم مِّن دِيَٰرِهِمْ
تَظَٰهَرُونَ عَلَيْهِم بِٱلْإِثْمِ وَٱلْعُدْوَٰنِ وَإِن
يَأْتُوكُمْ أُسَٰرَىٰ تُفَٰدُوهُمْ وَهُوَ مُحَرَّمٌ
عَلَيْكُمْ إِخْرَاجُهُمْ ۚ أَفَتُؤْمِنُونَ
بِبَعْضِ ٱلْكِتَٰبِ وَتَكْفُرُونَ بِبَعْضٍ ۚ
فَمَا جَزَآءُ مَن يَفْعَلُ ذَٰلِكَ مِنكُمْ
إِلَّا خِزْىٌ فِى ٱلْحَيَوٰةِ ٱلدُّنْيَا ۖ وَيَوْمَ
ٱلْقِيَٰمَةِ يُرَدُّونَ إِلَىٰٓ أَشَدِّ ٱلْعَذَابِ ۗ وَمَا ٱللَّهُ
بِغَٰفِلٍ عَمَّا تَعْمَلُونَ ﴿٨٥﴾

Such are the ones who buy the life of this world at the price of the life to come. Their suffering shall not be alleviated, nor shall they receive any succour. (86)

أُو۟لَٰٓئِكَ ٱلَّذِينَ ٱشْتَرَوُا۟ ٱلْحَيَوٰةَ ٱلدُّنْيَا
بِٱلْءَاخِرَةِ ۖ فَلَا يُخَفَّفُ عَنْهُمُ ٱلْعَذَابُ
وَلَا هُمْ يُنصَرُونَ ﴿٨٦﴾

We gave Moses the Book and caused a succession of messengers to follow him. To Jesus, son of Mary, We gave clear proofs and supported him with the Holy Spirit. Why is it that every time a messenger comes to you with a message that does not suit your fancies, you glory in your arrogance, charging some (messengers) with lying and slaying others? (87)

وَلَقَدْ ءَاتَيْنَا مُوسَى ٱلْكِتَٰبَ وَقَفَّيْنَا
مِنۢ بَعْدِهِۦ بِٱلرُّسُلِ ۖ وَءَاتَيْنَا عِيسَى ٱبْنَ
مَرْيَمَ ٱلْبَيِّنَٰتِ وَأَيَّدْنَٰهُ بِرُوحِ ٱلْقُدُسِ ۗ
أَفَكُلَّمَا جَآءَكُمْ رَسُولٌۢ بِمَا لَا تَهْوَىٰٓ
أَنفُسُكُمُ ٱسْتَكْبَرْتُمْ فَفَرِيقًا كَذَّبْتُمْ
وَفَرِيقًا تَقْتُلُونَ ﴿٨٧﴾

They say, 'Our hearts are sealed.' No! God has cursed them for their disbelief. They have but little faith. (88)

وَقَالُوا۟ قُلُوبُنَا غُلْفٌۢ ۚ بَل لَّعَنَهُمُ ٱللَّهُ
بِكُفْرِهِمْ فَقَلِيلًا مَّا يُؤْمِنُونَ ﴿٨٨﴾

And now that a Book confirming their own has come to them from God, and they had repeatedly forecast its coming to the unbelievers, they have denied what they know to be the truth. God's curse be upon the unbelievers! (89)

وَلَمَّا جَآءَهُمْ كِتَٰبٌ مِّنْ عِندِ ٱللَّهِ مُصَدِّقٌ
لِّمَا مَعَهُمْ وَكَانُوا۟ مِن قَبْلُ يَسْتَفْتِحُونَ
عَلَى ٱلَّذِينَ كَفَرُوا۟ فَلَمَّا جَآءَهُم
مَّا عَرَفُوا۟ كَفَرُوا۟ بِهِۦ ۚ فَلَعْنَةُ ٱللَّهِ عَلَى
ٱلْكَٰفِرِينَ ﴿٨٩﴾

Vile is that for which they have bartered their souls, because they have denied what God has revealed, grudging that He should, by His grace, send down His revelations to whom He chooses from among His servants. Thus they have incurred God's wrath over and over again. Ignominious suffering is in store for the unbelievers. (90)

بِئْسَمَا ٱشْتَرَوْا۟ بِهِۦٓ أَنفُسَهُمْ أَن
يَكْفُرُوا۟ بِمَآ أَنزَلَ ٱللَّهُ بَغْيًا أَن
يُنَزِّلَ ٱللَّهُ مِن فَضْلِهِۦ عَلَىٰ مَن يَشَآءُ
مِنْ عِبَادِهِۦ ۖ فَبَآءُو بِغَضَبٍ عَلَىٰ غَضَبٍ ۚ
وَلِلْكَٰفِرِينَ عَذَابٌ مُّهِينٌ ﴿٩٠﴾

When it is said to them, 'Believe in what God has revealed,' they say, 'We believe in what has been revealed to us.' They deny everything else, although it is the truth, corroborating the revelations they have. Say, 'Why, then, did you in the past kill God's prophets, if you were true believers?' (91)

وَإِذَا قِيلَ لَهُمْ ءَامِنُوا۟ بِمَآ أَنزَلَ ٱللَّهُ قَالُوا۟
نُؤْمِنُ بِمَآ أُنزِلَ عَلَيْنَا وَيَكْفُرُونَ بِمَا
وَرَآءَهُۥ وَهُوَ ٱلْحَقُّ مُصَدِّقًا لِّمَا مَعَهُمْ ۗ قُلْ
فَلِمَ تَقْتُلُونَ أَنۢبِيَآءَ ٱللَّهِ مِن قَبْلُ إِن كُنتُم
مُّؤْمِنِينَ ﴿٩١﴾

Moses came to you with clear proofs, but in his absence you transgressed, worshipping the calf. (92)

وَلَقَدْ جَآءَكُم مُّوسَىٰ بِٱلْبَيِّنَٰتِ ثُمَّ
ٱتَّخَذْتُمُ ٱلْعِجْلَ مِنۢ بَعْدِهِۦ وَأَنتُمْ
ظَٰلِمُونَ ﴿٩٢﴾

We accepted your solemn pledge, and We raised Mount Sinai above you, saying, 'Take with firmness and strength what We have given you and hearken to it.' They said, 'We hear but we disobey.' For their unbelief they were made to drink the calf into their hearts. Say, 'Vile is that which your faith enjoins upon you, if indeed you are believers.' (93)

وَإِذْ أَخَذْنَا مِيثَٰقَكُمْ وَرَفَعْنَا
فَوْقَكُمُ ٱلطُّورَ خُذُوا۟ مَآ ءَاتَيْنَٰكُم
بِقُوَّةٍ وَٱسْمَعُوا۟ ۖ قَالُوا۟ سَمِعْنَا وَعَصَيْنَا
وَأُشْرِبُوا۟ فِى قُلُوبِهِمُ ٱلْعِجْلَ
بِكُفْرِهِمْ ۚ قُلْ بِئْسَمَا يَأْمُرُكُم
بِهِۦٓ إِيمَٰنُكُمْ إِن كُنتُم مُّؤْمِنِينَ ﴿٩٣﴾

Say, 'If the ultimate abode with God is yours alone, to the exclusion of all others, then wish for death, if your claim is true.' (94)

قُلْ إِن كَانَتْ لَكُمُ ٱلدَّارُ ٱلْءَاخِرَةُ
عِندَ ٱللَّهِ خَالِصَةً مِّن دُونِ ٱلنَّاسِ فَتَمَنَّوُا۟
ٱلْمَوْتَ إِن كُنتُمْ صَٰدِقِينَ ﴿٩٤﴾

وَلَن يَتَمَنَّوْهُ أَبَدًۢا بِمَا قَدَّمَتْ أَيْدِيهِمْ ۗ
وَٱللَّهُ عَلِيمٌۢ بِٱلظَّٰلِمِينَ ﴿٩٥﴾

But they will never wish for it because of what their hands have wrought in this life. God is well aware of the wrongdoers. (95)

وَلَتَجِدَنَّهُمْ أَحْرَصَ ٱلنَّاسِ عَلَىٰ حَيَوٰةٍ وَمِنَ
ٱلَّذِينَ أَشْرَكُوا۟ ۚ يَوَدُّ أَحَدُهُمْ لَوْ يُعَمَّرُ أَلْفَ
سَنَةٍ وَمَا هُوَ بِمُزَحْزِحِهِۦ مِنَ ٱلْعَذَابِ أَن
يُعَمَّرَ ۗ وَٱللَّهُ بَصِيرٌۢ بِمَا يَعْمَلُونَ ﴿٩٦﴾

Indeed, you shall find that they cling to life more eagerly than any other people, even more than the idolaters. Each one of them would love to live a thousand years, although the grant of a long life could not save him from punishment. God sees all that they do. (96)

قُلْ مَن كَانَ عَدُوًّا لِّجِبْرِيلَ فَإِنَّهُۥ نَزَّلَهُۥ
عَلَىٰ قَلْبِكَ بِإِذْنِ ٱللَّهِ مُصَدِّقًا لِّمَا بَيْنَ
يَدَيْهِ وَهُدًى وَبُشْرَىٰ لِلْمُؤْمِنِينَ ﴿٩٧﴾

Say, 'Whoever is an enemy of Gabriel should know that he revealed it [the Qur'ān] to your heart by God's leave.' It confirms the Scriptures revealed before it, and is a guidance and joyful tidings for the believers. (97)

مَن كَانَ عَدُوًّا لِّلَّهِ وَمَلَٰٓئِكَتِهِۦ
وَرُسُلِهِۦ وَجِبْرِيلَ وَمِيكَىٰلَ فَإِنَّ
ٱللَّهَ عَدُوٌّ لِّلْكَٰفِرِينَ ﴿٩٨﴾

Whoever is an enemy of God, His angels, His messengers, and to Gabriel and Michael will surely find that God is indeed the enemy of the unbelievers. (98)

وَلَقَدْ أَنزَلْنَآ إِلَيْكَ ءَايَٰتٍۭ بَيِّنَٰتٍ ۖ
وَمَا يَكْفُرُ بِهَآ إِلَّا ٱلْفَٰسِقُونَ ﴿٩٩﴾

We have sent down to you clear revelations: none will deny them except the evildoers. (99)

أَوَكُلَّمَا عَٰهَدُوا۟ عَهْدًا نَّبَذَهُۥ فَرِيقٌ
مِّنْهُم ۚ بَلْ أَكْثَرُهُمْ لَا يُؤْمِنُونَ ﴿١٠٠﴾

Is it always to be the case that every time they make a solemn pledge some of them will violate it? The truth is that most of them do not believe. (100)

And now that a Messenger from God has come to them, confirming what is already in their possession, some of those who had been given the Scriptures cast God's Book behind their backs as though they know nothing. (101)

وَلَمَّا جَآءَهُمْ رَسُولٌ مِّنْ عِندِ
ٱللَّهِ مُصَدِّقٌ لِّمَا مَعَهُمْ نَبَذَ
فَرِيقٌ مِّنَ ٱلَّذِينَ أُوتُوا۟ ٱلْكِتَٰبَ
كِتَٰبَ ٱللَّهِ وَرَآءَ ظُهُورِهِمْ
كَأَنَّهُمْ لَا يَعْلَمُونَ ١٠١

They follow what the devils relate of Solomon's kingdom. Solomon never disbelieved, but the devils did. They instruct people in witchcraft which was certainly not revealed to the two angels, Hārūt and Mārūt, at Babylon. Yet these two [angels] never taught anyone without first declaring, 'We are but a temptation to evil, so do not renounce your faith.' From these two, people learned what they would use to cause discord between a man and his wife. However, with that knowledge they can harm no one except by God's leave. Indeed, they learn what harms them and brings them no profit. They knew full well that whoever contracted such a deal would have no share in the life to come. Vile indeed is what they had sold their souls for, if they but knew it! (102)

وَٱتَّبَعُوا۟ مَا تَتْلُوا۟ ٱلشَّيَٰطِينُ عَلَىٰ مُلْكِ
سُلَيْمَٰنَ ۖ وَمَا كَفَرَ سُلَيْمَٰنُ وَلَٰكِنَّ
ٱلشَّيَٰطِينَ كَفَرُوا۟ يُعَلِّمُونَ ٱلنَّاسَ
ٱلسِّحْرَ وَمَآ أُنزِلَ عَلَى ٱلْمَلَكَيْنِ
بِبَابِلَ هَٰرُوتَ وَمَٰرُوتَ ۚ وَمَا يُعَلِّمَانِ
مِنْ أَحَدٍ حَتَّىٰ يَقُولَآ إِنَّمَا نَحْنُ فِتْنَةٌ
فَلَا تَكْفُرْ ۖ فَيَتَعَلَّمُونَ مِنْهُمَا
مَا يُفَرِّقُونَ بِهِۦ بَيْنَ ٱلْمَرْءِ وَزَوْجِهِۦ ۚ
وَمَا هُم بِضَآرِّينَ بِهِۦ مِنْ أَحَدٍ
إِلَّا بِإِذْنِ ٱللَّهِ ۚ وَيَتَعَلَّمُونَ مَا يَضُرُّهُمْ
وَلَا يَنفَعُهُمْ ۚ وَلَقَدْ عَلِمُوا۟ لَمَنِ
ٱشْتَرَىٰهُ مَا لَهُۥ فِى ٱلْءَاخِرَةِ مِنْ خَلَٰقٍ ۚ
وَلَبِئْسَ مَا شَرَوْا۟ بِهِۦٓ أَنفُسَهُمْ ۚ
لَوْ كَانُوا۟ يَعْلَمُونَ ١٠٢

Had they embraced the faith and been God-fearing, God's reward would have been far better for them, if they but knew it. (103)

وَلَوْ أَنَّهُمْ ءَامَنُوا۟ وَٱتَّقَوْا۟ لَمَثُوبَةٌ مِّنْ عِندِ
ٱللَّهِ خَيْرٌ ۖ لَّوْ كَانُوا۟ يَعْلَمُونَ ﴿١٠٣﴾

Overview

The passage we discussed in Chapter 3 ended on a note reminding the Children of Israel of the many favours God had bestowed on them and their continued ingratitude. We witnessed a number of scenes, some drawn in general outline and some elaborate, showing God's favours and the Israelites' ungrateful response. This culminated in the description of their hearts as harder than rocks.

This passage addresses the Muslim community, giving it an outline of the machinations of the Children of Israel, and their devious, wicked scheming. The Muslims are warned that, with such history and nature, the Jews will always try to lead them astray. The length of this address, and the different styles and approaches it employs are indicative of the magnitude of the wicked schemes the Jews of Madinah employed to undermine the Muslim community.

Every now and then, the *sūrah* confronts the Children of Israel, in front of the Muslims, with the pledges they gave to God and how they violated them. They went as far as killing some of their Prophets when those Prophets would not comply with their wishes. It also describes their violation of divine law, their false arguments and distortion of their Scriptures.

The passage highlights their long arguments with the Muslim community, and the false claims they used. It instructs the Prophet on how to expose their claims and refute their arguments, putting forward the truth, clear and simple. One of their claims was that they would not be in hell for more than a small number of days, on account of their special position with God. God instructs His Messenger on how to refute this claim: *"Say: 'Have you received such a promise from God – for God never breaks His promise – or do you attribute to God something of which you have no knowledge?'"* (Verse 80)

When they were called upon to embrace Islam, *"they would say, 'We believe in what has been revealed to us.' They deny everything else, although it is the truth, corroborating the revelations they have."* (Verse 91) God tells the Prophet to expose as false their claim of believing in what was revealed to them. *"Say, 'Why, then, did you in the past kill God's prophets, if you were true believers?' Moses came to you with clear proofs, but in his absence you transgressed, worshipping the calf. We accepted your solemn pledge, and We raised Mount Sinai above you, saying, 'Take with firmness and strength what We have given you and hearken to it.' They said, 'We hear but we disobey. 'For their unbelief they were made to drink the calf into their hearts. Say, 'Vile is that which your faith enjoins upon you, if indeed you are believers.'"* (Verses 91–93)

They also alleged that paradise belongs to them alone, in preference to all people. God instructs the Prophet Muḥammad to challenge them to open appeal in which they and the Muslims would meet and pray to God together to destroy the party that is lying: *"Say: 'If the ultimate abode with God is yours alone, to the exclusion of all others, then wish for death, if your claim is true.'"* (Verse 94)

He also states very clearly that they would never wish for death. This proved to be true. When challenged for such a public appeal, they declined, because they realized that their claims were false.

The *sūrah* continues with this confrontation, exposure of the Israelites and instructions to the Muslims. Such a line was certain to weaken and foil the Jewish wicked schemes against the Muslims. All their devious designs were laid bare. Through knowledge of their old history, the Muslim community was able to expose their insidious methods.

Even today, the Muslim community continues to be the target of such Jewish methods. Unfortunately, the Muslim community today does not follow in the footsteps of its forefathers who implemented the Qur'ānic directives. It was only through such implementation that they were able to overcome the wicked schemes of the Jews of Madinah, even though the Muslim community was still in its infancy. Persisting with their wicked designs, the Jews continue to try to turn the Muslims away from the Qur'ān so that they would not derive from it their most effective weapons. As long as the Muslim community turns its back to its source of true power and pure knowledge, they feel safe. Therefore, anyone who tries to divert the Muslim community away from its faith and from the Qur'ān serves, knowingly and willingly or not, the Israeli aims. It is only through its true faith, its law and method of action that the Muslim community derives its true power. When it abandons these, its enemies are assured of their safety and victory.

Falsification of Scriptures

Do you hope that they will accept your message when some of them would listen to the word of God then, having understood them, knowingly distort it? When they meet the believers, they say, 'We believe,' but when they find themselves alone, they say to one another, 'Need you inform them that which God has disclosed to you? They will only use it in argument against you before your Lord? Will you not use your reason?' Do they not know that God is well aware of all that they conceal and all that they reveal? (Verses 75–77)

Towards the end of the last section, we were told about the rigid and relentless nature of the Israelites. It is a gloomy portrait that casts a bleak shadow of despair and hopelessness; it would seem impossible that any good would come out of them. With that in mind, the *sūrah* questions the grounds for any hope, as entertained by some Muslims, that the Jews would accept Islam.

Such a hope was ill-founded because the Jews seemed to lack the perception and the understanding that would lead them to acknowledge the truth and accept it. Faith and belief in God require a straightforward, refined and receptive nature that is free of deviousness and perversity. It requires a caring, sensitive nature that is truly sincere and fearful of God, that would not distort His words or try to obliterate the truth once it is declared.

The reference here is to the learned and the scholars among Madinah's Jews, the rabbis and religious elders, who were well versed in the Torah but were willing to tamper with it, and who would knowingly misrepresent and misquote it. This they would do out of jealousy and for their own selfish purposes. Since those people were predisposed to distorting their own Scriptures, they would be even more liable to misrepresent and reject what Muḥammad was teaching, and more than ready to oppose Islam and falsify its message.

When they meet the believers, they say, 'We believe,' but when they find themselves alone, they say to one another, 'Need you inform

> *them that which God has disclosed to you? They will only use it in argument against you before your Lord? Will you not use your reason?'* (Verse 76)

Besides distortion and misrepresentation of the truth, there is also cant and hypocrisy. In fulfilment of prophecies found in their own Scriptures and by virtue of the fact that they had been awaiting the coming of a prophet to lead them to salvation, some Jews would tell the Muslims at times that they too believed in Muḥammad (peace be upon him). Privately, to avoid giving the Muslims any evidence they could use to indict them before God, they would strongly reproach one another for overdoing their pretence of belief. Ludicrous as it may appear, they seemed to believe that as long as they did not divulge their true convictions to the Muslims publicly, they would succeed in concealing them from God and He would thereby not hold it against them. The *sūrah*, therefore, wonders what kind of logic they were using and, before moving to elaborate on their claims, asks in amazement: *"Do they not know that God is well aware of all that they conceal and all that they reveal?"* (Verse 77)

The *sūrah* continues with its education of the Muslims about the Israelites by saying that they fall into two groups. The first is the ignorant, illiterate masses who have no knowledge or understanding of the Scriptures, who live by superstition and wishful thinking, and who presume that the Jews will gain eternal salvation, on the fallacious grounds of being God's 'Chosen People', whose sins are forgiven and deliverance guaranteed.

The second group is those who exploit this ignorance and distort the Scriptures for material gain and in order to further and safeguard their own ambitions, power and influence: "*There are among them illiterate people who have no real knowledge of the Scriptures, entertaining only wishful beliefs and conjecture. Woe, then, to those who write down, with their own hands, [something which they claim to be of] the Scriptures, and then say, 'This is from God', in order to get for it a trifling price. Woe to them for what their hands have written and woe to them for what they earn.*" (Verses 78–79)

Neither group could be relied on to be truthful to their Scriptures or respond positively to the truth and guidance revealed by God to the Prophet Muḥammad. They are condemned to a deplorable end for distorting God's words, and for exploiting their own people and others for material gain and for the sake of religious and political dominance.

Reply to False Arguments

One of the most notorious claims made by the Israelites which stood in direct conflict with divine justice, and had no basis in logic or religious doctrine, was that they were immune to punishment no matter how much they erred or deviated. Hell fire, they said, would touch them for no more than a few days, if at all; after which they would abide in Paradise for ever.

What basis did they have for such a pompous claim? Nothing but sheer wishful thinking based on ignorance and the cunning lies of their elders. When people stray away and find themselves, over a long period, divorced from the true spirit of their religious belief, they end up with a mere façade, a superficial identity that means little in reality. Such people will continue to cherish the illusion of righteousness and salvation by paying lip service to their religious faith. They imagine that their claims of following the right faith will spare them God's punishment: "*They declare, 'The fire will not touch us except for a few days.' Say, 'Have you received such a promise from God – for God never breaks His promise – or do you attribute to God something of which you have no knowledge?'*" (Verse 80)

What a powerful rebuttal! What promise or assurance do they have from God to substantiate their claims? The truth is that they have no such thing. The question is a rhetorical one, carrying a whiff of sarcasm and reproach.

The next verse gives a definitive statement which represents one of the most fundamental concepts in Islam based on its overall view of man, life and the universe. Reward relates directly to action, both in quantity and quality: "*Indeed, those who earn evil and become engulfed by their sin are destined for the fire where they shall abide, but those who believe and do righteous deeds are destined for Paradise where they shall abide.*" (Verses 81–82)

What we have here is a superb artistic portrait of a particular mentality, leading to a clear-cut and decisive ruling. We learn that evil is earned. This goes beyond the mere act of committing a sin. We are presented with a psychological frame of mind: the sinners are deriving a certain degree of pleasure and satisfaction from their sins.

They somehow consider that as gainful and worthwhile behaviour, and so they become totally overcome by it. Had they not believed it to be so, they would have desisted and done their best to avoid such sinful conduct. The Qur'ānic Arabic expression is most graphic, so that the meaning is clear and immediately grasped. These people are totally enthralled with their wrongdoing and misguided behaviour. It practically engulfs them to the extent that their whole life is dominated by it and they live for nothing else.

The image of these sinners as eternal dwellers of hell is contrasted with that of those who *"believe and do righteous deeds"* and are destined for eternal bliss and endless happiness.

True faith finds genuine expression in good acts; a fact which believers, and Muslims in particular, ought to consider and realize. Belief loses its meaning unless it leads to constructive and worthwhile activity. Those who claim to be Muslims but perpetrate corruption, oppose the implementation of God's law in society, and resist the promotion of Islamic ethics and modes of moral conduct among people are seriously lacking in faith and loyalty to God and Islam. The efforts of such people are fruitless. They shall have no protection whatsoever against God's punishment, which is bound to come, keen as they may be to avoid it.

Going Back on Firm Pledges

The *sūrah* tells the Muslims more about the nature of the Jews and their crooked and devious ways while, at the same time, confronting the Jews themselves with these revelations.

> *We made this covenant with the Children of Israel: 'Worship none but God; show kindness to parents and kinsfolk and to the orphans and the poor; speak kindly to all people; attend regularly to your prayers and pay the obligatory alms.' But, except for a few, you turned away and paid no heed. We made a covenant with you that you shall not shed your own blood or drive yourselves out of your own homeland. You acknowledged all that and bore witness to it. Yet there you are, slaying yourselves, and driving some of your own people out of their homes, collaborating against them in sin and injustice. Had they come to you as captives you would have ransomed them. Their expulsion is indeed forbidden to you. Do you, then, believe in*

> *some parts of the Scriptures and deny others? Those of you who do this will have nothing for their reward other than ignominy in this life and, on the Day of Resurrection, they shall be committed to a most grievous suffering. For God is not unaware of what you do.* (Verses 83–85)

Reference has already been made to God's covenant with the Israelites, and here we learn of more details of this covenant.

Right at the outset, we learn that the covenant between God and the Israelites contained the fundamental and absolute tenets of Divine faith that were subsequently confirmed by Islam, which the Jews chose to oppose and deny.

It required that the Israelites submit to, and worship God, other than whom there is no deity. It advocated kindness to parents, relatives, orphans and the poor in society. It urged courtesy towards others, especially in teaching and preaching to them about right and wrong, good and evil. Furthermore, the covenant enjoined upon the Israelites the observance of regular prayer and the giving of alms; all of which are, indeed, the very basic principles and obligations set by Islam.

This leads to two definite conclusions. First, God's religion is one and the same throughout human history; its last version, Islam, confirms and endorses the fundamentals of all preceding ones. Second, there is no doubt about the arrogance and obstinacy of the Jews towards this universal religion of God and their refusal to acknowledge it, despite the fact that it advocated the same principles as their covenant with God.

The *sūrah* then turns to address the Israelites directly, highlighting the inherent contradiction in their attitude. It goes on to point out further contradictions between their present attitude and the terms of their covenant with God: "*We made a covenant with you that you shall not shed your own blood or drive yourselves out of your own homeland. You acknowledged all that and bore witness to it.*" (Verse 84)

But what have they done after that? "*Yet there you are, slaying yourselves, and driving some of your own people out of their homes, collaborating against them in sin and injustice. Had they come to you as captives you would have ransomed them. Their expulsion is indeed forbidden to you. Do you, then, believe in some parts of the Scriptures and deny others? Those of you who do this will have nothing for their reward other than ignominy in this life and, on the Day of Resurrection, they shall be committed to a most grievous suffering. For God is not unaware of what you do."* (Verse 85)

The *sūrah* is referring here to events that had occurred shortly before the advent of Islam. The city of Madinah was inhabited by two major Arab tribes, the Aws and the Khazraj, who had no formal religious beliefs of their own and worshipped various deities. They were bitter rivals, constantly at loggerheads. The Jews had settled in three well-defined areas of Madinah and made various agreements with their Arab neighbours from both tribes. The Jewish tribes of Qaynuqā' and al-Naḍīr allied themselves with the Khazraj tribe, while the Qurayẓah allied itself with the Aws. Whenever war broke out between the two major Arab tribes, the Jewish inhabitants would side with their respective allies, so that Jew killed Jew, in complete violation of their covenant with God. Jews would drive other Jews out of their homes, loot their possessions and take their women. As soon as hostilities ceased, Jews on both sides would hurry to exchange Jewish captives or buy their freedom, in fulfilment of the Torah teachings.

The contradiction underlying this behaviour is exposed and the Jews are strongly reproached: *"Do you, then, believe in some parts of the Scriptures and deny others?"* (Verse 85) This is the very violation of their covenant for which they are given a very stern warning: *"Those of you who do this will have nothing for their reward other than ignominy in this life and, on the Day of Resurrection, they shall be committed to a most grievous suffering. For God is not unaware of what you do."* (Verse 85)

The *sūrah* then addresses the Muslims, and mankind in general: *"Such are the ones who buy the life of this world at the price of the life to come. Their suffering shall not be alleviated, nor shall they receive any succour."* (Verse 86)

The motive behind their bartering away the life to come, and its rewards, for temporal gain in this life, in stark violation of their covenant with God, was their eagerness to fulfil the unholy alliances they had forged with the Arab idolaters, in contradiction to the teachings of their Scriptures. Siding with both rival camps at the same time was typical of the Jews of that time, consistent with their age-old policy of holding both ends of the stick and placing two-way bets on events in order to secure some gains and protect certain interests, whichever camp ends up the winner.

Such hypocrisy and cynical manipulation on the part of the Israelites betray a deep-seated mistrust of God Almighty and a lack of faith in His covenant with them. They undermine the very foundations of their belief in God and His powers, and expose their actions as driven wholly by materialistic self-interest, in total disregard for the precepts and teachings of their Scriptures.

A Long List of Contradictions

The *sūrah* then confronts the Israelites with their record of how they treated God's messages and messengers, including their own prophets: *"We gave Moses the Book and caused a succession of messengers to follow him. To Jesus, son of Mary, We gave clear proofs and supported him with the Holy Spirit. Why is it that every time a messenger comes to you with a message that does not suit your fancies, you glory in your arrogance, charging some (messengers) with lying and slaying others?"* (Verse 87)

The Israelites' main argument for not accepting Islam was that they were in possession of a great many such teachings that had been given to them by their own prophets. The Qur'ān, however, rejects that claim and exposes the disgraceful manner in which they had received those prophets and their teachings.

We have already been told of their encounter with Moses (peace be upon him), and here we learn of more prophets coming after him and receiving similar treatment, right up to Jesus, the son of Mary. Jesus (peace be upon him) came to them with clear evidence of the truth, including the performance of miracles, and was supported by the Holy Spirit, the Archangel Gabriel. But what was their attitude towards him? Their own Scriptures testify to a sad tale of rejection, denunciation and appalling ingratitude towards all the prophets who were sent to them: *"Why is it that every time a messenger comes to you with a message that does not suit your fancies, you glory in your arrogance, charging some (messengers) with lying and slaying others?"* (Verse 87)

The human tendency to manipulate rules and set double standards in order to achieve selfish ethnocentric, nationalist or sectarian objectives is a well-known phenomenon in society. It usually surfaces in corrupt societies that have lost the basic human sense of justice and fair-play. Laws, principles and standards ought to stem from a neutral, objective and a fair source that is not susceptible to the influence of human desires or prejudices. This agency must transcend human frailty and self-interest.

God relates these accounts of Israelite history as a warning to Muslims to avoid those pitfalls, to preserve their position of leadership on earth and live up to the trust God has placed in them. Thus we find that whenever Muslims have deviated from or abandoned the rule of Islam and persecuted the advocates of true faith, rejecting some and killing others, they have met a fate similar to that of the Israelites. They became weak, divided and humiliated, wallowing in ignominy and misery. This sad state will persist until they respond to the call of God and His messengers, submit to His will, and fulfil their covenant with God with clear resolve and determination.

Having confronted the Israelites with their attitude towards their own Prophets, the *sūrah* tackles their response to the new message, Islam, and its bearer, Prophet Muḥammad (peace be upon him):

> *They say, 'Our hearts are sealed.' No! God has cursed them for their disbelief. They have but little faith. And now that a Book confirming their own has come to them from God, and they had repeatedly forecast its coming to the unbelievers, they have denied what they know to be the truth. God's curse be upon the unbelievers! Vile is that for which they have bartered their souls, because they have denied what God has revealed, grudging that He should, by His grace, send down His revelations to whom He chooses from among His servants. Thus they have incurred God's wrath over and over again. Ignominous suffering is in store for the unbelievers. When it is said to them, 'Believe in what God has revealed,' they say, 'We believe in what has been revealed to us.' They deny everything else, although it is the truth, corroborating the revelations they have. Say, 'Why, then, did you in the past kill God's prophets, if you were true believers?' Moses came to you with clear proofs, but in his absence you transgressed, worshipping the calf. We accepted your solemn pledge, and We raised Mount Sinai above you, saying, 'Take with firmness and strength what We have given you and hearken to it.' They said, 'We hear but we disobey.' For their unbelief they were made to drink the calf into their hearts. Say, 'Vile is that which your faith enjoins upon you, if indeed you are believers.'* (Verses 88–93)

The words are fierce: it is as if thunderbolts or balls of fire are being thrown in their faces. The verses completely demolish their arguments and their bogus excuses; their malevolent attitude towards Islam and the Prophet Muḥammad is exposed fully.

"They say, 'Our hearts are sealed.' No! God has cursed them for their disbelief. They have but little faith." (Verse 88) They said that to Muḥammad and his followers to discourage them from presenting the new religion to them, and in order to justify their own refusal to accept Islam. But the real reason, according to the *sūrah*, is that God has rejected them because of their disbelief. This means that the initial step was theirs when they rejected the faith. Therefore, God punished them by His rejection, which means that they cannot benefit by His guidance, which they have already rejected. They have generally shown very little faith anyway, in all periods.

Their transgression was compounded, because they rejected a Prophet, Muḥammad, who had come to confirm the revelations they had already received, whom they were eagerly awaiting and about whom they had been boasting before the pagan Arabs. With him, they used to tell those Arabs, 'our victory would be complete.'

Such irresponsible and devious behaviour can only be met with divine wrath and condemnation: *"God's curse be upon the unbelievers!"* (Verse 89)

The *sūrah* exposes the hidden cause underlying their wicked attitude, stressing their loss and the failure of their pursuit. *"Vile is that for which they have bartered their souls, because they have denied what God has revealed, grudging that He should, by His grace, send down His revelations to whom He chooses from among His servants. Thus they have incurred God's wrath over and over again. Ignominous suffering is in store for the unbelievers."* (Verse 90)

It is vile indeed that they should barter away their souls for a denial of God's Revelations. The human soul may very well have a price, which can be high or low, but to sell oneself for such a demeaning reward as the denial of faith in God is the lowest a human being can achieve. By adopting this attitude, the Israelites have lost doubly: in this life and in the life to come, where a humiliating punishment is in store for them.

The main reason for all this is their envy of Muḥammad (peace be upon him) for being the Prophet they had been waiting for. They begrudge anyone else receiving the honour of carrying God's message to mankind, which reflects their arrogant, overweening mentality. This is totally unjust on their part, and it earns them God's wrath and punishment.

This typically grudging attitude of the Jews of Madinah betrays a deeply selfish and bigoted mind, which detests that any good or blessings should be given to other people, as if that would reduce their own share of such goodness. It reflects a total lack of sensitivity towards others and a tendency towards self-alienation, which explains the isolation experienced by the Jews throughout history. They have tended to look upon their race as separate from the rest of humanity. Indeed, they have often set themselves up against the rest, harbouring grudges and an insatiable desire for revenge, and exploiting other peoples' misfortunes. It is not surprising, therefore, that they have historically been portrayed as conspiring troublemakers who are prepared to instigate war and bloodshed among nations in order to advance and safeguard their own interests. This hideous tendency is traced back to their grudge *"that He should, by His grace, send down His revelations to whom He chooses from among His servants."* (Verse 90)

Claims Falsified by Actions

The *sūrah* then goes further in exposing their bigotry and deception. It says: *"When it is said to them, 'Believe in what God has revealed,' they say, 'We believe in what has been revealed to us.' They deny everything else, although it is the truth, corroborating the revelations they have."* (Verse 91)

This would be the reply of the Jews of Madinah whenever they were called upon to acknowledge Islam and the Qur'ān. They considered what their own Prophets had taught them sufficient and complete, and they rejected all else, including the revelations received by Jesus and Muḥammad, the last of all prophets (peace be upon them all). The Qur'ān takes great exception to this reaction by the Israelites to God's revelations, when these are *"the truth, corroborating the revelations they have."* (Verse 91)

But, why should they bother about the truth when it is not addressed to them alone, and what concern is it to them that revelations sent to other nations should corroborate their own? Their bigotry and narrow-mindedness were so extreme that they had even rejected what their own Prophets had preached, and dared even to kill some of them. *"Say: 'Why, then, did you in the past kill God's prophets, if you were true believers?'"* (Verse 91) How could they substantiate their claims to believe only in what had been revealed to them through their Prophets if they went as far as killing some of these prophets?

Worse still, they rejected the revelations Moses, their most senior Prophet and the saviour of their nation, had conveyed to them. *"Moses came to you with clear proofs, but in his absence you transgressed, worshipping the calf."* (Verse 92) Could their worship of the calf, with Moses still alive, ever be considered a sign of faith? Does it support their argument that they believe in what has been revealed to them?

Nor, indeed, was that the only instance of their transgression and rebellion. Earlier, God had made the covenant with them under Mount Sinai, but soon they were in clear breach of that covenant. *"We accepted your solemn pledge, and We raised Mount Sinai above you, saying, 'Take with firmness and strength what We have given you and hearken to it.' They said, 'We hear but we disobey.' For their unbelief they were made to drink the calf into their hearts."* (Verse 93)

The mode of expression changes from direct address to that of reporting past events. Thus, it confronts the Israelites with their past attitudes, and informs Muslims and mankind generally of these Jewish attitudes. It then instructs the Prophet Muḥammad to condemn utterly the bizarre faith they claimed to have if it would require them to flagrantly reject the truth: *"Say, 'Vile is that which your faith enjoins upon you, if indeed you are believers.'"* (Verse 93)

Two fascinating expressions immediately draw our attention here. The first is: *"They said: 'We hear but we disobey.'"* Indeed, they did not utter the words, *'but we disobey'*. How is it then that these words are attributed to them? It is simply a question of portraying an attitude as though it is fully expressive. Thus, their actual words said that they had heard the message, but their actions said that they had disobeyed it. This reality was a much more authentic and accurate statement of their attitude than the words they uttered. The *sūrah* here is emphasizing one of the most fundamental Islamic principles: actions lend validity to words. Actions must be in harmony with words in order for the words to have any meaning or value whatsoever.

The second expression is: *"For their unbelief they were made to drink the calf into their hearts."* The sarcasm and the severity of the image are unmistakable. They were forcibly made to drink something nasty;

but what is it? It is nothing other than the calf, which is shown to be forced into their hearts. It is easy to get carried away by this image so as to almost overlook the real significance of the metaphor used here. It shows their love and adoration for the calf to be so strong that it runs in their veins. Such powerful imagery is but one tool of the inimitable Qur'ānic style.

The Jews have made a great fuss claiming themselves to be 'God's chosen people', alleging that they enjoy an exclusive inherent right to divine guidance. They have further claimed that, unlike other communities, their salvation is guaranteed, both in this life and in the life to come.

By implication, these claims exclude Muḥammad's followers from God's grace in the hereafter. Their aim behind such claims was to undermine the Muslims' trust in their own religion and in the promises made to them by the Prophet and in the Qur'ān. God instructs Prophet Muḥammad to challenge the Jews to join the Muslims in an earnest prayer to God to destroy the party that fabricated lies. He says: *"Say, 'If the ultimate abode with God is yours alone, to the exclusion of all others, then wish for death, if your claim is true.'"* (Verse 94)

This is immediately followed by the assertion that the Jews would not take up such a challenge or pray for death because they were aware that they were the ones who were lying. Hence, they would be afraid that God might answer their prayers. They were well aware that their actions and their record did not qualify them for any grace in the hereafter. Were they to die straightaway, their loss would be complete: their life here would be cut short and they would come to grief in the life hereafter. This, the *sūrah* affirms, would only mean that they would fight tooth and nail to stay alive, putting them on a par with the idolaters: *"But they will never wish for it because of what their hands have wrought in this life. God is well aware of the wrongdoers. Indeed, you shall find that they cling to life more eagerly than any other people, even more than the idolaters. Each one of them would love to live a thousand years, although the grant of a long life could not save him from punishment. God sees all that they do."* (Verses 95–96)

In these verses, the Qur'ān points to another contemptible characteristic of the Jews: their craven desire to live, no matter at what price and regardless of quality, honour and dignity. This has been borne out by Jewish behaviour during all stages of their history;

their heads are raised only when the big stick of the tormentor is put away, but once the stick is wielded before them, their heads are bowed and they acquiesce in fear and servility, scurrying for life, any kind of life.

Each of them would wish to live a thousand years because they do not believe in a future life, after this present one is over. When one accepts that one's days on earth are numbered but supposes that life here does not lead to a future life, this life would then seem very short, no matter how many years it lasts. Therefore, to believe in life after death is a blessing and a source of inspiration that brings hope, since man naturally entertains hopes that go far beyond his numbered years of life. To discard the hopes of an immortal and happy existence reflects a lack of appreciation for the very meaning of life.

Besides being a belief in God's absolute justice and His most gracious reward, belief in the hereafter is an expression of the value and vigour of life itself, not confined to, or restricted by, the limits of this world. It links man's existence to a life that goes far beyond this one, to reach spheres and realms the edges of which are known only to God Almighty.

A Strange Enmity to an Angel

The *sūrah* goes on to direct Prophet Muḥammad to proclaim more challenging truths: *"Say, 'Whoever is an enemy of Gabriel should know that he revealed it [the Qur'ān] to your heart by God's leave.' It confirms the Scriptures revealed before it, and is a guidance and joyful tidings for the believers. Whoever is an enemy of God, His angels, His messengers, and to Gabriel and Michael will surely find that God is indeed the enemy of the unbelievers."* (Verses 97–98)

Another astonishing trait of the Israelites is revealed. The spite and envy they feel towards other recipients of God's grace are not only beyond belief, but have now landed them in a serious paradox. Because they knew that the Angel Gabriel conveyed God's revelations to Muḥammad, and in view of the hatred and the grudge they harboured against Muḥammad, they circulated the absurd tale that Gabriel was also an enemy of theirs because he was the Angel of death and destruction. This, they alleged, gave them a valid reason to reject Muḥammad and the revelations he was receiving. Had it been the Angel Michael who had conveyed the revelations, they claimed, they would have accepted it, because he was the angel of rain, fertility and prosperity.

It is a ludicrous argument brought about by blind hatred. They had no reason to be hostile towards Gabriel who, not being human himself, could not take sides for or against them. He was a messenger whom they disliked although he had no personal preference or choice in delivering that message. He only did as he was bid.

We note in this verse the point that the Qur'ān was lodged in Muḥammad's 'heart', a term used frequently in the Qur'ān to indicate a non-physical part of the human personality that receives and understands. It does not refer to the physical human organ known by that name. The heart, according to the Qur'ān, is the centre of human perception.

The Qur'ān was lodged in Muḥammad's heart, confirming *"the Scriptures revealed before it, and is a guidance and joyful tidings for the believers".* (Verse 97)

The Qur'ān confirms and endorses in general terms all divine revelations received before it. The religion of God, as expounded and preached by all revealed Scriptures, is basically one and the same. All divine revelations have come as guidance to man and as a source of joyful tidings for all believing hearts that are receptive and willing to have faith in God.

There is an aspect of religious experience which is important to emphasize. The effect of divine revelations on the believing heart is uniquely uplifting. The simple recitation of the Qur'ān fills the heart with tranquillity and solace, and opens up new vistas of meaning and knowledge. The study of this revelation can also be very inspiring, uncovering wider horizons of understanding and, therefore, guidance and achievement. Many verses include descriptions of the Qur'ān as *'guidance for the God-fearing'* (2: 2), or *'guidance and grace for people who believe'* (12: 111), or *'a cure... and mercy for all believers.'* (10: 57) These descriptions confirm that its guidance is the fruit of strong faith and trust in, and genuine fear of, God Almighty.

Such qualities were seen to be lacking among the Israelites. They have traditionally undermined the inherent unity of divine religion by discriminating between the prophets and between the angels themselves. The verse, therefore, insists that prophets and angels should be equally respected and revered, and that whoever opposes or is hostile to any of them shall have God's power to contend with.

"Whoever is an enemy of God, His angels, His messengers, and to Gabriel and Michael will surely find that God is indeed the enemy of the unbelievers." (Verse 98)

Casting God's Revelations Away

The *sūrah* then turns to reassure Prophet Muḥammad of the truth and validity of the revelations he had received, and to denounce those who reject or oppose his message. It specifically condemns the Israelites for not living up to their promises and commitments, whether made to God or to their own prophets, or to Muḥammad himself. That is manifest in their rejection of the Qur'ān, God's final revelation to man, which endorsed and reinforced the revelations they already had. *"We have sent down to you clear revelations: none will deny them except the evildoers. Is it always to be the case that every time they make a solemn pledge some of them will violate it? The truth is that most of them do not believe. And now that a Messenger from God has come to them, confirming what is already in their possession, some of those who had been given the Scriptures cast God's Book behind their backs as though they know nothing."* (Verses 99–101)

Here, then, we have the real reason behind the Israelites' rejection of God's revelations; it is their sheer wickedness and the corruption of their souls. Normal, healthy human nature could not but acknowledge and embrace the truth and principles expounded by divine revelations. The compelling logic in such revelations cannot fail to impress the human heart and mind. The fact that the Jews, or any other people for that matter, have refused to believe divine revelations is not a criticism of the validity or veracity of such revelations, but rather a reflection of those people's perverted and corrupt nature.

The *sūrah* then makes a public condemnation of the Jews, exposing their inconsistency and insincerity and showing them as a fragmented community with no unity or identity of purpose, despite their racial prejudice against others. Their chauvinism, ethnocentricity and their jealousy of any other favoured community did not stop them from being divided among themselves and mistrustful of each other. Whatever treaty or agreement they make with any other people, some of them are bound to break ranks and violate it.

This was evident when they broke the covenant God made with them at Mount Sinai, and in their reneging on pledges given to their prophets and patriarchs, as well as in their breach of the treaty they had with the Prophet Muḥammad and the Muslims, when he first arrived to settle in Madinah. That agreement provided for a framework of peaceful coexistence between Muslims and Jews, but the Jews were quick to undermine the new faith, lending support to the Prophet's enemies and sowing the seeds of strife and discord within the Muslim community in Madinah.

This is a well-known characteristic of the Israelites. In contrast, the lives of Muslims, as described by the Prophet Muḥammad "are of equal worth. All Muslims stand united against any hostile party. Even the weakest among them speaks on their behalf and honours their commitments." No Muslim would break a promise made by another on behalf of the whole community. Abū 'Ubaydah, the commander of a Muslim army, once wrote to the Caliph 'Umar ibn al-Khaṭṭāb, seeking advice concerning one of his soldiers, a slave, who had given a pledge of security to the citizens of a town in Iraq. The Caliph wrote back, saying, "God has praised the honouring of pledges very highly and you would not be faithful to your commitments unless you honour them. Therefore, you must honour your pledge to these people and leave them in peace." Such is the behaviour of a magnanimous, united and straightforward community – a far cry from that of those perfidious and conniving Jews.

"And now that a Messenger from God has come to them confirming what is already in their possession, some of those who had been given the Scriptures cast God's Book behind their backs as though they know nothing." (Verse 101) This is further evidence that every time the Israelites made a commitment, some of them reneged on it. Their covenant with God stipulated that they would accept, believe and support every messenger He sent, but some of them rejected the Qur'ān revealed by God to Muḥammad, which in fact amounted to rejecting their own Scriptures, since it endorsed and confirmed those Scriptures.

The verse is loaded with stinging sarcasm, castigating the very recipients of divine revelations for rejecting similar revelations simply because these have been given to someone else.

Had such a stance been adopted by the pagan Arabs, it would perhaps have been understandable. The Jews had the privilege of receiving divine messages and messengers and were presumed well versed in religious guidance and experience. Yet, as the verse very graphically puts it, they cast God's new revelations *"behind their backs".* They carelessly and recklessly rejected it out of hand. They closed their minds to it and discounted it from their life and thought.

Magic and Psychic Phenomena

Would that be the end of their transgression? Would they, having rejected the revelations sent down to Muḥammad, hold fast to the revelations given to their forefathers and show faith and loyalty to its laws and teachings? Definitely not. They cast God's revelations behind their backs and went in search of myths and superstitions: *"They follow what the devils relate of Solomon's kingdom. Solomon never disbelieved, but the devils did. They instruct people in witchcraft which was certainly not revealed to the two angels, Hārūt and Mārūt, at Babylon. Yet these two [angels] never taught anyone without first declaring, 'We are but a temptation to evil, so do not renounce your faith.' From these two, people learned what they would use to cause discord between a man and his wife. However, with that knowledge they can harm no one except by God's leave. Indeed, they learn what harms them and brings them no profit. They knew full well that whoever contracted such a deal would have no share in the life to come. Vile indeed is what they had sold their souls for, if they but knew it! Had they embraced the faith and been God-fearing, God's reward would have been far better for them, if they but knew it."* (Verses 102–103)

They abandoned Divine revelations which had come to confirm their Scriptures and gave credence to myths and legends from the time of Solomon, which falsely asserted that he practised sorcery and witchcraft and owed all his extraordinary powers to them.

The Qur'ān refutes this allegation completely and talks of sorcery and deliberate rejection of the divine faith, in the same vein. Thus, the Qur'ān treats sorcery as disbelief, and attributes it to devils: *"Solomon never disbelieved, but the devils did. They instruct people in witchcraft."* (Verse 102) It further refutes the allegation that the two angels of Babylon, Hārūt and Mārūt, were sorcerers. It confirms that witchcraft *"was certainly not revealed to the two angels, Hārūt and Mārūt, at Babylon."* (Verse 102) The Qur'ān makes the truth about these two angels clear. They were testing people's faith, for a purpose that has not been identified. Again associating sorcery, black magic and witchcraft with disbelief in God, the Qur'ān exonerates the two angels, confirming that they had explained the nature of their work to the people and given them fair warning: *"Yet these two [angels] never taught anyone without first declaring, 'We are but a temptation to evil, so do not renounce your faith.'"* (Verse 102) Nevertheless, some people persisted with learning and practising sorcery, thus falling to temptation and causing harm: *"From these two, people learned what they would use to cause discord between a man and his wife."* (Verse 102)

At this point, the Qur'ān establishes another fundamental Islamic principle of faith: nothing happens in this world without God's authority. *"However, with that knowledge they can harm no one except by God's leave."* (Verse 102) Cause and effect are only valid by the will of God. When you put your hand in the fire it is burnt, but the burning itself only occurs with God's leave; for it is He who gave fire the property to incinerate and gave human skin susceptibility to burn. This means that God is also capable at any moment of cancelling this property and rendering fire completely harmless, as was the case with the Prophet Abraham, when his people threw him into a blazing fire and he came out of it unscathed. (21: 69)

The same is true for such practices as sorcery and witchcraft: they can only work with God's will, as must all conventional physical and metaphysical phenomena of cause and effect.

The *sūrah* states clearly that what people learnt of practices that could bring discord between man and wife could only bring them harm: *"Indeed, they learn what harms them and brings them no profit."* (Verse 102) Since this thing that they learnt is described as disbelief in God, this is reason enough to make it pure evil that can bring no profit whatsoever. *"They knew full well that whoever contracted such a deal would have no share in the life to come."* When anyone makes such a deal, he realizes that he is assigning away every good share he could have in the life to come. That makes their deal a massive loss indeed: *"Vile indeed is what they had sold their souls for, if they but knew it! Had they embraced the faith and been God-fearing, God's reward would have been far better for them, if they but knew it."* (Verses 102–103)

This condemnation applies to those who took to practising sorcery and witchcraft at Babylon, and to those Israelites who gave credence to tales about Solomon and his kingdom and abandoned God's authentic revelations.

The Nature of Magic

Black magic, sorcery and witchcraft still hold deep fascination for many people today, while many others are taken in by the seemingly extraordinary powers of their practitioners.

It is true that some individuals are seen to possess special powers or abilities not explained by scientific evidence. Science has not been able to go farther than giving a description of some of these phenomena such as telepathy, the supposed communication of thoughts or ideas other than by the known senses; and hypnosis, artificially produced sleep or the sleep-like state in which the subject acts only on external suggestion.

While recognizing these powers and acknowledging their existence and effects, science has not been able to offer any satisfactory explanations as to what they are or how they come about.

This, of course, applies to numerous other psychic phenomena over which scientists are in dispute and which science is still unable to understand, either through lack of scientific evidence or because such phenomena cannot be verified by empirical methods. One such method is premonitory or "prospective" dreams which foretell the future and which Sigmund Freud, the founder of modern psychoanalysis who was well known for his rejection of spiritual powers, was not able to dismiss or deny. How is it possible that some people are able to sense and identify future events long before they actually occur?

It is presumptuous and naïve to dismiss these powers of extrasensory perception simply because science has not been able to understand or explain them.

This does not, however, give credence to myths or fairy tales. It is important that we should take an objective and open-minded attitude towards such experiences. While science cannot deny them completely, it should nevertheless continue to probe these phenomena and try to decipher their mystery. We have, therefore, to accept the fact that certain matters in the physical as well as the spiritual world will remain beyond human comprehension and that they must be taken into account when trying to understand life.

One of these matters is black magic, and all other feats and activities related to it, and the possibility of Satanic invasion of the human mind. The evident power possessed by some people to convey suggestions, and to psychologically influence and inspire others, mentally and physically, is quite striking. And, although the Qur'ān speaks of the sorcery performed by Pharaoh's magicians in their challenge to Moses as delusion (20: 66), we cannot dismiss the possibility that this type of trickery could be used to create discord and dissension between friends or husbands and wives. Naturally, people's emotions and feelings are determined by all kinds of influences and causes that are ultimately controlled by the will of God, as discussed earlier.

As to the identity of the two angels referred to here, Hārūt and Mārūt, and their location in Babylon, the story was well known in Jewish religious literature. The Jews of Madinah did not question the Qur'ānic account of their story. Qur'ānic accounts of this type, however, are often brief and general, since the aim is not to give detailed chronological or historic information, but rather to draw lessons and highlight the morals behind the events.

It is not our intention in this work to pursue the myths and legends woven around the events and personalities we come across in our study of the Qur'ān, not least because of lack of authentic historical information.

Human history is vastly rich in accounts of human endeavour, and the tests and tribulations people of different ages and generations encountered. The personalities and the details of those events that are cited may change in accordance with the circumstances and stage of cultural development of each human group or society, but the messages remain valid and valuable.

From this story we learn of the Israelites' misguided pursuit of myths and their preference for superstition and such-like activities, and we come to know that sorcery, black magic and witchcraft are works of the devil that undermine man's belief in God, negate his good deeds and deprive him of all favour and privilege in the hereafter.

5

Jewish Efforts to Undermine Islam

Believers, do not say [to the Prophet]: 'Listen to us,' but say: 'Have patience with us,' and hearken. Grievous suffering awaits the unbelievers. (104)

يَٰٓأَيُّهَا ٱلَّذِينَ ءَامَنُواْ لَا تَقُولُواْ
رَٰعِنَا وَقُولُواْ ٱنظُرۡنَا وَٱسۡمَعُواْۗ
وَلِلۡكَٰفِرِينَ عَذَابٌ أَلِيمٞ ﴿١٠٤﴾

Neither the unbelievers among the people of earlier revelations nor the idolaters would like to see any blessing ever bestowed upon you by your Lord. But God favours with His mercy whom He wills; His grace is infinite. (105)

مَّا يَوَدُّ ٱلَّذِينَ كَفَرُواْ مِنۡ أَهۡلِ
ٱلۡكِتَٰبِ وَلَا ٱلۡمُشۡرِكِينَ أَن يُنَزَّلَ
عَلَيۡكُم مِّنۡ خَيۡرٖ مِّن رَّبِّكُمۡۚ
وَٱللَّهُ يَخۡتَصُّ بِرَحۡمَتِهِۦ مَن يَشَآءُۚ
وَٱللَّهُ ذُو ٱلۡفَضۡلِ ٱلۡعَظِيمِ ﴿١٠٥﴾

Any revelation We annul or consign to oblivion We replace with a better or similar one. Do you not know that God has power over all things? (106)

مَا نَنسَخۡ مِنۡ ءَايَةٍ أَوۡ نُنسِهَا نَأۡتِ بِخَيۡرٖ
مِّنۡهَآ أَوۡ مِثۡلِهَآۗ أَلَمۡ تَعۡلَمۡ أَنَّ ٱللَّهَ عَلَىٰ كُلِّ
شَيۡءٖ قَدِيرٌ ﴿١٠٦﴾

Do you not know that God has sovereignty over the heavens and the earth, and that apart from God you have no one to protect you or give you help? (107)

أَلَمۡ تَعۡلَمۡ أَنَّ ٱللَّهَ لَهُۥ مُلۡكُ ٱلسَّمَٰوَٰتِ
وَٱلۡأَرۡضِۗ وَمَا لَكُم مِّن دُونِ ٱللَّهِ
مِن وَلِيّٖ وَلَا نَصِيرٍ ﴿١٠٧﴾

أَمْ تُرِيدُونَ أَن تَسْـَٔلُوا۟ رَسُولَكُمْ كَمَا
سُئِلَ مُوسَىٰ مِن قَبْلُ ۗ وَمَن يَتَبَدَّلِ
ٱلْكُفْرَ بِٱلْإِيمَٰنِ فَقَدْ ضَلَّ سَوَآءَ
ٱلسَّبِيلِ ﴿١٠٨﴾

Do you wish to ask of the Messenger who has been sent to you the same as was formerly asked of Moses? He who barters faith for unbelief has surely strayed away from the right path. (108)

وَدَّ كَثِيرٌ مِّنْ أَهْلِ ٱلْكِتَٰبِ
لَوْ يَرُدُّونَكُم مِّنۢ بَعْدِ إِيمَٰنِكُمْ
كُفَّارًا حَسَدًا مِّنْ عِندِ أَنفُسِهِم مِّنۢ
بَعْدِ مَا تَبَيَّنَ لَهُمُ ٱلْحَقُّ ۖ فَٱعْفُوا۟
وَٱصْفَحُوا۟ حَتَّىٰ يَأْتِىَ ٱللَّهُ بِأَمْرِهِۦٓ ۗ إِنَّ ٱللَّهَ
عَلَىٰ كُلِّ شَىْءٍ قَدِيرٌ ﴿١٠٩﴾

Many among the people of earlier revelations would love to lead you back to unbelief, now that you have embraced the faith. This they do out of deep-seated envy, after the truth has become manifest to them; so forgive and forbear until God makes known His decree. Indeed, God has power over all things. (109)

وَأَقِيمُوا۟ ٱلصَّلَوٰةَ وَءَاتُوا۟ ٱلزَّكَوٰةَ ۚ وَمَا
تُقَدِّمُوا۟ لِأَنفُسِكُم مِّنْ خَيْرٍ تَجِدُوهُ عِندَ
ٱللَّهِ ۗ إِنَّ ٱللَّهَ بِمَا تَعْمَلُونَ بَصِيرٌ ﴿١١٠﴾

Attend regularly to your prayer and pay *zakāt* (financial duty); for, whatever good you do for your own sake you shall find it with God. God sees all that you do. (110)

وَقَالُوا۟ لَن يَدْخُلَ ٱلْجَنَّةَ إِلَّا مَن كَانَ
هُودًا أَوْ نَصَٰرَىٰ ۗ تِلْكَ أَمَانِيُّهُمْ ۗ قُلْ
هَاتُوا۟ بُرْهَٰنَكُمْ إِن كُنتُمْ
صَٰدِقِينَ ﴿١١١﴾

They declare, 'None shall enter Paradise unless he is a Jew or a Christian.' Such are their wishful fancies. Say, 'Produce your proof, if what you say is true.' (111)

بَلَىٰ مَنْ أَسْلَمَ وَجْهَهُۥ لِلَّهِ وَهُوَ مُحْسِنٌ
فَلَهُۥٓ أَجْرُهُۥ عِندَ رَبِّهِۦ وَلَا خَوْفٌ عَلَيْهِمْ
وَلَا هُمْ يَحْزَنُونَ ﴿١١٢﴾

Indeed, whoever surrender themselves to God, while doing good works, shall have their reward with their Lord; they shall have nothing to fear nor shall they grieve. (112)

The Jews say the Christians have no basis for their faith and the Christians say the Jews have no basis for their faith. Yet they both recite the Scriptures. Those devoid of knowledge say likewise, and on the Day of Judgement God shall judge between them on all their disputes. (113)

وَقَالَتِ ٱلْيَهُودُ لَيْسَتِ ٱلنَّصَٰرَىٰ عَلَىٰ شَيْءٍ
وَقَالَتِ ٱلنَّصَٰرَىٰ لَيْسَتِ ٱلْيَهُودُ عَلَىٰ شَيْءٍ
وَهُمْ يَتْلُونَ ٱلْكِتَٰبَ ۗ كَذَٰلِكَ قَالَ ٱلَّذِينَ
لَا يَعْلَمُونَ مِثْلَ قَوْلِهِمْ ۚ فَٱللَّهُ يَحْكُمُ بَيْنَهُمْ
يَوْمَ ٱلْقِيَٰمَةِ فِيمَا كَانُوا۟ فِيهِ يَخْتَلِفُونَ ﴿١١٣﴾

Who is more unjust than he who forbids God's name to be mentioned in His places of worship, and seeks to destroy them? Such people have no right to enter them except with fear in their hearts. They shall suffer ignominy in this world and awesome suffering awaits them in the life to come. (114)

وَمَنْ أَظْلَمُ مِمَّن مَّنَعَ مَسَٰجِدَ ٱللَّهِ أَن يُذْكَرَ
فِيهَا ٱسْمُهُۥ وَسَعَىٰ فِى خَرَابِهَآ ۚ أُو۟لَٰٓئِكَ
مَا كَانَ لَهُمْ أَن يَدْخُلُوهَآ إِلَّا خَآئِفِينَ ۚ
لَهُمْ فِى ٱلدُّنْيَا خِزْىٌ وَلَهُمْ فِى ٱلْءَاخِرَةِ
عَذَابٌ عَظِيمٌ ﴿١١٤﴾

To God belong the east and the west: wherever you turn there will be the face of God. Truly, God is limitless in His bounty and He knows all. (115)

وَلِلَّهِ ٱلْمَشْرِقُ وَٱلْمَغْرِبُ ۚ فَأَيْنَمَا تُوَلُّوا۟ فَثَمَّ
وَجْهُ ٱللَّهِ ۚ إِنَّ ٱللَّهَ وَٰسِعٌ عَلِيمٌ ﴿١١٥﴾

They say, 'God has taken to Himself a son.' Limitless is He in His glory! His is all that is in the heavens and on earth; all things are obedient to Him. (116)

وَقَالُوا۟ ٱتَّخَذَ ٱللَّهُ وَلَدًا ۗ سُبْحَٰنَهُۥ ۖ
بَل لَّهُۥ مَا فِى ٱلسَّمَٰوَٰتِ وَٱلْأَرْضِ ۖ
كُلٌّ لَّهُۥ قَٰنِتُونَ ﴿١١٦﴾

He is the Originator of the heavens and the earth. When He wills something to be, He need only say, 'Be', and it is. (117)

بَدِيعُ ٱلسَّمَٰوَٰتِ وَٱلْأَرْضِ ۖ وَإِذَا قَضَىٰٓ
أَمْرًا فَإِنَّمَا يَقُولُ لَهُۥ كُن فَيَكُونُ ﴿١١٧﴾

Those devoid of knowledge say, 'Why does not God speak to us, nor is a sign shown to us?' The same demands were made by people before them: their hearts are all alike. We have made the signs very clear for those with firm conviction. (118)

وَقَالَ الَّذِينَ لَا يَعْلَمُونَ لَوْلَا يُكَلِّمُنَا اللَّهُ أَوْ تَأْتِينَا آيَةٌ ۗ كَذَٰلِكَ قَالَ الَّذِينَ مِن قَبْلِهِم مِّثْلَ قَوْلِهِمْ ۘ تَشَابَهَتْ قُلُوبُهُمْ ۗ قَدْ بَيَّنَّا الْآيَاتِ لِقَوْمٍ يُوقِنُونَ ﴿١١٨﴾

We have sent you with the truth; a bearer of glad tidings and a warner. You shall not be questioned about those who are destined for the blazing fire. (119)

إِنَّا أَرْسَلْنَاكَ بِالْحَقِّ بَشِيرًا وَنَذِيرًا ۖ وَلَا تُسْأَلُ عَنْ أَصْحَابِ الْجَحِيمِ ﴿١١٩﴾

Never will the Jews nor yet the Christians be pleased with you unless you follow their faith. Say, 'God's guidance is the only true guidance.' Should you follow their desires after all the knowledge that has come to you, you would have none to protect you from God, nor to give you help. (120)

وَلَن تَرْضَىٰ عَنكَ الْيَهُودُ وَلَا النَّصَارَىٰ حَتَّىٰ تَتَّبِعَ مِلَّتَهُمْ ۗ قُلْ إِنَّ هُدَى اللَّهِ هُوَ الْهُدَىٰ ۗ وَلَئِنِ اتَّبَعْتَ أَهْوَاءَهُم بَعْدَ الَّذِي جَاءَكَ مِنَ الْعِلْمِ ۙ مَا لَكَ مِنَ اللَّهِ مِن وَلِيٍّ وَلَا نَصِيرٍ ﴿١٢٠﴾

Those to whom We have given the Book, and who recite it as it ought to be recited, truly believe in it; those who deny it are utter losers. (121)

الَّذِينَ آتَيْنَاهُمُ الْكِتَابَ يَتْلُونَهُ حَقَّ تِلَاوَتِهِ أُولَٰئِكَ يُؤْمِنُونَ بِهِ ۗ وَمَن يَكْفُرْ بِهِ فَأُولَٰئِكَ هُمُ الْخَاسِرُونَ ﴿١٢١﴾

Children of Israel! Remember My favour which I bestowed on you, and that I have preferred you over all people. (122)

يَا بَنِي إِسْرَائِيلَ اذْكُرُوا نِعْمَتِيَ الَّتِي أَنْعَمْتُ عَلَيْكُمْ وَأَنِّي فَضَّلْتُكُمْ عَلَى الْعَالَمِينَ ﴿١٢٢﴾

Fear the day when no soul shall avail another in any way, nor shall ransom be accepted from any of them, nor shall intercession be of any benefit, and none shall receive help. (123)

وَٱتَّقُواْ يَوْمًا لَّا تَجْزِى نَفْسٌ عَن نَّفْسٍ شَيْـًٔا
وَلَا يُقْبَلُ مِنْهَا عَدْلٌ وَلَا تَنفَعُهَا شَفَٰعَةٌ
وَلَا هُمْ يُنصَرُونَ ﴿١٢٣﴾

Efforts to Undermine the New Religion

This new passage takes the exposition of Jewish intrigue against Islam and the Muslims a step further, revealing the reasons that lie behind their deep-seated hatred and their treachery and trouble-making. It gives Muslims strong warnings, requiring them to be on their guard in dealing with the hostile and malicious scheming of the Jews. Muslims are pointedly told not to emulate the behaviour of the Jews, or to fall for their trickery and deceit.

It appears that the Jews were making an issue of the modifications and amendments that had to be made to some Islamic rules and requirements during the formative years of Islam. They utilized this to raise doubts in Muslim minds, questioning the validity and veracity of their religion. Had those rules and ideas originated from God, the Jews argued, they would not have had to be changed or replaced.

This insidious campaign gathered strength when the direction faced by Muslims in prayer, the *qiblah*, was changed from Jerusalem to the Ka'bah in Makkah, sixteen months after the Prophet's arrival in Madinah in 622 CE.

On his arrival in Madinah, the Prophet instructed his followers to turn towards Jerusalem, the sacred city of Judaism, in prayer, which gave the Jews reason to argue that their faith was superior, the one and only true religion. This made the Prophet wish, although he never expressed his feelings in words, that prayers could be made facing the Ka'bah in Makkah. As time went by, this feeling grew even stronger until his unspoken wish was granted, as we shall see later in the *sūrah*.

Since the change of *qiblah* deprived the Israelites of the basis for their argument concerning the merits and status of their faith, they launched a malevolent and surreptitious campaign aimed at discrediting the divine origins of Islam and questioning its veracity. They went for the very foundations of Islam, arguing with the Muslims that if facing Jerusalem during Prayer had not been valid, their worship hitherto would have been in vain; but that if it had been valid, there would be no justification for a change of *qiblah*. They were hitting at the very roots of the Muslims' faith in God's reward and, more seriously, at the wisdom and insight of the Prophet's leadership.

More worrying were the indications that the anti-Islamic campaign instigated by the Jews of Madinah was having some success. Weak-minded Muslims began to question the Prophet demanding 'proof' and 'evidence' for what he taught and preached. Needless to say, such questioning is the opposite of complete trust in the Prophet's leadership and in the source of the Islamic faith. Therefore, the Qur'ān clarifies the principle and the wisdom behind the abrogation, replacement or amendment of some rulings, and warns the Muslims against the real aims of Jewish criticism of the Qur'ān and the Prophet. It tells them clearly that the ultimate aim of the Jews was to turn the clock back, so that the Arabs who believed in Islam would revert to their old pagan days. It was jealousy and malice that drove the Jews to those lengths. They deeply resented, and would not accept, the fact that God had favoured another people with the honour of His final mandate to man and chosen them as the advocates of His last message. The Qur'ān undertook to expose the perfidious and malevolent Jewish accusations and claims, citing examples of earlier conflicts between Jews and Christians in which accusations were exchanged and insults traded.

The *sūrah* then turns to highlight aspects of the *qiblah* issue, pointing out that the Jews were hell-bent on preventing the Muslims from turning towards the Ka'bah in prayer. The Qur'ān condemns this stance, branding it an attempt to prevent the mentioning of God's name in His places of worship and an effort to destroy such places.

As the passage draws to a close it brings the Muslims face to face with the real and underlying motives driving the Jews and Christians in their opposition to Islam. Their chief wish had been to turn the Muslims away from their beliefs and their religion altogether. They were never going to rest or be happy with Muḥammad until he abandoned his faith for theirs; otherwise, it would be war, intrigue and confrontation all the way.

Begrudging God's Grace

"Believers, do not say [to the Prophet]: 'Listen to us,' but say: 'Have patience with us,' and hearken. Grievous suffering awaits the unbelievers. Neither the unbelievers among the people of earlier revelations nor the idolaters would like to see any blessing ever bestowed upon you by your Lord. But God favours with His mercy whom He wills; His grace is infinite. Any revelation We annul or consign to oblivion We replace with a better or similar one. Do you not know that God has power over all things? Do you not know that God has sovereignty over the heavens and the earth, and that apart from God you have no one to protect you or give you help? Do you wish to ask of the Messenger who has been sent to you the same as was formerly asked of Moses? He who barters faith for unbelief has surely strayed away from the right path. Many among the people of earlier revelations would love to lead you back to unbelief, now that you have embraced the faith. This they do out of deep-seated envy, after the truth has become manifest to them; so forgive and forbear until God makes known His decree. Indeed, God has power over all things. Attend regularly to your prayer and pay zakāt *(financial duty); for, whatever good you do for your own sake you shall find it with God. God sees all that you do.* (Verses 104–110)

The opening verse of this passage addresses the believers, asking them not to emulate the Jews in their play on certain Arabic words when speaking to the Prophet. One such word is *rāʿinā*, which means "listen to us", but the sound of which could be subtly varied to convey the offensive meaning of 'an impulsive fool'. They would resort to this cowardly form of abuse because they would not dare insult the Prophet openly. The Muslims were advised to use synonymous words that could not be twisted to give an offensive meaning in their address to the Prophet.

This kind of behaviour not only shows the extent of Jewish resentment and envy towards the Muslims, it also shows the Jews as discourteous and underhand. The Qur'ān mentions these activities to indicate how caring and well disposed God is towards the Prophet and the Muslims, and how much He is willing to defend and protect them against their detractors.

The *sūrah* goes on to expose further Jewish ill-will and animosity towards the Muslims, so that they may beware of their malign influence and hold fast to what God has entrusted them with: *"Neither the unbelievers among the people of earlier revelations nor the idolaters would like to see any blessing ever bestowed upon you by your Lord. But God favours with His mercy whom He wills; His grace is infinite."* (Verse 105)

The verse speaks of Jews, Christians and idolaters in the same vein, describing them as unbelievers because they have all denied God's last and final message to man which was revealed to Muḥammad (peace be upon him). They share the same grudges and hatred towards the Muslims for being chosen by God as recipients of His revelation and as trustees and custodians of His religion on earth.

Earlier, we saw other manifestations of this jealousy and the blind hatred underlying it, and how it was extended even to angels such as Gabriel who was no more than a carrier of God's revelations to the Prophet Muḥammad.

In stating that *"God favours with His mercy whom He wills"*, the *sūrah* emphasizes that God's decisions in these matters are not arbitrary. If He chooses to bestow His mercy on Muḥammad and his followers, it is because He knows that they both deserve and are worthy of it. The comment at the end of this verse is: *"His grace is infinite"* (Verse 105).

The greatest of God's bounties is His message, and the advocacy of His faith. Thus, believers should realize in their hearts how favoured they have been. They would be able then to counter the hatred and doubt campaign led always by the Jews to weaken the faith in the hearts of Muslims, with awe and gratitude, coming as it does after they have been alerted to the unbelievers' intrigues and ill-will. All these feelings may be seen as an essential mobilization to counter the Jews' campaign against Islam.

The main reason for this impudent attack, as mentioned earlier, was the abrogation, replacement or amendment of certain Qur'ānic directives and rulings, especially the one regarding the *qiblah*. This last ruling instructed Muslims to face the Ka'bah in Makkah, rather than Jerusalem, in prayer.

Regardless of the immediate occasion, the *sūrah* at this point gives a definitive statement with regard to this important issue: *"Any revelation We annul or consign to oblivion We replace with a better or similar one. Do you not know that God has power over all things?"* (Verse 106)

Partial amendments of rulings in response to changing circumstances during the lifetime of Prophet Muḥammad could only be in the interest of mankind as a whole. As the originator of revelations, God, the Creator, is the final and absolute authority to decide such amendments. To cancel or replace any directive or principle is His exclusive prerogative. This point is emphasized in the next verse: "*Do you not know that God has sovereignty over the heavens and the earth, and that apart from God you have no one to protect you or give you help?*" (Verse 107)

We can clearly detect a hint of warning, and a reminder to Muslims that other than God they can call on no one for support or protection. The likely reason for this is the effect the Jewish campaign had had on some Muslims, whose trust and confidence in the Prophet showed signs of flagging. That is borne out by the following verse: "*Do you wish to ask of the Messenger who has been sent to you the same as was formerly asked of Moses? He who barters faith for unbelief has surely strayed away from the right path.*" (Verse 108)

Again there is a clear denunciation of the Jewish habit of questioning their prophets, disobeying them and asking for the impossible, as has been described at length earlier in the *sūrah*.

The verse also warns Muslims not to lose sight of their commitments and obligations towards God, as the Jews had done before them. Otherwise, they would lose faith in their own religion, as the Jews wish them to do: "*Many among the people of earlier revelations would love to lead you back to unbelief, now that you have embraced the faith. This they do out of deep-seated envy, after the truth has become manifest to them.*" (Verse 109)

That enmity towards Islam which filled, and continues to fill, the hearts of the Jews, has always been the real force that motivates their plotting and scheming. The Qur'ān makes this very clear as it describes the relentless Jewish efforts to shake the foundations of Islam and destroy the Muslim community throughout the world. It therefore calls on Muslims to rise above their opponents' level rather than meet evil with evil. It advises not mere restraint, but forgiveness and forbearance: "*so forgive and forbear until God makes known His decree. Indeed, God has power over all things.*" (Verse 109)

Muslims are urged to pursue the faith God has chosen for them and to invest their efforts and energies in the worship of God Almighty: "*Attend regularly to your prayer and pay* zakāt *(financial duty);*

for, whatever good you do for your own sake you shall find it with God. God sees all that you do." (Verse 110)

Thus we can see how the Qur'ān revitalizes the collective Muslim conscience, focuses on the real sources of danger to the community, and mobilizes Muslims' energy and feelings for closer contact with God and more gracious submission to His will and command. Until that will is revealed and God's word takes effect in life, Muslims are urged to exercise prudence and show tolerance and magnanimity towards detractors, envious people and ill-wishers.

Claims without Basis

The *sūrah* then deals with some general claims made by Jews and Christians, to the effect that they are the only righteous people who are assured of being admitted to heaven in the life to come. At the same time they continue to denounce and throw charges at each other. It then goes on to give God's final word on the matter. *"They declare, 'None shall enter Paradise unless he is a Jew or a Christian.' Such are their wishful fancies. Say, 'Produce your proof, if what you say is true.' Indeed, whoever surrender themselves to God, while doing good works, shall have their reward with their Lord; they shall have nothing to fear nor shall they grieve. The Jews say the Christians have no basis for their faith and the Christians say the Jews have no basis for their faith. Yet they both recite the Scriptures. Those devoid of knowledge say likewise, and on the Day of Judgement God shall judge between them on all their disputes."* (Verses 111–113)

Although, when the Qur'ān was being revealed, there was no strong Christian presence in Madinah, as compared to that of the Jews, the text refers to both groups as well as to the polytheists, dismissing their claims as baseless and challenging them to provide evidence to support their argument. *"They declare: None shall enter Paradise unless he is a Jew or a Christian."* This is a dual report of what both groups argued. Otherwise, the Jews used to claim that only they were destined for heaven, and the Christians claimed that for themselves. Both statements are boastful, without supporting evidence. Hence, God instructs the Prophet to challenge their claims: *"Say: 'Produce your proof, if what you say is true.'"* (Verse 111)

The *sūrah* then establishes another fundamental Islamic principle: that reward is commensurate with deed, without any preference for one nation, group or individual over another. Faith and submission to God, rather than title, ancestry or name, is the determining factor in this regard, and *"whoever surrender themselves to God, while doing good works, shall have their reward with their Lord; they shall have nothing to fear nor shall they grieve."* (Verse 112)

This complements the earlier principle concerning punishment, when they claimed that the fire of hell would only touch them for a very brief period. They were told: *"Those who earn evil and become engulfed by their sin are destined for the fire, where they shall abide."* (Verse 81) Thus, the complete Islamic concept of reward and punishment emerges.

Here again we find the most important feature of the Islamic faith: total, unconditional, mental and physical surrender to God. It is, however, a surrender that must be manifested in a practical form, expressed in the verse in the proviso, *'while doing good works,'* because Islam makes a direct functional link between abstract belief and everyday behaviour, between faith and action, inner convictions and outward deeds. In this way, religious faith becomes a complete way of life, and man's character and actions merge into a single entity – hence the generous reward granted by God Almighty to believers without discrimination or preference of one group over another. Those who willingly and completely surrender themselves to God *"shall have their reward with their Lord; they shall have nothing to fear no shall they grieve."* (Verse 112)

While the Jews and the Christians were making those inflated and self-righteous claims, they were accusing each other of having no basis for their respective beliefs, which caused the Arabs *"devoid of knowledge"* to refuse both of them and throw the same charge back at them both.

This last phrase clearly refers to the illiterate idolaters of Arabia, who observed with bewilderment the polemical religious arguments and the incessant barrage of accusations and counter-accusations hurled at each other by Jews and Christians. They viewed both religious groups with disdain, not least because of the myths and superstitions that had crept into Jewish and Christian theology, which did not greatly differ from the Arabs' own polytheistic beliefs, such as ascribing offspring to God. Accordingly, neither Judaism nor Christianity had much appeal for the people of Arabia.

The *sūrah* notes those accusations and controversies but leaves the final judgement to God, who *"on the Day of Judgement shall judge between them on all their disputes".* It is to Him that all matters are ultimately referred. This is the fairest and most satisfactory way of dealing with these irrational and futile arguments, which were made by people whose exclusive claim to salvation and guidance has already been refuted.

There follow further denunciations of the Jews' and Christians' attempts to raise doubts in Muslim minds about the veracity of the Prophet's teachings and instructions, especially those concerned with the change of the direction of prayer, or the *qiblah*. These attempts are considered tantamount to obstructing places of worship and keeping people out of them, or even seeking to destroy them. *"Who is more unjust than he who forbids God's name to be mentioned in His places of worship, and seeks to destroy them? Such people have no right to enter them except with fear in their hearts. They shall suffer ignominy in this world and awesome suffering awaits them in the life to come. To God belong the east and the west: wherever you turn there will be the face of God. Truly, God is limitless in His bounty and He knows all."* (Verses 114–115)

The immediate impression one gets from these two verses is that they relate to the *qiblah* issue and to Jewish efforts to dissuade the Muslims from turning in prayer towards the Ka'bah, in Makkah. Other accounts, however, speak of different circumstances for their revelation.

The verses are phrased in general terms and may therefore be interpreted generally. The same applies to the consequences of hindering the use of God's places of worship or destroying them. Those who perpetrate such acts deserve to be unceasingly pursued and relentlessly harassed, unless they seek refuge in the sanctuary of places of worship. It was in this spirit that on the day the Muslims conquered Makkah in August 630 CE, the Prophet Muḥammad ordered a general amnesty declaring that anyone who entered the sacred mosque would be safe. Many of the Arab enemies of Islam did exactly that. These were the very people who prevented the Prophet and his followers from entering the sacred mosque in Makkah, making it clear that they would go to war, if necessary, to stop the Muslims from entering. Furthermore, they are now warned of a double punishment: *"They shall suffer ignominy in this world and awesome suffering awaits them in the life to come."* (Verse 114)

However, another interpretation of the statement *"Such people have no right to enter them except with fear in their hearts"* emphasizes the fact that those who hinder or impede the use of places of worship should themselves only enter such places in fear of God and in total submission to Him. That would be the most appropriate way for them to show respect for these places and to acknowledge God's power and glory.

But what makes us favour the view that the two verses were revealed in connection with the *qiblah* issue is the verse that comes immediately after them, stating: *"To God belong the east and the west; wherever you turn there will be the face of God. Truly, God is limitless in His bounty, and He knows all."* (Verse 115) Clearly this verse comes as a response to Jewish lies and false contentions that prayers offered by Muslims facing Jerusalem were worthless and in vain. It is saying that in the final analysis prayer is valid whatever direction a worshipper faces, because God's face will be there. To specify a particular direction is no more than a matter of discipline. It does not mean that God's face is found in one direction rather than another. After all, God does not wish to make things difficult for people, nor would He want to take away their reward or devalue it: *"Truly, God is limitless in His bounty and He knows all."* (Verse 115)

Unbelief Is All One

The *sūrah* then discusses certain distorted concepts of Godhead held by Jews and Christians. It highlights the contrast between those and the beliefs held by the pagan Arabs, emphasizing the striking similarities, before it corrects those erroneous concepts and presents the true unitarian belief of Islam. *"They say, 'God has taken to Himself a son.' Limitless is He in His glory! His is all that is in the heavens and on earth; all things are obedient to Him. He is the Originator of the heavens and the earth. When He wills something to be, He need only say, 'Be', and it is. Those devoid of knowledge say, 'Why does not God speak to us, nor is a sign shown to us?' The same demands were made by people before them: their hearts are all alike. We have made the signs very clear for those with firm conviction."* (Verses 116–118)

Indeed, the totally misguided notion of "God the Father" was not restricted to the Christians who take Jesus to be the son of God; for some Jews also believed that Ezra was a son of God, while the Arab idolaters believed that the angels were God's daughters. The *sūrah* condemns these three groups, all fiercely antagonistic towards Islam in Arabia at the time, without going into details of their beliefs.

It is interesting to note here that those groups compare very closely with the three groups that are opposed to Islam today, as represented by world Zionism, the crusading Churches and international Communism, the last being even more hostile to Islam than the Arab idolaters ever were.

By grouping all three camps together, the Qur'ān equates the absurd Jewish and Christian beliefs with those of idolatry, and it implicitly refutes their claims to exclusive righteousness and salvation by putting forward the correct version of unitarian belief: *"Limitless is He in His Glory! His is all that is in the heavens and on earth; all things are obedient to Him. He is the Originator of the heavens and the earth. When He wills something to be, He need only say, 'Be', and it is."* (Verses 116–117)

Here we come to the pure and clear Islamic concept of the nature of God and His relationship with His creation, and how creatures come into being. This is the clearest and noblest understanding of all these facts.

The universe was created directly by God through an act of His free, absolute and omnipotent will, expressed in the simple word "Be". The mere intention of God to create anything would bring it instantaneously into existence in the form chosen for it, without the need for intermediaries of any kind. As to how this actually happens, this remains one of life's most profound mysteries. In fact, the human mind is not equipped to fathom the secret of life. Such understanding is not necessary for the fulfilment of man's role, which is to build human life on earth.

God has given man numerous skills, talents and resources that have enabled him to discover and unravel a great many of the natural laws that govern the world around him. But, much as man has been able to learn about the world and exploit that knowledge for his own progress and advancement, other aspects have been kept away from him, as these have no impact on man's role on earth.

Philosophers and thinkers throughout human existence have attempted to unravel the secrets of creation, and a number of theories of life and the universe have been advanced, including some absurd and ridiculous notions. Man's failure in this area has been due to the fact that human science and philosophy have ventured into a realm of thought for which man does not possess the necessary intellectual and analytical tools. They have merely been groping in the dark, adrift in uncharted waters.

Some Muslim thinkers and philosophers have also been lured into this controversial and complicated area of human thinking but failed to come up with any satisfactory conclusions. When some of them sought help in Greek philosophy, itself none the wiser, they were thrown into even deeper confusion. This has inevitably and surreptitiously found its way into Islamic thought but only as an alien body.

The Islamic view draws a distinct line between Creator and creation. The Creator is unique and matchless, which leaves no room in Islamic thought for the idea of "the unity of creation" or pantheism. Non-Muslim philosophy relies on this idea to indicate that creation and the Creator are one and the same; that creation is a mere reflection of the Creator and the physical manifestation of its Maker. A Muslim views existence as a unity in a different sense: it is created by one will, follows the same laws of nature, demonstrates absolute harmony and submits humbly to its Lord:

"His is all that is in the heavens and on earth; all things are obedient to Him." (Verse 116) This plain concept eliminates the need for the Creator to have offspring or have them ascribed to Him, since *"He is the Originator of the heavens and the earth. When He wills something to be, He need only say, 'Be', and it is."* (Verse 117) How this divine will operates cannot be known because it is beyond man's capacity to comprehend, and it would be futile for him to try or pretend to know.

Following this brief discussion, the *sūrah* cites another statement it attributes to the idolaters of Arabia, again having a strange resemblance to what the Jews and the Christians were saying: *"Those devoid of knowledge say, 'Why does not God speak to us, nor is a sign shown to us?' The same demands were made by people before them: their hearts are all alike. We have made the signs very clear for those with firm conviction."* (Verse 118)

The pagan Arabs had often challenged the Prophet Muḥammad to come up with some miraculous proof or an extraordinary act to convince them of Islam. The *sūrah* makes the point that Jews and Christians who lived before them had asked the same of their prophets. A case in mind is that when the Israelites asked Moses that they should be allowed to see God in person. All three groups seem to share the same attitudes, concepts and inclinations, and therefore belong together.

God emphasizes that He has *"made the signs very clear for those with firm conviction."* Conviction, or certainty of faith, is a function of the heart and not a reaction to astounding or spectacular demonstrations. With faith, man is capable of appreciating signs and miracles, and understanding their meaning and purpose, and drawing the necessary lessons and reassurance from them.

Jewish and Christian Arguments

Having dismissed the false claims of the Jews, the Christians and the Arab idolaters and revealed the real motives driving them to oppose Islam, the *sūrah* directly addresses the Prophet Muḥammad in order to define his mission and specify his responsibilities. It also exposes the true nature of the dispute between him and the Jews and Christians, who wanted to exact a very high price that Muḥammad neither possessed nor was able to afford. *"We have sent you with the truth; a bearer of glad tidings and a warner. You shall not be questioned about those who are destined for the blazing fire. Never will the Jews nor yet the Christians be pleased with you unless you follow their faith. Say, 'God's guidance is the only true guidance.' Should you follow their desires after all the knowledge that has come to you, you would have none to protect you from God, nor to give you help. Those to whom We have given the Book, and who recite it as it ought to be recited, truly believe in it; those who deny it are utter losers."* (Verses 119–121)

"We have sent you with the truth..." This opening statement in these verses gives strong reassurance to the Prophet that would help him to dispel any doubts or fears regarding the nature of his mission, and to foil any schemes or threats to undermine it. It is expressed very sharply and succinctly, giving it force and impact.

"A bearer of glad tidings and a warner." Muḥammad's mission was to deliver God's message, giving the good news to those who accept it and warning those who reject it. This is the total sum of his task. He would not be questioned about those who would end up in hell, because they would have met their fate as a result of their own actions.

The Prophet is also told that the Jews and the Christians would continue to oppose and scheme against him. They would never make peace with Islam, nor be satisfied unless Muḥammad abandoned Islam and took up their distorted beliefs and erroneous ideas, referred to earlier. It was not evidence or proof of credentials they were after; nor was it because they doubted his integrity or the truth of the revelations he had received. Nothing would seem to satisfy or convince them apart from an undertaking by Muḥammad that he was ready to relinquish his commission as Messenger of God and adopt their faith.

"Never will the Jews, nor yet the Christians be pleased with you unless you follow their faith." This is the bone of contention. What they are after is not evidence or conviction of the truth of Islam. Islam and Muḥammad have been a constant obsession with Jews and Christians throughout history. The faith of Islam has always been at the centre of the crusades and campaigns launched against the Muslim community all over the world. No matter how much the two camps may differ or quarrel between themselves, or how divided each of them may be, when it comes to fighting Islam and Muslims they are in full agreement and as united as they could be.

The conflict between the Judaeo-Christian world on the one side, and the Muslim community on the other, remains in essence one of ideology, although over the years it has appeared in various guises and has grown more sophisticated and, at times, more insidious. We have seen the original ideological conflict succeeded by economic, political and military confrontation, on the basis that 'religious' or 'ideological' conflicts are outdated and are usually prosecuted by 'fanatics' and backward people. Unfortunately, some naïve and confused Muslims have fallen for this stratagem and persuaded themselves that the religious and ideological aspects of the conflict are no longer relevant.

But in reality world Zionism and Christian Imperialism, as well as world Communism, are conducting the fight against Islam and the Muslim community, first and foremost, on ideological grounds and with the sole aim of destroying this solid rock which, despite their concerted and sustained efforts, they have not been able to remove.

The confrontation is not over control of territory or economic resources, or for military domination. If we believe that, we would play into our enemies' hands and would have no one but ourselves to blame for the consequences.

"Never will the Jews, nor yet the Christians be pleased with you unless you follow their faith." (Verse 120) That is the heavy price that would have to be paid. They will accept nothing less.

But God's instructions are very clear: *"Say: 'God's guidance is the only true guidance.'"* (Verse 120) The instruction is definite and emphatic: there is to be no negotiation or bargaining, no compromise or appeasement. The Prophet is warned that his wish to convey the message to those people and his eagerness for them to believe him, or his inclination to befriend them, should not distract him from the difficult but straight path he has taken: *"Should you follow their desires after all the knowledge that has come to you, you would have none to protect you from God, nor to give you help."* (Verse 120)

It is a stern, uncompromising warning, addressed to none other than Muḥammad, God's Messenger and beloved Prophet. His detractors are motivated by prejudice and narrow-minded self-interest, rather than by lack of proof or knowledge. Those of them who are able to rid themselves of such motives and who properly understand their own Scriptures will believe him. *"Those to whom We have given the Book, and who recite it as it ought to be recited, truly believe in it; those who deny it are utter losers."* (Verse 121)

Having delivered this decisive warning, the *sūrah* now addresses the Israelites with an amicable and sympathetic appeal, as a fitting end to this extensive debate concerning their history and religious conduct. They are offered a last chance before they are totally discredited and deprived of the privilege and honour of being the trustees and custodians of God's message to mankind.

The appeal opens with similar words as used earlier: *"Children of Israel! Remember My favour which I bestowed on you, and that I have preferred you over all people. Fear the day when no soul shall avail another in any way, nor shall ransom be accepted from any of them, nor shall intercession be of any benefit, and none shall receive help."* (Verses 122–123)

6

Universal Faith

When his Lord tested Abraham with certain commandments and he fulfilled them, He said, 'I have appointed you a leader of mankind.' Abraham asked, 'And what of my descendants?' God said, 'My covenant does not apply to the wrongdoers.' (124)

وَإِذِ ٱبْتَلَىٰٓ إِبْرَٰهِـۧمَ رَبُّهُۥ بِكَلِمَـٰتٍ فَأَتَمَّهُنَّ ۖ قَالَ
إِنِّى جَاعِلُكَ لِلنَّاسِ إِمَامًا ۖ قَالَ وَمِن ذُرِّيَّتِى ۖ
قَالَ لَا يَنَالُ عَهْدِى ٱلظَّـٰلِمِينَ ﴿١٢٤﴾

We made the House [i.e. the Ka'bah] a resort for mankind and a sanctuary: 'Make the place where Abraham stood as a place of prayer.' We assigned to Abraham and Ishmael the task of purifying My House for those who walk around it, those who sojourn there for meditation and those who bow down and prostrate themselves in prayer. (125)

وَإِذْ جَعَلْنَا ٱلْبَيْتَ مَثَابَةً لِّلنَّاسِ وَأَمْنًا
وَٱتَّخِذُوا۟ مِن مَّقَامِ إِبْرَٰهِـۧمَ مُصَلًّى ۖ
وَعَهِدْنَآ إِلَىٰٓ إِبْرَٰهِـۧمَ وَإِسْمَـٰعِيلَ
أَن طَهِّرَا بَيْتِىَ لِلطَّآئِفِينَ وَٱلْعَـٰكِفِينَ
وَٱلرُّكَّعِ ٱلسُّجُودِ ﴿١٢٥﴾

Abraham said, 'Lord, make this a land of security and make provisions of fruits for those of its people who believe in God and the Last Day.' God said, 'And as for he who disbelieves, I shall let him enjoy life for a while and then I shall drive him to suffering through the fire; and what a terrible end!' (126)

وَإِذْ قَالَ إِبْرَٰهِـۧمُ رَبِّ ٱجْعَلْ هَـٰذَا بَلَدًا ءَامِنًا
وَٱرْزُقْ أَهْلَهُۥ مِنَ ٱلثَّمَرَٰتِ مَنْ ءَامَنَ مِنْهُم
بِٱللَّهِ وَٱلْيَوْمِ ٱلْـَٔاخِرِ ۖ قَالَ وَمَن كَفَرَ فَأُمَتِّعُهُۥ
قَلِيلًا ثُمَّ أَضْطَرُّهُۥٓ إِلَىٰ عَذَابِ ٱلنَّارِ ۖ
وَبِئْسَ ٱلْمَصِيرُ ﴿١٢٦﴾

As Abraham and Ishmael raised the foundations of the House, [they prayed]: 'Our Lord, accept this from us; You are the One that hears all and knows all. (127)

وَإِذْ يَرْفَعُ إِبْرَٰهِـۧمُ ٱلْقَوَاعِدَ مِنَ ٱلْبَيْتِ
وَإِسْمَٰعِيلُ رَبَّنَا تَقَبَّلْ مِنَّآ ۖ إِنَّكَ أَنتَ
ٱلسَّمِيعُ ٱلْعَلِيمُ ﴿١٢٧﴾

Our Lord, make us surrender ourselves to You, and make out of our offspring a community that will surrender itself to You. Show us our ways of worship and accept our repentance; You are the One who accepts repentance, the Merciful. (128)

رَبَّنَا وَٱجْعَلْنَا مُسْلِمَيْنِ لَكَ وَمِن ذُرِّيَّتِنَآ
أُمَّةً مُّسْلِمَةً لَّكَ وَأَرِنَا مَنَاسِكَنَا وَتُبْ
عَلَيْنَآ ۖ إِنَّكَ أَنتَ ٱلتَّوَّابُ ٱلرَّحِيمُ ﴿١٢٨﴾

Our Lord, send them a Messenger from among themselves who shall declare to them Your revelations, and instruct them in the Book and in wisdom, and purify them. You are Mighty and Wise.' (129)

رَبَّنَا وَٱبْعَثْ فِيهِمْ رَسُولًا مِّنْهُمْ يَتْلُوا۟ عَلَيْهِمْ
ءَايَٰتِكَ وَيُعَلِّمُهُمُ ٱلْكِتَٰبَ وَٱلْحِكْمَةَ
وَيُزَكِّيهِمْ ۚ إِنَّكَ أَنتَ ٱلْعَزِيزُ ٱلْحَكِيمُ ﴿١٢٩﴾

Who but a foolish person would turn away from the faith of Abraham? We raised him high in this life, and in the life to come he shall be among the righteous. (130)

وَمَن يَرْغَبُ عَن مِّلَّةِ إِبْرَٰهِـۧمَ إِلَّا مَن
سَفِهَ نَفْسَهُۥ ۚ وَلَقَدِ ٱصْطَفَيْنَٰهُ فِى ٱلدُّنْيَا ۖ
وَإِنَّهُۥ فِى ٱلْـَٔاخِرَةِ لَمِنَ ٱلصَّٰلِحِينَ ﴿١٣٠﴾

When his Lord said to him, 'Submit yourself', he said, 'I have submitted myself to the Lord of all the worlds.' (131)

إِذْ قَالَ لَهُۥ رَبُّهُۥٓ أَسْلِمْ ۖ قَالَ أَسْلَمْتُ لِرَبِّ
ٱلْعَٰلَمِينَ ﴿١٣١﴾

Abraham enjoined the same on his children, and so did Jacob, saying, 'My children, God has given you the purest faith. Do not let death overtake you before you have submitted yourselves to God.' (132)

وَوَصَّىٰ بِهَآ إِبۡرَٰهِـۧمُ بَنِيهِ وَيَعۡقُوبُ يَٰبَنِيَّ
إِنَّ ٱللَّهَ ٱصۡطَفَىٰ لَكُمُ ٱلدِّينَ فَلَا تَمُوتُنَّ
إِلَّا وَأَنتُم مُّسۡلِمُونَ ١٣٢

Were you present when death approached Jacob? He asked his children, 'Whom will you worship when I am gone?' They replied, 'We will worship your God, the God of your forefathers Abraham, Ishmael and Isaac, the One God. To Him we submit ourselves.' (133)

أَمۡ كُنتُمۡ شُهَدَآءَ إِذۡ حَضَرَ يَعۡقُوبَ
ٱلۡمَوۡتُ إِذۡ قَالَ لِبَنِيهِ مَا تَعۡبُدُونَ مِنۢ
بَعۡدِي قَالُواْ نَعۡبُدُ إِلَٰهَكَ وَإِلَٰهَ ءَابَآئِكَ
إِبۡرَٰهِـۧمَ وَإِسۡمَٰعِيلَ وَإِسۡحَٰقَ إِلَٰهٗا وَٰحِدٗا
وَنَحۡنُ لَهُۥ مُسۡلِمُونَ ١٣٣

That community has passed away. Theirs is what they had earned and yours is what you have earned. You shall not be questioned about what they did. (134)

تِلۡكَ أُمَّةٞ قَدۡ خَلَتۡۖ لَهَا مَا كَسَبَتۡ
وَلَكُم مَّا كَسَبۡتُمۡۖ وَلَا تُسۡـَٔلُونَ عَمَّا كَانُواْ
يَعۡمَلُونَ ١٣٤

They say, 'Follow the Jewish faith – or, follow the Christian faith – and you shall be rightly guided.' Say, 'No. We follow the faith of Abraham, who was truly devoted to God, and was not of those who associated partners with God.' (135)

وَقَالُواْ كُونُواْ هُودًا أَوۡ نَصَٰرَىٰ تَهۡتَدُواْۗ
قُلۡ بَلۡ مِلَّةَ إِبۡرَٰهِـۧمَ حَنِيفٗاۖ وَمَا كَانَ مِنَ
ٱلۡمُشۡرِكِينَ ١٣٥

Say [all of you], 'We believe in God and in what has been revealed to us, and in what was revealed to Abraham, Ishmael, Isaac, Jacob and their descendants, and in what was given to Moses and Jesus, and in what all prophets have been given by their Lord. We make no distinction between any of them, and to God we have surrendered ourselves.' (136)

قُولُوٓا۟ ءَامَنَّا بِٱللَّهِ وَمَآ أُنزِلَ إِلَيْنَا وَمَآ أُنزِلَ
إِلَىٰٓ إِبْرَٰهِۦمَ وَإِسْمَٰعِيلَ وَإِسْحَٰقَ وَيَعْقُوبَ
وَٱلْأَسْبَاطِ وَمَآ أُوتِىَ مُوسَىٰ وَعِيسَىٰ
وَمَآ أُوتِىَ ٱلنَّبِيُّونَ مِن رَّبِّهِمْ لَا نُفَرِّقُ
بَيْنَ أَحَدٍ مِّنْهُمْ وَنَحْنُ لَهُۥ مُسْلِمُونَ ﴿١٣٦﴾

If they come to believe in the way you believe, they will be rightly guided; but if they turn away, they will be in schism, but God will protect you from them; He hears all and knows all. (137)

فَإِنْ ءَامَنُوا۟ بِمِثْلِ مَآ ءَامَنتُم بِهِۦ فَقَدِ
ٱهْتَدَوا۟ ۖ وَّإِن تَوَلَّوْا۟ فَإِنَّمَا هُمْ فِى شِقَاقٍ ۖ
فَسَيَكْفِيكَهُمُ ٱللَّهُ ۚ وَهُوَ ٱلسَّمِيعُ
ٱلْعَلِيمُ ﴿١٣٧﴾

[This message takes its] hue from God; who can give a better hue than God? Him alone do we worship. (138)

صِبْغَةَ ٱللَّهِ ۖ وَمَنْ أَحْسَنُ مِنَ ٱللَّهِ
صِبْغَةً ۖ وَنَحْنُ لَهُۥ عَٰبِدُونَ ﴿١٣٨﴾

Say, 'Would you dispute with us about God? He is our Lord and your Lord. To us our deeds shall be credited and to you, your deeds. To Him alone we are devoted.' (139)

قُلْ أَتُحَآجُّونَنَا فِى ٱللَّهِ وَهُوَ رَبُّنَا وَرَبُّكُمْ
وَلَنَآ أَعْمَٰلُنَا وَلَكُمْ أَعْمَٰلُكُمْ وَنَحْنُ لَهُۥ
مُخْلِصُونَ ﴿١٣٩﴾

Do you claim that Abraham, Ishmael, Isaac, Jacob and the Tribes were Jews or Christians? Say, 'Do you know better than God?' Who is more wicked than one who suppresses a testimony he has received from God? God is not unmindful of what you do. (140)

أَمْ تَقُولُونَ إِنَّ إِبْرَٰهِـۧمَ وَإِسْمَٰعِيلَ
وَإِسْحَٰقَ وَيَعْقُوبَ وَٱلْأَسْبَاطَ
كَانُوا۟ هُودًا أَوْ نَصَٰرَىٰ ۗ قُلْ ءَأَنتُمْ أَعْلَمُ
أَمِ ٱللَّهُ ۗ وَمَنْ أَظْلَمُ مِمَّن كَتَمَ شَهَٰدَةً
عِندَهُۥ مِنَ ٱللَّهِ ۗ وَمَا ٱللَّهُ بِغَٰفِلٍ عَمَّا
تَعْمَلُونَ ﴿١٤٠﴾

That community has passed away. Theirs is what they earned and yours is what you have earned. You shall not be questioned about what they did. (141)

تِلْكَ أُمَّةٌ قَدْ خَلَتْ ۖ لَهَا مَا كَسَبَتْ وَلَكُم
مَّا كَسَبْتُمْ ۖ وَلَا تُسْـَٔلُونَ عَمَّا كَانُوا۟
يَعْمَلُونَ ﴿١٤١﴾

Overview

So far in the *sūrah*, the debate with the people of earlier revelations, i.e. the Jews and the Christians, has mainly focused on the historical record of the Israelites and their response to the Prophets who came to lead them, the teachings that these Prophets preached, and the covenants and pledges to which the Israelites committed themselves. This covered a historical span from the era of Moses to the time of Muḥammad (peace be upon them both). The argument so far was in the most part with the Jews, shorter ones with the Christians, with a few references to the idolaters, particularly when they shared certain features with the other two groups.

In this section we are taken farther back in history, to the era of Abraham. The events and amount of detail presented here fall neatly into context with the subject matter of the *sūrah* as a whole. They are also immediately relevant to the long and hard debate that was taking place between the Muslims and the Jews in Madinah when these verses were revealed.

The people of earlier revelations trace their origins back to Abraham by way of his son Isaac (peace be upon them). Understandably, they have always been proud of this relationship, just as they have cherished the promises God made to Abraham to bless him and his seed, and the covenant God made with them. This has led them to make exclusive claims to righteousness and custodianship of God's message to mankind. It has also misled them into believing that heaven is exclusively theirs, whatever they do.

The Quraysh Arab tribe living in Makkah were also Abraham's descendants through his other son, Ishmael. They were also just as proud of their ancestry as the Jews were of theirs. It gave them the privilege of being the custodians of the sacred shrine of the Ka'bah in Makkah, which had, in turn, given them the religious authority, honour, power and position they enjoyed over the rest of the Arabs.

Towards the end of the last passage we saw how the Qur'ān refuted Jewish and Christian claims to exclusive righteousness and salvation: *"They declare: 'None shall enter Paradise unless he is a Jew or a Christian.'"* (Verse 111) Hard did they try to convert Muslims to Judaism or Christianity: *"They say: 'Follow the Jewish faith' – or, 'Follow the Christian faith' – 'and you shall be rightly guided.'"* (Verse 135) It also condemned those who prevent people from worshipping in God's places of worship – which, as we said, was probably linked to the issue of changing the direction Muslims face in prayer from Jerusalem to the Ka'bah in Makkah – and efforts to exploit that issue to create division and confusion within Muslim ranks.

In this section, and still within the same context of Jewish, Christian and pagan claims, the *sūrah* recounts parts of the history of Abraham and his sons Ishmael and Isaac, and gives a final ruling on the *qiblah* issue. The occasion is also used to establish the truth regarding the religion of Abraham, which was based purely on the belief in God's absolute oneness. Thus it remains at complete variance with the distorted beliefs adopted by those three groups, while its affinity to the message of the Prophet Muḥammad was total. It denounces the monopoly of religious righteousness by any nation or racial group, stressing that religion resides in the believer's heart; it is not inherited through blood or ancestral lineage. Religion belongs to God Almighty, who is not related through blood or ancestry to any human individual or group. Those who believe in His religion and practise it properly shall be its rightful custodians and trustees, at all times, regardless of their race or ethnic origin.

The Qur'ān presents these facts, which form some of the most basic tenets of Islamic belief, in a fine, clear and elegant style. It takes the reader step by step through the long span of history starting at the time God entrusted Abraham with the religious leadership of mankind, upon successfully completing the test to which God put him. It goes up to the early formation of the Muslim community which believes in the message of Muḥammad. Its rise is seen as fulfilment of Abraham's and Ishmael's prayers while they were laying the foundations of the Ka'bah. Thus, it is the Muslim community that is the legitimate heir to God's religion, solely by virtue of their faith in God and by their true and sincere following of Abraham's teachings. Those who depart from it, choosing to turn away from Abraham's faith in God's absolute oneness, renege on their commitments to God and, as such, cannot be the heirs to the divine faith.

The Qur'ān further establishes that Islam, in the sense of submission to God alone, was the first and the last divine message to mankind. It was the religion of Abraham and of Ishmael, Isaac, Jacob and the Hebrew tribes who came after him, and was handed down to Moses and Jesus until it was eventually inherited by the Muslims. All true and faithful followers of those and other prophets and messengers belong to the same nation and share in all the merits and rewards of following the religion of Islam in its wider, universal version. All those who reject the religion of Abraham or renege on any of their covenants with God forfeit their claim to those privileges and rewards.

Thus we can see how Jewish and Christian claims to an exclusive possession of God's true religion, by virtue of lineage to Abraham, are totally groundless. They lost that right the moment they deviated from the true faith based on total submission to God alone. For the same reason, the idolater Arabs of the Quraysh forfeited their claim to the exclusive custodianship of the Ka'bah. Likewise, the Jewish argument for opposing the designation of the Ka'bah as the *qiblah* for the Muslims falls apart, because the Ka'bah was the original *qiblah* of their forefather Abraham, and therefore it was theirs also.

Following this brief introduction, let us now take a closer look at the account of Abraham, his covenant with God, and its significance in the history of the religion of Islam.

Abraham's Covenant

> *When his Lord tested Abraham with certain commandments and he fulfilled them, He said, 'I have appointed you a leader of mankind.' Abraham asked, 'And what of my descendants?' God said, 'My covenant does not apply to the wrongdoers.'* (Verse 124)

The Prophet is here reminded of how God had imparted certain commandments and obligations to Abraham in order to test his faith, loyalty and resolve. Elsewhere in the Qur'ān, he is described as *"Abraham, who was faithful to his trust."* (53: 37) This is a recognition by God of Abraham's faithful and complete fulfilment of those obligations, according him a very high rank in God's estimation. Hence, God's promise: *"I have appointed you a leader of mankind."* Thus, Abraham becomes the leader to be followed, the one who shows people the way to all goodness.

Being human, Abraham is immediately prompted to wish for that blessing and privilege to be extended to his offspring. What Abraham expressed was a natural instinctive human reaction, because man is always eager to multiply and perpetuate his achievements and attainments. By the passing of knowledge and experience from one generation to the next, the human lot is improved and life is preserved. This natural and necessary human process has been a target for criticism and attack, while Islam recognizes its importance, and promotes it through its law of inheritance, so that it serves human society to the full.

The misguided efforts made in some societies to undermine this natural progression in fact try to suppress human nature altogether. Such efforts betray short-sightedness, inhumanity and arbitrary methods in tackling social and moral ills. Unless remedied, these will lead to the fragmentation and destruction of society. However, solutions that run contrary to human nature will inevitably end in failure. What is needed is a solution that rectifies deviation and social ills without contradicting human nature. Such methods can only be adopted and made to work within a framework of divine guidance and faith. They require a profound and enlightened understanding of human nature and the human mind, and an unbiased outlook, free of all grudges and destructive tendencies.

The answer to Abraham's question, *"And what of my descendants?"* reiterates an already stated major principle: that religious leadership and authority are granted purely on merit, in reward for sincere faith and diligent work. They are not inherited through ancestral lineage. God said: *"My covenant does not apply to the wrongdoers."*

"Wrongdoing" takes various forms: it might be directed at oneself, by associating partners with God, or it might be oppression directed at fellow human beings. The leadership denied to wrongdoers includes all the meanings covered by the Arabic term *imām*, which include prophethood, political authority, and the leading of congregational prayers. Equity and justice make up the foremost qualification for this lofty vocation, and no one who deviates from these qualities deserves any form of leadership, in its widest sense.

This is the clear essence of the covenant made with Abraham. According to it, the Jews, as a result of their repeated wrongdoing, self-indulgence and waywardness, could never have an exclusive monopoly of the leadership of mankind. Similarly, and for the same reasons, some so-called Muslims today would also be barred from that covenant.

Islam gives no credence to ties or relationships not based on faith and sincere action. It places a sharp distinction between one generation and another when the later one deviates from the faith, despite their common ancestry. Indeed, according to Islam, faith can separate father and son, and man and wife. Thus the Arabs who adopted Islam are distinguished from those who did not, just as Jews and Christians who believed in the religion of Abraham, Moses and Jesus are distinguished from those who deviated from them. Ancestors and offspring only become one family or nation when they are all believers united by the same faith, regardless of colour and geographic or ethnic origins.

Building the Kaʿbah

> *We made the House [i.e. the Kaʿbah] a resort for mankind and a sanctuary: 'Make the place where Abraham stood as a place of prayer.' We assigned to Abraham and Ishmael the task of purifying My House for those who walk around it, those who sojourn there for meditation and those who bow down and prostrate themselves in prayer.* (Verse 125)

The Sacred House, the Kaʿbah, was defiled by the Arabs of the Quraysh who were supposed to be its trusted caretakers and custodians. They harassed and persecuted the believers and drove them out of Makkah. Yet God wanted this House to be a sanctuary to which people of all races resort. In there people should find peace and security for all.

The Arabs had been directed to establish *"the place where Abraham stood"*, which is a reference to the whole area surrounding the Ka'bah, as a place for prayer, which makes its subsequent designation as a *qiblah*, a spot towards which Muslims turn in Prayer, a very natural progression raising no objections from anyone. After all, it had been the very first place to which Muslims, the legitimate heirs of Abraham's monotheistic religion, had turned in their prayer, because it had been dedicated to God and to no one else. Abraham and Ishmael, two pious and sincere servants of God, had been charged with cleansing it and preparing it for pilgrims who would come to it for worship and meditation. They would make no claim to its ownership, nor did they have it in their power to pass such ownership to anyone else. They were mere servants of God Almighty and keepers of His sacred and revered House.

> *Abraham said, 'Lord, make this a land of security and make provisions of fruits for those of its people who believe in God and the Last Day.' God said, 'And as for he who disbelieves, I shall let him enjoy life for a while and then I shall drive him to suffering through the fire; and what a terrible end!'* (Verse 126)

While still pleading for the House to be made a universal place of peace and security for posterity, Abraham has clearly heeded God's earlier admonition, as we now find him making the exception that only the believers should receive God's favour.

The *sūrah* then goes on to paint a lively picture of Abraham and Ishmael embarking on the job of constructing the House of God and preparing it for worshippers: *"As Abraham and Ishmael raised the foundations of the House, [they prayed]: 'Our Lord, accept this from us; You are the One that hears all and knows all. Our Lord, make us surrender ourselves to You, and make out of our offspring a community that will surrender itself to You. Show us our ways of worship and accept our repentance; You are the One who accepts repentance, the Merciful. Our Lord, send them a Messenger from among themselves who shall declare to them Your revelations, and instruct them in the Book and in wisdom, and purify them. You are Mighty and Wise.'"* (Verses 127–129)

Not only does this vivid account take the reader right into the scene of the action, but it also surrounds him with the mood and feeling of the occasion. It was a labour of love and devotion that those two pious people undertook, dedicated to God Almighty and carried out in expectation and hope that He would accept it and be pleased with it.

We almost hear the tone and music of their prayer, and we feel the atmosphere of heart-felt appeal to God. This is a special characteristic of the Qur'ānic style which brings a scene of an event long gone as though it is taking place here and now, right in front of us. In their prayer we cannot fail to note the sort of humility, devotion and profound faith that are worthy of prophets who understand the importance of true faith in this world. Such characteristics the Qur'ān tries to teach the advocates of faith and instil it in their hearts.

"'Our Lord, accept this from us; You are the One that hears all and knows all.'" (Verse 127) Their first aim is that their labour, which is dedicated purely to God, should be accepted by Him. Hence, they offer it with humility, hoping to earn God's pleasure through it, pinning their hopes on the fact that God listens to their prayers and knows their feelings and intentions.

"Our Lord, make us surrender ourselves to You, and make out of our offspring a community that will surrender itself to You. Show us our ways of worship and accept our repentance; You are the One who accepts repentance, the Merciful." (Verse 128) They turn to God seeking His guidance, fully aware that, without His help and support, they are powerless. Their prayer also shows the intrinsic solidarity of the community of believers over successive generations. *"Make of our offspring a community that will surrender itself to You."* This shows not only the fact that faith is the most important aspect in a believer's life, and appreciation of its great blessings, but also the instinctive natural feeling of wishing the best for one's children and descendants. Their main concern was that their offspring should be God-fearing, righteous and obedient to God. So they add a specific request: *"'Our Lord, send them a Messenger from among themselves who shall declare to them Your revelations, and instruct them in the Book and in wisdom, and purify them. You are Mighty and Wise.'"* (Verse 129)

That particular prayer was answered when the Prophet Muḥammad, a direct descendant of Abraham and Ishmael, was given his message several centuries later. We note that some time may elapse before

God answers a particular prayer. As human beings, we tend to be impatient and want our prayers answered immediately, forgetting that it is for God Almighty to choose how and when they should be answered and fulfilled.

This prayer by Abraham and Ishmael carries particular significance for the debate that was going on between the Muslims and the Jews in Madinah at the time. The two Prophets expressly request God to make out of their offspring a nation that would serve God, as the word 'Muslim', (meaning one who submits himself) implies. The prayer makes clear that the Muslim nation, followers of Muḥammad, are the recognized heirs to the legacy of Abraham; that is, the leadership of mankind and the custody of the House of God in Makkah. This, in turn, is an affirmation of the Muslims' right, over the idolater Arabs, to the Ka'bah, as well as of the latter's precedence over Jerusalem as the *qiblah* faced by Muslims in Prayer throughout the world.

Jews and Christians who claim a religious bond with Abraham, and the Quraysh Arabs who claim an ancestral relationship to Ishmael, are informed in clear, simple language that Abraham excluded the wrongdoers among his offspring from his covenant with God, and prayed for guidance and salvation only for the believers among them. Furthermore, when Abraham and Ishmael embarked on building a place dedicated to the worship of God on earth, they asked Him to make a nation from their offspring, the Muslim nation that would submit to God; and to send them a messenger of their own, Muḥammad, to instruct them in the true religion of God. These are the real and legitimate heirs of the legacy of Abraham and Ishmael.

Then comes a brief interjection condemning those who dispute Muḥammad's role as a prophet and messenger and argue about the essence of divine faith: *"Who but a foolish person would turn away from the faith of Abraham? We raised him high in this life, and in the life to come he shall be among the righteous. When his Lord said to him, 'Submit yourself', he said, 'I have submitted myself to the Lord of all the worlds.' Abraham enjoined the same on his children, and so did Jacob, saying, 'My children, God has given you the purest faith. Do not let death overtake you before you have submitted yourselves to God.'"* (Verses 130–132)

The essence of the religion of Abraham is pure submission to God, or Islam, which only a foolish or obstinate person would abandon or reject. Abraham and Jacob, or Israel as he is otherwise called, were determined to hand it down to their offspring, in perpetuity. This religion had been chosen for them by God Himself, as an act of grace and a boon to them; it was not of their making, and a better choice they would not have. With the coming of Muḥammad and the message of Islam, a fresh opportunity opened up for the Arabs and the Jews of Arabia to fulfil the wishes of their forefathers from whom they were proud to claim descent.

A Faith to Pass to Your Children

At this point we come to witness another awesome scene: Jacob on his deathbed, giving his last words of wisdom and advice to his children, gathered around him: *"Were you present when death approached Jacob? He asked his children, 'Whom will you worship when I am gone?' They replied, 'We will worship your God, the God of your forefathers Abraham, Ishmael and Isaac, the One God. To Him we submit ourselves.'"* (Verse 133)

It is indeed a tremendous and solemn occasion. The most important and only issue that concerned Jacob as he drew his last breath was the religion his children were to follow after his death. He was worried about the fate of his legacy and the future of the religion placed in his trust. His children's reply must have been most reassuring and gratifying for him. The chain would not be broken, and the legacy of Abraham was sure to live on for many generations to come.

Jacob asks his children: *"Whom will you worship when I am gone?"* (Verse 133) He thus tells them why he gathered them, and the issue he wanted to be sure of before his death. It is the trust and the heritage of that blessed house. His children reassure Jacob that they would be true to their trust. Thus, the same heritage of Abraham was safe with Jacob's children, who clearly state that they have submitted themselves to God.

The verse opens with a rhetorical question addressed to the Jews: *"Were you present when death approached Jacob?"* (Verse 133) It tells them what went on as witnessed by God Himself. They could not question the truth of what had happened or distort it after God has stated what went on.

In the light of these assertions, a clear distinction is established between that bygone generation and the one that was facing Islam in Madinah: *"That community has passed away. Theirs is what they had earned and yours is what you have earned. You shall not be questioned about what they did."* (Verse 134)

Every generation has its concerns and characteristics, and the record for which it shall be accountable. A corrupt and heedless generation shall bear no relation to a righteous one. The only durable link between generations of nations is that of faith and belief. From the Islamic point of view, a nation's characteristics are preserved and perpetuated through faith rather than race or blood, and generations are viewed as either believers or unbelievers, with every one seen in the light of their actions and record.

According to Islam, a nation is defined by its faith and beliefs, regardless of its constituent ethnic and racial groups, or how widely spread in the world they are. Having a common race or territory does not make a nation. This approach stems from Islam's universal view of mankind as a single race deriving its unique human qualities from the divine spirit God had breathed into man at the moment of creation, rather than from some acquired physical qualities that are of little concern.

The Argument Is Finally Settled

Against this historical background of God's covenant with Abraham, the building of the Ka'bah and the entitlement to the religious heritage of Abraham, the *sūrah* takes a closer look at some Jewish and Christian arguments and claims. It exposes the weakness in those arguments and the insidious ulterior motives behind them. The passage is rounded off by presenting Islam as man's comprehensive and universal religion, opposed and rejected only by those who are stubborn and ungrateful:

> *They say, 'Follow the Jewish faith – or, follow the Christian faith – and you shall be rightly guided.' Say, 'No. We follow the faith of Abraham, who was truly devoted to God, and was not of those who associated partners with God.' Say [all of you], 'We believe in God and in what has been revealed to us, and in what was revealed to Abraham, Ishmael, Isaac, Jacob and their descendants, and in what was given to Moses and Jesus, and in what all prophets have been given by their Lord. We make no distinction between any of them, and to God we have surrendered ourselves.' If they come to believe in the way you believe, they will be rightly guided; but if they turn away, they will be in schism, but God will protect you from them; He hears all and knows all.'* (Verses 135–137)

The Prophet is instructed here to confront the Jews and the Christians together with the same challenge, and call upon them equally to revert, together with the Muslims, to the original religion of Abraham, the founding father of the faith of Islam on earth. He was the one to make a covenant with God and he was true to his covenant.

Then the Muslims are called upon to acknowledge and declare an overall unity of faith, from that of Abraham right up to that of Jesus and Muḥammad.

The principle of the unity and universality of faith, and the unity of all prophets and messengers all through the ages, is the cornerstone of Islamic faith. It lends legitimacy to the Muslim community's claim to the legacy of Abraham and to the right of trusteeship for God's religion in this world. It is this principle as a fundamental backbone of Islam that gives it its universal characteristic, which brings people together under the same banner, free of all prejudice or discrimination. It makes the Muslim community open to all people in a spirit of genuine love and peace.

This leads to the conclusion that Islam, in its broad, universal sense, is the true guidance. Its followers shall succeed and prosper while its opponents will never find a firm basis to stand upon. On the contrary, they will live in constant turmoil and confusion.

This testimony from none other than God Almighty will give Muslims reassurance and make them proud of their faith and confident that they will overcome setbacks and tribulations and prevail over their enemies. God is on their side and *"will protect you from them; He hears all and knows all."* (Verse 137)

The duty of believers is to uphold the faith and take pride in it and wear the distinctive mark of the true servants of God which makes them stand out and surpass all others in the world: *"[This message takes its] hue from God; who can give a better hue than God? Him alone do we worship."* (Verse 138) He has given a very distinctive colour to the message He has chosen to be the last to mankind. It serves as a basis on which to establish an all-embracing human unity, free of all prejudices and fanaticism, giving no special status to any race or colour.

We need to reflect a little here about a unique and highly significant aspect of the Qur'ānic mode of expression. The beginning of this verse is a statement made by God: *"This message takes its hue from God; who can give a better hue than God?"* (Verse 138) The rest of the verse is a statement by the believers. The Qur'ān joins both statements without anything to separate or distinguish one from the other. This is a great honour to the believers when their statement is joined to that of God, indicating their very close link with their Lord. Examples of such highly significant type of expression are numerous in the Qur'ān.

The argument is then brought to its climax by posing the ultimate question: *"Say, 'Would you dispute with us about God? He is our Lord and your Lord. To us our deeds shall be credited and to you, your deeds. To Him alone we are devoted.'"* (Verse 139)

There can be no room for doubt about God's oneness and sovereignty over all creation. He is the Lord of all of us, and He shall judge everyone by their own deeds. As Muslims, we devote our life and existence totally to God alone. We seek no other beings with or beside Him; and to us, these are incontrovertible and indisputable facts on which the faith of Islam rests.

In terse and forceful language, the *sūrah* poses other rhetorical questions regarding the faith of earlier prophets, well known to the Jews and the Christians: *"Do you claim that Abraham, Ishmael, Isaac, Jacob and the Tribes were Jews or Christians?"* (Verse 140) These lived long before Moses, and their faith preceded both Christianity and Judaism. God states the truth about their faith: *"Say: 'Do you know better than God?'"* (Verse 140) No answer could be offered to such a rhetorical question. Besides, both Jews and Christians knew very well that these Prophets lived long before their faiths. They further have, in their own Scriptures, clear statements speaking of the Prophet who would be sent with a message of the pure monotheistic faith of Abraham, but they suppressed that. Hence, the warning that God is fully aware of what they suppress: *"Who is more wicked than one who suppresses a testimony he has received from God? God is not unmindful of what you do."* (Verse 140)

As the *sūrah* makes its final, irrefutable argument, showing the great gulf separating Abraham, Ishmael, Isaac, Jacob and his sons from the Jews who were the Prophet's contemporaries, it repeats the verse with which it concluded its discourse about Abraham and his descendants who submitted themselves to God: *"That community has passed away. Theirs is what they earned and yours is what you have earned. You shall not be questioned about what they did."* (Verse 141) With this powerful statement, all arguments are brought to their decisive conclusion.

7

Change of Direction

The weak-minded among people will say, 'What has turned them away from the direction of prayer which they have so far observed?' Say, 'To God belong the east and the west. He guides whomever He wills to a straight path.' (142)

سَيَقُولُ ٱلسُّفَهَآءُ مِنَ ٱلنَّاسِ مَا وَلَّىٰهُمْ
عَن قِبْلَتِهِمُ ٱلَّتِي كَانُواْ عَلَيْهَاۚ قُل لِّلَّهِ ٱلْمَشْرِقُ
وَٱلْمَغْرِبُۚ يَهْدِي مَن يَشَآءُ إِلَىٰ صِرَٰطٖ
مُّسْتَقِيمٖ ١٤٢

Thus We have made you the community [*ummah*] of the middle way, so that you may stand witness against the rest of mankind, and the Messenger shall be a witness against you. We appointed the direction of prayer which you formerly followed in order that We might distinguish those who follow the Messenger from those who turn on their heels. It was indeed a hard test except for those whom God has guided. God would never have let your faith be in vain. God is Compassionate and Merciful to mankind. (143)

وَكَذَٰلِكَ جَعَلْنَٰكُمْ أُمَّةٗ وَسَطٗا لِّتَكُونُواْ
شُهَدَآءَ عَلَى ٱلنَّاسِ وَيَكُونَ ٱلرَّسُولُ
عَلَيْكُمْ شَهِيدٗاۗ وَمَا جَعَلْنَا ٱلْقِبْلَةَ ٱلَّتِي
كُنتَ عَلَيْهَآ إِلَّا لِنَعْلَمَ مَن يَتَّبِعُ ٱلرَّسُولَ
مِمَّن يَنقَلِبُ عَلَىٰ عَقِبَيْهِۚ وَإِن كَانَتْ
لَكَبِيرَةً إِلَّا عَلَى ٱلَّذِينَ هَدَى ٱللَّهُۗ وَمَا كَانَ
ٱللَّهُ لِيُضِيعَ إِيمَٰنَكُمْۚ إِنَّ ٱللَّهَ بِٱلنَّاسِ
لَرَءُوفٞ رَّحِيمٞ ١٤٣

We have seen you often turn your face towards heaven. We shall, therefore, make you turn in prayer towards a direction you will be happy with. Turn your face, then, towards the Sacred Mosque; and wherever you all may be, turn your faces [in prayer] towards it. Those who have been granted revelations in the past know well that it is the truth from their Lord. God is not unaware of what they do. (144)

قَدْ نَرَىٰ تَقَلُّبَ وَجْهِكَ فِي ٱلسَّمَآءِ
فَلَنُوَلِّيَنَّكَ قِبْلَةً تَرْضَىٰهَاۚ فَوَلِّ وَجْهَكَ
شَطْرَ ٱلْمَسْجِدِ ٱلْحَرَامِۚ وَحَيْثُ مَا كُنتُمْ
فَوَلُّوا۟ وُجُوهَكُمْ شَطْرَهُۥۗ وَإِنَّ ٱلَّذِينَ أُوتُوا۟
ٱلْكِتَـٰبَ لَيَعْلَمُونَ أَنَّهُ ٱلْحَقُّ مِن رَّبِّهِمْۗ
وَمَا ٱللَّهُ بِغَـٰفِلٍ عَمَّا يَعْمَلُونَ ﴿١٤٤﴾

Were you to bring every possible sign before those who had been granted revelations, they would not follow your direction of prayer. And neither may you follow their direction of prayer, nor would they even follow one another's direction. If you were to follow their whims and desires after all the knowledge that has been given to you, you would certainly be among the wrongdoers. (145)

وَلَئِنْ أَتَيْتَ ٱلَّذِينَ أُوتُوا۟ ٱلْكِتَـٰبَ بِكُلِّ
ءَايَةٍ مَّا تَبِعُوا۟ قِبْلَتَكَۚ وَمَآ أَنتَ بِتَابِعٍ
قِبْلَتَهُمْۚ وَمَا بَعْضُهُم بِتَابِعٍ قِبْلَةَ بَعْضٍۚ
وَلَئِنِ ٱتَّبَعْتَ أَهْوَآءَهُم مِّنۢ بَعْدِ
مَا جَآءَكَ مِنَ ٱلْعِلْمِۙ إِنَّكَ إِذًا لَّمِنَ
ٱلظَّـٰلِمِينَ ﴿١٤٥﴾

Those to whom We granted revelation know it as well as they know their own children, but some of them knowingly conceal the truth. (146)

ٱلَّذِينَ ءَاتَيْنَـٰهُمُ ٱلْكِتَـٰبَ يَعْرِفُونَهُۥ كَمَا
يَعْرِفُونَ أَبْنَآءَهُمْۖ وَإِنَّ فَرِيقًا مِّنْهُمْ لَيَكْتُمُونَ
ٱلْحَقَّ وَهُمْ يَعْلَمُونَ ﴿١٤٦﴾

This is the truth from your Lord; never, then, be among the doubters. (147)

ٱلْحَقُّ مِن رَّبِّكَۖ فَلَا تَكُونَنَّ مِنَ
ٱلْمُمْتَرِينَ ﴿١٤٧﴾

Each one has a goal towards which he turns; so vie with one another in good works. Wherever you may be, God will bring you all together. God has power over all things. (148)

وَلِكُلٍّ وِجْهَةٌ هُوَ مُوَلِّيهَا ۖ فَاسْتَبِقُوا الْخَيْرَاتِ ۚ
أَيْنَ مَا تَكُونُوا يَأْتِ بِكُمُ اللَّهُ جَمِيعًا ۚ إِنَّ
اللَّهَ عَلَىٰ كُلِّ شَيْءٍ قَدِيرٌ ﴿١٤٨﴾

From wherever you may come forth, turn your face [in prayer] towards the Sacred Mosque. It is indeed the truth from your Lord. God is not unaware of what you do. (149)

وَمِنْ حَيْثُ خَرَجْتَ فَوَلِّ وَجْهَكَ شَطْرَ
الْمَسْجِدِ الْحَرَامِ ۖ وَإِنَّهُ لَلْحَقُّ مِن رَّبِّكَ ۗ
وَمَا اللَّهُ بِغَافِلٍ عَمَّا تَعْمَلُونَ ﴿١٤٩﴾

From wherever you may come forth, turn your face [in prayer] towards the Sacred Mosque; and wherever you all may be, turn your faces towards it, so that people may have no argument against you, except those who are bent on wrongdoing. Have no fear of them, but fear Me, so that I may perfect My grace on you, and that you may be rightly guided. (150)

وَمِنْ حَيْثُ خَرَجْتَ فَوَلِّ وَجْهَكَ شَطْرَ
الْمَسْجِدِ الْحَرَامِ ۚ وَحَيْثُ مَا كُنتُمْ فَوَلُّوا
وُجُوهَكُمْ شَطْرَهُ لِئَلَّا يَكُونَ لِلنَّاسِ
عَلَيْكُمْ حُجَّةٌ إِلَّا الَّذِينَ ظَلَمُوا مِنْهُمْ
فَلَا تَخْشَوْهُمْ وَاخْشَوْنِي وَلِأُتِمَّ نِعْمَتِي
عَلَيْكُمْ وَلَعَلَّكُمْ تَهْتَدُونَ ﴿١٥٠﴾

Thus We have sent forth to you a Messenger from among yourselves to recite to you Our revelations, purify you, and instruct you in the Book and in wisdom and teach you what you did not know. (151)

كَمَا أَرْسَلْنَا فِيكُمْ رَسُولًا مِّنكُمْ
يَتْلُوا عَلَيْكُمْ آيَاتِنَا وَيُزَكِّيكُمْ
وَيُعَلِّمُكُمُ الْكِتَابَ وَالْحِكْمَةَ
وَيُعَلِّمُكُم مَّا لَمْ تَكُونُوا تَعْلَمُونَ ﴿١٥١﴾

Remember Me, then, and I will remember you; give thanks to Me and never deny Me. (152)

فَاذْكُرُونِي أَذْكُرْكُمْ وَاشْكُرُوا لِي
وَلَا تَكْفُرُونِ ﴿١٥٢﴾

Overview

This passage is almost entirely devoted to a discussion of the change of the *qiblah*, or direction faced in prayer, which occurred sixteen or seventeen months after the Prophet's arrival in Madinah in 622 CE, and the controversy that attended it. The Jews of Madinah tried to exploit the *qiblah* issue to create division and confusion among the Muslims. The Qur'ān denounces their allegations, and warns of the damage they might cause to the more vulnerable members of the Muslim community. No reference can be found in the Qur'ān to the exact date of the change of the *qiblah*.

The main facts of the situation make it clear that prayer was made a daily religious duty for Muslims while they were still in Makkah. They faced the Ka'bah when they prayed. No specific order is given in the Qur'ān on this point. When the Muslims emigrated from Makkah to Madinah, the instruction was given to the Prophet that instead of the Ka'bah in Makkah, Muslims should face Jerusalem. The fact that in both cases the instruction had come from the Prophet rather than in Qur'ānic statements in no way diminishes its validity or authority.

This continued to be the practice until the revelation of the instructions in the present section, which superseded the previous ones. The Prophet, and the Muslims with him, were told to *"Turn your face, then, towards the Sacred Mosque, and wherever you all may be, turn your faces [in prayer] towards it."* (Verse 144)

Jerusalem happened to be the *qiblah* for the Jews and the Christians also, and the fact that the Muslims too had been instructed to use it as theirs gave the Jews of Madinah a ready excuse for refusing to recognize or accept Islam. They saw the fact that the Prophet and his companions faced Jerusalem when they prayed as proof that theirs was the true religion and their *qiblah* was the original and legitimate one. Muḥammad and his followers, they argued, should follow their religion and refrain from trying to convert them to Islam.

This was not easy for the Arab Muslims to accept, since they had always revered the Ka'bah and considered it their most sacred religious symbol. The Jewish arguments made the situation even harder for the Muslims.

The Prophet Muḥammad entertained a wish to turn towards the Ka'bah, and could be seen looking up to heaven anxiously, without uttering a word, trusting to God and His wisdom.

Not long afterwards instructions were revealed that the Muslims should turn towards the Ka'bah. Some Muslims were reportedly in the middle of performing their prayer when they heard the news, and immediately turned to face the Ka'bah.

The Jews resented that decision which deprived them of their argument. They began to question the wisdom of the Muslim leadership and to raise doubts about the validity of the religious basis of Islam. Did the change of *qiblah* from Jerusalem to the Ka'bah mean that the Muslims had been praying towards the wrong *qiblah* all that time? And, if Jerusalem was the right *qiblah*, and it was correct to pray towards it, then it must have been wrong to change to another one. Praying towards the new *qiblah*, the Ka'bah, would, in this case, not be valid. They further argued that such abrogation of earlier orders could not be done by God. Hence, the decision must have been made by Muḥammad himself, proving that he was not receiving any divine revelations.

The gravity of the controversy surrounding this event is clear from the considerable attention given in the Qur'ān to its ramifications and the effect it had on some rank-and-file Muslims. It is also clear in the way the *sūrah* deals with the concept of abrogation. This is discussed in full in Chapters 5 and 6, beginning with Verse 106. More on this later.

The change of the *qiblah* was a central event in the history of Islam with far-reaching long-term consequences. It gave Islam a new focus and identified the Muslim community as an independent nation with a *qiblah* of its own.

The earlier decision to declare Jerusalem rather than the Ka'bah as the *qiblah* was for specific educational reasons, as explained in Verse 143: *"We appointed the direction of prayer [i.e. the* qiblah*] which you formerly followed in order that We might distinguish those who follow the Messenger from those who turn on their heels."*

Before Islam, the Arabs revered the Ka'bah and considered it a symbol of their religious and cultural heritage and glory. But in order to test their sincerity in accepting Islam, and ensure that their hearts were totally free of narrow racial or tribal loyalties, God initially instructed the Prophet to command his followers to adopt Jerusalem as the direction they faced in prayer. It was a difficult instruction to carry out, but it was a crucial test of how much they really understood the nature and the spirit of their new religion. It was necessary in order to establish how far some of those early Muslims were still influenced by pre-Islamic racial and tribal traditions.

When the Muslims adopted their new direction, and the Jews had begun to exploit that situation, fresh divine instructions were received to revert to the Ka'bah as the direction to face in prayer. The basis for the new decision was, however, made clear. It stemmed from the fact that the Sacred Mosque at Makkah had, in the first instance, been established by Abraham and Ishmael as a monument to pure unadulterated monotheism. It was part of the heritage of Islam which had come about, as seen earlier in verses 124–141, in answer to Abraham's prayer that a Messenger should be sent to his descendants, the inhabitants of Makkah, with the pure faith based on complete submission to God.

That part of the *sūrah*, giving the background and the circumstances surrounding the construction of the Ka'bah, provided a fitting introduction to the issue of the *qiblah*. Changing the *qiblah* back to the Ka'bah seems the only logical conclusion from that discussion of the dispute between the Muslims on the one hand, and the Jews, Christians and polytheist Arabs on the other, concerning Abraham's covenant with God and the right to his heritage. That covenant bound Abraham and his descendants, from one generation to another, to total submission to God.

The construction of the Sacred Mosque at the Ka'bah was carried out by Abraham and his son Ishmael at God's specific instruction. It is, therefore, part of the heritage passed on to their offspring. Muḥammad, a direct descendant of Abraham and a beneficiary of his covenant with God, and his followers, are rightful and natural heirs to that heritage, of which the Ka'bah is an important part. The decision to declare it a permanent *qiblah* for Islam and the Muslims is the natural one that brings reality, history and feeling together in unison.

The decision could not have come sooner. Jewish hostility towards Islam and Muḥammad, despite the temporary declaration of Jerusalem as a *qiblah*, did not diminish. They could see that their right to Abraham's religious legacy was being forfeited as the days passed, and the time had come when the Muslims could emerge as independent and rightful claimants to that heritage, and move on to declare its universal and eternal message to the rest of the world.

It had become imperative for the Muslims to forge ahead in that way and to establish their distinct identity as a religious force for advocating the central principle of God's oneness, or *tawḥīd*. The symbolism of the Ka'bah as the exclusive and permanent direction in prayer for the Muslim community was most important.

Symbolism, ritual and form in religious practice can be easily misunderstood, if taken in isolation from the ideals and principles of the religious faith itself. Physical expression of feelings and emotions is a natural human tendency, because man has a material as well as a spiritual aspect to his nature. Emotions and feelings are only fulfilled when expressed in a physical or tangible form, through which they are released to one's happiness and satisfaction. This action brings about balance and harmony between the outer and inner aspects of the human soul, and provides a means of fulfilling man's desire to know what lies behind the apparent symbol and the outward physical form.

All Islamic religious rituals are based on this basic natural philosophy. Mere intention expressed privately, or abstract spiritual meditation, is not enough to satisfy the requirements of religious worship. These involve the participation of the senses, coordinated movement of the body, and position, direction, dress, and recitation of set text, as well as abstention at specified times from food and drink. In this way, every movement and bodily action will have a religious significance attached to it, while religious ritual assumes meaning and dignity, thus bringing soul and body into full harmony.

In those religious communities where this innate human craving for symbolism and physical expression and representation of religious devotion is misunderstood or abused, people have gone astray. Idolatry and the worship of inanimate objects such as stones, trees, planets and stars, as well as animals and birds, can be traced to such abuse and misunderstanding. Islam presents a unique, straightforward concept of the nature of God Almighty, who is not anthropomorphic and whose attributes cannot be defined or represented in physical form. Nevertheless, physical means, or symbols, such as the *qiblah*, that point man's senses, heart, soul and body towards God, are important. God cannot be restricted by the confines of space, but man needs the dimension of space to direct and concentrate his devotion and feelings towards God. That is how the important need for the *qiblah* arises.

Once that principle was understood, it was necessary for the new direction in prayer, *qiblah,* to be unique and exclusive to Islam, in order to underline Islam's distinction and eminence.

A corollary of this principle says that Muslims are specifically forbidden to emulate or adopt other, non-Muslim, religious and cultural customs. However, it would be wrong to put this down to bigotry or prejudice on the part of Islam, since outward religious and social behaviour is a reflection of the inner beliefs and ideals that motivate and determine behaviour and outlook. These beliefs and ideals are the main factors that distinguish between different nations, outlooks, ethical systems, moral values and ways of life.

Abū Hurayrah quotes the Prophet as saying, "The Jews and the Christians do not dye their hair. So, adopt a different line." [Related by Mālik, al-Bukhārī, Muslim and Abū Dāwūd] He was also reported to have told a group of his Companions who stood up to greet him, "Do not be like other communities who stand up in reverence to one another." [Related by Abū Dāwūd and Ibn Mājah] He also said, "Do not revere me in the same way the Christians revered Jesus, son of Mary. I am a mere servant of God. So refer to me as God's servant and messenger." [Related by al-Bukhārī]

The Prophet Muḥammad strongly advised against imitating non-Muslims in appearance, dress, manners, etiquette and behaviour. Behind all these outward aspects lie the emotions and convictions that shape man's outlook, character and way of life.

More importantly, the Prophet strongly rules out the adoption of ideas and concepts not emanating from, or reconcilable with, the world order God has commissioned the Muslim community to promote and establish. He warns against defeatism and feelings of inferiority among the Muslims who, being selected to lead mankind, should derive their values and traditions, and the basis of their faith, from the original source of their religion: God Almighty.

The Qur'ān describes the Muslim community variously as the leading community, a consummately upright nation and a paradigm of moderation. This special acclaim is only conferred upon them by virtue of the fact that they draw their philosophy, outlook, traditions and way of life from God's revelations.

It is not out of religious bigotry and intolerance that Islam presents itself to the world as a universal and most complete way of life. Islam sees itself as a unifying force in the world, because it advocates the unity of all mankind under one God-given social, political and economic way of life. It offers equality to all in the eyes of God, and does not recognize or advance the interests of one group at the expense of others.

Today, Muslims are called on once again to understand the significance of having their own exclusive *qiblah*. It is not merely a direction to which they turn in their Prayers, nor is it an empty symbol. It is a feature that distinguishes Islam's whole outlook on life, its concerns and aims, and its identity.

Muslims today, more than at any other time in their history, need to assert their identity. They need to set themselves apart in the world, which is suffering under the tyranny of false religions, oppressive and arrogant ideologies, flawed political and economic systems and heedless leadership. They have to offer new and effective remedies to save mankind and fulfil God's will, so that the world will acknowledge their community as the central and righteous nation commissioned by God to carry His message to all mankind.

Islam is a complete way of life. Through Islam, Muslims become fit to inherit God's trust and the leadership of mankind, and to stand witness before God for all humanity. But it is only when they adhere faithfully to Islam that they take on their distinctive and unique features and qualities. Without it they lose their way; and their influence and status in the world diminish and evaporate.

We will now look at the passage in more detail.

A Middle Community and a Pure Faith

> *The weak-minded among people will say, 'What has turned them away from the direction of prayer which they have so far observed?' Say, 'To God belong the east and the west. He guides whomever He wills to a straight path.' Thus We have made you the community [ummah] of the middle way, so that you may stand witness against the rest of mankind, and the Messenger shall be a witness against you. We appointed the direction of prayer which you formerly followed in order that We might distinguish those who follow the Messenger from those who turn on their heels. It was indeed a hard test except for those whom God has guided. God would never have let your faith be in vain. God is Compassionate and Merciful to mankind.* (Verses 142–143)

It is clear from the course of the discussion that 'the weak-minded' is a reference to the Jews of Madinah. They were the ones who stirred up the controversy about the change of *qiblah* from Jerusalem to Makkah, and questioned its validity and the wisdom behind it.

Al-Barā' ibn 'Āzib reported: "When the Prophet first arrived in Madinah, he stayed at his grandparents [or maybe he said at his maternal uncles] of the *Anṣār*.[1] The Prophet used to pray facing Jerusalem for the first sixteen or seventeen months, though he would have preferred to face the Ka'bah. The first prayer he offered [facing the Ka'bah] was *'Aṣr*, when he was joined by a group of people. One of them later passed by another group praying in a mosque and said to them, 'I bear witness before God that I have just prayed with the Prophet facing the Ka'bah.' They all turned towards it without interrupting their prayer. The Jews were happy while the Prophet faced Jerusalem in prayer, but when he now turned towards the Ka'bah they were dismayed. It was then that this verse was revealed describing the Jews as weak-minded." [Related by Mālik, al-Bukhārī, Muslim and al-Tirmidhī]

The way the Qur'ān deals with this issue clearly indicates the enormity of the effect that the Jewish campaign was then having on some ordinary Muslims. From the first few words one is made aware that a change of the direction to be faced in prayer is going to be announced. The tone is clearly meant to forestall the doubts and questions that were inevitably going to be raised by troublemakers. But the Qur'ān was ready with the appropriate reply to the argument they would put forward.

The Qur'ān goes on to direct the Prophet to the proper course of action in dealing with the questions that would arise and how to put the whole issue in its proper perspective.

"Say: 'To God belong the east and the west. He guides whomever He wills to a straight path.'" (Verse 142) Places and directions carry no intrinsic merit in themselves, except inasmuch as God assigns them such merit, and to whatever direction one turns, God will be there. It is God's prerogative to guide whomever He wishes to the right path.

1. It is well known that the Prophet stayed at the home of Khālid ibn Zayd, better known as Abū Ayyūb al-Anṣārī, who belonged to al-Najjār clan, to whom belonged the Prophet's maternal grandmother. According to the Arabian usage, all men of this clan are considered maternal uncles of the Prophet by virtue of his grandfather's marriage to one of its women – Editor's notes.

What He designates as the direction to be faced in prayer is the right and proper choice, and His designation of it is for the good of the community.

On such criteria Islam defines the relative merits of places and directions, and specifies the source of those criteria: God Almighty to whom all should turn and submit.

The *sūrah* goes on to outline the central position the Muslim community, or *ummah*, occupies in the world, and the great role it is destined to play in the history and development of mankind. A prerequisite of that status and role is that the Muslim *ummah* should have its own exclusive *qiblah* and distinct identity. It must, first and foremost, owe allegiance to none other than God Almighty, who has commissioned it for that great task.

"We have made you the community of the middle way, so that you may stand witness against the rest of mankind, and the Messenger shall be a witness against you." (Verse 143)

The Arabic term *wasaṭ,* used in this verse to describe the global Muslim community, is a vivid epithet which evokes a much wider range of meaning than is given by its literal equivalent of 'middle'. The term is used here in a very broad sense. Thus, the Muslim community, or *ummah*, to use the Qur'ānic term, is a middle-of-the-road community which stands witness against other nations and communities in the sense that it upholds and defends justice and equality for all people. It weighs up their values, standards, traditions, concepts and objectives, judging them as either true or false. It occupies the dual position of being a witness against mankind and an umpire administering justice among them. God's Messenger, Muḥammad, is in turn a witness against the Muslim community in the sense that, as its leader and guardian, he defines its aims, activities and obligations, and charts the direction it should take. His teachings, example and leadership stimulate the community to appreciate its role and position in the world, and live up to their requirements.

The Muslim community occupies the middle ground in its beliefs and outlook on life. It maintains a healthy and equitable balance between the two extremes of spiritual asceticism and materialism. It treats man as a balanced combination of body and soul, and allows him the opportunity and means to satisfy them both in such a way as to uplift the spirit and enhance the quality of human life. Within this framework of balance and moderation, every constructive talent, ability, aptitude, and activity is nourished and encouraged to grow and play its part in society.

The Muslim community is balanced in the sense that it is not rigid or dogmatic. It holds fast to its ideals and traditions, and to the sources of its religion and way of life, while fostering change and progress in all fields. It is an open society that welcomes new ideas and learns from the work and experience of other societies, cultures and civilizations. Its main objective is to seek the truth, wherever that may come from, and to adopt it with courage and confidence.

Balance and moderation are clear in the way Muslim society is run and organized. It is neither a permissive, undisciplined community nor a regimented one run by brute force or rigid rules. It is a society raised on learning, education and rich cultural and social traditions.

Within the Muslim 'middle' community, equitable and fair relationships are cultivated and regulated among all individuals and social groups in the community. Individual rights and liberties are guaranteed and protected in order to encourage innovation, production and growth, in a manner that will serve the common good without infringing upon the rights of the individual, or endangering society as a whole. Individual as well as collective rights and obligations are clearly defined to enable people to serve a society that will care for them and protect their rights and interests.

The Muslim community is also the middle nation geographically, because the part of the world where Islam first emerged, and which continues to represent the heart of the Muslim world, occupies a central position in the world as a whole. It has been a crucible of cultures and civilizations and a busy crossroads for trade from all corners of the earth. It has been, throughout history, a rich source of vital natural resources and raw materials of many kinds for nations and civilizations all over the world. This position has given the Islamic community a strategic and influential role to play on the world stage.

Islam emerged at a time that can be said to mark the beginning of maturity in human thinking. It brought a religious and social order that appealed to the human mind and rescued man from religions and philosophies founded on mythology, superstition, paganism or nihilistic thinking. It ushered in a new era of enlightenment that brought together genuine divine revelations, authentic philosophical thought and sound practical human experience to chart the proper course for man's progress, happiness and prosperity.

What stops Muslims today from assuming the position and role in the world that God has assigned to them is the fact that they have abandoned the religion God has chosen for them, and adopted social and political philosophies and systems that are inconsistent with it.

World leadership imposes its own demands and responsibilities. For the Muslim community to legitimately earn that position again, it must undergo severe trials and make great sacrifices, prove its loyalty and dedication to God and show total allegiance to its wise leadership.

Having announced that the Ka'bah was to be the permanent, universal direction of prayer for Muslims, the *sūrah* now reveals the purpose behind the previous choice of Jerusalem as a temporary *qiblah*.

"We appointed the direction of prayer which you formerly followed in order that We might distinguish those who follow the Messenger from those who turn on their heels." (Verse 143) From these few words one can immediately identify the divine approach in educating the Muslims and preparing them, from that early stage of their development, for the role of custodian of God's message and the leadership of mankind. As part of that transformation, it was essential for that nascent community to be freed of all traces of paganism and ethnocentricity, and to become totally obedient and dedicated to the new religion of Islam. The early Muslims had to realize that their values and standards in life must, from then on, be derived from the divine revelations being regularly communicated to the Prophet Muḥammad.

In pre-Islamic days, certain elements of polytheism and racism had crept into the Arabs' understanding of the faith of Abraham and the status of the Sacred House in Makkah. The Ka'bah had come to be venerated as an exclusively Arab shrine. This was contrary to its intended purpose, since it had been established by Abraham and his son Ishmael as a symbol of purely monotheistic faith and for the reverence and worship of God alone.

To correct the situation and to test their faith and loyalty to the Prophet Muḥammad, God commanded the Muslims to adopt Jerusalem as the direction they face in prayer. Although it was not clear to the Muslims at the time, the measure was meant to be a temporary one, specifically intended to decide where their allegiance would really lie.

It was a delicate decision, but Islam is a complete and self-sufficient religion. It does not need to be supplemented or augmented by other religious beliefs. It does not accept any lingering traces of un-Islamic ways, serious or trivial. This is indeed the point implied in the Qur'ānic statement: *"We appointed the direction of prayer which you formerly followed in order that We might distinguish those who follow the Messenger from those who turn on their heels."* (Verse 143) God certainly knows everything before it happens. However, He wishes that what is kept deep in people's hearts should first appear in action before He holds them accountable for it. His grace means that He does not hold man answerable for his thoughts and feelings; He only holds man accountable for what he does.

It was also a critical decision because God was aware that it was going to be a hard test for some Muslims, still fresh from idolatry. But He was also there to provide help and support for the sincere ones: *"It was indeed a hard test except for those whom God has guided."* (Verse 143) With God's guidance every difficulty becomes easy.

For yet further reassurance, God affirms that the prayers the Muslims had performed facing Jerusalem were valid and the reward for them guaranteed. *"God would never have let your faith be in vain. God is Compassionate and Merciful to mankind."* (Verse 143) God would have never burdened the Muslims with more than He knew they would be able to bear. As long as their intentions were genuine and their determination sincere, God was sure to come to their assistance and lighten the tasks expected of them. If a certain hardship or test is meant to reflect God's wisdom and purpose, passing such a test is indicative of His mercy and compassion.

Thus the Muslims could feel content, confident and free of worry about the past and the future.

Clarification of Issues

Next comes the indication that Muḥammad's unease with respect to the direction of prayer was soon to be over, as God decreed a permanent one which would satisfy his wishes. However, the announcement comes with a stern warning that the Jews would oppose it and try to exploit it to sow division and confusion among the Muslims.

> *We have seen you often turn your face towards heaven. We shall, therefore, make you turn in prayer towards a direction you will be*

happy with. Turn your face, then, towards the Sacred Mosque; and wherever you all may be, turn your faces [in prayer] towards it. Those who have been granted revelations in the past know well that it is the truth from their Lord. God is not unaware of what they do. Were you to bring every possible sign before those who had been granted revelations, they would not follow your direction of prayer. And neither may you follow their direction of prayer, nor would they even follow one another's direction. If you were to follow their whims and desires after all the knowledge that has been given to you, you would certainly be among the wrongdoers. Those to whom We granted revelation know it as well as they know their own children, but some of them knowingly conceal the truth. This is the truth from your Lord; never, then, be among the doubters. Each one has a goal towards which he turns; so vie with one another in good works. Wherever you may be, God will bring you all together. God has power over all things. From wherever you may come forth, turn your face [in prayer] towards the Sacred Mosque. It is indeed the truth from your Lord. God is not unaware of what you do. From wherever you may come forth, turn your face [in prayer] towards the Sacred Mosque; and wherever you all may be, turn your faces towards it, so that people may have no argument against you, except those who are bent on wrongdoing. Have no fear of them, but fear Me, so that I may perfect My grace on you, and that you may be rightly guided." (Verses 144–150)

We have a graphic description of the Prophet's strong desire that God might direct him to a *qiblah* other than that which the Muslims had hitherto followed, i.e. Jerusalem. The Jews attempted to mislead the Muslims and exploit that situation to their advantage. We can almost feel the restrained desire of the Prophet and his reluctance even to say a prayer that reflected his desire. This is a question on which no one could have a say. It is entirely up to God.

The divine decree, expressed here with compassion and love, comes in line with the Prophet's wish. The new direction of prayer is exactly the one he has been silently hoping for all those months: *"We shall, therefore, make you turn in prayer towards a direction you will be happy with. Turn your face, then, towards the Sacred Mosque."* (Verse 144) What is more, is that it is a permanent and universal one: *"Wherever you all may be, turn your faces [in prayer] towards it."* (Verse 144)

Thus the Ka'bah was reinstated as the original focus and symbol of religious unity for the whole world community of Islam. Muslims all over the world, with all their differences of race and language, would from then on perform their prayers facing the same spot on the globe. In doing so, Muslims would assert, and be reminded of, their human and religious unity, and of their membership of a single world community with a common way of life, a common religious legacy, and a common role and aim in the world.

The Muslim world community transcends race and language. The principle of God's oneness, the bedrock of Islam, is thus manifested in total subservience to God alone; allegiance to the same leadership, that of Muḥammad; adherence to the same religion, Islam; and adoption of the same direction of prayer. Despite all the superficial differences that may exist between people, they are one and equal in their faith. There is no other means by which a truly universal and equitable human society can be brought forth and successfully organized.

Turning to the people of earlier revelations, the *sūrah* confirms their certain knowledge of the history and religious status of the Sacred Mosque at the Ka'bah. They were well aware that it had been established by Abraham, the founding father of the community that had inherited the creed of God's oneness, and that its designation as the universal and permanent direction of Islamic prayer would be totally in line with the divine universal order.

Nevertheless, the *sūrah* points out, they would raise doubts and endlessly quibble over it. The Muslims should not be unduly concerned at that; God will take care of it, as He is fully aware of what they do.

There would be no point in reasoning with the Jews over the issue of the *qiblah*. Their problem was not lack of evidence or persuasion, but lack of faith and unwillingness to accept the truth. *"Were you to bring every possible sign before those who had been granted revelations, they would not follow your direction of prayer."* (Verse 145)

It was not ignorance or lack of understanding that was responsible for that stubborn attitude, but caprice and vested interests. This would also be the source of subsequent Jewish and Christian animosity towards Islam, which was to emerge in various forms in later centuries.

In response to that bigoted stance, the proper and natural attitude of the Prophet is stated: *"And neither may you follow their direction of prayer."* (Verse 145) This Qur'ānic statement implies, particularly in its Arabic phraseology, a strong sense of finality and permanence. It also conveys to the Muslims a clear instruction never to adopt any direction of prayer, distinctive symbol or a way of life other than what gives it its clear Islamic identity.

The *sūrah* further reveals that neither the bitterly divided Jewish and Christian sects, nor even the majority of the Jews and the Christians, could ever agree on the adoption of one direction of prayer: *"nor would they even follow one another's direction."* (Verse 145)

As the Prophet is made fully aware of the truth in this matter of worship, he is warned against falling in with those people and their desires: *"If you were to follow their whims and desires after all the knowledge that has been given to you, you would certainly be among the wrongdoers."* (Verse 145)

Having been addressed by his Lord with warmth and compassion, the Prophet is here given a strong warning. A grave matter of principle is involved here. There should be no hesitation in carrying out God's instructions; personal preferences or considerations must not be allowed to influence the Prophet's or the Muslims' response to God's will and command. A Muslim may not abandon the certain knowledge that is given by God to pick up what suits personal whims and desires.

This strong admonition also suggests that there could have been specific cases in which a certain degree of weakness had crept into Muslim minds, in the face of the vicious and insistent propaganda campaign launched by the Jews of Madinah.

The *sūrah* then asserts that the Jews and Christians were absolutely certain that what the Qur'ān has stated with respect to the *qiblah* issue, and other issues for that matter, and what the Prophet has ordered is the truth. However, they suppress the truth they know for their own self-interest: *"Those to whom We granted revelation know it as well as they know their own children, but some of them knowingly conceal the truth."* (Verse 146)

It is a very powerful simile, used among the Arabs to denote absolute certainty. The point here is that the Jews, despite their denials, were as certain of the truth of the revelations that Muḥammad was receiving, including the announcement of the new direction of prayer. Therefore, the Muslims should pay them no attention nor be influenced by their allegations and misleading interpretations.

The Final Say on the Direction of Prayer

Then the *sūrah* addresses the Prophet directly, saying: *"This is the truth from your Lord; never, then, be among the doubters."* (Verse 147) The Prophet never entertained any doubt about the veracity of his message. Elsewhere in the Qur'ān, the Prophet is told, *"If you are in any doubt regarding what has been revealed to you, then consult those who have read the Scriptures before your time."* (10: 94) On hearing this verse, the Prophet said: "I entertain no doubts, and I ask no one." But the fact that he is here addressed directly is a clear signal to those around him, and others who would come later, who might be influenced by those who may try to undermine Islam.

It is appropriate for Muslims today to reflect on this statement. Some Muslims display remarkable naïvety in relying on the authority of Jewish, Christian and Marxist Orientalists, for the interpretation and understanding of Islamic principles and texts of the Qur'ān and *ḥadīth*, or for the study and analysis of Islamic faith, literature, and history. It is a great pity that Muslim students have to be sent from Muslim countries to be educated in various Islamic disciplines in European and American universities, where some of them acquire a distorted and confused understanding of Islam and Islamic teachings and principles. We must never forget that the Qur'ān is the eternal book God revealed to the Muslim community, outlining what it should do and what it must refrain from. Unbelievers of any creed are not the ones to teach us our faith.

The *sūrah* gives us clear instructions not to rely on Jewish and Christian advice regarding Islamic principles and practices. It urges Muslims not to deviate from the path charted for them by Islam, and to compete among themselves in their pursuit of constructive and beneficial goals. They will, eventually, return to God, to whom all mankind will be gathered: *"Each one has a goal towards which he turns; so vie with one another in good works. Wherever you may be, God will bring you all together. God has power over all things."* (Verse 148) Thus God turns the minds of the Muslims away from the falsehood spread by the followers of other religions. They should disregard any schemes or ploys to thwart or undermine their status and role in the world. They should, instead, compete in doing what is good and beneficial.

The instruction to face the Sacred Mosque in Makkah is reiterated in the following verse: *"From wherever you may come forth, turn your face [in prayer] towards the Sacred Mosque. It is indeed the truth from your Lord. God is not unaware of what you do."* (Verse 149) The point here has nothing to do with the people of earlier revelations. It is an order to the Prophet to turn towards the Sacred Mosque wherever he offers his prayers, emphasizing that what God reveals to him is the truth. But the verse also implies a warning in the words *"God is not unaware of what you do"*, indicating yet again that there had been some weakness among some Muslims, which called for attention and remedy.

Then comes a third reiteration of the institution of the new direction of prayer, but this new statement has a different purpose, namely to refute the argument made by the Jews and other people that taking Jerusalem as the direction of prayer was a vindication of their claim that their religion was superior to that of Muḥammad. It was also meant to counter the argument of the polytheist Arabs who had exploited the situation to turn their fellow Arabs, who venerated the Ka'bah, away from Islam. *"From wherever you may come forth, turn your face [in prayer] towards the Sacred Mosque; and wherever you all may be, turn your faces towards it, so that people may have no argument against you, except those who are bent on wrongdoing. Have no fear of them, but fear Me, so that I may perfect My grace on you, and that you may be rightly guided."* (Verse 150)

This is a general order to the Prophet and the Muslims to turn in prayer towards the Ka'bah, wherever they happen to be. Thus, no one would have any argument against them. Any criticism of this decision is of no consequence, and its detractors, Jewish and Arab alike, are motivated only by stubborn hatred of Islam. But they need not be feared, because they can no longer pose any threat to Islam or Muslims. The Muslims in Madinah were reminded that God was on their side and would look after them until they were fully developed and transformed into the leading community they were destined to become.

The Muslims of that small community knew very well what God Almighty meant by the reminder: *"so that I may perfect My grace on you, and that you may be rightly guided."* (Verse 150) Only a few years earlier they had been wallowing in tribal ignorance, dogged by futile internecine conflicts, and preoccupied with worldly pursuits. The Arabs before Islam were a heathen, aimless society, plagued by corruption and absurd religious beliefs and practices. They had little or no influence outside their immediate traditional territory, and no ambitions or ideals to strive for.

But Islam changed all that and transformed those erratic and wayward people into an enlightened, mature, outward-looking and powerful community, charged with the momentous and historic role of custodians of God's message to the world, and poised to assume the leadership of mankind.

The Prophet's generation of Muslims could see tangible proof, in their personal as well as communal life, of God's infinite grace and favour. The reminder would raise their morale and boost their confidence and determination to move ahead.

That the instruction to adopt the new direction of prayer is mentioned three times stresses a different purpose each time. It was, first, to grant the Prophet Muḥammad his unspoken wish on this question; second, to assert that it was also the truth declared by God coinciding with the Prophet's wish; and third, to put an end to self-serving criticism and hostility from other groups.

Apart from those reasons, we can detect that there was real cause for concern about weakness and doubt among some Muslims, which called for the instruction to be stressed and reiterated. This suggests that the campaign of false allegations was quite vicious and had gone some way towards creating disruption and confusion within the Muslim community.

Although these statements deal with the immediate issue at the time, the principles and the basic advice that they impart remain relevant and applicable in other similar situations that might arise in the perennial confrontation between the Muslims and their enemies.

Abraham's Prayers Are Answered

The *sūrah* goes on to remind the Muslims of more divine favours reserved for them. By one such special favour God has sent them a Messenger, Muḥammad, in fulfilment of the prayer made by Abraham, the first custodian of the Sacred Mosque in Makkah, the permanent and universal *qiblah* of all Muslims.

> *Thus We have sent forth to you a Messenger from among yourselves to recite to you Our revelations, purify you, and instruct you in the Book and in wisdom and teach you what you did not know. Remember Me, then, and I will remember you; give thanks to Me and never deny Me.* (Verses 151–152)

The same words of Abraham's prayer (Verse 129) are used here, thus establishing a direct and significant link between the two Prophets and their religion. Islam was not, then, invented or born out of expediency, but had its origins firmly rooted in history. The direction of prayer that was being instituted had not been chosen haphazardly or without purpose. It was the answer to Abraham's passionate and sincere prayers.

As a result of this boundless divine grace, the Muslims were sent a messenger, one of their own number, who was to be the last human Messenger from God to mankind, and had their own exclusive direction of prayer designated for them by God, thereby giving them a distinctive character and a privileged status in the world.

Another aspect of God's favour is that, through Muḥammad, He was addressing the Muslims, a humble and insignificant band of believers, with His own words. Who were those people? What did they represent, for God and for mankind? What did they do or have to deserve God's attention and special favour?

"Thus We have sent forth to you a Messenger from among yourselves to recite to you Our revelations, purify you...."

The fact that Muḥammad had come from that society, and was chosen to receive God's revelations, the Qur'ān, represented God's limitless favour. God's Messenger, Muḥammad (peace be upon him) was also sent to cleanse the Arabs of the sad misconceptions, corruption and ignorance that went with their idolatrous beliefs and lax way of life. Those whose souls are not purged by submission to God, at whatever time or place they may live, sink into a stinking depth of worldly desires that are unbecoming of man. In such a condition, man sinks lower than animals, controlled as animals are by their desires. The Prophet also purges their society of usury, cheating, looting and illegal earnings; all of which are impurities that contaminate souls, feelings, society and human life altogether. He further purges their lives of injustice, putting in place a superior standard of justice to which their community aspires.

"... And instructs you in the Book and in wisdom..." This incorporates what has been mentioned earlier about reciting God's revelations included in His book, and emphasizes its essential subject matter, i.e. wisdom. Wisdom is acquired as the fruit of instruction in this book, i.e. the Qur'ān. It is a quality which ensures that anyone who has it views matters in their proper perspective and evaluates them correctly.

He has the necessary understanding to appreciate the aims behind God's commandments and teachings.

Before Islam, the Arabs were a heedless and xenophobic people, living in total darkness and moral corruption, given to inhuman practices such as usury, infanticide, slavery, piracy and other forms of crime. Islam had come to purge that vile and destructive way of life and transform the Arabs into a pioneering society that would uphold justice and strive to promote and preserve the humanity of man.

Muḥammad had also been sent to *"instruct you in the Book and in wisdom and teach you what you did not know"*. One of Muḥammad's duties was to teach his followers how to understand and interpret the Qur'ān, and translate it into a practical code for daily life. Through the Qur'ān they acquired the wisdom and the ability to appreciate and understand God's commands, evaluate ideas and concepts, and judge values and objectives.

It was through that slow and painstaking process of education and development that the first group of Muslims was raised out of an almost uncultured tribal desert people. Out of that community, within a phenomenally short time, came a nation with a rich ideology and a dynamic spirit, fit to assume a leading role in the world.

That pioneering generation was raised on the ideas and teachings of the Qur'ān and under the instruction of the Prophet Muḥammad, which was inspired by and derived from the Qur'ān. The Prophet's mosque in Madinah was the focal point of Muslim life and its centre of learning, which produced a unique civilization and a community that has been unrivalled throughout history.

That divine legacy and those teachings, which were responsible for raising the first generation of Islam, remain intact and accessible today. It is vital for Muslims to return to their original source of knowledge and greatness, and to look at the Qur'ān as a guide and an instrument for change, rather than as lyrics to be melodiously chanted for idle pleasure.

When God Remembers His Servants

This passage is concluded with yet another reminder of God's favours to the Muslim community. God calls on Muslims to remember and praise Him, and in return He will remember them: *"Remember*

Me, then, and I will remember you; give thanks to Me and never deny Me." (Verse 152)

What honour, what benevolence and compassion! God Almighty, in all His greatness and glory, exchanges these sentiments on an equal level with His humble servants. What grace and generosity!

"Remember Me, then, and I will remember you" – it is the greatest privilege any human being can receive from God, whose generosity is limitless and whose benevolence knows no bounds. The Prophet Muḥammad is reported to have quoted God as saying: "Whoever remembers Me privately to himself I will remember him to Myself; and whoever remembers Me in the company of people I will remember him in a better company."

The Prophet also quotes God as saying: "Son of Adam! When you remember Me to yourself, I will remember you to Myself. When you remember Me in the company of others I will remember you in a company of angels. When you draw closer to Me by a handspan, I will draw closer to you by an arm's length; and when you draw closer to Me by an arm's length, I will draw closer to you by a longer distance; and when you walk towards Me, I will run towards you."

No words could possibly describe the effects and scope of this divine grace. Man can only reciprocate such feelings through prayer, meditation and total submission to God Almighty. This will eventually lead him to see and recognize no other power in this world but that of God.

The recognition of God's power and the expression of one's gratitude to Him come in several stages. The least of them is to acknowledge God's grace and blessings and refrain from disobeying Him. The highest stage is that of total dedication of one's thoughts, talents, energies and actions to the service of God.

The words *"give thanks to Me and never deny Me"* also carry a warning that negligence of, ingratitude to, and rebellion against God would lead to denying Him altogether, which is a most hopeless and dismal end.

All the instructions and warnings conveyed in the above passage are extremely pertinent to the issue of the direction of prayer, the focus of Muslims and the distinctive symbol of acknowledging God's oneness. They are also pertinent to the confrontation with the Jews of Madinah, whose ultimate objective was to mislead the Muslims in the hope that they might revert to unbelief. Thus, they would deprive them of God's favours and blessings, the greatest and foremost of which is that of faith.

The Jews were aware that the Arabs without Islam would go back to their aimless tribal existence, with no influence on the rest of the world or role in history. A people without sound principles or creed, or a philosophy of life, would have no reason to assume a position of leadership in the world.

To be remembered by God, Muslims have to remember that Islam is more than a religion concerned only with the spiritual or personal aspects of life. It is a complete way of life with teachings, laws and practices for the organization and development of all human affairs. History tells us that whenever Muslims showed awareness of God and dedication to His cause, they progressed and achieved prominence, and their standing in the world rose high above all others; but when they neglected Islam and forgot God, they declined and were crushed and left behind.

Yet, the door will always remain open. In His blessed book, the Qur'ān, God calls on Muslims: *"Remember Me, then, and I will remember you; give thanks to Me and never deny Me."* (Verse 152)

8

Acquiring Real Strength

Believers, seek strength in patience and prayer. God is with those who are patient. (153)

يَٰٓأَيُّهَا ٱلَّذِينَ ءَامَنُوا۟ ٱسْتَعِينُوا۟ بِٱلصَّبْرِ
وَٱلصَّلَوٰةِ ۚ إِنَّ ٱللَّهَ مَعَ ٱلصَّٰبِرِينَ ﴿١٥٣﴾

Do not say of those who are killed in God's cause, 'They are dead.' They are alive, although you do not perceive that. (154)

وَلَا تَقُولُوا۟ لِمَن يُقْتَلُ فِى سَبِيلِ ٱللَّهِ
أَمْوَٰتٌۢ ۚ بَلْ أَحْيَآءٌ وَلَٰكِن لَّا تَشْعُرُونَ ﴿١٥٤﴾

We shall certainly try you with a certain measure of fear and hunger, and with diminution of wealth, lives and crops. But give glad tidings to those who remain patient in adversity. (155)

وَلَنَبْلُوَنَّكُم بِشَىْءٍ مِّنَ ٱلْخَوْفِ وَٱلْجُوعِ
وَنَقْصٍ مِّنَ ٱلْأَمْوَٰلِ وَٱلْأَنفُسِ وَٱلثَّمَرَٰتِ ۗ
وَبَشِّرِ ٱلصَّٰبِرِينَ ﴿١٥٥﴾

Who, when a calamity befalls them, say, 'To God we belong, and to Him we shall return.' (156)

ٱلَّذِينَ إِذَآ أَصَٰبَتْهُم مُّصِيبَةٌ قَالُوٓا۟
إِنَّا لِلَّهِ وَإِنَّآ إِلَيْهِ رَٰجِعُونَ ﴿١٥٦﴾

On such people, blessings and mercy are bestowed by their Lord; such people will be rightly guided. (157)

أُو۟لَٰٓئِكَ عَلَيْهِمْ صَلَوَٰتٌ مِّن رَّبِّهِمْ وَرَحْمَةٌ ۖ
وَأُو۟لَٰٓئِكَ هُمُ ٱلْمُهْتَدُونَ ﴿١٥٧﴾

Overview

Having established a permanent and universal *qiblah* for Islam, and having outlined the general features of the 'middle' Muslim community, distinguished by Islam and by its role of guardianship over the rest of mankind, the Qur'ān gives Muslims specific instructions to endure adversity with patience and to observe their prayers. These are the best help they may have in the fulfilment of their great role that requires great sacrifice.

These are the two most essential requisites for the Muslim *ummah* to be able to withstand the hardships and trials that were to come, and to fulfil its universal and historic role in this world. Lives would have to be sacrificed; poverty, death, famine and insecurity would have to be faced with courage and strength, for the *ummah* to establish and defend the Divine world order, make it a reality in human society on this earth, and assert God's unrivalled sovereignty over all its affairs.

In return, the Muslim community shall receive God's blessings, mercy and guidance, making it a most profitable bargain indeed, if only the Muslims would appreciate it.

The Power of Patience

"Believers, seek strength in patience and prayer. God is with those who are patient." (Verse 153) Patience is mentioned frequently in the Qur'ān. God is aware that patience is an essential element in maintaining a steady and balanced pace in the face of the inevitable hardships and adversities of life. It is a prime requirement for the Muslim community in its universal responsibility for establishing God's order on earth.

Patience is required on the personal level for observing one's religious duties, for resisting temptation, misfortune, poverty, oppression and injustice, and for carrying out one's responsibilities towards the establishment of the Islamic way of life in society. Patience and perseverance are required to remain always on the alert, ready to give whatever sacrifice may be needed. When those who are hostile to God's cause seem to wield power, when falsehood seems too strong, when help seems to be endlessly delayed and the destination too far away patience and perseverance are the most important qualities to have. They are also needed to face those who are deviant, erring, harsh and persistent in their opposition to the truth.

When victory seems far away and the going gets really tough, people tend to lose heart and give up. To avoid that state of despair, God links patience with prayer, as an inexhaustible source of strength and energy. The two combine to infuse the heart with boundless confidence and fortitude and to impart to the believer total tranquillity, happiness and inner peace.

When man, weak as he is, faces a task that seems beyond his limited resources, when he faces the powers of evil, when he finds temptations and allurements very hard to resist, when tyranny and corruption are too powerful, seeking support from God Almighty is the only way forward. As the goals of one's endeavour seem to recede and life becomes shorter and shorter, despair starts to creep into one's heart and mind. As the twilight of one's life approaches and all achievements seem trivial and meaningless, one realizes the value and significance of prayer. It is a spring that never ceases to flow with spiritual strength and tender compassion.

The value and role of prayer lie in its being the direct link between God and man. It is the means by which man, an insignificant mortal, draws strength, reassurance and help from God's infinite power and everlasting mercy. It is the source from which man, a frail creature, replenishes his energy and renews his power and strength to face and resist his own inner temptations and prejudices, as well as the temptations and pressures of the world around him. It is the key to the treasures of God's grace, and the fountain of light which illuminates man's heart with inner peace and tranquillity and leads him through the darkness of doubt and confusion to the certainty of faith and trust in God Almighty. It is an occasion for rest, serenity and peace of mind. It is no wonder, therefore, that the Prophet Muḥammad (peace be upon him) used to resort to prayer whenever things became difficult to cope with. He used to ask Bilāl, his Companion, to make the call to prayer, saying: "Bring us its comfort."

Worship is the essence of the Islamic way of life, which revolves around its mysteries and hidden qualities. It is a source of sustenance in the long journey of life; it purifies the heart and gives the human spirit its inner powers. It goes hand in hand with responsibility and obligation, because it is the key to our appreciation of our responsibilities and obligations in life and to the satisfaction and benefits we draw from fulfilling them.

When God Almighty commissioned Muḥammad for his great and historic task, He said to him: *"Stand up in prayer at night, all except for a small portion of it; or half the night or a little less, or a little more, and recite the Qur'ān in a calm and distinct manner. We are about to address you with words of surpassing gravity"* (73: 2–5)

Prayer during the night and recitation of the Qur'ān were the essential means of preparing Muḥammad for the stupendous task of conveying God's message to mankind. Prayer opens the human heart to hope and enlightenment, reinvigorates one's relationship with God, mitigates the struggle for life, and provides one with inspiration and confidence.

For the believers in that small fledgling Muslim community, poised to embark on their momentous task, the *sūrah* reinforces that reassurance by saying: *"God is with those who are patient."* God is always there to provide the believers with help and comfort, to lend them His support and replenish their sapping morale and fading enthusiasm. It is noteworthy that the verse starts by making its address exclusively to the believers, and concludes by reassuring them that patience ensures God's help.

Numerous reports have been handed down that tell us how highly the Prophet himself viewed the qualities of patience and perseverance, and how deeply he had thought about them. Some of them are quite relevant to our discussion.

The Prophet's Companion, Khabbāb ibn al-Aratt, said: "A group of us once appealed to God's Messenger while he was resting in the shade of the Ka'bah. We said, 'Would you please appeal to God to help us? Would you kindly pray for us?' He replied, 'In days gone by, believers like yourselves used to be put in ditches and have their heads sawed in halves, and have their flesh scraped off the bone with iron combs. They withstood all that torture, held on to their faith, and never wavered. I swear that God Almighty will establish this religion so that a man can travel from Ṣan'ā' [in western Yemen] to Ḥaḍramawt [in eastern Yemen] fearing none but God, and the wolf for his sheep. But you are impatient!'" [Related by al-Bukhārī, Abū Dāwūd and al-Nasā'ī]

Another Companion of the Prophet, 'Abdullāh ibn Mas'ūd says: "I can almost see God's Messenger in the same position as an earlier prophet who was beaten by his people until he bled. But even while he was wiping the blood off his face he said: "Lord, forgive my people, for they do not know the truth." [Related by al-Bukhārī and Muslim]

The Prophet is also quoted as saying: "A Muslim who mixes with people and puts up with their maltreatment is better than one who neither mixes with people nor suffers their abuse." [Related by al-Tirmidhī]

Sacrificing One's Life

The Qur'ān continues with its spiritual mobilization of the pioneering Muslim community of Madinah, as the latter braces itself for the crucial and momentous task of leading mankind back to God. It outlines the major demands and consequences of its hard and long struggle, or *jihād*, with its attendant sacrifices. It identifies the proper and correct criteria for the evaluation and appraisal of its outcome: *"Do not say of those who are killed in God's cause 'They are dead.' They are alive, although you do not perceive that."* (Verse 154)

The *sūrah* tells the Muslims that, in the fight to uphold God's universal truth, lives will have to be sacrificed. Those who risk their lives and go out to fight, and who are prepared to lay down their lives for the cause of God are honourable people, pure of heart and blessed of soul. But the great surprise is that those among them who are killed in the struggle must not be considered or described as dead. They continue to live, as God Himself clearly states.

To all intents and purposes, those people may very well appear lifeless, but life and death are not judged by superficial physical means alone. Life is chiefly characterized by activity, growth, and persistence, while death is a state of total loss of function, of complete inertia and lifelessness. But the death of those who are killed for the cause of God gives more impetus to the cause, which continues to thrive on their blood. Their influence on those they leave behind also grows and spreads. Thus, after their death they remain an active force in shaping the life of their community and giving it direction. It is in this sense that such people, having sacrificed their lives for the sake of God, retain their active existence in everyday life. They might, on the other hand, be alive in another level or mode of existence which we here cannot see or conceive of.

According to Islamic tradition, people who are killed "for the cause of God" are not washed or prepared for burial in the conventional way, but buried in the clothes they happen to be wearing, because they are considered clean and pure, and because in reality they are not dead.

Because they are alive, those who die for the cause of God should not be missed or grieved over by their relatives, friends and loved ones. There is no real sense of loss in their death, since they continue to live, enjoying the hospitality of their Lord, relishing His company and boundless rewards.

There are copious reports in the *ḥadīth* literature extolling the spirit of sacrifice and the status of martyrs. Muslim records a *ḥadīth* which says: "The souls of martyrs are carried in the bellies of green birds which fly at leisure in Paradise. They roost on lamps, placed near God's Throne. God casts a glance at them and says, 'What is your wish?' They would reply, 'Lord, what more can we wish for, when You have given us what You have not given any of Your creation.' God would ask them again and again until they realize they have to make a request, and they would say, 'We wish to be returned to live on earth so that we fight for Your cause and be killed a second time.' They say this since they have seen how great God's rewards are to those who attain martyrdom for God's cause. But God says, 'I have already decreed that people would not return to worldly life.'"

The Prophet's Companion, Anas ibn Mālik, reports that the Prophet said: "No one enters Paradise and wishes to return to worldly life, even if he was given everything on earth, except a martyr. He wishes to return to life and be killed in the cause of God ten times over, for the honour and privilege he receives." [Related by Mālik, al-Bukhārī and Muslim]

But who are the living martyrs? They are those killed in God's cause, and in God's cause alone. It is they who lay down their lives in defence of God's universal truth, rather than in the name of a king, nation or military honour. The sole objective of their struggle and sacrifice is to uphold God's world order and establish it as a social reality. The Qur'ān and the *ḥadīth* lay strong emphasis on this point, so as to leave no doubt about its meaning.

The Prophet's Companion, Abū Mūsā, reports that the Prophet was asked whether fighting out of bravery, or to support one's own ethnic group, or in pursuit of fame and glory, might be considered as fighting "for the cause of God." He replied: "Only the one who fights to keep God's word supreme fights for God's cause!" [Related by Mālik, al-Bukhārī and Muslim]

Another Companion of the Prophet, Abū Hurayrah, reported that a man asked God's Messenger three times about the fate of someone who fights 'in the cause of God,' but is also seeking worldly gain. Every time the Messenger replied: "He would receive no reward!" [Related by Abū Dāwūd]

Abū Hurayrah reports that God's Messenger said that God gives a guarantee to anyone who goes to battle for God's cause: "If he has set out for no purpose other than to fight for My cause, totally motivated by faith in Me and to confirm the veracity of My messengers, then I guarantee that he will either enter Paradise or return safely home, enjoying whatever reward or booty he might have gained." The Prophet continues this *ḥadīth*, saying: "By Him who holds Muhammad's soul in His hand, any wound he may have sustained in battle will look on the Day of Resurrection in the same way as on the day it happened, with the colour of blood, but with the smell of pure musk. By Him who holds Muhammad's soul in His hand, were it not for fear of making things too hard for Muslims I would have joined every single expedition going out in God's cause. However, I do not have the means to give them transport, nor do they have such means to follow me. In addition, it is trying for them to stay behind. By Him who holds Muhammad's soul in His hand, I would love to have fought and been killed for God's cause again and again." [Related by Mālik, al-Bukhārī and Muslim]

Martyrs, then, are those who set out to fight solely and purely for God's cause, out of faith in Him and an unshakeable belief in His messengers.

The Prophet Muḥammad expressed disapproval when he heard a Persian youth extolling his ancestry in the battlefield. 'Abd al-Raḥmān ibn Abī 'Uqbah reported that his father, a Persian 'ally' of the *Anṣār*, relates that he took part with the Prophet in the Battle of Uḥud. "As I struck an unbeliever, I shouted, 'Take it from me; I, a Persian youth!'. The Prophet turned to me and said, 'Would it not have been better for you to say, I, the *Anṣārī* youth. The nephew and the ally of any group of people belong to them.'" [Related by Abū Dāwūd]

The Prophet disliked the fact that the young man had chosen to express pride in anything other than being a supporter of God's Messenger and to fight under any banner other than that of the religion of Islam. That is the true meaning of *jihād*, for which men can give up their lives, earn martyrdom and ensure permanent life.

The *sūrah* continues to mobilize the believers for the hard, long struggle ahead and increase their understanding of things to come:

> *We shall certainly try you with a certain measure of fear and hunger, and with diminution of wealth, lives and crops. But give glad tidings to those who remain patient in adversity. Who, when a calamity befalls them, say, 'To God we belong, and to Him we shall return.'* (Verses 155–156)

Trials are part of the process of education. The believers' resolve to fight for the truth, and to bear in the process whatever they may have to face of fear, hardship, poverty, famine, and loss of life, must be rigorously tested. There is a price that believers have to pay in order to uphold their faith, and that price is their own lives. Unless one's faith becomes dearer to one than one's own life, that faith has no chance of survival at the very first serious test. This love and dedication to one's faith must be apparent to others on every occasion for them to appreciate its place and value in the believer's heart. Such sacrifice and perseverance demonstrate the believer's love for his faith, and inspire others to respect it, examine its merits and develop an interest in it. That can open the hearts and minds of many people to Islam.

Tests and trials bring out the best in people, renew their energies, reinforce their resolve, and unleash within them latent powers that they themselves knew nothing of. Moreover, such experiences refine one's perception and sharpen one's mental and emotional vision and judgement.

Underlying all this is the fact that, when subjected to pressure and the severe demands of the struggle, a believer will turn to no one else but God for help and solace, and will seek the support of no other power than God's. This will be done in full acknowledgement of God's sovereignty and total control over everything in this world.

"Give glad tidings to those who remain patient in adversity. Who, when a calamity befalls them, say, 'To God we belong, and to Him we shall return.'" (Verses 155–156) God is the ultimate sovereign and final arbiter. To Him we turn for guidance on every matter. This is the essence of true submission, which comes from full recognition of His control of our destiny and our fate.

Such are the true believers who show patience and endure with fortitude. God's Messenger gives them the happy news of having earned their reward from God, the most bounteous. The blessings they receive are guaranteed by God Himself: *"On such people, blessings and mercy are bestowed by their Lord; such people will be rightly guided."* (Verse 157) It is indeed a noble and honourable reward that they will receive. Indeed, they share in the same type of reward the Prophet himself receives. What is more is that they have a testimony by God making it clear that they are rightly guided. This, again, is an honourable status.

In the process of mobilizing the Muslims for their great struggle, or *jihād*, God Almighty makes it clear that the believers' only reward for making the sort of sacrifice involved in struggle in God's cause, which includes loss of life, property, hunger, worry, as well as depletion of numbers and resources, will be God's mercy and blessings.

No material victory, power or wealth whatsoever is promised here – only God's mercy and blessings. There is no promise of victory or having power in their own community. That pioneering Muslim community was being prepared for a role that is more valuable than the very life of its members. Members of that community had to be free of all personal ambitions and selfish desires, and the community's aims and objectives had to be free of all worldly considerations, including victory for Islam through its own efforts.

The Qur'ān teaches the Muslims to seek nothing in return for their obedience, struggle and hard work but God's pleasure, blessings and guidance. That is to be the ultimate goal of their endeavour, and these will be the sweet fruits of their labour. As and when the victory comes, it will not be a victory for them but for the religion and the way of life they represent and are striving to establish in society.

God's mercy and blessings are ample reward for the believers' perseverance and for the sacrifices they make. In fact, they are a better reward than any material or worldly gain they aspire to achieve.

The foregoing passage has given us a glimpse of God's amazing but effective approach in educating the Muslim community and preparing its ranks for upholding His order and carrying it on to the rest of mankind.

9

Setting the Record Straight

Ṣafā and Marwah are among the symbols set up by God. Whoever visits the Sacred House for Pilgrimage or *ʿUmrah*, would do no wrong to walk to and fro between them. He who does good of his own accord shall find that God is most thankful, All-Knowing. (158)

إِنَّ ٱلصَّفَا وَٱلْمَرْوَةَ مِن شَعَآئِرِ ٱللَّهِ ۖ فَمَنْ حَجَّ
ٱلْبَيْتَ أَوِ ٱعْتَمَرَ فَلَا جُنَاحَ عَلَيْهِ أَن
يَطَّوَّفَ بِهِمَا ۚ وَمَن تَطَوَّعَ خَيْرًا فَإِنَّ ٱللَّهَ
شَاكِرٌ عَلِيمٌ ﴿١٥٨﴾

Those who conceal the clear proofs and guidance We bestowed from on high, after We have expounded it clearly for mankind in the Book, shall be cursed by God and by others who curse. (159)

إِنَّ ٱلَّذِينَ يَكْتُمُونَ مَآ أَنزَلْنَا مِنَ ٱلْبَيِّنَٰتِ
وَٱلْهُدَىٰ مِنۢ بَعْدِ مَا بَيَّنَّٰهُ لِلنَّاسِ فِى
ٱلْكِتَٰبِ ۙ أُو۟لَٰٓئِكَ يَلْعَنُهُمُ ٱللَّهُ وَيَلْعَنُهُمُ
ٱللَّٰعِنُونَ ﴿١٥٩﴾

Excepted, however, shall be those who repent, mend their ways and make known the Truth: from these I shall accept their repentance; for I alone accept repentance and I am the Merciful. (160)

إِلَّا ٱلَّذِينَ تَابُوا۟ وَأَصْلَحُوا۟ وَبَيَّنُوا۟
فَأُو۟لَٰٓئِكَ أَتُوبُ عَلَيْهِمْ ۚ وَأَنَا ٱلتَّوَّابُ
ٱلرَّحِيمُ ﴿١٦٠﴾

Those who reject the faith and die unbelievers shall incur the curse of God, the angels and all mankind. (161)

إِنَّ ٱلَّذِينَ كَفَرُوا۟ وَمَاتُوا۟ وَهُمْ كُفَّارٌ أُو۟لَٰٓئِكَ
عَلَيْهِمْ لَعْنَةُ ٱللَّهِ وَٱلْمَلَٰٓئِكَةِ وَٱلنَّاسِ
أَجْمَعِينَ ﴿١٦١﴾

They shall remain under that curse for ever, their torment shall not be alleviated, nor shall they have a respite. (162)

خَٰلِدِينَ فِيهَا لَا يُخَفَّفُ عَنْهُمُ ٱلْعَذَابُ
وَلَا هُمْ يُنظَرُونَ ١٦٢

Your God is the One God: there is no deity but He, the Compassionate, the Merciful. (163)

وَإِلَٰهُكُمْ إِلَٰهٌ وَٰحِدٌ لَّآ إِلَٰهَ إِلَّا هُوَ
ٱلرَّحْمَٰنُ ٱلرَّحِيمُ ١٦٣

In the creation of the heavens and the earth; in the alternation of night and day; in the vessels that sail through the sea with what is useful for mankind; in the water God sends down from the sky giving life to the earth after it had been lifeless, causing all manner of living creatures to multiply on it; in the movement of the winds, and the clouds that run their courses between sky and earth: in all this there are signs for people who use their reason. (164)

إِنَّ فِى خَلْقِ ٱلسَّمَٰوَٰتِ وَٱلْأَرْضِ
وَٱخْتِلَٰفِ ٱلَّيْلِ وَٱلنَّهَارِ وَٱلْفُلْكِ
ٱلَّتِى تَجْرِى فِى ٱلْبَحْرِ بِمَا يَنفَعُ ٱلنَّاسَ
وَمَآ أَنزَلَ ٱللَّهُ مِنَ ٱلسَّمَآءِ مِن مَّآءٍ
فَأَحْيَا بِهِ ٱلْأَرْضَ بَعْدَ مَوْتِهَا وَبَثَّ
فِيهَا مِن كُلِّ دَآبَّةٍ وَتَصْرِيفِ
ٱلرِّيَٰحِ وَٱلسَّحَابِ ٱلْمُسَخَّرِ بَيْنَ
ٱلسَّمَآءِ وَٱلْأَرْضِ لَءَايَٰتٍ لِّقَوْمٍ
يَعْقِلُونَ ١٦٤

Yet there are people who worship beings other than God, giving them a status equal to His, loving them as God alone should be loved; whereas the believers love God more than all else. If the unbelievers could but see, as see they will when they are made to suffer, that all might belongs to God alone, and that He is stern in retribution. (165)

وَمِنَ ٱلنَّاسِ مَن يَتَّخِذُ مِن دُونِ ٱللَّهِ
أَندَادًا يُحِبُّونَهُمْ كَحُبِّ ٱللَّهِ وَٱلَّذِينَ
ءَامَنُوٓا۟ أَشَدُّ حُبًّا لِّلَّهِ وَلَوْ يَرَى ٱلَّذِينَ ظَلَمُوٓا۟
إِذْ يَرَوْنَ ٱلْعَذَابَ أَنَّ ٱلْقُوَّةَ لِلَّهِ جَمِيعًا
وَأَنَّ ٱللَّهَ شَدِيدُ ٱلْعَذَابِ ١٦٥

[On that day] those who were followed will disown their followers and they all shall see their punishment, while all their ties are severed. (166)

إِذْ تَبَرَّأَ ٱلَّذِينَ ٱتُّبِعُوا۟ مِنَ ٱلَّذِينَ
ٱتَّبَعُوا۟ وَرَأَوُا۟ ٱلْعَذَابَ وَتَقَطَّعَتْ
بِهِمُ ٱلْأَسْبَابُ ﴿١٦٦﴾

The followers will say, 'Would that we had another chance so that we can disown them as they have disowned us!' Thus will God show them their works [in a way which causes them] bitter regrets. They shall never come out of the fire. (167)

وَقَالَ ٱلَّذِينَ ٱتَّبَعُوا۟ لَوْ أَنَّ لَنَا كَرَّةً
فَنَتَبَرَّأَ مِنْهُمْ كَمَا تَبَرَّءُوا۟ مِنَّا ۗ كَذَٰلِكَ
يُرِيهِمُ ٱللَّهُ أَعْمَٰلَهُمْ حَسَرَٰتٍ عَلَيْهِمْ ۖ
وَمَا هُم بِخَٰرِجِينَ مِنَ ٱلنَّارِ ﴿١٦٧﴾

Mankind, eat of what is lawful and wholesome on earth and do not follow Satan's footsteps: he is indeed an open enemy for you. (168)

يَٰٓأَيُّهَا ٱلنَّاسُ كُلُوا۟ مِمَّا فِى ٱلْأَرْضِ حَلَٰلًا
طَيِّبًا وَلَا تَتَّبِعُوا۟ خُطُوَٰتِ ٱلشَّيْطَٰنِ ۚ إِنَّهُۥ
لَكُمْ عَدُوٌّ مُّبِينٌ ﴿١٦٨﴾

He enjoins you only to commit evil and indecency and to attribute to God something of which you have no knowledge. (169)

إِنَّمَا يَأْمُرُكُم بِٱلسُّوٓءِ وَٱلْفَحْشَآءِ وَأَن
تَقُولُوا۟ عَلَى ٱللَّهِ مَا لَا تَعْلَمُونَ ﴿١٦٩﴾

When it is said to them, 'Follow what God has revealed', they say, 'No; but we will follow only what we found our forefathers believing in.' Why, even if their forefathers did not use reason at all, and followed no guidance. (170)

وَإِذَا قِيلَ لَهُمُ ٱتَّبِعُوا۟ مَآ أَنزَلَ ٱللَّهُ قَالُوا۟ بَلْ
نَتَّبِعُ مَآ أَلْفَيْنَا عَلَيْهِ ءَابَآءَنَآ ۗ أَوَلَوْ كَانَ
ءَابَآؤُهُمْ لَا يَعْقِلُونَ شَيْـًٔا وَلَا
يَهْتَدُونَ ﴿١٧٠﴾

The unbelievers are like the one who shouts to that which hears nothing but a call and a cry. Deaf, dumb and blind, they understand nothing. (171)

وَمَثَلُ ٱلَّذِينَ كَفَرُوا۟ كَمَثَلِ ٱلَّذِى يَنْعِقُ
بِمَا لَا يَسْمَعُ إِلَّا دُعَآءً وَنِدَآءً ۚ صُمٌّۢ بُكْمٌ عُمْىٌ
فَهُمْ لَا يَعْقِلُونَ ﴿١٧١﴾

Believers, eat of the wholesome things We have provided for you, and give thanks to God, if it is truly Him that you worship. (172)

يَٰٓأَيُّهَا ٱلَّذِينَ ءَامَنُوا۟ كُلُوا۟ مِن طَيِّبَٰتِ
مَا رَزَقْنَٰكُمْ وَٱشْكُرُوا۟ لِلَّهِ إِن كُنتُمْ إِيَّاهُ
تَعْبُدُونَ ﴿١٧٢﴾

He has only forbidden you carrion, blood, the flesh of swine, and that on which a name other than God's has been invoked. But he who is driven by necessity, not intending to transgress nor exceeding his need, incurs no sin. God is much-Forgiving, Merciful. (173)

إِنَّمَا حَرَّمَ عَلَيْكُمُ ٱلْمَيْتَةَ وَٱلدَّمَ وَلَحْمَ
ٱلْخِنزِيرِ وَمَآ أُهِلَّ بِهِۦ لِغَيْرِ ٱللَّهِ ۖ فَمَنِ
ٱضْطُرَّ غَيْرَ بَاغٍ وَلَا عَادٍ فَلَآ إِثْمَ عَلَيْهِ ۚ
إِنَّ ٱللَّهَ غَفُورٌ رَّحِيمٌ ﴿١٧٣﴾

Those who suppress any part of the Scriptures God has revealed, and barter it away for a paltry price, eat nothing but fire in their bellies. God will not speak to them on the Day of Resurrection, nor will He purify them. A grievous suffering awaits them. (174)

إِنَّ ٱلَّذِينَ يَكْتُمُونَ مَآ أَنزَلَ ٱللَّهُ مِنَ
ٱلْكِتَٰبِ وَيَشْتَرُونَ بِهِۦ ثَمَنًا قَلِيلًا ۙ
أُو۟لَٰٓئِكَ مَا يَأْكُلُونَ فِى بُطُونِهِمْ
إِلَّا ٱلنَّارَ وَلَا يُكَلِّمُهُمُ ٱللَّهُ يَوْمَ ٱلْقِيَٰمَةِ
وَلَا يُزَكِّيهِمْ وَلَهُمْ عَذَابٌ أَلِيمٌ ﴿١٧٤﴾

It is they who barter guidance for error and forgiveness for suffering. How great is their endurance of the Fire! (175)

أُو۟لَٰٓئِكَ ٱلَّذِينَ ٱشْتَرَوُا۟ ٱلضَّلَٰلَةَ
بِٱلْهُدَىٰ وَٱلْعَذَابَ بِٱلْمَغْفِرَةِ ۚ فَمَآ
أَصْبَرَهُمْ عَلَى ٱلنَّارِ ﴿١٧٥﴾

That is because God has revealed the Book with the truth. Those who are at variance with the Book are most deeply in the wrong. (176)

ذَٰلِكَ بِأَنَّ ٱللَّهَ نَزَّلَ ٱلْكِتَٰبَ بِٱلْحَقِّ ۗ
وَإِنَّ ٱلَّذِينَ ٱخْتَلَفُوا۟ فِى ٱلْكِتَٰبِ لَفِى
شِقَاقٍۭ بَعِيدٍ ١٧٦

Righteousness is not that you turn your faces towards the east or the west, but truly righteous is he who believes in God, the Last Day, the angels, the Book, and the Prophets; and gives his money, much as he may cherish it, to his kinsfolk, orphans, the needy, a stranded wayfarer, beggars, and for the freeing of slaves; who attends to his prayers and pays *zakāt*; and [truly pious are] they who keep their promises once made, and are patient in misfortune and adversity and in time of peril. Such are those who have proved themselves true, and such are the God-fearing. (177)

لَّيْسَ ٱلْبِرَّ أَن تُوَلُّوا۟ وُجُوهَكُمْ قِبَلَ ٱلْمَشْرِقِ
وَٱلْمَغْرِبِ وَلَٰكِنَّ ٱلْبِرَّ مَنْ ءَامَنَ بِٱللَّهِ
وَٱلْيَوْمِ ٱلْءَاخِرِ وَٱلْمَلَٰٓئِكَةِ وَٱلْكِتَٰبِ
وَٱلنَّبِيِّۦنَ وَءَاتَى ٱلْمَالَ عَلَىٰ حُبِّهِۦ ذَوِى
ٱلْقُرْبَىٰ وَٱلْيَتَٰمَىٰ وَٱلْمَسَٰكِينَ وَٱبْنَ
ٱلسَّبِيلِ وَٱلسَّآئِلِينَ وَفِى ٱلرِّقَابِ وَأَقَامَ
ٱلصَّلَوٰةَ وَءَاتَى ٱلزَّكَوٰةَ وَٱلْمُوفُونَ
بِعَهْدِهِمْ إِذَا عَٰهَدُوا۟ ۖ وَٱلصَّٰبِرِينَ فِى
ٱلْبَأْسَآءِ وَٱلضَّرَّآءِ وَحِينَ ٱلْبَأْسِ ۗ أُو۟لَٰٓئِكَ
ٱلَّذِينَ صَدَقُوا۟ ۖ وَأُو۟لَٰٓئِكَ هُمُ ٱلْمُتَّقُونَ ١٧٧

Overview

This new passage aims at correcting certain principles and clarifying some misconceptions concerning the true faith. It also continues the confrontation with the Jews of Madinah, to which we were introduced earlier. They did not cease to try to present falsehood in the guise of truth, and to cause confusion among the Muslims. However, the tone this time is rather general, presenting principles that apply to the Jews of Madinah as well as other opponents of the new faith. It also identifies a number of pitfalls that the Muslims would do well to avoid.

To begin with, we have a reference to the pilgrimage ritual of walking between the two hills of Ṣafā and Marwah, near the Ka'bah, clarifying the confusion surrounding them as a result of pre-Islamic pagan traditions. To some extent, this is related to the institution of the Ka'bah as the universal direction of prayer for Muslims as well as to pilgrimage rituals.

This is followed by a fierce condemnation of Jews and Christians who conceal parts of their Scriptures, while making it clear that repentance and forgiveness remain open to those of them who wish to refrain from such practices. Those who persist will meet with harsh punishment.

Then comes a reaffirmation of the concept of God's oneness, and a reference to the marvels of the natural world that attest to it. Those who reject God's oneness are roundly condemned, while a scene from the Day of Judgement depicts how futile it will be for unbelievers to realize their wrongdoing when it is too late.

Referring to the Jewish arguments about what is lawful and unlawful of food and drink, the passage makes a general call to mankind to enjoy the wholesome and lawful things in life which God has provided for them. An account of things that are forbidden to eat and drink is also given in this section.

The passage resumes the attack on those who suppress or tamper with God's revelations, threatening them with God's wrath and their own humiliation, and a most severe punishment in the life to come.

As the passage is rounded off, we have a statement of the essential principles of faith and good works, highlighting the direct link between faith and action, and reiterating the fact that it stems from one's heart and emotions. It is no empty gesture or hollow ritual, but a deliberate and constant state of consciousness of God's existence and power.

The passage continues to educate and inform, and to raise the Muslims' understanding of the principles of their religion as well as their awareness of the hostile schemes and campaigns of their enemies to undermine their faith and sow chaos and confusion in their community.

A Very Significant Ritual

> *Ṣafā and Marwah are among the symbols set up by God. Whoever visits the Sacred House for pilgrimage or* 'umrah, *would do no wrong to walk to and fro between them. He who does good of his own accord shall find that God is most thankful, All-Knowing.* (Verse 158)

Several reports suggest a specific cause for the revelation of this verse; the most logical account, which is also the closest to the way of thinking Islam had cultivated in the minds of the early Muslims, is the following:

Walking between the two small hills known as Ṣafā and Marwah had been part of the pilgrimage rituals practised by the Arabs before Islam. However, two idols, Isāf and Nā'ilah, were erected on top of them, respectively. Hence, some Muslims felt uneasy about this walk because of the two idols that had been there, associating the two hills with polytheism.

Al-Bukhārī relates that, in answer to a question about walking between Ṣafā and Marwah, Anas, a Companion of the Prophet, said: "We used to consider them part of pre-Islamic ignorant tradition. With the advent of Islam, people stopped walking there as part of religious ritual. God then revealed the verse starting: *"Ṣafā and Marwah are among the symbols set up by God."*"

Al-Sha'bī says: "Isāf was placed on Ṣafā and Nā'ilah on the Marwah, and people used to revere these idols. Hence, after Islam they felt uneasy about walking in between the two hills. Hence this verse was revealed."

No specific date can be determined for the revelation of this verse, but it seems more probable that it was revealed later than the verses dealing with the change of the direction of prayer. Although Makkah was hostile territory for the Muslims for many years after their migration to Madinah, it was possible for some of them to visit it for pilgrimage or *'umrah*. It is most probably such individual Muslim pilgrims who were reluctant to include Ṣafā and Marwah in their rituals.

Their reluctance was the outcome of the long and rigorous process of education and purification they had undergone under their new faith. They developed a new sense of faith and religious understanding that made them question all the traditions and practices they had inherited from their pre-Islamic life, in case these were not sanctioned by Islam.

Islam shook the hearts of the Arabs who adopted it and penetrated the deepest recesses of their souls. It brought about a complete change in their psyche, perceptions and attitude. They began to view their pre-Islamic past with different eyes, and were inclined to divorce themselves from it completely. They no longer felt any affinity towards it; rather, it became a hateful legacy.

A closer study of that radical change brought about in the life of that generation by Islamic beliefs, principles and arguments would reveal how total and complete was the transformation they had undergone. It was as if the Prophet had shaken those people with an electric shock that reshaped their character and personality in a completely new form.

This is, in fact, the true essence of Islam: total departure from one's previous *jāhiliyyah*[1] convictions and outlook. One develops an acute sensitivity towards all that is un-Islamic, and all one's inherited habits, customs, practices and traditions. Both heart and soul must be given up to the new religion.

Once that stage was reached in the life of that pioneering Muslim society, Islam began to adopt and reform those traditions and practices it considered acceptable and in line with its own principles, objectives and outlook. The Muslims then readopted those traditions and practices as part of Islam, and not because they had inherited them from their forefathers.

The incorporation of Ṣafā and Marwah in the pilgrimage rituals is a good example of this process. Clarifying the issue, the Qur'ān begins by stating: *"Ṣafā and Marwah are among the symbols set up by God."* (Verse 158) When a person walks now from one to the other in the prescribed manner, he is fulfilling an Islamic ritual, devoted to God alone. It has been purified and cleansed of all its pagan associations and significance. Muslims can perform the ritual with no fear of doing anything wrong or un-Islamic. *"Whoever visits the Sacred House for pilgrimage or* 'umrah, *would do no wrong to walk to and fro between them."* (Verse 158)

This was the case with most rituals of the pilgrimage practised by the Arabs in pre-Islamic days. All aspects pertaining to idolatry were abolished. Now all the pilgrimage rituals have become linked to Islamic principles and restored to the original form practised by Abraham, as will be discussed in detail later in the *sūrah*. As for the *'Umrah*, its rituals are the same as the pilgrimage, except for attendance

1. This is an Islamic term that refers to the beliefs and concepts that prevailed in pre-Islamic Arabia, but it is often used by Islamic writers to refer to all non-Islamic social practices and traditions. The word is derived from the root *'jahl'* which means ignorance. Thus, it has come to mean a state of mind associated with ignorance.

at Arafāt and that it may be performed at all times. In both, walking between the two hills is a duty.

The verse ends with a statement praising voluntary acts of worship in general: *"He who does good of his own accord shall find that God is most thankful, All-Knowing."* (Verse 158) This statement affirms that God would welcome and appreciate such acts and would reserve generous rewards for their doers. By its very wording, this verse implies that walking between the two hills is a good action which earns reward from God.

The word *shākir*, which means "thankful", used in the Arabic original to describe God's response to voluntary acts, conveys a very friendly impression. It has the added connotation that God Almighty is very pleased with these acts and thanks His servants for doing them. This would surely demand respect and modesty towards God on the part of His human servants. If God describes Himself as thankful to His servant for any good action that servant does, how can we be sufficiently grateful to God in our praise of Him? The connotations of divine compassion and mercy implied here defy description in human language.

Suppressing the Truth

The verses that follow launch a sharp attack on those Jews who, as mentioned earlier, concealed facts that were revealed in their Scriptures, in the wake of the controversy they created over the change of the direction of prayer from Jerusalem to the Ka'bah. This suggests that they continued to exploit the situation, especially after Makkah was also instituted as the place of the pilgrimage for Muslims.

> *Those who conceal the clear proofs and guidance We bestowed from on high, after We have expounded it clearly for mankind in the Book, shall be cursed by God and by others who curse. Excepted, however, shall be those who repent, mend their ways and make known the Truth: from these I shall accept their repentance; for I alone accept repentance and I am the Merciful. Those who reject the faith and die unbelievers shall incur the curse of God, the angels and all mankind. They shall remain under that curse for ever, their torment shall not be alleviated, nor shall they have a respite.* (Verses 159–162)

The Jews and the Christians were already aware, on the basis of their own Scriptures, of the truth of Muḥammad's mission. They had little doubt of his honesty and integrity. Nevertheless, they spared no effort to conceal and suppress what their Scriptures had to say about him. Manipulation of religious text and tampering with revealed Scriptures have, for a variety of reasons, been encountered on numerous occasions in history. There have always been people with a propensity for evading the truth, or ignoring or suppressing it, or changing it to suit their own aims and ends. Thy knowingly conceal the truth, suppressing all evidence of the veracity of which they are most certain. They even suppress verses in God's book so that the truth they expound is kept away from people. They do all this in order to achieve some worldly gain. In fact, we often encounter examples of such uppression of the truth. Such people shall be cursed by God and man. They shall become pariahs, denied God's mercy and rejected by their fellow men.

Exception is, of course, made of those who come to realize their folly, repent and abandon such practices: *"Excepted, however, shall be those who repent, mend their ways and make known the Truth: from these I shall accept their repentance; for I alone accept repentance and I am the Merciful."* (Verse 160) The Qur'ān opens the door, as always, for those who repent and make amends, giving them another chance to see the light and make the change within themselves. To prove that the change is genuine, they are required to make up for the past by performing good deeds, being scrupulously honest in their actions, and championing the truth and abiding by it in all they say and do. They must have full confidence in God's mercy and be certain that He will forgive and reward their repentance.

Those who persist and refuse to repent, however, shall meet their nemesis in the worst possible way, because they rejected God's hospitality and consciously chose to perpetrate evil and falsehood: *"Those who reject the faith and die unbelievers shall incur the curse of God, the angels and all mankind. They shall remain under that curse for ever, their torment shall not be alleviated, nor shall they have a respite."* (Verses 161–162)

This general curse is considered a just reward for their abhorrent behaviour. They shall live as social outcasts, rejected by everyone and bereft of all dignity and respect. Worst of all, they shall incur the curse of God, which is the most devastating of all humiliations.

Following that, there is a reiteration of the basic aspects of the concept of God's oneness. To illustrate these, the *sūrah* cites a number of natural phenomena in the physical world that testify to God's power and overall sovereignty. It then portrays a scene from the Day of Resurrection, showing the despair and confusion of those who reject God and deny His power and existence.

> *Your God is the One God: there is no deity but He, the Compassionate, the Merciful. In the creation of the heavens and the earth; in the alternation of night and day; in the vessels that sail through the sea with what is useful for mankind; in the water God sends down from the sky giving life to the earth after it had been lifeless, causing all manner of living creatures to multiply on it; in the movement of the winds, and the clouds that run their courses between sky and earth: in all this there are signs for people who use their reason. Yet there are people who worship beings other than God, giving them a status equal to His, loving them as God alone should be loved; whereas the believers love God more than all else. If the unbelievers could but see, as see they will when they are made to suffer, that all might belongs to God alone, and that He is stern in retribution. [On that day] those who were followed will disown their followers and they all shall see their punishment, while all their ties are severed. The followers will say, 'Would that we had another chance so that we can disown them as they have disowned us!" Thus will God show them their works [in a way which causes them] bitter regrets. They shall never come out of the fire.* (Verses 163–167)

The oneness of God is the quintessence of faith. On the whole, the debate has never been about God's existence, however differently his entity, attributes or role in the universe might be viewed or defined by different societies and religions. Man's nature has always led him to the belief in God. But in recent human history, a new philosophy has emerged, never known in human thinking before, which totally denies the very notion of God. This intellectual monstrosity has very little chance of becoming universal, because it is self-defeating and is invalidated by the very nature and structure of the universe and our own existence in it.

The passage, therefore, affirms the principle of God's oneness as an essential part of true faith and a solid foundation for man's moral and social systems. The one God is the only deity to be adored and worshipped, and He is also the sole source of man's moral codes and norms, and the origin of all the laws and regulations that govern and control man's social, political and economic life and the life of the whole cosmos: *"Your God is the One God: there is no deity but He, the Compassionate, the Merciful."* (Verse 163) We cannot fail to note how the truth of God's oneness is emphatically stressed here in several ways. Thus, the Lord worshipped and obeyed by all creatures is the only God who legislates for all people making clear for them what moral values to uphold. It is from Him that they receive all their legislation.

This central concept of Islam is re-emphasized time after time in the Qur'ān, particularly in the parts revealed in Makkah. It is brought up here in the context of preparing the Muslim community for its crucial universal leadership role. The Qur'ān hammers home these concepts so as to leave people in no doubt that the principle of God's oneness permeates all aspects of life and all parts of existence.

God's sovereignty over this world and His active control of its affairs stem from His grace attributes. He is *"the Merciful, the Compassionate."*

Those Using Their Reason

> *In the creation of the heavens and the earth; in the alternation of night and day; in the vessels that sail through the sea with what is useful for mankind; in the water God sends down from the sky giving life to the earth after it had been lifeless, causing all manner of living creatures to multiply on it; in the movement of the winds, and the clouds that run their courses between sky and earth: in all this there are signs for people who use their reason.* (Verse 164)

This unique Qur'ānic approach in addressing the human mind and heart tends to heighten man's feelings and emotions and make him behold and contemplate the wonders of the Universe. Familiarity may have blunted man's appreciation of these marvels, but the verses invite him to reflect on the world around, as if for the first time, with open eyes and eager senses and a conscious heart. The physical world is full of beautiful mysteries and awe-inspiring events that have captivated many an eye and fascinated many a heart.

The world is a boundless festival of mystery, splendour and beauty. The Heavens, the Earth, the planets, the stars, the galaxies, are all floating along their decreed orbits with incredible harmony, in a vast expanse of limitless space of dizzying dimensions. Man has been fascinated by this vast gallery of wonders long before he was able to get a glimpse, through study and science, of how it works and what lies behind it.

The cycle of day and night and the alternation of light and darkness, dawn and dusk, have sent a million shivers through the hearts and souls of men everywhere. For the believing heart, it is a daily marvel to behold, despite its familiarity; a constant reminder of God's magnificence and glory.

As for *"in the vessels that sail through the sea with what is useful for mankind,"* I admit that I had not fully appreciated the import of this statement until the day I travelled on board a large ship, which seemed like a dot in the ocean. Waves were hitting us from all sides while we were engulfed in an almost surreal world of endless blue. Those who have experienced sea travel know that in the middle of the ocean one is entirely at God's mercy and that it is only with God's will and command that one is brought to the safety of the shore.

The *sūrah* highlights other natural phenomena: *"the water God sends down from the sky giving life to the earth after it had been lifeless, causing all manner of living creatures to multiply on it; in the movement of the winds, and the clouds that run their courses between sky and earth."* (Verse 164) All these phenomena deserve our attention, reflection and intelligent study. They are all manifestations of God's awesome power and infinite mercy. Life is the greatest mystery of all. How does it spring out of the earth when water makes it fertile? How does it come about, starting gently at first before manifesting itself with full vigour? By what incredible process is it carried in a seed, an egg or a gene?

It is a question that has to be asked. It is no good brushing it aside or ignoring it, as some agnostics have tried to do. Some have even gone further and claimed that life can be created by man, without the need for God's intervention! But even in the land where the ruling class prides itself on denying God altogether they have given up and were forced to admit that this is impossible without a Creator to give life. Leading Soviet scientists do now openly admit this as a fact beyond man's ability.[2] In the past Charles Darwin, the first to put forward the theory of evolution, tried hard to evade the question.

As for the wind and the clouds, and all other natural phenomena, it is not sufficient to advance a theory to explain or describe merely how winds blow, or how clouds form, or the process by which they function, or what their effects are. The central question, the real mystery, revolves around the origin of life itself: why has the world been created in the way it has, and by what methods? How did the universe come to exist in its present form which, in order to produce and sustain life, provides the right combination of elements such as wind, cloud, rain and soil, according to thousands upon thousands of perfectly balanced proportions and formulae? If any of these proportions were to change, life would not be possible. The secret lies in the intricate design and clear purpose of existence, and in the unity and compassion of the Creator.

"In all this there are signs for people who use their reason." (Verse 164) Indeed, all man needs to do is to shake off familiarity and apathy and look afresh at the world around with a discerning eye and an enlightened heart. He should study every movement, scrutinize every phenomenon, and probe all secrets and mysteries, and let his ingenuity and imagination be fired so that he can grasp the splendour of the universe and the brilliance of its Maker.

Such refined awareness, such sensitivity, and such appreciation of the beauty, balance and perfection of the universe are derived from true faith. Faith gives the believer a new insight into the world around him and a new understanding of beauty, and turns life into one continuous celebration of the creation and glory of God.

Nevertheless, there are still those who neither look nor understand. That is the reason they go astray and lose direction in life.

"Yet there are people who worship beings other than God, giving them a status equal to His, loving them as God alone should be loved." (Verse 165)

In those days these were idols carved out of stone or wood, or they were stars and planets, or angels and devils. In every age these deities take on different forms and sizes. Their common feature is that they are all forms of associating partners with God, whether they are

2. This was written in the early 1960s.– Editor's note.

invoked together with God, or treated merely as objects of adoration or on a par with God. In the worst case, they replace God altogether.

But the case is different with true believers: *"whereas the believers love God more than all else."* (Verse 165) Their love for God supersedes their love for everything else in the world. The use of the term "love" here is both touching and appropriate, because the relationship between God and true believers is one of love and spiritual affection. It is an intimate and private relationship, continuously renewed with an undying adoration.

Alliances Fall Apart

> *If the unbelievers could but see, as see they will when they are made to suffer, that all might belongs to God alone, and that He is stern in retribution. [On that day] those who were followed will disown their followers and they all shall see their punishment, while all their ties are severed. The followers will say, 'Would that we had another chance so that we can disown them as they have disowned us!' Thus will God show them their works [in a way which causes them] bitter regrets. They shall never come out of the fire.* (Verses 165–167)

Were these transgressors to look ahead to the Day of Resurrection, they would realize their folly in worshipping anything or anybody other than God. All power belongs to Him. He has neither equals nor partners. They would also see the hopelessness of their actions and the severity of the punishment awaiting them. The leaders shall disassociate themselves from their followers, and shall be exposed as powerless to help them, or even help themselves. The truth of God's oneness and His absolute power would be clearly manifest. The followers, on the other hand, would wish for a second chance of life in order to denounce and disown those false gods and leaders. The full extent of the fraud and the delusion under which they had been living would be exposed.

It is an awesome scene in which all the hypocrisy and the insincerity and futility of the relationship between the two groups is brought fully into the open. And then come the pain and the torment: *"Thus will God show them their works [in a way which causes them] bitter regrets. They shall never come out of the fire."* (Verse 167)

Which Path to Follow

This is followed by an invitation to all mankind to enjoy the good things in life and avoid the harmful ones. This is coupled with a warning against following the suggestions of Satan, who will only advise people to do evil and harmful things and to arrogate to themselves the right to legislate without reference to God. There is also a warning against following others blindly in matters of religion, and a denunciation of the worship of any deity other than God Almighty, neatly linking this passage with the preceding one.

> *Mankind, eat of what is lawful and wholesome on earth and do not follow Satan's footsteps: he is indeed an open enemy for you. He enjoins you only to commit evil and indecency and to attribute to God something of which you have no knowledge. When it is said to them, 'Follow what God has revealed', they say, 'No; but we will follow only what we found our forefathers believing in.' Why, even if their forefathers did not use reason at all, and followed no guidance. The unbelievers are like the one who shouts to that which hears nothing but a call and a cry. Deaf, dumb and blind, they understand nothing.* (Verses 168–171)

Having set out the argument for God's oneness and shown Himself as the Creator of all, and exposed the utter failure of those who worship gods other than Him, God Almighty states in these verses that He is also the provider and sustainer of life. Accordingly, He is the ultimate authority to decide what food is lawful and what is unlawful; an aspect of exercising His authority as the only God. The Creator who makes and provides is also the authority who decides what is lawful and what is not. The law, *Sharī'ah*, is thus inextricably intertwined with belief.

The verses give the whole of mankind permission to enjoy the food God has provided on earth, with the exception of what He has forbidden – which will be mentioned later in the *sūrah*. People are also instructed here that they should listen only to God concerning what may or may not be lawful for consumption. They should not listen to Satan's views in these matters, because, as their sworn enemy, he will not give them good advice. He will only mislead them and encourage them to decide what is and is not lawful of their own accord, with no reference to God's guidance, as the Jews used to do, and as the Arab idolaters used to claim.

These instructions show plainly how realistic and practical Islam is, and how genuinely aware of man's nature and needs. The rule is that everything is lawful with the exception of a few things, which are listed in the Qur'ān by name.

God has created the earth and all its products for man's free use, enjoyment and benefit. The exceptions and restrictions are made only to safeguard man's interests, and to ensure that he does not over-consume, or abuse the resources God has provided for him. The most important condition, however, is that man should not refer to anybody other than God for the identification of those items that are not permissible, and for the determination of the limits and the conditions under which the permissible ones should be consumed and used. If they do not, then they will be listening to Satan's promptings, and he is wont to bid people to commit only evil and indecency.

The *sūrah* derides the argument put forward by the Arab idolaters or the Jews, or both, who insist that they will only follow what their forefathers followed: *"Even if their forefathers did not use reason at all, and followed no guidance."* That is exactly what the Qur'ān condemns. When it comes to defining matters relating to faith, the Qur'ān rejects all authority other than God's, and flatly condemns those who follow blindly inherited traditions and practices.

The next verse gives a humiliating image of those blind followers of earlier generations, depicting them as herds of sheep that can hear the shouting and the sounds made by their shepherds but do not understand what those words actually mean. In fact, as the *sūrah* goes on we realize that they are worse. For while sheep can, at least, see, hear and bleat, while these are heedless and even worse: *"The unbelievers are like the one who shouts to that which hears nothing but a call and a cry. Deaf, dumb and blind, they understand nothing."* (Verse 171)

Such people may very well have ears, tongues and eyes of their own, but what good will these do them if not put to proper use? They might as well have none. That is indeed the lowest and the most contemptible state that human beings can reach: when they give up their intelligence and discerning faculties. No one other than God has the authority to ordain or pronounce over matters of religion, law or behaviour.

Things Forbidden to Eat

The *sūrah* then gives believers specific rules on the various types of animal meat that they may eat, denouncing the Jews, who argue over this matter although it has been adequately discussed in their own Scriptures.

> *Believers, eat of the wholesome things We have provided for you, and give thanks to God, if it is truly Him that you worship. He has only forbidden you carrion, blood, the flesh of swine, and that on which a name other than God's has been invoked. But he who is driven by necessity, not intending to transgress nor exceeding his need, incurs no sin. God is much-Forgiving, Merciful. Those who suppress any part of the Scriptures God has revealed, and barter it away for a paltry price, eat nothing but fire in their bellies. God will not speak to them on the Day of Resurrection, nor will He purify them. A grievous suffering awaits them. It is they who barter guidance for error and forgiveness for suffering. How great is their endurance of the Fire! That is because God has revealed the Book with the truth. Those who are at variance with the Book are most deeply in the wrong.* (Verses 172–176)

God addresses believers by their most important quality of having accepted the faith, clearly underlining their special relationship with Him and making it clear that they should accept only His instructions and guidelines with respect to what is or is not lawful and permissible. They are reminded that He alone provides for them and shows them what is permissible and what is not. Nothing good or wholesome has been forbidden, only what is harmful and corrupt. The purpose behind these few restrictions is not to deprive people or curb their enjoyment of the good things God has made available, and for which they should show gratitude. God directs them to thank Him if they truly worship Him alone. Thus, they are taught that thanksgiving is an act of worship. *"Believers, eat of the wholesome things We have provided for you, and give thanks to God, if it is truly Him that you worship."* (Verse 172)

Then comes a list of what has been forbidden for the Muslims to eat. It starts with an Arabic word which indicates that the restriction is limited to the given items: *"He has only forbidden you carrion, blood, the flesh of swine, and that on which a name other than God's has been invoked."* (Verse 173)

Both carrion – dead putrefying flesh – and blood are unhygienic and offensive to human taste. Centuries after this Qur'ānic statement was revealed, modern medical research has shown that both attract harmful germs and carry deadly substances. There could be many more reasons why they were forbidden by Islam, which modern medical science has yet to discover.

The next item is the flesh of swine, about the banning of which some have recently raised doubts. The pig is an unattractive animal with foul habits, and God has forbidden its flesh a very long time ago. Only recently, human knowledge has shown it to be singularly prone to infection with parasitic worms that are a serious health hazard to humans. Some may yet argue that advances in health care and modern cooking methods have reduced or even eliminated this risk. But this has only come to light several centuries after Islam, and there is no guarantee that pig's meat does not carry other risks of which we are yet to become aware. Islamic law has been well ahead of human science by many centuries. It deserves our unqualified trust. It must be considered the final arbiter in what is wholesome and what is not. It is the legislation revealed by the One who is wise and who knows all.

The meat of animals slaughtered in dedication to something or someone other than God is forbidden for Muslims to eat for that very reason. There is nothing physically wrong with the meat, but it is spiritually tainted by the fact that it was sacrificed in reverence of a creature of God. This impairs one's loyalty to, and faith in, God. This makes it akin to material impurity and dirtiness. Of all prohibited things this type is most relevant to faith.

It becomes clear, yet again, how strongly and closely the principle of God's oneness is linked to the source of religious guidance and lawmaking in Islam, God Almighty.

In establishing the above restrictions, however, Islam takes account of the circumstances under which they would apply. Necessities could arise which would entail a measured lifting or relaxation of those restrictions. These are dictated strictly by the need at the time, and on condition that consumption of forbidden meat is not, in any way, permitted for reasons of self-indulgence or in defiance of God's instructions.

"But he who is driven by necessity, not intending to transgress nor exceeding his need, incurs no sin. God is much-Forgiving, Merciful."

(Verse 173) This is a general Islamic principle in all matters of this kind, and can be extended to situations of a similar nature. Any life-threatening situation creates a necessity which would allow a person to eat or drink forbidden things if alternatives cannot be found, within the conditions mentioned above.

Scholars differ in their definition of what constitutes necessity. Are the situations in which necessity exists only those specifically cited by God, or could other, similar circumstances be included? Nor is there any consensus of opinion among scholars on what constitutes relieving the necessity: is it confined to the smallest of measures, or is it a full meal or drink? However, we are happy to confine our discussion here to pointing out the general principles that are of relevance in these matters, without discussing these differences in detail.

Suppression of God's Revelations

The Jews created considerable controversy around the Qur'ānic pronouncements on permissible and forbidden food and drink. Elsewhere, the Qur'ān informs us of other types of meat that had been forbidden to the Jews but which Muslims were allowed to eat: *"To those who followed the Jewish faith did We forbid all animals that have claws; and We forbade them the fat of both oxen and sheep, except that which is in their backs and entrails or what is mixed with their bones."* (6: 146) All these are lawful to Muslims.

The Jews might have disputed this relaxation of the earlier prohibition. They even argued about other forbidden things, although these were forbidden them in their own Scriptures. Their aim, of which they never lost sight, was to create doubts about Qur'ānic commandments and undermine the fact that they were revealed by God. This explains the strong denunciation of those who suppress what they know to be God's revelation. *"Those who suppress any part of the Scriptures God has revealed, and barter it away for a paltry price, eat nothing but fire in their bellies. God will not speak to them on the Day of Resurrection, nor will He purify them. A grievous suffering awaits them. It is they who barter guidance for error and forgiveness for suffering. How great is their endurance of the Fire! That is because God has revealed the Book with the truth. Those who are at variance with the Book are most deeply in the wrong.* (Verses 174–176)

The verses may be directed at people of earlier Scriptures, Jews and Christians, but the condemnation applies in the widest possible sense. All those who deliberately and systematically suppress the truth, especially religious truth, or manipulate it for power or worldly gains of any kind, stand condemned by God, and are doomed to incur His wrath and a stern punishment in the hereafter. Even if they were to gain this whole world for such suppression, it remains a paltry price when compared with what they lose of God's pleasure and His reward in the life to come.

They *"eat nothing but fire in their bellies."* (Verse 174) Here we have a description that is in perfect harmony with the scene being portrayed. Their gain for suppressing the truth is nothing but fire in their bellies. Indeed they are portrayed eating fire. Yet the description is factual. When they are in hell, the fire makes their clothes and their food. As an additional disgrace and humiliation, they are totally ignored in the life to come. Their isolation is given a very graphic description in the text: *"God will not speak to them on the Day of Resurrection, nor will He purify them. A grievous suffering awaits them."* (Verse 174)

Another expressive description tells us that they have made an utterly foolish choice by exchanging success for failure and making a losing deal. *"It is they who barter guidance for error and forgiveness for suffering. How great is their endurance of the Fire!"* (Verse 175)

The sarcasm is unmistakable, but it fits the vile actions of concealing the truth that God has revealed for the guidance and benefit of all mankind, and rightly castigates the folly of rejecting guidance and accepting humbug.

The result of deliberately concealing or disputing God's revealed truth is a life of constant turmoil, confusion and conflict with human nature. It is a life of permanent conflict and discord. *"That is because God has revealed the Book with the truth. Those who are at variance with the Book are most deeply in the wrong."* (Verse 176) Such an outcome has been seen time and again in human society, in accordance with God's true warning; history is evidence of its veracity.

What Constitutes Righteousness

This passage concludes with a verse that outlines the principles of true faith together with the rules of proper Islamic conduct:

Righteousness is not that you turn your faces towards the east or the west, but truly righteous is he who believes in God, the Last Day, the angels, the Book, and the Prophets; and gives his money, much as he may cherish it, to his kinsfolk, orphans, the needy, a stranded wayfarer, beggars, and for the freeing of slaves; who attends to his prayers and pays zakāt; *and [truly pious are] they who keep their promises once made, and are patient in misfortune and adversity and in time of peril. Such are those who have proved themselves true, and such are the God-fearing.* (Verse 177)

The subject of this verse is clearly linked to the issue of the direction of prayer and the controversy surrounding it, as discussed earlier. It now establishes a comprehensive principle that covers this issue and all matters that the Jews of Madinah were wont to dispute. These mostly centred on new religious rituals and forms of worship introduced by Islam and which differed from their own.

The purpose behind the change of the place Muslims face in prayers, and indeed all aspects of worship and ritual, has never been the direction people face, or indeed any outward form. These are not what gives worship its value or meaning, nor what makes people good and righteous. Righteousness is the result of a total feeling, an attitude and a mode of behaviour which shape the individual's conscience and the mind set of the community. It is a discipline whose effects are immediately and constantly apparent in one's life and the life of society as a whole. Without these aspects, facing east or west, or turning one's face to the right and to the left at the end of prayer or the performance of the various movements of prayer would have no effect or significance.

"*Truly righteous is he who believes in God, the Last Day, the angels, the Book, and the Prophets....*" Taken as a whole, the verse spells out the total sum of goodness, or righteousness. What, then, gives these beliefs and actions their value and meaning? What is the value of believing in God, the Last Day, the angels, the Book, and the Prophets?

Belief in God marks a definite turning point in one's life, at which one is freed from servitude and submission to all manner of powers, forces and desires, and submits to God alone. It is a transformation from chaos to order, from aimlessness to purpose, and from fragmentation to unity. It is a focal point around which all mankind stands equal in the eyes of God and which gives the whole of existence direction, balance, and coherence.

Belief in the Last Day is a belief in universal and divine justice. It is a testimony to the fact that human life on earth is not without purpose or value or order, and that good works that seem to go unrewarded shall certainly be rewarded.

Believing in the angels is an essential part of believing in a world that is beyond human perception. It is what distinguishes the way humans perceive the world and understand it from the way animals do. Animals perceive the world through their senses and instincts, while man believes in a world that lies beyond the reach of his perception.[3]

To believe in the Books and the Prophets means to attest, without reservation, to the truth, honesty, and integrity of all the revealed Books and all the Prophets and messengers God commissioned to deliver them at various times of human history. This leads to a belief in the unity of the human race, serving God alone, abiding by one and the same religion and adhering to one universal divine order. This outlook has a profound effect on the personality of the believer, who is seen as custodian of the heritage of God's messengers and divine messages.

The next element of righteousness is to spend money, dear as it may be, on one's near of kin, orphans, the needy, the stranded traveller, beggars, and for the freeing of slaves. The significance of this commendable act of charity and sacrifice is that it liberates man from stinginess, selfishness, greed and excessive love of wealth, which cripple one's ability to give and help those who are in need. It is a highly spiritual act of altruism when someone of means has the courage and the generosity to give away his dearest and most precious possessions. It is an act of liberation for the human soul when man rises above worldly desires and materialistic instincts. It is an admirable achievement, which Islam commends and values very highly.

It is characteristic of the Islamic approach that it aims, first and foremost, at liberating man from his own internal prejudices, weaknesses and desires before going on to liberate him from the pressures and influences of the society around him. Unless one

---

3. This is fully discussed in our commentary on the first few verses of this *sūrah*, pp.33–35

overcomes one's own egotism, one is not likely to stand up to evil and temptation in the world outside.

Charity is also a social value that strengthens the bonds of love and trust within the family unit, the vital nucleus of society, and preserves the dignity of its members. Charity towards orphans in society achieves social justice and helps to save the young and the weak from homelessness, corruption and abuse. For the needy and the destitute, charity provides the care and security by which their dignity is preserved, their standing in society may be enhanced, and their contribution to society assured. It ensures that not a single person in the community is lost, or left uncared for. For travellers who, for one reason or another, find themselves stranded in foreign lands or in societies where they feel alienated, charity can be a lifeline. It is an emergency measure to alleviate an unexpected hardship, and by which they are made to feel that they belong to the global human family.

Begging is a practice Islam abhors. It is forbidden to those who can earn a minimum of sustenance or have jobs. Charity by those who have the means aims to stop this evil practice.

Charity has played a vital role in Islam's fight against slavery. It provided the means to free those unfortunate enough to have been taken prisoner in wars against Islam. This is done by either buying slaves to set them free, or by giving a slave money to buy his own freedom, at a price he agrees with his master. Under Islam, slaves became entitled to their freedom as soon as they demanded it, and they were helped to regain their liberty and dignity by allocating them money from charity and *zakāt*. Slaves would then become wage earners, entitled to receive *zakāt*. Every effort would be made to speed up their total freedom.

The verse adds that the regular observance of prayer is another important aspect of righteousness. Prayer is more than a sequence of bodily movements, and there is more to it than facing in a certain direction, east or west. It is more than a simple act of spiritual meditation. Prayer, an act of total submission and dedication to God, epitomizes the entire Islamic outlook on life.

Islam recognizes the human being as a complex entity comprising body, mind and soul, and perceives no contradiction or conflict among their respective roles or needs. It, therefore, sees no need for suppressing the functions or needs of any one of them in order to satisfy any of the others. From this perspective we can clearly see how prayer combines the activity of all three elements in an integrated act of worship dedicated completely to the adoration and glorification of God Almighty. The bodily movements of standing (*qiyām*), bowing (*rukūʿ*) and prostration (*sujūd*), and the recitation of Qur'ānic verses and other prescribed text and the deliberate reflection required on that, and exclusive devotion to God, coalesce beautifully during prayer in a unique and splendid combination. Maintaining this standard in the performance of prayer is a reminder and a fulfilment of the essence and purpose of Islam as a whole.

Paying the *zakāt* duty is another aspect of righteousness. This is a social tax instituted by God Almighty, the ultimate provider, as a token of the entitlement of the poor to a share in the wealth of the rich. It is clear from the text that *zakāt* is separate from, rather than a substitute for, the charitable spending mentioned earlier. While giving to those causes is voluntary, payment of *zakāt* is a religious duty in its own right, and both are essential factors in attaining righteousness. Unless this was the case, obviously there would be no meaning in giving *zakāt* a separate mention in the same verse.

Keeping one's promises is another aspect of righteousness that the Qur'ān frequently highlights as a feature of true faith and humanity. It is a quality that stems from honesty to God and fulfilment of one's promises to Him. Furthermore, it is an essential requirement for creating an environment of mutual trust and confidence among individuals, societies and nations. History will readily testify to the Muslims' impeccable record in honouring agreements, promises and treaties with allies and enemies alike. Islam has given an unparalleled example of integrity that can never be surpassed.

Steadfastness and perseverance in times of adversity and hardship, and in the face of danger, are necessary qualities for the education and development of strong individuals with solid characters who will stand firm, come what may. Under such conditions the faithful never lose hope or confidence in God, nor will they seek help from any source other than Him.

For the Muslim community, or *ummah,* to fulfil its great role of universal leadership of mankind and its task of instituting justice and equality in the world, it is necessary to collectively acquire these qualities. All should have the resilience to withstand poverty, weakness, loss of friends and allies, shortage of manpower and resources, and the rigours and consequences of war and striving to serve God's cause.

The construction of this part of the verse in the Arabic original indicates that this quality is singled out as especially significant in the context of the verse as a whole. This gives added importance and a higher status in the sight of God to those possessing this quality.[4]

Thus we see how, in the inimitable style of the Qur'ān, a single short verse combines the essentials of faith and personal and financial Islamic obligations and presents them as a complete code under the all-embracing title of *al-birr*, which has been variously interpreted as 'righteousness', 'ultimate goodness' or, indeed, 'faith'. It is essentially a concise and complete statement of the basic philosophy of Islam and the principles of the Islamic code of living that must be evident in any Muslim society.

The verse ends with the words: *"Such are those who have proved themselves true, and such are the God-fearing."* (Verse 177) They will have been sincere in their faith and their commitment to God, and they will have proved themselves capable of translating that faith into a practical way of life. They are also God-fearing because they are conscious of God and of their bond with His power and grace, and they are conscientious in fulfilling their obligations towards Him.

In reflecting on the contents of this verse, one can clearly visualize the great heights to which God is aiming to raise human beings through Islam, His constitution. But as one looks at those who ignore Islam, or those who resist it and suppress or persecute its followers and supporters, and those who simply turn away from it, one cannot help being filled with sorrow.

Yet we must not despair. Our faith and trust in God fill our hearts with hope and confidence that the day is coming when humanity will come around to seeing the profound value, universal beauty and eternal qualities of Islam.

4. See the commentary on Verses 153–157 in this volume, pp.190–197

10

Social Justice and Fasting

Believers, just retribution is prescribed for you in cases of killing: a free man for a free man, a slave for a slave, and a female for a female. If something [of his guilt] is remitted to a person by his brother, this shall be pursued with fairness, and restitution to his fellow-man shall be made in a goodly manner. This is an alleviation from your Lord, and an act of His grace. He who transgresses thereafter shall face grievous suffering. (178)

يَٰٓأَيُّهَا ٱلَّذِينَ ءَامَنُوا۟ كُتِبَ عَلَيْكُمُ ٱلْقِصَاصُ
فِى ٱلْقَتْلَى ۖ ٱلْحُرُّ بِٱلْحُرِّ وَٱلْعَبْدُ بِٱلْعَبْدِ وَٱلْأُنثَىٰ
بِٱلْأُنثَىٰ ۚ فَمَنْ عُفِىَ لَهُۥ مِنْ أَخِيهِ شَىْءٌ
فَٱتِّبَاعٌۢ بِٱلْمَعْرُوفِ وَأَدَآءٌ إِلَيْهِ بِإِحْسَٰنٍ ۗ
ذَٰلِكَ تَخْفِيفٌ مِّن رَّبِّكُمْ وَرَحْمَةٌ ۗ فَمَنِ
ٱعْتَدَىٰ بَعْدَ ذَٰلِكَ فَلَهُۥ عَذَابٌ أَلِيمٌ ﴿١٧٨﴾

There is life for you, men of understanding, in this law of just retribution, so that you may remain God-fearing. (179)

وَلَكُمْ فِى ٱلْقِصَاصِ حَيَوٰةٌ يَٰٓأُو۟لِى ٱلْأَلْبَٰبِ
لَعَلَّكُمْ تَتَّقُونَ ﴿١٧٩﴾

It is prescribed for you, when death approaches any of you and he is leaving behind some property, to make bequests in favour of his parents and other near of kin in fairness. This is a duty incumbent on the God-fearing. (180)

كُتِبَ عَلَيْكُمْ إِذَا حَضَرَ أَحَدَكُمُ
ٱلْمَوْتُ إِن تَرَكَ خَيْرًا ٱلْوَصِيَّةُ
لِلْوَٰلِدَيْنِ وَٱلْأَقْرَبِينَ بِٱلْمَعْرُوفِ ۖ
حَقًّا عَلَى ٱلْمُتَّقِينَ ﴿١٨٠﴾

If anyone alters a will after having come to know it, the sin of acting thus shall fall only on those who have altered it. God hears all and knows all. (181)

فَمَنۢ بَدَّلَهُۥ بَعۡدَ مَا سَمِعَهُۥ فَإِنَّمَآ إِثۡمُهُۥ عَلَى ٱلَّذِينَ يُبَدِّلُونَهُۥٓۚ إِنَّ ٱللَّهَ سَمِيعٌ عَلِيمٞ ١٨١

If, however, one fears that the testator has committed a mistake or a wrong, and brings about a settlement between the parties concerned, he will incur no sin thereby. God is indeed much-Forgiving, Merciful. (182)

فَمَنۡ خَافَ مِن مُّوصٖ جَنَفًا أَوۡ إِثۡمٗا فَأَصۡلَحَ بَيۡنَهُمۡ فَلَآ إِثۡمَ عَلَيۡهِۚ إِنَّ ٱللَّهَ غَفُورٞ رَّحِيمٞ ١٨٢

Believers, fasting is decreed for you as it was decreed for those before you, so that you may be God-fearing. (183)

يَٰٓأَيُّهَا ٱلَّذِينَ ءَامَنُواْ كُتِبَ عَلَيۡكُمُ ٱلصِّيَامُ كَمَا كُتِبَ عَلَى ٱلَّذِينَ مِن قَبۡلِكُمۡ لَعَلَّكُمۡ تَتَّقُونَ ١٨٣

[Fast] on a certain number of days. But whoever of you is ill, or on a journey, shall fast instead the same number of days later on. Those who find fasting a strain too hard to bear may compensate for it by feeding a needy person. He who does good of his own account does himself good thereby. For to fast is to do good to yourselves, if you only knew it. (184)

أَيَّامٗا مَّعۡدُودَٰتٖۚ فَمَن كَانَ مِنكُم مَّرِيضًا أَوۡ عَلَىٰ سَفَرٖ فَعِدَّةٞ مِّنۡ أَيَّامٍ أُخَرَۚ وَعَلَى ٱلَّذِينَ يُطِيقُونَهُۥ فِدۡيَةٞ طَعَامُ مِسۡكِينٖۖ فَمَن تَطَوَّعَ خَيۡرٗا فَهُوَ خَيۡرٞ لَّهُۥۚ وَأَن تَصُومُواْ خَيۡرٞ لَّكُمۡ إِن كُنتُمۡ تَعۡلَمُونَ ١٨٤

It was in the month of Ramaḍān that the Qur'ān was revealed: a guidance for mankind and a self-evident proof of that guidance and a standard to distinguish

شَهۡرُ رَمَضَانَ ٱلَّذِيٓ أُنزِلَ فِيهِ ٱلۡقُرۡءَانُ هُدٗى لِّلنَّاسِ وَبَيِّنَٰتٖ

right from wrong. Therefore, whoever of you is present in that month shall fast throughout the month; but he who is ill or on a journey shall fast instead the same number of days later on. God desires that you have ease. He does not desire that you be afflicted with hardship. You are, however, required to complete the necessary number of days and to extol and glorify God for having guided you aright and to tender your thanks. (185)

مِّنَ ٱلْهُدَىٰ وَٱلْفُرْقَانِ ۚ فَمَن شَهِدَ
مِنكُمُ ٱلشَّهْرَ فَلْيَصُمْهُ ۖ وَمَن كَانَ
مَرِيضًا أَوْ عَلَىٰ سَفَرٍ فَعِدَّةٌ مِّنْ أَيَّامٍ
أُخَرَ ۗ يُرِيدُ ٱللَّهُ بِكُمُ ٱلْيُسْرَ وَلَا يُرِيدُ
بِكُمُ ٱلْعُسْرَ وَلِتُكْمِلُوا۟ ٱلْعِدَّةَ
وَلِتُكَبِّرُوا۟ ٱللَّهَ عَلَىٰ مَا هَدَىٰكُمْ
وَلَعَلَّكُمْ تَشْكُرُونَ ﴿١٨٥﴾

If My servants ask you about Me, well, I am near; I answer the prayer of the supplicant when he calls to Me. Let them then respond to Me, and believe in Me, so that they may follow the right way. (186)

وَإِذَا سَأَلَكَ عِبَادِى عَنِّى فَإِنِّى
قَرِيبٌ ۖ أُجِيبُ دَعْوَةَ ٱلدَّاعِ إِذَا دَعَانِ ۖ
فَلْيَسْتَجِيبُوا۟ لِى وَلْيُؤْمِنُوا۟ بِى لَعَلَّهُمْ
يَرْشُدُونَ ﴿١٨٦﴾

It is lawful for you to be intimate with your wives during the night preceding the fast. They are as a garment for you, as you are for them. God is aware that you have been deceiving yourselves in this respect, and He has turned to you in His mercy and pardoned you. So, you may now lie with them and seek what God has ordained for you. Eat and drink until you can see the white streak of dawn against the blackness of the night. Then

أُحِلَّ لَكُمْ لَيْلَةَ ٱلصِّيَامِ ٱلرَّفَثُ إِلَىٰ
نِسَآئِكُمْ ۚ هُنَّ لِبَاسٌ لَّكُمْ وَأَنتُمْ لِبَاسٌ
لَّهُنَّ ۗ عَلِمَ ٱللَّهُ أَنَّكُمْ كُنتُمْ تَخْتَانُونَ
أَنفُسَكُمْ فَتَابَ عَلَيْكُمْ وَعَفَا عَنكُمْ ۖ
فَٱلْـَٔـٰنَ بَـٰشِرُوهُنَّ وَٱبْتَغُوا۟ مَا كَتَبَ ٱللَّهُ
لَكُمْ ۚ وَكُلُوا۟ وَٱشْرَبُوا۟ حَتَّىٰ يَتَبَيَّنَ لَكُمُ ٱلْخَيْطُ
ٱلْأَبْيَضُ مِنَ ٱلْخَيْطِ ٱلْأَسْوَدِ مِنَ ٱلْفَجْرِ ۖ ثُمَّ

resume the fast till nightfall. Do not lie with your wives when you are in retreat in the mosques. These are the bounds set by God, so do not come near them. Thus God makes clear His revelations to people, that they may remain God-fearing. (187)

أَتِمُّوا۟ ٱلصِّيَامَ إِلَى ٱلَّيْلِ ۚ وَلَا تُبَٰشِرُوهُنَّ
وَأَنتُمْ عَٰكِفُونَ فِى ٱلْمَسَٰجِدِ ۗ تِلْكَ حُدُودُ
ٱللَّهِ فَلَا تَقْرَبُوهَا ۗ كَذَٰلِكَ يُبَيِّنُ ٱللَّهُ
ءَايَٰتِهِۦ لِلنَّاسِ لَعَلَّهُمْ يَتَّقُونَ ﴿١٨٧﴾

Do not devour one another's property wrongfully, nor bribe with it the judges in order that you may sinfully, and knowingly, deprive others of any part of what is rightfully theirs. (188)

وَلَا تَأْكُلُوٓا۟ أَمْوَٰلَكُم بَيْنَكُم بِٱلْبَٰطِلِ وَتُدْلُوا۟
بِهَآ إِلَى ٱلْحُكَّامِ لِتَأْكُلُوا۟ فَرِيقًا مِّنْ
أَمْوَٰلِ ٱلنَّاسِ بِٱلْإِثْمِ وَأَنتُمْ تَعْلَمُونَ ﴿١٨٨﴾

Overview

This passage covers a series of instructions relating to the social organization of the Muslim community during its formative period in Madinah. It also introduces certain aspects of Muslim religious worship. The two parts go hand in hand, and are linked with the notion of maintaining a sense of God-fearing, or *taqwā*, which is emphasized towards the end of each part. It is worth recalling that the same feature of *taqwā* was highlighted at the end of the previous verse (177), which outlined the fundamental elements of righteousness, incorporating aspects of faith and practical behaviour.

The passage discusses the legal aspects of just retribution (*qiṣāṣ*) in cases of killing. It outlines rulings on will and inheritance, and outlines provisions relating to fasting, prayer, retirement to a mosque for a certain period of time (*i'tikāf*), and rules governing financial claims.

The outline of each of these and other subjects in the passage is concluded with a direct or an indirect reference to *taqwā*.

This consistent and deliberate approach highlights the essential nature of the religion of Islam. It is an integral system, an indivisible whole. Its social systems, legislative codes, and religious rituals emanate from faith and the comprehensive world order it generates. These are all held together by a common goal of submission to, and veneration of God, the Creator and the Provider, who has instituted man as His vicegerent and custodian in this world. This trusteeship is conditional on man's worship of God alone and on receiving all his concepts, systems and laws from Him only.

The passage is a notable example of the cohesion of the various aspects of Islam.

The Law of Just Retribution

> *Believers, just retribution is prescribed for you in cases of killing: a free man for a free man, a slave for a slave, and a female for a female. If something [of his guilt] is remitted to a person by his brother, this shall be pursued with fairness, and restitution to his fellow-man shall be made in a goodly manner. This is an alleviation from your Lord, and an act of His grace. He who transgresses thereafter shall face grievous suffering. There is life for you, men of understanding, in this law of just retribution, so that you may remain God-fearing.* (Verses 178–179)

The passage begins with an address to the believers, highlighting their main quality of having accepted the faith, which means that they receive their laws from God. They are hereby informed that retribution in cases of killing is permitted to them, in accordance with the provisions laid down in these two verses. They are also called upon to reflect on the purpose and wisdom of this legislation, outlined in the second verse. They are reminded of the need to enhance their sense of God-fearing, which acts as a safety valve against any excess or injustice in punishing those accused of killing.

The statement clearly indicates how retribution ought to be exacted: a free man for a free man, a slave for a slave, a woman for a woman. But *"If something [of his guilt] is remitted to a person by his brother, this shall be pursued with fairness, and restitution to his fellow-man shall be made in a goodly manner."* (Verse 178) This situation would arise when the victim's relatives decide to accept financial compensation instead of insisting on the execution of the killer in retaliation. Once this is agreed, the victim's relatives are also under an obligation to seek a fair and amicable settlement, while the killer's guardian or representative must, on his part, settle readily and honourably. This serves to clear the air and to remove any ill-feelings or grudges that would have inevitably arisen between the two parties. It would also be conducive to a more friendly and pleasant relationship between the living members of both parties.

This provision has been laid down out of God's grace, as a special favour and an act of mercy towards believers: *"This is an alleviation from your Lord, and an act of His grace."* (Verse 178) The concession permitting the settlement of cases of killing by financial compensation paid to the victim's family was not given to the Jews in the Torah. For Islam, it has been set up as an alternative aiming to spare lives when agreement and amicable settlement can be reached.

He who transgresses thereafter shall face grievous suffering." (Verse 178) It is not merely the punishment in the hereafter that is certain to come; such aggression means that capital punishment becomes due and financial compensation no longer accepted. Reneging on the agreement constitutes a violation of the agreed settlement and could only fuel hatred, animosity and a desire for vengeance from both sides. Therefore, when the victim's closest relatives have accepted blood money, they can no longer seek retaliation by killing the killer.

We can appreciate the profound wisdom of the Islamic approach and its respect for, and understanding of, human nature and motivation. Islam recognizes anger as a very basic human reaction when one's relative is killed, and Islam satisfies this desire by legislating for just retribution in this way. Rigorous justice cools tempers and helps to remove grudges and deter the killer from offending again.

At the same time, however, Islam holds out the prospect of pardon and opens the way for mutual agreement, defining precisely the principles and rules which govern it. Islam advocates that the alternative of pardon should, therefore, come as a voluntary option accepted by both sides out of a genuine desire for reconciliation, rather than having it forced upon them.

Some commentators consider that this ruling was cancelled and superseded by that given in Verse 45 of *Sūrah* 5, which provides for retribution on the basis of *"a life for a life, an eye for an eye, a nose for a nose, an ear for an ear, a tooth for a tooth, and a similar retribution for wounds."* In his commentary on the Qur'ān, Ibn Kathīr quotes Sa'īd ibn Jubayr, an early scholar, explaining that the present verse was revealed with reference to fighting that broke out between two Arab clans, shortly before the advent of Islam, leading to widespread bloodshed on both sides. Among those killed were several slaves and women, but the dispute was not settled until much later, after both clans had embraced Islam. Excessive claims were made by both clans, demanding that a free man be killed for a slave and a man for a woman. They could not reach a settlement until this verse was revealed. But this verse has, in turn, been superseded by Verse 45 of *Sūrah* 5 revealed at a later date. The same version is supported in a report by Abū Mālik.

Nevertheless, it seems to me that the two verses are dealing with different aspects of the same issue, retribution for killing. Verse 5: 45, stating equal retribution is applicable in cases of premeditated murder of one specific person, or group of persons, by another, in which case conviction entails capital punishment. The verse we are discussing here, however, covers situations of assault by a group such as when a family, clan or community attacks another, as happened between those two Arab clans. As and when such conflicts come to be settled, just retribution would require that a free man be set against a free man, a slave against a slave, and a woman against a woman. How else in such cases, one may ask, can justice be seen to be done?

If this view is correct, then there is no conflict between the two verses, and the rulings of each remain valid without one superseding or replacing the other.

Revealing the profound wisdom underlying this ruling, and its objectives, the verse ends with the words: *"There is life for you, men of understanding, in this law of just retribution, so that you may remain God-fearing."* (Verse 179)

Vengeance, or the satisfaction of grudges, is not the prime goal of this legislation. Its objective is to promote and preserve human life. Furthermore, there is an invitation to reflect on the wisdom of this code and an endeavour to raise believers' consciousness and fear of God.

Life Preservation through Retribution

This is achieved by providing strong deterrence, preventing further crimes from being committed. When a person knows for certain that the price he will pay for committing murder is his own life, he is more likely to stop and think before deciding to go ahead. Life is also preserved by giving satisfaction to the victim's relatives in exacting justice on the offender, with the effect that they will neither seek, nor have the right to seek, further revenge on the offender's family. In pre-Islamic Arabia the desire for vengeance knew no limits, leading to protracted wars and conflicts that continued for years on end – the notorious al-Basūs[1] wars lasted, on and off, for forty years. There were other family, tribal and clan feuds in which vendettas and bloodshed continued for generations.

The law of just retribution promotes life in a wider and more comprehensive sense. Murder is an aggression on life and a criminal act against humanity as a whole. In preventing a single murder from being committed, the law upholds the inviolability of life as an absolute value. This is a far higher goal than saving the life of an individual or a group of people. It is a goal that enshrines life.

More importantly, the verse urges believers to reflect deeply on this matter and discover the wisdom behind the code, in order *"that you may remain God-fearing"*.

This is the real deterrent that can prevent murder being committed in the first instance, and stop vendettas being pursued endlessly. Without this measure of deterrence, no law can be successfully upheld and crime can never be effectively rooted out. Laws and regulations that lack such sensitivity, or do not evoke in people the fear and respect of an authority higher and more powerful than the human one, are inadequate and ineffective.

This explains the remarkably small number of cases in which capital punishment was carried out during the Prophet Muḥammad's era and that of his early successors. In most of those cases, conviction was based on confessions voluntarily made by the offenders themselves. Fear and consciousness of God, *taqwā*, were evident in the public conscience which, together with enlightened and wise legislation, served as a most effective deterrent. Legal codes and regulations were supplemented by religious discipline, education and exhortation to produce a balanced and virtuous society, with clear concepts of responsibility and justice.

The renowned contemporary scholar, Abū al-Ḥasan ʿAlī Nadwī puts it thus:

---

1. Al-Basūs is the name given to a series of tribal conflicts which took place in pre-Islamic Arabia, and continued sporadically over a period of some forty years.

> If anyone ever succumbed to beastly urges and fell into error, even though unobserved, he would make a confession thereof straightaway before the Prophet and undergo the severest punishment willingly to save himself from Divine Displeasure.[2]

The next piece of legislation introduced in the *sūrah* relates to personal wills: *"It is prescribed for you, when death approaches any of you and he is leaving behind some property, to make bequests in favour of his parents and other near of kin in fairness. This is a duty incumbent on the God-fearing. If anyone alters a will after having come to know it, the sin of acting thus shall fall only on those who have altered it. God hears all and knows all. If, however, one fears that the testator has committed a mistake or a wrong, and brings about a settlement between the parties concerned, he will incur no sin thereby. God is indeed much-forgiving, merciful."* (Verses 180–182)

Before the revelation of the verses in *Sūrah* 5 specifying the exact share of inheritance due to each heir, it was an incumbent duty on Muslims to make a will in favour of parents and other near of kin. The Arabic term *khayr*, translated here as "property", also means "good" and "goodness", and some commentators interpret it to denote wealth generally.

Scholars differ, however, as to the minimum amount of wealth for which drawing up a will becomes obligatory. The majority view is that this is decided by convention. Assets ranging in value between sixty and a thousand dīnārs have been mentioned, but surely this must differ from one generation to another and from one society to another.

The Qur'ānic verses, 4: 11, 12 and 176, specifying shares for the distribution of inheritance were revealed at a later date than those under discussion here. Those verses make parents legally entitled to specific shares of their departed children's wealth. Hence, no bequest by will may be made to them. The Prophet established the rule that no will may be made in favour of an heir. As for other relatives the present rule holds in general terms, except for relatives who are named as heirs in the relevant verses on inheritance in *Sūrah* 4. All other

2. Abū al-Ḥasan 'Alī Nadwī, *Islam and the World*. Academy of Islamic Research and Publications, Lucknow, 1980, p.56

non-inheriting relatives may be included in a will. This is the view of a number of the Prophet's Companions and their successors, to which we subscribe.

The provision of including non-inheriting relatives in one's will is extremely perceptive because it benefits, in particular, those relatives who are not assigned a share or entitled to any inheritance. Providing for them through a will strengthens family ties and promotes the welfare of the family.

In this way equitable distribution of wealth is guaranteed: heirs are not wronged, and other relatives are not ignored. A will should be made combining moderation, kindness and benevolence. As an additional measure, the Prophet specified that a maximum of one-third, and preferably a quarter, of the inheritance may be bequeathed by will. This ensures that the rights of natural heirs are not unfavourably affected by the will. These legal measures are reinforced, as is the case with all social legislation in Islam, by a positive fear and consciousness of God Almighty.

Anyone having knowledge of the contents of a will who, after the death of the testator, gives himself the right to alter any of its details will be guilty of grave misconduct. The deceased would bear no blame for such unauthorized alteration. *"If anyone alters a will after having come to know it, the sin of acting thus shall fall only on those who have altered it. God hears all and knows all."* (Verse 181) God will be the witness to the deceased's innocence as well as to the guilt of those who tamper with the will, and He will deal with each of them accordingly.

There is, however, one exceptional situation in which an executor may amend the contents of a will. This arises when the executor realizes that the will favours some beneficiaries at the expense of others or that it prejudices one or more of the heirs. *"If, however, one fears that the testator has committed a mistake or a wrong, and brings about a settlement between the parties concerned, he will incur no sin thereby. God is indeed much-Forgiving, Merciful."* (Verse 182) Here again, the action is closely linked to how conscientious and God-fearing the people involved are. This quality, as we saw earlier in our discussion of just retribution, is the basis of the Islamic concepts of justice and honesty, and of public responsibility in an Islamic society.

Fasting: Its Nature and Purpose

For the Muslim community, or *ummah,* duty-bound to undertake a campaign of struggle, i.e. *jihād,* as a means of establishing God's universal order, to assume the leadership of mankind, and to stand witness against the rest of mankind, it is only natural that fasting should be made obligatory. Fasting is a means of testing man's determination and will-power, and an important aspect of man's relationship with God. It is a discipline that teaches man how to rise above his physical needs and overcome the pressure of temptation in order to earn God's blessings and reward.

These are essential ingredients for the discipline and training of the believers so that they may carry God's message forward despite the temptations, the obstacles and hardships they are bound to encounter.

Although I am not in favour of justifying religious obligations and practices, especially in matters of worship, on the grounds of their immediate material benefits, which become apparent with experience or through scientific discovery, I would not deny that fasting has several obvious health benefits. But in my view, the whole purpose underlying religious obligations is far greater and more comprehensive than any physical advantages gained from them. The overall aim is to adequately equip man for the fulfilment of his role in this world and for the perfection he is intended to achieve in the life to come.

It is obvious that all religious practices and obligations are ordained by God with full consideration of man's physical needs and capabilities, but we should not justify them solely on the basis of what our knowledge, limited as it is, may discover. The scope of human knowledge remains limited and incapable of comprehending the divine wisdom behind the order and the system God has chosen for the discipline of man and the administration of the universe as a whole.

> *Believers, fasting is decreed for you as it was decreed for those before you, so that you may be God-fearing. [Fast] on a certain number of days. But whoever of you is ill, or on a journey, shall fast instead the same number of days later on. Those who find fasting a strain too hard to bear may compensate for it by feeding a needy person. He who does good of his own account does himself good thereby. For to fast is to do good to yourselves, if you only knew it.*

It was in the month of Ramaḍān that the Qur'ān was revealed: a guidance for mankind and a self-evident proof of that guidance and a standard to distinguish right from wrong. Therefore, whoever of you is present in that month shall fast throughout the month; but he who is ill or on a journey shall fast instead the same number of days later on. God desires that you have ease. He does not desire that you be afflicted with hardship. You are, however, required to complete the necessary number of days and to extol and glorify God for having guided you aright and to tender your thanks. (Verses 183–185)

This important announcement begins by addressing believers directly to remind them of who they are and of their status with God. God is aware that for believers to fulfil any religious obligation, regardless of its immediate benefits, they need encouragement and motivation. Hence they are addressed by their essential quality of having faith.

The verse establishes that fasting had been made obligatory for earlier believers, and that the aim behind it is to open their hearts to God and make them more conscious of Him. This, then, is the principal objective of fasting: to be God-fearing, or *taqwā*. Fasting, when observed in obedience to God and in pursuit of His pleasure, instils and revives this quality in the human heart and acts as a safeguard against evil and wrongdoing. True believers know and appreciate the value of being God-fearing in God's sight. Hence, they constantly seek to enhance their sense of it. Fasting is a means to achieve just that.

Fasting is prescribed for a specific number of days. It is not required the whole year round. Nevertheless, those who are ill or travelling are exempt from fasting until they recover or return home.

On the face of it, the type and extent of the illness and the travel to which the exemption applies are left unqualified. Therefore, any kind of illness or travel would exempt one from fasting, provided one makes up for it at some other time, after one has recovered or returned home. This would seem to be the most appropriate interpretation of the Qur'ānic statement, truly reflecting the overriding Islamic objective of mitigating hardship and relieving discomfort. The concession is not conditional on either the severity of the illness or on how arduous the journey is, because in all cases people should not have to undergo any undue strain as a result of fasting.

There could be other considerations, known only to God, for leaving the conditions so general. Fasting during illness or in the course of a journey could result in hardship or adverse effects that human beings cannot foresee or predict. We take the ruling as it is stated, in the certain belief that there are valid reasons behind it.

Some people may fear that such a view may encourage a more lax attitude that could lead to abuse of such concessions, rendering them an easy excuse for neglecting religious observances and practices. This concern is said to account for the strict terms set by Muslim scholars on the use of these concessions, but it should not, in my view, justify the need to restrict an unqualified Qur'ānic ruling such as the one under discussion.

Islam does not lead people to obedience by force. It guides them through their consciousness of God, which is the ultimate objective in this particular case. Those who use concessions to evade religious obligation merely bring their own faith under suspicion, because their attitude negates the very purpose of the obligation.

Above all, it is important to keep in mind that Islam is a religion laid down by God not by man, and He is best aware of how much tightening or relaxation is prudent in fulfilling its obligations. It must be the case, then, that a concession can under certain circumstances serve a particular purpose far more effectively than would strict adherence to the rule. From this we find that the Prophet Muḥammad instructed Muslims to avail themselves of the concessions and exemptions God has allowed them.

If it so happens that in certain generations people's behaviour tends to become corrupt, reform will not be achieved through a stricter application of religious rules. A better chance of reform would come through enlightenment, education and motivation in order to instil the quality of fearing God in people's hearts.

At times of social decline, a stricter application of religious rules would, indeed, be desirable as a deterrent in matters relating to public or collective behaviour. But the fulfilment of personal religious obligations is largely a matter between God and each individual, with little or no direct influence on the public interest. In public duties – unlike personal religious duties which are based on faith – appearance and form have considerable significance. Once *taqwā,* or the fear of God, takes its roots, one would not resort to concessions except when absolutely necessary, and with a clear conscience. A concession is thus exercised only when one is fully satisfied that it is conducive to achieving a higher degree of obedience to God.

Strictness in the application of the rules relating to acts of worship generally, and the tendency to restrict unqualified exemptions, can be counter-productive. Besides causing hardship and discomfort, they have little effect in dissuading those who want to evade the rules. It is far more appropriate to approach Islam and understand it within the terms and the framework in which it is presented by God, who is wiser and more aware of all the advantages to be gained from fulfilling its obligations.

Exemption from Fasting when Travelling

A number of reported incidents illustrate the Prophet's attitude towards the exemption from fasting in Ramaḍān while travelling. These give us a glimpse of how the early Muslims received and implemented such rules, long before scholars introduced legal technicalities. These reports reflect a realistic and dynamic approach to Islam which gives it, and life under it, a vigorous and agreeable meaning.

1. Jābir reports that it was in the month of Ramaḍān that the Prophet left Madinah for Makkah, the year it fell to Islam. He observed the fast until he reached Kurā' al-Ghamīm, and so did those who marched with him. Then he called for a glass of water, raised it for everyone to see, and drank from it. Later he was told that some people continued to fast. He said, "They are disobedient! They are disobedient!" [Related by Muslim and al-Tirmidhī]

2. Anas reports: "A group of us were once travelling with the Prophet in Ramaḍān. Some of us were fasting and some were not. On a hot day, we stopped to rest, with little or no shade available. The one who had maximum shade was a person who had a shirt to cover himself. Some used their hands as a cover from the sun. Those who were fasting collapsed of exhaustion while those who were not pitched the tents and gave water to the animals. Commenting, the Prophet said: "Those who are not fasting have run away with the whole reward today." [Related by al-Bukhārī, Muslim and al-Nasā'ī]

3. Jābir reports: "Once on a journey, the Prophet saw a group of people gathered to shade a fellow traveller. When he enquired what

was wrong with him, he was told that the man was fasting. The Prophet said, "It is not righteous to fast while on a journey." [Related by Mālik, al-Bukhārī, Muslim, Abū Dāwūd and al-Nasā'ī]

4. 'Amr ibn Umayyah al-Ḍamarī reports: "On arriving from a journey, I reported to the Prophet who invited me to stay for lunch. I apologised because I was fasting. The Prophet said, 'Then let me tell you about the traveller: God has exempted him from fasting and half his prayers.'" [Related by al-Nasā'ī]

5. A man from the clan of 'Abdullāh ibn Ka'b ibn Mālik, called Anas ibn Mālik, quotes the Prophet as saying, "God has reduced the prayer for the traveller by half and exempted him from fasting. He has also exempted from fasting the nursing mother and the pregnant woman if they fear for their babies" [Related by Abū Dāwūd, al-Tirmidhī, al-Nasā'ī and Ibn Mājah]

6. 'Ā'ishah reports that Ḥamzah ibn 'Amr al-Aslamī, who was frequently fasting, once asked the Prophet about fasting while travelling, to which the Prophet replied: "You may fast if you wish, or you may not." [Related by Mālik, al-Bukhārī, Muslim, Abū Dāwūd, al-Tirmidhī and al-Nasā'ī] Another version of this *ḥadīth* describes the man as 'one who had no difficulty with fasting'.

7. Anas reports: "A group of us were travelling with the Prophet: some were fasting and others were not. No fasting person criticized anyone for not fasting, nor did any criticize others for fasting." [Related by Mālik, al-Bukhārī, Muslim and Abū Dāwūd]

8. Abū al-Dardā' reports: "We travelled with the Prophet one very hot day in Ramaḍān. We would even cover our heads with our hands because of the instense heat. None of us was fasting except the Prophet and Ibn Rawāḥah." [Related by al-Bukhārī, Muslim and Abū Dāwūd]

9. Muḥammad ibn Ka'b reports: "I went in Ramaḍān to see Anas ibn Mālik as he was about to leave on a journey. When Anas was dressed and had his horse saddled and ready, he requested some food and ate. I asked whether this was the practice of the Prophet. Anas said, 'Yes.'" [Related by al-Tirmidhī]

10. 'Ubayd ibn Jubayr reports: "I was travelling from Fusṭāṭ by boat during Ramaḍān with Abū Baṣrah al-Ghifārī, a Companion of the Prophet (peace be upon him). As he set off on his journey, Abū Baṣrah asked for lunch to be brought to him. He said to me, 'Come

and join me.' I said, 'We can still see the buildings on the shore,' (meaning they had not gone past the city, as they were travelling in the Nile). Abū Baṣrah said, 'Are you unwilling to follow the Prophet's example, or *sunnah*?' He then started eating and I joined him." [Related by Abū Dāwūd]

11. Manṣūr al-Kalbī reports that Diḥyah ibn Khalīfah, a Companion of the Prophet, was travelling a distance of about five kilometres from a suburb of Damascus during Ramaḍān. Neither did he fast, nor did many of the people with him. Some, however, were reluctant to break the fast. When he returned to his home village, Diḥyah said, "By God, I have today seen something I thought I would never see: people unwilling to follow the example of God's Messenger and his Companions. My Lord, gather me to You!" [Related by Abū Dāwūd]

Taken together, these reports support the view that the option of not fasting while on a journey ought to be taken unconditionally to alleviate hardship. This is particularly clear in the last two reports. The incident reported by Abū al-Dardā', which relates that the Prophet and only one of his Companions continued to fast despite the severe heat, should be taken as an exceptional case. In certain religious matters, the Prophet was known to commit himself to a much more rigorous discipline than he would recommend to his Companions. He, for example, ordered that no one should fast two days running without the normal night break. Yet, he did so on some occasions. When he was asked about that, he said: "I am not like you; my Lord feeds me and gives me to drink." [Related by al-Bukhārī and Muslim] The first report cited above clearly shows that the Prophet broke his fast and described those who continued to fast as 'disobedient'. The incident happened around the time of the conquest of Makkah, which occurred towards the end of the Prophet's life. Hence, this *ḥadīth* is a better pointer to the option preferred by the Prophet.

The common thread in all these incidents is that in issuing any directive, mitigating circumstances are always taken into account. This is so whenever several *aḥadīth* referring to the same subject seem to point in different directions. The Prophet Muḥammad was a leader and a teacher dealing with real situations and giving practical rulings and solutions in each case.

As far as fasting while travelling is concerned, one gets the distinct impression that the ruling is strongly in favour of exemption from fasting without restricting the exemption to cases of hardship. As for the licence to break the fast during illness, apart from the different opinions of scholars, it also seems to be granted unconditionally and without qualification. Implicit in this ruling is the requirement that the missing days must be compensated for at a later date, with no requirement to make the compensatory fasting days consecutive.

The purpose of this detailed discussion and quotations is not to get involved in any legal discussion, but to highlight two important aspects in understanding rulings relevant to matters of personal worship. A paramount objective is to create a healthy attitude, in order to cultivate the worshipper's conscience, improve his performance, and raise the standards of his behaviour in life generally. Another consideration is that Islam must be adopted in its totality and as God has intended. All its instructions, the hard as well as the lenient, must be accepted in equal measure. They should be taken in total confidence in God's mercy and wisdom, always aiming to enhance our God-fearing sense.

Obligatory Fasting

Fasting was made obligatory for Muslims in the second year after the *Hijrah*, i.e. the Prophet's migration from Makkah to Madinah (which was to become the start of the Islamic lunar calendar). Thus, the obligation of fasting was decreed shortly before the ordinance of *jihād*, or striving for God's cause. As a new duty, fasting was at first hard for the Muslims to observe. Those who found it too strenuous were, therefore, given a concession, requiring them instead to feed one needy person for every day of fasting they miss. A general recommendation to feed the needy is then made, either as a voluntary act in itself or by feeding more than the minimum number of needy people in lieu of fasting. *"He who does good of his own account does himself good thereby."* (Verse 184) This is followed by the recommendation that, apart from cases of illness or travel, fasting would be more beneficial and preferable despite the hardship or discomfort it might cause: *"For to fast is to do good to yourselves, if you only knew it."* (Verse 184) There is here an obvious element of education and training of will-power to enable Muslims to make the effort to fast. This also highlights the health benefits of fasting, in spite of the strain, all of which are important factors in the Islamic self-education process.

These recommendations were a step towards the withdrawal of the exemption for non-travelling healthy people and making fasting in the month of Ramaḍān obligatory, as given in verse 185. The concession remained valid for elderly people who find fasting in Ramaḍān too strenuous and are not expected to be able to fast at a later date.

Imām Mālik reports that Anas ibn Mālik, a Companion of the Prophet Muḥammad, lived to a very advanced age and was not able to keep the fast. He used to compensate by feeding poor people instead. 'Abdullāh ibn 'Abbās, a cousin and learned Companion of the Prophet, was of the opinion that the exemption has not been completely abrogated by the ruling of verse 185; it remains applicable to the elderly who are not able to keep the fast.

Ibn Abī Laylā, a prominent scholar, says that he visited 'Aṭā' one day in Ramaḍān and found him eating. "'Aṭā' told me that, according to Ibn 'Abbās, the ruling of verse 185 superseded that of the one before it with respect to healthy non-travelling people, but the elderly were free not to fast if they fed instead one needy person for every day."

Fasting was made more appealing due to the fact that it is observed in Ramaḍān, the month in which the Qur'ān was revealed. This could be a reference to the fact that it was first revealed during Ramaḍān, or that most of it was revealed in it. It is a significant distinction since the Qur'ān is the definitive and timeless Book of the Muslim community, its guiding light, the source of its strength and security, from which it has drawn all the enduring qualities and elements that have made it great. Without the gifts that the Qur'ān has given the Muslim community, it would have become forgotten history long ago. As a token of gratitude to God Almighty, Muslims observe the fast in the month of Ramaḍān during which the Qur'ān was revealed.

> *It was in the month of Ramaḍān that the Qur'ān was revealed: a guidance for mankind and a self-evident proof of that guidance and a standard to distinguish right from wrong. Therefore, whoever of you is present in that month shall fast throughout the month; but he who is ill or on a journey shall fast instead the same number of days later on.* (Verse 185)

This verse establishes fasting in Ramaḍān as obligatory for all healthy non-travelling Muslims, with no concessions except for the elderly, as pointed out above: *"Whoever of you is present in that month shall fast throughout the month."* It has thus become binding on all Muslims who either see the new moon of the lunar month of Ramaḍān themselves or learn of it by any other reliable means, to observe the fast in Ramaḍān. But as this is a general order applicable to all, a reiteration of the concession given in special cases immediately follows: *"But he who is ill or on a journey shall fast instead the same number of days later on."*

The *sūrah* gives the Muslims yet another incentive to keep the fast: *"God desires that you have ease. He does not desire that you be afflicted with hardship."* (Verse 185) This statement encapsulates the fundamental principle on which all Islamic religious duties are founded. They are intended to be easy, not arduous. This indicates a generous and realistic outlook on life as a whole. It instils in the Muslim heart a tolerant, easy and agreeable attitude. Religious and social activities and responsibilities are discharged with ease, confidence and assurance, in the happy knowledge that God's purpose is to enable man to go through life with the minimum of hardship or discomfort.

To complete a whole month, sick people or those who travel in Ramaḍān and avail themselves of the special concession are required to make up for days missed by fasting an equal number of days at a later date in the year: *"You are, however, required to complete the necessary number of days."* (Verse 185)

Fasting is an occasion to celebrate God's guidance, glory and grace. Hence the requirement *"to extol and glorify God for having guided you aright and to tender your thanks."* (Verse 185) It is a time during which believers can feel and appreciate God's favours and reciprocate with thanks, submission and gratitude. In so doing, Muslims cultivate the precious and vital quality of *taqwā*, or God-fearing; a main objective of fasting.

Thus we can see how evident God's grace is in the imposition of the duty of fasting which, on the face of it, seems hard and demanding. We can clearly see its educational and disciplinary benefits for a nation being prepared for the leadership of mankind, guided by a genuine fear of God, a keen sense of accountability, and a vigorous conscience.

A Close Relationship with God

Interposed among the verses dealing with fasting comes a verse reflecting a profound insight into human nature. It reaches to the deepest recesses of the human psyche, offering solace and ample rewards for keeping the fast in response to God's commands: *"If My servants ask you about Me, well, I am near; I answer the prayer of the supplicant when he calls to Me. Let them then respond to Me, and believe in Me, so that they may follow the right way."* (Verse 186)

How kind and compassionate God truly is! Any hardship encountered in keeping the fast fades in comparison with this friendly and gentle reassurance. The choice of words creates an atmosphere of intimacy and accessibility, with God Himself stating a direct contact between Him and His servants. He does not give instructions to His Messenger, the Prophet Muḥammad on how to answer believers' questions about Him. He gives the answer Himself: *"I am near."* His closeness is not only to listen but also for immediate response: *"I answer the prayer of the supplicant when he calls to Me."* (Verse 186)

This verse fills a believer's heart with love, confidence and utter reassurance. In this atmosphere of friendliness and compassion, God, who has no need for anyone, directs believers to respond to Him and believe in Him, in the hope that this will guide them to wisdom and righteousness. *"Let them then respond to Me, and believe in Me, so that they may follow the right way."* (Verse 186) By earning God's generosity and guidance, believers end up winners on all counts.

Belief in God and response to His commands lead to true guidance. The way of life God has ordained for man is the only one truly worthy of adoption and adherence; all other ideologies lead only to ruin and frustration. When one responds to God's call, one must be confident that God will answer one's prayers (*du'ā'*). However, one should not hasten God's response, for He alone decides the most appropriate time to respond.

Salmān, the Persian, a Companion of the Prophet, quotes the Prophet as saying: "God would not like to see His servant holding out his arms pleading for help and turn him away empty handed." [Related by Abū Dāwūd, al-Tirmidhī and Ibn Mājah]

'Ubādah ibn al-Ṣāmit quotes the Prophet as saying: "God shall answer the prayer (*du'ā'*) of any Muslim anywhere on earth, or He will protect him against contrasting harm, as long as he does not ask for something evil or for the break-up of kinship relations." [Related by al-Tirmidhī on ibn Thawbān's authority and by ʿAbdullāh ibn Imām Aḥmad]

The Prophet is also reported to have said: "Your prayers shall be answered as long as you remain patient. Do not say, 'I have prayed but my prayer has never been answered!'" [Related by al-Bukhārī and Muslim]

He is also reported as saying: "Prayers [*duʿā'*] shall be answered unless one asks for something evil or the break-up of kinship relations, and as long as one does not become impatient." When the Prophet was asked to explain how one becomes impatient, he said: "One says, 'I have prayed many times but I have had no response,' then gives up hope and abandons praying [*duʿā'*] altogether." [Related by Muslim]

A fasting person has the best chance of his prayers being answered. Abū Dāwūd al-Ṭayālisī relates on the authority of ʿAbdullāh ibn ʿUmar that the Prophet said: "The prayer a fasting person says at the time when he is about to finish his fast shall be answered." Accordingly, ʿAbdullāh ibn ʿUmar, a learned Companion of the Prophet, used to gather his family together when breaking the fast and pray.

Ibn Mājah also relates a *ḥadīth* in which ʿAbdullāh ibn ʿUmar quoted the Prophet as saying: "On breaking the fast, the prayer of a fasting person is never turned down." This is supported by a *ḥadīth* in which Abū Hurayrah quotes the Prophet as saying: "Prayers by three people shall never be turned down: a just ruler, a fasting person until he breaks the fast, and the oppressed for whose prayer [*duʿā'*] the gates of heaven shall be opened wide and God shall say to him, 'By My power, I shall support you, even though it may be in due course.'" [Related by Imām Aḥmad, al-Tirmidhī, al-Nasā'ī and Ibn Mājah]

From these reports one can clearly see the close relationship between prayer and fasting.

Further Rules on Fasting

The *sūrah* then resumes its elaboration on the rules of fasting. It points out that, in addition to food and drink, married Muslims are permitted sexual intimacy with their spouses between sunset and dawn. It gives the exact time for the fasting which extends from dawn till sunset. It points out that during any period when people retire to a mosque for worship in Ramaḍān, i.e. *i'tikāf,* sexual intimacy is not permitted for married people.

> *It is lawful for you to be intimate with your wives during the night preceding the fast. They are as a garment for you, as you are for them. God is aware that you have been deceiving yourselves in this respect, and He has turned to you in His mercy and pardoned you. So, you may now lie with them and seek what God has ordained for you. Eat and drink until you can see the white streak of dawn against the blackness of the night. Then resume the fast till nightfall. Do not lie with your wives when you are in retreat in the mosques. These are the bounds set by God, so do not come near them. Thus God makes clear His revelations to people, that they may remain God-fearing.* (Verse 187)

When fasting was first instituted, once one got to sleep at night, one would not eat, drink or have sexual intercourse with his wife, even if one woke up before dawn. It so happened that some Muslims did not have anything to eat at the time of the evening meal. One person was overtaken by sleep before he could eat anything and had to fast the following day as well, which made the fast arduous. Likewise, some were inclined to have sexual intercourse and did so. The Prophet became acutely aware of the hardship the Muslims were experiencing. Soon afterwards, God eased the situation by revealing this verse as a token of His mercy and benevolence.

"It is lawful for you to be intimate with your wives during the night preceding the fast." (Verse 187) The Arabic expression translated here as 'to be intimate with one's wife' denotes the preliminaries of sex, or denotes sexual intercourse. In fact, both are intended here and made lawful. However, in setting out this rule, God does not overlook to describe the marital relationship in transparent and compassionate terms: *"They are as a garment for you, as you are for them."* The word used to describe the marital relationship in the Arabic original is *libās,* literally meaning garment. Marriage does indeed cover and protect both spouses. Islam fully takes into account man's natural drives, instincts and desires. It elevates man, treating him as one integral entity. Accordingly, Islam responds to the needs of the flesh, incorporating them into a decent and virtuous context.

The verse reveals the fact that some Muslims were finding it difficult to suppress their natural sexual desires, and some were even breaking the rules: *"God is aware that you have been deceiving yourselves in this respect, and He has turned to you in His mercy and pardoned you."* (Verse 187) The self deception mentioned here refers to suppressed desires, or to the breach of the rules, as happened in some cases. Whichever was the case, the Qur'ān affirms that God understood their weaknesses and forgave them. New rules are laid down: *"You may now lie with them and seek what God has ordained for you."* (Verse 187) It tells the Muslims that they are allowed to enjoy the intimacy of their spouses to satisfy their craving and to seek offspring, both of which are legitimate aspects of the relationship.

Thus, marriage is given a much wider dimension and higher objectives, over and above the mere satisfaction of the carnal sexual desire. It assumes an honourable status that must be cherished, treasured and protected.

These hints that the Qur'ān gives from time to time indicate the credit that should be given to the effort Islam dedicates to raising man's moral and ethical standards within the parameters of his human nature and disposition. This is what makes Islam such a unique, practical and effective way for education and development. It is, after all, God's way.

The verse goes on to define the parts of the day and night allocated for fasting and eating, respectively, which, when taken with reports from the Prophet's own practice, indicate that fasting begins not long before sunrise. However, it seems to me that we, in Egypt, start fasting sometime before it is due, perhaps as a precautionary measure.

Ibn Jarīr relates on the authority of Samurah ibn Jundub who quotes the Prophet as saying: "Do not take much heed of Bilāl's call for dawn Prayer or this whiteness; do not start the fast until dawn breaks fully." Another version quotes the Prophet as saying: "Do not abstain from eating if you hear Bilāl calling for the dawn Prayer, or when you see the elongated dawn light. But begin the fast when the dawn spreads over the horizon." This means the light spreading in the eastern sky a short while before sunrise. It is also important to recall here that Bilāl used to raise the call to prayer early to wake people up, while Ibn Umm Maktūm used to make a second call at a later time to indicate the beginning of the fast. Hence, the Prophet clarifies the point of starting the fast.

The *sūrah* then instructs the Muslims not to lie with their wives when they decide to retreat in the mosques. This is a reference to a special practice known in Arabic as *i'tikāf*. It is an act of devotion involving a stay in the mosque for several days during the last ten days of the month of Ramaḍān, for prolonged Prayer, recitation of the Qur'ān, reflection and spiritual rejuvenation. Once one decides to observe *i'tikāf*, one will only go home when it is necessary. The Prophet was known to observe this practice during the last ten days of the month. To enhance their sense of devotion and enable them to concentrate their hearts and minds on the worship of God during such retreat, or *i'tikāf*, Muslims are barred from sexual intercourse with their wives during such period.

The *sūrah* then links these rules and instructions directly with God, emphasizing that: *"These are the bounds set by God, so do not come near them."* (Verse 187) Although the Qur'ān uses the words *"come near"*, the warning is against the violation of these bounds. But a margin of safety has to be maintained, because man cannot always rely on his moral strength and self-control. It is far better to keep away from evil rather than walk into it, over-confident of resisting, and then failing to do so. Prudence is liable to develop and cultivate that very precious quality of God-fearing, one of the most fundamental goals the Qur'ān is coaching man to attain in his life: *"Thus God makes clear His revelations to people, that they may remain God-fearing."* (Verse 187)

Honesty at All Times

Within this context of fasting and abstention from food and drink, the *sūrah* sounds another warning, this time against usurping other people's possessions. The verse refers specifically to presenting false and fraudulent evidence before a judge or an arbiter in order to obtain a favourable judgement giving one the right to appropriate someone else's property. To reinforce the sense of deterrence, the warning follows immediately after reference to the bounds set by God and the call for more consciousness and fear of Him.

> *Do not devour one another's property wrongfully, nor bribe with it the judges in order that you may sinfully, and knowingly, deprive others of any part of what is rightfully theirs.* (Verse 188)

Commenting on this verse, Ibn Kathīr cites a report by Alī ibn Abī Ṭalḥah who quotes Ibn ʿAbbās, a cousin and Companion of the Prophet, as saying that the verse refers to someone owing money to another. Knowing that the creditor has no document to prove the debt, the debtor denies liability altogether. He would then put the matter before a judge, knowing very well that he is in the wrong, taking what is unlawful to him, and has no case whatsoever. He adds that Mujāhid, Saʿīd ibn Jubayr, ʿIkrimah, al-Ḥasan, Qatādah, al-Suddī, Muqātil ibn Ḥayyān, and ʿAbd al-Raḥmān ibn Zayd ibn Aslam have all warned against contesting a dispute when one knows oneself to be in the wrong. Ibn Kathīr also refers to accounts in al-Bukhārī and Muslim in which Umm Salamah quotes the Prophet as saying: "I am only human. When you come to me for judgement, some of you may have a clearer piece of evidence, and I might be inclined to rule in their favour. If I give someone anything which is not rightly his, it would be as if I have given him a brand of fire; it is up to him to take it or leave it."

Judges decide on *prima facie* evidence, and the onus of honesty is on the litigants. They are left to their own conscience.

Thus we can see how this matter is also closely linked to *taqwā*, or the sense of God-fearing, as was just retribution and fasting before it. These rulings represent parts of a harmonious and divinely-ordained way of life, firmly bound together in a common framework of maintaining the fear of God, or *taqwā*. This makes Islam a potent and well integrated system which cannot be fragmented or disconnected, taking some parts of it and discarding others. That would be a gross transgression and a most vile offence against God Almighty.

11

The Sacred Months, Fighting and Pilgrimage

They ask you about the new moons. Say, 'They are signs for people to mark fixed periods of time, and for the pilgrimage.' Righteousness does not mean that you enter houses from the rear, but truly righteous is he who fears God. Enter houses by their doors and fear God, so that you may be successful. (189)

يَسْـَٔلُونَكَ عَنِ ٱلْأَهِلَّةِ ۖ قُلْ هِىَ مَوَٰقِيتُ
لِلنَّاسِ وَٱلْحَجِّ ۗ وَلَيْسَ ٱلْبِرُّ بِأَن تَأْتُوا۟
ٱلْبُيُوتَ مِن ظُهُورِهَا وَلَٰكِنَّ ٱلْبِرَّ مَنِ
ٱتَّقَىٰ ۗ وَأْتُوا۟ ٱلْبُيُوتَ مِنْ أَبْوَٰبِهَا ۚ
وَٱتَّقُوا۟ ٱللَّهَ لَعَلَّكُمْ تُفْلِحُونَ ﴿١٨٩﴾

Fight for the cause of God those who wage war against you, but do not commit aggression. Indeed, God does not love aggressors. (190)

وَقَٰتِلُوا۟ فِى سَبِيلِ ٱللَّهِ ٱلَّذِينَ يُقَٰتِلُونَكُمْ
وَلَا تَعْتَدُوٓا۟ ۚ إِنَّ ٱللَّهَ لَا يُحِبُّ
ٱلْمُعْتَدِينَ ﴿١٩٠﴾

Slay them wherever you may come upon them, and drive them away from wherever they drove you away; for oppression is even worse than killing. Do not fight them near the Sacred Mosque unless they fight you there first. Should they fight you, then kill them. Such is the reward of the unbelievers. (191)

وَٱقْتُلُوهُمْ حَيْثُ ثَقِفْتُمُوهُمْ وَأَخْرِجُوهُم مِّنْ حَيْثُ
أَخْرَجُوكُمْ ۚ وَٱلْفِتْنَةُ أَشَدُّ مِنَ ٱلْقَتْلِ ۚ وَلَا تُقَٰتِلُوهُمْ
عِندَ ٱلْمَسْجِدِ ٱلْحَرَامِ حَتَّىٰ يُقَٰتِلُوكُمْ فِيهِ ۖ فَإِن
قَٰتَلُوكُمْ فَٱقْتُلُوهُمْ ۗ كَذَٰلِكَ جَزَآءُ ٱلْكَٰفِرِينَ ﴿١٩١﴾

فَإِنِ ٱنتَهَوْا۟ فَإِنَّ ٱللَّهَ غَفُورٌ رَّحِيمٌ ﴿١٩٢﴾

But if they desist, know that God is much-Forgiving, Merciful. (192)

وَقَٰتِلُوهُمْ حَتَّىٰ لَا تَكُونَ فِتْنَةٌ وَيَكُونَ
ٱلدِّينُ لِلَّهِ فَإِنِ ٱنتَهَوْا۟ فَلَا عُدْوَٰنَ إِلَّا
عَلَى ٱلظَّٰلِمِينَ ﴿١٩٣﴾

Fight them until there is no more oppression, and submission is made to God alone. If they desist, let there be no hostility except against the wrongdoers. (193)

ٱلشَّهْرُ ٱلْحَرَامُ بِٱلشَّهْرِ ٱلْحَرَامِ وَٱلْحُرُمَٰتُ قِصَاصٌ
فَمَنِ ٱعْتَدَىٰ عَلَيْكُمْ فَٱعْتَدُوا۟ عَلَيْهِ بِمِثْلِ
مَا ٱعْتَدَىٰ عَلَيْكُمْ وَٱتَّقُوا۟ ٱللَّهَ وَٱعْلَمُوٓا۟ أَنَّ ٱللَّهَ
مَعَ ٱلْمُتَّقِينَ ﴿١٩٤﴾

A sacred month for a sacred month: for just retribution also applies to the violation of sanctity. If anyone commits aggression against you, attack him just as he has attacked you. Have fear of God, and be sure that God is with those who are God-fearing. (194)

وَأَنفِقُوا۟ فِى سَبِيلِ ٱللَّهِ وَلَا تُلْقُوا۟ بِأَيْدِيكُمْ
إِلَى ٱلتَّهْلُكَةِ وَأَحْسِنُوٓا۟ إِنَّ ٱللَّهَ يُحِبُّ
ٱلْمُحْسِنِينَ ﴿١٩٥﴾

Give generously for the cause of God and do not with your own hands throw yourselves to ruin. Persevere in doing good, for God loves those who do good. (195)

وَأَتِمُّوا۟ ٱلْحَجَّ وَٱلْعُمْرَةَ لِلَّهِ فَإِنْ أُحْصِرْتُمْ فَمَا
ٱسْتَيْسَرَ مِنَ ٱلْهَدْىِ وَلَا تَحْلِقُوا۟ رُءُوسَكُمْ
حَتَّىٰ يَبْلُغَ ٱلْهَدْىُ مَحِلَّهُۥ فَمَن كَانَ مِنكُم مَّرِيضًا
أَوْ بِهِۦٓ أَذًى مِّن رَّأْسِهِۦ فَفِدْيَةٌ مِّن صِيَامٍ
أَوْ صَدَقَةٍ أَوْ نُسُكٍ فَإِذَآ أَمِنتُمْ فَمَن تَمَتَّعَ

Perform to their completion both the pilgrimage and the *'umrah* purely for God's sake. If you are prevented from doing so, then make whatever offering you can easily afford. Do not shave your heads until the offerings have reached their appointed destination. If any of you is ill or suffers from an ailment of the head, he shall redeem himself by fasting, or alms, or sacrifice. When you are in safety, then he who takes advantage of performing the *ʿumrah* before the pilgrimage shall make whatever offering he can easily afford; but he who lacks the means shall fast three days during the pilgrimage and seven more days on returning home; that is, ten days in all. All this applies to those whose families are not resident in the vicinity of the Sacred Mosque. Fear God, and know well that He is severe in retribution. (196)

بِٱلْعُمْرَةِ إِلَى ٱلْحَجِّ فَمَا ٱسْتَيْسَرَ مِنَ ٱلْهَدْيِ ۚ فَمَن
لَّمْ يَجِدْ فَصِيَامُ ثَلَٰثَةِ أَيَّامٍ فِى ٱلْحَجِّ وَسَبْعَةٍ إِذَا
رَجَعْتُمْ ۗ تِلْكَ عَشَرَةٌ كَامِلَةٌ ۗ ذَٰلِكَ لِمَن لَّمْ
يَكُنْ أَهْلُهُۥ حَاضِرِى ٱلْمَسْجِدِ ٱلْحَرَامِ ۚ
وَٱتَّقُوا۟ ٱللَّهَ وَٱعْلَمُوٓا۟ أَنَّ ٱللَّهَ شَدِيدُ
ٱلْعِقَابِ ﴿١٩٦﴾

The pilgrimage takes place in the months appointed for it. Whoever undertakes the pilgrimage in those months shall, while on pilgrimage, abstain from lewdness, all wicked conduct and wrangling. Whatever good you do God is well aware of it. Provide well for yourselves: the best provision of all is to be God-fearing. Fear Me, then, you who are endowed with insight. (197)

ٱلْحَجُّ أَشْهُرٌ مَّعْلُومَٰتٌ ۚ فَمَن فَرَضَ فِيهِنَّ
ٱلْحَجَّ فَلَا رَفَثَ وَلَا فُسُوقَ وَلَا جِدَالَ فِى
ٱلْحَجِّ ۗ وَمَا تَفْعَلُوا۟ مِنْ خَيْرٍ يَعْلَمْهُ ٱللَّهُ ۗ
وَتَزَوَّدُوا۟ فَإِنَّ خَيْرَ ٱلزَّادِ ٱلتَّقْوَىٰ ۚ وَٱتَّقُونِ
يَٰٓأُو۟لِى ٱلْأَلْبَٰبِ ﴿١٩٧﴾

It is no sin for you to seek the bounty of your Lord. When you surge downward from ʿArafāt, remember God at al-Mashʿar al-Ḥarām. Remember Him who has given you guidance. Before this you were certainly in error. (198)

لَيْسَ عَلَيْكُمْ جُنَاحٌ أَن تَبْتَغُوا۟
فَضْلًا مِّن رَّبِّكُمْ ۚ فَإِذَآ أَفَضْتُم
مِّنْ عَرَفَٰتٍ فَٱذْكُرُوا۟ ٱللَّهَ عِندَ
ٱلْمَشْعَرِ ٱلْحَرَامِ ۖ وَٱذْكُرُوهُ كَمَا
هَدَىٰكُمْ وَإِن كُنتُم مِّن قَبْلِهِۦ
لَمِنَ ٱلضَّآلِّينَ ﴿١٩٨﴾

Surge onward from the place where all other pilgrims surge and pray God to forgive you. He is much-Forgiving, ever Merciful. (199)

ثُمَّ أَفِيضُوا۟ مِنْ حَيْثُ أَفَاضَ
ٱلنَّاسُ وَٱسْتَغْفِرُوا۟ ٱللَّهَ ۚ إِنَّ ٱللَّهَ
غَفُورٌ رَّحِيمٌ ﴿١٩٩﴾

When you have fulfilled your sacred duties, remember God as you remember your fathers – nay with a yet keener remembrance. Some people say, 'Our Lord, give us abundance in this world.' They shall have no share in the rewards of the life to come. (200)

فَإِذَا قَضَيْتُم مَّنَـٰسِكَكُمْ
فَٱذْكُرُوا۟ ٱللَّهَ كَذِكْرِكُمْ ءَابَآءَكُمْ
أَوْ أَشَدَّ ذِكْرًا ۗ فَمِنَ ٱلنَّاسِ
مَن يَقُولُ رَبَّنَآ ءَاتِنَا فِى ٱلدُّنْيَا
وَمَا لَهُۥ فِى ٱلْـَٔاخِرَةِ مِنْ خَلَـٰقٍ ﴿٢٠٠﴾

There are others who say, 'Our Lord, grant us what is good in this world and what is good in the life to come and protect us from the torment of the fire.' (201)

وَمِنْهُم مَّن يَقُولُ رَبَّنَآ ءَاتِنَا
فِى ٱلدُّنْيَا حَسَنَةً وَفِى ٱلْـَٔاخِرَةِ
حَسَنَةً وَقِنَا عَذَابَ ٱلنَّارِ ﴿٢٠١﴾

These shall have their portion in return for what they have earned; for God is swift in reckoning. (202)

أُو۟لَـٰٓئِكَ لَهُمْ نَصِيبٌ مِّمَّا كَسَبُوا۟ ۚ وَٱللَّهُ
سَرِيعُ ٱلْحِسَابِ ﴿٢٠٢﴾

Give glory to God during certain appointed days. Those who hasten their departure after two days incur no sin, and those who stay longer incur no sin, provided that they are truly God-fearing. Have fear of God and know well that you shall all be gathered before Him. (203)

وَٱذْكُرُوا۟ ٱللَّهَ فِىٓ أَيَّامٍ مَّعْدُودَٰتٍ ۚ
فَمَن تَعَجَّلَ فِى يَوْمَيْنِ فَلَآ إِثْمَ عَلَيْهِ
وَمَن تَأَخَّرَ فَلَآ إِثْمَ عَلَيْهِ ۚ لِمَنِ ٱتَّقَىٰ ۗ
وَٱتَّقُوا۟ ٱللَّهَ وَٱعْلَمُوٓا۟ أَنَّكُمْ إِلَيْهِ
تُحْشَرُونَ ﴿٢٠٣﴾

Overview

This new passage resumes the elaboration of religious obligations and practical rules governing behaviour within the Muslim community and its relations with the outside world.

It explains the religious and practical significance of the phases of the moon. It dismisses the pre-Islamic Arab superstitious practice of entering houses through the back door on certain occasions. It outlines the rules governing war and fighting generally, as well as the prohibition of fighting in the four lunar months: Rajab (the seventh), Dhu'l-Qa'dah (the eleventh), Dhu'l-Ḥijjah (the twelfth) and Muḥarram (the first) and particularly in the vicinity of the Sacred Mosque in Makkah. It ends with a comprehensive description of the rituals of the pilgrimage and the *'umrah* (which may be described as a mini-pilgrimage) as prescribed by Islam, revising, modifying and replacing all the pagan and idolatrous concepts and practices of former times.

In one concise passage, and in a succinctly clear style, the Qur'ān lays down rules and principles relating to faith and belief, the regulation of religious rituals and practices, as well as war and fighting. These are all linked and interlaced with powerful admonitions and comments evocative of God and His power.

On correcting the Arab practice of entering houses through the back door, the *sūrah* points out that form, in itself, is not what really matters but it is one's consciousness and fear of God. It says: *"Righteousness does not mean that you enter houses from the rear; but truly righteous is he who fears God. Enter houses by their doors and fear God, so that you may be successful."* (Verse 189)

In dealing with war, the *sūrah* directs Muslims never to initiate aggression, affirming that *"God does not love aggressors."* (Verse 190)

Commenting on fighting during a sacred month, the *sūrah* urges: *"Fear God and be sure that God is with those who are God-fearing."* (Verse 194)

The *sūrah* calls on Muslims to spend of their wealth for the cause of God, exhorting them to *"Persevere in doing good, for God loves those who do good."* (Verse 195)

The *sūrah* again emphasizes consciousness and fear of God when dealing with the pilgrimage rituals. *"Fear God, and know well that He is severe in retribution."* (Verse 196) *"Provide well for yourselves: the best provision of all is to be God-fearing. Fear Me, then, you who are endowed with insight."* (Verse 197) *"Have fear of God, and know well that you shall all be gathered before Him."* (Verse 203)

It is quite clear that there is a common thread firmly binding these instructions and rulings together. Matters of faith, ritual and law, the spiritual and the mundane, the religious and the secular, the personal, national and international, are all intertwined and spun together in one comprehensive, universal religious and social system based on rules and laws laid down directly by God.

The Islamic Transformation

Beginning with this passage, we note a salient feature recurring in the rest of the *sūrah*. We find the Muslims addressing the Prophet Muḥammad with specific enquiries relating to a wide range of everyday issues and situations they were encountering in their new way of life. They reveal a genuine desire on the part of the new Muslims to find out what their new religion has to say about these matters. The believers wanted to learn more about how Islam viewed and interpreted the social and physical phenomena they were experiencing in the world around them.

They ask about the moon and the various phases it goes through. Why does it start as a fine crescent which becomes bigger until it develops into a full sphere, and then reverses the cycle until it disappears altogether before it is reborn in the shape of a thin crescent again?

They enquired about what part and how much of their wealth they should give away as charity. They enquired about war, and whether it would be allowed during the sacred months and in the vicinity of the Sacred Mosque in Makkah. They asked for Islamic rulings on alcoholic drinks and gambling, which were social habits in pre-Islamic Arabian life.

They enquired regarding menstruation, and whether sexual contact between spouses was allowed during such periods. They enquired about even more intimate and personal issues concerning matrimonial relations. These questions were sometimes raised by women.

Questions relating to other issues are to be found in several other *sūrahs* in the Qur'ān. The fact that they were raised is in itself significant in more ways than one.

To begin with, it indicates a high degree of enlightenment and dynamism in the Muslim society, which was already developing a distinct character. A sense of community was rapidly growing. The Muslims were no longer a set of isolated individuals, nor were they any longer separate tribes scattered all over Arabia. They had become a nation with its own identity, systems and relationships, in which every person was keen to assume his or her role and position. This new social, intellectual and emotional awareness was brought about by Islam, and was moulded by the Islamic outlook on life, its system and its pioneering views and concepts.

Second, this inquisitiveness also indicates a keen sense of religious consciousness emerging in the new society. It reflects the depth and strength of the hold the new faith had taken on the hearts and minds of its followers. Having discarded their old assumptions and attitudes, and wrenched themselves away from pre-Islamic customs and traditions, they lost confidence in the old order and began looking to their new religion for education and guidance in all aspects of life.

This state of emotional and intellectual awareness is generated by true faith. The believer is freed from all former beliefs and traditions. He begins to view with scepticism all previously held ideas, and to subject all his actions to fresh scrutiny. The believer becomes readily receptive to the directives of the new faith, and keen to reform his or her life accordingly. Even those former concepts and practices which are approved or adopted by the new order will assume a new context as they are integrated into the new faith.

The new order need not necessarily replace the old one in every detail, but it is important that those details adopted by the new faith should be assimilated and incorporated into it in substance as well as in spirit. This is very well illustrated by the pre-Islamic pilgrimage rituals which Islam transforms into a new set of rules, hardly bearing any resemblance to those formerly practised by the Arabs.

Third, some of the questions the Muslims were raising relate directly to the historical context of that period. The Jews in Madinah and the idolatrous Arabs in Makkah would often voice doubts as to the merits of Islamic teachings and principles. They would seize every opportunity to disparage Islam, exploiting certain occasions or events to wage a campaign of hostility and disinformation. One such occasion involved unwarranted criticism to the effect that a Muslim expedition, led by ʿAbdullāh ibn Jaḥsh, had violated the prohibition of fighting during the sacred months by attacking a Quraysh caravan.

The Muslims found it necessary to solicit answers and explanations to reassure themselves and to enable them to face the propaganda launched against them by their enemies.

This illustrates that the Qur'ān was keeping abreast of the confrontation between the Muslims and the non-Muslims, and providing the Muslims with guidance and leadership. This was happening in areas of faith and belief as well as in the real world, where the enemies of Islam were incessantly scheming and plotting against its followers.

The situation today is not very different: the same battles continue to rage on. Human nature has not changed, and the enemies of Islam can be found everywhere. But the Qur'ān is also there. Neither man nor the Muslim world community will be safe until the Qur'ān assumes conduct of the battle as it did for the first generation of Muslims. Unless Muslims realize this fact they cannot hope to succeed or prosper.

The least that results from such a realization is that Muslims would approach the Qur'ān with the same understanding and attitude. The Qur'ān would be seen as a dynamic, active force, formulating new concepts, facing up to anti-Islamic ideas, insulating Muslims against ignorance and deviation and helping them avoid the pitfalls. This would be far removed from the present approach many have adopted towards the Qur'ān, viewing it merely as a fine work of literature and going no farther than reciting it rhythmically or chanting its words like a melody on certain occasions.

The Qur'ān was revealed for a totally different purpose. God meant it as a blueprint for a complete way of life, a stimulus, a driving force guiding the Muslim community, charting its course through thick and thin, and helping it overcome and avoid all the difficulties and obstacles it is bound to encounter in this world.

The New Moon and its Significance

> *They ask you about the new moons. Say, 'They are signs for people to mark fixed periods of time, and for the pilgrimage.' Righteousness does not mean that you enter houses from the rear, but truly righteous is he who fears God. Enter houses by their doors and fear God, so that you may be successful.* (Verse 189)

Some reports suggest that the Prophet Muḥammad was asked why the moon goes through its various phases. Others say that he was asked why have the crescent moons been created, which seems to be more consistent with the answer given in the *sūrah*: *"They are signs for people to mark fixed periods of time, and for the pilgrimage."*

They serve as a means by which people fix and measure the time of important religious events and activities such as travel, pilgrimage, fasting, marriage and divorce, as well as trade transactions and loan periods.

Whatever the original enquiry, the answer had gone beyond mere abstraction and given practical, rather than 'scientific', information relating to the phases of the moon. The Qur'ān, without going into a detailed astronomical discussion, speaks of the function of the moon and its role in people's daily life. The Qur'ān did not embark on an explanation of the moon's position within the solar system or the relative movement of stars, planets and galaxies, although this is implied in the question.

What significance, then, does the answer given in the Qur'ān imply? The principal objective of the Qur'ān was the creation and promotion of a new conception of life in a new social, political and economic order. Indeed, it was working towards the creation of a new human community, with a special role of leadership in the world. It was developing a new model of human society, the like of which had not been known before, to uphold a new way of life that would firmly establish essential universal features and principles which the rest of mankind would look up to and emulate.

A scientific answer would undoubtedly have provided the Prophet's followers with theoretical knowledge about the universe, to add to their meagre understanding of it. Indeed, it is doubtful that the Arabs knew enough about astronomy at that time to be able to make use of further theoretical information, which would have required an understanding of basic principles and phenomena that were beyond all scientific progress achieved in the world up to that time.

The Qur'ān avoided a scientific answer because people were not ready for it, and it would have been of little use for the universal mission the Qur'ān was revealed to fulfil. Its role was far greater than the mere dissemination of detailed knowledge. The Qur'ān was never intended to be a book on astronomy, chemistry or medicine, as some of its admirers and detractors try, each for their own different purposes, to demonstrate.

These attempts betray a lack of understanding of the nature of the Qur'ān, its function and scope. It is mainly concerned with the human soul and the state and direction of the human condition. Its purpose is to establish a broad view of the world in which we exist and its relationship with the Creator, and a general outline of man's position in this world and his relationship with the Creator. On the basis of these broad concepts, the Qur'ān goes on to establish a way of life which enables man to apply all his skills and abilities, not least his intellectual faculties. Once these are properly and correctly developed, they are given full freedom, through observation, experiment and scientific research, to probe the mysteries of life and the universe and make the appropriate conclusions – which could never, in any case, be said to be final or absolute.

The basic raw material with which the Qur'ān is concerned is man himself: the way he views things around him, his beliefs, emotions and ideas, his behaviour and activity, and the ties and relationships that govern his life. The conduct and development of material science and innovation are left to man's mental and intellectual capabilities and his diligent endeavour to know and understand. It is this knowledge and understanding that are the essential prerequisites for man to fulfil his divinely ordained mission in the world, for which he is naturally fitted and qualified.

The Qur'ān nurtures man's basic nature and protects it against deviation and corruption. It provides man with the moral, social, political and economic foundations and mechanisms that enable him to put his talents and skills to full and proper use. It furnishes him with a broad and comprehensive view of the nature, the inherent harmony, and the delicate balance of the physical world, of which man himself is an important and integral part, and its relationship with the Creator.

The Qur'ān does not cover such topics in great detail, because that is man's task. He is expected to take the initiative to search, discover and use his environment in order to further and fulfil his supreme position in the world.

The attempt to make the Qur'ān what it was never meant to be often seems naïve and counter-productive. The fact that the Qur'ān is not a reference book for medicine or chemistry or astronomy takes nothing away from its power and glory.

The Qur'ān and Scientific Truth

The Qur'ān deals with something much wider and more comprehensive than all those sciences. It is concerned with man himself, the key to uncovering the facts and mysteries of the world around. The human mind is fully equipped to scrutinize and probe into man's surroundings, and to experiment with and apply the theories he formulates and the tools he invents. The Qur'ān concentrates on nurturing man's character, conscience and mind, and laying the sound foundations of the human environment which allows him to make full use of his own hidden potential and that of the world around. Having laid down the groundwork and given man the necessary mental tools and criteria, the Qur'ān leaves man free to seek and search, experiment, achieve and make mistakes, in all areas of life.

There is also a great risk in attempting to seek verification of facts of a scientific nature given occasionally in the Qur'ān through suppositions, theories or so-called 'scientific facts' arrived at through human empirical efforts.

The facts that the Qur'ān mentions are absolute and final truths, while those arrived at through human research are not, no matter how advanced or sophisticated the means or the approach used to arrive at them. The latter are constrained by the conditions of man's own environment, and they are limited by the nature and scope of the tools used. The absolute and final truths of the Qur'ān cannot, therefore, be qualified or authenticated by the inconclusive ones discovered by man.

In addition to 'scientific fact', this applies in the case of 'scientific theory'. This includes theories on the origin of the universe, the creation and evolution of man, and psychological and sociological theories. Even within the realm of human thought, these are not considered to express scientific facts. Indeed, they are no more than suppositions or speculative ideas which, at best, help explain a vast array of physical, biological, psychological or sociological phenomena. As more accurate instruments and more discoveries are made, these theories are constantly amended and developed, or superseded by others that give wider or more accurate explanations or interpretations.

The attempt to verify Qur'ānic facts by the changing findings of human science is fundamentally flawed. It reflects three negative aspects that should not be associated with the Qur'ān.

First, is an inner defeatism that science is somehow superior to the Qur'ān. This leads to an attempt to find scientific evidence to verify and corroborate what the Qur'ān says. But in fact, Qur'ānic statements are definitive, complete and conclusive, while human science remains in a constant state of flux and development. This is due to the constraints of the environment in which human research and experiment are conducted, and the inadequacy of the tools and methods used in those processes.

Second, is a misunderstanding of the true nature and function of the Qur'ān as the absolute definitive truth addressing man in his totality according to his basic nature and within the constraints of the physical world and its laws. Ideally, it aims to achieve perfect harmony between man and the physical world, avoiding a clash between man and nature. Such harmony enables man to unravel, through enquiry, observation, experiment and application, as many of the world's mysteries as he can and use its potential energies and resources to enhance his position and fulfil his role as God's vicegerent on earth.

Third, is the continuous interpretation and re-interpretation, with frequent resort to far-fetched and arbitrary methods, of Qur'ānic statements in a vain attempt to make them agree or coincide with speculative suppositions and tentative theories.

However, this should not prevent us from making full use of what human sciences uncover about man, life and the world, for a better understanding of the Qur'ān. God says: *"We shall show them Our signs across all horizons and within themselves, until they clearly see that this [revelation] is the truth."* (41: 53) This is a clear call to study closely and absorb what science discovers of God's signs and to use them to expand the meaning and application of the Qur'ānic injunctions, without undermining or demeaning the immutability and integrity of the Qur'ān.

This may be illustrated further by the following examples:

The Qur'ān says: *"And He created all things and ordained them in due proportion."* (25: 2) Scientific observation also has led to the conclusion that there are inherent harmony, very intricate interactions and consonances within the structure of the universe. The earth's shape and distance from both the sun and the moon, its size relative to theirs, its speed and axis of rotation, and countless other factors combine to make life on earth possible and sustainable. None of this may be attributed to chance or coincidence, or can be said to be without purpose.

These observations no doubt are useful in gaining a better understanding of the Qur'ānic statement. This is quite legitimate and should be encouraged. But here are other examples that are neither legitimate nor scientifically correct.

The Qur'ān says: *"We created man from an extraction of clay."* (23: 12) Centuries later, scientists such as Charles Darwin, proposed a theory of evolution which purports that life began in water as a single cell, and that human beings are the result of millions of years of evolution. Now, it would be pointless, indeed wrong, to attempt to show that this is precisely what the Qur'ān says.

To begin with, the theory is not conclusive and, within a century, it underwent several amendments and changes that have made it almost unrecognizable. There were flaws in the original theory, which was conceived at a time when nothing was known of the genes which carry hereditary properties and distinguish one species from another. Several aspects of Darwin's theory have since been disproved, and many others are still a matter of debate.

The Qur'ānic statement is conclusive as it establishes the origin of man without giving any details of the process involved. It does not aim at more than that and carries no other connotations or meaning.

The Qur'ān tells us: *"And the sun runs towards its resting place."* (36: 38) This is a statement of fact concerning the movement of the sun. Science has shown that the sun is indeed moving relative to other stars nearby and is part of a galaxy which itself is moving. Furthermore the speeds at which the sun and the galaxies move are measured. Such observations, relative and inconclusive as they are, do not affect the truth of the Qur'ānic statement, which is final.

The Qur'ān says: *"Are the unbelievers unaware that the heaven and the earth were once one single entity, which We then parted asunder?"* (21: 30) Some have tried to reconcile this statement with the theory that suggests that the earth was part of the sun and then they were separated. It is futile to try and limit Qur'ānic statements with human scientific theory. This particular theory is not the only one in its field and it is contested by many scientists, while the Qur'ānic statement is complete and conclusive. It merely states a fact without telling us what is meant by 'heavens' or how the fragmentation occurred. No scientific proposition should be used to corroborate Qur'ānic statements, no matter how apparently close or similar the conclusions may be.

Having established these principles, we may now return to the Qur'ānic text: *"Righteousness does not mean that you enter houses from the rear, but truly righteous is he who fears God. Enter houses by their doors and fear God, so that you may be successful."* (Verse 189)

This part of the verse and the preceding one relating to phases of the moon seem to be connected by the theme of pilgrimage: the new moon as an astronomical time marker for pilgrimage and other events, and the pre-Islamic Arab pilgrimage custom of entering houses from the rear.

Al-Bukhārī and Muslim relate a report by al-Barā', in which he said: "It was the custom of the *Anṣār* [i.e. Muslims from Madinah] that on returning from pilgrimage they would approach their houses from the rear. When one of them broke this tradition and entered by the front door, he was severely criticised. It was at this point that the verse was revealed." A similar report is related by Abū Dāwūd.

Whether this custom related to the pilgrimage only, which seems more probable, or to travelling in general, the Arabs had maintained the belief that it was a sign of piety and righteousness to uphold it. However, the Qur'ān refutes that as an empty gesture that could serve no religious purpose. It goes on to establish the proper religious concept of righteousness as consciousness of God and His presence at all times and in all situations, rather than as a routine gesture that had no meaning whatsoever. Therefore it gives the instruction that houses must be approached from the front, and re-emphasizes the importance of God-fearing as the road to success in this life.

The verse, then, focuses our minds and hearts on *taqwā,* God-fearing, as a basic fact of faith, and links it with the attainment of absolute success, both in this life and in the life to come. It repeals a useless, ignorant tradition and directs the believers to appreciate God's grace in providing them with the new moon at the beginning of every month to enable them to determine the time for pilgrimage and other human activities.

The First Order to Fight

This is followed with a statement on fighting in general, and on fighting around the Sacred Mosque in Makkah and during the sacred months in particular. Then follows an urgent call to spend of one's personal wealth for the promotion of God's cause, an activity which is closely related to the fundamental Islamic duty of *jihād*, or struggle for God's cause:

> *Fight for the cause of God those who wage war against you, but do not commit aggression. Indeed, God does not love aggressors. Slay them wherever you may come upon them, and drive them away from wherever they drove you away; for oppression is even worse than killing. Do not fight them near the Sacred Mosque unless they fight you there first. Should they fight you, then kill them. Such is the reward of the unbelievers. But if they desist, know that God is much-Forgiving, Merciful.*
>
> *Fight them until there is no more oppression, and submission is made to God alone. If they desist, let there be no hostility except against the wrongdoers.*
>
> *A sacred month for a sacred month: for just retribution also applies to the violation of sanctity. If anyone commits aggression against you, attack him just as he has attacked you. Have fear of God, and be sure that God is with those who are God-fearing.*
>
> *Give generously for the cause of God and do not with your own hands throw yourselves to ruin. Persevere in doing good, for God loves those who do good.* (Verses 190–195)

Some reports indicate that these were the first verses on the subject of fighting to be revealed. They were preceded only by verses 39–41 of *Sūrah* 22: *"Permission to fight is given to those against whom war is being wrongfully waged. Most certainly, God has the power to grant them victory. These are the ones who have been driven from their homelands against all right for no other reason than their saying, 'Our Lord is God!' Were it not that God repels some people by means of others, monasteries, churches, synagogues and mosques – in all of which God's name is abundantly extolled – would surely have been destroyed. God will most certainly succour him who succours God's cause. God is certainly most Powerful, Almighty. They are those who, if We firmly establish them on earth, attend regularly to their prayers, give in charity, enjoin the doing of what is right and forbid the doing of what is wrong. With God rests the final outcome of all events."*

These verses had given the Muslims permission to fight those unbelievers who had oppressed them, and they understood them to be a prelude to the institution of *jihād,* or striving for God's cause, as a religious duty. Further, they realized that because they had been oppressed, they were given permission to fight back and restore justice, after they had been restrained from doing so all the time they were in Makkah. Their instructions then were to *"hold back your hands [from fighting], and attend regularly to prayer, and pay your* zakāt." (4: 77) This restraint had been imposed by God for a purpose He had determined. We may try to discern some of the reasons behind this order.

The first of these reasons is a disciplinary one, aimed at taming the insubordinate and rebellious nature of the early Arab Muslims. They had to learn to be patient and await instructions, rather than act impulsively and recklessly, as they used to do in pre-Islamic days. For the new Muslim community to fulfil its great universal role, the desire for revenge and heedless reaction had to be brought under control, and left to the discretion of a trusted leadership which gave its decisions careful consideration and was duly obeyed – even though to do so would test the Arabs' impatient and impetuous nature.

Such discipline enabled people such as 'Umar ibn al-Khaṭṭāb and Hamzah ibn 'Abd al-Muṭṭalib, and other independent and strong personalities among the early Muslims, to show a great deal of patience in the face of the persecution and oppression being inflicted upon their fellow Muslims. They would await Prophet Muḥammad's instructions and the commands of the Supreme Authority which had ordered them to *"hold back your hands [from fighting], and attend regularly to prayer, and pay your* zakāt." (4: 77) Thus a balance was struck in the consciousness of that pioneering community, between rashness and restraint, impulse and deliberation, passionate reaction and rational compliance.

Another reason for restraining the Muslims from fighting in Makkah was that in Arabian society, rushing to help an oppressed person was highly commendable. Despite their ability to hit back hard, the Muslims showed a large degree of restraint. This was demonstrated during the boycott imposed by the rest of the Quraysh against the Prophet's Hāshimite clan in order to force them to withdraw their support and protection of the Prophet and his followers. When this persecution, which lasted for three years, became unbearable, their re-awakened sense of justice caused some non-Muslim Arabs to break ranks and end the boycott. It seems from a study of the Prophet's history at this time that, in adopting this policy of passive resistance, the Muslim leadership in Makkah was aware of the crucial role played by social and tribal factors.

This is strongly borne out by the fact that the Muslim leadership had no wish to unleash internecine feuds within the Makkan clans. Muslim converts fell victim to moral and physical torture and abuse to force them to renounce their new faith, even at the hands of members of their own families. These were self-appointed tormentors, with no central authority directing their battles against the Muslims. Had the Muslims been allowed to hit back, fighting would have broken out in every Makkan household, and blood would have been shed in every family. That would have made Islam, in the eyes of Arabian society, seem a divisive religion, advocating strife and destruction within Arab clans.

After the *Hijrah,* or emigration to Madinah, however, the Muslims emerged as an independent community, prepared to face up to the Makkan leadership which was actively recruiting fighters and organizing military expeditions against it. The situation had changed; instead of individual persecutors targetting individual victims, a collective and deliberate campaign was being organized.

To these reasons one may add the fact that the Muslims in Makkah were a dangerously exposed minority. Had they engaged the unbelievers in armed conflict as an organized group, they would have faced total annihilation. God's will was that they should first gather in a safe place before He granted them permission to go into battle.

However, the rules governing fighting were issued gradually, as and when the need arose, and as dictated by the needs of the development of Islam, first within Arabia and later outside it as well.

The present verses contain some of those rules which were relevant to that stage of development of the community, when hostility was just beginning to set in between the Muslim and non-Muslim camps. These rules also represent part of the permanent code that has come to govern war in Islam generally. They have undergone slight modifications, given at a later stage in *Sūrah* 9.

It might well be useful at this point to give a general synopsis of the concept of *jihād* in Islam, which can form the basis for the interpretation and understanding of Qur'ānic statements on fighting and war.

Islam represents the final and complete version of faith, revealed as the basis of a universal and comprehensive human order on earth. The Muslim community was raised to assume the leadership of humanity in accordance with this order, which derives in its entirety from the comprehensive Islamic concept of the purpose of existence as a whole and of human existence in particular. The Muslim community would lead humanity to ultimate success and to all that is good and noble (*khayr*), which no man-made order can provide. It would raise mankind to unprecedented moral and material standards. Conversely, no greater harm could be inflicted upon humanity than to deprive it of seeking to attain those levels of nobility, purity, happiness and perfection God wants it to achieve.

It is, therefore, a basic human right to be addressed with the message of Islam. No authority should deny mankind that right and under no circumstances should any obstacles be allowed to prevent that divine message from being delivered.

Having received the message, people have the right to freely accept the religion of Islam, and be under no pressure from any quarter to dissuade or prevent them from taking it up. Those who choose not to accept Islam are expected not to impede its progress. Indeed, they are required to guarantee Islam's freedom of action and to leave the Muslim community a clear road to fulfil its task, free from any threat of aggression.

Those who adopt the religion of Islam also have the right not to be intimidated or subjected to oppression, in any way whatsoever, so that they abandon their faith. No impediments may be placed to turn people away from Islam. The Muslim community, if subjected to any such aggressive designs, has the right to defend itself by force, in order to protect the community's freedom and security. This would further the establishment of God's order on earth and guarantee humanity the opportunity and the right to receive God's message.

It also results in another obligation that the Muslim community must undertake: to oppose any power that would stand in its way and prevent it from conveying the message freely to the public, or would threaten its followers. The Muslim community must pursue this course of *jihād*, or struggle for God's cause, until all threat of oppression is eliminated and people are free to believe in Islam and practise it. This does not imply any sense of compulsion, but it does mean allowing Islam to prevail in society to the extent that everyone is free to accept it and tell others about it without any fear of persecution or intimidation.

These are the parameters within which the principles of *jihād* have been laid down. These are the real objectives for which it has been instituted. It has no other purpose and serves no other end.

Jihād in Islam is pursued to protect the faith against outside attacks as well as internal strife. Its aim is the preservation of the Islamic way of life, establishing it as a force to be respected and reckoned with in the world. Anyone who willingly wishes to enter the fold of Islam should have no fear of being prevented from doing so and should not have to suffer for making that choice.

This is the true *jihād*, as recognized and endorsed by Islam. Those who take part in it are richly rewarded and rank among the noblest of believers, and those who give their lives in doing so are the true martyrs.

Jihād: When and Against Whom?

The present passage addresses the situation of the Muslim community in Madinah as it was in confrontation with the pagan Arabs of the Quraysh. Those unbelievers had persecuted the Muslims for their religious beliefs, drove them out of their homes and were trying hard to turn them away from their faith. It also lays down the fundamental rules of *jihād* in Islam.

It begins with the precise instruction that Muslims should fight those who had been fighting them and to meet with force any attacks against them by anyone, without committing aggression. *"Fight for the cause of God those who wage war against you, but do not commit aggression. Indeed, God does not love aggressors."* (Verse 190)

The aims of war in Islam are clearly defined right at the outset: *"Fight for the cause of God those who wage war against you ..."* Fighting should, therefore, be undertaken for the sake of God, and for no other purpose that may be defined by human desires or motivations. War should not be pursued for glory or dominance, nor for material aggrandisement, nor to gain new markets or control raw materials. It should not be pursued to give one class, race or nation of people dominance over another. Fighting in Islam must be undertaken only to promote the aims defined by Islam: to make God's word supreme in the world, to establish His order, and to protect the believers against persecution, coercion, corruption, and all efforts to force them to betray their faith or abandon it. According to Islam, all other types of war are unjust, and those who take part in them should expect no rewards or blessings from God.

Having defined the objective, the verses also define the limits of war: *"... but do not commit aggression. Indeed, God does not love aggressors."* (Verse 190) 'Aggression' implies attacks on non-combatants and peaceful, unarmed civilians who pose no threat to Muslims or to their community as a whole. This includes women, children, the elderly, and those devoted to religious activity, such as priests and monks, of all religious and ideological persuasions. Aggression also entails exceeding the moral and ethical limits set by Islam for fighting a just war. These limits outlaw the atrocities perpetrated in wars outside Islam, past and present. Such atrocities are totally repugnant to Muslims and can never be sanctioned or committed by people who honour and fear God.

The Ethics of War

Here is a selection of these principles and conventions, as laid down by the Prophet Muḥammad and outlined in the instructions of some of his Companions. They clearly reveal the nature of the Islamic approach to a just war, hitherto unknown to human society.

'Abdullāh ibn 'Umar reports that when, in one of the battles, the Prophet was told that a woman was found among those killed, he immediately ordered that women and children should not be killed during combat. [Related by Mālik, al-Bukhārī, Muslim, Abū Dāwūd and al-Tirmidhī]

Abū Hurayrah quotes the Prophet as saying: "When you fight, avoid striking your opponent in the face." [Related by al-Bukhārī and Muslim]

Abū Hurayrah reports that the Prophet sent him with an expedition instructing them to burn two men from the Quraysh he had named, but as they were about to depart the Prophet said: "I have ordered you to burn these two people, but only God may punish with fire. If you capture them, just kill them." [Related by al-Bukhārī, Abū Dāwūd and al-Tirmidhī]

ʿAbdullāh ibn Masʿūd quotes the Prophet as saying: "True believers are those who strictly observe their moral code when they kill." [Related by Abū Dāwūd]

ʿAbdullāh ibn Yazīd al-Anṣarī reports that the Prophet has strictly forbidden looting and the mutilation of dead bodies. [Related by al-Bukhārī]

Ibn Yaʿlā reports that on one expedition, the leader, ʿAbd al-Raḥmān ibn Khālid ibn al-Walīd, was brought four enemy fighters. He ordered that they be tied and put to death slowly. When Abū Ayyūb al-Anṣārī, a close Companion of the Prophet, heard of this, he said: "I heard the Prophet forbid slow killing. I swear by God that I would not inflict slow death even on a chicken." When ʿAbd al-Raḥmān heard this he immediately sought to free four slaves in compensation. [Related by Abū Dāwūd] We may add here that freeing a slave is part of the prescribed compensation for accidental killing.

Al-Ḥārith ibn Muslim ibn al-Ḥārith quotes his father as saying that the Prophet sent him with others on an expedition. As they approached their target he hurried his horse and reached the village ahead of the rest of the expedition. He said that the inhabitants gave him a noisy reception and that he told them that if they were to declare their acceptance of Islam they would be spared and their safety would be assured. They followed his advice declaring their acceptance of Islam. Some of his Companions reproached him for what he did, saying that he had deprived them of the spoils of war. But when they returned and the Prophet learnt of what had happened, he commended him for his action and said: "God Almighty has given you such and such reward for every one of them." [Related by Abū Dāwūd]

Buraydah reports: "Whenever God's Messenger appointed a commander to lead an expedition or an army, he would urge him to fear God and to show kindness towards his fellow Muslims. He would then instruct him as follows: 'Proceed to fight in God's name and for His cause. Fight those who deny God. Take the initiative but do not commit any acts of treachery, do not mutilate your victims, and do not kill any children." [Related by Muslim, Abū Dāwūd and al-Tirmidhī]

Mālik quotes Abū Bakr as saying in his farewell address to one of his armies: "You will come across people who claim to have devoted themselves to the service of God, so leave them to their claim. Do not kill any women, children or elderly people."

Such is the code that governs war in Islam, and such are its objectives, which derive directly from the Qur'ānic statement: *"Fight for the cause of God those who wage war against you, but do not commit aggression. Indeed, God does not love aggressors."* (Verse 190)

The Muslims were well aware that they would not prevail as a result of their numerical strength or superior armament; they were hopelessly deficient on both counts. The main secret of their victory lay in their faith in, and obedience to, God, and the support they received from Him. To ignore God's commands and the Prophet's instructions would have deprived them of the only force that could ensure their victory. These principles had to be strictly observed, even with those enemies who had persecuted them and inflicted unspeakable atrocities on them. Even though at one point the Prophet, overcome by rage, had ordered that two Qurayshī men be put to death by burning, he immediately retracted that order, because only God punishes with fire.

The *sūrah* goes on to reaffirm the rightness of war against those who had subjected the Muslims to campaigns of terror and persecution, and driven them out of their homeland. The Muslims were urged to confront their enemies and kill them wherever they happen to be, except within the vicinity of the Sacred Mosque in Makkah unless their enemies were to attack them there first. Those orders would stand unless the unbelievers accepted Islam, in which case it was forbidden to fight them, regardless of any killings or atrocities they might have perpetrated against Muslims earlier.

"Slay them wherever you may come upon them, and drive them away from wherever they drove you away; for oppression is even worse than killing. Do not fight them near the Sacred Mosque unless they fight you there first. Should they fight you, then kill them. Such is the reward of the unbelievers. But if they desist, know that God is much-Forgiving, Merciful." (Verses 191–192)

Forced religious conversion is the worst violation of a most inviolable human right. It is, therefore, a much more heinous offence than murder, regardless of the form that coercion takes or how it is exerted.

Suppression of religious freedom can be imposed by threats and the direct use of force. But it can also be practised through the imposition of corrupt or totalitarian regimes and oppressive social systems that deprave the masses, drive them away from God's path, and encourage and force them to reject the divine faith and break away from it. The best example to illustrate this is Communism, which banned religious instruction, openly advocated atheism, legislated for prostitution and drinking, promoted vice and discouraged virtue almost to the point of direct compulsion.

The Islamic view of freedom of belief assigns it a great status as a social and human value, and stems from the Islamic view of the ultimate purpose of life and of the whole of human existence: the worship of God in its widest sense which encompasses all constructive human activity. Freedom of belief is man's most precious right in this world, and ought to be cherished and protected. Any infringement of this right, direct or indirect, must be fought even if one has to kill for it. This is borne out by the significant term used in the Qur'ān, which is *"slay them* [rather than 'fight them'] *wherever you may find them"*. This signifies that, if you have to, you may resort to any means to slay those who infringe upon your right of freedom of belief, while heeding those other Islamic principles mentioned earlier.

Violation of Sanctities

The other restriction is that no fighting was allowed within the vicinity of the Sacred Mosque in Makkah, which God, in response to the Prophet Abraham's prayers, had declared a safe haven and an inviolable house of peace. However, those who desecrate the sanctity of the Sacred Mosque and commit aggression against Muslims there must be fought and should not be spared. Their vile actions and their persecution of Muslims, committed as they are within the vicinity of the Sacred Mosque, can only be rewarded with severe punishment.

"But if they desist, know that God is much-Forgiving, Merciful." (Verse 192) To earn God's forgiveness and mercy, they should not simply desist from waging war against the Muslims and trying to force them to abandon their faith. They would be required to renounce their denial of God and their rejection of His Message. The most they can expect in return for refraining from attacking the Muslims and persecuting them would be a truce, but that would not be sufficient to merit God's forgiveness and mercy. The unbelievers are, therefore, invited and encouraged to believe so that they may enjoy God's mercy and forgiveness.

What a commendable gesture! Islam spares its staunchest enemies punishment and retribution, and instead offers them forgiveness and mercy in return for the simple act of joining the ranks of the believers. That would absolve them of all their previous misdemeanours, and cancel out the damage and the atrocities they had wrought against the Muslims.

The aim of war in Islam is to let people be free to uphold Islam and practise it, and never find themselves, by virtue of either direct force or the type of social, political or economic system they live under, compelled to renounce it. The growth and spread of Islam must not be hampered or restricted, and the Muslim community must be allowed the means to defend itself and deter its enemies from taking advantage of it. No one who wishes to adopt Islam should feel threatened. If such threats are made, the Muslim community is collectively obliged to do all it can to eliminate that threat and secure the success of Islam.

"Fight them until there is no more oppression, and submission is made to God alone. If they desist, let there be no hostility except against the wrongdoers." (Verse 193) These statements were revealed to deal with a specific situation in Arabia, when the pagan Arabs were persecuting an incipient Muslim community and stifling the spread of Islam. Nevertheless, they remain valid, and *jihād* is incumbent on Muslims until the end of time. Whenever a tyrant or an oppressive power emerges and prevents people from upholding Islam or seeks to prevent them from knowing about it, the Muslim community must rise against it and secure for all the right of freedom to know the truth, listen to it, and have the choice to accept it freely.

It is clear how severely these verses condemn oppression. It is considered a more repugnant evil than murder. This emphasis makes it clear that Islam views this matter most gravely. It establishes another crucial universal principle, heralding a rebirth of mankind, according to which man's value is determined by his faith. Man's life is always outweighed by his religious beliefs.

This principle also identifies the true enemies of humanity in this world. They are those who persecute believers and inflict suffering on a Muslim for no reason other than his being a Muslim. They are those who stand between mankind and God's truth and guidance. It is these that Muslims are obliged to fight and destroy *"until there is no more oppression, and submission is made to God alone."* (Verse 193)

This fundamental Islamic principle remains as valid today as it was when these verses were revealed. Islam remains a target for attack and vilification from various quarters. Muslims everywhere continue to be victims of aggression, oppression and religious intolerance as individuals and groups and, in some cases, as whole communities. All victims of oppression and aggression have the right and duty to defend themselves and seek to destroy their enemies, in fulfilment of this great Islamic principle which marked a rebirth of humanity.

It is only when the aggression or the persecution ceases or is eliminated that fighting must come to an end. *"If they desist, let there be no hostility except against the wrongdoers."*[1] (Verse 193)

Having ruled on fighting during the sacred months, the *sūrah* now gives the ruling on fighting in the vicinity of the Sacred Mosque in Makkah. *"A sacred month for a sacred month: for just retribution also applies to the violation of sanctity. If anyone commits aggression against you, attack him just as he has attacked you. Have fear of God, and be sure that God is with those who are God-fearing."* (Verse 194)

Those who violate the sacred months cannot expect guarantees of peace and immunity from attack during it. God had declared the Sacred Mosque a safe haven and a place of peace, and designated the sacred months a time of truce and security. During these months no blood shall be shed, all sacred places and property shall be immune, and the safety of every living thing is guaranteed. Those who are bent on infringing this peace must not escape unpunished. The Muslims are instructed to retaliate in a measured way and within the limits dictated by the type and extent of the initial aggression. *"If anyone commits aggression against you, attack him just as he has attacked you."* (Verse 194)

There should be no excessive retribution. Muslims are here left to their own conscience and their consciousness of God. They realize that their own victory depends on God's help and support, and are therefore reminded that God is on the side of those who fear Him – a supremely effective safeguard.

---

1. This ruling was later amended by verses in the first passage of *Sūrah* 9, which instructed the Muslims to liberate the whole of the Arabian Peninsula from idolatry and paganism. This was a necessary measure to give Islam a solid and secure base in Arabia. Muslims would thus be safe from any rearguard attack as they moved to face the hostile powers of the Byzantines to the north and the Persians to the east.

Jihād requires money as much as it requires men. In those early days of Islam, fighters would provide their own fighting equipment, their own transport and their own food. They received no remuneration for their work, and freely offered their own possessions as well as their lives. This can only happen when the political, social and economic system in society is based on faith. The community would not need to appropriate funds to defend itself against internal or external enemies. Leaders and soldiers volunteer their efforts and their possessions to defend the faith and the community.

However, some of the less well-to-do Muslims who were keen to join the fighting but could not provide their own means of transport would go to the Prophet pleading to be taken to the battlefront. The Qur'ān tells us that when the Prophet did not have the necessary transportation or equipment to give them: *"They turned away with tears in their eyes, sad that they did not have the means to contribute."* (9: 92)

For this reason, we find numerous exhortations in the Qur'ān and the *sunnah* urging financial contribution, whenever necessary, to the war effort. The call to *jihād* is almost always accompanied by a call to contribute materially and financially.

The passage goes as far as describing the reluctance to contribute financially as folly leading to self-destruction. It says: *"Give generously for the cause of God and do not with your own hands throw yourselves to ruin. Persevere in doing good, for God loves those who do good."* (Verse 195) Miserliness and greed are indeed a form of self-destruction for the individual as well as for society as a whole. They result in deprivation and weakness of the whole community, especially one whose affairs are dependant on voluntary, self-motivated contributions.

The Qur'ān goes on to recommend even a higher state of excellence: *"Persevere in doing good, for God loves those who do good."* (Verse 195) The Arabic term used here is *iḥsān*, whose Islamic connotations are difficult to convey in translation. It is the highest level of altruism and self-denial. The Prophet Muḥammad defines it as: "worshipping God as if you see Him with your own eyes; for, though you cannot see Him, He certainly sees you". [Related by al-Bukhārī and Muslim] Once this stage of piety is reached, one will become a consummate devotee, utterly obedient to God in everything; and all one's resources, energies and life will be entirely dedicated to God Almighty.

This closing comment is a befitting end for a passage dealing with fighting and giving for God's cause. It urges believers to aspire to the level of *iḥsān*, the highest grade of religious excellence.

A Symbol of Islamic Unity

The *sūrah* then gives an outline of the rituals of the pilgrimage and the *ʿumrah* (lesser pilgrimage). This follows quite naturally from the earlier account dealing with lunar changes and phases, and the admissibility of fighting during the sacred months of the year and in the vicinity of the Sacred Mosque in Makkah.

> *Perform to their completion both the pilgrimage and the ʿumrah purely for God's sake. If you are prevented from doing so, then make whatever offering you can easily afford. Do not shave your heads until the offerings have reached their appointed destination. If any of you is ill or suffers from an ailment of the head, he shall redeem himself by fasting, or alms, or sacrifice. When you are in safety, then he who takes advantage of performing the ʿumrah before the pilgrimage shall make whatever offering he can easily afford; but he who lacks the means shall fast three days during the pilgrimage and seven more days on returning home; that is, ten days in all. All this applies to those whose families are not resident in the vicinity of the Sacred Mosque. Fear God, and know well that He is severe in retribution.*
>
> *The pilgrimage takes place in the months appointed for it. Whoever undertakes the pilgrimage in those months shall, while on pilgrimage, abstain from lewdness, all wicked conduct and wrangling. Whatever good you do God is well aware of it. Provide well for yourselves: the best provision of all is to be God-fearing. Fear Me, then, you who are endowed with insight.*
>
> *It is no sin for you to seek the bounty of your Lord. When you surge downward from ʿArafāt, remember God at al-Mashʿar al-Ḥarām. Remember Him who has given you guidance. Before this you were certainly in error. Surge onward from the place where all other pilgrims surge and pray God to forgive you. He is much-forgiving, ever merciful. When you have fulfilled your sacred duties, remember God as you remember your fathers – nay with a yet keener remembrance. Some people say, 'Our Lord, give us abundance in*

this world.' They shall have no share in the rewards of the life to come. There are others who say, 'Our Lord, grant us what is good in this world and what is good in the life to come and protect us from the torment of the fire.' These shall have their portion in return for what they have earned; for God is swift in reckoning.

Give glory to God during certain appointed days. Those who hasten their departure after two days incur no sin, and those who stay longer incur no sin, provided that they are truly God-fearing. Have fear of God and know well that you shall all be gathered before Him. (Verses 196–203)

The exact date of the revelation of these verses is not known, except for one report indicating that verse 196 was revealed at al-Ḥudaybīyah during the sixth year after *Hijrah*, 628 CE. Nor can we be precise as to when the pilgrimage was made obligatory in Islam, whether we take that to have been established by verse 196 of this *sūrah* or verse 97 of *Sūrah* 3 which says: *"Pilgrimage to this House is a duty owed to God by all people who are able to undertake it."*

In his book *Zād al-Ma'ād*, Imām Ibn al-Qayyim says that the pilgrimage was instituted during the ninth or tenth year of the Prophet's migration to Madinah. This is based on the fact that the Prophet himself performed the pilgrimage in 10 AH. This, however, is not sufficient evidence to support that view. There could have been other reasons that made the Prophet delay going on pilgrimage until the tenth year, especially when we know that he delegated Abū Bakr to head the pilgrimage during the ninth year.

It is also well established that on his return from the campaign of Tabūk, the Prophet intended to go for pilgrimage. However, he later decided not to do so, because non-Muslim Arabs were still doing the pilgrimage to Makkah and he did not wish to join them, not least because some of them would be going round the Ka'bah naked, as was their custom. At that point *Sūrah* 9, which brought the truce with the polytheist Arabs to an end, was revealed and the Prophet dispatched 'Alī ibn Abī Ṭālib to Makkah to proclaim its provisions to the pilgrims. He charged him with the task of announcing at Minā, when all the pilgrims were gathered, that: "No unbeliever shall enter paradise; no idolater may henceforth perform the pilgrimage; no one may go round the Ka'bah naked. All treaties signed with God's Messenger shall run their course." Accordingly, the Prophet did not go to Makkah for pilgrimage until the Ka'bah was cleared of all symbols and manifestations of idolatry.

One could point out certain texts as evidence indicating that the pilgrimage was instituted in principle much earlier. Indeed some reports suggest that this took place when the Prophet was still in Makkah, before the migration to Madinah. But this would not hold water. Nevertheless, verses 26–37 of *Sūrah* 22 list most of the pilgrimage rituals as they were communicated to the Prophet Abraham. These include:

> *When We assigned to Abraham the site of the [Sacred] House, [We said], 'Do not associate anything as partner with Me. Purify My House for those who will walk around it, and those who will stand before it, and those who will bow down and prostrate themselves in prayer. Proclaim to all people the duty of pilgrimage. They will come to you on foot and on every kind of fast mount. They will come from every far-away quarter, so that they might experience much that shall be of benefit to them, and that they might extol the name of God on the days appointed [for sacrifice], over whatever heads of cattle He may have provided for them. Eat, then, of such [sacrificed cattle] and feed the unfortunate poor. Thereafter let them complete the rites prescribed for them, fulfil their vows, and again walk around the Ancient House...*
>
> *Anyone who honours the symbols set up by God [shows evidence of] God-consciousness in people's hearts. You have benefit in them for a term appointed; and in the end their place of sacrifice is near the Ancient House...*
>
> *The sacrifice of camels We have ordained for you as one of the symbols set up by God, in which there is much good for you. Hence, extol the name of God over them when they are lined up [for sacrifice]; and after they have fallen lifeless to the ground, eat of their meat, and feed the poor who is contented with his lot, as well as the one who is forced to beg. It is to this end that We have made them subservient to your needs, so that you might have cause to be grateful. Never does their meat or their blood reach God; it is your piety that reaches Him. It is to this end that He has made them subservient to your needs, so that you might glorify God for all the guidance with which He has graced you. Give good news to those who do good.*

These verses make specific reference to offering animals for sacrifice, walking around the Ka'bah (*ṭawāf*), the rites of *iḥrām*[2] (consecration), and the invocation of God's name, all of which constitute the basic rites of the pilgrimage. The Muslims were addressed with these words as the heirs of Abraham, indicating that the pilgrimage had been instituted at an early stage as part of the legacy of Abraham. The fact that Muslims, for various practical reasons, had not been able to perform the pilgrimage is beside the point. However, as mentioned earlier in this volume, individual Muslims had been able to perform the pilgrimage since the Ka'bah was re-instituted as the *qiblah* in the second year of the Islamic calendar.

Let us now take a closer look at the verses on pilgrimage in this *sūrah* and the instructive message they convey.

> *Perform to their completion both the pilgrimage and the 'umrah purely for God's sake. If you are prevented from doing so, then make whatever offering you can easily afford. Do not shave your heads until the offerings have reached their appointed destination. If any of you is ill or suffers from an ailment of the head, he shall redeem himself by fasting, or alms, or sacrifice. When you are in safety, then he who takes advantage of performing the 'umrah before the pilgrimage shall make whatever offering he can easily afford; but he who lacks the means shall fast three days during the pilgrimage and seven more days on returning home; that is, ten days in all. All this applies to those whose families are not resident in the vicinity of the Sacred Mosque. Fear God, and know well that God is severe in retribution.* (Verse 196)

The first thing to notice about this verse is the precision with which it treats the subject. It is divided into a number of short, well-defined instructions. Any exceptions or provisions relating to each ruling are made immediately before moving on to the next. The passage is rounded off with a strong emphasis on God-fearing.

---

2. *Iḥrām*, or consecration, involves that men discard their normal clothes and wear simple unsewn garments, refraining from shaving or cutting one's hair, covering the head, clipping one's nails, hunting, and sexual contact with one's spouse. This state is assumed at specified locations outside Makkah, each known as *mīqāt*, and for the main part of the pilgrimage and the whole of the *'Umrah*. Women observe the same restrictions but wear their normal clothes.

The first article stresses the fact that once one has decided to perform the pilgrimage or the *'umrah*, one must do so in full and dedicate one's actions to God: *"Perform to their completion both the pilgrimage and the 'umrah purely for God's sake."* Some scholars have taken this statement as instituting the pilgrimage as a religious duty, while others have understood it to be a mere instruction that once one begins performing the pilgrimage, one should go on to complete its rites. The latter interpretation seems more accurate, since the *'umrah* is not universally considered by scholars an obligatory duty. Nevertheless, the order to complete the rites, once begun, applies equally to the pilgrimage and the *'umrah*. The latter involves the same rites with the exception of attending at 'Arafāt, but differs in that it can be performed any time throughout the year.

Exemption from completing the pilgrimage or the *'umrah* is granted when one is prevented from doing so either by an enemy or, by illness or other exceptional circumstances. This is universally accepted by all schools of thought. The same applies to the case of being prevented from completing the rites. *"If you are prevented from doing so, then make whatever offering you can easily afford."* (Verse 196) If prevented by force, a pilgrim offers a sacrifice within the means at his disposal. He would then be able to terminate his state of consecration, or *iḥrām,* at the point he reached, even though he might not have performed any of the rituals other than going into the state of consecration.

Such a situation arose in the sixth year of the Islamic calendar when the pagan Arabs prevented the Prophet and his Companions from entering Makkah and visiting the Sacred Mosque. The Muslims had camped at al-Ḥudaybīyah, about 25 kilometres west of Makkah, where eventually the famous truce agreement was signed between the Quraysh and the Muslims. It stipulated that the Prophet and his followers would be free to return for *'umrah* the following year. Some reports indicate that this verse was revealed at that time, and, accordingly, the Prophet ordered his Companions to make their sacrifices at al-Ḥudaybīyah and terminate their state of consecration, or *iḥrām*. Some of them showed reluctance, finding it difficult to release themselves from *iḥrām* before making the offerings at the appropriate place. But once the Prophet took the initiative and offered his sacrifice there, the rest followed suit.

The verse refers to *"whatever offering you can easily afford"*. This includes animals such as camels, cows, sheep, or goats. A pilgrim should sacrifice whatever he can easily afford, and several people may share in a single camel or cow. In the *ʿumrah* of al-Ḥudaybīyah, as many as seven people shared in the sacrifice of one camel. On the other hand, one person may choose to offer a sheep or a goat, which would suffice. The exemption serves to mitigate hardship such as that encountered at al-Ḥudaybīyah, or which might arise as a result of illness.

The essential aim of such a religious practice is to revive one's awareness of God and draw closer to Him. If this is disrupted by threats from a hostile quarter, a disabling illness or the like, pilgrims are not deprived of the rewards they would have received had they completed the pilgrimage or the *ʿumrah*. They are, therefore, instructed to proceed with making the offerings as if they had completed the intended rituals. This compassionate attitude is well in line with the spirit of Islam and its view of the purpose of worship.

Then follows another rule relating to the performance of pilgrimage and *ʿumrah*: *"Do not shave your heads until the offerings have reached their appointed destination."* (Verse 196)

This, of course, applies under normal peaceful conditions. A pilgrim is not to shave his head, which precedes the termination of the state of consecration, or *iḥrām*, until he has made his offerings at the designated place and time. This is done at Minā on the tenth day of Dhu'l-Ḥijjah, after attendance the previous day at the plain of ʿArafāt. Once the offerings are made, a pilgrim may release himself from consecration.

Here we have another exemption: *"If any of you is ill or suffers from an ailment of the head, he shall redeem himself by fasting, or alms, or sacrifice."* (Verse 196) Islam is a practical and humane religion, and if there are grounds of health that would require shaving one's head, one would be permitted to do so while in the state of *iḥrām*, even before the destination for offering the sacrifice is reached or the appropriate rituals are completed. The concession, however, is balanced with a compensation which has been set as a three-day fast from dawn to dusk, the feeding of six needy people, or slaughtering a sheep and giving its meat to the poor.

This is supported by what the Prophet Muḥammad said to Kaʿb ibn ʿAjrah when the latter was brought to him during the pilgrimage, having suffered a severe infection so that lice were crawling all over his face. The Prophet said: "I would not have thought you could have reached such a dire state. Can you afford a sheep?" Ka'b said he could not. The Prophet said to him: "Fast for three days, or feed six needy people, giving each half a *ṣā'* of food, and shave your head." (One *ṣā'* is an Arabian measure equivalent to four times the fill of a man's hands cupped together.)

The *sūrah* gives another ruling relating to the pilgrimage and the *'umrah*: *"When you are in safety, then he who takes advantage of performing the 'umrah before the pilgrimage shall make whatever offering he can easily afford."* (Verse 196) The sacrifice is required of those who are able to complete the rituals of both duties. Let us look at the matter in more detail.

One form of *tamattu'*, which is referred to in this verse as 'taking advantage of performing both duties of pilgrimage and *'umrah,* involves the performance of the *'umrah* separately, prior to performing the pilgrimage. To do this, one sets off for *'umrah*, goes into *iḥrām* at the appointed location, performs the rites of *'umrah*, which include *ṭawāf* around the Ka'bah and *sa'ī* between Ṣafā and Marwah, and shaving one's head or trimming one's hair to release oneself from consecration. One then waits for the time of the pilgrimage to re-enter into *iḥrām,* or consecration, for the pilgrimage. This is valid only if the *'umrah* is offered within the appointed months of pilgrimage: Shawwāl, Dhu'l-Qa'dah and the first ten days of Dhu'l-Ḥijjah.

Another form of *tamattu'* is when one goes into *iḥrām*, at the appointed location, with the intention of combining both *'umrah* and pilgrimage. On arrival in Makkah, the *'umrah* is performed, after which the pilgrim maintains his *iḥrām* until he has performed the rest of the rites of the pilgrimage at the proper time.

In both cases, pilgrims are required to make such offerings as they can afford and are available. Animals such as camels, cows, sheep and goats can be offered for this purpose.

Those who lack the means need to fulfil an alternative requirement. *"He who lacks the means shall fast three days during the pilgrimage and seven more days on returning home; that is, ten days in all."* (Verse 196) It is recommended that fasting should be undertaken over the three days before attendance at 'Arafāt on the ninth day of Dhu'l-Ḥijjah. The other seven days of fasting are undertaken following one's arrival back home, a total of ten days in all, as the Qur'ān clearly points out.

The idea here apparently is to keep the pilgrims' hearts and minds attached to God during the interval between the *'umrah* and the pilgrimage. The requirement of sacrifice or fasting perhaps aims to maintain the feeling of being closer to God in the period between the *'umrah* and pilgrimage. Thus, lifting the restrictions of consecration, or *iḥrām,* after performing the *'umrah* would not lead people away from the highly spiritual atmosphere that the pilgrimage generates.

Since those who live close to the Sacred Mosque are required to perform the pilgrimage only, and not the *'umrah,* they cannot have the option of *tamattu'*. They have no sacrifice to offer and, consequently, the ruling of fasting ten days instead does not apply to them, either: *"This applies to those whose families are not resident in the vicinity of the Sacred Mosque."* (Verse 196)

At this juncture the *sūrah* draws attention to a vital and fundamental aspect of man's relationship with God. It exhorts: *"Fear God, and know well that He is severe in retribution."* (Verse 196) The requirement for proper observance of these rulings would be an ever-present sense of God-fearing, and an appreciation of the awesome power of His retribution. By its very nature, *iḥrām* invokes a high sense of awareness of God and an eagerness not to incur His displeasure, which must be maintained, with equal vigour and sincerity, during the interval when the pilgrims are relieved from the restrictions of *iḥrām.* Pilgrims are expected to remain vigilant and self-controlled throughout the whole period.

The *sūrah* proceeds to give further details of the pilgrimage rituals. It defines the time of the year in which it is valid and explains further the values to be observed in its performance. Like the preceding passage, it closes with an exhortation to fear God at all times.

"The pilgrimage takes place in the months appointed for it. Whoever undertakes the pilgrimage in those months shall, while on pilgrimage, abstain from lewdness, all wicked conduct and wrangling. Whatever good you do God is well aware of it. Provide well for yourselves: the best provision of all is to be God-fearing. Fear Me, then, you who are endowed with insight." (Verse 197)

The text is clear that pilgrimage may be undertaken only within a specified period of the year, which extends over the months of Shawwāl, Dhu'l-Qa'dah and the first ten days of Dhu'l-Ḥijjah, the last three months in the Islamic lunar year. Accordingly – and this is the view held by the Shāfiʿī school of thought and attributed to the reputable scholars Ibn ʿAbbās, Jābir, ʿAṭāʾ, Ṭāwūs and Mujāhid – *iḥrām* for the purpose of pilgrimage is valid only when undertaken during this specified period, known as the "pilgrimage months". However, Mālik, Abū Ḥanīfah and Aḥmad ibn Ḥanbal, as well as Ibrāhīm al-Nakhaʿī, al-Thawrī and al-Layth ibn Saʿd, hold that *iḥrām* for pilgrimage is valid all the year round. Nevertheless, they restrict the actual performance of the pilgrimage rituals to the period of the year specified in the *sūrah*. The former view appears to reflect more closely the meaning of the Qur'ānic text.

Once a commitment is made to perform the pilgrimage, by entering into the state of *iḥrām* during the pilgrimage months, the would-be pilgrim *"must abstain from lewdness, all wicked conduct and wrangling."* This is a call for total abstinence from all interests, preoccupations and behaviour that are in conflict with, or distract from, the spirit of total devotion and obedience to God which should prevail during pilgrimage. It entails rising above worldly pursuits, total devotion to God alone, and seeking to acquire the necessary humility when conducting oneself at His Sacred Mosque. Donning the unsewn garments of *iḥrām* is the signal that the pilgrim has discarded all that relates to worldly position or possession, including ordinary clothes.

Having pointed out what should be avoided, the *sūrah* conveys the reassurance that *"Whatever good you do, God is well aware of it."* (Verse 197) This would be the greatest incentive for the believer to perform more good deeds, and to have God witness more of his devotion, which is in itself a source of contentment and recompense.

God then calls on the pilgrims to provide for themselves, physically and spiritually, in preparation for the challenging and demanding experience of pilgrimage.

It has been reported that a group of Yemeni pilgrims set off for pilgrimage without carrying any provisions for the journey, claiming that, since they were intending to visit God's Sacred House, He would surely provide for them. This conflicts directly with Islamic teaching that while one should rely on God and put one's trust in Him, one should also seek the necessary practical means and take all measures to look after oneself. Furthermore, such an attitude smacks of impertinence towards God; the implication that God is obliged to provide is one of condescending arrogance.

Hence the emphatic exhortation: *"Provide well for yourselves: the best provision of all is to be God-fearing. Fear Me, then, you who are endowed with insight."* (Verse 197) The fear of God is a real source of both material and spiritual sustenance. It provides the human mind and body with strength, refinement and physical and moral support. Those with insight and understanding would be the first to appreciate this directive and benefit from divine provision.

The *sūrah* outlines more pilgrimage rules. It explains that it is permitted for pilgrims to engage in trade or employment during the pilgrimage period. It also adds further elaboration of rituals.

"It is no sin for you to seek the bounty of your Lord. When you surge downward from 'Arafāt, remember God at al-Mash'ar al-Ḥarām [the sacred landmark of Muzdalifah]. Remember Him who has given you guidance. Before this, you were certainly in error. Surge onwards from the place where all other pilgrims surge and pray God to forgive you. God is much-Forgiving, ever-Merciful." (Verses 198–199)

Al-Bukhārī reports that Ibn 'Abbās said that this verse was revealed because people used to feel uneasy about conducting trade during the pilgrimage as they did in pre-Islamic days in such markets as 'Ukāẓ, Mijannah and Dhu'l-Majāz. Abū Dāwūd also quotes Ibn 'Abbās as saying that the verse was revealed because people used to avoid trading during the pilgrimage season, as they considered it a time for worship and devotion.

Abū Umāmah al-Taymī asked 'Abdullāh ibn 'Umar: "While on pilgrimage we offer transport services for hire. Is our pilgrimage valid?" Ibn 'Umar said, "Do you not make *ṭawāf* around the Ka'bah, do good deeds, throw the stones, and shave your heads?" When Abū Umāmah replied that they did all those things, Ibn 'Umar said, "When the Prophet was asked the same question, he gave no answer until the angel Gabriel conveyed to him the verse which states: *"It is no sin for you to seek the bounty of your Lord.* "

Abū Ṣāliḥ, an attendant of 'Umar, the second Caliph, is reported to have asked him whether people used to conduct trade during the pilgrimage season. 'Umar replied, "Indeed! People had no other way of earning a living!"

This reluctance to conduct trade and business during the pilgrimage season is but one aspect of the new sensitivity and awareness that Islam had brought to people's minds, giving them a new attitude towards their pre-Islamic way of life. Muslims would seek to know the view of Islam, or await instructions, before performing certain actions or adopting certain modes of behaviour, as explained earlier with reference to the ritual of *sa'ī* between the two hills of Ṣafā and Marwah.

Thus, trading and commercial activity, including letting and leasing, are permitted during pilgrimage. In fact, the Qur'ān describes such activities as a means of seeking *"the bounty of your Lord"*. Thus, anyone who seeks to earn some income through trade and business in pilgrimage should feel that he only seeks God's bounty and that whatever he receives is given to him by God. It is not his own efforts that give him his earnings. It is God, the generous giver who gives us all we have. Once this is appreciated by the pilgrim, he will realize that even as he is trading, he is in a state of devotion to God which in no way violates or defiles his observance of the pilgrimage duties. Once this principle is established in believers' hearts and minds, Islam allows them total freedom to pursue their interests, every one of which would in itself be considered a valid act of worship.

It is not by chance, therefore, that a verse dealing with the rituals of pilgrimage should also include instructions on earning through trade and commercial activities.

"When you surge downward from 'Arafāt, remember God at al-Mash'ar al-Ḥarām. Remember tHim who has given you guidance. Before this you were certainly in error." (Verse 198) Attendance at 'Arafāt is the central duty of the pilgrimage. It is authentically reported on the authority of 'Abd al-Raḥmān al-Daylamī that the Prophet Muḥammad said: "The pilgrimage is attendance at 'Arafāt. [He repeated this three times.] He who arrives at 'Arafāt before the break of dawn [on the tenth day of Dhu'l-Ḥijjah] will have fulfilled this duty. The days of Minā are three; those who depart after only two days incur no sin, nor do those who stay longer."

The scheduled time for attendance at 'Arafāt begins at noon on the Day of 'Arafāt, the ninth day of the Muslim lunar month of Dhu'l-Ḥijjah, and ends at the break of dawn the following morning, the Day of Sacrifice. Aḥmad ibn Ḥanbal, however, is of the opinion that the time begins at the break of day, rather than at noon, on the Day of 'Arafāt. This is based on the report by 'Urwah al-Ṭā'ī that he had gone up to the Prophet, as he was going to prayer at Muzdalifah, and explained to him that having come from a long way away both he and his camel were on the point of exhaustion, and that he had done his best to stand at every hill he had passed, and wanted to know whether his pilgrimage would still be valid. The Prophet replied: "Anyone who has joined us in the prayer today and stands with us until we move on, having already been present in 'Arafāt at any time, night or day, has completed the pilgrimage and fulfilled his obligations."

Perfect Devotion at Every Move

The Prophet laid down this rule and extended the time to the break of dawn on the Day of Sacrifice, the tenth of Dhu'l-Ḥijjah, in order to distinguish Islamic practice from that of the pagan Arabs.

Al-Musawwar ibn Makhramah, a Companion of the Prophet reports that, in his address at 'Arafāt, the Prophet began with praising and glorifying God before saying: "This is the grand day of pilgrimage. The polytheists and the idolaters used to leave 'Arafāt before the sun had set, when it was still visible over mountain tops looking like men's turbans. But we depart before the sun rises, our practice being distinctly different to theirs."

The established tradition adopted by the Prophet was to depart from 'Arafāt after sunset. In an authentic *ḥadīth* related by Muslim, Jābir ibn 'Abdullāh reports that "the Prophet remained at 'Arafāt until the sun began to set, the sky reddened and the sun's disc completely disappeared. With Usāmah behind him on the same camel, he was pulling hard on the reins of his she-camel until her head would hit the saddle. He motioned with his right hand, saying, 'Stay calm! Stay calm!' He relaxed his grip on the reins at every hill so that the camel could climb with ease. On arrival at Muzdalifah, he prayed *maghrib* and *'ishā'* with a single *adhān* and two separate *iqāmahs*. He did not separate the two obligatory prayers with any glorification of God. After that he lay down to rest until dawn, when he got up and offered the *fajr* prayer when the light of day began to appear. The prayer was preceded by *adhān* and *iqāmah*. The Prophet then mounted his camel and headed towards al-Mash'ar al-Ḥarām. There he faced the *qiblah* and embarked on a lengthy devotional prayers and praise of God until the light of day was bright. He then set off before the sun had risen." This is the practice outlined in the *sūrah* as it says:

"When you surge downward from 'Arafāt, remember God at al-Mash'ar al-Ḥarām. Remember Him who has given you guidance. Before this you were certainly in error." (Verse 198)

The Qur'ān exhorts Muslims to invoke God's name following their departure from 'Arafāt. It reminds them that this is part of the guidance God favoured them with, and that their actions are an expression of gratitude for that favour. They are also reminded of the gloom and despair that had marked their way of life prior to Islam: *"Remember Him who has given you guidance. Before this you were certainly in error."*

Those early Muslims were fully aware of this profound truth. They were only a few years away from the pagan Arab way of life, with its lamentable religious ignorance and its worship of idols, *jinn* and angels, who were also conceived to be daughters of God, while the jinn were thought to be His in-laws. Such foolish superstitions had in turn led to confusion in religious practices. These included the unjustified and unexplained prohibition of the meat of certain animals, or the meat from their backs, and the sacrifice of children to idols, gods or *jinn*.

Pre-Islamic Arab life was plagued with a host of socially unjust and morally corrupt practices. The *sūrah* points specifically to one of them here, class distinction, by commanding: *"Surge onwards from the place where all other pilgrims surge."*

The Arabs' decadence was also shown in the senseless and bloody tribal conflicts which at the time had totally undermined their position in the world. It was further reflected in the near-total confusion of their sexual mores, marriage customs, and family relationships in general. It was apparent in the injustice inflicted upon the weak by the strong, in the total absence of ethical or legal guarantees to restore the balance. Above all, it was manifested in the Arabs' marginal existence and insignificance on the world stage, which had only begun to be redressed with the advent of Islam.

The Qur'ānic words, *"Remember Him who has given you guidance. Before this you were certainly in error,"* brought all that dark history back to the Muslims' minds, and led them to consider their new life under Islam, to reflect on God's grace in guiding them, and to appreciate its value and role in shaping their existence. This remains true for Muslims of all nations and generations. Without Islam they would fall into utter insignificance.

Islam has been the main force that has transformed Muslims' lives and lifted them from tiny, subservient and confused communities to a great pioneering nation. Muslims appreciate this transformation only when they sincerely and diligently adopt Islam and build their whole way of life on its principles. In fact, all mankind needs Islam's guidance and blessings. This is confirmed, and highly appreciated, by those who come into the fold of Islam after having lived a different life. They find the contrast immeasurable.

As a believer in Islam reflects on the social philosophies and ideologies developed and adopted by various societies throughout human history, he is usually astonished by their triviality, misery, pettiness and confusion when compared with Islam. In some societies man, to his great disadvantage, seems to have chosen the reckless course of denying his instinctive need for God and His care and guidance. That is precisely what is being emphasized in this *sūrah* when God says: *"Remember that He has given you guidance. Before this you were certainly in error."* (Verse 198)

Returning to the main theme of this passage, one can also describe the pilgrimage as the greatest gathering of Muslims from all over the globe. They are brought together under the single banner of Islam, abandoning all their former racial, cultural and national ties. The unsewn *iḥrām* garments they don when they are in the state of consecration are symbolic in more senses than one. All pilgrims wearing these garments stand on the same level, with no distinctions of tribal or ethnic kinship. Islam is the only unifying factor.

In pre-Islamic days, the Quraysh used to give themselves certain privileges to distinguish them from the rest of the Arabs during the pilgrimage. They arrogantly referred to themselves as *al-ḥums*, or the pure. One such privilege the Quraysh had granted themselves was that they did not attend at 'Arafāt, and so approached Muzdalifah from a different direction to that of other pilgrims. These Qur'ānic instructions eliminated this anomaly and bound the Quraysh to observe the same pilgrimage rituals as the rest of the Muslims, removing all false distinction: *"Surge onwards from the place where all other pilgrims surge and pray God to forgive you. God is much-Forgiving, ever-Merciful."*

Al-Bukhārī relates a report by 'Ā'ishah, the Prophet's wife, in which she said, "The Quraysh and those who followed its lead used to attend at Muzdalifah, and they were known as *al-ḥums*, while the rest of the

Arabs attended at 'Arafāt. But God's Messenger was instructed to go to 'Arafāt, spend the day there, and then leave it for Muzdalifah, and this is what the verse refers to."

Islam transcends kinship and class distinction, and treats all human beings as belonging to one nation; the sole distinction being their fear of, and obedience to, God Almighty. The pilgrimage ritual of *iḥrām* requires all pilgrims to abandon their usual clothing in order to appear equal, and it would be inconsistent to allow them to boast of their lineage or ancestry.

All prejudices and manifestations of pride and vanity must be discarded during the pilgrimage. Pilgrims are instructed to direct their devotion, praise and pleas to God, to pray for forgiveness for their errors and excesses, large and small. They ought to keep their minds, hearts and souls pure of all thoughts of lewdness, transgression, wicked conduct and wrangling of any kind. Through the pilgrimage, Muslims are educated in the wide fundamental principles of Islam: the equality of man and the rejection of discrimination on the basis of caste, race, language, or any other differences. Should they deviate or become negligent, they are urged to seek God's guidance and forgiveness.

The Journey Approaches Its End

> *When you have fulfilled your sacred duties, remember God as you remember your fathers – nay with a yet keener remembrance. Some people say, 'Our Lord, give us abundance in this world.' They shall have no share in the rewards of the life to come. There are others who say, 'Our Lord, grant us what is good in this world and what is good in the life to come and protect us from the torment of the fire.' These shall have their portion in return for what they have earned; for God is swift in reckoning.* (Verses 200–202)

Prior to Islam, the Arabs had no mission or message to take them outside the confines of the Arabian Peninsula. They would throng to the famous market places of 'Ukāẓ, Mijannah, and Dhu'l-Majāz, not only to trade and exchange material goods, but also to display their tribal pride, eulogize their ancestors and celebrate their past glories. These were occasions for showing off their poetic and literary prowess. They had no other culturally or nationally significant pursuits to attract their interest or encourage them to mix with or explore other cultures and societies.

With the advent of Islam, however, they acquired a fresh outlook on life, a great responsibility, and a definite purpose. The Qur'ān prompted them in their new direction: *"When you have fulfilled your sacred duties, remember God as you remember your fathers – nay with a yet keener remembrance."* (Verse 200)

The irony of this statement would not have escaped them. It ridicules their infatuation with their forefathers and instructs them to correct their behaviour by devoting their attention completely to God, and with far greater diligence. Just as they are required to abandon their normal dress for the untaylored, plain garments of *iḥrām*, they are directed to break free from their racial and ethnic prejudices. It is made clear to them that devotion to God alone, and not to their ancestral glory, will take them to higher attainments in this world.

Man's destiny is determined, and his credentials evaluated, according to how close his way of life is to God. *"Some people say, 'Our Lord, give us abundance in this world.' They shall have no share in the rewards of the life to come. There are others who say, 'Our Lord, grant us what is good in this world and what is good in the life to come and protect us from the torment of the fire.' These shall have their portion in return for what they have earned; for God is swift in reckoning."* (Verses 200–202)

There are two types of people: those who care only for the here and now and devote their energies to nothing else, and those with a wider vision and more far-reaching concerns, who are conscious of God and who seek happiness in this life without forfeiting their share of life to come.

Ibn 'Abbās reported that this verse was revealed with reference to those Arabs who, on pilgrimage day, would pray for rain, or a good harvest, or a successful breeding season, but ask nothing of the rewards of the hereafter. Of course, its message is timeless and applies much more generally. Such people, who remain preoccupied with this worldly life even as they pray to God, are to be found in all human societies and generations. God, in His infinite wisdom, may well grant them some or all of what they wish for, but their share in the life to come will amount to nothing.

But those who say, *"Our Lord, grant us what is good in this world and in the life to come and protect us from the torment of the fire,"* are assured their full share of happiness and reward. They are polite enough not to specify the type of reward they seek, but will be content with whatever God grants them. His generosity is neither withheld nor delayed. The temperate and reasonable tone of their prayer assures them success and a generous response from God Almighty.

These divine statements clearly point to the direction man ought to take in seeking help and success. By wholeheartedly submitting oneself to God and accepting His judgement without doubt or hesitation, one's good fortune is guaranteed both in this life and in the life to come. Only those who devote all their love and energy to life in this world will forfeit their reward in the Hereafter.

Islam does not require believers to abandon worldly pursuits altogether. Man has a vital role to play on this Earth. But in taking charge of the world's affairs, man must be guided by God in order to see life in its wider dimension. Islam aims to free man from the shackles of material living, and help him rise above its limits and restrictions. Man is encouraged to apply his energies and abilities as the master of the world rather than its slave, and to transcend its trivial ephemera.

The passage on pilgrimage rituals closes with more exhortations to praise God and be conscious of His power: *"Give glory to God during certain appointed days. Those who hasten their departure after two days incur no sin, and those who stay longer incur no sin, provided that they are truly God-fearing. Have fear of God and know well that you shall all be gathered before Him."* (Verse 203)

These special days are widely believed to be the day of ʿArafāt (the ninth day of Dhu'l-Ḥijjah), the day of sacrifice (the tenth day), and the following three days. Ibn ʿAbbās suggests that the 'appointed days' are the eleventh to the thirteenth. ʿIkrimah, however, interprets the verse as referring to the glorification of God following the regular daily prayers on the three days following the tenth of Dhu'l-Ḥijjah.

In the *ḥadīth* quoted earlier, ʿAbd al-Raḥmān ibn Muʿammar al-Daylamī quotes the Prophet as saying: "The days of Minā are three; those who depart after only two days incur no sin, nor do those who stay longer." Indeed, the days from the ninth to the thirteenth of Dhul-Ḥijjah are all equally suitable for devotional prayers and glorification of God, regardless of whether one includes the first or the last two days. The common prerequisite is that one should *"truly fear God"*.

The passage ends on a significant note, reminding the believers of the Day of Judgement, to which reference is made in some of the verses on pilgrimage, thus arousing in their hearts a healthy fear of God. *"Have fear of God and know well that you shall all be gathered before Him."* (Verse 203)

The preceding verses demonstrate clearly how Islam transformed the pagan Arab customs of the pilgrimage into a rich and meaningful Islamic ritual, ridding it of all idolatrous, sectarian and exclusive practices. It turned it from a narrow Arab tradition into a truly universal one: a typical Islamic form of worship dedicated to the praise and service of God Almighty. This is yet another example of how Islam can overcome and transcend all differences and distinctions that divide mankind.

12

The Nature of Islamic Society

There is a kind of man who pleases you greatly in the present life by what he says, and he cites God as witness to what is in his heart, whereas he is the most hostile of adversaries. (204)

وَمِنَ ٱلنَّاسِ مَن يُعۡجِبُكَ قَوۡلُهُۥ فِي
ٱلۡحَيَوٰةِ ٱلدُّنۡيَا وَيُشۡهِدُ ٱللَّهَ عَلَىٰ مَا
فِي قَلۡبِهِۦ وَهُوَ أَلَدُّ ٱلۡخِصَامِ ٢٠٤

Yet, no sooner does he turn his back than he strives to spread corruption in the world, destroying crops and progeny. God does not love corruption. (205)

وَإِذَا تَوَلَّىٰ سَعَىٰ فِي ٱلۡأَرۡضِ لِيُفۡسِدَ
فِيهَا وَيُهۡلِكَ ٱلۡحَرۡثَ وَٱلنَّسۡلَۗ
وَٱللَّهُ لَا يُحِبُّ ٱلۡفَسَادَ ٢٠٥

When it is said to him, 'Have fear of God', his false pride drives him into sin. Therefore, hell will be his allotted portion, and how vile a resting place. (206)

وَإِذَا قِيلَ لَهُ ٱتَّقِ ٱللَّهَ أَخَذَتۡهُ ٱلۡعِزَّةُ
بِٱلۡإِثۡمِۚ فَحَسۡبُهُۥ جَهَنَّمُۖ وَلَبِئۡسَ
ٱلۡمِهَادُ ٢٠٦

But there is also a kind of man who would willingly sell himself, seeking God's pleasure. God is most Compassionate to His servants. (207)

وَمِنَ ٱلنَّاسِ مَن يَشۡرِي نَفۡسَهُ
ٱبۡتِغَآءَ مَرۡضَاتِ ٱللَّهِۚ وَٱللَّهُ رَءُوفُۢ
بِٱلۡعِبَادِ ٢٠٧

Believers, submit all of you to God and do not follow Satan's footsteps. He is indeed your open foe. (208)

يَٰٓأَيُّهَا ٱلَّذِينَ ءَامَنُوا۟ ٱدْخُلُوا۟ فِى ٱلسِّلْمِ
كَآفَّةً وَلَا تَتَّبِعُوا۟ خُطُوَٰتِ ٱلشَّيْطَٰنِ ۚ
إِنَّهُۥ لَكُمْ عَدُوٌّ مُّبِينٌ ﴿٢٠٨﴾

If you should stumble after all evidence of the truth has come to you, then know that God is Almighty, Wise. (209)

فَإِن زَلَلْتُم مِّنۢ بَعْدِ مَا جَآءَتْكُمُ
ٱلْبَيِّنَٰتُ فَٱعْلَمُوٓا۟ أَنَّ ٱللَّهَ عَزِيزٌ
حَكِيمٌ ﴿٢٠٩﴾

Are they waiting for God to reveal Himself to them in the shadows of clouds, together with the angels? The case will have been settled then. To God shall all things return. (210)

هَلْ يَنظُرُونَ إِلَّآ أَن يَأْتِيَهُمُ
ٱللَّهُ فِى ظُلَلٍ مِّنَ ٱلْغَمَامِ
وَٱلْمَلَٰٓئِكَةُ وَقُضِىَ ٱلْأَمْرُ ۚ وَإِلَى
ٱللَّهِ تُرْجَعُ ٱلْأُمُورُ ﴿٢١٠﴾

Ask the Children of Israel how many a veritable sign We have given them. He who alters the grace of God after it has been bestowed on him [should know that] God is severe in retribution. (211)

سَلْ بَنِىٓ إِسْرَٰٓءِيلَ كَمْ ءَاتَيْنَٰهُم مِّنْ ءَايَةٍۭ
بَيِّنَةٍ ۗ وَمَن يُبَدِّلْ نِعْمَةَ ٱللَّهِ مِنۢ بَعْدِ مَا جَآءَتْهُ
فَإِنَّ ٱللَّهَ شَدِيدُ ٱلْعِقَابِ ﴿٢١١﴾

The life of this world has been made alluring to the unbelievers; hence, they scoff at those who believe; but those that fear God shall be above them in rank on the Day of Resurrection. God grants sustenance to whom He wills beyond all reckoning. (212)

زُيِّنَ لِلَّذِينَ كَفَرُوا۟ ٱلْحَيَوٰةُ ٱلدُّنْيَا وَيَسْخَرُونَ
مِنَ ٱلَّذِينَ ءَامَنُوا۟ ۘ وَٱلَّذِينَ ٱتَّقَوْا۟ فَوْقَهُمْ
يَوْمَ ٱلْقِيَٰمَةِ ۗ وَٱللَّهُ يَرْزُقُ مَن يَشَآءُ بِغَيْرِ
حِسَابٍ ﴿٢١٢﴾

All mankind were once one single community. Then God sent forth Prophets to give them good tidings and to warn them, and with them He sent down the Book, setting forth the truth, to judge between people over all on which they differed. Yet none other than those who had been given the Book started, out of injustice to one another, to dispute it after clear evidence of the truth had come to them. God, by His will, guided the believers to the truth concerning which they had differed. God guides whom He will to the straight path. (213)

كَانَ ٱلنَّاسُ أُمَّةً وَٰحِدَةً فَبَعَثَ ٱللَّهُ ٱلنَّبِيِّـۧنَ
مُبَشِّرِينَ وَمُنذِرِينَ وَأَنزَلَ مَعَهُمُ
ٱلْكِتَٰبَ بِٱلْحَقِّ لِيَحْكُمَ بَيْنَ ٱلنَّاسِ فِيمَا
ٱخْتَلَفُوا۟ فِيهِ ۚ وَمَا ٱخْتَلَفَ فِيهِ إِلَّا ٱلَّذِينَ
أُوتُوهُ مِنۢ بَعْدِ مَا جَآءَتْهُمُ ٱلْبَيِّنَٰتُ بَغْيًۢا
بَيْنَهُمْ ۖ فَهَدَى ٱللَّهُ ٱلَّذِينَ ءَامَنُوا۟ لِمَا
ٱخْتَلَفُوا۟ فِيهِ مِنَ ٱلْحَقِّ بِإِذْنِهِۦ ۗ وَٱللَّهُ يَهْدِى
مَن يَشَآءُ إِلَىٰ صِرَٰطٍ مُّسْتَقِيمٍ ﴿٢١٣﴾

Do you reckon that you will enter paradise while you have not suffered like those [believers] who passed away before you? Affliction and adversity befell them, and so terribly shaken were they that the Messenger and the believers with him would exclaim, 'When will God's help come?' Surely, God's help is close at hand. (214)

أَمْ حَسِبْتُمْ أَن تَدْخُلُوا۟ ٱلْجَنَّةَ وَلَمَّا
يَأْتِكُم مَّثَلُ ٱلَّذِينَ خَلَوْا۟ مِن قَبْلِكُم ۖ
مَّسَّتْهُمُ ٱلْبَأْسَآءُ وَٱلضَّرَّآءُ وَزُلْزِلُوا۟ حَتَّىٰ
يَقُولَ ٱلرَّسُولُ وَٱلَّذِينَ ءَامَنُوا۟ مَعَهُۥ مَتَىٰ
نَصْرُ ٱللَّهِ ۗ أَلَآ إِنَّ نَصْرَ ٱللَّهِ قَرِيبٌ ﴿٢١٤﴾

Overview

Within the body of Qur'ānic directives and legislative statements, which cumulatively constitute the all-embracing divine code of living, one often comes across elements of a complete theory of personal and social education and enlightenment, based on a full and deep understanding of human nature in its totality. This theory introduces us to different types of human beings with such lucidity and in such detail that almost bring them to life before our eyes. It would be natural to point to real individuals we know from personal experience and say, "These are the very people the Qur'ān talks about!"

In this passage the Qur'ān presents us with two distinct types of human personalities. One is the ostentatious and smooth-talking but malevolent person, outwardly charming but self-centred and usually concealing evil intentions. If called on to fear God and heed His message such a person will not respond, but will arrogantly persist in his misdeeds and wanton intrigues, mischief-making and oppression.

The other type is the sincere and genuine believer whose life is totally devoted to seeking the pleasure of God Almighty. This type of person is sanguine, benevolent and entirely selfless.

The passage then continues with an earnest call to the believers to submit themselves completely to God, unconditionally and without any doubt or hesitation. Muslims are urged to submit themselves to God, emphasizing the vast reality of the essence of faith in God and the divine code of living based on it. There are further reproofs of the Israelites for their betrayal of God's cause. The passage also highlights the fundamental flaws in the unbelievers' outlook on life and their derision of those who believe in God, stressing that *"those that fear God shall be above them in rank on the Day of Resurrection".*

This is followed by a brief reference to the differences that have beset mankind, and the criteria human beings ought to use in judging or settling those differences. The role of the Qur'ān, as the ultimate word of God's universal truth, in that regard is then explained. The passage goes on to elaborate the demands of upholding that truth, and the difficulty in delivering the message that God has entrusted to believers. This serves as a warning and an incentive for the Muslims to live up to the demands and standards of their new global mission, fully confident in God's unfailing support.

Thus, even as the Qur'ān deals with religious and legislative aspects of Islamic life, it provides an overall view of the Divine method in guiding, educating and preparing Muslims for the role of custodians of God's universal message.

Two Different Types of People

> *There is a kind of man who pleases you greatly in the present life by what he says, and he cites God as witness to what is in his heart, whereas he is the most hostile of adversaries. Yet, no sooner does he turn his back than he strives to spread corruption in the world, destroying crops and progeny. God does not love corruption. When it is said to him, 'Have fear of God', his false pride drives him into sin. Therefore, hell will be his allotted portion, and how vile a resting place. But there is also a kind of man who would willingly sell himself, seeking God's pleasure. God is most Compassionate to His servants.* (Verses 204–207)

This fascinating insight into human nature is in itself sufficient proof that the inimitable style in which it is presented cannot be human. The precision, clarity and depth we find here cannot be matched by any human expression.

The words are like the strokes of a master painter's brush, delivered with outstanding vigour and confidence. No sooner are the strokes laid down than the true personality emerges, distinctive and lifelike. We can easily recognize the type that we may exclaim, "Yes, we know the very person the Qur'ān is talking about!" It is a process no less creative than the physical creation of man.

The passage introduces a person who portrays himself as the epitome of goodness, sincerity, dedication, love, innocence, and undoubted willingness to spread goodness, compassion, happiness, and purity of heart all around him. *"There is a kind of man who pleases you greatly in the present life by what he says."* (Verse 204) Such people enchant you with their turn of phrase; their tone of sincerity and claims of integrity and righteousness can easily mislead; and, for good measure, they would cite God as witness to what is in their hearts.

In reality, however, such people are *"the most hostile of adversaries".* Their hearts are filled with malice and hatred, with no room for love, compassion or tolerance. Such two-faced people are capable of the most vicious lies; they are treacherous and totally dishonest. When put to the test, their true personality is revealed: evil, spiteful, and malevolent.

"Yet, no sooner does he turn his back than he strives to spread corruption in the world, destroying crops and progeny. God does not love corruption." (Verse 205) As they go about their daily work, these people do nothing but spread evil and plunder the material and human resources of society. Their actions are a true and accurate reflection of the grudges they harbour and the evil contained inside them. But God is fully aware of the corruption these hypocrites spread in society and throughout the world, and utterly condemns them.

As we read on, more features of this type of people are revealed: *"When it is said to him, 'Have fear of God', his false pride drives him into sin. Therefore, hell will be his allotted portion, and how vile a resting place."* (Verse 206) Intent on pursuing their vile deeds, these people become resistant to advice and reform; if anything, they grow more obstinate and arrogant. They begin to take pride in spreading evil and corruption, with no remorse, sense of guilt or fear of God. The portrait is thus complete. The example is clear, true to life, and instantly recognizable, at any time and in every society.

This snobbery, contention and lack of shame are met with a most swift and appropriate punishment: *"Hell will be his allotted portion, and how vile a resting place."* (Verse 206) That would be more than sufficient retribution. For hell is the most terrible of all punishments: it is a fire fuelled by men and stones; it consumes everything thrown into it. With unmistakable irony, the verse describes hell as their *"resting place"*.

By way of contrast, the *sūrah* presents the other type of human being: *"But there is also a kind of man who would willingly sell himself, seeking God's pleasure. God is most Compassionate to His servants."* (Verse 207) These people are willing to dedicate their souls and bodies to God Almighty, for nothing in return other than His pleasure. It is a deal they conclude without a moment's hesitation, desiring nothing else but divine blessing and approval.

The Arabic expression used here may be interpreted differently to give the same message. The Arabic term denoting 'sell' is also used to mean 'buy'. Thus such people buy themselves by giving up all the pleasures of this world, dedicating themselves purely to God. They are ready and willing to sacrifice all worldly success and pleasure so that they may be accepted by God and admitted into the divine fold.

In his commentary on the Qur'ān, Ibn Kathīr cites several reports suggesting that this verse was revealed with reference to one of the Prophet's Companions, Ṣuhayb ibn Sinān, who was of Byzantine origin. He had accepted Islam when the Prophet was still in Makkah, but when the migration to Madinah took place and he wanted to join the Muslims, the Arab unbelievers prevented him from taking his belongings and his money with him. He decided to give it all up in return for the right to leave Makkah.

He was met at the outskirts of Madinah by a group of Muslims, including 'Umar ibn al-Khaṭṭāb, who greeted him with the words: "Well done! You have struck a profitable bargain!"

He returned the compliment, saying, "And may God make your trade always profitable. What might be the cause of your felicitations?"

They gave him the good news that a verse of the Qur'ān, a great honour, was revealed in tribute to his deal with the Arabs of Makkah.

It is also reported that the Prophet Muḥammad had commented, "Ṣuhayb has struck a profitable deal."

Whether the verse was revealed with reference to this particular incident, or it was simply applicable to it, it certainly covers a range far beyond a single person or event. It portrays a type of person to be found again and again in human societies.

We have two contrasting portraits. One is that of the hypocrite, silver-tongued who is essentially brutal, ill-mannered, contentious, and corrupt. The other is that of the true believer whose whole life is dedicated to the service of God, and who has conquered the temptations of life.

These two living portraits, which reveal some extraordinary aspects of the Qur'ānic style, are for us to study and marvel at. We cannot but stand in awe of God's inimitable power of creation, as we learn how not to be taken in by soft-spoken words or false pretences. We are directed to look deeper into the essence of things, rather than be deceived by outward appearances. The verses also draw our attention to the values and criteria, based on faith in God, which should be used to judge people.

The True Meaning of Islam

Against this background, the *sūrah* addresses the Muslim community, the believers, with a very special and unique instruction:

> *Believers, submit all of you to God and do not follow Satan's footsteps. He is indeed your open foe. If you should stumble after all evidence of the truth has come to you, then know that God is Almighty, Wise.* (Verses 208–209)

The call is addressed to the true adherents of Islam, whose faith sets them apart and links them directly to God. The invitation entails, first of all, total submission to God Almighty in all matters, simple or grave. Believers must surrender to God their intentions, actions, desires, and their whole destiny, and accept His judgement without hesitation, and with total trust and self-assurance. They will submit in full certainty and confidence that God will lead them to happiness and self-fulfilment, in both this life and the life to come.

The fact that the call was made at that particular stage of the development of the Muslim community suggests that there were Muslims who fell short of the required degree of obedience and submission to God, in their public as well as their private life. This in itself is not unusual, and could explain the need for such a call to be made from time to time, in order to create the required discipline in the community and enable it to function as a coherent, self-assured, and forward-looking body.

Heeding this call takes the Muslim into a realm of peace and security. The world of Islamic faith radiates tranquillity, harmony, reassurance and clarity of vision. A believing Muslim lives in total peace with himself, with his conscience and his mind, with other people and with his whole environment. He lives in peace with all the world and everything in it. He enjoys peace on earth and peace in heaven.

This peace emanates, first and foremost, from a clear, simple and compelling understanding of the essence and nature of the Divine Being. There is but one God, to whom every Muslim believer turns for guidance. Freed from paganism and idolatry, a Muslim believer happily and honestly devotes his loyalty and energy to God alone, to whom there is but one straight path.

He is mighty, omnipotent, supreme. Turning to Him for help and guidance is turning to the ultimate power that controls all existence.

Having thus sought His succour, the believer is totally secure and confident, having no cause or reason to fear anyone or anything else. Submission to the all-powerful and supreme God is a sufficient guarantee of perpetual sustenance, which spares the believer the need to seek livelihood and support anywhere else.

God is also just and wise, unlike pagan and man-made deities. His might and omnipotence are a safeguard against injustice, inequity and bias. To seek His protection is to seek dependable justice, care and security.

He is also merciful and compassionate, generous and benevolent, forgiving and responsive to those who repent and seek His protection. Under God's protection a believer feels total peace, security, understanding and sympathy.

Islam reveals to Muslims that every attribute of God Almighty inspires an overwhelming feeling of added intimacy and renewed tranquillity, bringing about an unshakeable sense of protection, compassion, self-esteem, stability and peace.

A believer's heart is filled with peace as a result of the clear and robust understanding of the nature of the relationship between God and man, between Creator and creation and between man and the world around him. God has created the world and everything in it according to a sound scheme and for a definite purpose. The creation of man is a deliberate and carefully considered act, and he does not stand alone; all the natural prerequisites for his existence and well-being are present in nature and the world around him, and available for his benefit. As God's representative on earth, man is given honour by God and enjoys a privileged position in the divine order of things. In discharging his mission, he receives God's unstinted support and the support of the world around, with which, through submitting to the will of God Almighty, he shares a harmony of bonding. Man is invited to partake in a cosmic festival of divine creation, to reflect on its marvels, to interact and become intimate with everything and every being in this vast, rich and dynamic universe.

The faith that teaches its followers to reflect on the tiniest plants, and promises to reward them for watering them and looking after them and helping them grow and flourish, is a beautiful and noble one. It fills man's heart with peace and releases him to embrace the whole cosmos and everything in it, promoting peace, mercy, love, compassion, and security all around him.

Belief in the hereafter plays a fundamental role in radiating peace throughout a believer's surroundings, and prevents anxiety, resentment and despair. It makes it clear that the final reckoning and the real and just reward are reserved for another time, when full justice shall be guaranteed. One need not regret the good deeds and the sacrifices and the struggles that may go unrewarded in this life, nor should one lose hope that justice will be done when in this brief journey of life one encounters hatred, wrongdoing or oppression. God harbours no grudges against anyone, and His justice shall be done.

Belief in the hereafter saves believers from following the frenetic rat-race of mankind, in which values and sanctity are brazenly trampled upon and violated. This belief gives real promise of abundance, magnanimity and recompense for all victims, and can turn that contentious and selfish race into a peaceful and fair contest, assuaging the frenzied feeling that this transient life is man's only chance to have, hold and enjoy.

The conviction that the ultimate purpose of human existence is to worship and serve God can elevate man's conscience and consciousness, his activity and performance, to wider and more glorious horizons. It purifies and develops his methods and techniques; all his pursuits and activities and his whole vocation as God's vicegerent on earth become means of worship of, and devotion to, God and the establishment of His order. Man will thus shun treachery, deceit, law breaking, arrogance, oppression, and all such foul and vile behaviour. He will avoid haste and recklessness, shortcuts and aimless wandering; the sincerity of his intentions and his diligence are the best guarantee of success. Man will be free of fear and anxiety throughout his life, because he is aware that at every step he is asserting his own role and serving God Almighty. Every action he takes will bring him closer to God.

A believer's feeling that he is moving according to God's order, in obedience to, and in fulfilment of, His will, and the security, peace and tranquillity such a feeling generates, fill his heart and soul with inner peace. Even during armed combat against his and God's enemies, he continues to feel and enjoy such peace because he is conscious that he is fighting in the cause of God and to establish His order, not for worldly or personal gain, privilege or ambition.

The believer's feeling that he is living in harmony with God's order and the laws of nature, and acting in unison with all other creatures and forces around him, brings a state of peace and tranquillity. His existence is reinforced by the world around him, and together they move in harmony and union, without conflict or contradiction, guided by God's light and devoted to Him.

The obligations prescribed by Islam are in full harmony with human nature and aim to keep that nature on the right path. They are well within man's capabilities and take full account of his aptitudes and disposition. They leave no human talent or ability untapped, enhancing and promoting them, and fulfilling man's physical and spiritual needs. In discharging these obligations, man faces no hardship or distress, but seeks God's pleasure with confidence and peace of mind.

The society which Islam creates existed once in its purest and best form. Islam then continued to give different examples of it in varying degrees of purity, in various parts of the world. It is a society established on the principles of love, compassion, unity, solidarity and care. Whatever its degree of purity, it remains the best and most shining social experiment the world has known.

It is a society brought together by the single bond of religious faith, which is greater than any bond of race, origin, colour or language. Muslims are described in the Qur'ān as the community of 'brothers,' (49: 10) and by the Prophet Muḥammad as 'one body; if any part suffers any pain all other parts share in its complaint, feeling sleepless and feverish.' [Related by Aḥmad and Muslim]

It is a society with a strong code of social morality based on Qur'ānic teachings and exhortations, some of which are outlined in the statements:

> *When a greeting is offered you, answer it with an even better greeting, or [at least] with its like.* (4: 86)
>
> *Never turn your face away in disdain to others, and do not walk haughtily on the ground, for God does not like the arrogant and vain-glorious.* (31: 18)
>
> *Repel [evil] with something that is better. Thus, a person with whom you had enmity may become as though he has always been close to you and a true friend.* (41: 34)
>
> *Believers! No men shall deride other men: it may well be that those [whom they deride] are better than themselves. And no women [shall deride other] women: it may well be that those [whom they*

> *deride] are better than themselves. And neither shall you defame yourselves, nor insult one another by [opprobrious] epithets. Ill-seeming is a name connoting wickedness [to be used of one] after he has believed. Those who do not repent are indeed wrongdoers... Do not spy on one another, nor backbite one another. Would any of you like to eat the flesh of his dead brother? Surely you would loathe it. And remain God-fearing. God is certainly the One who accepts repentance, and He is Merciful.* (49: 11–12)

It is a society protected by solid guarantees enshrined in the Qur'ān: *"Believers! If any evildoer comes to you with a piece of news, make sure of it first, lest you should wrong others unwittingly and then regret your action."* (49: 6) *"Believers! Avoid suspicion as much as possible, for, some such suspicion is a sin. And do not spy on one another."* (49: 12) *"Believers, shun most suspicions, for in some cases suspicion is injustice, and do not spy on one another"* (49: 12) *"Believers, do not enter houses other than your own unless you have obtained their residents' permission and greeted them."* (24: 27) The Prophet Muḥammad clearly states: "All that belongs to a Muslim is inviolable and forbidden to any other Muslim: his blood, personal honour and property." [Related by Mālik, al-Bukhārī and Muslim]

It is a clean and virtuous society, where promiscuity and loose sexual conduct are stringently outlawed, and where lewd and indecent behaviour is given no room to thrive. It is well protected against all forms of over-indulgence, and against unrestricted exploitation and manipulation of people's sensual and sexual desires common in many non-Muslim societies, past and present. The principles of this social morality are derived from a host of Qur'ānic directives, a few of which may be cited below.

> *Those who delight in spreading immoral slander against the believers shall face grievous punishment in this life and in the life to come. God knows, whereas you do not know.* (24: 19)
>
> *As for the adulteress and the adulterer: flog each of them with a hundred lashes, and let no compassion for them hold you from [carrying out] this law of God, if you truly believe in God and the Last Day; and let their punishment be witnessed by a group of believers.* (24: 2)

As for those who accuse chaste women [of adultery] and are unable to produce four witnesses: flog them with eighty lashes. Do not accept their testimony ever after, for they are transgressors. (24: 4)

Tell the believing men to lower their gaze and to be mindful of their chastity: this will be most conducive to their purity. God is aware of all they do. And tell the believing women to lower their gaze and be mindful of their chastity and not to display their charms in public beyond what may decently be apparent thereof. Hence, let them draw their head-covering over their bosoms. And let them not display their charms except to their husbands, or their fathers, or their husbands' fathers, or their sons, or their husbands' sons, or their brothers, or their brothers' sons, or their sisters' sons, or their womenfolk, or those whom they rightfully possess, or such male attendants as are beyond all sexual desire, or children who are yet unaware of women's nakedness. And let them not walk in such a way as to draw attention to their hidden charms. Believers, turn all of you to God in repentance, so that you may be successful. (24: 30–31)

The Qur'ān addresses the Prophet's wives, the purest women ever to grace this earth, living in the purest house at the purest place in the purest time, saying: *"Wives of the Prophet, you are not like any other women, provided you maintain your fear of God. Do not be over-soft in your speech, lest any whose heart is diseased should be moved to desire [you], and always speak in a kindly way. Abide quietly in your homes, and do not flaunt your charms as women used to flaunt them in the old days of pagan ignorance. Attend regularly to your prayers, pay zakāt [the purifying alms], and obey God and His Messenger. Women of the Prophet's household, God wishes only to remove from you all that might be loathsome, and to totally purify you."* (33: 32–33)

A Caring and Peaceful Society

In such a society husbands and wives grow to trust each other, and people feel that their families and their honour are safe and respected. All society is free from stress and anxiety. There are no salacious or lurid temptations that might lead people to violate the moral codes and norms of society. It is a tranquil and peaceful society.

A Muslim society gives every able-bodied member the opportunity to work and earn a decent living. The infirm and invalid are cared for and helped to lead a dignified life. It provides for those who seek to marry and start a family. It is a society where the residents of a locality are collectively responsible for the death of any one of them through hunger. Some Muslim jurists would charge them with negligence and require them to pay indemnity for manslaughter to his family.

Under the laws of Islam, all basic rights and freedoms are protected and guaranteed; no one may be condemned on suspicion alone. According to Islamic law, illegal entry into homes or private property, invasion of privacy, homicide, theft, or robbery of any kind are strictly forbidden and are punishable crimes.

A Muslim society is built on mutual consultation and cooperation among its members, on equality and rigorous justice, where everyone feels that their rights are subject only to God's law and not to the fancy or prejudice or interests of any individual or group.

It is, further, the only human society in which people are not subjected to the rule of other people. The whole society, the rulers as well as the ruled, are subordinate to God and His laws, and comply willingly and confidently with His will and order. All stand equal before God, the just Lord of all creation.

These are some aspects of the peace the *sūrah* invites the believers to enter into in submitting themselves completely to God. The significance of such peace can only be appreciated when one considers the extent of confusion and mental stress plaguing non-Muslim societies as well as societies that have cast Islam and its teachings aside. Despite all the material comfort and progress these societies may achieve, their life remains aimless, confused and miserable.

In a highly developed country like Sweden, for example, people enjoy a high per capita income, free health care and sickness benefit, free education and an array of state grants and easy loans for students. Newly married couples receive financial assistance to help them set up homes. Indeed, in Sweden there are numerous other manifestations of true material affluence. But where is it all leading to in a country where the majority have abandoned their faith in God? It is a society with incurable ills, living under the threat of a rapidly declining birth rate, rampant promiscuity, a high divorce rate (one in six marriages ends in divorce!),[1] alcohol and drug addiction, widespread psychological and mental disease and disturbed behaviour, and a rising rate of suicide. The same can be said about the United States or Russia.

Such wretchedness can only be the result of lack of belief in God, without which souls are deprived of happiness, security and peace of mind.

As God calls upon the believers to submit themselves to Him alone, He warns them against following *"Satan's footsteps; he is indeed your open foe."* (Verse 208) There is no third way; it is either God's Guidance or Satan's confusion; either the way of Islam or the way of ignorance and foolishness. A Muslim has to be very clear on this point and permit no doubt or hesitation.

In life there can be no compromises or half measures; the choice is between right and wrong, guidance and confusion, order and chaos, Islam and unbelief, the way of God and the way of Satan. God invites believers to peace and obedience and warns them against following Satan, in an effort to arouse their emotions and inspire their conscience and to make them conscious of Satan's avowed enmity to believers. It is a hostility of which the believing heart is ever aware.

The *sūrah* goes on to point to the consequences of taking that warning lightly, saying: *"If you should stumble after all evidence of the truth has come to you, then know that God is Almighty, Wise."* (Verse 209)

The reminder carries awesome power. Those who disregard God's advice, challenge His power and question the wisdom of His guidance, expose themselves to condemnation and destruction.

At this point the *sūrah* adopts a different approach to emphasize its previous warnings and speaks in the third person, saying: *"Are they waiting for God to reveal Himself to them in the shadows of clouds, together with the angels? The case will have been settled then. To God shall all things return."* (Verse 210)

It condemns those who waver and are reluctant to submit and come into the fold of God's peace. It questions their motives and the reasons that hold them back, and asks whether they will remain fixed in their obstinacy until such time as God, flanked by angels, should appear to them in person. In other words, are they waiting for the fearful

1. The author wrote this in the early 1960s, when such divorce rate was considered very high. Now it is much higher throughout Europe. Other social ills are also at higher peaks. – Editor's note.

Day of Judgement to arrive? That day will indeed come, and the *sūrah* moves at once to that momentous day to tell us that everything has been settled. Time has come to a stop. The opportunity to believe and repent has gone for ever. No one could be saved now, as all stand facing their Lord to whom *"shall all things return"*.

This is an illustration of the unique and effective style of the Qur'ān, which brings to life the scenes it describes, and makes the reader or listener feel, see and hear what is going on as if it were happening now.

How much longer will they dither when the chance to come into the fold of God's peace is calling, and the final judgement is so close? God's invitation is a promise of peace and happiness both in this life and the life to come.

A Question Put to the Israelites

The *sūrah* then addresses the Prophet Muḥammad, ordering him to inquire of the Israelites, described earlier in the *sūrah* as dithering and hesitant in their response to God's call: how many signs they chose to disregard and how they abused the privileges God had bestowed upon them and how much they distorted His Message: *"Ask the Children of Israel how many a veritable sign We have given them. He who alters the grace of God after it has been bestowed on him [should know that] God is severe in retribution."* (Verse 211)

Referring back to the experience of the Israelites at this juncture is a timely warning to Muslims not to follow their example. Muslims are urged not to hesitate in responding to God's call, or show any reluctance or stubbornness, or insist on miracles as proof of its authenticity. By avoiding these pitfalls, Muslims will be sure to avoid the Israelites' fate. The instruction to *"ask the Children of Israel"* is not meant literally, of course, but purely to introduce the next point: the profusion of evidence presented to them, either at their request or directly given by God, and their persistent refusal to accept and believe in God, or submit themselves to Him.

Having drawn attention to the Israelites' example, the *sūrah* makes a general reference to the 'grace' of faith and peace, and warns: *"He who alters the grace of God after it has been bestowed on him [should know that] God is severe in retribution."* (Verse 211)

Whenever a society turns away from God's grace and denies His favour, it is beset by tension and strife, as manifested all over the world today in the inordinate spread of stress and depression, social and military conflict, alcohol and drug abuse, and the emergence of extreme and bizarre alternatives to religious faith.

The strange trends in fashion, the arts, entertainment and general social behaviour, which appear almost every day in modern society, as well as the changing social norms relating to marriage and the family, to sexual relations and attitudes, are all indications of social alienation, insecurity, discontent and a lack of direction in life. Modern life seems almost like a demented attempt to escape, where individuals and groups tend to break away from the norm and reject everything, but have no idea what they are looking for. That is the outcome of renouncing God's teachings, and ignoring His call to enter the fold of faith.

The *sūrah* then contrasts believers and unbelievers, and the difference in their outlook: *"The life of this world has been made alluring to the unbelievers; hence, they scoff at those who believe; but those that fear God shall be above them in rank on the Day of Resurrection. God grants sustenance to whom He wills beyond all reckoning."* (Verse 212)

This life, with its transient concerns and ephemeral interests and enjoyments, is all that the unbelievers know and aspire to. They are unable to see beyond the here-and-now; they know of no greater values or aspirations other than those of life on this earth. Consequently, their scope is limited, their vision is blurred, and they are deprived of the higher understanding and greater reward experienced by believers.

A believer in God may look with disdain at material and worldly things, but that is not due to a negative or pessimistic view of life. It is because a believer seeks more from life than mere material or sensual enjoyment. A believer aims to establish God's order in society and lead his community towards a better and more fulfilled way of life.

Believers are altruistic in their approach to life; they have high hopes for humanity, and they care for the progress and well-being of others. They look beyond their selfish egotistic needs and desires and make tremendous personal sacrifices for the sake of their beliefs and ideals. From the point of view of a person who only thinks of this life's concerns and worldly affairs, that might seem strange or even ludicrous. Hence it may evoke scorn and derision from unbelievers.

But what justification could there be for such a reaction? The unbelievers' opinion is erroneous and utterly false. It is the view of unbelief and ignorance. The true measure is that of God who confirms that *"those that fear God shall be above them in rank on the Day of Resurrection"*. (Verse 212) Believers should uphold their faith and disregard the mockery and scorn of the unbelievers. They have God's word that they shall occupy a higher position than those unbelievers on the Day of Resurrection, and that shall be the real test and the final judgement.

What God has in store for believers is far better and far more favourable. They shall be rewarded in abundance, according to God's wish and wisdom, either here in this life or in the life to come, for *"God grants sustenance to whom He wills beyond all reckoning."*

God is the gracious giver who gives directly, generously and with no restriction. In His infinite wisdom, He may give to those who do not believe much of the comforts and allurements of this world. What He grants them is not based on any merit they may have. He also gives to the believers whatever He chooses to grant them both in this life and in the life to come. He is the sole benefactor and His choice is right, wise and most durable.

The two types of human being – believers who take their guidance and advice from God, and others for whom this life is the be-all and end-all, can be found in every age and every generation. The former rise above the trivialities of life to fulfil their humanity and become masters of their world and their destiny, while the latter shall ever be attached to, and enslaved by, the prurient and lewd aspects of life.

Believers will always look from their elevated position on unbelievers, no matter how affluent or influential these may be. Unbelievers, who think they are more fortunate and privileged, may well be contemptuous of the faithful, but it is they who deserve pity and commiseration.

A Single Community and Divergent Views

The *sūrah* continues to elaborate on the differences among human beings in their beliefs, outlook, values and standards, concluding with a statement identifying the ultimate judgement and criteria to pronounce on those differences.

> *All mankind were once one single community. Then God sent forth Prophets to give them good tidings and to warn them, and with*

them He sent down the Book, setting forth the truth, to judge between people over all on which they differed. Yet none other than those who had been given the Book started, out of injustice to one another, to dispute it after clear evidence of the truth had come to them. God, by His will, guided the believers to the truth concerning which they had differed. God guides whom He will to the straight path. (Verse 213)

That is it in a nutshell! Humanity emerged as a single community, living according to the same code and upholding similar beliefs. This may be taken as reference to the very first nucleus of human beings to live on earth, consisting of Adam, Eve and their offspring, before they multiplied and adopted various beliefs and ways of life. What the Qur'ān asserts here, however, is that mankind shares the same origin and that we are members of the same human family. Such was the will of God, to instil the family principle in human life and establish it as the cornerstone of the human community. Time was when that early group remained close-knit and uniform in its outlook and understanding, but it was later to grow, multiply and scatter in various directions; their way of life evolved in different ways, and so did their mental and cultural abilities and norms. New trends, fresh ideas and advanced social and cultural forms emerged which, as God knew, would be useful and advantageous to human society.

With progress and diversity came differences, disagreements and divisions. New beliefs, traditions and ideologies appeared and were accepted in various degrees by various communities. It was then that God, in His infinite wisdom, decided to send forth Prophets to convey the promise of success and to warn against deviation. With the Prophets, God *"sent down the Book, setting forth the truth, to judge between people over all on which they differed."* (Verse 213)

Here is a profound truth: it is in the nature of human beings to differ and disagree. Such a propensity is fundamental to the human disposition, and essential for the fulfilment of man's role as God's vicegerent on earth. This task calls for a divergence of functions, aptitudes and talents that are compatible and complementary to one another and come together in harmony, according to God's universal scheme and wisdom. Different needs require different abilities.

Differences of ability and function lead to differences in perception, outlook, interests, approach and method. These differences and variations, however, are harmonized and regulated within the wide, all-embracing framework of the divine order of faith where abilities, faculties and resources are given the best chance to grow and develop for the good of the individual and the community, as well as for the benefit of humanity at large.

However, it is essential that there should be a proper and valid standard by which differences and divisions may be judged and evaluated. Such a point of reference is alluded to in the *sūrah* when it says that God: *"sent down the Book, setting forth the truth, to judge between people over all on which they differed".* (Verse 213)

It is worth pausing here to consider the statement that the Book is *"setting forth the truth".* This is an affirmation that the Book, the revelation from God to mankind, has come with the definitive and absolute truth. It is the ultimate, pre-eminent and sole arbiter and judge of all human thought and behaviour. Without this authority society would be at a loss, life would descend into chaos, confusion and strife, and mankind would know no peace or happiness.

This is vital in determining the source of human values, thought and understanding, and for defining the laws that govern human relations. The source is God, and God alone, who has sent down revelations, the Book, to establish the truth and maintain harmony, justice and peace in the world.

The Book is, in essence, one and the same, whose message all Messengers had delivered. Its teachings convey a faith based on belief in one God and the same set of laws and values for all mankind. As time goes on, changes occur according to peoples' needs from generation to generation, and from one stage of development to another, culminating in the ultimate version of God's message represented by the Islamic faith. Under the caring eye of God Almighty and the vibrant and dynamic laws and teachings of divine revelation, Islam took the scope of human experience to new horizons, enabling man to reach new heights of progress and achievement within the all-embracing framework of values provided by the faith.

What the Qur'ān states here is the definitive Islamic view of the origin and development of religion and religious ideology in the world. Briefly stated, this says that every Prophet came with teachings based on the fundamental principle of God's absolute oneness. Inevitably, after some time, deviations and myths crept in, causing people to depart from the original authentic traditions and teachings, thereby precipitating the need for a new Prophet and a new set of teachings to revive and restore the preceding one, taking into account the mental, cultural and material developments and changes society had undergone and the new conditions prevailing. This is a far more estimable theory of the history of religion than others advanced by secular thinkers, and unwittingly adopted by some Muslim students of religion.

The united kinship of religious faith is congruous with the role and function of the Book God has revealed to mankind at every phase through all the Prophets and messengers, throughout human history.

The fact is that it was necessary for a definite and firm standard to exist as a reference point for all mankind. It was likewise necessary that this standard should come from a source above the human mind and independent from it. It had to come from an impartial source, not encumbered or swayed by human prejudices or shortcomings.

Such a responsibility requires an infinite and comprehensive knowledge of past, present and future events, not restricted by the limitations of time and space. It also requires perfection, total self-sufficiency, and freedom from all the needs, instincts, ambitions, desires and fears that constrain and control human beings. It can then be given only by God who is influenced neither by personal purpose, prejudice or desire, nor by weakness or shortcoming.

Man's role is one of facing change and coping with new circumstances and needs that arise as a result of it, and of adapting to them within the prevailing conditions. The divine criteria act as a reference point and a guide, directing mankind to what is best and most advantageous. Thus life proceeds along proper lines, and people are confident that their fate and destiny are in the hands of an impartial, fair and caring God.

The Book was not revealed in order to eliminate or restrict the differences and variety in human talent, ability or inclination, but it is there as an arbiter and a reference point whenever disputes and controversies arise.

This argument gives rise to another fundamental aspect of the Islamic view of human history. Islam considers the Book revealed by God as a criterion and an arbiter for mankind, a foundation for human life on which it can rise or fall. Society will progress and improve as long as it adheres to the teachings of God's Book, and it will falter and deviate when it neglects them, even if this was the choice of the majority in society. Right and wrong are not to be decided by human individuals or through a ballot box. The Islamic view is that the norms, traditions, systems, and laws people may adopt and accept as a way of life for human society at any particular time in history have no merit or consistency if they are at variance or in contradiction with God's Book. The whole philosophy on which such a way of life is based would be discredited, no matter how durable it might prove in practice.

This argument is important in protecting the foundations of religious thought against human interference. In Muslim society, for example, serious deviations have occurred at certain stages of its history, and such deviation continued to move further away. But it would be a travesty of the truth to argue that these darker chapters are in any way representative of the true image or spirit of Muslim life. Islam, as a religion and a way of life, will remain unsullied by that inauspicious history, which must be discredited and renounced. For genuine Islamic life to be resumed and a distinctive Muslim society to be rebuilt, deviant practices that might have occurred at certain periods of Muslim history have to be cast aside. Reference should be made again directly to the Book that God has revealed, containing the whole truth as arbiter and guide for all mankind.

The *sūrah* goes on to explain why people allowed their whims and prejudices to cause them to neglect God's Book and turn away from the truth and the guidance it had brought them: *"Yet none other than those who had been given the Book started, out of injustice to one another, to dispute it after clear evidence of the truth had come to them."* (Verse 213) Jealousy, greed, caprice and self-aggrandizement were some of the motives behind the divisions, disagreements and conflict that have beset mankind throughout history.

No two people could disagree over the veracity and authenticity of God's revelations unless one or both of them are adversely motivated. True believers are in full agreement: *"God, by His will, guided the believers to the truth concerning which they had differed. God guides whom He will to the straight path."* (Verse 213)

God guides believers to the true and straight path outlined by His revelations, for their sincerity and devotion and for their genuine desire to seek the truth and live by the truth. God, in His infinite wisdom, bestows such grace and privilege on those who earn it with their passion and enthusiasm for the truth. Those are they who shall be liberated to enjoy peace and happiness and the favour of God Almighty. They are the ones who submit themselves totally to God, and they are the ones who are granted the highest position by God. This is true even though people who are ignorant of God's standards may think them to lead a deprived sort of life in this world. It is true even though they may be derided or scoffed at by foolish unbelievers.

When Will God's Help Arrive?

As it comes to a close, this highly instructive passage addresses the fearful adversity the believers encountered as a result of their disagreement and confrontation with the Arab unbelievers on the one hand, and with the followers of earlier religions, such as the Jews, on the other. The *sūrah* reassures the believers that what they faced was part of the experience and education they needed to qualify for God's reward in paradise. Believers must defend their faith and, in doing so, have to face up to numerous challenges and much hardship. They will experience triumphs as well as setbacks. If they persevere and stand firm and hold on to their beliefs and convictions, they will earn God's succour and trust. They will deserve to be the custodians of God's message in this world. Their reward will be in paradise in the life to come. It is a fitting reward for their courage in defeating their own selfishness and greed, resisting all manner of temptation, and refusing to surrender their life and destiny to any other power or authority except that of God Almighty.

> *Do you reckon that you will enter paradise while you have not suffered like those [believers] who passed away before you? Affliction and adversity befell them, and so terribly shaken were they that the messenger and the believers with him would exclaim, 'When will God's help come?' Surely, God's help is close at hand.* (Verse 214)

With these poignant and profound words, and in this direct manner, God addresses the founding community of Islam, drawing their attention to the experiences of their fellow believers before them who were entrusted with the same task of establishing the divine code of living on earth. Nevertheless, the message in these words is timeless. It is directed to all human groups to whom God assigns that honourable task.

It is an awesome experience that drives God's own Messenger and those who have accepted the faith close to despair and makes them cry out with frustration: " *'When will God's help come?'* " It is a picture of great trepidation and unimaginable apprehension that cause a believer's faith to be tested so severely and shaken in such a profound manner. However, with determination and steadfastness, God's help is sure to arrive, for *"Surely, God's help is close at hand."*

God's support that ensures victory is reserved for those who earn it: those who persevere and stand firm to the end in the face of all adversity and misfortune, never wavering but always certain that God's help is on its way. No matter how severe the ordeal may become, true believers will always look to God, and to God alone, for salvation and support. By displaying such faith and trust in God, believers are deservedly rewarded by being admitted into paradise.

The dynamic of social and religious struggle reinforces the human spirit and encourages man to rise above his own ego and so emerge purer and stronger, ready to uphold the faith with greater energy and vigour. Thus, believers become a shining role model even for their most ardent adversaries, some of whom are liable to be impressed and join ranks with the believers, as witnessed throughout human history.

But even if this were not the case, something else much greater and much more admirable happens: advocates of God's order are liberated from subordination to any worldly power or temptation. Life and its comforts become of no real consequence, and man assumes control of his world, which can only mean a triumph for humanity and the human spirit as a whole.

The ingredients of success are faith, hard work, sacrifice, and perseverance. With those, victory is guaranteed and the road to greater, everlasting rewards, to eternal bliss, is direct and clear.

13

Worse Than Murder

They ask you what they should spend [in charity]. Say, 'Anything good you spend of your wealth should go to parents and the near of kin, to orphans and the needy, and to travellers in need. God is well aware of whatever good you do.' (215)

يَسْـَٔلُونَكَ مَاذَا يُنفِقُونَ ۖ قُلْ مَآ أَنفَقْتُم
مِّنْ خَيْرٍ فَلِلْوَٰلِدَيْنِ وَٱلْأَقْرَبِينَ وَٱلْيَتَٰمَىٰ
وَٱلْمَسَٰكِينِ وَٱبْنِ ٱلسَّبِيلِ ۗ وَمَا تَفْعَلُوا۟ مِنْ
خَيْرٍ فَإِنَّ ٱللَّهَ بِهِۦ عَلِيمٌ ﴿٢١٥﴾

Fighting is ordained for you, even though it is hateful to you. But it may well be that you hate a thing while it is good for you, and it may well be that you love a thing while it is bad for you. God knows, whereas you do not know. (216)

كُتِبَ عَلَيْكُمُ ٱلْقِتَالُ وَهُوَ كُرْهٌ لَّكُمْ ۖ
وَعَسَىٰٓ أَن تَكْرَهُوا۟ شَيْـًٔا وَهُوَ خَيْرٌ لَّكُمْ ۖ
وَعَسَىٰٓ أَن تُحِبُّوا۟ شَيْـًٔا وَهُوَ شَرٌّ لَّكُمْ ۗ
وَٱللَّهُ يَعْلَمُ وَأَنتُمْ لَا تَعْلَمُونَ ﴿٢١٦﴾

They ask you about fighting in the sacred month. Say, 'Fighting in it is a grave offence, but to turn people away from God's path, to disbelieve in Him and in the Sacred Mosque, and to expel its people from it – [all this] is far more grave in God's sight.' Religious persecution is worse than killing. They shall not cease to fight you until they

يَسْـَٔلُونَكَ عَنِ ٱلشَّهْرِ ٱلْحَرَامِ قِتَالٍ فِيهِ ۖ
قُلْ قِتَالٌ فِيهِ كَبِيرٌ ۖ وَصَدٌّ عَن سَبِيلِ
ٱللَّهِ وَكُفْرٌۢ بِهِۦ وَٱلْمَسْجِدِ ٱلْحَرَامِ
وَإِخْرَاجُ أَهْلِهِۦ مِنْهُ أَكْبَرُ عِندَ ٱللَّهِ ۚ
وَٱلْفِتْنَةُ أَكْبَرُ مِنَ ٱلْقَتْلِ ۗ وَلَا يَزَالُونَ
يُقَٰتِلُونَكُمْ حَتَّىٰ يَرُدُّوكُمْ عَن دِينِكُمْ

إِنِ ٱسْتَطَٰعُوا۟ ۚ وَمَن يَرْتَدِدْ مِنكُمْ عَن
دِينِهِۦ فَيَمُتْ وَهُوَ كَافِرٌ فَأُو۟لَٰٓئِكَ
حَبِطَتْ أَعْمَٰلُهُمْ فِى ٱلدُّنْيَا وَٱلْءَاخِرَةِ ۖ
وَأُو۟لَٰٓئِكَ أَصْحَٰبُ ٱلنَّارِ ۖ هُمْ فِيهَا
خَٰلِدُونَ ﴿٢١٧﴾

force you to renounce your faith, if they can. But whoever of you renounces his faith and dies an unbeliever, his works shall come to nothing in this world and in the world to come. Such people are destined for hell, wherein they shall abide. (217)

إِنَّ ٱلَّذِينَ ءَامَنُوا۟ وَٱلَّذِينَ هَاجَرُوا۟
وَجَٰهَدُوا۟ فِى سَبِيلِ ٱللَّهِ أُو۟لَٰٓئِكَ يَرْجُونَ
رَحْمَتَ ٱللَّهِ ۚ وَٱللَّهُ غَفُورٌ رَّحِيمٌ ﴿٢١٨﴾

Those who have believed and those who have forsaken their homeland and striven hard for God's cause are indeed the ones who may look forward to God's mercy. God is much-Forgiving, Merciful. (218)

يَسْـَٔلُونَكَ عَنِ ٱلْخَمْرِ وَٱلْمَيْسِرِ ۖ
قُلْ فِيهِمَآ إِثْمٌ كَبِيرٌ وَمَنَٰفِعُ لِلنَّاسِ
وَإِثْمُهُمَآ أَكْبَرُ مِن نَّفْعِهِمَا ۗ
وَيَسْـَٔلُونَكَ مَاذَا يُنفِقُونَ قُلِ ٱلْعَفْوَ ۗ
كَذَٰلِكَ يُبَيِّنُ ٱللَّهُ لَكُمُ ٱلْءَايَٰتِ
لَعَلَّكُمْ تَتَفَكَّرُونَ ﴿٢١٩﴾

They ask you about intoxicants and games of chance. Say, 'In both there is great evil although they have some benefits for people, but their evil is far greater than their benefit.' They ask you what they should spend in charity; say, 'Whatever you can spare.' Thus God makes plain His revelations so that you may reflect (219)

فِى ٱلدُّنْيَا وَٱلْءَاخِرَةِ ۗ وَيَسْـَٔلُونَكَ عَنِ
ٱلْيَتَٰمَىٰ ۖ قُلْ إِصْلَاحٌ لَّهُمْ خَيْرٌ ۖ وَإِن تُخَالِطُوهُمْ
فَإِخْوَٰنُكُمْ ۚ وَٱللَّهُ يَعْلَمُ ٱلْمُفْسِدَ مِنَ

upon this life and the life to come. They ask you about orphans; say, 'To improve their conditions is best. If you mix their affairs with yours, remember that they are your brothers.

God knows him who spoils things and him who improves. Had God so willed, He would indeed have overburdened you. God is indeed Almighty, Wise.' (220)	ٱلْمُصْلِحِ وَلَوْ شَآءَ ٱللَّهُ لَأَعْنَتَكُمْ إِنَّ ٱللَّهَ عَزِيزٌ حَكِيمٌ ﴿٢٢٠﴾

Overview

The most notable feature of the next passage is that it deals with specific religious rulings. These come in the form of answers to questions, reflecting a degree of alertness in the Muslim community, and an eagerness to know and understand the requirements and obligations of their new faith. It shows a desire on their part to live up to the demands of Islam in every aspect of everyday life. This is indeed the mark of a true Muslim: to learn Islamic rulings with respect to every detail, no matter how trivial. No action is taken before establishing the position of Islam on it: if sanctioned and approved, it becomes part of a Muslim's way of life; otherwise, it is shunned and avoided. This sensitivity is second nature to every true Muslim.

Questions were raised as a result of hostile propaganda spread by some Arabian Jews, hypocrites, and unbelievers among the Arabs. Muslims would then put those questions to the Prophet Muḥammad, either to seek clarification or to dispel doubts stirred by that poisonous propaganda. Revelation would often be received by the Prophet giving comprehensive and final answers. This process informs and educates the Muslims about their religion and pre-empts any hostile schemes or designs being contemplated against them.

This illustrates the dynamics of the battles the Qur'ān was fighting to enlighten individual Muslims and to reinforce the Muslim community in combating outside threats.

This passage covers questions relating to charity: what and how much should be given and to whom. There are questions on fighting during the sacred months, drinking and gambling, and the treatment of orphans. We will discuss the reasons that gave rise to these questions as we discuss the relevant verses.

Balancing Kindness and Personal Preferences

> *They ask you what they should spend [in charity]. Say, 'Anything good you spend of your wealth should go to parents and the near of kin, to orphans and the needy, and to travellers in need. God is well aware of whatever good you do.* (Verse 215)

The subject of charity had already been dealt with in several Qur'ānic passages that preceded the revelation of the present verse. The circumstances that witnessed the birth of Islam made voluntary financial contributions by Muslims absolutely essential in order for the community to emerge and consolidate its position, considering the great difficulties and threat of war it was facing. It was also essential as an expression of solidarity and cohesion within the community, and to eliminate inequality and reinforce loyalty and self-sufficiency. All these are indispensable qualities for building up a true and practical sense of community among the Muslims.

At this point we are told that some Muslims asked *"what they should spend [in charity]."* (Verse 215) The question is about the type of money Muslims may give in charity. The reply speaks of the nature of charitable spending and defines the most important beneficiaries. The phraseology of the answer, *"Say, 'Anything good you spend of your wealth,'"* indicates, first of all, that whatever is given in charity is good for the donor, the recipient and the community as a whole. It is good in itself and it is done for good reasons. It also implies that people should give from the best of what they have and share it with others. As well as benefitting the needy, this would purify the donor's heart and soul and give charity and altruism real meaning.

However, giving from the best of what one has is not a condition of generosity, as the Qur'ān urges elsewhere that people should give from neither the best nor the worst, but from the average, of what they have. In its inimitable style, the Qur'ān in the present passage is aiming to persuade people to rise to a higher level of excellence and generosity by giving what is closer and dearer to their hearts.

As to whom charity should be directed, the verse explains: *"to parents and the near of kin, to orphans and the needy, and to travellers in need."* The verse gives a list of categories of people brought together through ties of family, kinship, compassion, and an integral strong framework of human social welfare, nurtured and promoted by religious faith.

This relationship was further defined by the Prophet who was reported to have said: "Start by being charitable to yourself. If you have something left, then to your immediate family. When you have something left after having looked after your family, then give to your relatives. If you have more, then to all others." [Related by Muslim]

This example reveals the Islamic highly effective and common sense approach in guiding human individuals. It begins from man's natural aptitudes and inclinations and takes him gradually and gently upwards to where it wants him to be. As he progresses and improves his human condition, he would not find himself over-strained or being forcibly dragged to fulfil his duties, or find that his natural needs and talents are being suppressed or thwarted. While his eyes and aspirations are cast as high as possible, and his heart and soul reach out towards God Almighty, man's feet would be set firmly on the ground.

God knows that human beings tend to be selfish, and so He directs them to see to their own needs before those of others. God allows man to enjoy the good things of life, in moderation, and only when man has looked properly after himself does God direct him to be charitable towards others. The Prophet Muḥammad is quoted as saying: "The most noble charity is that made once one's own needs are fulfilled; the upper (giving) hand is better than the lower (receiving) hand. Start with your dependants." [Related by Muslim] Jābir ibn 'Abdullāh, a Companion of the Prophet, reports: "A man once offered a lump of gold, the size of an egg, to the Prophet saying that he is giving it for charity and that it was all he had, but the Prophet turned away from him. The man came to the Prophet again from the right, then from the left, then from the back, saying the same thing. Every time the Prophet turned away from him. At last the Prophet took the lump of gold and threw it at him. Had it hit him, he would have been hurt. The Prophet then said, 'A person would come with all he possesses and say he wants to give it away to charity. He then goes to beg from others. The best charity is that made when one's own needs have been fulfilled." [Related by Abū Dāwūd]

God also knows that human beings favour their immediate family and relatives, their parents and children, and so He urges them to give willingly to these relatives, thereby satisfying a natural human tendency, which is both legitimate and sensible, while benefitting a section of the community. For, unless these relatives are helped they would continue to be a burden on the rest of society, and it is far more dignified for them to be cared for by members of their own family. This is bound to bring people closer together and spread love and harmony within immediate and extended families, the vital nucleus of the larger human society.

Beyond that, man is required to show generosity towards a whole range of other human groups such as young orphans and those members of society who are helpless but are too sensitive to ask for help. Another group are those stranded travellers or immigrants, some of whom may be well-off but for reasons beyond their control are unable to have access to their money. The first Muslim community in Madinah had a sizeable section of such people, most of whom were migrants from Makkah who had left all their belongings behind.

All these are members of the Muslim community and Islam urges the well-off to act charitably towards them. It encourages people's natural kindness and good-will to purify the hearts and souls of the donors, who give generously and willingly, and to ensure the welfare of those in need, thereby achieving greater cohesion and solidarity among the community in a smooth, fair and equitable manner.

The verse goes on to link such commendable charity with God Almighty, saying: *"God is well aware of whatever good you do."* (Verse 215) God is aware of the deed as well as of the intention behind it. Thus, it will not go to waste. He has taken note of it and, being just, He will give a suitable reward for it.

This educational approach directs man's heart and soul towards God Almighty with ease and deliberation. It picks man up from wherever he is and takes him to far wider horizons of civility and humanity which he would never reach without God's guidance and grace.

What Things We May Love

The next verse deals with the duty of taking up arms for a legitimate cause: *"Fighting is ordained for you, even though it is hateful to you. But it may well be that you hate a thing while it is good for you, and it may well be that you love a thing while it is bad for you. God knows, whereas you do not know."* (Verse 216)

To take up arms in support of a cause blessed by God is a demanding duty, but is nevertheless necessary because it serves the good of Muslim individuals and communities as well as that of mankind as a whole. It also underpins what is good and right.

As with all the obligations it prescribes, Islam takes into account the limits of human nature. In the case of war, it does not only acknowledge the efforts and the sacrifices it demands, but also man's instinctive reluctance to prosecute it. Islam does not deny, contradict or suppress human nature, but always seeks an appropriate approach to deal with the issues it proposes. It clearly allows for the fact that certain obligations in this life are demanding, unappealing or even detestable, but at the same time it indicates that there is a greater cause to be served by fulfilling them, which might not be readily obvious to the human mind, finite as it is. It opens up new avenues of hope and achievement. For, no one can tell for certain whether there is not some unforeseen good beyond an impending evil. Only God, the omniscient, knows the future outcome of present actions, and man cannot even pretend to have that privilege.

This comforting thought revives man's hopes and optimism, drawing him closer to God with more self-confidence and reassurance.

By this effective educational approach, Islam nurtures in man a deeper sense of loyalty and readiness to sacrifice and to scale greater heights of excellence and achievement. It allows him to face his reponsibilities with courage and enthusiasm, safe in the knowledge that God's blessings and support are not far behind. This motivates him to persevere in the face of adversity, because a pleasant and favourable outcome might be waiting for him. It also restrains man's cravings so that he is not carried away by his pleasures and desires, which could end in pain and sorrow.

It is a remarkably simple, but profound, approach that is in harmony with human nature and honest in addressing it. It is undeniable that man, weak and short-sighted as he is, would reject something which is in fact good for him, or covet something which is in fact evil and harmful. The fact is that God alone has knowledge of everything; people are often ignorant or hampered by prejudice and their own shortcomings.

This opens up a whole new world, hitherto unknown, and brings to light new factors of cause and effect, into which man's fears, hopes and behaviour blend smoothly, under God's benevolent and omniscient presence. By accepting the fact that whatever God ordains is always for the best, man enters a world of total serenity, security and faith. It is the world of peace which God has recommended to the believers even as He calls upon them to take up arms and fight, because real peace is that of the soul and the conscience that one experiences in the heat of battle.

The implications of this Qur'ānic principle are not limited to fighting, which is only one example of a necessary evil that may ultimately result in something good, but extend to all aspects of a believer's life. The Muslims who left Madinah, on the eve of the Battle of Badr in 624 CE, to intercept the Quraysh trade caravan travelling from Syria to Makkah, were hoping that they would take it over without having to fight. However, God willed it that the caravan would escape and the Muslims find themselves facing the Quraysh army which was intent on subduing them. The outcome was a resounding victory for Islam and the Muslims which was infinitely better than the trade caravan and its valuable commodities. What the Muslims aimed for was much inferior to what God had in store for them. God knows and people do not.

In an episode involving the Prophet Moses, the Qur'ān tells us how, as he embarked on a journey accompanied by his boy servant, the boy unwittingly left their provisions of fish behind and it found its way back into the sea. The narrative goes on, saying: *"And after they had marched on for some distance, Moses said to his servant: 'Bring us our mid-day meal; we are indeed worn out by this our journey.' Said [the servant]: 'Do you recall when we betook ourselves to that rock for rest. There I forgot the fish – and none but Satan made me thus forget to mention it! – and it took its way into the sea. How strange! [Moses] said: 'That is [the place] we are seeking!' So they turned back, retracing their footsteps, and found one of Our servants, on whom We had bestowed Our mercy and whom We had endowed with knowledge of Our own."* (18: 62–65) What seemed an oversight by the servant turned out to be a fortunate turn of events that brought Moses into contact with the learned man, which was the very purpose of the journey.

We could all recall instances, from personal experience, in which we dreaded certain situations that had turned out to be of great benefit, as well as others which looked appealing and lucrative but ended in disaster. Often, people bitterly regret missing out on certain things, but as time goes by they realize that God had spared them certain adverse consequences; while others undergo intense suffering that could drive them to the edge of despair, but would eventually bring opportunities of incredible happiness and prosperity.

Man simply cannot pretend to know where his good lies, but God knows for certain, a fact that man must accept and act upon by submitting himself to God alone. This is what the Qur'ān teaches, and this is the approach it adopts to convince people to submit to the will and judgement of God Almighty.

Fighting in the Sacred Months

> *They ask you about fighting in the sacred month. Say, 'Fighting in it is a grave offence, but to turn people away from God's path, to disbelieve in Him and in the Sacred Mosque, and to expel its people from it – [all this] is far more grave in God's sight.' Religious persecution is worse than killing. They shall not cease to fight you until they force you to renounce your faith, if they can. But whoever of you renounces his faith and dies an unbeliever, his works shall come to nothing in this world and in the world to come. Such people are destined for hell, wherein they shall abide.* (Verse 217)

Several reports indicate that these verses were revealed in connection with an expedition of eight Muslims from the *Muhājirūn* [i.e. those who migrated with the Prophet to Madinah], led by ʿAbdullāh ibn Jaḥsh, dispatched by the Prophet Muḥammad prior to the great Battle of Badr, with sealed instructions and ordered not to open them before the company had travelled for two nights. When opened, the instructions read as follows: "When you have read this letter of mine proceed until you reach the Nakhlah valley, between Makkah and Ṭā'if. Once there, monitor the movements of the Quraysh and gather news of their activities. Do not force any of your men to go with you."

On reading those instructions, ʿAbdullāh ibn Jaḥsh, the group commander, said, "To hear is to obey." He informed his Companions, giving them the choice to join him or return to Madinah. They all agreed to go ahead. They took a route through the Hijaz, but on the way the camel mounted by Saʿd ibn Abī Waqqāṣ and ʿUtbah ibn Ghazwān went missing and they stayed behind to look for it. The other six went on and, as they reached the valley, a small trade caravan belonging to the Quraysh, passed by. Four people, including ʿAmr ibn al-Ḥaḍramī, were travelling with it. The task force attacked it, killing ʿAmr ibn al-Ḥaḍramī and apprehending two of the other three men, while the fourth escaped. They did this thinking it was the last day of Jumādā II, whereas in fact it was the first day of Rajab, one of the months recognized as sacred by the Arabs, when no fighting may take place, and whose sanctity was endorsed by Islam.

When the expedition returned to Madinah, the Prophet said to them, "I never ordered you to fight during the sacred month," and refused to accept the caravan or the two prisoners. Members of the expedition were reproached by their fellow Muslims and they were in despair, while the Quraysh accused the Prophet and his followers of violating a sacred month by killing one man, abducting two others, and seizing the caravan. Some Jews in Madinah saw the incident as an omen of impending war between the Muslims and the Quraysh.

The atmosphere became charged with intrigue and propaganda. The Muslims were depicted as self-serving renegades who would not hesitate to violate age-old sanctities. It was at that point that the revelations were received confirming the sanctity of the sacred months and condemning all acts of killing during them, but putting the whole episode involving the expedition in the right perspective.

It was the unbelievers who had declared war against the Muslims, rather than the other way round. They obstructed the spread of Islam, and spared no effort in turning people away from it, resorting to oppression and persecution. They refused to believe in God or respect the Sacred Mosque. Over a period of thirteen long years, they repeatedly violated the sanctity of Makkah by their relentless and violent opposition to Islam and by persecuting Muslim converts whom they had eventually driven out of their homes and families.

These vile and shameless acts the pagan Arabs had perpetrated against Islam and the Muslims were far more grievous violations of the sanctity of the Sacred Mosque and the sacred months. They persecuted people in order to force them to renounce their faith. That is a much more grievous crime. The smoke screen had fallen down, and the pagan Arabs could no longer hide behind a wall of false piety, putting the Muslims on the defensive and accusing them of the very aggressions they themselves had committed.

Islam is a practical and realistic way of life which is not based on rigid idealistic dogma. It takes life as it is and deals with the realities of problems and situations as and when they arise, and provides practical, effective and realistic solutions.

In this instance, the idolater Arabs were the aggressors, who were seen to treat sanctities of religion and tradition with utter contempt.

They stood in active opposition to Islam, using all forms of intimidation and enticement to disconcert the Muslims, break up their ranks, drive them out of their homes and bar them from their land. At the same time, they falsely claimed the higher moral ground, protesting in the name of religion and accusing Muḥammad and his followers of breaching the sanctity of the sacred months.

How should Islam deal with such people? Should it recommend a utopian approach? It could not possibly advise its followers to stand idle while their opponents were using every available means to stifle them. Islam aims to stamp out oppression and evil, and curtail the powers of aggression and injustice, to allow the good and righteous to prevail and prevent religious sanctities being used as a shield for the perpetration of tyranny and corruption.

Islam assiduously respects those who honour religious sanctities, but it would not allow such sanctities to be used as a pretext for the persecution or suppression of the believers, or to deprive them of their legitimate rights. It further affirms that such acts should not go unpunished.

By the same token, Islam forbids backbiting, slander and injustice, for instance, but makes it clear that this does not apply in cases of people who are known for their corruption or bad reputation, or who commit an injustice. To protect such behaviour is liable to be misconstrued as weakness, and could only encourage further corruption and injustice.

Nevertheless, Islam maintains its own high moral principles and does not recommend resort to the same obscene methods used by its detractors. It simply directs the Muslims to stand up to those who offend against them, and reserves for them the right to appropriately and publicly punish them. It is only when justice is established and wrongdoing is contained that sanctities can be protected and preserved.

Islam is utterly unequivocal on this point. It makes no excuses, nor allows anyone to take advantage of its lenient and tolerant attitude. The Qur'ān, in this instance, provides the Muslim community with the solid ground on which to stand in its fight against evil and corruption. It gives Muslims clear and definite principles to allow them to forge ahead with their mission with certainty, self-assurance and total peace of conscience.

The Ultimate Aim of Islam's Enemies

The verse then goes on to state, in no uncertain terms, how determined the unbelievers are in pursuing their goal of destroying the Muslims' faith, saying: *"They shall not cease to fight you until they force you to renounce your faith, if they can."* (Verse 217)

This objective is common to all enemies of Islam everywhere, to whom its very existence and success seem to be a source of deep resentment and consternation. They are profoundly alarmed by Islam's inherent strength and resilience. The clarity of its ideas and the rigour of its principles seem to evoke their displeasure and hostility because Islam represents a bedrock of resistance against falsehood, tyranny and corruption. This morbid attitude towards Islam lies behind most of the hostile and bigoted policies and designs directed against Muslim groups and communities in many parts of the world.

The methods and means of achieving this unholy goal may vary from one case to another, but the aim remains constant: to force Muslims to abandon their faith. This campaign never abates or relaxes. Fresh impetus is added at every stage, and greater resources are deployed whenever deemed necessary.

Hence, the Qur'ān urges caution and persistence, warning of dire consequences if Muslims give in to pressure or relinquish their position. It says: *"But whoever of you renounces his faith and dies an unbeliever, his works shall come to nothing in this world and in the world to come. Such people are destined for hell, wherein they shall abide."* (Verse 217)

The Arabic term, *ḥabiṭat*, used to describe the futility of the works of those who renounce their faith, conjures up an image very familiar to the Arabs. It is what happens to a camel that grazes in polluted pastures and ends up with an inflated belly, and dies. The impact of this metaphor could not have been lost on them.

It is almost inconceivable for someone who has truly experienced the faith of Islam to renounce it completely, unless that person has been irredeemably corrupted. Renouncing the faith of Islam, no matter how severe a pressure one is subjected to, can only result in total loss, both in this world as well as in the world to come. This is not to say that it is not justifiable under extreme duress, when one could feign desertion of one's faith to save oneself from danger or death, while one continues to believe in one's heart and conscience.

Deliberate and conscious apostasy, on the other hand, is a gross and loathsome offence.

The warning given in this verse remains true for the rest of time. Muslims are exhorted never to desert their faith, no matter what difficulties they have to put up with. When they are in difficulty, they should persevere, endure and look to God for help and salvation. No matter what hardships they undergo, Muslims are guaranteed one of two ends: victory or martyrdom.

Above all, there is God's grace and mercy, reserved for those who struggle for His cause. No one with true faith can ever despair of God's mercy: *"Those who have believed and those who have forsaken their homeland and striven hard for God's cause are indeed the ones who may look forward to God's mercy. God is much-Forgiving, Merciful."* (Verse 218)

As long as a believer continues to trust in God's grace, he shall never be disappointed. Those early Muslims from Makkah, who had given up everything for their faith, lived up to their belief, strove hard, and received the appropriate rewards. They deservedly won God's forgiveness and mercy, pointing the way to those who would come after them.

The Qur'ānic Method of Education

The *sūrah* goes on to give the Islamic rulings on drinking and gambling, two of the most popular indulgences among the Arabs at the time, who had little else of importance to occupy their minds or their time:

> *They ask you about intoxicants and games of chance. Say, "In both there is great evil although they have some benefits for people, but their evil is far greater than their benefit.* (Verse 219)

Prior to the revelation of this verse, drinking and gambling were tolerated but never condoned. We do not have a single statement in the Qur'ān which may be construed as making them permissible. God, however, carefully charted the way He wanted the newly born Muslim community to take, marking it step by step, so that it would be able to fulfil the role He has assigned to it. The time had to come when such wasteful pastimes would be condemned and rooted out of the Muslim community whose role in the life and history of mankind demanded the dedication and full conscious participation of everyone in that community. Unlike godless societies, past, present and future, a Muslim community has no room for escapism or excessive diversions. The Qur'ānic approach in banning these practices was measured and deliberate.

This statement was the first step towards a universal ban on drinking and gambling in Muslim society. While good and evil could often intermingle and be confused with one another, making it impossible in the human world for things to be purely good or purely evil, the main criteria for whether something could be permissible or prohibited is the preponderance of good or evil associated with it. This statement is a good example of the judicious Qur'ānic approach discernible in many Islamic legal and practical rulings and teachings.

We often find that in matters of faith or abstract belief, Islam gives specific and definite pronouncements, but when it comes to matters of tradition or complex social practices, it takes a more pragmatic and measured approach, preparing the ground for smoother adoption and implementation.

On the question of God's oneness, for example, Islam gave its final ruling right at the outset, without any hesitation or room for compromise. That is an essential question of faith. Unless the concept of God's oneness is firmly established in a community, it cannot be truly Islamic.

Drinking and gambling are well-entrenched social habits that require careful treatment. The first step was to raise in people's minds an inner consciousness of their harmful effects, advising that they would be better avoided. The second step came later on, which directed Muslims: *"Believers, do not attempt to pray when you are drunk, [but wait] until you know what you are saying."* (4: 43)

There are five prayers to be performed at set times every day. The time interval between one prayer and the next is not long enough for a drinking person to regain sobriety. This restricts the opportunity to drink and helps habitual drinkers to give it up altogether.

The third and final step in banning drinking came in the verse which says: *"Believers, intoxicants, games of chance, idolatrous practices and divining arrows are abominations devised by Satan. Therefore, turn away from them, so that you may be successful."* (5: 90)

Dealing with Slavery

At the advent of Islam, slavery was an established social and economic practice known all over the world. Any movement towards the abolition of slavery would require radical social change and far-reaching economic reforms and adjustments, as well as international treaties and conventions to govern the treatment of war prisoners. Islam never condoned slavery. There is not a single statement in the Qur'ān that recommends or approves of slavery or the enslavement of war prisoners. Slavery was a widespread practice with considerable bearing on the world economy. Moreover, it was an international tradition that prisoners of war were made slaves. Hence, there was no alternative but to phase it out gradually and progressively.

Apart from war captives and slave children, Islam opted for eliminating the root causes and drying up the sources of slavery, with an overriding objective to avoid social upheaval, and it strove to provide the basic guarantees of a decent living and dignity for freed slaves.

As for war captives, Islam could not unilaterally forgo imposing slavery on war prisoners since non-Muslim states continued to do so with Muslim prisoners in times of war. Were it to do so, it would have immediately put the Muslims at a disadvantage *vis-à-vis* their enemies. If any Muslim soldiers were taken prisoners, they would be certain to be made slaves, while prisoners taken by Muslims would remain free. On the other hand, were Islam to require that children born in slavery be immediately freed before creating the right social and economic environment that would absorb them as free citizens, they would have been left stranded, thrown into society with no means of living or welfare. They would have had no families to protect them against descending into poverty or moral delinquency.

For these, and other, reasons it would have been premature for Islam to immediately and unilaterally abolish slavery. However, taking the well-entrenched social conditions into account and while not banning the enslavement of war captives, the Qur'ān did not specifically order that they should be held in bondage. Instead, the Qur'ān advises the Muslims: *"when you meet the unbelievers [in war] smite their necks until you overcome them fully, then bind [the captives] firmly. Thereafter, [set them free,] either by an act of grace or against ransom, so that war lays down its burdens."* (47: 4) This gave the Muslim authorities the choice to deal with war captives according to the prevailing circumstances and the nature of the conflict and the enemy they were facing. War captives could be released, exchanged or, if necessary, held in bondage.

Other ways of enslavement, and they were many, were totally banned. That was sure to minimize the number of slaves in society. Islam began by integrating those slaves as soon as they joined the Muslim community. It gave them the full right to buy their freedom through an agreement a slave would make with his master, who may not refuse him such a deal. Once an agreement of this sort is made, a slave has the right to work, own property, earn an independent income, and seek employment with other employers, in order to be able to raise the money to secure his freedom. That made it possible for slaves to gradually acquire an independent status in society and enjoy all the basic citizenship rights of the community, and they would become eligible for state welfare aid, which consists mainly of *zakāt* revenue. Furthermore, Islam urged its followers to help slaves financially to secure their freedom and incorporated the freeing of slaves into the legal code as a form of atonement for certain offences including manslaughter, reneging on an oath, and the ancient Arabian practice of a husband banishing his wife and saying that he considers her, for marital purposes, like his mother. With time, slavery was bound to be phased out, whereas a drastic or draconian approach to abolish it would have resulted in unnecessary social turmoil and disintegration.

The subsequent proliferation of slavery in Muslim societies had come about as a result of a gradual decline of the authority of Islam. This is a historical fact for which Islam may not be blamed. Islam cannot be held responsible for its incorrect implementation in certain periods or societies. Islam was, and remains, unchanged, but what had changed was people's understanding of it and the way they translated its principles into social reality, which was often an aberration and a travesty of Islam for which it cannot be held accountable.

Any revival of Islamic life should, therefore, start from the authentic and established sources and principles of Islam and not be a continuation of a certain distorted historical legacy. This is an essential truth, both in abstract as well as practical terms, that cannot be over-emphasized. Grossly mistaken conclusions are made regarding the Islamic view of history and on understanding the historic reality of Islam and how it operates in society. The leading culprits in this field are the so-called Orientalists, or Western scholars of Islam, and their students, including some sincere but very naïve Muslim scholars who were misled by them.

More Questions by Believers

The *sūrah* continues, answering other questions and laying down more fundamental Islamic principles. *"They ask you what they should spend in charity; say, 'Whatever you can spare.' Thus God makes plain His revelations so that you may reflect upon this life and the life to come."* (Verses 219–220)

The answer given to this question the first time round, in verse 215, identified what could be given in charity and to whom, and here it identifies quantities. Anything above one's basic reasonable personal needs should be considered available for donation to others, starting with those eligible among one's nearest of kin, as already pointed out.

The present statement implies that the obligatory *zakāt* is not by itself sufficient as a means of wealth distribution, and this ruling, in my view, has not been overruled by the imposition of *zakāt*. Payment of *zakāt* by those liable to it does not exempt them from making additional donations and contributions to good causes. *Zakāt* is a duty levied by the ruling Muslim authority for allocation to the various causes specified in the Qur'ān (9: 60), beyond which Muslims continue to have an obligation towards God and fellow-Muslims in society. It may not exhaust one's ability to give, or one's desire to gain further blessings and pleasure from God Almighty. The Prophet Muḥammad is quoted in al-Jaṣṣāṣ's *Aḥkām al-Qur'ān* as having said: "There is a duty on wealth other than *zakāt*." If this duty is not discharged voluntarily, which is obviously more gracious and laudable, Muslim authorities have the power to collect funds over and above the obligatory *zakāt*, for spending in the public interest, in order to curb wastage or hoarding of wealth.

Muslims are then reminded that: *"God makes plain His revelations so that you may reflect upon this life and the life to come."* (Verses 219–220) It would not suffice to consider only the realities of this life, which represents the more immediate and shorter part of the whole picture of human existence and all the responsibilities and relationships associated with it. That would only give a distorted understanding of the values and the criteria upon which life is built which would bring about the wrong kind of human behaviour.

The distribution and allocation of wealth, in particular, calls for total awareness of accountability in this life and in the life to come. One is always substantially rewarded, spiritually and morally, for what one gives in charity. Further reward comes in the contribution one makes to the welfare and well-being of society. These rewards may not, however, be readily apparent to everyone, which makes the rewards of the hereafter even more of an incentive to give generously and willingly and away from ostentation and pomposity.

Treatment of Orphans

The *sūrah* then raises the question of how orphans ought to be treated. *"They ask you about orphans; say, 'To improve their conditions is best.' If you mix their affairs with yours, remember that they are your brothers. God knows him who spoils things and him who improves. Had God so willed, He would indeed have overburdened you. God is indeed Almighty, Wise."* (Verse 220)

Social welfare is the bedrock of Muslim society which has a responsibility to care for the weaker among its members and protect their interests. Having lost either or both of their parents at a young age, orphan children would come at the top of the list of social groups that deserve care and protection. Some guardians of orphan children used to incorporate any possessions or wealth those children might have inherited into their own, for trading or other purposes, which did not always work in the children's favour. As the Qur'ān denounced such actions, some conscientious people began to feel guilty and went too far the other way in caring for orphans, to the extent that they separated their own food from that of the orphans in their care. This led to subsequent revelations being sent down to moderate the situation and put the whole issue in a proper perspective. Muslims were urged to do what would be in the best interest of the orphan children they were caring for. Being members of the larger family of Islam, orphans should be treated in a spirit of fraternity and brotherhood. God is the judge of people's motives and intentions. He recognizes those who are genuine and, being all-powerful and compassionate, He does not wish to overburden them.

The Qur'ān refers all actions ultimately to God. Faith and life revolve on the central pivot of belief in God. It is notable that Islamic teachings and precepts are based on an inner conscious conviction that acts as a solid guarantee for their success and effectiveness.

14

The Family: The Foundation of Human Society

Do not marry women who associate partners with God unless they embrace the true faith. Any believing bondwoman is certainly better than an idolatress, even though the latter may well please you. And do not give your women in marriage to men who associate partners with God unless they embrace the true faith. Any believing bondman is certainly better than an idolater, even though the latter may well please you. These invite to the fire; whereas God invites to paradise and to the achievement of forgiveness by His leave. He makes plain His revelations to mankind so that they may bear them in mind. (221)

وَلَا تَنكِحُوا۟ ٱلْمُشْرِكَٰتِ حَتَّىٰ
يُؤْمِنَّ ۚ وَلَأَمَةٌ مُّؤْمِنَةٌ خَيْرٌ مِّن
مُّشْرِكَةٍ وَلَوْ أَعْجَبَتْكُمْ ۗ
وَلَا تُنكِحُوا۟ ٱلْمُشْرِكِينَ حَتَّىٰ
يُؤْمِنُوا۟ ۚ وَلَعَبْدٌ مُّؤْمِنٌ خَيْرٌ مِّن
مُّشْرِكٍ وَلَوْ أَعْجَبَكُمْ ۗ أُو۟لَٰٓئِكَ
يَدْعُونَ إِلَى ٱلنَّارِ ۖ وَٱللَّهُ يَدْعُوٓا۟
إِلَى ٱلْجَنَّةِ وَٱلْمَغْفِرَةِ بِإِذْنِهِۦ ۖ
وَيُبَيِّنُ ءَايَٰتِهِۦ لِلنَّاسِ لَعَلَّهُمْ
يَتَذَكَّرُونَ ﴿٢٢١﴾

They ask you about menstruation. Say: 'It is an unclean condition; so keep aloof from women during menstruation, and do not draw near to them until they are cleansed. When they have cleansed themselves,

وَيَسْـَٔلُونَكَ عَنِ ٱلْمَحِيضِ ۖ قُلْ هُوَ
أَذًى فَٱعْتَزِلُوا۟ ٱلنِّسَآءَ فِى ٱلْمَحِيضِ ۖ
وَلَا تَقْرَبُوهُنَّ حَتَّىٰ يَطْهُرْنَ ۖ فَإِذَا تَطَهَّرْنَ

فَأْتُوهُنَّ مِنْ حَيْثُ أَمَرَكُمُ ٱللَّهُ ۚ إِنَّ ٱللَّهَ يُحِبُّ ٱلتَّوَّٰبِينَ وَيُحِبُّ ٱلْمُتَطَهِّرِينَ ﴿٢٢٢﴾

you may go in unto them in the proper way, as God has bidden you. God loves those who turn to Him in repentance, and He loves those who keep themselves pure.' (222)

نِسَآؤُكُمْ حَرْثٌ لَّكُمْ فَأْتُوا۟ حَرْثَكُمْ أَنَّىٰ شِئْتُمْ ۖ وَقَدِّمُوا۟ لِأَنفُسِكُمْ ۚ وَٱتَّقُوا۟ ٱللَّهَ وَٱعْلَمُوٓا۟ أَنَّكُم مُّلَٰقُوهُ ۗ وَبَشِّرِ ٱلْمُؤْمِنِينَ ﴿٢٢٣﴾

Your wives are your tilth; go, then, to your tilth as you may desire, but first provide something for your souls. Fear God and know that you shall meet Him. Give the happy news to the believers. (223)

وَلَا تَجْعَلُوا۟ ٱللَّهَ عُرْضَةً لِّأَيْمَٰنِكُمْ أَن تَبَرُّوا۟ وَتَتَّقُوا۟ وَتُصْلِحُوا۟ بَيْنَ ٱلنَّاسِ ۗ وَٱللَّهُ سَمِيعٌ عَلِيمٌ ﴿٢٢٤﴾

Do not allow your oaths in the name of God to become an obstacle to your being kind and God-fearing, or to promoting peace among people. God hears all and knows all. (224)

لَّا يُؤَاخِذُكُمُ ٱللَّهُ بِٱللَّغْوِ فِىٓ أَيْمَٰنِكُمْ وَلَٰكِن يُؤَاخِذُكُم بِمَا كَسَبَتْ قُلُوبُكُمْ ۗ وَٱللَّهُ غَفُورٌ حَلِيمٌ ﴿٢٢٥﴾

God shall not take you to task for oaths which you may have uttered without thought, but He will take you to task for what your hearts have conceived in earnest. God is much-Forgiving, Forbearing. (225)

لِّلَّذِينَ يُؤْلُونَ مِن نِّسَآئِهِمْ تَرَبُّصُ أَرْبَعَةِ أَشْهُرٍ ۖ فَإِن فَآءُو فَإِنَّ ٱللَّهَ غَفُورٌ رَّحِيمٌ ﴿٢٢٦﴾

Those who take an oath that they will not approach their wives shall have four months of grace. If they go back on their oaths, God is much-Forgiving, Merciful; (226)

and if they are resolved on divorce, [let them remember that] God hears all and knows all. (227)

وَإِنْ عَزَمُوا۟ ٱلطَّلَٰقَ فَإِنَّ ٱللَّهَ سَمِيعٌ
عَلِيمٌ ٢٢٧

Divorced women shall wait, by themselves, for three monthly courses. It is unlawful for them to conceal what God might have created in their wombs, if they believe in God and the Last Day. During this period, their husbands are entitled to take them back, if they desire reconciliation. Women shall, in all fairness, enjoy rights similar to those exercised against them, although men have an advantage over them. God is Almighty, Wise. (228)

وَٱلْمُطَلَّقَٰتُ يَتَرَبَّصْنَ بِأَنفُسِهِنَّ
ثَلَٰثَةَ قُرُوٓءٍ ۚ وَلَا يَحِلُّ لَهُنَّ أَن يَكْتُمْنَ
مَا خَلَقَ ٱللَّهُ فِىٓ أَرْحَامِهِنَّ إِن كُنَّ يُؤْمِنَّ
بِٱللَّهِ وَٱلْيَوْمِ ٱلْـَٔاخِرِ ۚ وَبُعُولَتُهُنَّ أَحَقُّ بِرَدِّهِنَّ
فِى ذَٰلِكَ إِنْ أَرَادُوٓا۟ إِصْلَٰحًا ۚ وَلَهُنَّ مِثْلُ
ٱلَّذِى عَلَيْهِنَّ بِٱلْمَعْرُوفِ ۚ وَلِلرِّجَالِ عَلَيْهِنَّ
دَرَجَةٌ ۗ وَٱللَّهُ عَزِيزٌ حَكِيمٌ ٢٢٨

Divorce may be [revoked] twice, whereupon a woman may either be retained in fairness or released with kindness. It is unlawful for you to take back from women anything of what you have given them [as dowry], unless they both [husband and wife] fear that they may not be able to keep within the bounds set by God. If you have cause to fear that they would not be able to keep within the bounds set by God, it shall be no offence for either of them if she gives up whatever she may in order to free herself.

ٱلطَّلَٰقُ مَرَّتَانِ ۖ فَإِمْسَاكٌۢ بِمَعْرُوفٍ
أَوْ تَسْرِيحٌۢ بِإِحْسَٰنٍ ۗ وَلَا يَحِلُّ لَكُمْ
أَن تَأْخُذُوا۟ مِمَّآ ءَاتَيْتُمُوهُنَّ شَيْـًٔا
إِلَّآ أَن يَخَافَآ أَلَّا يُقِيمَا حُدُودَ ٱللَّهِ ۖ
فَإِنْ خِفْتُمْ أَلَّا يُقِيمَا حُدُودَ ٱللَّهِ
فَلَا جُنَاحَ عَلَيْهِمَا فِيمَا ٱفْتَدَتْ بِهِۦ ۗ

These are the bounds set by God; do not, then, transgress them. Those who transgress the bounds set by God are wrongdoers indeed. (229)

تِلْكَ حُدُودُ ٱللَّهِ فَلَا تَعْتَدُوهَا ۚ وَمَن يَتَعَدَّ حُدُودَ ٱللَّهِ فَأُو۟لَٰٓئِكَ هُمُ ٱلظَّٰلِمُونَ ﴿٢٢٩﴾

Should he divorce her [a third time], she shall not thereafter be lawful for him to remarry until she has wedded another husband. If the latter then divorces her it shall be no offence for either of the two if they return to one another, if they feel that they will be able to keep within the bounds set by God. Such are the bounds set by God. He makes them plain for people who have knowledge. (230)

فَإِن طَلَّقَهَا فَلَا تَحِلُّ لَهُۥ مِنۢ بَعْدُ حَتَّىٰ تَنكِحَ زَوْجًا غَيْرَهُۥ ۗ فَإِن طَلَّقَهَا فَلَا جُنَاحَ عَلَيْهِمَآ أَن يَتَرَاجَعَآ إِن ظَنَّآ أَن يُقِيمَا حُدُودَ ٱللَّهِ ۗ وَتِلْكَ حُدُودُ ٱللَّهِ يُبَيِّنُهَا لِقَوْمٍ يَعْلَمُونَ ﴿٢٣٠﴾

When you have divorced women and they have reached the end of their waiting-term, either retain them with fairness or let them go with fairness. Do not retain them out of malice in order to hurt them. He who does so wrongs his own soul. Do not take God's revelations in a frivolous manner. Remember the blessings God has bestowed upon you, and all the revelation and wisdom He has bestowed upon you from on high in order to admonish you. Fear God and know well that He has full knowledge of everything. (231)

وَإِذَا طَلَّقْتُمُ ٱلنِّسَآءَ فَبَلَغْنَ أَجَلَهُنَّ فَأَمْسِكُوهُنَّ بِمَعْرُوفٍ أَوْ سَرِّحُوهُنَّ بِمَعْرُوفٍ ۚ وَلَا تُمْسِكُوهُنَّ ضِرَارًا لِّتَعْتَدُوا۟ ۚ وَمَن يَفْعَلْ ذَٰلِكَ فَقَدْ ظَلَمَ نَفْسَهُۥ ۚ وَلَا تَتَّخِذُوٓا۟ ءَايَٰتِ ٱللَّهِ هُزُوًا ۚ وَٱذْكُرُوا۟ نِعْمَتَ ٱللَّهِ عَلَيْكُمْ وَمَآ أَنزَلَ عَلَيْكُم مِّنَ ٱلْكِتَٰبِ وَٱلْحِكْمَةِ يَعِظُكُم بِهِۦ ۚ وَٱتَّقُوا۟ ٱللَّهَ وَٱعْلَمُوٓا۟ أَنَّ ٱللَّهَ بِكُلِّ شَىْءٍ عَلِيمٌ ﴿٢٣١﴾

And when you have divorced women and they have reached the end of their waiting-term, do not prevent them from marrying their husbands if they have agreed with each other in a fair manner. This is an admonition for everyone of you who believes in God and the Last Day. That is more virtuous for you, and purer. God knows, whereas you do not know. (232)

وَإِذَا طَلَّقْتُمُ ٱلنِّسَآءَ فَبَلَغْنَ أَجَلَهُنَّ
فَلَا تَعْضُلُوهُنَّ أَن يَنكِحْنَ أَزْوَٰجَهُنَّ
إِذَا تَرَٰضَوْا۟ بَيْنَهُم بِٱلْمَعْرُوفِ ۗ ذَٰلِكَ
يُوعَظُ بِهِۦ مَن كَانَ مِنكُمْ يُؤْمِنُ بِٱللَّهِ
وَٱلْيَوْمِ ٱلْءَاخِرِ ۗ ذَٰلِكُمْ أَزْكَىٰ لَكُمْ
وَأَطْهَرُ ۗ وَٱللَّهُ يَعْلَمُ وَأَنتُمْ لَا تَعْلَمُونَ ﴿٢٣٢﴾

Mothers may breast-feed their children for two whole years; [that is] for those who wish to complete the suckling. The father of the child is responsible to provide in a fair manner for their sustenance and clothing. No human being shall be burdened with more than he is well able to bear. Neither shall a mother be allowed to cause her child to suffer, nor shall a father cause suffering to his child. The same shall apply to the father's heir. If, by mutual consent and after due consultation, the parents choose to wean the child, they will incur no sin thereby. Nor shall it be any offence on your part if you engage wet nurses for your children, provided that you hand over what you agreed to pay, in a fair manner. Fear God, and know that God sees all that you do. (233)

وَٱلْوَٰلِدَٰتُ يُرْضِعْنَ أَوْلَٰدَهُنَّ حَوْلَيْنِ
كَامِلَيْنِ ۖ لِمَنْ أَرَادَ أَن يُتِمَّ ٱلرَّضَاعَةَ ۚ وَعَلَى
ٱلْمَوْلُودِ لَهُۥ رِزْقُهُنَّ وَكِسْوَتُهُنَّ بِٱلْمَعْرُوفِ ۚ
لَا تُكَلَّفُ نَفْسٌ إِلَّا وُسْعَهَا ۚ لَا تُضَآرَّ
وَٰلِدَةٌۢ بِوَلَدِهَا وَلَا مَوْلُودٌ لَّهُۥ بِوَلَدِهِۦ ۚ
وَعَلَى ٱلْوَارِثِ مِثْلُ ذَٰلِكَ ۗ فَإِنْ أَرَادَا
فِصَالًا عَن تَرَاضٍ مِّنْهُمَا وَتَشَاوُرٍ فَلَا جُنَاحَ
عَلَيْهِمَا ۗ وَإِنْ أَرَدتُّمْ أَن تَسْتَرْضِعُوٓا۟ أَوْلَٰدَكُمْ
فَلَا جُنَاحَ عَلَيْكُمْ إِذَا سَلَّمْتُم مَّآ ءَاتَيْتُم
بِٱلْمَعْرُوفِ ۗ وَٱتَّقُوا۟ ٱللَّهَ وَٱعْلَمُوٓا۟ أَنَّ ٱللَّهَ
بِمَا تَعْمَلُونَ بَصِيرٌ ﴿٢٣٣﴾

Those of you who die leaving wives behind, their wives shall wait, by themselves, for four months and ten days. When they have reached the end of their waiting-term, you shall incur no sin in whatever they may do with themselves in a lawful manner. God is aware of all that you do. (234)

وَٱلَّذِينَ يُتَوَفَّوْنَ مِنكُمْ وَيَذَرُونَ أَزْوَٰجًا
يَتَرَبَّصْنَ بِأَنفُسِهِنَّ أَرْبَعَةَ أَشْهُرٍ وَعَشْرًا ۖ
فَإِذَا بَلَغْنَ أَجَلَهُنَّ فَلَا جُنَاحَ عَلَيْكُمْ
فِيمَا فَعَلْنَ فِىٓ أَنفُسِهِنَّ بِٱلْمَعْرُوفِ ۗ وَٱللَّهُ
بِمَا تَعْمَلُونَ خَبِيرٌ ﴿٢٣٤﴾

You will incur no sin if you give a hint of a marriage offer to [widowed] women or keep such an intention to yourselves. God knows that you will entertain such intentions concerning them. Do not, however, plight your troth in secret; but speak only in a decent manner. Furthermore, do not resolve on actually making the marriage tie before the prescribed term [of waiting] has run its course. Know well that God knows what is in your minds, so have fear of Him; and know that God is much-Forgiving, Forbearing. (235)

وَلَا جُنَاحَ عَلَيْكُمْ فِيمَا عَرَّضْتُم بِهِۦ مِنْ
خِطْبَةِ ٱلنِّسَآءِ أَوْ أَكْنَنتُمْ فِىٓ أَنفُسِكُمْ ۚ
عَلِمَ ٱللَّهُ أَنَّكُمْ سَتَذْكُرُونَهُنَّ وَلَٰكِن
لَّا تُوَاعِدُوهُنَّ سِرًّا إِلَّآ أَن تَقُولُوا۟ قَوْلًا
مَّعْرُوفًا ۚ وَلَا تَعْزِمُوا۟ عُقْدَةَ ٱلنِّكَاحِ
حَتَّىٰ يَبْلُغَ ٱلْكِتَٰبُ أَجَلَهُۥ ۚ وَٱعْلَمُوٓا۟ أَنَّ
ٱللَّهَ يَعْلَمُ مَا فِىٓ أَنفُسِكُمْ فَٱحْذَرُوهُ ۚ
وَٱعْلَمُوٓا۟ أَنَّ ٱللَّهَ غَفُورٌ حَلِيمٌ ﴿٢٣٥﴾

You will incur no sin if you divorce women before having touched them or settled a dowry for them. Provide for them, the rich according to his means and the straitened according to his means. Such a provision, in an equitable manner, is an obligation binding on the righteous. (236)

لَّا جُنَاحَ عَلَيْكُمْ إِن طَلَّقْتُمُ ٱلنِّسَآءَ
مَا لَمْ تَمَسُّوهُنَّ أَوْ تَفْرِضُوا۟ لَهُنَّ
فَرِيضَةً ۚ وَمَتِّعُوهُنَّ عَلَى ٱلْمُوسِعِ قَدَرُهُۥ
وَعَلَى ٱلْمُقْتِرِ قَدَرُهُۥ مَتَٰعًۢا بِٱلْمَعْرُوفِ ۖ
حَقًّا عَلَى ٱلْمُحْسِنِينَ ﴿٢٣٦﴾

If you divorce them before having touched them but after having settled a dowry for them, then give them half of that which you have settled, unless they forgo it or he in whose hand is the marriage tie forgoes it. To forgo what is due to you is closer to being righteous. Do not forget to act benevolently to one another. God sees all that you do. (237)

وَإِن طَلَّقْتُمُوهُنَّ مِن قَبْلِ أَن تَمَسُّوهُنَّ
وَقَدْ فَرَضْتُمْ لَهُنَّ فَرِيضَةً فَنِصْفُ
مَا فَرَضْتُمْ إِلَّآ أَن يَعْفُونَ أَوْ يَعْفُوَا۟
ٱلَّذِى بِيَدِهِۦ عُقْدَةُ ٱلنِّكَاحِ ۚ وَأَن
تَعْفُوٓا۟ أَقْرَبُ لِلتَّقْوَىٰ ۚ وَلَا تَنسَوُا۟
ٱلْفَضْلَ بَيْنَكُمْ ۚ إِنَّ ٱللَّهَ بِمَا تَعْمَلُونَ
بَصِيرٌ ﴿٢٣٧﴾

Attend regularly to your prayers, particularly the middle prayer, and stand up before God in devout obedience. (238)

حَٰفِظُوا۟ عَلَى ٱلصَّلَوَٰتِ وَٱلصَّلَوٰةِ
ٱلْوُسْطَىٰ وَقُومُوا۟ لِلَّهِ قَٰنِتِينَ ﴿٢٣٨﴾

If you are in fear, pray walking or riding. When you are again secure, remember God, since it is He who has taught you what you did not know. (239)

فَإِنْ خِفْتُمْ فَرِجَالًا أَوْ رُكْبَانًا ۖ فَإِذَآ أَمِنتُمْ
فَٱذْكُرُوا۟ ٱللَّهَ كَمَا عَلَّمَكُم مَّا لَمْ
تَكُونُوا۟ تَعْلَمُونَ ﴿٢٣٩﴾

Those of you who die leaving their wives behind, shall bequeath to their wives provisions for one year without their being obliged to leave [their deceased husbands' homes]. Should they leave home [of their own accord], you shall incur no sin for what they may do with themselves in a lawful manner. God is Almighty, Wise. (240)

وَٱلَّذِينَ يُتَوَفَّوْنَ مِنكُمْ وَيَذَرُونَ
أَزْوَٰجًا وَصِيَّةً لِّأَزْوَٰجِهِم مَّتَٰعًا إِلَى
ٱلْحَوْلِ غَيْرَ إِخْرَاجٍ ۚ فَإِنْ خَرَجْنَ فَلَا
جُنَاحَ عَلَيْكُمْ فِى مَا فَعَلْنَ
فِىٓ أَنفُسِهِنَّ مِن مَّعْرُوفٍ ۗ وَٱللَّهُ
عَزِيزٌ حَكِيمٌ ﴿٢٤٠﴾

Divorced women shall have a provision according to what is fair. This is an obligation on the God-fearing. (241)

وَلِلْمُطَلَّقَٰتِ مَتَٰعٌۢ بِٱلْمَعْرُوفِ ۖ حَقًّا عَلَى ٱلْمُتَّقِينَ ﴿٢٤١﴾

Thus God makes clear to you His revelations that you may understand. (242)

كَذَٰلِكَ يُبَيِّنُ ٱللَّهُ لَكُمْ ءَايَٰتِهِۦ لَعَلَّكُمْ تَعْقِلُونَ ﴿٢٤٢﴾

Overview

The following section of the *sūrah* deals with the family, the nucleus and the foundation of Muslim society, to which Islam has extended notable attention and effort, regulating its essential aspects and ensuring its safety and protection against abuse and disintegration. Such attention is reflected in several Qur'ānic *sūrahs* and addresses all necessary elements to ensure the strong foundation of the family in Muslim society.

The Islamic social order is family-based by virtue of its being a divinely-ordained system for human society that takes full account of the essentials of human nature and its basic requirements.

Its ingredients originate with the very essence of life itself, as stated in the Qur'ān when it says: *"Of all things We have created a pair [male and female], so that you may give thought."* (51: 49) *"Limitless in His glory is He who has created pairs of whatever the earth produces, of your own kind, and of that which they [people] have no knowledge."* (36: 36)

Human life began with one person, out of whom came a spouse, and then offspring from the pair of them, and so on. The result is this numerous multitude of human beings. The Qur'ān says: *"Mankind, fear your Lord, who created you from a single soul, and from it created its mate, and from the two of them spread abroad so many men and women."* (4: 1) *"Mankind! We have created you all out of a male and a female, and have made you into nations and tribes, so that you might come to know one another."* (49: 13)

The Qur'ān also highlights the special inherent attraction between the male and the female of the human species which is vital for setting up and supporting the family unit: *"And of His signs is that He creates for you mates from your own selves, so that you may incline towards them, and He engenders between you love and compassion."* (30: 21) *"They [your wives] are a garment and you are a garment to them."* (2: 187)

"Your wives are your tilth; go, then, to your tilth as you may desire, but first provide something for your souls, and fear God and know that you shall meet Him." (2: 223)

"And God has made for you in your homes, a place of rest." (16: 80)

As ever, Islam strongly emphasizes the harmony and compatibility between the philosophy and the spirit upon which the system of the natural universe is built and that upon which the human social order is based.

The family is the natural environment in which children can be raised and protected, and allowed to grow and develop, mentally and physically. Within the family, they receive love, kindness and care, and gain the values, ideals and behaviour patterns that will accompany them for the rest of their lives, and according to which they will know life, understand it and deal with it.

Humans have the longest childhood period of all species, extending to several years. It is the formative period during which children acquire all the essential skills that will enable them to chart their way through life and find a suitable role in society. It is made longer in order to ensure that adequate training, education and discipline are imparted to children to prepare them sufficiently for the future, especially in view of man's heavy responsibility in this world. Furthermore, children need to be cared for and brought up by their own parents in a happy and stable environment.

Experience has shown that no other arrangement can adequately compensate for the role of the family as the proper setting for bringing up children. In fact, the alternatives have proved extremely harmful and damaging to both the individual and society. These alternatives, such as the children's homes which emerged in Europe after the Second World War or as a result of social pressures created by the need for mothers to go out to work, have deprived children of the love and care that only mothers can provide within a secure family atmosphere. Thousands of children, brought up in children's homes, grew up to develop numerous chronic and disturbing mental and psychological problems.

What is most amazing is that prevailing misconceptions lead people to consider the fact that women are today forced to seek work a symbol of progress and emancipation. It is in fact this system that is responsible for much of the deprivation and suffering witnessed in many countries. It sacrifices the psychological health of society's most precious resources, young children, for nothing other than an increase in the family's income or giving a young mother an income to live on. It is modern ignorance that refuses to look after young mothers to allow them to rear their children. This is indeed one of the most reprehensible failures of modern society.

Studies have shown that during the first two years of life, a child shows an instinctive need to have the exclusive care and attention of its parents, particularly its mother. After that stage, a child needs to be with its parents in a caring family atmosphere. Both of these needs are impossible to meet under any arrangement other than a stable family, without which children are bound to grow up with all kinds of mental and psychological deficiencies and ailments.

The social system of Islam as a religion of peace and harmony is based on the family, to which it accords proper and adequate attention. As we see in this *sūrah*, numerous Qur'ānic passages have been dedicated to emphasizing the importance of the family and to setting out the principles and foundations upon which it is based.

This section of the *sūrah* puts forward the principles of marriage and the rules governing essential aspects of divorce and its repercussions, desertion of wives by their husbands, alimony, breast-feeding, and the custody of children.

These principles and rules are not given in abstract legalistic language, but within a broader context, as part of God's universal code of living and as a fundamental dimension of the Islamic faith. The *sūrah* emphasizes the strong link between these principles and God's ultimate will and purpose.

One is immediately aware of the weight of the whole matter, and of how meticulously it is being dealt with. Every aspect of it is there to serve a greater objective in the overall scheme of things which is being guided and protected by God Almighty. It is the system He has perfected for implementation in human life. Hence, He gives His reward to those who implement it, and punishes those who discard or abuse it.

The *sūrah* makes a very detailed and rational presentation of these rules and principles, of which there are twelve altogether, intermittently prodding the human conscience to be aware of its responsibility and accountability. These rules cover a very wide area directly related to marriage and divorce, beginning with the prohibition of marriage with unbelievers, followed by the prohibition of sexual intercourse between married couples when the woman is in menstruation. Here we note how even this aspect is elevated from a purely physical attraction to a human function that serves important goals. Then follow rulings on faith, suspension of marital relations, a divorcee's waiting period, repeated divorce and the refund of the dowry, the finalization of divorce, breast-feeding when divorce has taken place, a widow's waiting period, hints of a marriage proposal during such a period, divorce before the consummation of marriage and free gifts to a widow or a divorcee. The final comment on all these rulings is: *"Thus God makes clear to you His revelations that you may understand."* (Verse 242)

We note that in all these, the emphasis is on the worship of God. Thus, the Qur'ān relates man's behaviour in all these situations to worship, which is, from the Islamic point of view, not confined to prayers and rituals. Thus, to further relate prayer to aspects of worship in practical life situations, the *sūrah* mentions, along with these rulings regulating marriage and divorce, a couple of rulings on prayer in times of fear and security. (Verses 238–239)

What is worthy of note is that while all these rulings spread an air of worship on all these affairs, no aspect of practical life, human nature or the needs of human life is overlooked. Islam enacts its laws for a community of human beings, who are neither angels nor flying aliens. As it elevates people to the pure atmosphere of worship through its rulings and directives, it does not ignore their human nature, prejudices, preferences, weaknesses, feelings, reactions and moments of clear thinking and pure feeling. It works on all these, directing them in a congenial atmosphere to a better human status.

Thus we see that Islam allows the suspension of marital relations but restricts it to a maximum of four months. It allows divorce, but regulates it fairly and tries hard to strengthen the foundations of the family in a balanced way that makes of ideal principles a daily practice. It is a smooth approach designed to facilitate things, for both man and woman, in the case when this great institution of the family meets with failure. God Almighty, who knows His creation better than they know themselves, does not wish the marriage bond to become a prison when the two parties are unsuited to each other. If their natures clash, then it is better for them to part and try again with different spouses. But before reaching this point, it would have made every effort to save the family. Furthermore, it provides every legal and compassionate guarantee to ensure that no harm comes to husband, wife, child or infant.

Compare the principles of the Islamic family system God has enacted for human life, and the balanced and peaceful society it produces, with what prevailed in human life prior to Islam, or what prevails today in non-Islamic societies everywhere, and you are bound to recognize the high standard of peace and dignity God wants for mankind. Women in particular will appreciate the extent of care God takes of them. I am absolutely certain that no woman could understand this manifestly caring approach without feeling the love of God fills her heart.

Marriage to Unbelievers

> *Do not marry women who associate partners with God unless they embrace the true faith. Any believing bondwoman is certainly better than an idolatress, even though the latter may well please you. And do not give your women in marriage to men who associate partners with God unless they embrace the true faith. Any believing bondman is certainly better than an idolater, even though the latter may well please you. These invite to the fire; whereas God invites to paradise and to the achievement of forgiveness by His leave. He makes plain His revelations to mankind so that they may bear them in mind.* (Verse 221)

Marriage is the deepest and most enduring bond that can exist between two human beings. It calls for the widest possible range of mutual and intimate responses and, therefore, requires the most firm emotional commitment that can be made. For this to be achieved, a clear common objective must exist between the two parties, and what is better than religious faith to provide such affinity and unity of purpose. This profound influence of religion on human thought has often been ignored or overlooked and some societies have made the mistake of trying to replace religious faith with one social philosophy or another.

During the early days of Islam in Makkah, although the Muslims had succeeded in detaching themselves spiritually and ideologically from the rest of society, it was not possible for them to totally disengage themselves socially. This transformation required time and a measured pace of change. In Madinah, however, where Muslims were to acquire an independent social as well as religious identity, the new social order rapidly began to take shape, with these Qur'ānic verses prohibiting any new marriage of Muslims and idol worshippers. Existing marriages remained valid, however, until the sixth year of the Islamic calendar when verses 9 and 10 of *Sūrah* 60 were revealed, annulling such marriages once and for all.

From then on, marriages involving Muslims and pagans were prohibited, as such unions were considered devoid of spiritual meaning and non-deserving of God's blessings or consecration, since the parties involved did not share the same beliefs and outlook on life. Having honoured mankind, God does not want marriage to be based on mere physical attraction. It is a bond that is closely related to the divine system for human life.

Hence, we have a clear, definitive injunction: *"Do not marry women who associate partners with God unless they embrace the true faith."* (Verse 221) Were the unbelieving woman to embrace the faith, the barrier would be removed and the hearts of the two people concerned would fall into harmony and could be united in marriage as they are united in belief.

"Any believing bondwoman is certainly better than an idolatress, even though the latter may well please you." (Verse 221) Such attraction would normally be physical, rather than spiritual, and therefore superficial. It is the attraction of the soul that really matters, even if the Muslim girl is a slave, because it would be infinitely more enduring and profound.

"And do not give your women in marriage to men who associate partners with God unless they embrace the true faith. Any believing bondman is certainly better than an idolater, even though the latter may well please you." (Verse 221) The same rule applies to Muslim women who wish to marry unbelieving men, and for the same underlying reason: *"These invite to the fire; whereas God invites to paradise and to the achievement of forgiveness by His leave. He makes plain His revelations to mankind so that they may bear them in mind."* (Verse 221)

Believers and unbelievers move along two different paths: how can they meet together in a unit that is the foundation of life? The unbelievers take the route that leads to the fire, while those who believe in God take the way leading to His forgiveness and to heaven. The gap between the two is an ever-widening one.

The question arises here: do these people really call to the fire? Would anyone knowingly take himself or others towards the fire? What is highlighted here is the outcome, shown to be the advocated objective. Hence, God warns against such advocacy that leads to perdition and makes plain His revelations so that people may bear them in mind. Whoever fails to take heed can blame none other than himself.

It is noteworthy that Muslim men are not prohibited from marrying Christian or Jewish women, despite certain important differences in religious belief and practice. This is because Muslims, Christians and Jews share a fundamental belief in God's oneness.

As for marrying Christian women who believe in the doctrine of the Trinity, or in Jesus as the Lord, and Jewish women who believe Ezra was the son of God, Muslim jurists take various views. The question is whether such women should be considered idolaters, and therefore outlawed from marriage with Muslims, or whether they are covered by the general Qur'ānic ruling which says: *"Today, all the good things of life have been made lawful to you. The food of those who were given revelations is lawful to you, and your food is lawful to them. And the virtuous women from among the believers and the virtuous women from among those who were given revelations before you [are also lawful to you] when you give them their dower."* (5: 5) The majority of jurists are of the opinion that they are lawful for Muslims to marry, but I am more inclined to support the view that they are not. Al-Bukhārī quotes 'Abdullāh ibn 'Umar, a scholar Companion of the Prophet Muḥammad, as saying: "To my mind, there could be no greater polytheism for a woman than to believe that Jesus is the Lord."

Muslim women, however, are forbidden from marrying Jewish or Christian men. The two cases are different, meriting different verdicts. Under Islamic law, children are called by their father's names. It is the practice in all societies that, after marriage, a woman joins the household of her husband. If a Muslim man married a Christian or Jewish woman, she would move to the town or country where he lived, and join the rest of his family, and their children would take the father's name and grow up in his religious and cultural environment. The situation would be reversed in the case of a Muslim woman marrying a Jewish or Christian man, where the children would be raised in a non-Muslim culture and most likely grow up to be non-Muslims.

There are, however, other practical considerations that would discourage the marriage of a Muslim man to a Christian or Jewish woman, which is otherwise permissible. Some of these were pointed out by the second Caliph, 'Umar ibn al-Khaṭṭāb.

In his commentary on the Qur'ān, Ibn Kathīr quotes Ibn Jarīr al-Ṭabarī as saying that despite unanimity over the marriage of Muslim men to Jewish or Christian women, 'Umar ibn al-Khaṭṭāb was not in favour of it, lest Muslim men should turn away from marrying Muslim women.

He also reports that when Hudhayfah married a Jewess, 'Umar wrote ordering him to divorce her. Hudhayfah wrote back, asking: "Is it because you claim that she is forbidden for me to marry that I should divorce her?" 'Umar replied: "No, I do not, but I fear that people may turn away from marrying Muslim women."

More recent experiences provide further evidence that such marriages undermine the faith and Muslim identity of the new generations of Islam, especially in view of the fact that our societies today are only nominally Muslim.

Purity in Sexual Relations

The next point the *sūrah* deals with is a delicate and most private one, but here again marital relations are elevated above the physical contact, even when the discussion is concerned with the most physical aspect of married life, namely, sexual relations:

> *They ask you about menstruation. Say: 'It is an unclean condition; so keep aloof from women during menstruation, and do not draw near to them until they are cleansed. When they have cleansed themselves, you may go in unto them in the proper way, as God has bidden you. God loves those who turn to Him in repentance, and He loves those who keep themselves pure.' Your wives are your tilth; go, then, to your tilth as you may desire, but first provide something for your souls. Fear God and know that you shall meet Him. Give the happy news to the believers.* (Verses 222–223)

Within marriage, sex is not an end in itself, but a means to achieving much more profound goals in life, not least of which is reproduction and the continuation of human life. While it may satisfy the physical desire, sex during menstruation is not only unclean and carries health risks for both man and woman, but also fails to serve its fundamental objective. As a matter of fact, sex during menstruation is not very attractive to normal healthy people because it is not conducive to reproduction. Sound human nature tends to avoid it. On the other hand, during cleanliness sex fulfils the natural desire and achieves a natural objective. Therefore, the question raised is given a clear answer of prohibition: *"They ask you about menstruation. Say: 'It is an unclean condition; so keep aloof from women during menstruation, and do not draw near to them until they are cleansed.'"* (Verse 222)

However, that is not the end of the matter. Sexual behaviour outside the menstruation period must conform to certain manners and standards of decency and propriety: *"When they have cleansed themselves, you may go in unto them in the proper way, as God has bidden you."* (Verse 222) Here the *sūrah* points out that sexual intercourse is allowed only at the place where fertilization may take place. The immediate physical pleasure is not the only purpose of sexual intercourse; its higher purpose is the continuity of human life. God points out what He has made lawful, and a Muslim seeks what is lawful. Moreover, God's laws are meant to purify His servants. Hence the statement: *"God loves those who turn to Him in repentance, and He loves those who keep themselves pure."* (Verse 222)

The *sūrah* then defines this aspect of the marital relationship in the most poignant and affectionate terms, saying: *"Your wives are your tilth; go, then, to your tilth as you may desire, but first provide something for your souls. Fear God and know that you shall meet Him. Give the happy news to the believers."* (Verse 223)

There can hardly be a more accurate and eloquent description of the nature and purpose of this aspect of the relationship between husband and wife. It is by no means a complete description of the marital relationship. Elsewhere in the Qur'ān we find other similarly befitting and powerful descriptions, such as: *"They [your wives] are a garment and you are a garment to them."* (2: 187) *"And of His signs is that He creates for you mates from your own selves, so that you may incline towards them, and He engenders between you love and compassion."* (30: 21)

Each of these statements describes an aspect of this most profound and important of human relationships. The use of the Arabic word *ḥarth*, rendered here as 'tilth', with its connotations of tillage and production, is most fitting, in a context of fertility and procreation. Within this healthy, warm and conducive atmosphere, couples may seek each other's comfort in any manner that will give them the greatest and most fulfilling pleasure.

Sexual fulfilment must, therefore, be sought as part of an overall objective which serves to please God Almighty, and is beneficial to the individuals concerned. They will be further rewarded by God for respecting His teachings and abiding by them.

We have here a good example of the generosity and kindness of Islam. It is a religion that does not deny man any of his natural tendencies or instincts, or pretend to achieve human purity by suppressing or destroying man's basic physical needs. Rather, Islam disciplines, guides and fosters these desires and needs in a manner that reinforces man's humanity and invigorates his consciousness of, and relationship with, God. It seeks to blend physical and sensual tendencies with human and religious emotions, thus bringing together the transient pleasures and the immutable values of human life into one harmonious and congruent system that will render man worthy of being God's vicegerent on earth. Being a system ordained by the Creator Himself, it will never clash with human nature or cause any human misery or unhappiness.

Oaths and Atonements

The *sūrah* then moves on to the subject of renouncing wives on oath and abstaining from sexual contact with them as a form of punishment. By way of introduction, it begins with talking about oaths in general, saying:

> *Do not allow your oaths in the name of God to become an obstacle to your being kind and God-fearing, or to promoting peace among people. God hears all and knows all. God shall not take you to task for oaths which you may have uttered without thought, but He will take you to task for what your hearts have conceived in earnest. God is much-Forgiving, Forbearing. Those who take an oath that they will not approach their wives shall have four months of grace. If they go back on their oaths, God is much-Forgiving, Merciful; and if they are resolved on divorce, [let them remember that] God hears all and knows all.* (Verses 224–227)

The accepted interpretation of the opening part of this passage is that attributed to 'Abdullāh ibn 'Abbās who is quoted as saying: "Do not allow the fact that you have made an oath prevent you from doing what is good and righteous; rather, do what is right and atone for your oath." According to Ibn Kathīr, a similar view is attributed to a host of leading scholars.

To support this interpretation, the Prophet's statement, reported by Abū Hurayrah and related by Muslim, is often quoted. The Prophet said: "Whoever made an oath and later realized that it would be better to do something different, let him atone for his oath and do what is better." Al-Bukhārī cites the statement reported by Abū Hurayrah that the Prophet said: "For someone to insist on honouring his oath concerning his relationship with his wife is, in God's sight, far worse than to relent and pay the atonement God has prescribed for going back on an oath."

It may, therefore, be concluded that the main import of the statement is that oaths should not be an excuse for not doing what is best under the circumstances. One should not hesitate to revoke an oath one has taken if it becomes clear that revoking it is better from the Islamic point of view. The promotion of goodness and reconciliation takes precedence over one's commitment to an oath.

A case in point is the vow made by Abū Bakr, the Prophet's leading Companion, that he would never forgive one of his relatives, Misṭaḥ, for taking part in the campaign to slander the Prophet's wife, 'Ā'ishah, who was also Abū Bakr's daughter.

On that occasion a passage was revealed, declaring 'Ā'ishah's innocence of what was said against her. Then a verse follows in the same *sūrah* calling on believers to always choose the better course of action. This verse may be translated as follows: *"Let not those of you who have been graced with God's favour and are well-off withhold their generosity from their relatives, or the needy, or those who leave their homes for the cause of God. Let them forgive and forebear. Do you not wish that God should forgive you your sins? God is much-Forgiving, Merciful."* (24: 22) Abū Bakr relented and atoned for his oath, and reinstated his generous help to Misṭaḥ.

God is even more gracious in offering this concession not only for inadvertent vows that need no atonement, but also for vows made in earnest and with full intention. The Prophet was reported to have often overlooked off-hand or casual vows made out of habit or in the heat of the moment. Premeditated vows must be revoked and atoned for, if keeping them results in, or leads to, something evil, harmful or inequitable. Some jurists, however, are of the opinion that making a false vow, knowing that it is false, can never be atoned for. Mālik says in his famous book, *al-Muwaṭṭa'*: "The best I have heard on this subject is that a casual vow is made in total good faith. If it is subsequently proven to be false, it requires no atonement. If a false vow is made deliberately, with the intention of appeasing someone, or for material gain, that is too grave to be atoned for."

The *sūrah* emphasizes that God knows all and hears all, and that He is forgiving and lenient, in order to establish in people's minds the fact that these matters are ultimately referred to God Almighty for judgement, and to urge them to be conscious of Him and seek His pleasure and grace in all such matters.

Having established the general rule with respect to vows, the *sūrah* goes on to deal with the specific vows by husbands to abstain from sexual contact with their wives, either indefinitely or for a specified but long period of time: *"Those who take an oath that they will not approach their wives shall have four months of grace. If they go back on their oaths, God is much-forgiving, merciful; and if they are resolved on divorce, [let them remember that] God hears all and knows all."* (Verses 226–227)

There are times in married life when spouses, for one reason or another, find themselves drawn away from one another. In such cases, some men swear not to sleep with their wives as a form of punishment, which can be humiliating for the wife and psychologically extremely hard on her. It is also a negation of the very essence of marriage and can be detrimental to the well-being and stability of the whole family.

This behaviour was not forbidden outright to begin with because it could be effective with vain, spiteful or quarrelsome women. It could, indeed, act as a safety valve for the relief of certain pressures that build up within a married relationship. Nor was the advantage left completely on the man's side, who could sometimes be at fault, intent on humilating his wife or coercing her to submit to his terms or demands. He thus tries to deny her the chance to live happily with him, refusing, at the same time, to release her to seek happiness with someone else.

To balance all relevant factors and all practicalities, Islam has limited the duration of such estrangement to four months. This period seems to be the maximum an average normal woman can go before feeling the need for a man's comfort.

'Umar ibn al-Khaṭṭāb, the second Caliph, was reported to be patrolling the streets of Madinah one night when he heard a woman reciting a few lines of poetry expressing her loneliness and desire for her husband who was away fighting with one of the Muslim armies. She complained of sleeplessness which she attributed to the fact that she had no one to frolic with, affirming that only her fear of God prevented her from seeking pleasure with someone else.

'Umar then enquired from his daughter, Ḥafṣah, the Prophet's wife, how long a woman could stand the absence of her husband. She replied: "Six months;" or she said four months, according to some reports. 'Umar then declared that he would never let soldiers stay away from their wives for more than that period.

People's temperament and will-power vary, but four months seem to be a reasonable test period, after which a husband should either resume normal marital relations with his wife or insist on his rejection of her. In this latter case the relationship must be dissolved by divorce and the wife given her freedom, whether by the husband or through the courts. This would enable both parties to start a new life with another spouse, thereby preserving the dignity and integrity of the wife and taking the pressure off the husband. Such a solution would be more just to both people and would safeguard the institution of marriage, which God has ordained for the enhancement and advancement of human life.

Rules of Divorce

Having reached in the previous verse a point when divorce becomes a possibility, the *sūrah* goes on to outline in some detail the rules governing divorce and all matters relating to it, such as the waiting period and maintenance: *"Divorced women shall wait, by themselves, for three monthly courses. It is unlawful for them to conceal what God might have created in their wombs, if they believe in God and the Last Day. During this period, their husbands are entitled to take them back, if they desire reconciliation. Women shall, in all fairness, enjoy rights similar to those exercised against them, although men have an advantage over them. God is Almighty, Wise."* (Verse 228)

The three monthly courses referred to here are variously understood as three menstrual periods, or three periods of cleanliness from menstruation. The idea is that a divorced woman should not seek another marriage within that period.

The original Arabic expression uses a most delicate and sensitive language when advising divorced women to *"wait, by themselves, for three monthly courses."* It conveys a mixed sense of eagerness and apprehension. It suggests that a divorced woman would have a strong desire to start a new marital relationship in order to reassure herself, and show others, that the failure of her marriage was not due to any weaknesses or shortcomings on her part, and that she remained attractive to men and capable of starting her life afresh. Being the one who had initiated the divorce, the husband would naturally have no such feelings.

Furthermore, the Qur'ān appeals to the woman's faith in God and the Last Day, urging her not to conceal the fact if she were pregnant by the divorcing husband. Reminding her of the Last Day, the time for punishment and reward, is especially pertinent here as it is meant to arouse her conscience and make her totally scrupulous over such a grave matter. After all, God knows the truth and there is no point in hiding it from Him.

The waiting period also acts as a period of grace during which the estranged couple can test their feelings and emotions. They may still have feelings for each other, and their mutual compassion might have been overshadowed by a temporary moment of heated emotions, or a misunderstanding, or personal pride. Once tempers are cooled and fury gives way to common sense, the couple might reconsider their situation and decide that it would be more sensible to forget their disagreement and resume their life together.

Divorce is the least preferable solution in God's eyes; it should only be used as a last resort, when all else has failed. Elsewhere, the Qur'ān urges that divorce must be preceded by attempts at reconciliation and that it must not take place during the menstrual period. It is only possible in a period of cleanliness from menstruation during which no sexual intercourse has taken place between the divorcing couples. This gives yet more time for reflection and reconsideration.

When a first divorce between a married couple is initiated, the waiting period acts as a test for their feelings, and if they discover during this time that reconciliation is possible, that option is available to them. As the *sūrah* says: *"their husbands are entitled to take them back, if they desire reconciliation."* (Verse 228) The condition here is that, in coming back together again, the couple should be seriously seeking reconciliation. The aim should never be to undermine the wife's right to marry someone else or put any pressure on her to resume an unhappy relationship.

"Women shall, in all fairness, enjoy rights similar to those exercised against them ..." (Verse 228) The divorced woman is required to wait for a certain period before she can marry someone else, and is obliged to declare whether she is carrying a baby by her divorced husband. The husband is equally required to show good faith if he wishes to take her back, making sure that he intends to cause her no harm. He is further obliged, as we shall see later, to provide maintenance for his divorced wife during the waiting period.

The *sūrah* goes on to say: *"... although men have an advantage over them."* (Verse 228) This advantage, in my view, is in no way absolute but is contingent, within the present context, upon the fact that it is the man who initiates the divorce and would, therefore, have the prerogative to take his wife back, a decision that could not be left to her to take. This advantage, indeed a useful and proper one, is by no means universal, as some have erroneously concluded, but is simply dictated by the nature and the circumstances of the dispute.

The verse then concludes by asserting: *"God is Almighty, Wise."* He lays down rules with force and authority, as well as prudence and compassion.

Fair and Balanced Divorce Systems

The next set of rules relates to the number of times divorce can take place and the wife's full entitlement to her dowry, except in the case when a wife buys herself out of a marriage she feels she could not sustain for fear that she might commit an act of disobedience to God. Under such circumstances, a wife may forgo part of her dowry or make an agreed settlement in order to release herself when her husband is unwilling to divorce her.

The *sūrah* says: *"Divorce may be [revoked] twice, whereupon a woman may either be retained in fairness or released with kindness. It is unlawful for you to take back from women anything of what you have given them [as dowry], unless they both [husband and wife] fear that they may not be able to keep within the bounds set by God. If you have cause to fear that they would not be able to keep within the bounds set by God, it shall be no offence for either of them if she gives up whatever she may in order to free herself. These are the bounds set by God; do not, then, transgress them. Those who transgress the bounds set by God are wrongdoers indeed."* (Verse 229)

Couples are allowed to divorce and revoke their divorce twice before the condition stated in the next verse applies. Under this provision, remarriage with a three-times divorced wife cannot take place except in the case when she legally marries another husband who may subsequently, and in the normal course of events, divorce her. Should this take place normally, without it being pre-arranged, the woman and her first husband may be re-married, if they believe that by now they are able to make their marriage successful.

The background to this ruling is that in pre-Islamic Arabia no limitation was set on the number of times divorce could take place. Men would marry, divorce and remarry the same woman, virtually at will. When a man from Madinah had fallen out with his wife and grew to dislike her intensely, he vowed that he would neither keep her nor let her go; he would divorce her and then take her back just before her waiting period had elapsed. The woman complained to the Prophet Muḥammad, to whom this verse was then revealed.

This is another example of the prudent and propitious method the Qur'ān had adopted in providing the Muslims with the rulings and directions they needed to organize their community. This approach continued throughout the period of the revelation of the Qur'ān until all the main provisions of the Islamic code were fully laid down, enabling succeeding generations of Muslims to live by their guidance and principles.

Limiting the number of times divorce can be revoked prevents its abuse. The first time a man divorces his wife he would be entitled, without the need for any formalities, to take her back anytime during her waiting period. If this period elapses, the divorce would become final and a fresh marriage contract, with a fresh dowry, would have to be entered into. In both cases, the husband is allowed one additional divorce if matters again go wrong. The third time a divorce takes place, it is final and irrevocable. The only way a three-times divorced couple could resume a married relationship would be if the ex-wife married a different man who subsequently dies or, in the normal course of events, divorces her and she completes her waiting period without the marriage being re-instated.

The first divorce, as we said earlier, would put the whole relationship to the test, the second one would provide a second and final chance to reassess the situation before judging whether it is irreconcilable. If the marriage could be saved, well and good. A third divorce would, however, be evidence of a total breakdown of the relationship, and that the marriage was unworkable.

In any case, divorce should only be a last resort option to remedy a situation which could not otherwise be saved. Once divorce takes place twice, it would only be fair to either maintain the relationship with honour and dignity and resume as happy a life as possible, or to amicably bring it to an end without pain or acrimony. This would be the third divorce, after which both man and woman are free to start afresh with a different spouse. This is an extremely realistic approach, providing practical solutions. It neither denies the problem nor condemns it, nor attempts to re-create human nature to suit it, nor, indeed, does it ignore the problem altogether or try to sweep it under the carpet.

If the marriage proved unsustainable, the woman would be entitled to everything that had come to be hers during the marriage including the dowry. She would not have to reimburse the man for any upkeep or other costs he had incurred, unless it was her decision to end the marriage, for reasons of her own which had convinced her that life with that particular husband was no longer tolerable or would drive her to transgress the limits of decency, with herself or in her relationship with her husband. In this case the woman may ask for a divorce but would be obliged to compensate the man for the break-up of his marriage home, through no fault of his own, by giving him back the dowry he had paid her, or reimbursing him for all or some of the costs he had incurred while keeping her and enabling her to preserve her honour and dignity.

These realistic and scrupulous measures take account of all possible situations and feelings, ensuring that a wife will never have to accept an unhappy marriage under duress, and that a husband does not forgo any of his rights if his marriage breaks up through no fault of his own.

The merits of this approach may be illustrated by an event during the Prophet Muḥammad's lifetime. Mālik reports in *al-Muwaṭṭa'* that one morning, at dawn, the Prophet found Ḥabībah bint Sahl, wife of

Thābit ibn Qays, waiting at his door. He asked her what she wanted and she replied: "I can no longer live with Thābit ibn Qays."

The Prophet sent for her husband and told him what Ḥabībah had said. Ḥabībah then turned to the Prophet and said: "I still have all that he had given me," upon which the Prophet said to Thābit: "Take it back"; which he did and Ḥabībah went back to her people.

The version related by al-Bukhārī mentions that Ḥabībah said to the Prophet: "I take nothing against Thābit's religious or moral behaviour, but as a Muslim I cannot live with him and be ungrateful." The Prophet asked her: "Would you give him back his orchard?" (The orchard being the dowry Thābit had given her.) She agreed and the Prophet said to Thābit: "Take back the orchard and divorce her once."

Another version related by al-Ṭabarī mentions that Abū Jarīr had asked 'Ikrimah how the *khul'* had been instituted. He said that Ibn 'Abbās used to say that the first case of *khula'* was when 'Abdullāh ibn Ubayy's sister went to the Prophet and said: "Nothing could ever make me put my head next to his! I lifted my curtain and saw him with a group of men. He was the darkest, shortest and the least handsome of them all." Her husband then said: "But I have given her the best of what I have: my orchard. If she gives it back to me, I shall let her go." She agreed and offered to give him more, if he so wished. The Prophet annulled their marriage.

These incidents show how the Prophet took into consideration the psychological and emotional state of the wife, and settled the matter fairly and forthrightly, in full appreciation of human nature and consideration of family relations and personal feelings.

To put these rulings within their proper religious context, the verse ends with a powerful reminder, saying: *"These are the bounds set by God; do not, then, transgress them. Those who transgress the bounds set by God are wrongdoers indeed."* (Verse 229)

We pause here to reflect on a subtle difference in the use of two Qur'ānic expressions denoting a similar meaning in two different contexts.

Verse 187 of this *sūrah* may be given in translation: *"It is lawful for you to be intimate with your wives during the night preceding the fast. They are as a garment for you, as you are for them. God is aware that you have been deceiving yourselves in this respect, and He has turned to you in His mercy and pardoned you. So, you may now lie with them and seek what God has ordained for you. Eat and drink until you can see the white streak of dawn against the blackness of the night. Then resume the fast till nightfall. Do not lie with your wives when you are in retreat in the mosques. These are the bounds set by God, so do not come near them. Thus God makes clear His revelations to people, that they may remain God-fearing."*

We note here that the verse closes with the words: *"These are the bounds set by God, so do not come near them"*, while the present verse uses the expression: *"These are the bounds set by God; do not, then, transgress them."* While one warns against drawing near to the act of wrongdoing itself, the other warns against transgression.

In the first instance, the warning was against being attracted or tempted by certain desires and it was appropriate to talk of resisting those temptations and keeping away from them. In the second instance, the subject matter involves conflict and acrimonious disputes, and the danger here is of either party overreaching or exceeding their limits, so it is more pertinent to advise restraint and steering away from transgression.

This is a good example of the remarkably precise diction of the Qur'ān.

The *sūrah* continues, giving more rulings relating to divorce: *"Should he divorce her [a third time], she shall not thereafter be lawful for him to remarry until she has wedded another husband. If the latter then divorces her it shall be no offence for either of the two if they return to one another, if they feel that they will be able to keep within the bounds set by God. Such are the bounds set by God. He makes them plain for people who have knowledge."* (Verse 230)

If a third divorce takes place in a marriage, it could only be a sign of serious and irreversible deterioration within that relationship. The best solution in this case would be permanent separation, and for each partner to seek happiness with someone else. However, if any or all of the three divorces were pronounced by the man lightly, or out of spite, or in the heat of the moment, here again, a drastic measure must be taken to prevent men abusing their divorce privilege. Such an unhappy relationship should not be perpetuated, since the man has no appreciation for it, nor is keen to protect it.

The question may here be put, therefore, as to why the woman should have to suffer the consequences of a rash utterance by her husband, thereby jeopardizing her life, peace and security? The answer is that the ruling has to be realistic. Let us look at this more closely and ask: What would be the alternative solution? Should the man be forced to live with a woman in a marriage he has little or no respect for? Should he be told that his repeated divorcing of his wife is not enforceable and that his wife is his responsibility, whether he likes it or not? This, in fact, would be far more humiliating for the wife, and degrading to the marriage itself, neither of which Islam would condone. A more proper censure of the man's behaviour would be to deprive him of the right to his wife and make him in the first and second divorces liable to pay a new dowry, under a new marriage contract, after he had failed to take her back before the passing of the waiting period. The third time a man resorts to divorce, the separation shall be deemed final and the woman has to marry someone else and be legally divorced by him before being able to return to her former husband. The first husband would stand to forfeit the dowry he had paid as well as all the costs he had incurred during the marriage. He will also, in any case, be liable for alimony payments. This is a practical and workable manner in which to approach this delicate and emotionally-charged situation.

If, after the third divorce, the woman marries someone else and this marriage is then terminated, in the normal course of events, by divorce or by the husband's death, she may be reunited with the first husband as long as *"they feel that they will be able to keep within the bounds set by God."* (Verse 230) This indicates very clearly that the matter is not left to the couple to decide as they please, but it is regulated by terms and conditions set out by God for a proper social order that conforms to His will. These terms and conditions are fully expounded in the Qur'ān for all who are capable of learning and understanding.

Kindly Retention or Amicable Separation

Having detailed the divorce procedure, the *sūrah* goes on to give directions to divorcing couples, urging them to show kindness, compassion and consideration during the post-divorce period, regardless of how the rift came about:

> *When you have divorced women and they have reached the end of their waiting-term, either retain them with fairness or let them go with fairness. Do not retain them out of malice in order to hurt*

them. He who does so wrongs his own soul. Do not take God's revelations in a frivolous manner. Remember the blessings God has bestowed upon you, and all the revelation and wisdom He has bestowed upon you from on high in order to admonish you. Fear God and know well that He has full knowledge of everything. And when you have divorced women and they have reached the end of their waiting-term, do not prevent them from marrying their husbands if they have agreed with each other in a fair manner. This is an admonition for everyone of you who believes in God and the Last Day. That is more virtuous for you, and purer. God knows, whereas you do not know. (Verses 231–232)

Married life must be built on a spirit of mutual kindness, fairness and compassion, and this spirit must be evident even if the relationship has to be severed. Malice and ill-will must not be allowed to cloud this relationship. But, this can only be attained if the parties concerned are guided by faith in God and are conscious of their accountability to Him in the hereafter. They ought to acknowledge God's grace and blessings in allowing them to marry and enabling them to seek happiness elsewhere when the marriage fails, and providing both parties with necessary and fair guarantees for compensation and redress. These principles of kindness and fairness must be observed under all circumstances.

In pre-Islamic society, women faced a great deal of oppression and abuse. Female infanticide was widespread in Arabia, and those who survived would suffer cruelty and degradation throughout their lives. Women were bought and sold like animals; mares and she-camels were sometimes considered more precious! They would suffer when they were married; and they received grossly unfair treatment when divorced. Divorced women were not allowed to remarry without their former husband's permission, nor were they allowed by their families to return to their husbands if they wished to be reconciled. Generally, women were looked down upon in Arabia, as indeed in other societies.

When Islam came, it brought fresh principles and values that recognized women and afforded them a status comparable to that of men. It elevated marriage to a religious duty, preserved women's human dignity, and established for them specific rights when they were married and when they were divorced. These principles and values were a gift from God to both men and women, guaranteeing for them fundamental human, social and legal rights they had neither demanded nor even thought possible.

Thus, as the end of the waiting period approaches, a husband should either take his wife back into the marriage, with no ill-feelings and with a sincere intention to treat her kindly and sympathetically; or allow the waiting period to elapse and the divorce to take effect without causing any harm or injustice to the divorced wife or demanding any compensation from her.

This would ensure that a man would not be able to abuse his prerogative to divorce at the expense of his estranged wife, as with the case of the man from Madinah referred to earlier, and as seems to have been the custom among Arabian men before Islam.

To emphasize this further and purge men's hearts of evil and selfishness, the Qur'ān appeals to the noblest of feelings and to man's sense of shame and honour and fear of God: *"Do not retain them out of malice in order to hurt them. He who does so wrongs his own soul. Do not take God's revelations in a frivolous manner. Remember the blessings God has bestowed upon you, and all the revelation and wisdom He has bestowed upon you from on high in order to admonish you. Fear God and know well that He has full knowledge of everything."* (Verse 231)

Keeping a wife against her will, or mistreating her, would be akin to harming oneself, because she is a fellow human being, with dignity and feelings. A man would be doing himself injustice, too, by allowing himself to act in defiance of God's guidance and teachings.

When it comes to marital relations and divorce, Islamic teachings are straightforward and clear, aimed at building social life on complete honesty and integrity. Men who abuse divorce, which God has permitted a last resort solution, in order to malign or ill-treat their estranged wives, are violating God's will and subverting His instructions. Regrettably, such blatant abuse is quite widespread in many Muslim communities today, where men tend to do all they can to evade the proper conduct taught by Islam.

The Qur'ānic words evoke man's sense of integrity and gratitude to God. They remind that first generation of Muslims of the very special grace and favour God bestowed upon them through the revelation of Qur'ānic guidance, which had elevated every aspect of their daily life.

One of the most evident favours God had extended to the Arabs was to transform them from obscure, fragmented, uncouth and backward hordes, with no influence or role to play in the world. They had nothing, whether material or spiritual, to provide for themselves, let alone to offer to humanity. A small minority of them lived in riches, while the overwhelming majority lived in dire poverty. They also suffered mental and spiritual deprivation, with an absurd set of beliefs and a primitive concept of life. Their interests were little more than looting raids, vengeance killings, drinking, gambling and similarly trivial enjoyments.

Islam transformed them into a great, united, mature and pioneering nation with a profound religious faith. Under Islam they could offer to the world a faith that provided a superior concept of existence. That same nation went on to lead the world and influence its development and progress in all fields. They became a power to reckon with, whereas previously they were subordinated by neighbouring empires or an ingnored community with little consequence. Islam also gave them power and wealth.

Above all else, Islam gave the Muslim nation peace: peace within the minds of individual Muslims, and peace within the home and within society as a whole. It gave Muslims a greatly enhanced sense of pride, decency and nobility, which in turn gave them cultural maturity and self-confidence that made their civilization stand out in the history of mankind.

Muslims of that generation did not require much persuasion that they were a favoured nation because they were aware of their pre-Islamic past and the vast leap they had taken with Islam. They knew and appreciated fully the value of the Qur'ān and its wisdom for the well-being and stability of their community and, in particular, of family life which formed the cornerstone of their society.

Finally, the Qur'ān touches Muslims' hearts with a warning that they should fear God who *"has full knowledge of everything."* This warning evokes a sense of fear and caution, in addition to the sense of gratitude and integrity already revived, in order to use every means of focusing their attention on the right course of action and behaviour.

The *sūrah* directs Muslims not to stand in the way of an estranged wife, whose waiting period has elapsed, if she wants to remarry her divorced husband and they have come to an amicable and honourable agreement to do so: *"And when you have divorced women and they have reached the end of their waiting-term, do not prevent them from marrying their husbands if they have agreed with each other in a fair manner. This is an admonition for everyone of you who believes in God and the Last Day. That is more virtuous for you, and purer. God knows, whereas you do not know."* (Verse 232)

Al-Tirmidhī reported that Maʿqil ibn Yasār gave his sister in marriage to a Muslim man who later divorced her and she remained divorced until her waiting period had elapsed. After some time they both felt they would like to marry again and the man went to Maʿqil, asking to marry her. Maʿqil was furious and reprimanded the man for divorcing her in the first place, and swore that he would never marry her if he were to live for ever. Al-Tirmidhī adds that, nevertheless, it was God's will that the couple should have the chance to be reunited. Thus, this verse was revealed. On hearing it, Maʿqil said: "I hear and I obey." He then called the man and said to him: "You have my blessings to marry her."

This highly compassionate divine gesture towards people's feelings and emotions is evidence of God's boundless mercy towards mankind. The verse as a whole aims to mitigate the trauma of divorce and to educate Muslims in organizing their social affairs realistically and with compassion.

The verse closes with more exhortations, calling upon the Muslims to be conscious of their accountability to God and to look beyond the objectives of this transient life. They should realize that in ordaining these rules God, who knows all, wishes to elevate their aspirations and bring their society more happiness and harmony. Thus, every action is linked to God and serves as an act of worship aimed at cleansing the individual and all society from immediate materialistic considerations.

Child Care in Broken Homes

The following ruling concerns the fostering and breast-feeding of infants after divorce. When a marriage breaks up, certain ties, commitments and relationships continue to exist between the divorced couple, foremost among which is the well-being and upbringing of children. The *sūrah* covers all possible eventualities:

> *Mothers may breast-feed their children for two whole years; [that is] for those who wish to complete the suckling. The father of the child is responsible to provide in a fair manner for their sustenance and clothing. No human being shall be burdened with more than he is*

well able to bear. Neither shall a mother be allowed to cause her child to suffer, nor shall a father cause suffering to his child. The same shall apply to the father's heir. If, by mutual consent and after due consultation, the parents choose to wean the child, they will incur no sin thereby. Nor shall it be any offence on your part if you engage wet nurses for your children, provided that you hand over what you agreed to pay, in a fair manner. Fear God, and know that God sees all that you do. (Verse 233)

A divorced mother continues to have a God-given duty towards her infant, no matter how acrimonious the separation from her husband. God's mercy and compassion dictate that under no circumstances should the children be made to suffer, especially during the early years of life when they are still being breast-fed. Modern scientific research has shown that the mother's milk is essential for the first two years of life for the healthy physical and psychological development of the child. Mankind needed to know this important fact and hence God, out of His infinite mercy, revealed it in the Qur'ān more than fourteen centuries ago.

In return, the mother has secured the right that the father must provide for her maintenance with fairness and good-will, as partners in their responsibility towards the infant and within their respective means.

"No human being shall be burdened with more than he is well able to bear." (Verse 233) The child should not be used by either parent as a pretext to put pressure on the other, and: *"Neither shall a mother be allowed to cause her child to suffer, nor shall a father cause suffering to his child."* (Verse 233)

Neither parent should resort to emotional blackmail or coercion to extort concessions from the other. Were the child's father to die: *"The same shall apply to the father's heir."* (Verse 233) The father's heir takes over the responsibility to provide for the suckling mother in a fair manner. This is a case where gains and liabilities are shared within the family: the heir receives his share of inheritance and discharges the liabilities of the deceased. It is essential that this right of the mother, and that of her child, is respected and fulfilled in all situations.

"If, by mutual consent and after due consultation, the parents choose to wean the child, they will incur no sin thereby." (Verse 233) If, for health or other reasons, the parents, or the mother and the father's

heir, jointly decide that it would be in the child's interest to take him off his mother's milk before he has reached two years of age, they shall have the right to do so, provided they have had sufficient consultation over the matter, and act in the child's interest.

Similarly, if the father chooses to have the baby suckled by someone other than the natural mother, and can show the distinct advantage of such action, he may do so provided that he ensures that the suckling mother receives her wages: *"Nor shall it be any offence on your part if you engage wet nurses for your children, provided that you hand over what you agreed to pay, in a fair manner."* (Verse 233) This ensures that the wet nurse would take good care of the child.

The verse closes with yet further exhortation to all concerned to fear God and take account of His presence and overall authority. *"Fear God, and know that God sees all that you do."* (Verse 233) This, above all else, is a firm guarantee of proper and fair conduct by all.

The Case of Widows

The *sūrah* then turns to introduce the rules governing widows; their waiting period and whether and when they can entertain new proposals for marriage:

> *Those of you who die leaving wives behind, their wives shall wait, by themselves, for four months and ten days. When they have reached the end of their waiting-term, you shall incur no sin in whatever they may do with themselves in a lawful manner. God is aware of all that you do. You will incur no sin if you give a hint of a marriage offer to [widowed] women or keep such an intention to yourselves. God knows that you will entertain such intentions concerning them. Do not, however, plight your troth in secret; but speak only in a decent manner. Furthermore, do not resolve on actually making the marriage tie before the prescribed term [of waiting] has run its course. Know well that God knows what is in your minds, so have fear of Him; and know that God is much-Forgiving, Forbearing.* (Verses 234–235)

In pre-Islamic Arabia, widows suffered a great deal of injustice at the hands of their own families, their in-laws and society in general. When a husband died, his widow would be confined to a drab part of the home and made to wear her shabbiest clothes and refrain from using any perfume or incense for a whole year. At the end of that period, she would be required to perform a series of degrading and meaningless rituals which included casting animal faeces into the air and riding an ass or a sheep through the town or village. Islam did away with all those worthless customs and alleviated the suffering of widows who, in addition to the grief of losing their husbands, had to endure the humiliation and persecution of their families and were deprived of the opportunity to resume a happy and decent family life.

Islam set a waiting period of four months and ten days, which is slightly longer than that for a divorced wife, unless a woman is pregnant, in which case her waiting period extends until she has delivered. The purpose of the waiting period is to determine whether the woman is pregnant and to avoid hurting the feelings of the family of her deceased husband by leaving his home immediately after his death. During this period, the widow wears modest clothes, and does not wear the sort of make-up that encourages suitors to propose marriage to her. Once the waiting period is over, no one, from either her family or that of her deceased husband, has the right to dictate to her what to do with her life. She is totally free to decide for herself within the established traditions and teachings of Islam. She is free to wear all the adornments permitted for Muslim women, to receive marriage proposals, and to give her consent to marrying anyone she chooses, unimpeded by any antiquated or unreasonable traditions or customs. She has only God to please and fear. For: *"God is aware of all that you do."*

As for men who wish to marry a widow before the end of her waiting period, the *sūrah* gives a most perceptive ruling, based on the observance of principles of decency and propriety, ethical and social values, and the feelings and sensibilities of all concerned while taking account of the overall needs and interests of the community as a whole: *"You will incur no sin if you give a hint of a marriage offer to [widowed] women or keep such an intention to yourselves."* (Verse 235)

During the waiting period, the memory of the deceased husband is still fresh in his widow's mind. She may be overwhelmed by the grief she shares with his family, and anxious to find out whether she is carrying his child. If she already knows that she is pregnant, she is bound to be under stress, and would have to wait until she gives birth before she may marry again. All these considerations make any entertainment of a new marriage rather premature, or even inappropriate and hurtful.

Nevertheless, this should not prevent prospective suitors from expressing an interest in marrying a widow once her waiting period had elapsed, short of directly and officially proposing to her.

Al-Bukhārī relates that Ibn 'Abbās, the Prophet's cousin and learned Companion, is reported to have suggested that statements such as: "I wish to get married," or, "I need to have a woman around me," or "I wish I had a good wife," are appropriate.

The *sūrah* also makes it clear that God is always aware of any unexpressed feelings or intentions by some men in wishing to marry a certain widow. It casts no aspersions on such feelings, which it implicitly recognizes as natural and normal, but urges that no practical steps be taken, or secretive arrangements agreed, before the waiting period is over. Thus, Islam regulates and tames human natural desires rather than condemning or suppressing them. *"God knows that you will entertain such intentions concerning them. Do not, however, plight your troth in secret; but speak only in a decent manner."* (Verse 235)

Arrangements or agreements of marriage made in secret during the waiting period are seen as contrary to decent social propriety and impertinent towards God, who has designated that period as a positive division in a widow's life.

None of this should prevent a decent contact with the woman, provided the subject of conversation falls within the decent religious and social norms as dictated by Islam. No intention of marriage is expressed directly lest the woman's feelings are hurt at such a delicate time in her predicament, as pointed out earlier.

"Do not, however, plight your troth in secret; but speak only in a decent manner. Furthermore, do not resolve on actually making the marriage tie before the prescribed term [of waiting] has run its course." (Verse 235) Once again we note the delicate touches with which the Qur'ān approaches sensitive subjects. It does not warn against making marriage contracts before the end of the waiting period; it warns against making a commitment, plighting one's troth.

The choice of words at the end of the verse is significant: *"Know well that God knows what is in your minds, so have fear of Him; and know that God is much-Forgiving, Forbearing."* (Verse 235) These closing words refer the whole matter to God's grace and generosity, appealing directly to Muslims' respect and fear of God Almighty in conducting their personal and social affairs. This fear and respect are, in themselves, the ultimate guarantee of God's forgiveness and tolerance towards those who earnestly and sincerely strive to observe and implement His directives and rulings.

Kindness after Divorce

The *sūrah* then tackles a different, but frequently met, situation, in which a woman is divorced before the consummation of the marriage. It outlines the respective rights and obligations of both spouses.

> *You will incur no sin if you divorce women before having touched them or settled a dowry for them. Provide for them, the rich according to his means and the straitened according to his means. Such a provision, in an equitable manner, is an obligation binding on the righteous. If you divorce them before having touched them but after having settled a dowry for them, then give them half of that which you have settled, unless they forgo it or he in whose hand is the marriage tie forgoes it. To forgo what is due to you is closer to being righteous. Do not forget to act benevolently to one another. God sees all that you do.* (Verses 236–237)

Two situations are outlined here. The first involves a woman who is divorced before her marriage had been consummated or a dowry agreed. In this case, the husband is obliged to recompense her according to his means. Such a gesture would have an immense psychological impact on the woman, who would be devastated at having her marriage dissolved before it has even begun. It would go a long way towards dissipating any bitterness or acrimony left in her heart. The unfulfilled marriage would be understood as an unfortunate mistake rather than a reflection on her suitability or integrity. The aim would be to diffuse the tension and conduct the severance of the relationship amicably, in a spirit of fairness and with no hard feelings. Meanwhile, the size of the gift offered in this case is left to the man's discretion and conscience, within his financial ability: *"the rich according to his means and the straitened according to his means. Such a provision, in an equitable manner, is an obligation binding on the righteous."* (Verse 236)

The second possibility arises if a dowry has been agreed and settled, in which case half of it must, in principle, be paid unless the wife, or her guardian if she is young, choose, without any pressure, to forgo such a payment. Forgoing such a claim is the attitude of one who has the power of the law on her side but she declines to touch the money of a man with whom she no longer has any relation.

Nevertheless, the Qur'ān goes on to urge more fear of God, tolerance, magnanimity and benevolence on the part of all involved. It exhorts: *"To forgo what is due to you is closer to being righteous. Do not forget to act benevolently to one another. God sees all that you do."* (Verse 237)

A Question of Worship

Having evoked an atmosphere of submission to, and consciousness of, God, the *sūrah* interjects with a short passage on prayer, the main act of worship in Islam, before it deals with other aspects of divorce. The inference here, in the inimitable style of the Qur'ān, is that obedience to God in matters of marriage and divorce is an act of worship no less reverent or commendable than prayer itself. This is in total harmony with the comprehensive Islamic concept of worship (*'ibādah*) which encompasses all human activity and is seen as the central purpose of human existence, expressed in the Qur'ān: *"I have not created the jinns and human beings to any end other than that they may worship Me.* (51: 56)

The *sūrah* says: *"Attend regularly to your prayers, particularly the middle prayer, and stand up before God in devout obedience. If you are in fear, pray walking or riding. When you are again secure, remember God, since it is He who has taught you what you did not know."* (Verses 238–239)

This is a clear instruction to Muslims to attend regularly to the five daily prayers, offering them in the proper manner, in the correct form, and at their appointed times. The middle Prayer is generally taken to refer to *'Aṣr*, or mid-afternoon prayer, on the basis of reports that on the day of the Battle of the Moat (627 CE), the Prophet Muḥammad was heard cursing the enemy forces for "causing us to miss the middle prayer of *'Aṣr*. May God engulf their hearts and homes in fire." The reason for a specific mention of the *'Aṣr* prayer is perhaps because it falls during that part of the afternoon when people take a short rest and may easily miss it.

The *sūrah* also emphasizes total devotion during prayers, because in the early days, Muslims used to, if they felt the need, talk and break away from the prayer to attend to urgent business. When this verse was revealed, it became clear that nothing should distract one from prayer and that worshippers must stand before God in a state of complete submission and devotion.

The *sūrah* points out that even in times of danger and war, Muslims must not neglect the obligatory prayers. They may perform them in the most convenient way possible under the circumstances. They are permitted to perform the prayer in whatever posture they find themselves in, walking or riding, without having to face the *qiblah*, the direction of the Ka'bah, or follow the prescribed procedure. This is not to be confused with *Ṣalāt al-khawf* or 'prayer while in a state of fear', referred to in *Sūrah* 4, which relates specifically to the performance of prayer in the battlefield. If fighting actually breaks out, or an enemy attack is imminent, the ruling given in the present *sūrah* will apply.

The great importance God attaches to prayer is very clear. It is seen as a source of inspiration and moral support, and should not be neglected no matter how dangerous or threatening the situation may be. In times of war, it is another weapon a Muslim may use in facing the enemy. It is a supply line from God Almighty at a most crucial moment.

Islam is a religion founded upon the worship of God, in various forms and in all circumstances. Prayer is the foremost manifestation of man's submission to God. Through the worship of God, man attains the highest level of purity, gains divine support and direction, and achieves total peace of mind. Hence, prayer must never be neglected, even if one is in the line of fire.

When safety and security prevail, prayer must be observed in the normal way, as taught to Muslims by God Almighty in the Qur'ān and through the *sunnah* of the Prophet Muḥammad. The *sūrah* stresses this fact: *"When you are again secure, remember God, since it is He who has taught you what you did not know."* (Verse 239) Indeed, human beings would not have known anything if it were not for the fact that God teaches them in every minute of their lives.

More Rights for Widows and Divorcees

This interjection, with its fine spiritual touch, serves as a fitting interlude before the remaining rules on the rights of widows and on divorce are given:

> *Those of you who die leaving their wives behind, shall bequeath to their wives provisions for one year without their being obliged to leave [their deceased husbands' homes]. Should they leave home [of their own accord], you shall incur no sin for what they may do with themselves in a lawful manner. God is Almighty, Wise. Divorced women shall have a provision according to what is fair. This is an obligation on the God-fearing. Thus God makes clear to you His revelations that you may understand.* (Verses 240–242)

The first of these three verses establishes the right of a widow to a bequest by her deceased husband, allowing her to stay in his home with a provision for her maintenance. She does not need to leave his home or marry again during that period if that is what she chooses to do. This does not exclude her right to leave the house after four months and ten days, the waiting period, as laid down earlier. While the waiting period is an obligation upon the widow, her staying in her late husband's home for a year is her right. Some jurists are of the opinion that this ruling is overruled by the one given in Verse 234. Such a conclusion is not justified since the two rulings refer to two different matters: one establishes a widow's right while the other states an obligation binding upon her.

The *sūrah* goes on to state that: *"Should they leave home [of their own accord], you shall incur no sin for what they may do with themselves in a lawful manner."* (Verse 240) The use of the plural 'you' in this context is significant because it indicates a collective communal responsibility for the welfare of widowed women, and a need for all members of the community to respect and observe Islamic rules and norms.

The concluding phrase, *"God is Almighty, Wise,"* draws attention to God's power and wisdom in laying down such rules, with a hint of warning that they should not be taken lightly.

The next verse institutes a divorcee's right to provisions, in general, and links the observance of this to righteousness and God-fearing.

Some scholars are of the view that the right given in this verse was superseded by those outlined earlier, which is again difficult to justify because the 'provisions' referred to here are not the same as maintenance. The context and the spirit of these Qur'ānic passages suggest that such provisions are a right of all divorced women irrespective of whether the marriage was consummated or a dowry agreed and settled. These provisions are designed to mitigate the bitterness and acrimony normally associated with divorce, and to offset some of the sadness and disappointment that follow the separation. The *sūrah* again evokes the couple's fear of God as the best guarantee of fairness and generosity.

The final verse in this section asserts: *"God makes clear to you His revelations that you may understand."* (Verse 242) God lays down rules clearly, fairly and effectively, inviting people to reflect on their value and purpose and to appreciate God's blessings and mercy, implicit in them. They should not lose sight of the fact that they are aimed to bring about conciliation and accord. They are straightforward, easy and beneficial to put into practice, but rigorous and decisive at the same time.

There is a great need for mankind to take heed of the divinely-inspired social order of Islam and put it into effect in their daily life, which will surely bring peace, stability and harmony into their hearts and minds, and into their lives as a whole.

15

A Timeless Message

Are you not aware of those who left their homes in their thousands for fear of death? God said to them: 'Die,' and later He brought them back to life. Surely, God grants limitless bounty to mankind, but most people are ungrateful. (243)

أَلَمْ تَرَ إِلَى ٱلَّذِينَ خَرَجُوا۟ مِن دِيَٰرِهِمْ
وَهُمْ أُلُوفٌ حَذَرَ ٱلْمَوْتِ فَقَالَ لَهُمُ ٱللَّهُ
مُوتُوا۟ ثُمَّ أَحْيَٰهُمْ ۚ إِنَّ ٱللَّهَ لَذُو فَضْلٍ
عَلَى ٱلنَّاسِ وَلَٰكِنَّ أَكْثَرَ ٱلنَّاسِ
لَا يَشْكُرُونَ ﴿٢٤٣﴾

Fight for the cause of God and know that God hears all and knows all. (244)

وَقَٰتِلُوا۟ فِى سَبِيلِ ٱللَّهِ وَٱعْلَمُوٓا۟ أَنَّ ٱللَّهَ
سَمِيعٌ عَلِيمٌ ﴿٢٤٤﴾

Who will offer God a generous loan, which He will repay multiplied many times over? It is God who straitens people's circumstances and it is He who gives abundantly; and to Him you shall all return. (245)

مَّن ذَا ٱلَّذِى يُقْرِضُ ٱللَّهَ قَرْضًا حَسَنًا
فَيُضَٰعِفَهُۥ لَهُۥٓ أَضْعَافًا كَثِيرَةً ۚ وَٱللَّهُ
يَقْبِضُ وَيَبْصُۜطُ وَإِلَيْهِ تُرْجَعُونَ ﴿٢٤٥﴾

Are you not aware of those elders of the Children of Israel, after the time of Moses, when they said to one of their Prophets, 'Appoint for us a king, and we shall fight for the cause of God.' He said, 'Would you, perchance,

أَلَمْ تَرَ إِلَى ٱلْمَلَإِ مِنۢ بَنِىٓ إِسْرَٰٓءِيلَ مِنۢ
بَعْدِ مُوسَىٰٓ إِذْ قَالُوا۟ لِنَبِىٍّ لَّهُمُ ٱبْعَثْ
لَنَا مَلِكًا نُّقَٰتِلْ فِى سَبِيلِ ٱللَّهِ ۖ
قَالَ هَلْ عَسَيْتُمْ إِن كُتِبَ

refuse to fight if fighting is ordained for you?' They said, 'Why should we not fight for the cause of God when we have been driven out of our homes and our children?' Yet, when fighting was ordained for them, they turned back, save for a few of them. God is fully aware of the wrongdoers. (246)

عَلَيۡكُمُ ٱلۡقِتَالُ أَلَّا تُقَٰتِلُواْۖ قَالُواْ
وَمَا لَنَآ أَلَّا نُقَٰتِلَ فِي سَبِيلِ ٱللَّهِ
وَقَدۡ أُخۡرِجۡنَا مِن دِيَٰرِنَا وَأَبۡنَآئِنَاۖ
فَلَمَّا كُتِبَ عَلَيۡهِمُ ٱلۡقِتَالُ
تَوَلَّوۡاْ إِلَّا قَلِيلٗا مِّنۡهُمۡۚ وَٱللَّهُ عَلِيمُۢ
بِٱلظَّٰلِمِينَ ٢٤٦

Their Prophet said to them, 'God has appointed Saul [Ṭālūt] to be your king.' They said, 'How can he have the kingship over us when we are better entitled to it than he is? Besides, he has not been given abundance of wealth.' He said, 'God has chosen him in preference to you, and endowed him abundantly with knowledge and physical stature. God grants His dominion to whom He will. He is Munificent, All-Knowing.' (247)

وَقَالَ لَهُمۡ نَبِيُّهُمۡ إِنَّ ٱللَّهَ قَدۡ بَعَثَ
لَكُمۡ طَالُوتَ مَلِكٗاۚ قَالُوٓاْ أَنَّىٰ
يَكُونُ لَهُ ٱلۡمُلۡكُ عَلَيۡنَا وَنَحۡنُ أَحَقُّ
بِٱلۡمُلۡكِ مِنۡهُ وَلَمۡ يُؤۡتَ سَعَةٗ
مِّنَ ٱلۡمَالِۚ قَالَ إِنَّ ٱللَّهَ ٱصۡطَفَىٰهُ
عَلَيۡكُمۡ وَزَادَهُۥ بَسۡطَةٗ فِي
ٱلۡعِلۡمِ وَٱلۡجِسۡمِۖ وَٱللَّهُ يُؤۡتِي
مُلۡكَهُۥ مَن يَشَآءُۚ وَٱللَّهُ وَٰسِعٌ
عَلِيمٞ ٢٤٧

Their Prophet also said to them, 'The portent of his kingship is that a casket shall be brought to you, wherein you shall have peace of reassurance from your Lord, and a legacy left behind by the House of Moses and the House of Aaron. It will be borne by angels. That will be a sign for you, if you are true believers.' (248)

وَقَالَ لَهُمۡ نَبِيُّهُمۡ إِنَّ ءَايَةَ
مُلۡكِهِۦٓ أَن يَأۡتِيَكُمُ ٱلتَّابُوتُ
فِيهِ سَكِينَةٞ مِّن رَّبِّكُمۡ
وَبَقِيَّةٞ مِّمَّا تَرَكَ ءَالُ مُوسَىٰ
وَءَالُ هَٰرُونَ تَحۡمِلُهُ ٱلۡمَلَٰٓئِكَةُۚ
إِنَّ فِي ذَٰلِكَ لَأٓيَةٗ لَّكُمۡ إِن
كُنتُم مُّؤۡمِنِينَ ٢٤٨

And when Saul set out with his troops, he said, 'God will now put you to the test by a river. He who drinks from it will not belong to me, but he who does not taste its water will indeed belong to me, except him who takes a scoop with his hand.' They all drank [their fill] of it, except for a few of them. When he and those who kept faith with him crossed the river, they said, 'No strength have we today to stand up to Goliath and his forces.' But those of them who were certain that they would meet their Lord said, 'How often has a small host triumphed over a large host by God's grace. God is with those who remain patient in adversity.' (249)

فَلَمَّا فَصَلَ طَالُوتُ بِٱلْجُنُودِ قَالَ إِنَّ
ٱللَّهَ مُبْتَلِيكُم بِنَهَرٍ فَمَن شَرِبَ
مِنْهُ فَلَيْسَ مِنِّى وَمَن لَّمْ يَطْعَمْهُ فَإِنَّهُۥ
مِنِّىٓ إِلَّا مَنِ ٱغْتَرَفَ غُرْفَةًۢ بِيَدِهِۦ ۚ
فَشَرِبُوا۟ مِنْهُ إِلَّا قَلِيلًا مِّنْهُمْ ۚ فَلَمَّا
جَاوَزَهُۥ هُوَ وَٱلَّذِينَ ءَامَنُوا۟ مَعَهُۥ
قَالُوا۟ لَا طَاقَةَ لَنَا ٱلْيَوْمَ بِجَالُوتَ
وَجُنُودِهِۦ ۚ قَالَ ٱلَّذِينَ يَظُنُّونَ
أَنَّهُم مُّلَٰقُوا۟ ٱللَّهِ كَم مِّن فِئَةٍ
قَلِيلَةٍ غَلَبَتْ فِئَةً كَثِيرَةًۢ بِإِذْنِ
ٱللَّهِ ۗ وَٱللَّهُ مَعَ ٱلصَّٰبِرِينَ ﴿٢٤٩﴾

And when they came face to face with Goliath and his troops, they prayed, 'Our Lord, grant us patience in adversity, make firm our steps, and grant us victory over the unbelievers.' (250)

وَلَمَّا بَرَزُوا۟ لِجَالُوتَ وَجُنُودِهِۦ
قَالُوا۟ رَبَّنَآ أَفْرِغْ عَلَيْنَا صَبْرًا
وَثَبِّتْ أَقْدَامَنَا وَٱنصُرْنَا
عَلَى ٱلْقَوْمِ ٱلْكَٰفِرِينَ ﴿٢٥٠﴾

They routed them, by God's will. David slew Goliath, and God bestowed on him the kingdom and wisdom, and taught him whatever He willed. Had it not been for the fact that God repels one group of people

فَهَزَمُوهُم بِإِذْنِ ٱللَّهِ وَقَتَلَ دَاوُۥدُ
جَالُوتَ وَءَاتَىٰهُ ٱللَّهُ ٱلْمُلْكَ
وَٱلْحِكْمَةَ وَعَلَّمَهُۥ مِمَّا يَشَآءُ ۗ
وَلَوْلَا دَفْعُ ٱللَّهِ ٱلنَّاسَ بَعْضَهُم

by another, the earth would have been utterly corrupted. God is limitless in His bounty to all the worlds. (251)

بِبَعْضٍ لَّفَسَدَتِ ٱلْأَرْضُ وَلَٰكِنَّ ٱللَّهَ ذُو فَضْلٍ عَلَى ٱلْعَٰلَمِينَ ﴿٢٥١﴾

These are the revelations of God. We recite them to you in all truth, for you are indeed one of Our messengers. (252)

تِلْكَ ءَايَٰتُ ٱللَّهِ نَتْلُوهَا عَلَيْكَ بِٱلْحَقِّ ۚ وَإِنَّكَ لَمِنَ ٱلْمُرْسَلِينَ ﴿٢٥٢﴾

Overview

We can better appreciate the value of this passage and the experience of past nations and communities it relates when we bear in mind that the Qur'ān is the inspiring book of the Muslim community, its sincere counsellor and guide through life. It was with the Qur'ān that God moulded the first Muslim community to which He assigned the task of implementing the Islamic code of living. After the Prophet's death, the Qur'ān remains the guide which prepares future Muslim generations for their role of leadership of mankind. This is the role God has promised the Muslim community whenever it fulfils its pledges to follow His guidance, giving the Qur'ān supremacy over all man-made laws and methods.

The Qur'ān is not merely fine verses to be recited for enchantment. It is a comprehensive constitution providing education and guidance through life. Hence, it provides examples of the experience of past communities for the benefit of the new generations of Muslims. It lays special emphasis on past experience in the advocacy of faith, highlighting its interaction with people in practical life. Such wealth of experience portrayed in the Qur'ān is of great value in the enlightenment of the advocates of Islam.

This is the reason why the Qur'ān includes a wealth of highly inspiring historical accounts. The history of the Children of Israel provides the majority of these stories for a variety of reasons which we discussed in Chapter 3. We may add here that the prominence given to the Jewish history is perhaps due to God's prior knowledge that some Muslim generations will be going through situations similar to those experienced by the Israelites. Therefore, He alerts them to the slips that may lie in their way by highlighting the lessons they could learn from such history.

Muslim generations should read the Qur'ān very carefully, treating it as guidance provided today to show us how to deal with our present problems and to chart our future course. Its historical accounts are not provided for inconsequential academic study.

We will not benefit by the Qur'ān unless we read it with the aim of seeking guidance for our present and future life, in the same way as the first Muslim community did. When we approach the Qur'ān in this way, we are certain to find in it what we are looking for, and we shall have something far more remarkable than we can imagine. Its words, expressions and instructions will come alive, giving us all the guidance we need. It will point out to us what to do and what to avoid, what precautions to take, who is our friend and who is our enemy. It will give us a long, elaborate discourse touching on everything that may occur to us. Thus, we will find in the Qur'ān both life and enjoyment. God's words will ring in our ears: "*Believers, respond to the call of God and the Messenger when he calls you to that which will give you life.*" (8: 24)

The present passage gives an account of two episodes in the history of past nations to add to the practical lessons given to the Muslim community, as part of its preparation to face what may lie ahead on its way. The first is outlined briefly, but adequately, without even mentioning the people involved. They are a large group who tried to flee from death, leaving their homes to no avail. God caused them to die and brought them back to life, rendering their efforts to evade death futile, and giving them a new life without any effort on their part. As it shows them this example, the Qur'ān urges the believers to fight and donate for the cause of God who gives and takes away both life and wealth.

The second lesson is derived from an episode in the history of the Israelites after the death of Moses. Having abandoned divine guidance, they suffered the loss of their kingdom, violation of their sacred places and personal humiliation at the hands of their enemies. But then their sense of faith reawakened and they were eager to fight for God's cause. They asked their prophet to appoint for them a king to lead them in such a fight.

The way the Qur'ān portrays this episode is highly inspiring and particularly significant for all Muslim generations, let alone the first Muslim community. The total sum of what had taken place on this occasion is that, despite all the weaknesses shown by the Israelites, leading to one group's desertion after another, the steadfastness of even a small group of believers achieved very great results for the whole community. They were able to turn the tables on their enemies, shaking off their long humiliation by their enemies to achieve victory and establish the kingdom of David and Solomon. That was the beginning of the Israelites' golden age. All this was the result of the new impetus given to faith after it remained long forgotten, and the steadfastness of a small group facing the large army led by Goliath.

A number of significant facts are highlighted here. The first is that public enthusiasm can be dangerously deceptive. Therefore, those in the position of leadership must put it to the test before going into a decisive battle. A group of wise and respected elders of the Israelites requested their prophet to choose for them a king who could lead them in their struggle for God's cause. They wanted to fight those enemies who had ravaged their kingdom and looted their property, including what was left by their prophets, Moses and Aaron, and their household. Trying to gauge their determination, their prophet suggested that, once a battle loomed large, they might not be up to the task. Here their enthusiasm reached its highest point, and they expressed their attitude, feeling that they had every reason to fight: *"Why should we not fight for the cause of God when we have been driven out of our homes and our children?"* (Verse 246) Nevertheless, their enthusiasm was short lived: *"Yet, when fighting was ordained for them, they turned back, save for a few of them."* (Verse 246) Although the Israelites habitually reneged on their promises, such an attitude remains a human weakness often encountered in communities whose strength of faith remains suspect.

Another aspect of the moral of the story is that when public enthusiasm for action is at a high pitch, the first test of its substance should be the final. The great majority of the Israelites in the present case turned away once their expressed desire to fight was accepted. Only a few of them remained true to the promise they gave to their prophet. These were the soldiers that formed Saul's army after the long arguments about his choice as king and commander, and after they were clearly shown that it was God's choice. Nevertheless, the majority of these soldiers failed the very first test to which Saul put them, when he ordered them not to drink from the river they were about to cross. Even then, the minority that remained did not persevere; they were overawed by the great numbers of the enemy force and declared that they were no match for their opponents. But a very small group kept faith with God and stood firm. It was this small group that tilted the balance. They were granted victory and were worthy of their achievement.

As the story unfolds, we appreciate the importance of a resolute leadership motivated by faith. All fine leadership qualities are shown by Saul: knowledge of human nature, repeated testing of commitment of his soldiers, getting rid of the weak elements, unlimited trust in God's promise to those who remain steadfast in the face of adversity.

Moreover, we clearly see how true believers have their own standards and values, because they look at the present situation in a way that relates it to the greater reality of God's will and His power. The great disparity with the large enemy forces was not lost on the small group of believers who persevered with Saul to the end. The difference, however, was that those believers also recognized that victory is granted by God. Hence, they turned to Him in a sincere prayer: *"Our Lord, grant us patience in adversity, make firm our steps, and grant us victory over the unbelievers."* (Verse 250)

With such unshakeable faith, and such a proper understanding, they deserved the victory given by the One who is always able to grant victory. We will now look at the passage in more detail.

Fleeing from Death

We need not go into the plethora of interpretations with regard to the identity or the time and place of the people referred to in this verse. Had these details been of any particular importance in understanding the moral and the message of the story, they would most certainly have been given in the Qur'ānic account.

The aim of this verse is simply to establish that life and death are determined by the will of God, and that human beings should fulfil their obligations in life with complete trust in God's will and total reassurance that what befalls them is an integral part of God's order of things.

No precautions could ever prevent death or impede God's will, nor could fear or despair prolong life. Life and death are entirely in God's hands. He dispenses them according to reasons known only to Him, and His grace and mercy are evident in both. *"Surely, God grants limitless bounty to mankind, but most people are ungrateful."*

Such a mass exodus, with thousands of people fleeing at the same time, whether from a hostile attack or the outbreak of disease, could only occur in a state of total panic. Nevertheless, running away could not save those people from meeting their death, for *"God said to them: 'Die.'"* (Verse 243)

No details are given as to the manner in which God spoke to those people or how they met their death, because these bear no relevance to the objective of the story, which is that their despairing desertion of their homes did not change the destiny God had already willed for those panic-stricken people. They needed to persevere, be patient and freely put their trust in God.

Nor are we given any details of how God brought those people back to life, or on whether this is a reference to a later generation of the same community who did not panic or despair, and who accepted what God had chosen for them. There would be no point in speculating over these matters; nor can we accept the various unsubstantiated accounts of some commentaries. The essential message here is that God gave those people life, and their own efforts could not prevent their death. Life is a gift from God which He bestows on human beings with no effort or reason on their part. They, on the other hand, can do nothing to prevent what God has predestined.

Multiplied Loan Repayment

As the *sūrah* continues, we begin to understand the significance of the story and partly appreciate God's purpose in citing this episode quite early on in the history of the Muslim nation. The next verse says: *"Fight for the cause of God and know that God hears all and knows all."* (Verse 244)

This verse tells the Muslims very clearly that neither their love of life nor their fear of death should stop them from fighting for God's cause. Death and life are determined by God, and those who believe should fight for His cause and under His banner alone. They should be mindful that God is aware of what they do and is there to respond to their needs and appreciate and reward their actions.

To fight for the cause of God, which is the ultimate form of *jihād*, requires devotion and sacrifice. In the Qur'ān, *jihād* is frequently associated with financial contribution, especially in the early days of Islam when fighting was voluntary and fighters were required to finance their own participation in it. There would be eager and capable ones who were prevented from going out with the Muslim army only by their lack of means. The emphasis on financial sacrifice was, therefore, essential, as the *sūrah* strongly states: *"Who will offer God a generous loan, which He will repay multiplied many times over? It is God who straitens people's circumstances and it is He who gives abundantly; and to Him you shall all return."* (Verse 245)

God bestows life and takes it away, and one may go to battle and survive, if that is God's will. Wealth is not lost when spent in a good cause. It is a form of loan to God whose generous repayment is guaranteed, both in this world and in the life to come.

Poverty and wealth are also due to God's will rather than the outcome of one's financial acumen or frugality or philanthropy. *"It is God who straitens people's circumstances and it is He who gives abundantly; and to Him you shall all return."* (Verse 245) People and all their possessions shall one day return to God, and so death and poverty no longer pose any threat. Believers shall go ahead and sacrifice their lives, their wealth and all their possessions in the cause of God who has already charted their course and destiny in this world. They shall live their lives to the full, in dignity and freedom, in the service of God Almighty.

This short passage is a fine example of the power of the Qur'ānic language and style. We are immediately taken into a scene of panic and confusion, with thousands of people fleeing in all directions to avoid death and annihilation. Suddenly, they meet the very fate they are trying to escape; no measures or precautions they have taken will avail them. And, just as suddenly and without further explanation, they are brought back to life by the mighty hand of God, who controls everything and whose power is overwhelming. Thus, we realize that life and death are in the hands of God Almighty, as are wealth and fortune, which complement the theme of the passage.

A Test of Genuine Faith

The *sūrah* goes on to cite another episode of the story of the Israelites after the death of Moses, God's messenger to them: *"Are you not aware of those elders of the Children of Israel, after the time of Moses, when they said to one of their Prophets, 'Appoint for us a king, and we shall fight for the cause of God.' He said, 'Would you, perchance, refuse to fight if fighting is ordained for you?' They said, 'Why should we not fight for the cause of God when we have been driven out of our homes and our children?' Yet, when fighting was ordained for them, they turned back, save for a few of them. God is fully aware of the wrongdoers."* (Verse 246)

The reference here is to a group of the Israelite elders who had asked one of their numerous Prophets, whose identity has not been given as it is not essential in this context, to appoint for them a king to lead them into battle "for the cause of God". The narrative suggests a time of religious revival among the Israelites, and a strong desire to uphold the truth and defend it against the ungodly enemies.

Resolve takes a fighter halfway to victory. He must be certain of the legitimacy of his cause, and the falsehood of that of his enemy, and his objective to uphold the cause of God must also be clear in his mind.

The wise prophet needed reassurance that the elders' enthusiasm for fighting was not mere bravado, and that they were sincere in their resolve and committed to the requirements of fighting for God's cause. He did not wish his efforts to be in vain. Would they flinch or retreat once fighting had been made obligatory for them?

The elders gave reasons of their own for wishing to fight: *"They said, 'Why should we not fight for the cause of God when we have been driven out of our homes and our children?'"* Their motives were clear: they had been wronged. So was their objective: they wanted to fight for the cause of God, and their determination was not open to question.

Nevertheless, as soon as the time had come for them to face their enemy, *"Yet, when fighting was ordained for them, they turned back, save for a few of them."* (Verse 246) Here the *sūrah* highlights the propensity of some Israelites to breach agreements, break promises and disobey God. It also points to their tendency to display disunity and to betray their cause. This is not only true of those Israelites, but it is true of many other human communities and groups who lack cultural maturity and a strong and enlightened tradition. Such characteristics need to be taken into account by those who have to lead these communities through difficult times.

The verse concludes with the comment: *"God is fully aware of the wrongdoers."* (Verse 246) This comment deplores the dereliction of responsibility and accuses the large group of betraying themselves, their leader and their cause. No group of people could be so certain of the legitimacy of their cause, and of God's support for their case, and then go on to flagrantly relinquish their obligations. People who are certain of the truth they follow, like those Israelites were, could not just turn away from their responsibilities. If they do, they are certain to have the punishment reserved for wrongdoers.

The *sūrah* points to another disturbing streak in the Israelites' character, cited a number of times in the *sūrah*. The group had asked for a king to be appointed to lead them into battle, claiming to be ready to fight for "the cause of God". But, as soon as he was appointed, they began to question the wisdom of his choice and his eligibility to rule over them. They argued that some of them were better suited for the task because he did not come from a noble background, nor was he wealthy enough to be a king and leader.

Here is how the *sūrah* relates what happened: *"Their Prophet said to them, 'God has appointed Saul [Ṭālūt] to be your king.' They said, 'How can he have the kingship over us when we are better entitled to it than he is? Besides, he has not been given abundance of wealth.' He said, 'God has chosen him in preference to you, and endowed him abundantly with knowledge and physical stature. God grants His dominion to whom He will. He is Munificent, All-Knowing.'"* (Verse 247)

Their Prophet had to explain that the king was chosen by God, which should have been enough reason for his people to accept him, because God is powerful and generous and would only choose what would be in their best interest. Moreover, he was endowed with knowledge and physical strength, providing him with a greater quality of leadership and ability.

This should have been enough to convince them to accept Saul as king over them; but, it seems, nothing short of a miracle would persuade them. *"Their Prophet also said to them, 'The portent of his kingship is that a casket shall be brought to you, wherein you shall have peace of reassurance from your Lord, and a legacy left behind by the House of Moses and the House of Aaron. It will be borne by angels. That will be a sign for you, if you are true believers.'"* (Verse 248)

In the post-Moses era, the Israelites, during the reign of Joshua, were driven out of the Holy Land and most of their sacred heritage was pillaged and looted. This included a casket that was said to contain many relics of Moses and Aaron. More significantly, it also contained a copy of the tablets given by God to Moses on Mount Sinai. The reappearance of that casket, carried by angels, would be, their Prophet said, a sign from God and material proof of Saul's kingship. Once they saw it they would be reassured and, if they were true believers, would accept him as their leader.

The narration suggests that the miracle did take place and, completely reassured, the Israelites went on to confront their enemy.

Keeping Faith with God

Despite the lack of narrative details, we can gather that Saul had organized his fighting force of willing men and had gone ahead to do battle, and that as soon as they were on their way, he put their loyalty to the test. *"And when Saul set out with his troops, he said, 'God will now put you to the test by a river. He who drinks from it will not belong to me, but he who does not taste its water will indeed belong to me, except him who takes a scoop with his hand.' They all drank [their fill] of it, except for a few of them."* (Verse 249)

The leadership qualities of Saul are now coming to light. He was leading an army of a vanquished nation who had experienced defeat many times in its history, and was about to meet a formidable enemy, and had therefore to test the will of his troops. He had to be sure of their ability to overcome their desires and endure hardship and deprivation. Above all, he had to test their loyalty and obedience, and their ability to shoulder responsibility. He put them to the test at the river, having established that they were getting very thirsty, to find out who would obey him and who would not.

"They all drank [their fill] of it, except for a few of them." (Verse 249) He allowed them a single scoop with the hand to quench their thirst, but most of them drank their fill and were left behind because they had failed the test. It was better for the rest of the fighting force as weaklings would have been a liability on the battlefield. Military prowess is not determined by size or numbers, but is measured by the will and moral strength and faith of the troops.

This example shows that good intentions, by themselves, are not sufficient unless they are tested in practice. It also demonstrates the strength of a leader who is not swayed by the fall of most of his troops at the first hurdle, but who forges ahead with the rest of them.

Saul's forces were to encounter more trials of loyalty and strength: *"When he and those who kept faith with him crossed the river, they said, 'No strength have we today to stand up to Goliath and his forces.'"* (Verse 249)

Their numbers had dwindled, and they were aware that they were outnumbered by Goliath's forces. Certainly, they had the advantage of faith in their cause and trust in their leader, but the harsh reality of the situation told them they were the weaker side, and that their faith would be put to the test. Would that invisible force of faith triumph? How strong was their faith in God, and would they be able to harness that force in their favour and prevail?

At that decisive moment, a small group of true believers stood up to express their faith: *"But those of them who were certain that they would meet their Lord said, 'How often has a small host triumphed over a large host by God's grace. God is with those who remain patient in adversity.'"* (Verse 249)

To the believer's mind, that is the way it should be: believers are always numerically less than their enemies, because they need to sacrifice more and work harder to earn God's grace and pleasure. But they triumph because they draw their strength from God Almighty and their faith in Him. The believers are aware that their victory comes from God as a reward for their patience and perseverance.

The *sūrah* goes on to confirm that, despite their material disadvantage, the small, devoted, faithful band of believers prevailed and overran their formidable enemy: *"And when they came face to face with Goliath and his troops, they prayed, 'Our Lord, grant us patience in adversity, make firm our steps, and grant us victory over the unbelievers.' They routed them, by God's will. David slew Goliath, and God bestowed on him the kingdom and wisdom, and taught him whatever He willed."* (Verses 250–251)

Their prayers are deeply sincere and poignant. The Arabic words depict patience as an endless shower poured down upon the believers by God Almighty, filling their hearts with reassurance and tranquillity and providing them with the power and energy to face their superior enemy. They plead for strength to stand firm and to triumph over their adversary. It was clearly a confrontation between truth and falsehood in which God's intervention was indispensable to ensure a decisive victory for His allies.

And so it was: *"They routed them, by God's will."* The emphasis here is on "God's will" in order to reassure the believers, and to establish that what goes on in this world is determined and controlled by this will. Believers are only the means by which God's will comes to pass. They are His servants, with little power of their own, chosen to perform a certain predestined role in the universal divine scheme. Believers are granted this privileged status through the grace of God and as a result of their sincerity, their determination to serve God and their unstinted devotion to Him.

"David slew Goliath, and God bestowed on him the kingdom and wisdom, and taught him whatever He willed." (Verse 251) At the time of these events, David was a young man and Goliath a powerful king and a fearful commander, but God wished to demonstrate to the Israelites that they should not judge matters at face value, and should look deeper into the reality of things. Their side of the bargain was to keep their pact with God and prepare themselves for battle, leaving the rest to God who knows the essence of all things and how they come about. The outcome would be decided by God, in accordance with His will and wisdom. It was God's will that a youth such as David should slay a powerful giant-of-a-man such as Goliath as proof that physical power by itself is not the decisive factor. The other divine objective, not obvious at the time, was that David was destined to inherit the kingdom of Saul, and that David would be succeeded by his son, Solomon, who reigned over what became the golden era in the whole history of the Israelites, a period of great religious revival which came after their return from the wilderness.

Different Manifestations of God's Favours

David was a king and a Prophet, who excelled in the craft of making iron tools and implements of war, as the Qur'ān tells us elsewhere (21: 80). The purpose behind relating this story is revealed in the closing sentence of the verse: *"Had it not been for the fact that God repels one group of people by another, the earth would have been utterly corrupted. God is limitless in His bounty to all the worlds."* (Verse 251)

This powerful statement takes us beyond the limited narrative and its personalities and events to reveal the fundamental divine wisdom underlying the constant contention, power struggles and battles among the multitudes of mankind in the tumult of life. It depicts the incessant strife and the spirit of competition and rivalry that drive human beings to their various ends and objectives in this world, according to the overall divine scheme under God's wise hand which leads them all towards progress and higher standards of life.

Were it not for this spirit of struggle and competition, life would be dull and stale. The conflict of interests and the variety of objectives that people seek in this world are the means by which human talent and energy are released and brought into play to reinvigorate and revitalize the human experience for the good of mankind. This dynamic movement produces the true human force of goodness, brings truth to the fore, enhances man's sense of right and wrong, and firmly establishes justice on earth. It enables true and sincere believers to identify their noble role in life. It provides them with the will and strength to persevere and fulfil that role in total obedience to God's order and tireless pursuit of His pleasure and blessings.

God then intervenes on the side of the believers so that the truth they are upholding will prevail. Human conflict becomes a positive and constructive struggle for the good of mankind and a better life in this world. The fact that the smaller group of believers have placed their trust in God, and are devoted to fulfilling His ultimate will in protecting life and establishing the truth and defending it, enables them to eventually triumph and prevail.

The passage is rounded off with a final verse: *"These are the revelations of God. We recite them to you in all truth, for you are indeed one of Our messengers."* (Verse 252)

These noble revelations emanate directly from God, itself an august fact that deserves man's understanding and reflection. They convey the truth and outline a complete code for human life, unrivalled and unmatched by any other code or system. Any attempts to substitute God's code, or declare it obsolete, are bogus and futile; God alone should be served and obeyed.

The fact that Muḥammad is a Messenger chosen by God Almighty qualifies him to receive God's revelations and to learn from the experiences of previous generations, and adequately equips him to convey those revelations to the rest of mankind.

16

The Nature of God and Faith

Those are the Messengers! We have exalted some of them above others. To some God spoke directly, and some He raised in rank. We gave Jesus, the son of Mary, clear signs and strengthened him with the Holy Spirit. Had God so willed, those who succeeded them would not have fought against one another after the clear proofs had come to them. But they differed with one another: some of them accepted the faith and some rejected it. Yet had God so willed, they would not have fought one another. But God does whatever He wills. (253)

تِلْكَ ٱلرُّسُلُ فَضَّلْنَا بَعْضَهُمْ عَلَىٰ بَعْضٍ
مِّنْهُم مَّن كَلَّمَ ٱللَّهُ وَرَفَعَ بَعْضَهُمْ
دَرَجَٰتٍ وَءَاتَيْنَا عِيسَى ٱبْنَ مَرْيَمَ
ٱلْبَيِّنَٰتِ وَأَيَّدْنَٰهُ بِرُوحِ ٱلْقُدُسِ
وَلَوْ شَآءَ ٱللَّهُ مَا ٱقْتَتَلَ ٱلَّذِينَ
مِنۢ بَعْدِهِم مِّنۢ بَعْدِ مَا جَآءَتْهُمُ
ٱلْبَيِّنَٰتُ وَلَٰكِنِ ٱخْتَلَفُوا۟ فَمِنْهُم
مَّنْ ءَامَنَ وَمِنْهُم مَّن كَفَرَ وَلَوْ شَآءَ
ٱللَّهُ مَا ٱقْتَتَلُوا۟ وَلَٰكِنَّ ٱللَّهَ يَفْعَلُ
مَا يُرِيدُ ﴿٢٥٣﴾

Believers, spend [for God's cause] out of that with which We have provided you before there comes a day when there will be no trading, or friendship or intercession. Truly, the unbelievers are the wrongdoers. (254)

يَٰٓأَيُّهَا ٱلَّذِينَ ءَامَنُوٓا۟ أَنفِقُوا۟ مِمَّا رَزَقْنَٰكُم
مِّن قَبْلِ أَن يَأْتِىَ يَوْمٌ لَّا بَيْعٌ فِيهِ
وَلَا خُلَّةٌ وَلَا شَفَٰعَةٌ وَٱلْكَٰفِرُونَ هُمُ
ٱلظَّٰلِمُونَ ﴿٢٥٤﴾

God: there is no deity but Him, the Ever-Living, the Eternal Master of all. Neither slumber nor sleep overtakes Him. His is all that is in the heavens and all that is on earth. Who is there that can intercede with Him, except by His permission? He knows all that lies open before them and all that lies hidden from them; whereas they cannot attain to anything of His knowledge save as He wills. His throne extends over the heavens and the earth, and the preservation of both does not weary Him. He is the Most High, the Most Great. (255)

ٱللَّهُ لَآ إِلَٰهَ إِلَّا هُوَ ٱلْحَىُّ ٱلْقَيُّومُ ۚ لَا تَأْخُذُهُۥ سِنَةٌ وَلَا نَوْمٌ ۚ لَّهُۥ مَا فِى ٱلسَّمَٰوَٰتِ وَمَا فِى ٱلْأَرْضِ ۗ مَن ذَا ٱلَّذِى يَشْفَعُ عِندَهُۥٓ إِلَّا بِإِذْنِهِۦ ۚ يَعْلَمُ مَا بَيْنَ أَيْدِيهِمْ وَمَا خَلْفَهُمْ ۖ وَلَا يُحِيطُونَ بِشَىْءٍ مِّنْ عِلْمِهِۦٓ إِلَّا بِمَا شَآءَ ۚ وَسِعَ كُرْسِيُّهُ ٱلسَّمَٰوَٰتِ وَٱلْأَرْضَ ۖ وَلَا يَـُٔودُهُۥ حِفْظُهُمَا ۚ وَهُوَ ٱلْعَلِىُّ ٱلْعَظِيمُ ﴿٢٥٥﴾

There shall be no compulsion in religion. The right way is henceforth distinct from error. He who rejects false deities and believes in God has indeed taken hold of a most firm support that never breaks. God hears all and knows all. (256)

لَآ إِكْرَاهَ فِى ٱلدِّينِ ۖ قَد تَّبَيَّنَ ٱلرُّشْدُ مِنَ ٱلْغَىِّ ۚ فَمَن يَكْفُرْ بِٱلطَّٰغُوتِ وَيُؤْمِنۢ بِٱللَّهِ فَقَدِ ٱسْتَمْسَكَ بِٱلْعُرْوَةِ ٱلْوُثْقَىٰ لَا ٱنفِصَامَ لَهَا ۗ وَٱللَّهُ سَمِيعٌ عَلِيمٌ ﴿٢٥٦﴾

God is the Patron of the believers. He leads them out of darkness into the light. As for the unbelievers, their patrons are false deities who lead them out of light into darkness. Those are the people destined for the fire, therein to abide. (257)

ٱللَّهُ وَلِىُّ ٱلَّذِينَ ءَامَنُوا۟ يُخْرِجُهُم مِّنَ ٱلظُّلُمَٰتِ إِلَى ٱلنُّورِ ۖ وَٱلَّذِينَ كَفَرُوٓا۟ أَوْلِيَآؤُهُمُ ٱلطَّٰغُوتُ يُخْرِجُونَهُم مِّنَ ٱلنُّورِ إِلَى ٱلظُّلُمَٰتِ ۗ أُو۟لَٰٓئِكَ أَصْحَٰبُ ٱلنَّارِ ۖ هُمْ فِيهَا خَٰلِدُونَ ﴿٢٥٧﴾

The Unity of the Divine Message

The first thing we note in this passage is its opening phrase, which carries special significance: "Those are the Messengers!" The Qur'ān does not refer to them as, 'these messengers', as we would normally refer to a group of people. Reference to them is started in a rather unusual way to highlight certain strong implications.

"Those are the Messengers!" They are a special group of people, with a special nature, but they are at the same time ordinary human beings. Who are they, then? What is the nature of their message? How are they given it? And why are only these people made Messengers? These are questions I have always felt reluctant to try to answer, because when I consider the significance of a divine message given to man, I experience a host of feelings and identify several meanings which I cannot adequately express in words. Yet put them in words I must, in order to explain the concept involved, however inadequately.

The world we live in has certain basic laws supporting its existence. These are the laws of nature which God has set in operation. They govern everything in the universe. Man discovers certain peripheral aspects of these laws as his knowledge increases. But what he discovers remains naturally within the scope of his faculties of perception and understanding. These are suitable to the role assigned to him during his life duration on earth. His efforts to discover these laws rely on two basic methods: observation and experiment. By nature, both are partial, and their conclusions are by no means absolute. They occasionally lead to the discovery of some aspects of natural laws, but this takes place very infrequently and over long periods of time. Whatever man discovers remains of a temporary and partial nature, neither conclusive nor absolute. That is because the overall law that governs the inter-relationship and harmony between all natural laws will remain hidden from man: it cannot be discovered by human observation, which remains limited, over any period of time. The point here is that the ultimate factor in this respect is not time; rather, it is man's limitations within his constitution and role in life. Since this role is only limited, its restriction is compounded by the fact that the time of life on earth given to the human race is also limited. Hence, all means of discovery at man's disposal in this world, and all the conclusions they arrive at, remain within this restricted area.

Now we can identify the role of the message, and the special nature God has given to His messengers so that they may respond to the central law that governs the whole universe. How they respond remains unknown to us, but we can see the effects of their response. This special nature is able to receive God's revelations, as it has been specially equipped for the task. This means that it receives the same signal as the rest of the universe, because it has a direct link with that central and governing law. How does it receive that signal, and by what faculty of perception? To answer such questions we need to have the same nature which God grants to His chosen messengers, but *"God knows best whom to entrust with His message."* (6: 124) The basis of His choice is a far more serious matter than the greatest secrets of the universe.

All messengers were sent with the essential message of the oneness of God and they fully understood it. That has been possible because the effect of the single law governing the universe on their whole being directed them clearly to its one and only source. It cannot be anything but a single source, because there would otherwise be more than one law, giving more than one effect on them. Their understanding of this truth was made very early in the history of humanity, when knowledge based on observation and experiment was still in its early days, before many human discoveries concerning the laws of the universe were made and all confirmed this oneness. Every one of God's messengers called on people to worship God alone. That is the truth he received and was commanded to convey to people. Their fulfilment of their mission, which is simply to convey the message, was a natural result of their absolute conviction of its truth, as they have received it from God, the one and only God in the universe who has no equals or partners.

They were strongly committed to this truth and to the fulfilment of their mission. We note their commitment in some of their statements reported in the Qur'ān, or in the way they are described in God's revelations. One such example is evident in what Noah (Nūḥ) says to his people: *"Think, my people! If I take my stand on a clear evidence from my Lord and He has favoured me with grace from Himself, to which you have remained blind, can we force it upon you when you are averse to it? And, my people, I do not seek of you any money for it: my reward rests with none but God. Nor will I drive away those who believe; they will surely meet their Lord, whereas in you I see a people that are ignorant. Were I to drive them away, my people, who would protect me from God? Will you not reflect?"* (11: 28–30)

It is similarly evident in the statement of Prophet Ṣāliḥ, quoted in the Qur'ān: *"Think, my people! If I take my stand on clear evidence from my Lord who has bestowed on me His grace, who will save me from God should I disobey Him? You are, in such a case, only augmenting my ruin."* (11: 63)

We also see it in Abraham's argument with his people: *"Do you argue with me about God, when it is He who has given me guidance? I do not fear those beings you associate with Him, [for no evil can befall me] unless my Lord wills it. My Lord embraces all things within His knowledge. Will you not, then, reflect? And why should I fear anything you worship side by side with Him, when you are not afraid of associating with God partners without His ever giving you any warrant? Which of the two parties has a better right to feel secure, if you happen to know?"* (6: 80–81)

Another example is that we note in the story of Shu'ayb, when he says to his community: *"Think, my people! If I take my stand on clear evidence from my Lord and He has provided me with goodly sustenance which He alone can give? I have no desire to do behind your backs that which I ask you not to do. All that I desire is to set things right so far as I am able to do so. My success rests with God. In Him I have put my trust, and to Him I turn repentant."* (11: 88)

We find a similar example in what Jacob says to his sons when they remonstrated with him over his continued sorrow: "*It is only to God that I complain and express my grief. For I know of Him what you do not know.*" (12: 86)

In all these statements we find that their very nature has been strongly affected by the single law governing the whole of the universe. They feel that effect deep in their consciences.

Day after day, man was able to discover certain phenomena which pointed rather remotely to the central unifying law in the universe. Scientists were able to discern the unity of formation and the unity of movement throughout this vast universe. It was discovered, within the limited scope of human knowledge, that the atom is the basic unit of the whole universal structure and that the atom is energy. Thus matter and power were combined in this basic unit, the atom. Since matter is formed of a mass of atoms, it becomes energy when nuclear fission takes place. It was further discovered that there is continuous movement within the atom, which consists of electrons orbiting a nucleus in a continuous movement. Thus, as a poet has recently put it, every atom is like a complete solar system, with planets orbiting a sun.

What man has been able to discover, through observation and experiment, of the unity of formation and unity of movement in the universe, pointing to the single governing law, is something that the special nature of God's messengers, endowed with whatever He has given it, has understood at the outset. Their nature receives direct inspiration which enables it to grasp this truth. God's messengers have not gathered indicators and measured them, like what happens in a scientific experiment. They have used their special faculty of perception, which receives directly the messages of the single unifying and governing universal law. They were thus able to conclude that the single law which gives such consistent messages must come from a single source. Their special faculty of perception was thus able to make a far more accurate and comprehensive conclusion, realizing that beyond the single source, combining both will and action in the universe, there must be a single divine entity that controls the universe. Hence, they readily, unhesitatingly and completely believed in God.

I have not written this because modern science claims to have been able to understand one or two phenomena pointing to the unity of the universe. Science has an area of investigation in which it may prove or disprove anything. Whatever 'truth' it concludes remains partial and limited. It simply cannot arrive at a single truth that is final and absolute. Besides, whatever theories science makes are always liable to change, amendment and refutation. Nor have I mentioned the unity of formation and unity of movement so as to endorse the accurate perception by God's messengers of the single unifying law of the universe. My aim is totally different. I simply wish to point out the only reliable source for the formation of the right, comprehensive concept of the truth of existence.

The special nature of God's messengers has been able to identify this source, and its conclusion is correct, whether it is corroborated by science or not. Scientific conclusions remain subject to review and amendment through scientific experiment. They are neither final nor absolute. Hence, we cannot use scientific conclusions to judge whether God's message is correct or not. Our measure must be true, final and subject to no change or modification. Hence, it is God's message that provides such ultimate measure.

This leads to another truism of vital importance. The special nature of the messengers, which responds directly to the single law governing the universe, is the one which is able to define the direction humanity should take in order to be on the same line with the nature of the universe and its constant laws. It receives its inspiration directly from God, so it cannot make a mistake or deviate. It tells no lies and hides no information. It is not hindered by any factor of time or place from seeing the truth clearly, because it receives that truth directly from God, who is not bound by time or place.

The divine will has determined to send messengers, from time to time, to give mankind a clear vision of the absolute truth, of which they cannot hope to learn a few aspects through observation or experiment for hundreds of centuries to come. They would certainly never attain it in full, through these methods, at any time. Through the divine message human beings can achieve complete harmony between their direction, movement and nature and those of the universe.

This means that there is only one source from which people can receive a true, complete and comprehensive concept of the truth and purpose of existence in general and human existence in particular. It is this concept that can lay the basis for the only proper and true code of living which is in harmony with the universe. It is a code of living that leads to true and genuine peace with their own nature and with the universe around them. That gives them peace with one another that governs their activity, direction and progress. That source is God's messages. Everything else is false and erroneous, because it does not derive from the only true source.

What we need to understand is that all means of knowledge that man uses, other than the divine message, work within their respective limitations. They have been given to man so that he may be able to discover some phenomena and laws of the universe, as he needs these for the fulfilment of his role on earth, and to allow human life to progress and prosper. He may go very far indeed in this respect, but whatever progress he achieves will not get him anywhere near the absolute truth he needs to shape his life in accordance with the constant universal laws and with the overall objective of human existence. This objective is clearly determined by God, but remains unknown to man who is subject to the limitations of time and place.

Only the one who sees the whole road ahead can formulate a plan to follow the road to the ultimate destination. But man cannot see the whole length of the road. Indeed he cannot see what will happen in the next moment. That immediate future is completely hidden behind a thick curtain that is not drawn aside for anyone to see. How can man, then, plan the way ahead when that way is unknown to him? There are only two options for man: either confusion and error, or acceptance of the code defined by God's messengers, whose nature responds directly to the inspiration they receive from God, the Creator of all.

God's messages came in succession to take humanity by the hand and guide it along to new horizons of guidance and light. People and communities often tried to deviate from the way of God, going this way or that. They closed their ears and their minds to the tender call addressed to them by a messenger of God. They would sink into error until a new call is addressed to them by a new messenger. Each time the same truth is given to them in a new and more advanced form to suit their greater experience. The final message, given when humanity reached its maturity, addresses the human mind with all fundamentals of the whole truth, providing it with broad lines to determine its footsteps with certainty and reassurance. The lines it has painted for the ultimate truth were so clear that humanity would need no further message in future. Man will find in it what he needs over the coming centuries.

Now the choice open to humanity is a simple one. It can conduct its life within the framework provided by the divine message which can accommodate its progress and, at the same time, shows it the absolute truth it cannot achieve through any other means. The other option open to humanity is to go the wrong way and to be in utter loss.

The Ranks of God's Messengers

> *Those are the Messengers! We have exalted some of them above others. To some God spoke directly, and some He raised in rank. We gave Jesus, the son of Mary, clear signs and strengthened him with the Holy Spirit. Had God so willed, those who succeeded them would not have fought against one another after the clear proofs had come to them. But they differed with one another: some of them accepted the faith and some rejected it. Yet had God so willed, they would not have fought one another. But God does whatever He wills.* (Verse 253)

This verse summarizes the essence of the mission of God's messengers, whom it speaks of as a distinct group of human beings. It asserts that God has placed some of the messengers higher than others, pointing out some of the reasons for, and signs of, doing so. It refers to the dissension and disagreement among their followers and successors, which in some cases escalated to fighting, confirming that some of those successors believed while others did not. It points out that the fighting was part of God's scheme in order to establish the truth and defeat evil.

"Those are the Messengers! We have exalted some of them above others ..." (Verse 253) The relative elevation of God's messengers is determined by the environment, the nature and the scope of their respective missions. Some messengers were sent to single tribes, some to larger nations, some to single generations, and some to all nations and all generations. It also relates to the various distinctions they had received or brought to their people.

The verse makes a general reference to all messengers, and mentions two of them: Moses and Jesus, saying: *"... to some God spoke directly, and some He raised in rank. We gave Jesus, the son of Mary, clear signs and strengthened him with the Holy Spirit."* (Verse 253)

When reference is made to a messenger to whom God spoke directly, the immediate conclusion is that the reference is made to Moses. Hence, he is not mentioned by name.

Most Qur'ānic references to Jesus describe him as the "son of Mary", for obvious reasons. When the Qur'ān was being revealed, numerous myths surrounding the birth, sonship, and dual divine-human nature of Jesus had found their way into the culture and folklore of the time. Christian churches and councils of the Byzantine, and the Roman, empires were immersed in endless doctrinal disputes, some of which turned to bloody conflict, over the nature and status of Jesus. The Qur'ān often makes the point of emphasizing the human nature of Jesus, underlining the fact by relating him to his mother, Mary. In the Qur'ān, the 'holy spirit' always refers to the Archangel Gabriel (Jibrīl), who conveyed God's revelations to human messengers. He would inform them of their commissions and instructions, and act as aide and ally to the messengers in their demanding and arduous task of preaching God's Message. He would, as in the case of Jesus, provide them with reassurances and encouragement.

The 'clear signs' given to Jesus include the revealed Gospel and the miracles he was able to perform, detailed elsewhere in the Qur'ān, as supporting evidence of his claim to be God's Messenger to the obstinate Israelites with whom he had to deal.

Muḥammad is not mentioned here by name because these verses are addressed to him, as is clear from the preceding verse which says: *"These are the revelations of God. We recite them to you in all truth, for you are indeed one of Our messengers."* (Verse 252)

From whichever angle one looks at the merits of God's messengers, Muḥammad always occupies the highest position by virtue of the universal and all-inclusive nature of his Message as well as its scope.

Islam offers by far the most perfect understanding of the greatest and most fundamental truth in the world: the oneness of God (*tawḥīd*). This oneness epitomizes the unique nature of God and the divine will, which is done at the mere mention of the word: 'be.' That is indeed the cause of all existence. This existence, and all the laws governing it, form an integral whole.

This oneness is manifested in all aspects of existence: in human life which starts from a simple single cell; in the unity of humanity from Adam to the last human being on earth; in the synthesis of the system of beliefs revealed by God to mankind, in the unanimity of the messengers commissioned to champion and preach those beliefs; and in the integrity of the community of believers who uphold God's message. It is reflected in the patterns of human behaviour that constitute worship and are aimed at the pleasure and glorification of God; in the complementarity of life in this world, as a period of activity, and life in the hereafter, as a time for accountability; in the integrity of the divine world order to which all human beings are bound; and in the single source from which all knowledge and wisdom flow.

Muḥammad has shown full and complete response to the great universal truth of God's oneness. He fully absorbed its meaning and significance and was able to interpret its principles in his daily life in full view of all his people.

He was the one Messenger sent with a message addressed to all mankind in his and all future generations. The advent of his mission marked the maturity of the human mind. Hence, it is addressed to the human intellect in a rational, persuasive manner without compulsion or the need for worldly and fantastic miracles.

For these reasons, Muḥammad was the last and final Prophet and his message, Islam, was the last and final message which brought divine revelations to an end. Islam became the greatest unifying Message for all mankind, encompassing the entire gamut of human activity and providing the framework within which the human intellect and potential could be exercised to the full, without need for further divine revelations.

God Almighty, the Creator who knows all, has willed that the final message of Islam, and the entire way of life based upon it, are the most competent to guarantee the growth, development and progress of human life. Anyone who presumes for himself a better knowledge of where the human good might lie, or alleges that Islam is no longer appropriate for the organization of human life, or claims to have a better system than the one God has laid down – anyone making any or all of these assertions is undoubtedly and undeniably an unbeliever who wishes to bring the worst upon himself and the whole of mankind. He stands in open defiance to God Almighty and to humanity, towards whom God has shown great mercy and generosity by presenting it with a universal divine order that preserves and regulates life for all time to come.

Endless Disputes over a Single Truth

Despite the unity of 'those messengers' and the continuity of their messages, their followers quarrelled and fought among themselves. *"But they differed with one another: some of them accepted the faith and some rejected it. Yet had God so willed, they would not have fought one another. But God does whatever He wills."* (Verse 253)

Conflict among human groups, evident throughout history, has not come about in spite of God's will, for nothing in this whole world happens in spite of God's will. Man is created with the dual ability to accept guidance or to reject it, and is given the freedom to go one way or the other. All actions resulting from this human disposition are, therefore, determined and governed by the will of God.

The variance in aptitudes and abilities from one individual human being to another is an essential feature of God's scheme of creation. Despite the unity of human origin, such diversity is necessary to fulfil the requirements of the complex multifarious role man is destined to play as God's representative on earth. God does not wish for human beings to be clones of one another, especially in view of the diversity of functions and roles required for the construction, development and growth of life. It is a complementary, self-fulfilling process, in which every individual is urged to seek his or her route to guidance and faith, fully applying their latent disposition in that direction and benefitting from all the facilities and evidence available throughout the universe, as well as from divine revelations received by God's messengers all through the ages.

Nevertheless, people over the generations "... *differed with one another: some of them accepted the faith and some rejected it.*" (Verse 253) Once disagreements among people develop into a dispute over faith and belief in God, use of force becomes inevitable in order that the struggle between good and evil can be settled, and the truth clearly established. There is no room for confusion, ambiguity or obfuscation, nor would it suffice for any group of people to plead their following of, or association with, one messenger or another.

When these verses were revealed, the pagan Arabs of Makkah claimed to be the true followers of the religion of Abraham, while the Jews of Madinah professed to practise the religion of Moses and the Christians that of Jesus. In fact, all three groups were far removed from the teachings and principles of the faiths they declared themselves to uphold. Some of them could be fairly said to have abandoned their declared faith altogether.

At that time also, the Muslims were already in conflict with the idolatrous Arabs. They were about to be ordered to confront the Jews and Christians. These Qur'ānic statements came to affirm that such conflict among proponents of various religious faiths was part and parcel of God's will and scheme of life.

"*Had God so willed, they would not have fought one another. But God does whatever He wills.*" (Verse 253) It was God's will, therefore, that good and evil should clash in order to reinforce the principles of true faith, preached and upheld by all messengers. God, in His infinite wisdom, knew that evil would not relent or stand idle, and that for His order to be established, evil had to be confronted and driven back.

God's will is absolute and unconditional, and His power to make things happen is totally unrestricted. He has predetermined that human beings shall vary in their abilities and aptitudes; that they shall be free to decide their own destiny in life; that those who do not follow the right path shall deviate and fall; that evil will strive to prevail; that conflict between good and evil is inevitable; that faithful believers will have to struggle and make sacrifices in order to establish the truth and the integrity of their beliefs; that idle claims to following God's messengers is of no consequence and will not prevent one's faith being questioned and challenged.

These facts which God reasserted through revelations are timeless and universal, and not restricted to the Muslims of Madinah at that time. The use of a single incident to illustrate an absolute principle is a device used frequently in the Qur'ān.

The *sūrah* then addresses believers directly, urging them to give part of their wealth, which God has bestowed upon them, for the cause of God, complementing the earlier call to fight for God's cause and reinforcing it. *"Believers, spend [for God's cause] out of that with which We have provided you before there comes a day when there will be no trading, or friendship or intercession. Truly, the unbelievers are the wrongdoers."* (Verse 254)

God addresses the Muslims in a most intimate and touching way, using the title they most love and value: believers. He calls on them to give out of the wealth He has given them, before it is too late, in order to secure the greatest gain and the highest reward. He calls upon them to give for His cause; to uphold and defend His way of life and to subdue and uproot wrongdoing and injustice.

The unbelievers *"are the wrongdoers"* by virtue of their denial of the truth. They wrong themselves by choosing a doomed course in life. They wrong others by misleading and confusing them, depriving them of God's generosity and compassion which brings them peace, security, reassurance and serenity of faith.

People who stand in opposition to God's world order, and employ their energy to persuade others not to believe or to prevent God's laws from taking root in society, are undoubtedly the vilest enemies of mankind. Their efforts must be resisted and frustrated by all means available. Muslims are expected to be at the forefront of this fundamental and highly commendable duty.

God's Unique Attributes

Then follows a verse that summarizes, in powerful and succinct words, the basic principles of the Islamic faith, citing those attributes of God that most aptly assert the meaning and significance of the basic Islamic principle of *tawḥīd*: the oneness of God. *"God: there is no deity but Him, the Ever-Living, the Eternal Master of all. Neither slumber nor sleep overtakes Him. His is all that is in the heavens and all that is on earth. Who is there that can intercede with Him, except by His permission? He knows all that lies open before them and all that lies hidden from them; whereas they cannot attain to anything of His knowledge save as He wills. His throne extends over the heavens and the earth, and the preservation of both does not weary Him. He is the Most High, the Most Great."* (Verse 255)

Every one of these attributes reflects a fundamental aspect of the universal Islamic view of the world. Although the subject matter of this verse would normally be expected to fall within the themes of the Qur'ānic parts received by the Prophet in Makkah, we do find that on several occasions, parts received in Madinah also cover these most important aspects of Islam. For the overall Islamic system to be understood and appreciated, the fundamentals have to be established and firmly implanted in the minds of the believers.

In our commentary on *Sūrah al-Fātiḥah*, we pointed out the crucial importance of clearly and fully appreciating the significance of God's attributes. The religious and doctrinal confusion preceding the advent of Islam was almost entirely due to misinterpretation or distortion of God's position and attributes. Not until Islam had presented its clear view were the concept and identity of God distinguished from myth and superstition and from the blurred philosophical polemics that had enshrouded them.

The *sūrah* most clearly and unequivocally states: *"God: there is no deity but Him ..."* This statement clearly and definitively distinguishes the Islamic concept of God from that of the Trinity, adopted and advanced by Christian church councils long after Jesus, and from the pagan beliefs of the ancient Egyptians who confused God with the sun and recognized the existence of lesser gods beside Him.

This clear and uncompromising concept is the foundation of Islamic belief and of the whole Islamic system of life. It defines the object of worship and submission for all, so that man submits to none other than God, who alone should be worshipped, obeyed and revered. It gives rise to the principle that God alone should be the source of law and legislation for human life on this earth. The laws and rules that people may lay down should derive from those that

God has laid down. This would in turn imply that values and concepts originate with God and that all ethics, traditions and moral systems must be judged in relation to them.

The verse describes God as *"the Ever-Living, the Eternal Master of all"*. This implies a self-generating, self-sustaining being that is unique and independent of everything else. It is also a being without a beginning or an end, totally outside the dimension of time which defines the beginning and end of other ephemeral beings. Furthermore, this being, God Almighty, is absolute and cannot be defined in conventional terms applicable to all creation. He is unique in every respect, and nothing can be compared with Him. Thus, all other definitions or representations of God, conjured up by the human mind throughout the ages, are false and inadequate.

"The Eternal Master of all", implies that God has power over all things and that He is the supreme and ultimate cause, the *raison d'être*, of everything, without whom there can be no existence or action. This is diametrically opposite to the misguided view of Aristotle, the most eminent of Greek philosophers, that God takes no interest in His creation, because He is too great to preoccupy Himself with anything else. Aristotle took this to be a glorification of God, but in effect it means the elimination of God from the daily affairs of the world He created. The Islamic view of God, on the other hand, is a positive one, based on the principle that God is actively and constantly sustaining all existence, and that the existence of everything emanates from His will and design.

The Islamic view of God gives total assurance and relates a Muslim's conscience and being, as well as everything around him, directly to God, the power that controls all existence, according to the divine scheme and order. A believer thus draws all his values, norms and standards from God's order and watches God in all his actions and behaviour.

"Neither slumber nor sleep overtakes Him." This statement reinforces, in simpler and more graphic terms, the preceding one: that God is the everlasting power sustaining everything in existence. It also distinguishes God from other beings by pointing out that He is not affected by sleep to any degree, in any shape or form.

God's unique being and His total and absolute control over all things, large and small, at all times, are awesome concepts to comprehend. No matter how much the limited human mind may be able to grasp the size and variety of creatures and events of this vast universe, it would not be possible for man to adequately perceive how God exercises His power and control over the world. What we are able to appreciate is bound to fill us with amazement, and also give us endless reassurance of God's presence and protection over us.

"His is all that is in the heavens and all that is on earth." God's claim over the cosmos is total and absolute; unconditional and incontestable. This is another aspect of the principle of God's oneness which confirms that God is supreme, ever-present, eternal, master and owner of all. It completely invalidates the assumption that God has partners in His power or actions.

This concept gives a new definition of ownership as applied to individual human beings. For, since God is the ultimate owner of all that exists, no one else can claim ownership of anything in this world. People are, therefore, mere custodians of what they possess, which is entrusted to them by God. Accordingly, they are bound by the terms of that custodianship, as set out by God Almighty, the ultimate owner, in the divine code of living revealed to mankind. Any violation of these terms leads to disqualification and censure of the trustee.

Here we can see how Islamic principles are directly translated into law for immediate application in life. When God says: *"His is all that is in the heavens and all that is on earth,"* He is not merely stating a principle of faith, but also laying down a fundamental rule of the order of life He envisages for mankind.

Once the belief is firmly established in our consciousness that everything in this world belongs to God and that what we own is merely on loan for a limited period of time, greed and lust to accumulate wealth and worldly possessions by any means will not be difficult to hold in check. This belief is bound to fill our hearts with contentment, humility, tolerance, and magnanimity. One will face wealth and poverty with equal ease and steadfastness, and if impoverished will not be in the least bitter or grudging.

"Who is there that can intercede with Him, except by His permission?" This statement underlines yet another aspect of the concept of God's oneness, distinguishing clearly the Supreme Being, God, and His subordinate creation. All creatures stand in total humility and submission to the Master, never arrogating to themselves powers or authorities not delegated to them by Him. Above all, they are not to intercede on behalf of anyone without God's permission, and when

they are granted such permission, they will act within its limits, as set out by God Almighty. Some will certainly attain a higher degree of approval than others, but none of them will overstep their set limits.

The tone of the statement is plainly one of divine majesty and authority, enhanced by its rhetorical form which seems to question the legitimacy of the proposition that anyone can intercede on behalf of another without God's permission and authority.

In the light of this fact, the vulgar absurdity of certain religious notions of God and godhead, upheld by some communities to whom God has sent messengers, becomes glaringly obvious, often verging on the grotesque and outrageous. Some of these allege that God has partners, sons or others, who share His authority, or associates whose intercession He will not refuse. Others recognize certain human individuals as divine representatives of God who, in some mysterious way, draw their earthly powers from Him directly.

The Islamic concept of God is crystal-clear and unambiguous. It makes a sharp distinction between God, the Master, and all creation, His subordinates, leaving no room whatsoever for any confusion or overlap between the essence or status of the two. Islam complements this distinction by emphasizing God's merciful, caring, compassionate and munificent attitude towards His creation. All believers can enjoy His grace without the need for distorting their conception of God's omnipresence and omnipotence, or perverting the nature of their relationship with Him.

"He knows all that lies open before them and all that lies hidden from them; whereas they cannot attain to anything of His knowledge save as He wills." (Verse 255) This statement expresses God's omniscience. He has full and total knowledge of the present, the past and the future, which human beings cannot possibly know or perceive. He is ever aware of what human beings know and what they do not, and will not, know. They can learn only what He allows them to learn.

The fact that God knows our present, past and future actions and deeds, and beyond, ought to fill us with dread and awe, for being totally and permanently exposed before God Almighty. It inspires total humility and submission to the one omniscient God. It is also poignant to reflect on the corollary of this principle, that *"... they cannot attain to anything of His knowledge save as He wills"*. Human beings may learn only what God wills them to know and learn –

which, in an age of such tremendous expansion of scientific knowledge, is a compelling truth to ponder.

God alone possesses full and absolute knowledge of all existence. He is able, in His infinite wisdom, to impart whatever He chooses of His knowledge to mankind, as He has promised: *"We will show them Our signs in all the regions of the earth and in their own souls, until they clearly see that this is the truth."* (41: 53)

This fact is often forgotten, and so is the fact that whatever knowledge God imparts to man, whether relating to the physical or to the metaphysical world, entails a certain degree of responsibility and accountability. Despite this, men often forget that God is the source of the knowledge they have acquired, while others deny the fact altogether.

God has been giving man knowledge ever since the day He appointed man His vicegerent on earth and undertook to guide him and show him the way forward, unfolding before him the secrets of the physical world and all the principles, laws and tools that facilitate human life and progress on earth.

While God has generously enabled man to acquire vast amounts of knowledge and made him privy to many of the world's mysteries, He has withheld many others. These are not required for man to know in order to fulfil his role on earth. These include the secret of life, which continues to elude human knowledge and which man continues to pursue with zeal but little success. The same applies to knowledge of the future, which remains hidden behind an impregnable wall, despite man's persistent efforts to predict and determine the future. Occasionally, however, with God's permission certain individuals are given glimpses of the future, but the curtain soon falls, leaving that world firmly inaccessible.

All the stores of knowledge that are not necessary for man's role in this world remain locked, and the great leaps man has made have barely reached beyond planet earth, a mere speck in a vast immeasurable universe. Nevertheless, man is beguiled and overwhelmed by the little knowledge he has acquired, which he owes to God's grace and generosity, and has assumed for himself a quasi-divine status, a demigod, denying the very existence of God, the Creator. In recent decades, scientists have begun to show a certain degree of humility in recognizing the inadequacy and shortcomings of human knowledge. There are, however, many fools who continue to think that they know everything there is to know.

"His throne extends over the heavens and the earth, and the preservation of both does not weary Him. He is the Most High, the Most Great." (Verse 255) Here we have another example of the unique style of the Qur'ān in expressing an abstract idea by means of a visual image, in order to make the meaning clear and accessible. The word *kursī*, meaning 'seat' or 'chair' and translated here as "throne", is usually used to denote realm or sovereignty. The idea here is that God's sovereignty and authority extend over the entire cosmos, and the image makes it clear, easy to grasp and comprehend.

Likewise, the phrase, *"the preservation of both does not weary Him,"* is an expression of God's omnipotence, depicting in simple but powerful terms how easy it is for God to sustain and preserve the heavens and the earth.

Qur'ānic expressions of this kind have provoked a great deal of controversy, largely because commentators ignored the Qur'ānic syntax and leaned heavily on alien and absurd philosophies which distorted much of the clarity and simplicity of the Qur'ān.

I would also add here that I have not come across any authentic statements of the Prophet that explain precisely the meanings of 'seat, chair or throne' as used in the Qur'ān, and I would, therefore, rather not speculate further on their meaning.

The verse ends with two more attributes of God: *"He is the Most High, the Most Great,"* exalting God above all else. The Arabic words make it clear that these attributes are exclusive to God Almighty. No human being, or any other creature, could aspire to these qualities, and those who try shall be humbled and disgraced. Elsewhere in the Qur'ān, God says: *"As for the [happy] life to come, We grant it exclusively to those who seek neither to exalt themselves on earth nor yet to spread corruption."* (28: 83) It also castigates Pharaoh for being *"a tyrant and a transgressor"* (44: 31)

No matter how powerful or great a human being may grow, he can never rise above being a servant of God. Once this fact is firmly established in man's mind, it will enhance his status as subordinate to God and restrain his pride and transgression. He will truly fear God and appreciate His majesty and power, and will seek to be more humble towards God and less haughty in dealing with his fellow human beings.

Here again, we see how a tenet of faith is immediately translated into a code of conduct in real life.

Freedom of Belief Guaranteed

Having outlined some of the most essential and detailed aspects of faith, and having precisely defined the status of God and the nature of His relationship with the rest of creation, the *sūrah* goes on to describe the proper behaviour of the believers as they adopt this faith and pass it on to others, and assume the leadership of mankind.

> *There shall be no compulsion in religion. The right way is henceforth distinct from error. He who rejects false deities and believes in God has indeed taken hold of a most firm support that never breaks. God hears all and knows all. God is the Patron of the believers. He leads them out of darkness into the light. As for the unbelievers, their patrons are false deities who lead them out of light into darkness. Those are the ones destined for the fire, therein to abide.* (Verses 256–257)

Islam looks at religious faith as a matter of conviction, once the basic facts are provided and explained. Faith is never a matter of coercion or compulsion. To achieve this conviction, Islam addresses the human being in totality. It addresses the human mind and intellect, human common sense, emotions and feelings, the innermost human nature, and the whole human conscious being. It resorts to no coercive means or physical miracles that confound the mind or that are beyond human ability to rationalize and comprehend.

By the same token, Islam never seeks converts through compulsion or threats or pressure of any kind. It deploys facts, reasoning, explanation and persuasion.

In contrast, we find that Christianity, the last revealed religion before Islam, was imposed by force after Constantine, the Roman Emperor, made Christianity the official religion throughout his empire. He adopted the same brutal means his predecessors had used against Christian minorities. These were not restricted to subjects who did not convert to Christianity, but were also used against Christians who would not accept the official doctrine sanctioned by the emperor.

Islam came to declare and establish the great universal principle that: "*There shall be no compulsion in religion. The right way is henceforth distinct from error.*" (Verse 256) This reflects the honour God has reserved for man and the high regard in which man's will, thought and emotions are held, and the freedom he is granted to choose his beliefs, and the responsible position he is afforded to be judge of his own actions. Here lies the essence of human emancipation which 20th-century authoritarian and oppressive ideologies and regimes have denied mankind. Modern man has been deprived of the right to choose and live other than according to what is dictated by the state, using the full force of its colossal machinery, laws and powers. People are today given the choice only to adhere to the secular state system, which does not allow for a belief in God as the Creator and Master of the world, or to face annihilation.

Freedom of belief is the most basic right that identifies man as a human being. To deny anyone this right is to deny him or her humanity. Freedom of belief also implies the freedom to express and propagate one's belief without fear of threat or persecution; otherwise, that freedom is hollow and meaningless.

Islam, undoubtedly the most enlightened view of life and the world, establishing a most sensible human and social system, takes the lead in declaring this most fundamental principle. It teaches its adherents, before anyone else, that they are forbidden to compel others to embrace Islam. This Islamic approach stands in total contrast to that of man-made systems and regimes which, despite all their inherent shortcomings, impose their beliefs and policies by the force of the state and deny their opponents the right to dissent or even live.

The Arabic text, using a generic negative, imparts a negation of the very idea of compulsion. When it comes to matters of belief, not only should these never be imposed by coercion or compulsion, but there cannot even be an option to use such a means of conversion or persuasion.

The *sūrah* reinforces the principle with a gentle, but firm, touch to arouse the human conscience and guide it along the path of enlightenment, saying simply: *"The right way is henceforth distinct from error."* (Verse 256)

Belief in God is the right path man should seek and follow, and denial of His existence and sovereignty is the path of error that man should avoid and guard against. Belief in God is indeed a blessing. It gives the human mind a clear view of the world around, and gives the heart peace and assurance. It sets for man higher goals and noble concerns and aspirations, and for society as a whole a sound system of values and ideals that improve the quality of life. A moment's reflection is sufficient to verify the truth of this Qur'ānic statement, which could only be rejected by the ignorant and the foolish who would choose cynicism, confusion and insecurity over peace, certainty and high aspirations.

The *sūrah* elaborates the theme further, saying: *"He who rejects false deities and believes in God has indeed taken hold of a most firm support that never breaks."* (Verse 256) It is false deities that must be rejected, while faith must be reserved for God, who alone deserves faith and trust.

The Arabic term for 'false deities' is *ṭāghūt*, meaning tyranny, a word denoting anything or anyone that takes hold of the mind or suppresses the truth, or transgresses the laws and limits set by God. It refers to forces and systems that disregard the divine religious, moral, social and legal order and operate in this life on values and principles not sanctioned by God or derived from His guidance and teachings. To resist such forces, in all their manifestations, and to believe in God's oneness is the only certain path to success and salvation.

The *sūrah* presents us, yet again, with another vivid image to express an abstract truth. Faith in God provides the believer with a strong and unshakeable support that guarantees him certain liberation. In its essence, faith is a recognition of the most fundamental truth, the existence of God, upon which all reality stands, and acknowledgement of the laws God has laid down for the world and by which the world exists and operates. Believers who hold to God's Guidance are assured of never drifting away from God's path or losing their way.

"God hears all and knows all." (Verse 256) He hears what is uttered and knows what is in people's innermost souls. Those who believe in God will never be denied justice or be disappointed.

The *sūrah* then goes on to present a vivid and graphic scene depicting the two paths of guidance and error. It indicates how God kindly and gently takes the believers by the hand and leads them out of the darkness, into the light, and how the false deities sponsor the unbelievers and lead them, too, by the hand, but out of the light into the darkness.

It is a fascinating and inspiring scene, full of life and imagination, and far more eloquent and effective than any polemic or rational exposition. One would be hard pressed to find an alternative way of expressing the same ideas without losing spirit, rhythm, and dynamism. The Qur'ānic style is not only very articulate and beautiful, it is also precise as it describes, in the original Arabic syntax, faith and belief in the singular as light, and describes disbelief as darkness, in the plural. This is a succinct, profound and enduring statement.

Faith is light that permeates man's soul and conscience to radiate from within his being and illuminate all things, ideas and values around him. It gives the believer a clear vision and a steady and confident understanding that enable him to identify, discern and choose. It lights his route to God, His laws and teachings, putting man in perfect concord with the world around him. He proceeds through life in total harmony, free of all conflict and at peace with his human nature.

The light of faith and truth is one and unique, leading to the one straight path; while darkness, in the sense of evil, can take various shapes and forms. There is darkness in caprice and uncontrolled desire; in deviation, conceit and tyranny; and there is darkness in abject acquiescence and servility; as well as in ostentation and hypocrisy, in lechery and greed, and in cynicism and scepticism. All these forms of darkness stem from the evil of abandoning God's guidance and submitting to powers and laws other than His. Leaving the light that radiates from God plunges man into darkness and despondency, and the ultimate end is even worse: *"As for the unbelievers, their patrons are false deities who lead them out of light into darkness. Those are the people destined for the fire, therein to abide."* (Verse 257)

The statement *"There shall be no compulsion in religion,"* raises the question of whether this principle can be reconciled with the obligatory duty of *jihād*, or taking up arms for the defence and protection of the faith, which Islam has openly advocated and the Qur'ān has established in verses such as: *"Fight them until there is no more oppression, and submission is made to God alone."* (Verse 193)

Some biased writers have accused Islam of double standards, claiming that it was spread and imposed by the sword while, at the same time, advocating non-coercion and freedom of religion. Others have been rather more insidious and used this argument apparently to defend Islam; but in fact they have undermined the very meaning and significance of *jihād* in Islamic culture and history. Their tempting, but specious, arguments lead to the conclusion that *jihād* is a matter of history and is no longer valid or necessary.[1]

Many Orientalists approach this subject with hostility and a tendency to distort and belittle the dynamic aspects of Islam. They perceive Islam as a threat, and seek to resist and destroy it. In effect, they argue that the Muslim peoples' conflict with Western colonialism was dictated by trade, raw materials and power, rather than by religion, a view which would make *jihād* totally unnecessary.

There is no denying that, throughout its long history, Islam has advocated the use of force, not to impose its doctrines, but to guarantee certain objectives that are necessary for human prosperity.

Islam advocates *jihād* to protect its followers against attacks and threats and to ensure their security and freedom. As indicated in Verse 193 of this *sūrah*, Islam considers religious persecution and any threat to religion more dangerous for the future stability and existence of Islam than actual war. According to this great Islamic principle, the survival and prosperity of the faith take precedence over the preservation of human life itself. Islam justifies the defence and protection of life and possessions by force, and allows even greater justification for the use of force in defence of the faith. Muslims have been the target of religious persecution on many occasions and in various parts of the world. In Spain, they, together with non-Catholic Christians, suffered waves of genocide and brutality, wiping them out of that part of Europe altogether. In Jerusalem and its surroundings, Muslims were the target of relentless Crusader campaigns designed to uproot Islam and destroy the Muslims. The Muslims resisted and fought, and prevailed, in the name of Islam sparing their land and people a fate similar to that of the Muslims in Spain. Today, Muslims continue to be the target of religious persecution under a host of Christian, Zionist and secular regimes in many parts of the world. This situation makes *jihād* an incumbent duty on Muslims.

Islam also advocates *jihād* to guarantee the right and freedom of expression and propagation of the faith. Islam has a comprehensive understanding of life. Its highly refined social order dwarfs all systems that have existed before or since. Its global message is addressed to all mankind. In order for individual human beings to

---

1. A leading exponent of this argument is Sir T.W. Arnold, in his book *The Preaching of Islam*, Sh. Muhammad Ashraf, Lahore, Reprinted in 1968.

make the choice of whether they believe in Islam or not, nothing should stand between them and God's message. They should in any way be prevented from having full and free access to it. Once they are informed, they are free to make their choice under no duress, pressure or coercion of any kind.

Of the many obstacles that stand between Islam and people, foremost are the tyrannical political regimes that oppress and persecute religious believers. Islam takes a clear stand against such regimes, striving to topple them. It urges its followers to try to replace them by tolerant and liberal ones that respect and guarantee religious freedom as well as freedom of expression. This remains an on-going objective of Islam, and the duty of *jihād* continues to be a valid and urgent obligation on Muslims.

Another objective of *jihād* is to establish the Islamic social order and defend it. It is an order that frees man from tyranny, in all its forms, by urging the submission of all to God, the supreme master of all. No single person, class or group has the right to dictate laws or moral standards to other people or control their lives through ideology or legislation. The authority of individuals or institutions can only be valid or legitimate if they are representing or implementing God's law, and have had that duty entrusted to them by the community. Individuals have no authority invested in them to introduce ethical or legal concepts, principles or rules on the basis of their own preferences, because that is the prerogative of God alone.

This is the basic Islamic principle upon which a truly civilized social and ethical order is built, guaranteeing individual freedom for every member of society, including non-Muslims. It protects their privacy and personal dignity and respects their civil and religious rights, regardless of creed or conviction. Under Islamic law, no one is compelled or coerced to convert to the religion of Islam.

Islam has justifiably urged its followers to strive for the establishment of this society and to stand firm against man's domination of his fellow human beings. Hence, the hostility and aggression with which tyrannical and totalitarian regimes have responded to Islam were inevitable. Also inevitable was the determination of Islam to stamp out such regimes and assert its legal, social, ethical, and economic world order. That notwithstanding, Islam undertakes to respect and guarantee the religious and personal freedom of everyone under its jurisdiction, in accordance with its ethical principles and social norms and regulations.

It is to continue the fight against religious tyranny and persecution, and establish the tolerant and magnanimous principles of Islam that *jihād* remains valid and necessary today.

It is clear, therefore, that Islam has not used force to impose its beliefs. Nor was it force, as some would have us believe, that has been responsible for the phenomenal success and spread of Islam. Its main objective has been the establishment of a stable society in which all citizens, including those who follow other religious creeds, may live in peace and security.

Power was essential for the survival and continuity of the Islamic order, and for the peace and security of its followers. *Jihād* has been, and continues to be, a significant and necessary means for the establishment and protection of Muslim society. Islam, by definition, is a comprehensive order for the organization of human life that must take root in the world, and power is needed to sustain and promote its existence. *Jihād* is the sinew of that power, without which it would not survive.

The principle of *'no compulsion in religion,'* should be read in conjunction with another one that states: *"Make ready against them whatever force and war mounts you can muster, so that you may strike terror into the enemies of God who are also your own enemies, and others besides them of whom you may be unaware, but of whom God is well aware."* (8: 60)

These principles present the correct perspective of Islam from which its followers should view and understand it. Muslims need not be on the defensive nor have to justify Islam's stance, but should be confident and proud of its teachings and its history compared with those of all other cultures and philosophies. Muslims ought not to be taken in by those who claim to defend Islam but, in reality, only seek to undermine it and subvert the right of Muslims to strive to be powerful and to undertake *jihād* to protect their faith and spread its teachings to all mankind.

Those who stand in the way of Islam's progress are the real enemies of humanity who ought to be pursued, and whose efforts should be frustrated. This task falls upon the believers who have the benefit of God's grace and blessings which they are obliged to value and pass on to others.

17

Causing Life and Death

Are you not aware of him who argued with Abraham about his Lord simply because God had given him kingship? Abraham said, ‘My Lord gives life and causes death.’ ‘I, too,’ said he, ‘give life and cause death.’ Abraham said, ‘Well, God causes the sun to rise in the east; cause it, then, to rise in the west.’ Thus the unbeliever was dumbfounded. God does not guide the wrongdoers. (258)

أَلَمْ تَرَ إِلَى ٱلَّذِى حَآجَّ إِبْرَٰهِـۧمَ فِى رَبِّهِۦٓ
أَنْ ءَاتَىٰهُ ٱللَّهُ ٱلْمُلْكَ إِذْ قَالَ إِبْرَٰهِـۧمُ
رَبِّىَ ٱلَّذِى يُحْىِۦ وَيُمِيتُ قَالَ أَنَا۠ أُحْىِۦ
وَأُمِيتُ ۖ قَالَ إِبْرَٰهِـۧمُ فَإِنَّ ٱللَّهَ يَأْتِى
بِٱلشَّمْسِ مِنَ ٱلْمَشْرِقِ فَأْتِ بِهَا مِنَ
ٱلْمَغْرِبِ فَبُهِتَ ٱلَّذِى كَفَرَ ۗ وَٱللَّهُ
لَا يَهْدِى ٱلْقَوْمَ ٱلظَّٰلِمِينَ ﴿٢٥٨﴾

Or, [are you not aware] of him who, passing by a township which had fallen into utter ruin, exclaimed: ‘How can God bring this town back to life now that it is dead?’ Thereupon God caused him to be dead for a hundred years, then brought him back to life, and said, ‘How long have you remained thus?’ He said, ‘I have remained thus a day or part of a day.’ God said, ‘No. You have remained thus for a hundred years. Just look

أَوْ كَٱلَّذِى مَرَّ عَلَىٰ قَرْيَةٍ وَهِىَ خَاوِيَةٌ عَلَىٰ
عُرُوشِهَا قَالَ أَنَّىٰ يُحْىِۦ هَٰذِهِ ٱللَّهُ بَعْدَ
مَوْتِهَا ۖ فَأَمَاتَهُ ٱللَّهُ مِا۟ئَةَ عَامٍ ثُمَّ بَعَثَهُۥ
قَالَ كَمْ لَبِثْتَ ۖ قَالَ لَبِثْتُ يَوْمًا أَوْ بَعْضَ
يَوْمٍ ۖ قَالَ بَل لَّبِثْتَ مِا۟ئَةَ عَامٍ فَٱنظُرْ

at your food and drink: none of it has rotted. And look at your ass. We will make you a sign for mankind. Look you at the bones, how We put them up and then clothe them with flesh.' When it had all become clear to him, he said, 'I know now that God has power over all things.' (259)

إِلَىٰ طَعَامِكَ وَشَرَابِكَ لَمْ يَتَسَنَّهْ ۖ
وَانظُرْ إِلَىٰ حِمَارِكَ وَلِنَجْعَلَكَ آيَةً
لِّلنَّاسِ ۖ وَانظُرْ إِلَى الْعِظَامِ
كَيْفَ نُنشِزُهَا ثُمَّ نَكْسُوهَا
لَحْمًا ۚ فَلَمَّا تَبَيَّنَ لَهُ قَالَ أَعْلَمُ أَنَّ
اللَّهَ عَلَىٰ كُلِّ شَيْءٍ قَدِيرٌ ﴿٢٥٩﴾

When Abraham said, 'My Lord, show me how You give life to the dead,' He replied, 'Have you, then, no faith?' 'Indeed, I have', said Abraham, 'but I only wish to set my heart fully at rest to be fully reassured.' God said, 'Take four birds and draw them close to you, then [having cut them into pieces] place a part of them on each mountain. Then call them back and they will come to you in haste. Know that God is Almighty, Wise.' (260)

وَإِذْ قَالَ إِبْرَاهِيمُ رَبِّ أَرِنِي كَيْفَ
تُحْيِي الْمَوْتَىٰ ۖ قَالَ أَوَلَمْ تُؤْمِن ۖ قَالَ بَلَىٰ
وَلَٰكِن لِّيَطْمَئِنَّ قَلْبِي ۖ قَالَ فَخُذْ
أَرْبَعَةً مِّنَ الطَّيْرِ فَصُرْهُنَّ إِلَيْكَ ثُمَّ
اجْعَلْ عَلَىٰ كُلِّ جَبَلٍ مِّنْهُنَّ جُزْءًا ثُمَّ
ادْعُهُنَّ يَأْتِينَكَ سَعْيًا ۚ وَاعْلَمْ أَنَّ
اللَّهَ عَزِيزٌ حَكِيمٌ ﴿٢٦٠﴾

Overview

This passage, composed of only three verses deals with the subject of life and death, presenting an important aspect of Islamic belief, to complement the principles established in the preceding passage, with an obvious direct relationship to Verse 255, known as the 'Verse of the Throne', or *āyat al-kursī*, which outlines a number of fundamental attributes of God.

These three verses form part of the consistent and relentless drive that the Qur'ān pursues to establish in Muslim minds, hearts and consciousness a true and accurate understanding of the Islamic view of life and the world. This understanding is essential in order to approach life with full knowledge and an enlightened perception, built on confidence and an unshakeable faith.

Actions, modes of behaviour and moral values are not divorced from people's beliefs, but are in fact firmly based upon them. Life cannot be well and securely organized unless it is linked to faith and a comprehensive and cohesive view of the world and the relationship it has with its originator who brought it into existence. This explains the great emphasis in the Qur'ān on the fundamental concepts of Islamic belief. Indeed, the entire part of the Qur'ān revealed to the Prophet Muḥammad over thirteen years in Makkah is devoted to this subject. These concepts continue to receive ample and frequent attention in the parts of the Qur'ān revealed in Madinah, with every new legislation these parts outline and with every directive dealing with any aspect of life affairs.

An Easily Settled Argument

The first verse in this passage relates an argument between the Prophet Abraham and a contemporary king who disputed his belief in God. The *sūrah* does not mention the king's name, because mentioning it will not add to the moral of the story. This argument is related to the Prophet and the Muslim community in a way that invites amazement at this person who disputes the truth of God. We listen as though the argument is taking place now, before our eyes: *"Are you not aware of him who argued with Abraham about his Lord simply because God had given him kingship? Abraham said, 'My Lord gives life and causes death.' 'I, too,' said he, 'give life and cause death.' Abraham said, 'Well, God causes the sun to rise in the east; cause it, then, to rise in the west.' Thus the unbeliever was dumbfounded. God does not guide the wrongdoers."* (Verse 258)

We learn from the text that the king who argued with Abraham did not, in fact, deny God's existence, but he denied that He was the only God or that He had sole sovereignty and control over mankind's affairs. This belief was prevalent among the Arabs during their Dark Ages, or *Jāhiliyyah*. They assigned lesser gods as partners to God and denied that God had any concern with, or authority over, worldly and daily human affairs.

The arrogant, stubborn king denies God for the very reason that he should acknowledge Him, as it was God who had made it possible for him to become king and ruler, in the first place. Power in the hands of those who do not believe or appreciate God's grace and generosity corrupts and leads to tyranny and despotism. Rulers govern by God's authority, and He never empowers them to enslave and oppress their people, or impose their own ideas and laws. Like their subjects, they are servants of God and subject to His authority. Their power is delegated by Him. They have no right to initiate or devise teachings and legislation of their own.

The king's attitude seems to evoke astonishment, as the interrogative form indicates. How could one who is given power and sovereignty by God arrogate to himself the right to question those of God, or claim independent powers of his own?

Abraham challenged the king, saying: *"My Lord gives life and causes death."* (Verse 258) Life and death are two of the greatest wonders of this world which we witness every day. Thinking about them compels the human mind to seek a non-human cause behind them. There is, therefore, no escaping the conclusion that the supreme omnipotent power of God, and no other, lies behind the secrets of life and death. We remain ignorant of the true essence of life and death, but we perceive their manifestations in the world around us, and we are forced to seek their origin and cause with a power unlike any power known to man, and that is the power of God Almighty.

Abraham's reply, *"My Lord gives life and causes death,"* (Verse 258) cites an attribute that is unique to God Almighty, with no one else able to claim a share of it for himself. The statement implies, too, that God rules and legislates over all. It is clear that in his reply Abraham, a noble Prophet, was not seeking to establish God's power in the mere acts of originating life and taking it away. Both are prerogatives of God alone.

Abraham's interlocutor saw his sovereign position over his subjects and his ability to kill them or let them live as evidence of his having more than temporal authority over them. His reply, *"I, too, give life and cause death,"* (Verse 258) implies having absolute power and authority over the affairs and destiny of his people, who are obliged to submit to his rule.

Abraham did not wish to pursue the argument about the meaning of originating life and causing death, with someone who twists facts.

He simply took the argument to a different sphere, citing another familiar event and challenging the obdurate king to alter a natural phenomenon, the movement of the sun, to make him realize that godhead could not be assumed merely by having absolute power over a group of people in a small corner on earth. God, by definition, controls all the affairs of the whole universe, and He is the source of legislation for mankind.

Abraham said: *"God causes the sun to rise in the east; cause it, then, to rise in the west"* (Verse 258) Another familiar daily occurrence is portrayed as a visible proof of God's existence and power, even for those who are not familiar with the principles of astronomy or laws of physics. This statement comes as a direct challenge to man's basic nature by expressing a fact that cannot be disputed. God's Revelations often address human nature at various stages of human intellectual, cultural and social development to lead man from wherever he is to a higher state of consciousness. *"Thus the unbeliever was dumbfounded."* (Verse 258)

The challenge was real, clear, and unambiguous, and the stubborn king would have been better advised to give in, but his pride had the better of him and prevented him from submitting to the truth. He could do no more than be astounded and stupefied, thereby forfeiting the opportunity to believe and win God's guidance. *"The unbeliever was dumbfounded. God does not guide the wrongdoers."* (Verse 258)

This encounter, which God cited for His Messenger and his community of followers, remains today an example for obstinacy and ignorance, and a lesson from which they learn how to confront those who deny the truth.

The passage presents two simple but profound truths: one taken from within man's being, that God *'gives life and causes death',* and the other from the natural world around, that *'God causes the sun to rise in the east'*, and not in the west. These are familiar occurrences, available for all to see and contemplate, requiring little knowledge or effort to perceive or understand. Man only needs to allow his inner nature to respond and react to these imposing phenomena, the impact of which cannot be mistaken or escaped, unless one is being deliberately stubborn or bent on rejecting the truth.

God is too kind to demand His recognition by means that may not be available to all people. Belief in God is an indispensable ingredient of man's being, without which human life would lose all sense of direction and order, and man would have no source of values, legislation or moral standards.

This can be said about all other essential aspects of human life. Man seeks food, drink, air and procreation by his natural instincts. He does not need to attain certain levels of intellectual or cultural maturity to acquire the right to satisfy these desires. Were he to need these, man would perish without moving one step forward. Belief in God, is equally essential to human life, and it is easily attained by responding honestly and naturally to the compelling evidence present throughout the universe and within man's own being and existence.

Where Life Originates

Still on the subject of the miraculous nature of life and death, the *sūrah* relates another brief tale: *"Or, [are you not aware] of him who, passing by a township which had fallen into utter ruin, exclaimed: 'How can God bring this town back to life now that it is dead?' Thereupon God caused him to be dead for a hundred years, then brought him back to life, and said, 'How long have you remained thus?' He said, 'I have remained thus a day or part of a day.' God said, 'No. You have remained thus for a hundred years. Just look at your food and drink: none of it has rotted. And look at your ass. We will make you a sign for mankind. Look you at the bones, how We put them up and then clothe them with flesh.' When it had all become clear to him, he said, 'I know now that God has power over all things.'"* (Verse 259)

Again, the Qur'ān does not give details of the identity of the man or the ruined township because such details add little to the significance and impact of the story. Were these necessary, they would not have been omitted in the Qur'ān. Despite the absence of detail, however, the scene comes to life and stirs the imagination with great clarity and power. It is a scene of death, desolation and destruction; a town in ruins, with walls and columns caved in on their foundations, the effect of which is eloquently expressed in the man's incredulity as he exclaims: *"How can God bring this town back to life now that it is dead?"* (Verse 259)

The man is perfectly aware of God's presence, but the impact of that scene of devastation is so powerful that he wonders in disbelief how life could ever be returned to that rubble. It is a most evocative and moving impression which the Qur'ān, in its inimitable style, depicts with eloquence and awesome brilliance. *"Thereupon God caused him to be dead for a hundred years, then brought him back to life, and said, 'How long have you remained thus?' He said, 'I have remained thus a day or part of a day.' God said, 'No. You have remained thus for a hundred years. Just look at your food and drink, none of it has rotted. And look at your ass. We will make you a sign for mankind. Look you at the bones, how We put them up and then clothe them with flesh.'"* (Verse 259)

The man was not given a rational argument as to how a dead body could be brought to life again, but was himself made to undergo that experience. Such a personal direct approach is often more effective than any logical or visible demonstration. It involves one's senses, emotions and feelings. Its impact is sharp and overwhelming.

While he was dead, the man naturally lost all sense of time and could not tell how long he had been in that state. This is easy to understand, since human beings can misjudge things even when they are in control of their senses. Our material senses are not the only or the most accurate means of perception.

God said: *"No. You have remained thus for a hundred years."* (Verse 259) But the man had no way of telling. His provisions remained in good condition.

"'And look at your ass. We will make you a sign for mankind. Look you at the bones, how We put them up and then clothe them with flesh.'" (Verse 259) Which bones are referred to here: the man's own bones, as some commentators maintain? Had it been so, he would have immediately noticed, and would not have thought that he remained in that state for only a few hours or a day. Therefore, we are inclined to uphold the view that the reference here is to the bones of the ass whose gathering together and covering with flesh, before the man's own eyes, was a compelling sign of God's power. The fact that the man, the ass, and the provisions were affected in different ways under the same physical and environmental conditions is another sign of that absolute, limitless and unrestricted divine power. Thus the man was made to understand how God could bring that desolate town back to life again.

As to how this miracle was achieved, the answer is: in the same way as every other miracle, including the creation of life itself, which we often tend to overlook, forgetting how totally ignorant we are of its reality. All we know is that life comes from God, in the way He wills it to be.

In his study *The Origin of Species*, Charles Darwin, the eminent British biologist, traces life back to the amoeba, a simple single-celled organism, but goes no further in explaining the origin of life. For most unscientific reasons, relating to the historic conflict between science and the Christian Church in Europe, Darwin's theory does not acknowledge the logical and evident truth that life must originate with a creator. Darwin claims that to explain life's affairs by the notion of the existence of a creator is to introduce an unnatural element into a purely mechanical situation.

The situation, in fact, is far from being a purely mechanical one. What we need to look for is an explanation for this mystery that stares us in the face. It is indeed evident for all to see.

Darwin himself is compelled by the force of natural common sense to refer the whole phenomenon of life to 'the first cause', without telling us what this cause was. It is the power capable of initiating life in the first instance and, according to Darwin's own controversial thesis, is capable of directing the descendants of the first living cell in the direction Darwin supposed they had taken in the process of natural selection. It is pure evasion, obfuscation and muddle.

Going back to the parable of the man and the ruined city, one wonders what could explain the fact that things can exist in the same place and under the same environmental conditions but be affected differently. It could not be explained in terms of the creation or restoration of life. The explanation lies in the limitless and unrestrained nature of the divine will, which is bound by none of the laws or needs we consider absolute and incontrovertible.

Human beings fall into grave error when they apply human rational or 'scientific' assumptions to God Almighty or His actions, for a number of reasons. How can God or His actions be subjected to laws based on man's limited knowledge and experience, and on his imperfect understanding and interpretation of that experience? Even if we assume that the laws man has discovered are final and conclusive, how can we be certain that they are the ultimate and overriding truth? The absolute divine power of God creates laws but is not restricted by them. It is completely free to decide.

We learn from this passage that in addition to granting life and causing death, God's power and will are absolute. The Qur'ān lays particular emphasis on this fact and seeks to instil it in the hearts of believers in order to refer them directly to God, whom they should seek beyond the visible material world. The man in our present story had come to the right conclusion when he said: *"I know now that God has power over all things."* (Verse 259)

How God Raises the Dead

Then follows another episode, involving the Prophet Abraham and the phenomena of life and death. *"When Abraham said, 'My Lord, show me how You give life to the dead,' He replied, 'Have you, then, no faith?' 'Indeed, I have', said Abraham, 'but I only wish to set my heart fully at rest to be fully reassured.' God said, 'Take four birds and draw them close to you, then [having cut them into pieces] place a part of them on each mountain. Then call them back and they will come to you in haste. Know that God is Almighty, Wise.'"* (Verse 260)

It is the usual tale of curiosity about the great mystery of life and creation. When this curiosity is expressed by a devoted and pious person like the Prophet Abraham, it proves that there are times when even the most favoured and believing of God's servants experience a passionate urge and ambition to discover the secrets of creation.

Here curiosity is not motivated by lack of conviction or the demand for proof to confirm one's faith, but has a different flavour, excited by a spiritual yearning to see and share one of God's most fascinating secrets. This privilege, even for someone like Abraham, has a unique honour and a flavour of its own, different even to that of faith itself. It is a natural and spontaneous desire to know and learn how the divine will operates, not in order to believe or obtain proof, but to experience total peace and gain reassurance.

Abraham's experience and the short dialogue which accompanied it reveal several perceptions of faith which the human heart, if it so desires, can experience and enjoy.

Abraham was seeking the reassurance of seeing God's hand at work and the satisfaction of seeing a hidden mystery unfold before him. God was aware that Abraham was a devout believer and that his inquisitiveness had arisen out of the quest for knowledge. The episode also serves to inform and educate and reveal God's compassion and benevolence towards a faithful and curious servant.

God responds favourably to Abraham's request and exposes him to a direct personal experience to satisfy his curiosity, giving him the following instructions: *"Take four birds and draw them close to you, then [having cut them into pieces] place a part of them on each mountain. Then call them back and they will come to you in haste. Know that God is Almighty, Wise."* (Verse 260)

The instructions meant that Abraham should choose four birds and make sure of having them close to him so that he would be able to know every little detail of their appearance so that he could unmistakeably identify them at any time. He would then have to kill them and cut them into pieces before placing different parts of their bodies on the surrounding mountains. He would then call them to come over to him, and their parts will join again, life is breathed into them and they could speedily come to him. All this took place in reality.

Thus Abraham was able to witness the secret of breathing life into the dead unfolding before his own eyes. It is the secret that occurs all the time, but people only see its effects after its process has been completed. It is the greatest mystery of life, which was created in the first instance by God out of nothing, and which renews itself an infinite number of times in every new living thing. Abraham saw with his own eyes the birds he killed and placed portions of their bodies far apart, returned to life and moving in full vigour.

How could all this take place? It is the one mystery that continues to elude human perception. Even if one was to undergo Abraham's experience and witness the actual act of creation, one would not comprehend its reality or how it is accomplished. It is the prerogative of God Almighty, of whose perfect and absolute knowledge man can acquire nothing, except by His will. It is God's will that this sphere should remain beyond the bounds of human knowledge, possibly because it is beyond man's comprehension and is not required for the fulfilment of man's mission on earth.

Until God allows the curtain to be raised on this issue, man's aspiration to grasp the coveted secret of life shall remain unfulfilled. If, however, he were to persist in his defiance of God's authority and continue to trespass in regions that are the exclusive domain of the Divine, his efforts would for ever be in vain and yield nothing.

18

An Islamic Model of Social Security

The case of those who spend their property for the cause of God is like that of a grain that brings forth seven ears, each bearing a hundred grains. God gives manifold increase to whom He wills. God is Munificent, All-Knowing. (261)

مَّثَلُ ٱلَّذِينَ يُنفِقُونَ أَمْوَٰلَهُمْ فِي سَبِيلِ
ٱللَّهِ كَمَثَلِ حَبَّةٍ أَنۢبَتَتْ سَبْعَ سَنَابِلَ
فِي كُلِّ سُنۢبُلَةٍ مِّاْئَةُ حَبَّةٍۗ وَٱللَّهُ يُضَٰعِفُ
لِمَن يَشَآءُۗ وَٱللَّهُ وَٰسِعٌ عَلِيمٌ ﴿٢٦١﴾

Those who spend their property for the cause of God and do not follow their spending by vaunting their own generosity, or by hurting others, shall have their reward with their Lord. They have nothing to fear, nor shall they grieve. (262)

ٱلَّذِينَ يُنفِقُونَ أَمْوَٰلَهُمْ فِي سَبِيلِ ٱللَّهِ ثُمَّ
لَا يُتْبِعُونَ مَآ أَنفَقُواْ مَنًّا وَلَآ أَذًى لَّهُمْ
أَجْرُهُمْ عِندَ رَبِّهِمْ وَلَا خَوْفٌ عَلَيْهِمْ
وَلَا هُمْ يَحْزَنُونَ ﴿٢٦٢﴾

A kind word with forgiveness is better than charity followed by injury. God is free of all wants, clement. (263)

قَوْلٌ مَّعْرُوفٌ وَمَغْفِرَةٌ خَيْرٌ مِّن صَدَقَةٍ
يَتْبَعُهَآ أَذًىۗ وَٱللَّهُ غَنِيٌّ حَلِيمٌ ﴿٢٦٣﴾

Believers, do not render your charitable deeds worthless by boasting about your benevolence and causing injury to others, as does he who spends his wealth to impress people, while he

يَٰٓأَيُّهَا ٱلَّذِينَ ءَامَنُواْ لَا تُبْطِلُواْ
صَدَقَٰتِكُم بِٱلْمَنِّ وَٱلْأَذَىٰ كَٱلَّذِي
يُنفِقُ مَالَهُۥ رِئَآءَ ٱلنَّاسِ وَلَا يُؤْمِنُ

believes neither in God nor in the Last Day. Such a person is like a smooth rock covered with earth. Then heavy rain falls on it and leaves it hard and bare. Such as these shall gain nothing from their works. God does not guide the unbelievers. (264)

بِٱللَّهِ وَٱلْيَوْمِ ٱلْـَٔاخِرِ ۖ فَمَثَلُهُۥ كَمَثَلِ
صَفْوَانٍ عَلَيْهِ تُرَابٌ فَأَصَابَهُۥ وَابِلٌ
فَتَرَكَهُۥ صَلْدًا ۖ لَّا يَقْدِرُونَ عَلَىٰ
شَىْءٍ مِّمَّا كَسَبُوا۟ ۗ وَٱللَّهُ لَا يَهْدِى
ٱلْقَوْمَ ٱلْكَـٰفِرِينَ ﴿٢٦٤﴾

But those who give away their money out of a genuine desire to please God, and out of their own inner certainty, are like a garden on a hillside. When heavy rain falls on it, it yields up twice its normal produce. If no heavy rain falls on it, then a light drizzle [will suffice]. God sees all that you do. (265)

وَمَثَلُ ٱلَّذِينَ يُنفِقُونَ أَمْوَٰلَهُمُ
ٱبْتِغَآءَ مَرْضَاتِ ٱللَّهِ وَتَثْبِيتًا
مِّنْ أَنفُسِهِمْ كَمَثَلِ جَنَّةٍۭ بِرَبْوَةٍ
أَصَابَهَا وَابِلٌ فَـَٔاتَتْ أُكُلَهَا
ضِعْفَيْنِ فَإِن لَّمْ يُصِبْهَا وَابِلٌ
فَطَلٌّ ۗ وَٱللَّهُ بِمَا تَعْمَلُونَ
بَصِيرٌ ﴿٢٦٥﴾

Would any of you wish to have a garden of palm-trees and vines, through which running waters flow, bringing forth all kinds of fruits, then to be well advanced in age, with helpless offspring; and then a fiery whirlwind smites it and leaves it all burnt down? Thus God makes plain to you His revelations, so that you may reflect. (266)

أَيَوَدُّ أَحَدُكُمْ أَن تَكُونَ لَهُۥ جَنَّةٌ مِّن
نَّخِيلٍ وَأَعْنَابٍ تَجْرِى مِن تَحْتِهَا
ٱلْأَنْهَـٰرُ لَهُۥ فِيهَا مِن كُلِّ ٱلثَّمَرَٰتِ
وَأَصَابَهُ ٱلْكِبَرُ وَلَهُۥ ذُرِّيَّةٌ ضُعَفَآءُ
فَأَصَابَهَآ إِعْصَارٌ فِيهِ نَارٌ فَٱحْتَرَقَتْ ۗ
كَذَٰلِكَ يُبَيِّنُ ٱللَّهُ لَكُمُ ٱلْـَٔايَـٰتِ
لَعَلَّكُمْ تَتَفَكَّرُونَ ﴿٢٦٦﴾

Believers, spend on others out of the good things you have earned, and out of that which We bring forth for you from the earth. Do not choose for your spending the inferior things which you yourselves would not accept without turning your eyes away in disdain. Know that God is free of all want, ever to be praised. (267)

يَٰٓأَيُّهَا ٱلَّذِينَ ءَامَنُوٓا۟ أَنفِقُوا۟ مِن طَيِّبَٰتِ
مَا كَسَبْتُمْ وَمِمَّآ أَخْرَجْنَا لَكُم مِّنَ
ٱلْأَرْضِ ۖ وَلَا تَيَمَّمُوا۟ ٱلْخَبِيثَ مِنْهُ تُنفِقُونَ
وَلَسْتُم بِـَٔاخِذِيهِ إِلَّآ أَن تُغْمِضُوا۟ فِيهِ ۚ
وَٱعْلَمُوٓا۟ أَنَّ ٱللَّهَ غَنِىٌّ حَمِيدٌ ﴿٢٦٧﴾

Satan promises you poverty and bids you to commit indecency, whereas God promises you His forgiveness and bounty. God is Munificent, All-Knowing. (268)

ٱلشَّيْطَٰنُ يَعِدُكُمُ ٱلْفَقْرَ وَيَأْمُرُكُم
بِٱلْفَحْشَآءِ ۖ وَٱللَّهُ يَعِدُكُم مَّغْفِرَةً
مِّنْهُ وَفَضْلًا ۗ وَٱللَّهُ وَٰسِعٌ عَلِيمٌ ﴿٢٦٨﴾

He grants wisdom to whom He wills. He who is granted wisdom has indeed been granted abundant good. Yet only those with sound minds would take heed. (269)

يُؤْتِى ٱلْحِكْمَةَ مَن يَشَآءُ ۚ وَمَن يُؤْتَ
ٱلْحِكْمَةَ فَقَدْ أُوتِىَ خَيْرًا كَثِيرًا ۗ
وَمَا يَذَّكَّرُ إِلَّآ أُو۟لُوا۟ ٱلْأَلْبَٰبِ ﴿٢٦٩﴾

Whatever alms you give or vows you make are known to God. The evildoers shall have none to help them. (270)

وَمَآ أَنفَقْتُم مِّن نَّفَقَةٍ أَوْ نَذَرْتُم مِّن
نَّذْرٍ فَإِنَّ ٱللَّهَ يَعْلَمُهُۥ ۗ وَمَا لِلظَّٰلِمِينَ
مِنْ أَنصَارٍ ﴿٢٧٠﴾

If you give alms openly, that is well; but if you give them to the needy in private, it is even better for you, and will atone for some of your bad deeds. God is aware of all you do. (271)

إِن تُبْدُوا۟ ٱلصَّدَقَٰتِ فَنِعِمَّا هِىَ ۖ وَإِن
تُخْفُوهَا وَتُؤْتُوهَا ٱلْفُقَرَآءَ فَهُوَ خَيْرٌ
لَّكُمْ ۚ وَيُكَفِّرُ عَنكُم مِّن سَيِّـَٔاتِكُمْ ۗ
وَٱللَّهُ بِمَا تَعْمَلُونَ خَبِيرٌ ﴿٢٧١﴾

لَّيْسَ عَلَيْكَ هُدَىٰهُمْ وَلَٰكِنَّ ٱللَّهَ
يَهْدِى مَن يَشَآءُ ۗ وَمَا تُنفِقُوا۟ مِنْ
خَيْرٍ فَلِأَنفُسِكُمْ ۚ وَمَا تُنفِقُونَ
إِلَّا ٱبْتِغَآءَ وَجْهِ ٱللَّهِ ۚ وَمَا تُنفِقُوا۟
مِنْ خَيْرٍ يُوَفَّ إِلَيْكُمْ وَأَنتُمْ
لَا تُظْلَمُونَ ﴿٢٧٢﴾

It is not for you to make people follow the right guidance. It is God who guides whom He wills. Whatever good you may spend in charity is for your own good. You should only spend out of pure dedication to God. And whatever good you give in charity will be repaid to you in full, and you shall not be wronged. (272)

لِلْفُقَرَآءِ ٱلَّذِينَ أُحْصِرُوا۟ فِى
سَبِيلِ ٱللَّهِ لَا يَسْتَطِيعُونَ
ضَرْبًا فِى ٱلْأَرْضِ يَحْسَبُهُمُ
ٱلْجَاهِلُ أَغْنِيَآءَ مِنَ ٱلتَّعَفُّفِ
تَعْرِفُهُم بِسِيمَٰهُمْ لَا يَسْـَٔلُونَ
ٱلنَّاسَ إِلْحَافًا ۗ وَمَا تُنفِقُوا۟
مِنْ خَيْرٍ فَإِنَّ ٱللَّهَ بِهِۦ عَلِيمٌ ﴿٢٧٣﴾

[Alms are] for the needy who, being wholly preoccupied with God's cause, are unable to go about earning their livelihood. The unthinking take them for men of wealth on account of their restrained behaviour. You can recognize them by their special mark: they do not importune people for alms. Whatever good you give is certainly known to God. (273)

ٱلَّذِينَ يُنفِقُونَ أَمْوَٰلَهُم بِٱلَّيْلِ
وَٱلنَّهَارِ سِرًّا وَعَلَانِيَةً فَلَهُمْ
أَجْرُهُمْ عِندَ رَبِّهِمْ وَلَا خَوْفٌ
عَلَيْهِمْ وَلَا هُمْ يَحْزَنُونَ ﴿٢٧٤﴾

Those who give their property by night and by day, in private and in public, shall have their reward with their Lord. They have nothing to fear and they shall not grieve. (274)

Overview

The last three passages centred mainly on ideological concepts of the Islamic faith, clarifying its aspects and ensuring its firm establishment in people's hearts. These passages constituted an interval in the line followed in this long *sūrah* which prepares the Muslim community to undertake its role of leadership of mankind.

From this point and up to its concluding verses, the *sūrah* is largely devoted to setting out some fundamental features of the socio-economic system that the Muslim community should adopt. It is a system based on social cooperation and welfare through the established financial obligation of *zakāt* and other unspecified voluntary contributions and donations. We learn in this passage that, in contrast to the system prevalent in pre-Islamic Arabia, the Islamic socio-economic system is fundamentally opposed to usury and encourages fundamentally different financial dealings. Thus, the *sūrah* speaks of a proper method of charity, denounces usury and outlines the Islamic principles of lending and trade which complement the social and economic principles according to which Islamic social life is organized and conducted. All this is spread over three closely interrelated passages.

In the present passage we learn that contributing financially to charitable causes is akin to *jihād*, in the sense that its purpose is to serve the cause of God. *Jihād* is prescribed for Muslims to fulfil their duty of implementing God's message and conveying it to the rest of mankind and protecting its followers against persecution and oppression.

The call to spend of one's money is frequently made in this *sūrah*, and this part of it lays down the basic principle underlying that call. Its social and psychological ethics are presented in terms of both compassion and benefit, so that charity becomes a means of financial and spiritual exaltation and refinement for both donor and recipient. It is an act that spreads the spirit of brotherhood, empathy and cooperation among members of the community and makes them feel and behave as equal members of the same family.

It is important to point out that although the directives given in this section of the *sūrah* are universal and general, one can, nevertheless, detect that they were revealed in response to specific situations faced by the Muslims at the time, though these often recur. It is clear that a Muslim community may include selfish and parsimonious individuals who need rigorous discipline and convincing arguments and examples to absorb the facts.

Besides the sincere and generous people, there were miserly individuals who would exact a steep price for lending or donating their money. There were those who would give for charity with much difficulty and reluctance or merely for ostentatious reasons, and there were those who would use their money to demonstrate their superiority, and others who would give only what they disdained.

It is important to acknowledge these facts because they help us understand the nature and role of the Qur'ān as a dynamic and active force within the developing Muslim community. It was revealed to deal with actual situations and to lead, inform and educate the Muslims to whom it was addressed.

This is how the Qur'ān should be viewed by Muslims today: a living dynamic agent in society, especially in view of the widening gap between Islam and the reality of their daily life. We seem to view the Qur'ān as an abstract thing that has no historical living reality. We no longer perceive of it as the force that once shaped Islamic life and society, or the source of the daily orders that Muslims used to receive and act upon. Our perception of the Qur'ān has died, or at least has gone into a coma, and its true original image has faded from Muslim minds today. We have grown accustomed to listening to the Qur'ān recited by beautiful voices in melodious ways and to being moved and affected by the experience. Or we have become satisfied by simply reading it for spiritual or emotional stimulation, or to gain some esoteric or mystical comfort – all of which the Qur'ān does, indeed, evoke and provide.

We need to approach the Qur'ān in a way that restores its dynamic role in society and breathes life and consciousness into Muslim minds, and leads Muslim life and moves it forward. Muslims today need to turn back to the Qur'ān for advice, enlightenment and direction, as their predecessors did, and to understand its teachings on all aspects and areas of life. They need to see and learn the historic process through which Islam and the first Muslim community came to be established, to appreciate that process and accept it as part of their own formation and existence, and to recognize their life as an extension of that of their pioneering predecessors.

It is important for Muslims today to identify with the struggle and achievements of the early generations of Islam, and see the Qur'ān as equally and directly addressed to them in their present situation, and that they should let it guide all their plans and activities as a comprehensive code of life and a universal body of law and wisdom.

Reading the Qur'ān in this way helps us to recognize the human natural response to faith and the duties it imposes. We can see such response in reality through the Qur'ānic references to the life of the first Muslim community. Although that community was the first recipient of the Qur'ān and the immediate beneficiary of the Prophet's special care, it had certain weaknesses that needed to be addressed and remedied. Yet such weaknesses did not stop that community from achieving its rank as the best generation in the history of mankind. Thus we can see human communities in their reality, unlike the exaggerated images often given to them. We also learn not to despair as we see ourselves well below the high standards Islam calls on people to seek. It is enough that we are making a sincere effort to improve ourselves and achieve a higher standard. Moreover, we learn an important fact, namely that the urge to work towards perfection must continue all the time, unaffected by people's shortcomings and weaknesses. By nature, people will respond gradually as they are constantly reminded of their virtue, duty and goodness. They will also respond to repeated reminders showing the beauty of goodness and the horrible nature of evil. They need a helping hand whenever they slacken as they travel along the road leading to the sublime goal.

Such an intelligent reading of the Qur'ān will put before our eyes an often overlooked simple fact: it is the same people, the same divine message and the same battle fought throughout history. First and foremost, it is a battle against human weakness and parsimony of the individual, and against evil, falsehood, error and tyranny in human life. The fight must be engaged; there can be no way of averting it. The rulers of the Muslim community must fight this battle in both domains, just like the Qur'ān and the Prophet fought it the first time. It is inevitable that some slips and errors would occur; weakness would surface at some points. But a remedy must be found whenever a weakness appears. It is imperative that people should be guided to God in the same Qur'ānic method. This brings us back to what we said at the beginning: we must consult the Qur'ān before embarking on any course of action. It must be seen to mould our lives like it moulded the life of the first Muslim community.

Ethics of Islamic Charity

The present passage opens with gentle exhortations, touching inner, deep-seated human feelings and senses. It depicts a vigorous, flourishing picture of life, with grains sprouting and growing to yield multitudes of grains and return many times what has been invested. This verdant and lush image, the *sūrah* says, represents a model for those who spend of their own money for the cause of God. *"The case of those who spend their property for the cause of God is like that of a grain that brings forth seven ears, each bearing a hundred grains."* (Verse 261)

By simple arithmetic, a single grain of corn or wheat yields seven hundred grains, but we are presented with a much more inspiring and moving picture that leaves a profound and lasting impression on our minds and consciences. It is a picture of life itself, growing abundantly, and giving many times over.

With that vivid image, the Qur'ān directs the human conscience to giving and to charity. By giving away what one dearly loves to retain, one is in fact earning; and the more one gives, the more one gains, in a perpetual process which, with God's blessing, can continue without any limits or restrictions. *"God gives manifold increase to whom He wills. God is Munificent, All-Knowing."* (Verse 261) God's grace never runs out, nor is it withheld. God is aware of people's thoughts, intentions and feelings, and nothing escapes His knowledge.

The question here is: What kind of spending is made to grow in such a phenomenal way, and is rewarded so generously by God, both in this life and in the life to come?

The spending that is generously rewarded is that motivated by the purest and highest human feelings, and which enhances such feelings. It is not intended to degrade or spite or hurt. It is purely done for the sake of God Almighty: *"Those who spend their property for the cause of God and do not follow their spending by vaunting their own generosity, or by hurting others, shall have their reward with their Lord. They have nothing to fear, nor shall they grieve."* (Verse 262)

To give for the sake of vanity or ostentation is a vulgar and odious act. Those who brag about what they give to charity seek nothing but false prestige or the humiliation of the recipients, or to draw attention to themselves in order to win public praise rather than God's pleasure. Such self-seeking desires are alien to the pure heart of a true believer.

Boasting about one's own generosity is pernicious and hurtful to both giver and recipient. It is offensive to the giver because it inflates his ego and satisfies his sense of superiority as he savours the deference of the recipient of his awards. It also makes him arrogant and draws him further away from God. It is hurtful to the recipient because it draws attention to his need and his humble condition, and may make him jealous and desirous of revenge.

Giving, from the Islamic point of view, is not seen merely as an act of condescension, induced by pity, to hand over to the needy a paltry gift or a piece of bread; but as a means to purify the soul of the giver, revive his humanitarian feelings, reinforce the human bond with his less fortunate fellow human beings, and impress upon him the value of God's grace and favour and his obligation to employ his wealth, dispense of it sensibly and share it gratefully with others, in the service of God's cause. Giving for God's cause also acts as a consolation to the recipient and a means to strengthen the ties of humanity and fraternity. It also promotes love, cooperation and welfare among members of the community and furthers its cohesion and unity of purpose.

Flaunting one's wealth and philanthropy undermines social unity and fuels jealousy and mistrust that could only tear society apart.

Some modern psychologists have suggested that man's natural reaction to charity is hostility and hatred, at some time in the future. They explain this by saying that charity puts the recipient in a position of inferiority and weakness *vis-à-vis* the giver, a feeling that may ferment within him until it grows into total rejection and latent hostility. The more the giver reminds the recipient of his favour, the more painful it is for the recipient and the more antagonistic he grows.

This may well be the case in non-Muslim societies that have not been shaped or disciplined by Islam. Under Islam, people are taught that wealth belongs to God and He gives of it to those who are well-off. Only those who are ignorant of how wealth is acquired dispute this. Wealth and fortune are given by the grace of God, and man is helpless when it comes to earning them. The creation of a single grain of wheat involves a process in which a combination of energies from the sun and the soil, as well as water and air, come together to play their vital respective roles. This process is totally outside man's realm of control, and it applies to a whole range of similar processes of growth and procreation.

Hence, when those who have give, they do so from the wealth God has given them. Indeed, this act of charity is, in the Islamic sense, a loan given to God which is then returned multiplied manifold. Recipients of charity are there to provide the giver with an opportunity to earn a greater reward from God. The terms which the *sūrah* lays down in this passage emphasize these values, seeking to dissuade givers from flaunting their generosity, and encouraging the needy to abandon any feelings of inferiority or inadequacy. Both are beneficiaries of God's bounty, and both shall receive their respective rewards so long as they observe the ethics and the terms laid down by God.

"They have nothing to fear, nor shall they grieve." (Verse 262) Givers should not fear poverty, jealousy or injustice, nor should they regret their actions or have any concern regarding their fate in the hereafter.

Charity Coupled with Good Manners

The next verse reasserts the idea that a charitable act followed by wicked behaviour is worthless: *"A kind word with forgiveness is better than charity followed by injury. God is free of all wants, clement."* (Verse 263)

A pleasant word or a kind-hearted gesture would be far more favourable and likely to spread trust, confidence and love and to calm the hearts and souls. Charity, after all, is not a favour from the giver to the recipient, but an obligation towards God who is: *"free of all wants, clement."* He neither needs these pitiful donations nor is He anxious to exact punishment on the ungrateful. All people owe their very existence to God Almighty. He overlooks many of their shortcomings, and they ought to learn from Him by showing forgiveness and compassion towards the poor and the needy.

The Qur'ān always reminds people of the attributes of God, which provide the perfect ideal Muslims should try to emulate, as far as they can, in their behaviour, and in their values and aspirations.

When the previous verses have given the believers a keen sense of their role and the need to give freely, for no purpose other than to earn God's pleasure, the *sūrah* advises them not to undermine their charitable deeds with condescension or by hurting other people's feelings. Again, it gives a vivid and lively illustration from nature, in which ideas and concepts are reflected in exciting movement and vivid scenery.

Believers, do not render your charitable deeds worthless by boasting about your benevolence and causing injury to others, as does he who spends his wealth to impress people, while he believes neither in God nor in the Last Day. Such a person is like a smooth rock covered with earth. Then heavy rain falls on it and leaves it hard and bare. Such as these shall gain nothing from their works. God does not guide the unbelievers. But those who give away their money out of a genuine desire to please God, and out of their own inner certainty, are like a garden on a hillside. When heavy rain falls on it, it yields up twice its normal produce. If no heavy rain falls on it, then a light drizzle [will suffice]. God sees all that you do. (Verses 264–265)

We are presented here with a complete portrait, which is the composite of two perfectly contrasting scenes. Each is full of detail and contrast, beautifully reflecting ideas and feelings in elegant strokes of colour and imagination.

The first of these two scenes is arid, harsh and barren, but with a superficially attractive exterior; the other welcoming and fertile. The first reflects nothing of the warmth of faith; its harshness is concealed under a thin layer of soil, like the thin layer of hypocrisy that shields the real personality of the unbeliever. As soon as rain falls, the veneer disappears and the barren interior is revealed, and so it is with *"he who spends his wealth to impress people, while he believes neither in God nor in the Last Day. Such a person is like a smooth rock covered with earth. Then heavy rain falls on it and leaves it hard and bare."* (Verse 264)

The other scene depicts the believers who *"give away their money out of a genuine desire to please God, and out of their own inner certainty."* (Verse 265) Such people's hearts are filled with happiness and reassurance. They are full of confidence in the value and goodness of their actions. These are portrayed like a fertile garden with thick, rich soil, as opposed to the thin layer in the previous scene, set on a hillside. Rain revives and reinvigorates it to yield *"twice its normal produce."* (Verse 265) In fact it does not need heavy rain. Only *"a light drizzle [will suffice]. God sees all that you do."* (Verse 265) That is exactly the effect charity has on the believer. It rejuvenates him and enhances his relationship with God who, in turn, would reward him and make his wealth grow even more, thereby raising the quality of social welfare and the life of the community as a whole.

In the inimitable style of the Qur'ān, the *sūrah* presents a fully integrated and harmonious picture, with exquisite detail and elegant contrast of mood and colour, depicting every feeling and every emotion, and reflecting every idea and meaning with clarity and ease. The verse concludes by stressing that God is aware of the real motives and intentions behind people's actions.

The scene that follows depicts the outcome of flaunting one's charity and generosity, and how He thus causes their effect to be totally and irreversibly wiped out. In vivid and powerful terms, the *sūrah* paints a depressing and violent picture. *"Would any of you wish to have a garden of palm-trees and vines, through which running waters flow, bringing forth all kinds of fruits, then to be well advanced in age, with helpless offspring; and then a fiery whirlwind smites it and leaves it all burnt down? Thus God makes plain to you His revelations, so that you may reflect."* (Verse 266)

Charity, in essence, is given a tangible picture: it is just like *"a garden of palm-trees and vines, through which running waters flow, bringing forth all kinds of fruits ..."* It is fresh, opulent, luxuriant, bountiful and fertile. Thus is charity in its effect on the life of the giver and the recipient alike, and on the life of the community. It is blessed, purifying, ever-growing.

How could anyone, in their right mind, wish for such a wonderful gift to be squandered, blown away or burnt down? And for this to happen at the time when he is most in need of its fruits and good yield to look after his weak, helpless, young children! The boasting and flaunting of one's generosity and the injury caused to the recipient wipe out the benefit of charity, just like a fiery whirlwind burns down a whole beautiful garden.

We can see clearly from this passage how the Qur'ānic style achieves a perfect harmony between expression and meaning, in the individual scene as well as in the overall picture. The great truth behind this presentation is the common origin of human beings and the soil of the earth, and the attributes, strengths and weaknesses that they share.

Giving Away the Best

The *sūrah* goes on to outline the nature of charity, its methods, manners and outcome: *"Believers, spend on others out of the good things you have earned, and out of that which We bring forth for you from the earth. Do not choose for your spending the inferior things which you yourselves would not accept without turning your eyes away in disdain. Know that God is free of all want, ever to be praised."* (Verse 267)

Following the ethics and principles of charity outlined in the preceding verses, one should give of the best in one's possession, rather than of the less worthy, which one would not accept if offered in trade, unless one could strike a bargain price. God has no need to accept charity out of people's second-rate possessions.

This is a broad principle, valid for all time and all types of property, whether earned, cultivated, extracted or mined, whether known at the time of the Prophet Muḥammad or not. Not a single kind of earnings or capital, acquired at any time, is exempt from the obligation of charity, and *zakāt* accrues on it all, in accordance with the rates and proportions specified by the Prophet for the various types of capital known then. These form the standard by which percentages and proportions are determined for new types of wealth, capital or earnings.

By way of illustration, and to appreciate the realities the Qur'ān was dealing with at the time of its revelation, it would be instructive to recall the circumstances in which this verse was revealed to the Prophet. Ibn Jarīr al-Ṭabarī reports on the authority of al-Barā' ibn 'Āzib that the verse was revealed with reference to the *Anṣār* (the Muslims from Madinah). As the harvest season for dates approached, people would take bunches of dates that had just turned colour but had not fully ripened and tie them to posts in the Prophet's Mosque, for the poor among the *Muhājirūn* (the Muslims from Makkah) to eat. Some, however, would take dates of the worst quality and mix them with good ones and think nothing of it. It was then that God revealed the verse, which said: *"Do not choose for your spending the inferior things which you yourselves would not accept without turning your eyes away in disdain."*

Similar reports were related by al-Ḥākim and Ibn Abī Ḥātim, all of which go to show that, as well as having assiduous and exemplary members, a Muslim community may also have members who need to be educated and informed of their duties and obligations. The *Anṣār*'s commendable record of tireless sacrifice and support for the cause of Islam did not preclude them from being criticized and censured when some of them failed to live up to the standards and obligations of Islam.

God, after all, *"is free of all want, ever to be praised."* (Verse 267) People donate for their own good, as their donations are of no benefit to God in any way. So they should give willingly and with a clear conscience. When they do, God will accept their generosity and reward them for it, although it is He who has bestowed the wealth on them in the first place.

The *sūrah* goes on to reveal to the believers that niggardliness and the tendency to give to charity out of one's inferior possessions are motivated by lack of faith in God and by fear of poverty. Such fear is only entertained by those who have no trust in God and their accountability to Him. It identifies these motives clearly, pointing to their original instigator: *"Satan promises you poverty and bids you to commit indecency, whereas God promises you His forgiveness and bounty. God is Munificent, All-Knowing. He grants wisdom to whom He wills. He who is granted wisdom has indeed been granted abundant good. Yet only those with sound minds would take heed."* (Verses 268–269)

The *sūrah* is telling the believers that Satan insinuates into their minds a fear of poverty in order to arouse their selfishness and greed, and that it is he that entices them to transgress and commit indecencies. This fear was responsible for the practice of burying one's young daughters alive in pre-Islamic Arabia, while greed and excessive lust for wealth led some to gorge themselves on usury – both abhorrent and shameful practices.

In contrast to Satan's destructive exhortations, God promises forgiveness and generosity and provides sustenance and livelihood for everyone, in return for their generosity, because He is beneficent and fully aware of people's innermost thoughts and intentions. Furthermore, *"He grants wisdom to whom He wills. He who is granted wisdom has indeed been granted abundant good."* (Verse 269) God grants wisdom and common sense to enable people to reason and evaluate their actions and to seek moderation and forethought in their attitudes and behaviour. What a great gift, indeed!

"Yet only those with sound minds would take heed." (Verse 269) They are the ones who appreciate and understand and judge matters sensibly. As in all matters, it is up to God's absolute will to determine who deserves to receive the gift of wisdom, but the *sūrah* reassures those who sincerely strive for wisdom and guidance that they shall not be denied these gifts.

"Satan promises you poverty and bids you to commit indecency, whereas God promises you His forgiveness and bounty." (Verse 268) This statement asserts the fundamental truth that, in this life, there are only two clear choices to make: God's way or the way of Satan. Man can either heed God's advice or act on Satan's promises; rejecting one way means following the other. Only one way, the way of God, leads to the truth and all other routes belong to Satan.

This truth is frequently and deliberately emphasized in the Qur'ān in order to leave those who reject God's path with no argument or excuses. The path of truth is one and well defined, and people are free to take it or turn away from it. They will face the consequences of their choice.

The *sūrah* continues with the theme of charity, emphasizing that God is fully aware of what people give and how they give. He will reward them for both the act of giving and the intention behind it: *"Whatever alms you give or vows you make are known to God. The evildoers shall have none to help them. If you give alms openly, that is well; but if you give them to the needy in private, it is even better for you, and will atone for some of your bad deeds. God is aware of all you do."* (Verses 270–271)

Giving, in this sense, refers to all kinds of alms and charity, voluntary as well as obligatory, for private or public causes. Vows and pledges are made by individuals for personal reasons and must be made for the sake of God and for no other cause. Offerings made by unbelievers to individuals or bogus deities are totally unacceptable and condemned by Islam.

The fact that God is aware of one's intentions and actions is reassuring to the believer, arousing within him feelings of respect and eagerness to shun greed and ostentation, as well as total ease that comes from having fulfilled his obligations of giving for God's sake and of showing gratitude to God for His generosity and beneficence.

Honouring one's obligations is fair, and the opposite is evil and unjust. In this respect, people are two types. There are those who fulfil their obligations towards God, and live enjoying God's blessings. On the other side, those who deny God's generosity and show no gratitude for what He gives them, and withhold it from those in need, are condemned as evildoers who have violated their covenant with God and done wrong to themselves as well as to others, and they *"shall have none to help them"*.

The *sūrah* urges that voluntary charity is best given in private, to ensure that it is free from all traces of flaunting and pretension. However, publicizing the giving of obligatory charity could in fact be beneficial because it would promote the practice and help establish it in society. Hence, both ways are acceptable: *"If you give alms openly, that is well; but if you give them to the needy in private, it is even better for you."* (Verse 271) This statement covers both cases, giving each its appropriate weight, promising atonement from sin for both of them: *"and will atone for some of your bad deeds."* (Verse 271) It also evokes consciousness of God on the one hand, and confidence and reassurance on the other. Furthermore, it confirms that all actions and intentions are known to God, who is aware of all that people do.

We cannot fail to note the elaborate and extensive way in which the ethics of giving for charity are covered in the *sūrah*, from which two important conclusions can be drawn.

First is the fact that Islam recognizes human nature, its propensity to be selfish and tight-fisted and its constant need for motivation and encouragement. Only in this way can human nature overcome these tendencies and aspire towards the noble and benevolent spheres God wishes man to reach.

Second is the nature of the community the Qur'ān was addressing. The Arabs were particularly known for their hospitality and generous disposition, but these were tarnished by their tendency to flaunt their generosity and by their pursuit of fame, acclaim and recognition. It would not, therefore, have been easy to teach them to give all that up and give of their wealth purely for the sake of God. The task required extensive education and motivation to instruct them in self-denial and dedication to God's cause, in which Islam has achieved unparalleled success.

Charity Benefits the Charitable

At this point the *sūrah* addresses the Prophet personally, setting out a number of essential facts bearing on the formulation of Islamic principles and scope of behaviour: *"It is not for you to make people follow the right guidance. It is God who guides whom He wills. Whatever good you may spend in charity is for your own good. You should only spend out of pure dedication to God. And whatever good you give in charity will be repaid to you in full, and you shall not be wronged."* (Verse 272)

Ibn Abī Ḥātim reports on the authority of Ibn 'Abbās that until this verse was revealed, the Prophet (peace be upon him) used to instruct the Muslims to give in charity only to fellow Muslims, but then he ordered that charity should be extended to all who need it, regardless of their religion.

Guidance is a matter for God alone. Not even the Messenger of God could be held responsible for whether individuals heed the truth or not. God is the Creator, and He alone has power over people's hearts and minds. The mission of God's Messenger is to convey His message, and then it is up to God how He gives guidance to individual human beings, as they deserve to be guided. In taking this crucial issue out of the human domain, an important principle is established that a believer should seek and receive guidance from God alone. It also impresses upon the Messenger a need to show understanding, tolerance and perseverance in the face of any rejection or resistance he meets in conveying God's message to the public. He is to appeal to God to grant them guidance and show them the light.

"It is not for you to make people follow the right guidance. It is God who guides whom He wills." (Verse 272) Prophet Muḥammad is directed to open his heart to people, to show kindness, and to offer all possible help, leaving judgement and reward to God Almighty.

With such tenets and principles, Islam opens the widest possible horizons of compassion and tolerance. It goes beyond the recognition of religious freedom and rejection of compulsion and coercion. It demands universal human compassion and establishes the right of all needy members of society to help and support, regardless of their religious faith, as long as they do not pose any threat to the community. It further asserts that the rewards of those who give for the sake of God are safely guaranteed. No other religious faith has risen to or achieved such high standards of human or social morality.

The *sūrah* emphasizes that: *"Whatever good you may spend in charity is for your own good. You should only spend out of pure dedication to God. And whatever good you give in charity will be repaid to you in full, and you shall not be wronged."* (Verse 272) Only a believer gives for the sake of God and no other. He does not give to charity in order to gain influence or praise, nor does he exploit his generosity to achieve personal ends or satisfy his ego, nor does he seek the favour or pleasure of people in power or authority. A believer gives to charity in the full knowledge and satisfaction that he will be rewarded by God; and that his life, character, and standing will be enhanced and that, furthermore, God's generosity in the hereafter is guaranteed and will be all the more fulfilling.

The *sūrah* then refers to a specific form of giving, the beneficiary of which is an honest and honourable section of society who are not ashamed of being poor and who are prevented by their dignity and self-esteem from degrading themselves by begging: *"[Alms are] for the needy who, being wholly preoccupied with God's cause, are unable to go about earning their livelihood. The unthinking take them for men of wealth on account of their restrained behaviour. You can recognize them by their special mark: they do not importune people for alms. Whatever good you give is certainly known to God."* (Verse 273)

The description fitted a group of Makkan Muslims (*Muhājirūn*) who had migrated with the Prophet to Madinah, leaving behind all their belongings and members of their families. They settled in Madinah; some of them, known as *Ahl al-Ṣuffah*, lived in and around the Prophet's Mosque, and devoted their lives completely to the service of the community, volunteering for military missions and expeditions or guarding the Prophet and his household and mosque. These people were not able to work and earn a living, but behaved with dignity and propriety, refusing to beg or ask for charity, so much so that only a few people were aware of their plight.

Nevertheless, the directive has a universal application. In every generation there will be people not able, for various reasons, to earn their livelihood, but who insist on preserving their modesty and personal dignity by not becoming a burden on anyone else. They do their utmost to hide their poverty and distress, and only a few people are able to detect and appreciate their predicament.

Thus, in its unique and inimitable style, the Qur'ān depicts in a few words a full and deeply poignant picture of human dignity and self-respect. The highly expressive syntax brings the features of those people gradually to life, and puts the reader face to face with their human characters.

Those honourable people who hide their want, as eagerly as they would their nakedness, could only be offered assistance privately and in such a way as would not offend their dignity. The verse closes with the appropriate comment that: *"Whatever good you give is certainly known to God."* (Verse 273) He will certainly not let it go unrewarded.

Finally, the next verse gives a concise summary of the whole subject of charity and reiterates, reassuringly, the pledge made to those who give out of sheer humanity and altruism: *"Those who give their property by night and by day, in private and in public, shall have their reward with their Lord. They have nothing to fear and they shall not grieve."* (Verse 274) They will have their reward which includes an increase of what they have in this life, other life blessings, and a reward in the hereafter. But they also have what is more than that, namely earning God's pleasure. Hence they need fear nothing whatsoever in this life or in the life to come.

There is a striking harmony between this closing comment and the earlier detailed statements. It provides a fitting final note for the Islamic ethical code of charity which represents a vital aspect of Islamic community and social life.

A Perfectly Integrated System

Despite the attention given to charity, life under Islam is in no way based or dependent on it. Social and economic life in Islam is based, first and foremost, on the provision of work and a decent means of earning a living for all those who are able to do so. It is also based on the fair and equitable distribution of wealth in the community, with the aim of achieving a proper balance between input and reward. Nevertheless, there will always be times when people fall short for various exceptional reasons, and it is these that need to be dealt with through charity. This comes in two forms: obligatory and voluntary.

Obligatory contributions are levied only by Muslim state authorities that implement Islamic law in its entirety. They form an important source of public revenue for the Islamic state, although it is allocated for a specified purpose which cannot be exceeded.

Giving to charity voluntarily is not limited or restricted. It is up to those who can afford it to make directly to the poor and needy, following the ethics and codes given earlier so that the recipients may preserve their dignity and self-esteem, as the *sūrah* illustrates very clearly.

Al-Bukhārī relates on the authority of Abū Hurayrah that the Prophet said: "A needy person is not the one who is satisfied with a date or two, or a mouthful or two; but it is he that refrains from begging," and cited the words of verse 273: *"You can recognize them by their special mark: they do not importune people for alms."*

Aḥmad ibn Ḥanbal reports that a mother asked her son to go and ask the Prophet for some money, as other people were doing. The son went and found the Prophet addressing a crowd of people, saying: "He who refrains from begging, God shall spare him the need to beg, and he who refrains from taking charity will be amply provided for by God. If you beg while you possess the equivalent of five ounces of silver, you will be importuning for alms." The man thought for a moment and remembered that he owned a she-camel and his servant owned a she-camel, each of which was worth far more than five ounces of silver. He went away without asking the Prophet for anything.

Al-Ṭabarānī relates that a man from the Quraysh called al-Ḥārith was in Syria and heard that Abū Dharr al-Ghifārī, a Companion of the Prophet, was in need of help, so he sent him three hundred dīnārs. When the money arrived, Abū Dharr was taken aback and asked, "Did this man not find anyone else less fortunate than myself? I heard the Prophet say, 'If someone begs and he has forty dirhams, he is importuning for alms.' My family has forty dirhams, a sheep and two servants."

Islam has a fully integrated and comprehensive socio-economic system whose rules and ethics work harmoniously together, supporting and reinforcing each other. It was this feature of Islam that enabled it to establish that unique and pioneering society, the like of which the world has yet to see.

19

The Evil of Usury

Those who gorge themselves on usury cannot rise up except as he may rise up whom Satan has confounded with his touch. That is because they say, 'Trade is just the same as usury;' whereas God has made trade lawful and usury forbidden. He who receives an admonition from his Lord, and thereupon desists [from usury] may retain his past gains, and it will be for God to judge him. Those who revert to the practice [of usury] are indeed the inmates of the fire, wherein they shall abide. (275)

ٱلَّذِينَ يَأْكُلُونَ ٱلرِّبَوٰا۟ لَا يَقُومُونَ
إِلَّا كَمَا يَقُومُ ٱلَّذِى يَتَخَبَّطُهُ ٱلشَّيْطَـٰنُ
مِنَ ٱلْمَسِّ ۚ ذَٰلِكَ بِأَنَّهُمْ قَالُوٓا۟ إِنَّمَا ٱلْبَيْعُ
مِثْلُ ٱلرِّبَوٰا۟ ۗ وَأَحَلَّ ٱللَّهُ ٱلْبَيْعَ وَحَرَّمَ ٱلرِّبَوٰا۟ ۚ
فَمَن جَآءَهُۥ مَوْعِظَةٌ مِّن رَّبِّهِۦ فَٱنتَهَىٰ فَلَهُۥ
مَا سَلَفَ وَأَمْرُهُۥٓ إِلَى ٱللَّهِ ۖ وَمَنْ عَادَ
فَأُو۟لَـٰٓئِكَ أَصْحَـٰبُ ٱلنَّارِ ۖ هُمْ فِيهَا
خَـٰلِدُونَ ٢٧٥

God blots out usury and causes charitable offerings to grow and increase. God does not love confirmed unbelievers who persist in wrongdoing. (276)

يَمْحَقُ ٱللَّهُ ٱلرِّبَوٰا۟ وَيُرْبِى ٱلصَّدَقَـٰتِ ۗ
وَٱللَّهُ لَا يُحِبُّ كُلَّ كَفَّارٍ أَثِيمٍ ٢٧٦

Those that have faith and do good deeds, attend regularly to their prayers and pay *zakāt*, shall have their reward with their Lord. They shall have nothing to fear, nor shall they grieve. (277)

إِنَّ ٱلَّذِينَ ءَامَنُوا۟ وَعَمِلُوا۟ ٱلصَّـٰلِحَـٰتِ
وَأَقَامُوا۟ ٱلصَّلَوٰةَ وَءَاتَوُا۟ ٱلزَّكَوٰةَ لَهُمْ
أَجْرُهُمْ عِندَ رَبِّهِمْ وَلَا خَوْفٌ عَلَيْهِمْ وَلَا هُمْ
يَحْزَنُونَ ٢٧٧

Believers, fear God and give up what remains outstanding of usury gains, if you are true believers. (278)

يَـٰٓأَيُّهَا ٱلَّذِينَ ءَامَنُوا۟ ٱتَّقُوا۟ ٱللَّهَ وَذَرُوا۟
مَا بَقِىَ مِنَ ٱلرِّبَوٰٓا۟ إِن كُنتُم مُّؤْمِنِينَ ﴿٢٧٨﴾

If you do not, then war is declared against you by God and His Messenger. If you repent, however, you shall remain entitled to your principal. Thus, you shall commit no wrong, nor suffer any wrong yourselves. (279)

فَإِن لَّمْ تَفْعَلُوا۟ فَأْذَنُوا۟ بِحَرْبٍ مِّنَ ٱللَّهِ وَرَسُولِهِۦ ۖ
وَإِن تُبْتُمْ فَلَكُمْ رُءُوسُ أَمْوَٰلِكُمْ
لَا تَظْلِمُونَ وَلَا تُظْلَمُونَ ﴿٢٧٩﴾

If [the debtor] is in straitened circumstances, grant him a delay until a time of ease. And if you waive [the debt entirely] as a gift of charity, it will be better for you, if you but knew it. (280)

وَإِن كَانَ ذُو عُسْرَةٍ فَنَظِرَةٌ إِلَىٰ مَيْسَرَةٍ ۚ
وَأَن تَصَدَّقُوا۟ خَيْرٌ لَّكُمْ ۖ إِن كُنتُمْ
تَعْلَمُونَ ﴿٢٨٠﴾

Fear the day when you shall all return to God; when every soul shall be repaid in full for what it had earned, and none shall be wronged. (281)

وَٱتَّقُوا۟ يَوْمًا تُرْجَعُونَ فِيهِ إِلَى ٱللَّهِ ۖ ثُمَّ
تُوَفَّىٰ كُلُّ نَفْسٍ مَّا كَسَبَتْ وَهُمْ
لَا يُظْلَمُونَ ﴿٢٨١﴾

Overview

The preceding passage discussed the ethics of charity and its role in society; the present passage deals with the opposite, dark side of the circulation of money, namely, usury, or to use the Islamic term, *ribā*.

While charity denotes giving, generosity, purification, growth, cooperation and mutual social welfare, usury signifies stinginess, greed and self-aggrandizement.

Charity is giving of one's wealth without any expectation of recompense or repayment, while usury is the exaction of a charge over and above money owed, which is usually paid for out of the sweat and blood of the borrower, regardless of whether he profits as a result of the loan or not.

It is perhaps significant that the *sūrah* should discuss usury immediately after dealing with a pleasant subject such as charity, in order to highlight the sharp contrast between the two, and their effects on people and society.

No other issue has been condemned and denounced so strongly in the Qur'ān as has usury; nor has any practice come in for stronger warnings, spelling out fearful doom. Infinite is God in His wisdom. For, although it was one of the most pervasive evils during the pre-Islamic Dark Ages, most of its destructive aspects have only become better known in our modern society. Only today, in the light of widespread human suffering, can we appreciate the reasons behind the Qur'ān's determined onslaught on this evil practice. Today, we are better placed than even the people of pre-Islamic Arabia to understand God's wisdom underlying these principles, and the suitability of Islam for the organization of human society. In today's world, we have all the signs and evidence we need to explain and confirm the words of the Qur'ān. We can see what havoc and what misery a usury-based financial system has brought upon the world, as well as the insidious destruction it has caused to the morals, religion, health and economic strength of modern society. As the Qur'ān says, we are witnessing a divinely-inspired war against all individuals, groups, nations and states that persist in defying God's commands concerning the practice of usury in its various disguises.

The passage discussed in Chapter 18 laid down the basic principles for giving to charity, for the sake of God, as an important part of the Islamic social and economic system God has chosen for the Muslim community. It serves as a model for the rest of mankind to emulate and enjoy. It is presented as an alternative to a wicked and inhumane system based on usury.

We, thus, have two contrasting socio-economic systems: the Islamic system and the usury-based un-Islamic system. They are based on totally different value systems and views of the world. They can never be reconciled, as each leads in a completely opposite direction to the other and aims to achieve different ends.

The economic system Islam advocates, like its overall view of life, is based on the fundamental concept that God is the Creator and the undisputed master of all that exists. God has struck a deal with mankind and delegated to man certain duties and responsibilities on earth. He provided him with the tools, the materials and the means by which he can exercise his authority and free will. The main proviso of God's covenant with man is that man should live and behave according to God's laws. Only actions, morals, dealings or religious activities conducted according to God's law will be sanctioned and valid. The imposition of such activities by duress is rejected and condemned as injustice. God is the ultimate ruler and arbiter, and temporal human authority is derived from adherence to His law and code of living, to which human beings are bound by their covenant with Him.

Another provision of God's covenant with man stipulates that believers must look after one another's welfare and share the benefits of what God has provided for all of them. This does not mean common ownership in the Marxist sense, but responsible and regulated private ownership. Those who have should share with those who have not and all are equally required to seek work and earn their living according to their ability. No capable member of society should live off someone else or become a burden on the community. To support this system of social welfare, Islam has set up *zakāt* as a fixed obligation on the well-off and encouraged voluntary charity without limits.

God has also advised man to seek moderation and avoid lavish spending and extravagant living. This would ensure sensible employment of wealth and a surplus of funds for the payment of *zakāt* and a contribution to charitable causes.

Muslims are required to invest their money and seek the growth and development of their wealth, by scrupulous and legitimate means, without exploiting others or encroaching on their rights. Besides, it is not allowed to try to pervert, in any way, the fair and healthy circulation of capital and wealth in society. The Qur'ān stresses that wealth *"should not be left to circulate only among the rich of you."* (59: 7)

God has also enjoined honesty of intention and action and the integrity of ends and means. He has laid down rules and ethics that should be observed in the investment and development of wealth so as not to compromise the conscience or morals of the individual, or undermine the life and welfare of the community. These principles are laid down in accordance with Islam's overall philosophy of life and worldview, and in line with the terms and conditions of God's covenant with man that governs the whole range of human actions and activities in this world.

Thus we can see that usury as an economic instrument conflicts directly with the very basic concepts of Islam, because it is based on the total rejection of God's role and the dismissal of all the principles and aims on which the divine code of living is founded.

A usurious or interest-based system assumes a total divorce between the divine will and human life, leading to the conclusion that man is the absolute master of this world, not bound by any responsibility towards God or any obligation to respect His teachings or commands. It also implies that man is free as to how he accumulates, enjoys and uses wealth, and that in this regard he has no obligation whatsoever towards God or, indeed, any liability to others; it would not matter if thousands or millions of people were to suffer in the process.

Of course man-made laws may occasionally intervene to curb this freedom by setting the rates of usury or banning certain fraudulent and illegal practices, but this is usually dictated by expediency and popular convention rather than by considerations of the principle laid down by a higher divine authority.

A usury-based system is founded on the erroneous concept that the accumulation and enjoyment of wealth, regardless of the means, is the ultimate objective of human life, which explains the resulting reckless and vicious rush for money-making and prodigality.

Such a system brings nothing but misery and suffering upon individuals, communities, and nations, while it benefits only a few moneylenders. It undermines the moral and psychological fabric of society and creates a detrimental imbalance in the distribution of wealth and economic development, leading, as it is doing at present, to the concentration of power and influence in the hands of a few greedy, unscrupulous, and malevolent individuals and institutions, at national and international level, that reap the highest benefits but have no respect or regard for human values and human effort.

These powerful individuals and institutions not only control the world economy and international wealth, but they also wield enormous influence in several other walks of life with the aim of enhancing their role and position in the world. Since they are unscrupulous and unprincipled and look with disdain on religion and morality, it is to their advantage to undermine religious belief and encourage moral degradation, promiscuity and excessive spending. They manipulate the world economy for their own benefit, manufacturing and fuelling regular economic crises in various parts of the world and diverting economic and industrial production away from the common world interest to areas that will give them the greatest advantage and control of international wealth.

This catastrophic situation has been further exacerbated by the success of these powerful finance centres and groups, through their strong influence in the political, economic, media and entertainment worlds, to create the universal popular myth that usury is a good and natural aspect of the economy, without which there would be no economic prosperity or growth. It has been alleged that an interest-based economy is the one responsible for the tremendous achievements and progress of modern Western civilization, and that those calling for the abolition of usury are unrealistic dreamers and idealists motivated by moralistic and religious considerations that are capable, if given the chance, of corrupting the whole modern economic system. What is more is that those who criticize the interest-based economic system on these grounds are ridiculed by people who are in reality victims of this very system. Another victim of the system of usury is world economy which is forcibly set on the wrong course by international usurers. Thus, it suffers periodic, stage-managed crises to ensure that all its benefits are reaped by such usurers, rather than by humanity as a whole.

Some Western economists have recognized the fact that a usurious system is a threat, from the purely economic point of view. One leading critic of the system, Dr. Schacht, a former Governor of the German Central Bank, in a speech given in 1953 in Damascus, said that with an infinite mathematical operation it would be possible to show that the total sum of all liquid money in the world ends up in the hands of a few usurers, because a usurer-lender gains in every deal while the borrower is equally liable to gain or lose. Logically, therefore, money will ultimately end up with the one who always gains. The majority of capital today is under the real control of a few thousand people; while landlords, industrialists, farmers and traders who borrow from the banks, as well as workers and ordinary consumers, are no more than labourers working for the benefit of those in possession and control of capital.

That is not all that is wrong with a usury-based economy. The relationship between capitalists on the one hand, and those working in commerce and industry on the other, is based on mistrust, strife and resentment. Moneylenders try to make maximum gains by lending their money, and therefore favour a squeeze on the money supply to cause a rise in the cost of borrowing. This eventually leads to a slowdown in the economy, a rise in unemployment, and a fall in the purchasing power of the individual. This creates a fall in industrial loans which, in turn, forces the moneylenders to reduce the cost of borrowing, and a new cycle of growth and prosperity begins, only to lead to another recession and more misery for borrowers and consumers. It is this vicious circle of boom and bust that brings about the regular international economic crises.

In such an economy, every consumer pays part of the price of goods to the moneylenders albeit indirectly. Industrialists and traders take the extra cost of borrowing out of consumers' pockets by raising the prices of goods and services, thus spreading the burden over the widest possible area. Government borrowing to finance public projects is also met by ever-rising taxes imposed on the earning sections of the population, spreading the cost again over large numbers of people. This led to the rise of colonialism, and remains the root cause of war and conflict in the world today.

When considering the Islamic attitude to usury, we must bear in mind a number of essential facts.

The teachings and ethics of Islam, as we have seen, are in total conflict with a usurious economy. All the rulings, issued by the official 'clergy' in Muslim countries, and the arguments advanced to show that usury may be accommodated into the Islamic system, are pure humbug aimed at deceiving the public.

The usury system is a curse on all humanity, not only ethically and religiously, but also economically and practically. It is a system that creates unhappiness and restricts the growth of harmony and stability in society, despite its deceptive promise of prosperity.

Moral and practical considerations are inextricably linked. In all his actions, man is governed by the terms of God's covenant; he is here with a mission and a responsibility and will have to account for his actions in the hereafter. An Islamic economic system must be built on moral and ethical principles. Such principles are not a merely desirable addition that can be done without in people's life.

A usury-based economic system is bound to undermine the moral and ethical character of individuals, their feelings and their desire to help each other. It encourages greed, selfishness, lechery and speculation. In the modern world, it has opened the gates for the most sinister and corrupting forms of investment ever known, such as the drug trade, pornography, prostitution, all in pursuit of guaranteed astronomical profits. Borrowed money is not used in the service of humanity but for maximizing profit, regardless of the nature of the trade or the methods by which that profit is realized.

Islam is a comprehensive way of life. Its economic system completely discounts the need for usury and organizes the social life of the community in such a way as to eliminate usury altogether. At the same time it maintains the balance and progress of economic, social and human development in society.

Under Islam, there is no need for the abolition or removal of existing economic and financial institutions, such as banks and commercial companies, which play a vital role in modern economic development. Islam can reform these institutions and enable them to function along the sound and constructive rules and regulations it lays down.

Most importantly, Muslims must realize that it is a conceptual impossibility that God Almighty should prohibit something that is vital for the perpetuation and preservation of human life. By the same token, no practice that is inherently corrupt could ever be essential for the organization and progress of human life. A Muslim who truly believes in God as the creator, preserver and controller of life and the world cannot conceive that God would forbid anything that is vital, or prescribe anything that is vile or obscene. The reasons for widespread belief in usury-based economic and financial systems can be traced to ignorance and the obnoxious propaganda systematically waged by capitalist and moneylending lobbies and institutions. These continue to exert their pervasive influence on governments, international political organizations, and private and public media and information establishments.

The claim that the international economic and financial systems cannot exist or function without usury is simply a myth and a monstrous lie sustained by big business and international vested interests. Usury-free economies have existed and performed very successfully. To revive them today requires determination and a concerted, well-considered international effort by at least the Muslim countries of the world, in order to revive some hope of future stability, prosperity, happiness and real peace and justice in our world.

It is beyond the scope of this commentary to discuss in detail the practical methods of implementing the Islamic system. We will only look more closely at how Islam succeeded in the eradication of that abominable practice of usury.

The Horrific Image of Usury

> *Those who gorge themselves on usury cannot rise up except as he may rise up whom Satan has confounded with his touch. That is because they say, 'Trade is just the same as usury;' whereas God has made trade lawful and usury forbidden. He who receives an admonition from his Lord, and thereupon desists [from usury] may retain his past gains, and it will be for God to judge him. Those who revert to the practice [of usury] are indeed the inmates of the fire, wherein they shall abide. God blots out usury and causes charitable offerings to grow and increase. God does not love confirmed unbelievers who persist in wrongdoing.* (Verses 275–276)

It is a frightening image, far more effective than any threat or admonition. The image of a person possessed by the devil is an evocative and terrifying one, most effective in deterring usurers and in conveying the message to others. It shakes the human conscience and brings home the horrible reality of the effects of usury on individuals as well as society as a whole.

Most commentators have suggested that the *sūrah* refers to rising before God on the Day of Judgement, but I am of the view that this is a metaphor for what actually happens in life on this earth. This interpretation is supported by a later passage warning usurers of an impending war against them by God and His Messenger which, in my view, we can see going on in the world today. The whole world is currently reeling under the dire consequences of a pervasive international usury-based financial system.

However, before we study the Qur'ānic text in detail, let us review the different types of usury, or *ribā,* known at the time of revelation and how the Arabs of the pre-Islamic *jāhiliyyah,* or Dark Ages, viewed the whole practice of usury. There were two main types, known in Arabic as *ribā al-nasī'ah*, increase related to deferment, and *ribā al-faḍl*, increase based on difference in quality.

Ribā al-nasī'ah, according to Qatādah, applies to selling goods on credit for an agreed term. When the term expires, and the buyer finds himself unable to settle, the seller raises the price in lieu of extending the settlement term. According to Mujāhid, if a borrower fails to settle a debt, he agrees to make an additional payment, over the original loan, to the lender in return for an extension of the settlement period. According to Abū Bakr al-Jaṣṣāṣ, *ribā al-nasī'ah* was no more than a deferred loan conditional on an implied premium, the deferment being granted in return for the additional payment over the original amount.

In his commentary, Imām al-Rāzī says that *ribā al-nasī'ah* was the more widely known in the pre-Islamic days. People would advance money for a fixed term in return for an agreed monthly fee, keeping the original amount unchanged. At the end of the fixed term, the borrower would either pay back the original loan in full or be granted an extension with higher monthly payments.

Usāmah ibn Zayd quotes the Prophet as saying: "*Ribā al-nasī'ah* [i.e. increase related to deferment] is the only real form of usury." [Related by al-Bukhārī and Muslim]

Ribā al-faḍl [i.e. increase based on difference in quality] applies to premiums on spot transactions involving the exchange of quantities of the same commodity, with something extra: gold for gold, silver for silver, wheat for wheat, and so on. Such transactions are considered usurious because they bring exploitation, a feature common to all types of usury. This fact will be of great importance in our discussion of the contemporary situation.

Abū Sa'īd al-Khudrī quotes the Prophet as saying: "Gold for gold, silver for silver, wheat for wheat, barley for barley, dates for dates and salt for salt; may be exchanged, measure for measure, from hand to hand [on the spot]. If either party gives or seeks an increase, both parties are equally guilty of usury." [Related by al-Bukhārī and Muslim]

Abū Sa'īd al-Khudrī also reports that when Bilāl, the Abyssinian Companion of the Prophet, once brought the Prophet some dates of excellent quality, the Prophet immediately asked where he had obtained them. Bilāl said he had received them in exchange for some dates of lower quality that were in his possession, two measures for one. The Prophet was extremely displeased and said: "This is stark usury! It is the very thing! Do not ever do it. If you wish to buy good dates, sell your dates in some other way and then buy the good ones with what you receive." [Related by al-Bukhārī and Muslim]

That *ribā al-nasī'ah* is usurious is self-explanatory: it involves an increased payment and time extension, the two essential elements of usurious transactions. In *ribā al-faḍl* there have to be real differences in quality of the same commodity which give rise to an increase in the quantity of one over the other. This is clear in Bilāl's transaction, condemned by the Prophet as usurious, since it assigned different values to the two types of dates. Hence the Prophet ordered that one type of dates should be sold for cash, which is then used by the seller to buy the other type, thus removing all suspicion of usury.

The requirement to exchange traded goods simultaneously, "hand to hand", is important in order to avoid any difference in the two quantities due to a lapse in time which could affect their respective values. It also indicates how sensitive the Prophet was to any suspicion of usury, and how sagacious was his approach in uprooting it.

There are those today, overwhelmed by the triumph of Western capitalism, who wish to limit the definition of usury to *ribā al-nasī'ah* only, basing their reasoning on the report by Usāmah and definitions of usury in pre-Islamic Arabia given by some early scholars. Later and new forms of usury that do not precisely fit those definitions are, according to these pundits, allowed by Islam.

This is a symptom of spiritual and intellectual defeatism, because Islamic rules are not decided merely on technicalities but on sound and firm concepts and principles. Islam did not condemn one particular form of usury, but stood against it entirely in theory and practice. It went so far as to forbid *ribā al-faḍl* in order to eliminate all semblance of usury from Islamic monetary and economic systems.

This could only mean that all usurious dealings are forbidden, whether similar to those known in pre-Islamic Arabia or it has a new shape. Wherever the essential elements of usury are present in a transaction, it becomes forbidden. Similarly, any transaction tainted by extortion, greed or an element of gambling, or otherwise driven by the evil desire to make a profit by any means, is strictly outlawed.

Divine Admonition Remains Unheeded

"Those who gorge themselves on usury cannot rise up except as he may rise up whom Satan has confounded with his touch." (Verse 275) This is a reference not only to those who take interest or charge a usurious gain, but also to society as a whole.

Jābir ibn 'Abdullāh reports that the Prophet has cursed the person who charges usury, the one who pays it, the two witnesses and the one who writes the contract, saying: "They bear the same responsibility." [Related by Muslim, Aḥmad, Abū Dāwūd and al-Tirmidhī]

These rules apply to private, one-to-one transactions, while the whole community is condemned to the onslaught of God's wrath in societies where usury forms the basis for financial transactions. Such a society lives in turmoil and constant insecurity; and if there were doubts about this fact during the early days of the capitalist system, some four centuries ago, its record since then totally vindicates it.

The world we live in today is full of anxiety, instability and fear. Western leaders, intellectuals and scientists themselves admit to the frightening spread of nervous and psychological diseases in the West, despite its spectacular industrial, scientific and economic success. The other frightening aspect of today's Western-dominated world is the spread of conflict and strife, and the imminent threat of global war and mass destruction.

As a result, a dark cloud of depression and despair hangs over this world of ours which Western civilization, with all its achievements and capabilities and wealth cannot remove. What, then, is the point of material progress if it does not bring happiness, peace and security to individuals and societies?

It is a fact that no fair-minded person could ever deny: the majority of people in the most affluent and materially advanced countries, such as the United States of America or Sweden, lead the most miserable lives. Anxiety, depression and boredom are eating into people's lives who, despite their affluence and energy, are driven to a culture of fads and mental and sexual perversions, and all kinds of anti-social escapist behaviour that allows them no peace or security.

The fundamental cause of this pervasive unhappiness is the spiritual wilderness in which Western societies are living today. For, in spite of the prosperity and material well-being they enjoy, these societies lack the spiritual reassurance and faith that can only come with belief in God and placing our full trust in Him. They no longer have any universal goals or aims to aspire to. They have lost faith in human life and man's mission and role in the world as defined in God's covenant with mankind.

From that fundamental cause springs the curse of usury which undermines the whole economic edifice of society in such a way that the economy inflates but never seems to grow in a healthy and equitable manner or benefit all sections of the community. A usury-based economy is a lopsided one, in which the faceless privileged few prosper to the most obscene extent at the expense of the industrial and commercial resources of the community. Financiers and moneylenders control the flow of money into the market and thereby impose their wishes and interests rather than seek to meet the needs of the people or serve the public interest. Their aim is not to provide regular employment or long-term security of income, leading to happiness and social stability, but to maximize their own profits, even if that means the suffering and deprivation of millions, or the destruction of the security and welfare of the rest of mankind.

Those with vested interests objected to the condemnation and abolition of usury, claiming that *"'Trade is just the same as usury;' whereas God has made trade lawful and usury forbidden."* (Verse 275) Their argument rested on the false assumption that the objective of both trading and usury was to secure gains, but trading is open to the risk of loss as well as to making profit. It also requires real tangible input from the trader. Usury transactions, on the other hand, are aimed at bringing guaranteed gains for the lender in any case. That is the crucial difference between the two. Any transactions involving a guaranteed return for the lender, under all circumstances, are usurious and, hence, forbidden. There can be no argument on this point. God has permitted trading for many reasons that make it beneficial for human life, and the absence of guaranteed returns is first among them.

However, Islam faced the situation existing at the time with realism, averting any kind of economic or social upheaval. It declared its new rules effective immediately and turned a new page with respect to what had been going on previously: *"He who receives an admonition from his Lord, and thereupon desists [from usury] may retain his past gains, and it will be for God to judge him."* (Verse 275)

It seems to suggest that exoneration for previous usurious activities would be left to God's grace, thereby providing individuals with a stronger incentive to desist and seek to conduct their trade without usury. Nevertheless, it goes on to warn those who go back to such practices that they *"are indeed the inmates of the fire, wherein they shall abide."* (Verse 275) It affirms with power and authority for the benefit of those who might delude themselves that the hereafter was a long way away, that: *"God blots out usury and causes charitable offerings to grow and increase. God does not love confirmed unbelievers who persist in wrongdoing."* (Verse 276)

God's words have come true. There is evidence that no society has built its economy on usury and seen real prosperity, peace, security or happiness. A society may indeed be outwardly wealthy, productive and affluent, but these are not necessarily the signs of a blessed and fortunate society. Social welfare, integrity and cohesion are only found in societies constructed on altruism, charity, tolerance, compassion and open-handedness, and in which people vie only for the pleasure and grace of God Almighty.

There are, of course, those who refuse to see these facts, because they are either consumed by greed and self-interest or blinded by the falsehood and the propaganda perpetrated by those who have a real vested interest in the promotion and spread of the odious practice of usury and the whole system based on it.

"God does not love confirmed unbelievers who persist in wrongdoing." (Verse 276) This statement clearly indicates that those who persist with usury, after all that has been said about it, are guilty of grave wrongdoing and condemned by God. Evidently, those who legalize what God has forbidden are guilty and damned, even if they assert their belief in Islam with all the power at their disposal.

Islam is not mere words one utters, but a comprehensive way and system of life. To reject a part of it is to reject it all. In this case, there is not the slightest doubt that usury is totally forbidden. Hence, to legalize it and build the life of society on it is tantamount to unbelief.

In Perfect Contrast with Usurers

In contrast to the preceding example of disbelief and wrongdoing, the *sūrah* presents the case of faith and righteousness, highlighting the essential attributes of the community of believers and the basis of the economic system which disavows usury and has the firm foundation of the important institution of *zakāt*: *"Those that have faith and do good deeds, attend regularly to their prayers and pay* zakāt, *shall have their reward with their Lord. They shall have nothing to fear, nor shall they grieve."* (Verse 277)

The main element in this verse is that of *zakāt* which denotes giving willingly, expecting nothing from any human being in return. The verse also introduces a feature of the community of believers and one of its important pillars, before it goes on to describe the total reassurance, tranquillity and happiness such a community enjoys.

The institution of *zakāt* represents the foundation of a caring, sympathetic and supportive society, which has no cause to resort to usury in any aspect of its life. The image of *zakāt* has faded somewhat in the minds of those unfortunate generations of Muslims who have had no experience of life under Islam. They have not seen Islamic laws, ethics and principles shaping the daily lives of people, and creating a healthy, virtuous, decent society. They have had no experience of how *zakāt* works in practical terms to bring about economic growth and prosperity as a reward for individual diligence and honest cooperation.

These generations have become accustomed to the odious effects of the materialist usurious system, which promotes greed, unashamed self-interest and social antagonism. They have come to accept that economic and commercial life cannot be run without usury, although under this system, the transfer of wealth is often accompanied by exploitation, while people who have no money have no security in life, and industry and commerce become hostages to the moneylenders.

To contemporary eyes, *zakāt* appears as an outdated form of charity that does not fit into modern economic or financial systems. Yet *zakāt* is paid out by people educated by Islam to implement Islamic laws and regulations, and to establish a system that can hardly be imagined by those who have never experienced it. *Zakāt* is levied by Muslim authorities at the yearly rate of 2.5 per cent on liquid money (or 5–10 per cent on crops, and 20 per cent on mineral resources), as an incumbent duty rather than optional charity. The authorities then distribute the proceeds among those in need in the community as widely as possible, in order for the beneficiaries to meet their basic necessities and alleviate their hardships. Debtors who are insolvent are helped with *zakāt* money to settle their debts, whether these are personal or commercial. Poor people are helped to find appropriate work that makes them self-sufficient.

The form in which such a system operates is of secondary importance: what is important is the spirit in which the system and society come together and function as a whole to bring about genuine care and effective social welfare.

God promises those who conduct themselves according to the ethics and principles of faith, in submission to the divine will and in a spirit of cooperation, that they *"shall have their reward with their Lord. They shall have nothing to fear, nor shall they grieve."* (Verse 277)

On the other hand, God threatens the advocates of usury that they will live in fear, confusion, and insecurity, and that their society will disintegrate. History has witnessed the benefits of the Islamic, non-usury system and its results in human society. It is today witnessing the disastrous and oppressive effects of the usury-based system that forms the core of contemporary civilization. We Muslims only wish we could make others see the force of our argument against the evils of usury, but all we can do is present the facts and hope that people will listen and heed our warnings and advice.

Total War against the Usurers

Having evoked an atmosphere of calm and peace, the *sūrah* makes a final passionate appeal to the true believers to eradicate usury and rid their society of it completely, or face a relentless war waged against them by none other than God Almighty and His Messenger: *"Believers, fear God and give up what remains outstanding of usury gains, if you are true believers. If you do not, then war is declared against you by God and His Messenger. If you repent, however, you shall remain entitled to your principal. Thus, you shall commit no wrong, nor suffer any wrong yourselves."* (Verses 278–279)

This passage makes the rejection of usury a condition of true faith; Muslims shall only become true believers when they fear God and reject any usury money they are owed. No faith could be claimed, even as a mere form of words, without total acceptance of, and submission to, God's will and command. The Qur'ān is very explicit on this point and leaves no room for confusion. There is no chance for anyone wishing to declare their faith and belief in God verbally, only to adopt a way of life that is the antithesis of His laws and teachings. Those who separate religious belief from their daily affairs of life are deluding themselves if they think they are true believers, no matter how much they insist they are, or how regularly they observe religious rituals.

The *sūrah* exonerates Muslims of all previous dealings involving usury, making it clear that there would be no appropriation of property previously gained or acquired through usurious transactions. Islam has laid down an important rule that everything is permissible unless it is specifically declared otherwise, and no rules may be retroactively applied. Everything done previously would be suspended and left to God to judge and assess. Thus Islam ensured that the transition to a usury-free system was smooth and with little, if any, social or economic difficulty. Only very recently has this approach been incorporated into modern laws. Islamic legislation deals with practical human situations, while always aiming at purifying society and directing and promoting human progress and prosperity.

God also makes it a condition that Muslims, in order to be true believers, should accept this legislation and implement it in their daily life as soon as they become aware of it. The *sūrah* also stresses that fear of God and consciousness of Him are a necessary corollary to following His teachings and implementing His laws. This fear of God is an important safeguard for the enforcement of the laws and regulations, reinforcing the guarantees inherent in them. Thus, Islamic laws have a far better chance of being obeyed and adhered to than man-made laws. The enforcement of the latter is solely contingent upon the force of external authority which is easily evaded and circumvented in the absence of the inner incentives and convictions of a vigilant conscience.

The alternative is far more gloomy. *"If you do not, then war is declared against you by God and His Messenger. If you repent, however, you shall remain entitled to your principal. Thus, you shall commit no wrong, nor suffer any wrong yourselves."* (Verse 279) What a terrifying prospect! How could the frail and powerless humans even contemplate going to war against God and His Messenger; the outcome is a foregone conclusion.

Following the revelation of these verses, the Prophet instructed his governor in Makkah to use force against the wealthy clan of al-Mughīrah if they refused to cease dealing with usury. In his farewell speech in ʿArafāt, about three months before his death, the Prophet also declared that all usury originating in pre-Islamic times, and still due at the time, is written off, starting with that of his own uncle al-ʿAbbās. This crucial step in the transition into a fully-fledged, mature Islamic life came only many years after the start of the Islamic mission, when the ideological and ethical foundations of the society were firmly established.

In that speech, the Prophet said: "Every usury gain accrued according to the un-Islamic practices of *jāhiliyyah* is under my feet, and I start with that of al-ʿAbbās." He did not, however, order repayment of any gains made during the pre-Islamic era.

Every Muslim ruler is required to combat usury and those who pursue it, even if they declare themselves to be Muslims. The Prophet's successor, Abū Bakr, used force to crush groups of Muslims who, following the Prophet's death, refused to pay the *zakāt* they owed to the Muslim treasury, without renouncing any other precepts or obligations of Islam. A person who refuses to implement God's law in daily life is certainly not a Muslim.

The war that God and His Messenger are ready to wage against the perpetrators of usury is much wider in concept than the use of armed force by a worldly ruler. It is a warning of a total condemnation of all societies adopting usury as a basis for their social and economic life. It is a war affecting the psychological, economic, and emotional aspects of life. It is the social strife, acrimony and antagonism brought about by the exploitative usurious system, as well as the regional and international conflict and instability suffered in consequence by all humanity. It is a war instigated, directly or indirectly, by moneylenders and international capitalists who, like sharks, prey on corporations, businesses, industries, commerce, governments and states. Their predatory activities are the root cause of runaway inflation, high taxation, crippling international debts, recession and poverty, all of which are capable of starting wars and fuelling bloodshed and destruction all over the world. The outcome of this vicious circle of misery is economic deprivation, moral degradation, social disintegration and the inevitable collapse of human civilization.

It is a relentless war that spares nothing, and it is currently eating into the very fabric of human society as a result of the domination of the usury-based capitalist system, even though this is registering astronomical levels of industrial production and material consumption. This unprecedented industrial and material success should have ensured man's happiness, progress and well-being, but it has proved suffocating and destructive for all mankind, except for the small section of privileged financiers and capitalists, who are relatively unaffected by this misery and suffering.

Nevertheless, as it once called on that first community, Islam continues to call on every generation of mankind to desist from the evil of usury and adopt clean and wholesome monetary and commercial practices, assuring them that: *"If you repent, however, you shall remain entitled to your principal. Thus, you shall commit no wrong, nor suffer any wrong yourselves."* (Verse 279)

The objective of the persistent campaign against usury is to rid human society of this universal evil and take life back to God's pristine way, that humanity may be spared the psychological, moral and social effects of the exploitation and injustice that inevitably set in under a usury-based socio-economic system.

Recovery of the principal capital in commercial dealings cannot be said to be unfair to either lender or borrower. There are countless legitimate ways and means for investment, growth and development of capital, employing one's own entrepreneurial skills or by working in partnership with others, in which all parties proportionately share in the loss and profit of the enterprise. These would include many profitable and equitable forms of business such as trading in shares of companies whose profits are fairly distributed among the shareholders, cooperative banks that invest in commercial and industrial projects and share profits and losses among depositors, rather than give a fixed rate return on deposits – such banks would be entitled to charge appropriate service or management fees.

Kind Treatment of Insolvent Debtors

This passage dealing with lending and borrowing is concluded with advice on how to deal with insolvent debtors. In such cases, the solution would not be to impose further penalties in lieu of deferred payment, but the debtor should be granted a reprieve until he is able to settle his debt, or the lender should be magnanimous enough to write off the debt completely. *"If [the debtor] is in straitened circumstances, grant him a delay until a time of ease. And if you waive [the debt entirely] as a gift of charity, it will be better for you, if you but knew it."* (Verse 280)

The words evoke an atmosphere of tolerance and benevolence. They provide a respite from the harshness and severity of greed and selfishness. They call for clemency and compassion on the part of creditor and borrower, as well as by society as a whole.

These words may not make a great deal of sense to those 'rationalists' who apply purely materialistic criteria. It makes even less sense to moneylenders, individuals as well as faceless institutions, that justify their exploitative and extortionate practices on utterly amoral and inhuman principles and considerations. These Qur'ānic exhortations may never reach their hearts. But, as believing Muslims, we recognize that these are words of truth that are certain to bring about happiness and security for all mankind: *"If [the debtor] is in straitened circumstances, grant him a delay until a time of ease. And if you waive [the debt entirely] as a gift of charity, it will be better for you, if you but knew it."* (Verse 280)

Under Islam, a debtor is never put under duress by either the creditor or the law, but is always given another chance to settle his debt. Furthermore, society at large will not stand idly by when a borrower is suffering genuine hardship because of his indebtedness. God calls on the creditor to willingly waive the debt, and if he does so it will be good for him and for the debtor, and for the welfare and cohesion of the community as a whole.

The abolition of usury would lose much of its purpose if the creditor were allowed to harass and squeeze the debtor while he was not able to settle the debt. Thus the *sūrah* urges that he should be given time to settle, and advises the creditor to waive the debt, in full or in part. Other Qur'ānic statements (9: 60) specify that insolvent debtors, who borrow money for legitimate purposes and are unable to pay it back, qualify for help from *zakāt* funds to clear their liabilities and alleviate their situation, provided that their debts were incurred for legitimate purposes.

Then, in a highly inspiring comment, the *sūrah* recalls the fearful Day of Judgement when people shall stand defenceless before God to account for their actions. These words cannot fail to move a thoughtful and conscientious person to write off any money he might be owed by some helpless borrower. *"Fear the day when you shall all return to God; when every soul shall be repaid in full for what it had earned, and none shall be wronged."* (Verse 281)

The day to be feared is awesome indeed. Believers' hearts dread the events of that day when all will be made to stand in front of God to face the reckoning of their deeds. This verse serves as a fitting comment on a passage devoted to the liquidation of past unfair dealings.

This fear is the powerful 'voice within' which Islam kindles in the deepest recesses of people's minds and hearts to act as a potent guiding force in life. Thus Islam proves yet again how vigorous, well-integrated, practical and merciful it is, and demonstrates that its overriding aim and objective is the happiness and well-being of man as an individual, and of human society as a whole.

20

Safeguards for Financial Transactions

Believers, when you contract a debt for a fixed term, put it in writing, and let a scribe write it down for you with fairness. No scribe shall refuse to write as God has taught him. So he shall write. And let the one who incurs the liability [i.e. the debtor] dictate; and [in so doing] let him be conscious of God his Lord and not diminish anything of it. If he who incurs the liability is weak of mind or body, or unable to dictate himself, then let his guardian dictate with fairness. Call in two of your men to act as witnesses, but if two men are not available, then a man and two women, whom you consider acceptable as witnesses, so that if either of them should make a mistake, the other will remind her. Witnesses must not refuse when they are called in. Do not be averse to writing down debts, be they small or great, together with the time when they fall due; that is more equitable in the sight of

يَـٰٓأَيُّهَا ٱلَّذِينَ ءَامَنُوٓا۟ إِذَا تَدَايَنتُم بِدَيْنٍ إِلَىٰٓ
أَجَلٍ مُّسَمًّى فَٱكْتُبُوهُ ۚ وَلْيَكْتُب
بَّيْنَكُمْ كَاتِبٌۢ بِٱلْعَدْلِ ۚ وَلَا يَأْبَ كَاتِبٌ
أَن يَكْتُبَ كَمَا عَلَّمَهُ ٱللَّهُ ۚ فَلْيَكْتُبْ
وَلْيُمْلِلِ ٱلَّذِى عَلَيْهِ ٱلْحَقُّ وَلْيَتَّقِ ٱللَّهَ
رَبَّهُۥ وَلَا يَبْخَسْ مِنْهُ شَيْـًٔا ۚ فَإِن كَانَ
ٱلَّذِى عَلَيْهِ ٱلْحَقُّ سَفِيهًا أَوْ ضَعِيفًا
أَوْ لَا يَسْتَطِيعُ أَن يُمِلَّ هُوَ فَلْيُمْلِلْ وَلِيُّهُۥ
بِٱلْعَدْلِ ۚ وَٱسْتَشْهِدُوا۟ شَهِيدَيْنِ مِن
رِّجَالِكُمْ ۖ فَإِن لَّمْ يَكُونَا رَجُلَيْنِ فَرَجُلٌ
وَٱمْرَأَتَانِ مِمَّن تَرْضَوْنَ مِنَ ٱلشُّهَدَآءِ أَن
تَضِلَّ إِحْدَىٰهُمَا فَتُذَكِّرَ إِحْدَىٰهُمَا
ٱلْأُخْرَىٰ ۚ وَلَا يَأْبَ ٱلشُّهَدَآءُ إِذَا مَا دُعُوا۟ ۚ
وَلَا تَسْـَٔمُوٓا۟ أَن تَكْتُبُوهُ صَغِيرًا أَوْ كَبِيرًا
إِلَىٰٓ أَجَلِهِۦ ۚ ذَٰلِكُمْ أَقْسَطُ عِندَ ٱللَّهِ

God and lends greater credence to the testimony and is more likely to spare you any doubt. In the case of a commercial deal transacted on the spot, you shall incur no sin by not writing it down. Have witnesses when you make business deals; but let no harm be suffered by scribe or witness; if you do [harm them], that is sinful on your part. Have fear of God, for it is God who teaches you. God has knowledge of all things. (282)

وَأَقْوَمُ لِلشَّهَٰدَةِ وَأَدْنَىٰٓ أَلَّا تَرْتَابُوٓا۟ ۖ إِلَّآ
أَن تَكُونَ تِجَٰرَةً حَاضِرَةً تُدِيرُونَهَا
بَيْنَكُمْ فَلَيْسَ عَلَيْكُمْ جُنَاحٌ أَلَّا تَكْتُبُوهَا ۗ
وَأَشْهِدُوٓا۟ إِذَا تَبَايَعْتُمْ ۚ وَلَا يُضَآرَّ
كَاتِبٌ وَلَا شَهِيدٌ ۚ وَإِن تَفْعَلُوا۟ فَإِنَّهُۥ
فُسُوقٌۢ بِكُمْ ۗ وَٱتَّقُوا۟ ٱللَّهَ ۖ وَيُعَلِّمُكُمُ
ٱللَّهُ ۗ وَٱللَّهُ بِكُلِّ شَىْءٍ عَلِيمٌ ﴿٢٨٢﴾

If you are on a journey and cannot find a scribe, pledges taken in hand [are sufficient]. If you trust one another, let him who is trusted fulfil his trust, and let him fear God, his Lord. You shall not withhold testimony, for he that withholds testimony is sinful at heart. God has full knowledge of all you do. (283)

وَإِن كُنتُمْ عَلَىٰ سَفَرٍ وَلَمْ تَجِدُوا۟ كَاتِبًا
فَرِهَٰنٌ مَّقْبُوضَةٌ ۖ فَإِنْ أَمِنَ بَعْضُكُم
بَعْضًا فَلْيُؤَدِّ ٱلَّذِى ٱؤْتُمِنَ أَمَٰنَتَهُۥ
وَلْيَتَّقِ ٱللَّهَ رَبَّهُۥ ۗ وَلَا تَكْتُمُوا۟ ٱلشَّهَٰدَةَ ۚ
وَمَن يَكْتُمْهَا فَإِنَّهُۥٓ ءَاثِمٌ قَلْبُهُۥ ۗ وَٱللَّهُ
بِمَا تَعْمَلُونَ عَلِيمٌ ﴿٢٨٣﴾

To God belongs all that is in the heavens and the earth. Whether you make known what is in your minds or conceal it, God will bring you to account for it. He will then forgive whom He wills and punish whom He wills. God has power over all things. (284)

لِّلَّهِ مَا فِى ٱلسَّمَٰوَٰتِ وَمَا فِى ٱلْأَرْضِ ۗ وَإِن
تُبْدُوا۟ مَا فِىٓ أَنفُسِكُمْ أَوْ تُخْفُوهُ
يُحَاسِبْكُم بِهِ ٱللَّهُ ۖ فَيَغْفِرُ لِمَن يَشَآءُ
وَيُعَذِّبُ مَن يَشَآءُ ۗ وَٱللَّهُ عَلَىٰ كُلِّ
شَىْءٍ قَدِيرٌ ﴿٢٨٤﴾

Overview

Having condemned usury as an unhealthy, inequitable economic practice, the *sūrah* resumes by outlining provisions governing trade, loans, loan securities, and usury-free lending and transactions.

As one reads these verses, one cannot fail to marvel at the superb style of the Qur'ān, which combines precise legal language with eloquence and great literary merit. It achieves that delicate and elusive balance between clarity of meaning and pungency of expression, thereby gently but most effectively enhancing the appeal of the legal provisions to the religious conscience, without prejudicing the moral stance of the text or the precision of the wording. In the case of commercial contracts, for instance, all potential influences are brought into play with respect to the two parties to the contract, the witnesses and the executors, taking great care to consider all eventualities. Each point is thoroughly dealt with before moving on to the next, thereby avoiding unnecessary repetition, superfluous expressions, or the labouring of any aspect of the topic under discussion.

In these highly legalistic discussions, the Qur'ān maintains the same quality of literary excellence and beauty as in those passages that deal with moral or religious exhortations. Indeed, it is even more so, because precision is of the essence in these cases and one inappropriate word could affect the whole meaning with unfortunate consequences. Yet in its pioneering role in establishing these principles almost ten centuries before civil and commercial laws, as legal experts would willingly admit, the Qur'ān achieves its objective of penetrating the human mind and heart with immense ease and elegance.

Loan Arrangement and Documentation

Let us now take a closer look at the principles that Islam establishes with respect to loans: *"Believers, when you contract a debt for a fixed term, put it in writing, and let a scribe write it down for you with fairness."* (Verse 282)

The general rule, therefore, is that details of all fixed-term loans must be in writing, for reasons that will become clear later, and that a third party must do the recording in order to ensure total impartiality and fairness. The writer is required to record the agreed terms of the loan faithfully, without interference, bias or prejudice. He is obliged to do his job fully and competently as a duty to God who has blessed him with the ability to write, and for which he will be appropriately rewarded: *"No scribe shall refuse to write as God has taught him. So he shall write."* (Verse 282)

Having established that the terms of loans should be committed to writing by an independent document writer, the *sūrah* goes on to explain how the writing should be carried out: *"... and let the one who incurs the liability [i.e. the debtor] dictate; and [in so doing] let him be conscious of God his Lord and not diminish anything of it. If he who incurs the liability is weak of mind or body, or unable to dictate himself, then let his guardian dictate with fairness."* (Verse 282)

The party incurring the liability, the borrower, is the one to dictate to the writer, acknowledging the amount borrowed and his commitment to the terms and conditions of the loan, as a safeguard against any injustice to him. As the weaker party to the transaction, he would be less liable to alter the terms and conditions. This would reinforce the borrower's commitment to the liability. For, were the creditor to dictate, there would be no guarantee that he might not tamper with the terms and conditions of the loan to his advantage. Furthermore, the *sūrah* appeals to the borrower's conscience to be scrupulous and faithful in dictating the terms of the loan. It goes on to advise that if the borrower is feeble-minded, under age, or unable to dictate through ignorance or an impediment of speech, or any other reason, his guardian, attorney or trustee, may do so on his behalf, showing the same, if not greater, scrupulous fairness.

The *sūrah* gives detailed instructions concerning the witnessing of the contract: *"Call in two of your men to act as witnesses, but if two men are not available, then a man and two women, whom you consider acceptable as witnesses, so that if either of them should make a mistake, the other will remind her."* (Verse 282)

For the contract to be valid, it must be witnessed by two men or, if these are not readily available, one man and two women, all of whom should be of good standing in the community and deemed *"acceptable as witnesses"* by both parties. The reason for recommending men witnesses in the first instance is that, in a Muslim society, the majority of marketplace attendants are normally men, since women, generally, do not have to seek work to earn a living and their main preoccupation is the family home and the raising of society's new generation. Nevertheless, if two men cannot be found to witness a contract, a man and two women will do. But why two women? Since this is a legal matter, the *sūrah* does not leave the answer to speculation; and explains: "*... so that if either of them should make a mistake, the other will remind her.*" (Verse 282)

Such a mistake may occur for a number of reasons, such as lack of experience or knowledge, or failure to understand the subject matter or the ramifications of the contract. A woman's impulsive nature tends to make her impressionable and more easily influenced or swayed. This emotional, sympathetic nature is necessary and, indeed, advantageous for women in their role as mothers. Human nature being indivisible, it would be present whenever women are called upon to witness or judge anything requiring deliberation, reflection and strict impartiality. Having two women rather than one, provides a greater assurance that they will balance each other and provide an objective testimony.

The *sūrah* calls on people not to refuse to act as witnesses if invited to do so, as it did with the writer earlier, saying: "*Witnesses must not refuse when they are called in.*" (Verse 282) It is an obligation, rather than a privilege, because it is a means of establishing justice and preserving rights. Witnesses must carry out their duty willingly, honestly and without any condescension or deference towards either of the parties.

The *sūrah* moves on to another, more general, aspect of legal and business transactions: "*Do not be averse to writing down debts, be they small or great, together with the time when they fall due; that is more equitable in the sight of God and lends greater credence to the testimony and is more likely to spare you any doubt.*" (Verse 282)

The text displays a remarkable perception of human nature, as people are often inclined to judge that certain small debt transactions are not worth writing down, but the *sūrah* stresses the fact that recording all debt transactions is seen by God as preferable and more fair. A written contract gives greater force to the testimony of the witnesses, since a written statement carries more weight than one based totally on memory, and it "*is more likely to spare you any doubt*". Thus, the wisdom underlying these instructions becomes clear and they appear more convincing, practical and reassuring.

In spot trading, executed immediately and frequently, there is no need for writing dawn the details and the mere presence of witnesses will suffice: "*In the case of a commercial deal transacted on the spot, you shall incur no sin by not writing it down. Have witnesses when you make business deals."* (Verse 282)

At face value, the statement seems to allow the concession of not recording spot transactions while making it a condition that witnesses should be present; but, according to some considered opinion, the latter is strongly recommended rather than obligatory. Nevertheless, the weightier view is that witnesses are necessary for spot trading as well.

The *sūrah* proceeds to specify the rights of contract writers and witnesses, assuring them of the protection they deserve: *"But let no harm be suffered by scribe or witness; if you do [harm them], that is sinful on your part. Have fear of God, for it is God who teaches you. God has knowledge of all things."* (Verse 282)

Scribes and witnesses should come to no harm in the course of fulfilling their obligations towards God, and any wrongdoing they may suffer would be a gross violation of God's law. This is a necessary precaution, for scribes and witnesses often incur the displeasure of one or the other of the contracting parties and must, therefore, be protected and reassured so that they fulfil their obligations fairly, honestly and with absolute objectivity.

Finally the *sūrah*, in keeping with the Qur'ānic way of igniting the inner powers of the human conscience, calls on believers to fear God and reminds them of His grace and favour in giving them knowledge and understanding, so that they may conduct their affairs in accordance with His will and guidance: *"Have fear of God, for it is God who teaches you. God has knowledge of all things."* (Verse 282)

The *sūrah* rounds off the subject of loans by dealing with the special case of borrowing money while on a journey, when scribes may be difficult to find. Under these circumstances, to facilitate the transaction and ensure repayment of the loan, a verbal agreement is valid and binding provided a tangible article is given, and accepted, as security for the loan: *"If you are on a journey and cannot find a scribe, pledges taken in hand [are sufficient]. If you trust one another, let him who is trusted fulfil his trust, and let him fear God, his Lord."* (Verse 283)

Both creditor and borrower are trustees: the former entrusted with the security and the latter with the money he has borrowed, and they are both called upon to fulfil their trust and fear God, the ultimate master and ruler and judge over all.

We do not subscribe to the view advanced by some jurists that this ruling supersedes the one given in the preceding verse which makes the writing down of loan agreements obligatory. We believe that written documentation is essential except when the two parties are on a journey, in which case security must be provided for the loan and both parties are under an obligation to fulfil their part of the verbal agreement.

With all these principles in mind, the *sūrah* speaks about giving evidence in cases of litigation: *"You shall not withhold testimony, for he that withholds testimony is sinful at heart. God has full knowledge of all you do."* (Verse 283)

Transgression in this instance is attributed to the heart, where man's intention to do or not to do things originates, but the statement contains a veiled threat in stressing that *"God has full knowledge of all you do."* God will certainly recompense people according to His knowledge which uncovers any sinful intention.

Where Ultimate Authority Lies

The *sūrah* goes on to elaborate this point further, arousing deeper fear and consciousness of God, to whom everything belongs and who is aware of every thought, whether concealed or stated. He is sure to bring everyone to account, and He has full control over people's ultimate destiny: *"To God belongs all that is in the heavens and the earth. Whether you make known what is in your minds or conceal it, God will bring you to account for it. He will then forgive whom He wills and punish whom He wills. God has power over all things."* (Verse 284)

One of the most distinctive features of the Qur'ānic legislative approach is that it combines purely legalistic directives with emotional and spiritual exhortations. Thus, it links the rules to be implemented in human life to their source, the Creator of all life, within a context rich with fear of, and hope in, God Almighty. Islam moulds individual hearts and souls, as well as society as a whole, to which it addresses its legislation in order to achieve perfect harmony between morality and law, piety and authority. It is a code of life designed and laid down for man by his Creator, which can never be rivalled by anything that man, with his limited knowledge, perception and life duration, can ever hope to produce or achieve. After all, human beings always differ in their views and perspectives. Why, then, does humanity try to run away from its Creator who knows best what suits His creation in every case, time or situation?

The modern wilderness in which humanity suffers today originated in Europe with the breakaway from the oppression of the Church and the "God" it claimed to represent, and the shackles it put on human thought. The Church in Europe imposed steep taxes on ordinary people, levied tithes, sold indulgences for sins committed, and imposed very harsh tyranny. As people rose to challenge and discard these inhuman practices, they denounced the Church and rejected its teachings and authority. Regrettably, they did not stop there but went on to reject the "God of the Church" and His authority and to completely turn away from religion itself. That was a crucial development in human history that was to prove the cause of most of the misery and suffering seen in the world ever since.

The question is why should Muslims reject their religious way of life or turn away from it? Unlike the Church in Europe, Islam has been a religion largely associated with tolerance, progress and universal human well-being. The objective Islam has always worked for is to lighten the burden of human suffering and eradicate oppression, cruelty and injustice for all mankind. What reason, then, do we have to banish it from our life, imitating the West, when we have always been free from the problems that the West has had with the Church?

21

One Divine Message

The Messenger believes in what has been revealed to him by his Lord, and so do the believers. Each one of them believes in God, His angels, His books, and His messengers. We make no distinction between any of His messengers. And they say, 'We hear and we obey. Grant us Your forgiveness, our Lord; to You we shall all return.' (285)

ءَامَنَ ٱلرَّسُولُ بِمَآ أُنزِلَ إِلَيۡهِ مِن رَّبِّهِۦ
وَٱلۡمُؤۡمِنُونَۚ كُلٌّ ءَامَنَ بِٱللَّهِ وَمَلَٰٓئِكَتِهِۦ
وَكُتُبِهِۦ وَرُسُلِهِۦ لَا نُفَرِّقُ بَيۡنَ أَحَدٖ
مِّن رُّسُلِهِۦۚ وَقَالُواْ سَمِعۡنَا وَأَطَعۡنَاۖ
غُفۡرَانَكَ رَبَّنَا وَإِلَيۡكَ ٱلۡمَصِيرُ ٢٨٥

God does not charge a soul with more than it can bear. In its favour shall be whatever good it does, and against it whatever evil it does. Our Lord, do not take us to task if we forget or unwittingly do wrong. Our Lord, do not lay on us a burden such as that You laid on those before us. Our Lord, do not burden us with what we do not have the strength to bear. Pardon us, and forgive us our sins, and bestow Your mercy on us. You are our Lord Supreme; grant us victory against the unbelievers. (286)

لَا يُكَلِّفُ ٱللَّهُ نَفۡسًا إِلَّا وُسۡعَهَاۚ لَهَا
مَا كَسَبَتۡ وَعَلَيۡهَا مَا ٱكۡتَسَبَتۡۗ رَبَّنَا
لَا تُؤَاخِذۡنَآ إِن نَّسِينَآ أَوۡ أَخۡطَأۡنَاۚ رَبَّنَا
وَلَا تَحۡمِلۡ عَلَيۡنَآ إِصۡرٗا كَمَا حَمَلۡتَهُۥ
عَلَى ٱلَّذِينَ مِن قَبۡلِنَاۚ رَبَّنَا وَلَا تُحَمِّلۡنَا
مَا لَا طَاقَةَ لَنَا بِهِۦۖ وَٱعۡفُ عَنَّا وَٱغۡفِرۡ لَنَا
وَٱرۡحَمۡنَآۚ أَنتَ مَوۡلَىٰنَا فَٱنصُرۡنَا عَلَى
ٱلۡقَوۡمِ ٱلۡكَٰفِرِينَ ٢٨٦

Overview

These two verses make up the final passage of this comprehensive and remarkable *sūrah*, the longest in the Qur'ān. Its subject matter covers a wide range of issues and fundamental Islamic concepts, rules and principles. It outlines the nature and role of the Muslim community in the world, and identifies its enemies and detractors, their attitudes and the methods they use to undermine and weaken it, and the means the community has to use in order to combat their intrigues and thwart their schemes. The *sūrah* then elaborates on the nature and scope of man's role in the world, as well as his weaknesses and shortcomings.

These closing verses give a concise and appropriate summary of the major themes of the *sūrah*, and form an inspiring conclusion to its grand message.

The *sūrah* opened with the statement: *"This is the Book; there is no doubt about it, a guidance for the God-fearing. Those who believe in what lies beyond the reach of human perception, observe prayer and give of what We bestow upon them. Those who believe in what has been revealed to you and what was revealed before you, and are certain of the Hereafter. Those follow their Lord's guidance, and they shall surely prosper."* (Verses 1–5)

Throughout the *sūrah* we have found frequent references to the recognition and endorsement by Islam of all divine messages revealed to earlier prophets and messengers. Now the *sūrah* gives the final summation: *"The Messenger believes in what has been revealed to him by his Lord, and so do all the believers. Each one of them believes in God, His angels, His Books, and His Messengers. We make no distinction between any of His messengers."* (Verse 285) The two passages coalesce beautifully as if to form the frame of a single work of art.

The *sūrah* covers quite extensively many of the laws and rules governing all aspects of personal and communal life. It has described at length the excesses and the impertinence of some Israelite communities. Here it concludes with a clear statement regarding the fulfilment, or otherwise, of one's obligations in this life. It stresses that God neither wishes to overburden the believers who uphold the faith; nor to favour them with any concessions or privileges, as some Israelites had claimed for themselves. Nor does He leave them to their own devices. *"God does not charge a soul with more than it can bear. In its favour shall be whatever good it does, and against it whatever evil it does."* (Verse 286)

The *sūrah* has related various episodes of Israelite history, pointing out the grace God accorded them and how some of them had received that grace with insolence and ingratitude, for which they had to pay a heavy price amounting, in certain cases, to their own lives. Here it concludes with a moving and passionate prayer in which believers plead with God Almighty: *"Our Lord, do not take us to task if we forget or unwittingly do wrong. Our Lord, do not lay on us a burden such as that You laid on those before us. Our Lord, do not burden us with what we do not have the strength to bear. Pardon us, and forgive us our sins, and bestow Your mercy on us. You are our Lord Supreme; grant us victory against the unbelievers."* (Verse 286)

The *sūrah* has instituted *jihād* and generous donations for God's cause to combat aggression. It ends with believers seeking God's help and support, saying: *"You are our Lord Supreme; grant us victory against the unbelievers."* (Verse 286)

These concluding verses are precisely formulated, and every word has its place and significance in the text. Taken as a whole, they reflect the central aspects of faith and define the position of believers, their relationship with God and their perception of His will and purpose in the world, which they accept and willingly submit themselves to Him. The verses are a superb example of the excellence of the Qur'ānic style and approach, which remain fascinating even to those who are well acquainted with the Qur'ān. Let us now look more closely at these two verses.

One True Faith

> *The Messenger believes in what has been revealed to him by his Lord, and so do the believers. Each one of them believes in God, His angels, His books, and His messengers. We make no distinction between any of His messengers. And they say, 'We hear and we obey. Grant us Your forgiveness, our Lord; to You we shall all return.'* (Verse 285)

The Qur'ān refers to that privileged community of believers who are the archetype of faith, and to all succeeding communities modelled on their example. This community is honoured by, and greatly appreciates, being mentioned in the same breath as God's Messenger.

The Messenger's faith springs directly from the revelations he receives from God, the ultimate truth. It is a degree of faith that cannot be described except by one who has experienced it; it remains beyond comprehension for those mortals who have not experienced divine revelation and is, therefore, totally unique and exclusive to God's Messenger himself. That is why it is such an honour for ordinary believers to be mentioned side by side with God's Messenger.

The *sūrah* defines the nature and parameters of this faith. It is a comprehensive and universal faith, commensurate with the far-reaching and historic role the Muslim community is destined to inherit and take on in the world. It is a commitment that identifies humanity, throughout its history, as being of only two main groups: the believers who represent the party of God, and the unbelievers who constitute the party of Satan.

"Each one of them believes in God ..." According to Islam, belief in God is the foundation of a Muslim's understanding of life, and of the code governing his life, morals, economic and all other activities. It means believing in God as the Supreme Being, the Lord of everything and the sole object of reverence and worship. He is the ultimate authority over man's conscience and behaviour in every single aspect of his life.

God has no partners in His Godhead and Lordship over the world. He is the Creator and the active ruler of the whole cosmos, and no other power interferes with His organization and running of the physical world or of life in it. He is the sole provider of life and sustenance for all creation. He is the only and ultimate cause of what befalls the world, without whose will and knowledge nothing, great or small, happens or comes into being in this world.

Nothing and no one but God Almighty should be adored and worshipped, in any sense of the word. God is the supreme authority to be obeyed, and all temporal authority is derived from Him, and from total adherence to His teachings and commands and the laws He lays down. An imperative of faith in God is submission to, and acceptance of, the principles and values He has set out for the moral, social, legal and economic spheres of life. Faith in this sense sets man free from control and manipulation by all other forces, powers and authorities, and from the fetters of obligation or submission to anyone or anything other than God Almighty.

"... and His angels ..." This is an important aspect of belief in the unseen, the unknowable which lies beyond human perception or understanding, or, to use the Islamic term *ghayb*, as already discussed at the beginning of the *sūrah*. Man's ability to perceive and accept a world above and beyond the physical world whose existence he can discern and verify sets him above the rest of creation and confers on him his human qualities. This belief puts into proper perspective man's natural curiosity for what lies beyond the material physical world, which he instinctively and clearly perceives to exist. Without this clear perspective and vision, man resorts to myth and superstition, leading to imbalance and instability.

Angels are a fact of *ghayb* that humans cannot perceive by conventional sensory or intellectual means. But man has an instinctive urge to look beyond the world that he can see; and God, in His infinite wisdom, has seen to it that this natural and legitimate human urge is satisfied in order to save man the frustration and suffering he would otherwise inevitably encounter. There is sufficient evidence to show that those individuals and communities who have chosen to defy human nature and reject all notion of a world beyond have fallen victim to utterly farcical and fallacious superstitions that have blurred their vision, undermined their mental well-being, and turned their lives into a series of negative and destructive obsessions.

Like other aspects of *ghayb*, belief in the angels widens man's perception and understanding of the world around him. It is no longer restricted to what he can see and feel, which is only a small part of reality. He feels safer in the company of these faithful creatures, fellow believers in God's oneness, who pray constantly for man's redemption, and in the comforting thought that they are there to help and guide him spiritually. Furthermore, the mere knowledge of this fact is a blessing from God to those who believe in Him and His angels.

"... and His books and His messengers. We make no distinction between any of His messengers." According to the Islamic view, belief in God's books and messengers follows logically and naturally from belief in God Himself. To believe in God is to believe in the truth of all that is revealed by Him, and in the honour and integrity of all the

messengers He has commissioned, and in the unity of the source of the messages they have preached. A Muslim has no notion of discrimination between God's messengers. They all preached Islam in various versions, suited to the circumstances of the communities they addressed. Muḥammad, (peace be upon him), was the last and final of those Prophets and messengers who has delivered the final, complete and universal version of Islam, which will remain valid for the rest of time.

The Muslim community, therefore, inherits the legacy of God's religion on earth in its totality, which places a grave responsibility on Muslims. As bearers of God's banner on earth, they are the custodians of the greatest gift to mankind. Their mission is to promote and establish the Islamic order, and to stand up to chauvinistic, oppressive and totalitarian ideologies of all kinds, whenever they are advocated, anywhere in the world.

The Muslim community, or *ummah,* is undoubtedly the legitimate heir to the greatest treasure of guidance, light, confidence and fulfilment, as well as certainty and knowledge, ever made available to mankind. Those deprived of its benefits and blessings might as well be living in darkness and confusion. Their life is inevitably plagued with scepticism, cynicism, unhappiness, spiritual suffering and deprivation.

The history of mankind has seen countless individuals and communities deprived of the sustenance and happiness of faith. The agony and miserable experiences of many a sensitive and troubled heart have been most eloquently and passionately preserved for posterity in poetry, literature and art. There are those, however, who are immune to religious faith and have no desire for knowledge beyond the material world. They go through life with little or no humanity, hardly better than animals. They eat and survive and fend for themselves ruthlessly. They oppress, tyrannize and corrupt others in order to further their own interests and desires. They are despised by God and by their fellow human beings.

Human societies deprived of the grace and blessings of faith in God are miserable despite their affluence, barren despite their wealth, and restive despite their apparent freedom, security and peace. There are, even today, obvious examples of such unfortunate societies, a fact denied only by the arrogant.

The Ultimate End

Those who truly believe in God and His angels, books and messengers, know well that they shall return to their Lord, and so they turn to Him in obedience and submission, seeking His mercy and forgiveness. *"And they say, 'We hear and we obey. Grant us Your forgiveness, our Lord; to You we shall all return.'"* (Verse 285)

This submission is an expression of their faith. They heed and obey every commandment received from God in affirmation of His oneness and in recognition of the validity of His order in every aspect of life. No submission can be sincere without adherence to God's guidance and implementation of His rule in every sphere. Man's faith cannot be complete if he turns his back on God's teachings and seeks moral, social, economic or political guidance elsewhere. Faith is a quality firmly entrenched in man's heart and is only given credence when expressed in actions.

With submission and obedience to the Lord comes a feeling of inadequacy and deficiency in paying one's dues towards God. Thus believers appeal to the merciful God to overlook their failures and shortcomings: *"... Grant us Your forgiveness, our Lord ..."* (Verse 285)

The appeal for forgiveness follows the assertion of total submission and obedience. It is then followed by certainty in one's fate here in this life and in the life to come. God's word is the final and ultimate truth; everything shall return to Him; He is omnipotent; His will is done and His power unchallenged; His forgiveness, mercy and grace provide the way to escape punishment for sins we commit.

"To You we shall all return." (Verse 285) This statement implies belief in the hereafter, which, from the Islamic point of view, is another essential aspect of faith in God. Islam asserts that God has created man and made him His vicegerent on earth on the basis of a clear covenant encompassing all man's activities on earth. Throughout his earthly existence man is on probation. When his probation is over, he shall be judged and made accountable for his actions. Thus belief in the Day of Judgement and man's accountability for his deeds is a correlative of belief in God. This faith plays a central role in shaping and guiding a believer's conscience and behaviour, and his perception of values and consequences in this life. A believer will live in obedience to God, promoting good and supporting the truth, regardless of whether the result of his endeavour in this world is happiness or

suffering, gain or loss, victory or defeat, recompense or deprivation, or even death. The reward he seeks for passing the test of life is in the hereafter. Were the whole world to stand in opposition to him in this pursuit, and were his very life to be threatened, it would not dissuade him. He is dealing directly with God Almighty, fulfilling his obligation towards Him and looking forward to the reward He has in store for him.

This short Qur'ānic verse encapsulates the basic concept of the unity and integrity of the Islamic belief. It is a simple and clear belief in the unity of God, His angels, His books and messengers, with no distinction among those messengers whatsoever, based on total obedience and submission to God and an unshakeable faith in the Day of Judgement.

Such is Islam, a faith perfectly suited to epitomize the full and final divine message. It reflects the procession of faith which began with the creation of man and continued throughout the generations. It has been expounded and elucidated by messenger after messenger, according to the intellectual and social development of the recipient communities. With the Prophet Muḥammad (peace be upon him), the message is brought to full maturity and its complete unity is declared, leaving man with the task of understanding its principles and details, and implementing it in his life.

Islam is a religion that recognizes man as a unique being; neither animal nor inanimate, neither angelic nor Satanic. Islam takes a holistic, rather than a fragmented, view of man. It allows for his weaknesses as well as his strengths, treating him as an integrated being comprising a physical aspect with instincts, impulses and natural drives, and a discerning intellectual power, and a soul with spiritual passions and yearnings. It requires of man only such tasks as he is able to fulfil, maintaining that delicate balance between obligations and abilities, with fairness and without duress, satisfying the needs of body, mind and soul in perfect harmony. The corollary to that concept is man's freedom to choose and bear full responsibility for his choice.

Individual Responsibility

The *sūrah* continues: *"God does not charge a soul with more than it can bear. In its favour shall be whatever good it does, and against it whatever evil it does."* (Verse 286) It is within this framework of divine mercy and justice that a Muslim views, with total confidence and satisfaction, his obligations as God's vicegerent on earth, the challenges he faces in fulfilling those obligations, and the ultimate reward he receives. He is content in the belief that God is fully aware of his abilities and limitations, and will not overburden him or subject him to any duress or coercion. Not only does this fill a believer's heart with contentment and peace of mind, but it also inspires him to discharge his duties to the best of his ability. He is fully aware that any weakness he may experience is not because the task is excessive, but due to his own shortcomings, and this, in turn, motivates him to strengthen his resolve and strive for excellence in his actions.

The second part of the statement emphasizes individual responsibility for action: "*... In its favour shall be whatever good it does, and against it whatever evil it does.*" (Verse 286) Every individual is accountable for his own actions. No responsibility can be transferred from one person to another, nor can any person come to the aid of another in the matter of accountability. Once people appreciate this principle, each and every one of them becomes a positive and active force in society. They become responsible human beings ready to defend God's right over them, unwilling to concede it to anyone else. They will resist submission to temptation, tyranny, transgression and corruption, and submit their whole physical and spiritual being to God Almighty. Those who give in to powers other than God's, except those people subjected to duress or coercion, have only themselves to blame and shall have to face the full consequences of their actions.

On the Day of Judgement, no one shall intercede on behalf of anyone else, and everyone shall stand alone to face God's judgement. This inspires healthy individualism, spurring every member of society to fulfil his or her obligations towards the community, which derive from their obligations towards God. Individuals are obliged to share their wealth, labour and wisdom, and the responsibility to bring about good and fight evil and falsehood, and earn their respective reward individually and directly from God Almighty.

A Final Prayer

As the believers understand and appreciate the significance and implications of these principles, they make their earnest plea to God. The Qur'ān, in its fine and highly expressive style, quotes their moving, passionate prayer. The reader can almost see the multitudes of believers reciting in unison throughout the generations this prayer, evoked by a dual feeling of hope and fear: *"Our Lord, do not take us to task if we forget or unwittingly do wrong. Our Lord, do not lay on us a burden such as that You laid on those before us. Our Lord, do not burden us with what we do not have the strength to bear. Pardon us, and forgive us our sins, and bestow Your mercy on us. You are our Lord Supreme; grant us victory against the unbelievers."* (Verse 286)

It is a prayer that clearly defines the relationship between the believers and their Lord. In its soft tone and poignant rhythm it implies an admission of weakness and helplessness, and a recognition of the need for God's aid, support, forgiveness and grace.

"Our Lord, do not take us to task if we forget or unwittingly do wrong." (Verse 286) Error and forgetfulness are two defining characteristics of human behaviour. In recognition of this, a Muslim never boasts of his faults, nor deliberately exploits them, nor places himself above God's will, but always seeks God's help and turns to Him in repentance. The answer to this prayer is given by the Prophet who says: "God has pardoned my followers anything they do through a genuine mistake, forgetfulness or by compulsion." [Related by al-Ṭabarānī and others]

"Our Lord, do not lay on us a burden such as that You laid on those before us." (Verse 286) This plea stems from an appreciation of the gravity of the responsibility placed upon the Muslim community as heirs and custodians of God's message to mankind. It also reflects full absorption of the lessons and experiences of earlier nations who had received God's revelations, as related in the Qur'ān. We have seen, for example, earlier in this *sūrah* that the Israelites were castigated and penalized on several occasions, and in various ways, for their stubbornness and intransigence. Elsewhere in the Qur'ān, we read that, for similar reasons, they were forbidden certain foods: *"To those who followed the Jewish faith did We forbid all animals that have claws; and We forbade them the fat of both oxen and sheep, except that which is in their backs and entrails and what is mixed with their bones. Thus did We requite them for their wrongdoing."* (6: 146) On a certain occasion, they were ordered to kill one another in atonement for their worship of the calf, as stated in Verse 54 of this *sūrah.* They were also forbidden to conduct any business or to hunt on the Sabbath.

Hence, believers appeal to God not to burden them in the same way as He imposed on earlier communities. The Prophet Muḥammad was sent with a tolerant and benevolent religion that is fully cognizant of human nature, and is aimed at relieving mankind of all the burdens and encumbrances placed upon them. The Prophet is told by God: *"We shall smooth your way to perfect ease."* (87: 8)

The heaviest, most arduous burden placed on mankind, which Islam came to lift, is man's submission and subjugation to man. This is manifested in one man's capitulation to the will or power of another, or to the power of clan or class. Submission to God alone is true emancipation and represents real freedom from this oppression.

Submission to God entails recognition of Him as the ultimate source of values, standards and laws. It liberates man from the hegemony and oppression of all political, social and religious institutions, and from the power of myth and superstition. It delivers him from the grip of his whims and desires and equips him to resist any ungodly power that seeks to subjugate him or control his life and destiny.

The plea reflects the believers' gratitude for the freedom God has provided, as well as their fear of relapse.

"Our Lord, do not burden us with what we do not have the strength to bear." (Verse 286) This is not an excuse for negligence or a justification for dereliction of duty, but a plea by the weak to the powerful, for consideration and forbearance. A conscientious believer does not wish to fail in serving his Lord and Creator, and so he asks for leniency and tolerance. While acknowledging his weakness, a true believer remains vigilant and tries to compensate for his shortcomings by seeking more of God's grace and forgiveness.

"Pardon us, and forgive us our sins, and bestow Your mercy on us." (Verse 286) This is the only true guarantee of success and deliverance. No matter how hard a man strives to live up to his obligations and responsibilities towards God, he will not fulfil them satisfactorily. God shows grace by treating man with mercy and forgiveness. 'Ā'ishah, the Prophet's wife, reported that the Prophet had said, "No man shall enter Paradise by virtue of his deeds alone." When asked, "How about you?" he replied, "Not even I, unless God bestows mercy on me." [Related by al-Bukhārī]

The essence of a believer's attitude towards God revolves around an unflinching effort to strive to the best of his ability, tinged with a feeling of deficiency, of not doing enough, and with genuine hope and confidence in God's mercy and benevolence.

The *sūrah* closes with a statement asserting that believers put their full trust in God to come to their help in establishing His order on earth and defending it against its foes. God is the source of their strength and their ultimate triumph.

"You are our Lord Supreme; grant us victory against the unbelievers." (Verse 286) These words encapsulate the essence of the *sūrah* as well as the faith of Islam. They reflect the mind of true believers and define the eternal relationship between them and their Supreme Lord.

Index

F

G

H

I

J